EVOLUTION AND SOCIAL LIFE

Evolution is among the most central and most contested of ideas in the history of anthropology. This book charts the fortunes of the idea from the mid-nineteenth century to recent times. By comparing biological, historical, and anthropological approaches to the study of human culture and social life, it lays the foundation for their effective synthesis. Far ahead of its time when first published, the book anticipates debates at the forefront of contemporary thinking. Revisiting the work after almost thirty years, Tim Ingold offers a substantial new preface that describes how the book came to be written, how it was received and its bearing on later developments. Unique in scope and breadth of theoretical vision, *Evolution and Social Life* cuts across the boundaries of natural science and the humanities to provide a major contribution both to the history of anthropological and social thought, and to contemporary debate on the relationship between human nature, culture, and social life.

Tim Ingold is Professor of Social Anthropology at the University of Aberdeen, UK. His books for Routledge include *Lines: A Brief History* (2007), *The Perception of the Environment* (reissued 2011), *Being Alive* (2011), *Making: Anthropology, Archaeology, Art and Architecture* (2013), and *The Life of Lines* (2015).

Routledge Classic Texts in Anthropology

EVOLUTION AND SOCIAL LIFE

Tim Ingold

Routledge
Taylor & Francis Group

LONDON AND NEW YORK

This reissue published 2016
by Routledge
2 Park Square, Milton Park, Abingdon, Oxon OX14 4RN

and by Routledge
711 Third Avenue, New York, NY 10017

Routledge is an imprint of the Taylor & Francis Group, an informa business

First published 1986 by the Press Syndicate of the University of Cambridge.

British Library Cataloguing-in-Publication Data
A catalogue record for this book is available from the British Library

Library of Congress Cataloging-in-Publication Data
Names: Ingold, Tim, 1948– author.
Title: Evolution and social life / Tim Ingold.
Description: Abingdon, Oxon ; New York : Routledge, [2016] | Series:
    Routledge classic texts in anthropology ; 2 | Originally published:
    Cambridge : Cambridge Univesity Press, 1986. With new introduction. |
    Includes bibliographical references and index.
Identifiers: LCCN 2016003982 | ISBN 9781138675858
    (hardback : alk. paper) | ISBN 9781138675841 (pbk. : alk. paper) |
    ISBN 9781315560397 (ebk)
Subjects: LCSH: Social evolution. | Culture. | Human evolution.
Classification: LCC GN360 .I54 2016 | DDC 303.4—dc23
LC record available at http://lccn.loc.gov/2016003982

ISBN: 978-1-138-67585-8 (hbk)
ISBN: 978-1-138-67584-1 (pbk)
ISBN: 978-1-315-56039-7 (ebk)

Typeset in Bembo
by Swales & Willis Ltd, Exeter, Devon, UK

To
Christopher, Nicholas and Jonathan

Could it be that the specific subject of anthropology is the interrelation of what is biological in man and what is social and historical in him? The answer is Yes.

Kroeber, Anthropology

CONTENTS

FIGURES

PREFACE TO THE 2016 EDITION

Before writing this new Preface, I sat down to read *Evolution and Social Life* (henceforth ESL) from cover to cover. It was not something I had ever done since the book was published, and I found it an odd and slightly unnerving experience. Moving back into the past while meeting my earlier self travelling in the opposite direction, I caught myself reacting with a mixture of pleasant surprise at the extent to which the work anticipates much of my thinking for the subsequent three decades, and puzzlement over my obsession with conceptual delineations that, even then, must have seemed moribund. Then of course there were the gaps in my reading, only later to be filled with works that have become such a staple part of how I think these days that it is difficult to imagine what it can have been like to be without them. The biggest gap was in the field of psychology, and above all in the psychology of perception. At that time, I had scarcely heard of the ecological approach to perception of James Gibson, while studies in phenomenology were not even on my radar – I knew the names of characters like Maurice Merleau-Ponty and Martin Heidegger, but that was about it. And of course the biology of ESL was almost entirely evolutionary; the challenges of developmental biology that played such a major part in my later thinking had yet to cross the threshold of awareness. Unbeknownst to me, as I was labouring with my book, Susan Oyama was at work on what was to become the foundational text of developmental systems theory, *The Ontogeny of Information*. Though published a year before ESL, in 1985, the importance of this text would sink in only many years later.

However the work that was destined to have the deepest and most long-lasting influence of all was Henri Bergson's *Creative Evolution*. Though over seven decades had passed since its first publication, in 1911, the book burst in upon the scene somewhere in the middle of my writing Chapter 3 of ESL, on 'The substance of history'. I had stumbled upon it in the John Rylands Library of the

University of Manchester quite by accident, as I was looking for something else. No-one, apparently, had borrowed the book for decades, and its pages exuded that musty smell that comes from prolonged lack of exposure to the air. Yet the words imprinted on these pages spoke to me with the force of revelation. Here, expressed in incomparable prose, was everything that I had been struggling to articulate. It led to a complete change of direction. For it opened up the possibility of understanding the evolutionary process from within, and of thinking about organisms and persons not as self-contained individuals destined only to enact – and in so doing to transmit – the traits already bestowed upon them, but as loci of creative growth within an ever-unfolding field of relations. Life, then, is another word for the potential of this field to bring forms into being: its creativity is that of the growth or becoming of forms, not of the kaleidoscopic reconfiguration of what already is; its time is the duration of this becoming, not an axis upon which can be plotted the sequential combinations and permutations of being. In ESL I devoted two entire chapters (4 and 5) to working out these different understandings of creativity and time, to tracing their appearances in the literature, and to following through their implications. These chapters, more than any others, have laid the foundations for future work.

To read *Evolution and Social Life* now is rather like watching a traveller reeling under such a load of ill-assorted baggage that every step calls for almost insuperable effort. It had all seemed so simple at the outset. I thought I knew where I was going, and had packed two suitcases for the trip, one for each hand. The first case was labelled 'singular progressive movement', and in it I had packed the works of numerous theorists who thought that this was the way to think about the career of humanity. Some called it evolution, others history, but the idea was the same. The second case was labelled 'multiple, non-progressive and changeful sequences'. This, too, I packed with the works of assorted theorists who thought that this was the better way to tell the human story. Again, some called it evolution, and others called it history. As I went along through the first two chapters, proceeding from the general idea of evolution in biology to its more human-centred applications in anthropology, I picked up more and more works, packing each into the appropriate case. And for a while, despite the increasing heaviness of the load, everything proceeded according to plan. There was, indeed, a certain logic to it. For example, if one author's view of history was in the same case as another's of evolution, and if a third had contrasted their view of evolution to the former, and a fourth their view of history to the latter, then the 'evolution' of the third and the 'history' of the fourth would also end up packed in the same case – namely the one I was carrying in my other hand.

This procedure did lead to some surprising discoveries. That the cultural history of Franz Boas should be packed alongside Charles Darwin's idea of biological evolution, as 'descent with modification', was plain enough. If for Darwin, species evolved through the mutation and recombination of inherited characters in the selective environment of nature, so for Boas, the history of human cultures was played out in the assembly and reassembly of heritable traits, in countless permutations and combinations, within the selective environment of the human mind. But who would have thought that the work of a diehard scientific materialist such as Leslie White, author of *The Evolution of Culture*, could have so much in common with R. G. Collingwood's *The Idea of History*? White had gone out of his way to distinguish his monistic view of the evolutionary process from the particularism of Boas's cultural history; Collingwood, humanist and idealist to the core, had insisted that history can only be grasped from *within*, as a continuous process of mind or consciousness, and that it was in this sense utterly distinct from the reconstruction of phylogenetic sequences as understood in Darwinian evolutionary biology. Both, however, claimed to be dealing with process rather than events; for both the continuity of process was a real continuity of life and mind, rather than reconstructed from the eventful appearances of discrete individuals; for both what mattered was the unfolding of the whole process in its moments; for both, moreover, some kind of agency was at work, whether this be understood as an inherent evolutionary drive towards increasing systemic complexity or as the *telos* of an unfolding historical consciousness.

Nor did the parallels end there, for in comparing history with social anthropology Collingwood's intellectual heir, E. E. Evans-Pritchard, proposed an approach to generalisation virtually identical to White's, while borrowing his idea of anthropology as 'timeless history' verbatim from Alfred Kroeber, who had also set out his stall in explicit opposition to Boas. History, for Kroeber, had nothing to do with chronological sequencing and was all about capturing those moments in which the entire curve of a civilizational process could be encompassed, as if in a crystal ball. Even Edward Tylor, the acknowledged great-grandfather of cultural anthropology, contrived at one and the same time both to compare the laws of cultural evolution to those of physics and chemistry and to recommend that in seeking to understand people of the past (or the 'primitives' of today who were supposed to resemble them) one should endeavour to enter into their own imaginative worlds and to think things out as they would have done. Thus, as my triangulation proceeded, and as ever more authors were packed into my now bulging and oddly misshapen holdalls – prominent among them A. R. Radcliffe-Brown, Claude Lévi-Strauss, José Ortega y Gasset and of course Henri Bergson – the very ground of my inquiry began to shift. It was Bergson who brought the problem to a head. For the issue, it transpired, was not so much about progress, in any absolute or law-like sense, as about the role of consciousness in history and evolution, and about how one might intuit one's way into it.

In an idiom that was conventional for its time but which I would no longer accept today, the question was posed in terms of a dichotomy between subjective and objective dimensions of existence. Are we to regard human beings objectively as *individuals*, the carriers of particular cultural traits that are fixed and given from the outset, or subjectively, as *persons* – that is as real historical agents who continually grow themselves and one another in the conduct of lives lived together? At the time, this did not appear to me as an either/or question. One could focus on the properties, for example, of language, but equally one could focus on the conversations that are carried on by means of it. More generally, my argument was that the objective forms of culture provided necessary instruments for the ongoing conduct of purposive intersubjective life – that is, for the kind of life that we can call social. Just as you could have no conversations without language, so, I argued, there can be no social life without culture. It turned out, then, that in the course of my travels my baggage had been relabelled. The case originally tagged 'singular progressive movement' now carried the label 'social', while the case that had formerly been tagged 'multiple, non-progressive and changeful sequences' was now marked 'cultural'. And the problem was to figure out how, over time, the equipmental forms of culture are conditioned by the unfolding social life for which they serve as mediators. Or in short, what is the relation between social evolution and cultural adaptation? This question set the agenda for the final two chapters of ESL which, by then, had morphed into a very different kind of inquiry.

For a start, I had to show how social life, in my understanding, goes beyond any form of determination by culture. As individuals, perhaps, human beings may be seen to behave in conformity with a cultural programme or code, in the way that speakers of a language, for example, obey (up to a point) its rules of syntax. But just as there is more to a conversation than the aggregate of speech events and the grammar that governs them, so there is more to social life than the statistical summation of behavioural interactions and the regulative structures of culture to which they accord. For in social life, every person participates in the ongoing lives of others with whom he or she relates, in a process that I called *mutual constitution*. Today the idea that persons-in-relations are 'mutually constituted' is so well-established as to have become almost a cliché. In the early 1980s, however, as I was composing Chapter 6 of ESL, it was still a novelty. So was the idea, with which I was preoccupied in Chapter 7, that social action – though it may be carried on by way of symbolic representations of ends to be achieved, framed in the idioms of culture – *is not itself a symbolic praxis*. It is, I insisted, presentational, not representational; driven by an intention that lies in the action itself rather than by any prior intention that might be affixed in advance of it. Social life, as I put it, is the intentional presentation of that which is represented in culture. One could say that it is a process of production, but only so long as the verb 'to produce' is understood in a sense that is intransitive rather than transitive. Production, in this sense, does not begin with an idea and end with its realisation. Indeed it does not begin anywhere, but – like life itself – continually carries on. For in living socially, I argued, people produce not articles to consume but themselves and one another. That is why, whether viewed as a process of history or of evolution, social life continually overflows the bounds of any acquired tradition.

This theory of social life as an ongoing, productive and relational accomplishment is one that I would still endorse. However the theory of culture that complemented it is not. What I lacked at the time but has since become central to my thinking was an adequate understanding of *ontogenesis* – that is, of the growth and becoming of persons. It is all very well to say that persons grow themselves and one another in social relationships, but what does it mean to grow a person when everything about the way they do things has been hived off onto an instrumental armature, called 'culture', which appears to be transmitted more or less ready-made? What is left of the person once shorn of the cultural apparatus? The answer that comes from the pages of ESL is a 'consciousness' that is in itself ethereal and unmoored, floating free from the forms that it animates. It is this purification of consciousness – its decontamination from all worldly encumbrance – that leads to its equation with *subjectivity*, and to its opposition to the *objective* equipment through which it is rendered manifest in practice. Once we acknowledge, however, that to grow a person is to produce not to an unworldly consciousness but a whole being in a world, then it is necessary to admit, also, that in this growth also lies the production of everything that enables the person to carry on their life: their skills of perception and action, their language, their dwellings and tools, their institutions, and so forth. And if we are to use a word like 'culture' to refer to all these things or facilities, then there can be no holding apart the process of social life from the ongoing generation of cultural forms. And by the same token, any division between the respective domains of subjectivity and objectivity becomes untenable. In a world of life there are only goings-on; no subjects or objects, only verbs.

It is for this reason that the social and the cultural, initially introduced to denote complementary aspects of human being, respectively purposive and instrumental, came instead to stand for contrary approaches to the comprehension of being human, forced into a partnership that became increasingly unstable as the work proceeded, to the point that – by the end of the book – they were irreconcilable. While my theory of social life, inspired as it was by the philosophy of Bergson, called for an approach that would join with the process in its temporal unfolding, as it were from the inside, I was trying to combine it with a theory of culture, based on its analogue in Darwinian biology, that demanded just the opposite. For it required of the cultural analyst a kind of exterior double-take that would first read 'off' the patterns of culture from manifest behaviour, only then to read these same patterns 'in' to the minds of culture-bearing individuals, such that the behaviour itself could be seen to issue from instructions or representations already installed at the outset. As Susan Oyama pointed out in *The Ontogeny of Information*, this circularity is the Achilles' heel of the Darwinian paradigm. It lies in the fallacy, as she concisely put it, of supposing that forms precede the processes that give rise to them. Only when I came to read her book, some years after ESL was completed, did I realise that I had fallen headlong for the fallacy myself.

Indeed it is there in every proposition with which I would now profoundly disagree, for example (following an influential statement by Clifford Geertz) that culture provides the elements of a programme for living which fills the gaps left by a genetic programme that, in humans as compared with other animals, leaves much of its determinations under-specified. It is there in my innocent acceptance – which now seems astonishing – that learning can be understood as a process of enculturation, by which these programme elements are transmitted across generations, in a channel of inheritance that runs in parallel to the genetic, independently and in advance of their expression in practice. And it is there in my assumption that in any act of making or building, a conceptual form already implanted in the mind of the enculturated individual is imposed upon an initially formless material substrate. I have devoted much of my later work to repudiating these propositions: to demonstrating that human becoming is a developmentally open-ended process of enskilment, as much biological as cultural, rather than the supplemental acquisition of culture upon a universal baseline of human nature; to refuting the model of transmission of pre-coded information that underpins the notions of both genetic inheritance and cultural heritage, and with them the now fashionable theory of gene-culture coevolution; to showing how in processes of making or building, the forms of things are not given in advance but generated in the course of an engagement with active materials. In every instance, what distinguishes the way I think now from what was going through my head as I was writing ESL, is the primacy of ontogenesis. Whether our concern be with persons or with things, their coming into being has to be understood as a process of growth or development, and the forms and capacities they may have are to be seen as outcomes of this process.

Criticism is never more unforgiving than when it is directed against one's former self, and I have often been surprised by the harshness of my critique of positions that I would once have staunchly defended. Perhaps this is one reason, too, why I find so much contemporary writing on the themes of social and cultural evolution hard to put up with. For the fact is that faced with a choice between irreconcilable theoretical alternatives, I have gone down one path, while the mainstream of evolutionary anthropology has followed the other. While I have cleaved to Bergson, the mainstream has remained with Darwin. It is true that Bergson's vitalism, having languished for so long in the wilderness wherein I accidentally discovered it, has more recently been given new momentum through the extensive philosophical texts of Gilles Deleuze and Félix Guattari, and these have been inspirational for me too. Nevertheless, it is a direction that remains obstinately heterodox. Meanwhile Darwinian orthodoxy, marching to the flag of 'neo-Darwinism', has taken an increasingly rigid, doctrinaire turn. These two directions are now so far apart that communication between their respective champions seems to have terminally broken down. They inhabit different worlds, speaking mutually unintelligible languages. Indeed the polarisation has never been more extreme.

Thankfully, however, recent developments in fields ranging from molecular biology, epigenetics and neuroscience to ecological and developmental psychology, linguistics and the philosophy of mind, offer hope of a new synthesis. These developments challenge us to think afresh about all the key terms of our inquiry: humanity, evolution, culture and social life. They demand that we think of humanity not as a fixed and given condition but as a relational achievement; of evolution not as change along lines of descent but as the developmental unfolding of the entire matrix of relations within which forms of life arise are sustained; and of these forms as neither genetically nor culturally configured but as emergent outcomes of the dynamic self-organisation of developmental systems. This rethinking, I believe, could herald a paradigm shift in the human sciences of the twenty-first century of no less consequence than that which the Darwinian paradigm had for the sciences of the twentieth.

When *Evolution and Social Life* was first published it attracted little attention, and my hopes that it would represent a turning point in the human sciences were disappointed. Indeed the book was not a success. Looking back, it is easy to see why. Overlong and unwieldy, it was like an ill-designed flying machine with parts so heavy, unbalanced and ill-assorted that it had no hope of lifting off the ground. It was in some ways far ahead of its time, in other ways anachronistic; its jarring approaches pointed at once backwards and forwards. But above all, it fell between the two stools of social anthropology and evolutionary biology, and was largely disowned by both. So far as my anthropological colleagues were concerned, any work that gave space to evolutionary theory, or that dwelled on the biological aspects of human life, was automatically suspected of harbouring sympathies towards sociobiology. The suspicion was not entirely unfounded, given that nearly all the work being published around that time on the relations between social and biological phenomena was of this singularly and crudely reductionist bent. As for evolutionary biologists, it was probably my deference to Bergson, and my temerity in taking his ideas on evolution as seriously as Darwin's, that placed my book beyond the pale. It is one thing to write as an historian about the discredited figures of the past, but to evolutionary theorists basking in the promised land of neo-Darwinism, digging up the past was simply irrelevant to current endeavours. We all know, they would say, that Darwin has been proved magnificently right and Bergson disastrously wrong. Why waste time and effort on a lost cause?

For the new Darwinians, if ever evidence were needed of social anthropology's sluggishness, of its persistent errors, and of its failure to cast off old ways and move with the times, then ESL was it! Perhaps the best that could be said for it, in their estimation, was that it clarified the difference between the (incorrect) pre-Darwinian sense of evolution as progressive movement and its (correct) post-Darwinian sense as changeful sequence – a difference, it is often alleged, that social anthropologists have still not fully grasped. The irony of this, of course, is that sociobiologists of neo-Darwinian persuasion – along with their intellectual successors in evolutionary psychology – have consistently been in the forefront of those who insist on reading social evolution as a progressive development underwritten by the common genetic capital of the species. It is ironic, too, that evolution only came to mean what it does for most biologists today because of a colossal blunder perpetrated by the unacknowledged father of sociobiology, Herbert Spencer, who thought that Darwin's 'descent with modification' was a manifestation, in the domain of living organisms, of a law of progress at work throughout the cosmos. By the time twentieth century biology caught up with the mistake, it could only blame the error on social scientists who had never fallen for it in the first place and who continued, quite reasonably and properly, to use 'evolution' its original sense. One consequence of this for biology has been to render unthinkable the possibility that descent with modification, while taking place *within* the evolutionary process, may not be an evolutionary process in itself. For the most part, it is simply assumed that changes in gene frequencies in populations of organisms map onto changes in their morphological and behavioural specifications. Changes in gene frequencies, however, are one thing; changes in morphology and behaviour are quite another. That natural selection may explain the former does not mean that it explains the latter as well. Indeed it does not, unless or until it is embedded in a comprehensive theory of ontogenetic development.

I vividly recall one occasion, during the writing of ESL, when I presented a draft of one of my chapters to an anthropology seminar – it was, I think, the chapter on 'Mankind ascending'. I was curtly told, by one questioner in the seminar, that I should 'historicise my problematic'. What he meant, I think, is that I should have restored the principal *dramatis personae* of my account, the authors of the ideas I was talking about, to the contexts and currents of their times, so as to help explain why they came up with the ideas they did. But how could I do that, I responded, at the same time as triangulating the ideas themselves? It was not possible to do both things simultaneously. For me, treating these ideas seriously meant taking them at face value, as a critical interlocutor, rather than regarding them as objects of mere historical or antiquarian interest. Ideas matter, they are not just surrogates for their creators, and in ESL I wanted to write a history of ideas in its most literal sense, by tracing their genealogical connections, their affinities and their contradictions, and by allowing them to wrestle with one another directly. To place ideas in their historical context, by contrast, is to quell their discord, to disarm them, to make them safe and lay them finally to rest. It is perhaps because of their overwhelming desire to put ideas to bed that the disciplines of the humanities, in the eyes of many scientists, seem so backward-looking, and so incapable of moving on.

In contrast to the ever-lengthening memory of the humanities, the duration of recall in the natural sciences has attenuated to the point that no work can stand the test of time. More or less instant obsolescence has become the order of the day. Ostensibly, relentless overtaking is a mark of progress. Why bother with precedent, say scientists, when this is always already superseded? A science without precedent, however, is like a marooned spacecraft, heading off into the unknown but without the slightest recollection of where it has come from. Running in order to stay still, in a paralysis of perpetual self-invention, it ends up going nowhere. But between the somnambulant contextualising of the humanities and the restless decontextualisation of natural science, between sinking ever back into plenary substance and the perpetual escape into empty formalism, there is surely a third way. It is to understand the world we inhabit, and its constitutive processes, from within, recognising that we ourselves are no more capable of watching from the sidelines than are creatures of any other kind, and that like them, we participate with the whole of our being in the continuum of organic life. This, for me, is the way of anthropology.

Tim Ingold
Aberdeen, October 2015

PREFACE TO THE 1986 EDITION

One day in the spring of 1982, I jotted down an outline for the first chapter of a projected book on the material conditions of social life. In this chapter I intended to sort out some of the ambiguity that has surrounded the concept of evolution throughout the development of anthropology, to clarify the question of how—if at all—evolution is to be separated from history, and to argue for a thoroughgoing distinction between processes of social evolution and cultural adaptation. All this was meant as no more than a preliminary clearing of the ground for a more extended inquiry, and my jottings occupied barely a page. They have grown, however, into the present book. It has taken over two years to write, and is already twice as long as was originally planned. It is the most difficult and certainly the most ambitious job I have attempted, and on many occasions I have felt quite unequal to the task and ready to give up. In retrospect, however, it has proved to be an intellectual journey so exciting, and so full of unexpected revelations, that I would not have missed it for anything. I offer this book as an account, and a testimony, of that journey, in the hope that others might profit as much as I did in following the same course.

If wisdom lies in recognizing the true extent of one's own ignorance, then I am immeasurably the wiser for having written this volume. For whereas I started out in the belief that I knew most of the answers, which had merely to be transferred onto paper, I have now discovered at least some of the questions, and more important, how these questions are interconnected. That, I suppose, indicates some progress. The major problems that must confront anyone embarking on the study of a subject as all-embracing as evolution, and which certainly confronted me, are first, that there is not much to be said that has not been said before and second, that almost everything of significance that has been written in the natural and social sciences, or in the arts and humanities, touches on the subject in one way or another. Our ignorance, then, lies in how little we know of what is already known, that limitation of perspective that leads yesterday's old hat to be innocently paraded as today's novelty, and which causes different disciplines to sail past one another in opposite directions, like ships lost in a fog, their respective crews convinced that they are on course for a new world. To overcome this limitation, it is necessary to abandon some of the normal canons of fundamental research. One such canon is that one should begin with a survey of the relevant literature, which otherwise stated, means 'stay on board your own ship, but never mind where the others are going'. But once *all* literature is defined as potentially relevant, such advice is clearly worthless. One must be prepared to follow almost any lead, knowing however that not all leads can be followed and that with every decision *not* to follow a lead one may be ignoring something that could radically alter one's entire outlook. It is embarrassing but noteworthy that I came across many of the works that have most profoundly influenced the present project completely by accident, most often whilst looking for something else on the library shelf. This says much for the role of serendipity in scholarship, but is not altogether reassuring for one who would like to be confident that, in pursuing his inquiry, he has left no stone unturned. Indeed, the sight of rows of unread (and often unreadable) books, any one of which just might contain some fundamental revelation, is agonizing enough; the thought that one's own might eventually join the queue is even more so.

A second canon of research that had to be abandoned is the one that demands direct familiarity with all the most recent work in the field. Cynically, it could be said that the way to keep a step ahead of everyone else is to go back and reread the works of those who were writing in the period just after the one modern scholars are currently (and unwittingly) recapitulating. Anthropologists have as short a memory as the practitioners of any other discipline and are inclined to spend much effort groping towards conclusions already elaborated by their predecessors, in incomparable prose, a long time ago. For this reason I have considered it just as important to look closely at what these earlier authors actually said, as to keep abreast of the latest trends. What I found was often surprising and bore very little relation to the caricatures that are often paraded so as to impress a stamp of legitimacy on current inquiry. It is perhaps worth emphasizing that our disciplinary forbears were neither fools nor heroes, but intelligent and sophisticated people who were writing—as do we—to advance human knowledge and understanding, not to provide conveniently packaged modules for future use in teaching the history of the subject. It would be an admission of our own ignorance, not theirs, to fail to take their works with the seriousness they deserve.

There is a problem, however, in deciding how far back we should go. Every predecessor has predecessors, and the problems we address are timeless. I have, in this book, quite deliberately set my historical baseline around the middle of the last century, thus excluding a great many major thinkers who have exercised a formative influence on what later became the study of culture and social life: I mean figures of the stature of Kant, Herder, Hume, Rousseau, and above all, Vico. No doubt their presence can be felt between the lines. I have chosen, however, not to dwell on their contributions to human understanding for three reasons. First, there exist already a great many fine works by philosophers and intellectual historians that cover this ground, and to which anyone wishing to pursue the subject further could well refer. It is simply not a field I am qualified to enter. Second, I did not conceive this study purely as an exercise in the history of ideas, but rather as a contribution to contemporary debate; therefore it was imperative to go back only so far as would leave me still within reach of the present. Third, it made sense to start from the point when anthropology began to constitute itself as a distinct domain of knowledge. For this was a time when the various facets of humanity, variously grouped under the rubrics of human nature and history, had yet to be disentangled; and when anthropologists had to fight for recognition of the autonomy of cultural processes as the absolute pre-eminence of human beings in the animal kingdom met its severest challenge in the demonstration of evolutionary continuity. The problem this posed was not so much resolved as shelved with the coming-of-age of social and cultural anthropology, which as branches of the science of man came to rely on certain assumptions about human uniqueness that were dogmatically asserted rather than actively debated. To reopen the debate is naturally to call into question the delineation of the boundaries of the discipline, and this can only take us back to the days when these boundaries were as yet ill defined.

I have produced, here, a work of the kind that my anthropological colleagues are wont to call 'disembodied theory', meaning the sort of book of which they thoroughly disapprove. It is not something I have attempted before, my previous efforts having been limited to the more conventional business of analysing first-hand field observations and the comparative reanalysis of secondary ethnographic material. However, I reached a point, not only in research but also in teaching, when I felt that I could not advance without confronting some rather pressing uncertainties that, in the conduct of empirical work, are more conveniently left unattended. I do not believe that any apology is needed for theory. A science of man that ceases to address the most fundamental questions concerning the human condition, contenting itself with the ever more penetrating analysis of specific ethnographic situations (in which the people generally disappear behind a haze of symbols), is a sterile and introverted exercise; worse still, it leaves a vacuum that practitioners of other disciplines, whose knowledge of anthropology is rudimentary or non-existent, are only too happy to fill. We live in an age when the split between natural science and the humanities is as wide, and as damaging, as ever: The mission of anthropology, as I see it, is to bridge the divide; but to bridge it, not like philosophy, in a would-be world concocted in the ivory tower, but on the basis of an understanding of what, for ordinary folk, everyday life is all about. The perpetual tension between the construction of human beings as they might be, and the knowledge of them as they really are, is what keeps us always on our toes and prevents our inquiry from spinning off at a tangent into the intellectual equivalent of outer space. The subjects of our inquiry are human beings, and not abstract entities fabricated by our imaginations, and of which we say: 'Suppose that these be men . . . '

I advocate, in this book, an evolutionary approach to culture and social life. By and large, recent anthropology has turned its back on evolution for all the wrong reasons. Of these, the most commonly cited is the one that equates the evolution-ary paradigm with the establishment of a rank-order of societies that invariably places ourselves at the top. This is not, however, an essential aspect of the para-digm; what *is* essential to it is the idea that all human groups (ourselves included) are fellow passengers in the same overall movement, one that is irreversible and progressive, and hence that the differences between them must be relative to where they stand in it. But relativist anthropology, rejecting the notion of evolutionary progress and substituting the many worlds of culture for the one human world, in fact turned the imputed superiority of ourselves over others, observers over observed, into an *absolute* one. The enlightened few, liberated from the illusions of ethnocentrism with which all others were supposed to be afflicted as a condition of their belonging to one culture or another, could claim complete emancipation from the humdrum existence of ordinary people. It is my view that the redefini-tion of anthropology from 'the study of humanity' to 'the study of other cultures' has constituted no less than an abdication of our own position in the world, and with it of our moral responsibility for what goes on in it. The world we live in is continuous; what happens to others, however remote, inevitably has a bearing on every one of us, just as our own actions rebound on them. To justify an attitude of studied indifference to the fate of others on the grounds of the avoidance of eth-nocentrism, or the maintenance of total objectivity, is neither scientifically credible nor ethically acceptable.

It is characteristic of the evolutionary approach adopted here that it deals not only with mankind as a whole but with the Whole Man: not merely a carrier of culture but an unusual kind of animal, a creature of flesh and blood, endowed with feelings and passions, who acts purposively and creatively through whatever instru-ments are available to achieve concrete, practical results. It cannot be emphasized too often that humans, with the advent of culture, did not cease to be animals; for culture *completes* the human animal, it does not replace him with something differ-ent. It certainly will not do to reduce all social experience to the effects of innate biopsychological dispositions, thereby turning anthropology and history into sub-disciplines of evolutionary biology. But nor can we put human nature in brackets, or write as though there were no such thing, as some of the more extreme expo-nents of cultural idealism are inclined to do. No theory of culture or history can be adequate that is unable to countenance the fact of our existence as biological organisms and that fails to recognize the very considerable innate component of behavioural disposition. And yet, in facing up to the implications of human nature, we must do so in a way that does justice to the reality of intersubjective life. I believe that the need to relate, as Kroeber said, 'what is biological in man and what is social and historical in him' must once more unite the fields of human biology and social and cultural anthropology, after their long and increasingly unfortunate separation, around the central problems of evolution.

It is, to be sure, an uphill task. Faced with the crippling naïvety of contemporary biological thought when it comes to matters social and cultural, anthropologists have tended to respond either by preferring to remain ignorant of the biological challenge, considering it not worth the effort of bothering about, or by counteracting it with arguments even more lacking in sophistication and theoretical vision, which simply substitute one (cultural) fatalism for another (biogenetic). One cannot expect much support from either quarter, for where one side thinks itself on the point of knowing all, the other simply does not want to know. Moreover, as anyone with more than a superficial knowledge of the literature on evolution will be aware, the line between the deepest profundity and utter lunacy is thin and indistinct, and is drawn by different people in different ways. I have read much, by scientists of eminence and repute, which has struck me as being on the lunatic fringe, or at least downright silly. Although I have done my best to keep to the other side, there will doubtless be those who will want to commit what I have to say to the same category. This is a risk that simply has to be taken if one is to exercise any imagination at all; the safe course is always to remain ignorant. But no one, thank goodness, has been standing over me as I write, dictating what I should think and threatening me with damnation and physical torture should I put a word wrong. For that freedom, hard-won by our intellectual forbears, and still being fought for by a great many distinguished contemporaries, we may indeed be thankful.

In an age dedicated to the generation of 'facts', in which intellectual work is assimilated to industrial production, nothing is more needed than measured understanding and synthesis. And to achieve it, a first requirement is that we straighten out our concepts, so that we know at least when we are talking about the same and about different things. Doubtless there are contradictions and inconsistencies in this work that I have failed to iron out, or even to spot; but I have done my utmost to avoid the temptation to treat concepts like pieces of Plasticine, malleable to any purpose. I remain in envy of the matchless verbal agility of the prima donnas of anthropology, beside which my own efforts seem pretty pedestrian. However, I insist that real intellectual puzzles can *never* be solved by a neat turn of phrase, nor can their solution be confirmed simply through frequent citation. Facing contradictions head-on when they appear, rather than skirting them (or making a virtue out of paradox), is the best way to novel theoretical insight. To this end, I have endeavoured to write as simply, clearly and precisely as possible, in the hope that others will understand rather than merely repeat what I have to say. It has not been easy. There have been moments of exhilaration when all seems revealed, as when the skies open on a clear day, followed closely by feelings of despair when the clouds close in again. Infuriatingly, the total vision tends to evaporate like a dream on waking as soon as pen is put to paper. Only a fraction of it is ever regained.

Many of the ideas developed in this work were roughly sketched out in a notebook I kept during a six-week stay, in spring 1982, at the University of Umeå in Sweden. I owe a great deal of gratitude to everyone there for the hospitality and stimulus I received during that visit. At Manchester, my thanks are due to many of my students in the Department of Social Anthropology, who have put up patiently with my theoretical predilections and have always responded with insight and encouragement. The book was completed during the first two months of a period of sabbatical leave granted by the University of Manchester, for which I am extremely grateful, as I am to my colleagues who agreed to cover my teaching and administrative duties during my absence. Jean Monastiriotis, Mary Lea and Margaret Timms typed the manuscript to perfection, on top of a heavy load of other work, and to a tight schedule—my thanks to all three. The greatest debt of gratitude remains to my wife Anna, who for the last two years has had to put up with a husband who has been more than usually absent-minded and irritable, and who has certainly not done his fair share of household chores. The book is dedicated to my children, without whose 'continual interruptions' I doubt whether I would ever have completed it at all.

One final note. The word 'man' appears a great many times in what follows, the word 'woman' hardly at all. No sexist bias is intended. I am concerned a good deal, in this book, with the differences between human beings and other animals, but *not* with differences of sex or gender. Unfortunately, alternative terms such as 'individual' and 'person' have quite specific sociological connotations and cannot be employed with the same generality. In the circumstances, I have had no alternative but to comply with the conventions of the English language.

T.I.
Manchester

1

THE PROGRESS OF EVOLUTION

No-one should make sweeping claims concerning evolution in fields outside the biological world without first becoming acquainted with the well-seasoned concepts of organic evolution and, furthermore, without a most rigorous analysis of the concepts he plans to apply.

Mayr, The growth of biological thought.
Copyright © 1982 by Ernst Mayr.

Do societies, or cultures, evolve? It all depends, you will say, on what I mean by evolution. An anthropologist would probably interpret the question as one about progress, thus: 'Is it reasonable to envisage an overall movement from the primitive to the civilized in human modes of life?' Most likely the anthropologist's answer would be negative, but even were it affirmative he would surround it with qualifications—if only to avoid the charge of ethnocentrism. But how would a biologist construe the question? Most biologists consider evolution a proven fact, yet many balk at applying the idea of progress to living nature, just as do anthropologists in relation to culture and society (Lesser 1952:136–8). According to one recent definition, designed to embrace social phenomena within a biological framework, evolution is 'any gradual change' (Wilson 1980:311)—a definition that must strike anthropologists (and perhaps many biologists too) as too broad to be useful. Surely all societies are changing all the time. But paradoxically, so long as anthropologists were content to regard their subject as the study of 'primitive' forms, with the implicit connotation that others had progressed to a more advanced state, these forms were treated as essentially *changeless*. Are we, then, to regard evolution as progress without history, or as history without progress? These alternatives can be traced to the two major exponents of evolutionary thinking in Victorian England: Herbert Spencer and Charles Darwin. My purpose in this chapter is to isolate the critical points of difference between the two perspectives. Their clarification is essential to my subsequent project, which will be to link the difference to an opposition between the social and the cultural dimensions of human experience.

It is still widely believed that the 'evolutionism' that dominated nineteenth-century social thought was a unitary paradigm that owed its foundation to the publication, in 1859, of Darwin's *The origin of species*. This paradigm is largely a fabrication constructed and maintained by those who claim to reject it (Hirst 1976:15). There was not one theory of social evolution but many, and all stemmed from ideas current long before Darwin. As Burrow has remarked, 'The history of Darwin's influence on social theory belongs . . . to the history of the diffusion of ideas rather than of their development' (1966:114). And as we shall see, this diffusion did not take place without a great deal of distortion. These facts have been pointed out often enough in the literature.[1] Their obfuscation can be put down in part to the belief amongst some biologists and much of the lay public that Darwinian theory provides the key not only to the evolution of life, but also to the past and future of humanity. Many distinguished scientists, whose careful consideration of the facts of nature leads them to reject the idea of inevitable ascent from 'lower' to 'higher' forms, have thought fit to pronounce on the progress of mankind in tones reverberant with the ideals of bourgeois enlightenment, and backed by no solid evidence whatsoever. Darwin did this (see Bock 1980:37–60), and so do many of his latter-day sociobiological followers (e.g. Wilson 1978). Anthropologists have good reason to protest against such naïve speculations. Yet if their protestations are to carry any weight, and if they are to produce a theory of social or cultural evolution that avoids the pitfalls identified by biologists decades ago, they must be clear about the epistemological status of the concepts they intend to apply. For this reason Mayr's admonition (1982:627), with which I headed this chapter, must be taken seriously. In its fulfilment, we shall inevitably have to stray rather far into the realms of biological thought. But let me begin with a word about the origin of 'evolution'.[2]

The verb 'to evolve' comes from the Latin *evolvere,* which literally means to roll out or unfold. Already in the seventeenth century it was being extended metaphorically to refer to the revelation or working out of a preformed idea or principle. However, this usage was occasional and unsystematic (Williams 1976:103). The history of 'evolution' took an odd turn when it became the central concept of the theory of preformation in embryology, advocated by Charles Bonnet in 1762. According to this theory, every embryo grows from a tiny image of itself—a homunculus—present in the egg or sperm, which in turn contains an even tinier image of its future progeny, and so on. By extension, the very first homunculus—supposedly inhabiting the ovum of Eve—must have contained a programme for the development of all future generations, which would appear in the course of time as the homunculi were 'unpacked' one after another (Gould 1980:35, 203). However bizarre the idea, it did conform to the original, literal meaning of evolution (Bowler 1975:96–7). By the middle of the nineteenth century, Bonnet's theory of preformation was defunct, but the concept of evolution had been revived in quite another guise by that dinosaur of Victorian philosophy, Herbert Spencer. The connotation had ceased to be one of the unfolding or unpacking of qualities immanent in the thing evolving and had become linked instead to the idea of *progressive development* towards an enlightened future. As a prognosis for mankind, this was hardly a new idea in Western philosophy, for its roots go back at least to the early seventeenth century (Bury 1932:35–6; Bock 1955:126). It reached a climax in Condorcet's *Progress of the human mind,* published in 1795, which in turn became the inspiration for the work of Saint-Simon and his disciple, August Comte. From Comte, Spencer admitted to having adopted the term 'sociology' but little else (Burrow 1966:189–90; Carneiro 1967:xxi–xxii, xxxii). Despite their differences, which were indeed profound, both Comte and Spencer sought to establish natural laws by which human civilization might be ordained to progress (Mandelbaum 1971:89). It was Spencer's self-proclaimed achievement, however, to have welded a conception of the development of society ('the superorganic') into a grand synthesis that embraced the temporal progression of all organic and inorganic forms as well.

The intellectual climate of Spencer's day was particularly conducive to such a synthesis. At that time the dominant concern was to discover and explain how things had come to be as they are, a concern that grew in proportion to the steady decline in the authority of orthodox religious doctrines of creation, and to the concomitant advance of natural science. Thus the reconstruction of human development in its various aspects came to be conceived as but part of a wider enterprise, the reconstruction of life, which in turn was to be fitted into a picture of the history of the earth and even of the entire cosmos. Spencer found the inspiration for his synthetic philosophy through his acquaintance—at second hand—with the work of the German embryologist von Baer (1828), who had observed that every stage in the development of an organism constitutes an advance from homogeneity of structure to heterogeneity of structure (Mayr 1982:473). In an article entitled 'Progress: Its law and cause' (1857), Spencer endeavoured to show that 'this law of organic progress is the law of all progress' (1972:40). With one sweep of his cosmic pen, everything from the earth through all forms of life to man and human society was brought within the scope of a single principle of epigenetic development, as applicable in astronomy and geology as in biology, psychology and sociology. Shortly after the appearance of this article, Spencer decided to substitute 'evolution' for 'progress', on the grounds that the latter entailed too anthropocentric a vision (Carneiro 1967:xvii; Bowler 1975:107–8). His celebrated definition of evolution, appearing in *First principles* (1862), ran as follows: 'Evolution is definable as a change from an incoherent homogeneity to a coherent heterogeneity, accompanying the dissipation of motion and integration of matter' (1972:71). The grandeur of this conception captured the Victorian imagination. Before long, Spencer had a considerable following, and evolution had become a catchword. It still is, yet Spencer and his voluminous works are today all but forgotten. Although his intellectual death was pronounced almost fifty years ago by Talcott Parsons (1937:3), there are faint signs of a contemporary resurrection (e.g. Parsons 1977: 230–1; Carneiro 1973).

How are we to account for this curious turn of fate? In brief, the concept of evolution was extended—largely through the efforts of Spencer himself—to cover what Lamarck had called the 'transformism' of living forms, and the process to which Darwin came to refer as 'descent with modification'. Spencer remained throughout his life a committed Lamarckian (Freeman 1974), a point of some significance to which we shall return in Chapter 6. But he also became a strong advocate and publicist of Darwin's views, which he regarded as accessory to his own. For the principle of natural selection he substituted the catch-phrase 'survival of the fittest', which he had first hinted at in 1852, seven years before Darwin published *The origin of species*. The co-discoverer of natural selection, A. R. Wallace, later persuaded Darwin to adopt Spencer's phrase, believing that it would be less conducive to the misinterpretation of nature as a wilful agent selecting forms to suit its purposes (Carneiro 1967:xx; Mayr 1982:519). Yet in the doctrine of 'survival of the fittest' the theories of Darwin and Wallace were equally exposed to distortion, for the essential connotation of differential reproduction was obscured (Goudge 1961:116–18). It was all too easy to regard the 'fittest' not as those who left relatively more offspring but as those who managed—with 'tooth and claw'—to eliminate their rivals in a direct competitive struggle. Moreover, to avoid tautology, 'the fittest are those that survive'; the victorious parties were considered a priori to be the most advanced on a general scale of progress. For this distortion, Spencer and subsequent 'Social Darwinists' must be held principally responsible. In reality, the process of variation under natural selection that Darwin invoked to account for the diversification of living forms, far from providing confirmation from within the field of biology of Spencer's evolutionary 'laws', rested on principles wholly incompatible with the axiom of progressive development inherent in these laws. Today Darwinian theory has triumphed, in a form remarkably close to the original, and more or less purged of its Spencerian accretions (Ghiselin 1969). It has not, however, been stripped of the title Spencer bestowed on it—'the theory of evolution' (Bowler 1975:112–13). Therefore, to understand the difference between the social evolutionism of the nineteenth century and the biological evolutionism of the twentieth (as well as contemporary theories of cultural evolution constructed on the biological model), we must look more closely at the logical premises of Darwin's theory of descent with modification.

The most fundamental axiom on which Darwin built his theory was not the progression but the *variability* of living forms. Without variability there could be no natural selection, since there would not be the material on which it could operate. In fact, Darwin's conception of variability contained three components, two of which were not original to him. First, there was the idea of *continuity* or insensible gradation. Darwin himself refers to the precept *natura non facit saltum* (nature never makes leaps) as 'that old canon in natural history' (1872:146, 156). It had indeed been around for a long time, in the form of the classical doctrine of the 'Great Chain of Being'. According to this doctrine, which enjoyed widespread popularity from the Renaissance until the late eighteenth century (Oldroyd 1980:9–10), all the multitudinous forms of life are locked in place along a grand scale from the lowliest to the most exalted (human beings), such that not a single position in the scale remains unfilled (Bock 1980:10; Mayr 1982:326). Thus Leibniz, in a letter published in 1753, spoke of the 'law of continuity' that requires 'that all the orders of natural beings form but a single chain, in which the various classes, like so many rings, are so closely linked one to another that it is impossible for the senses or the imagination to determine precisely the point at which one ends and the next begins' (cited in Lovejoy 1936:145). If there is an evolution in such a system, it consists in the forward displacement of the entire chain, such that the hierarchical relations between its parts are preserved intact. Beings do not give rise one to another, as the less advanced to the more advanced; the monkey of the future—as Bonnet conjectured—may have the intellect of a Newton but will still be a monkey and not a human being, occupying its appointed place between mankind and beings lower on the scale, all of which will have undergone a concurrent advance (see Foucault 1970:151–2).

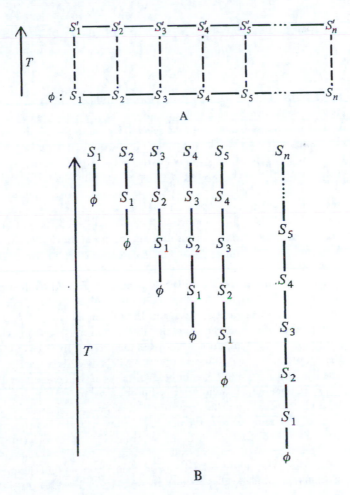

FIG. 1.1 *(continued on page 6)*

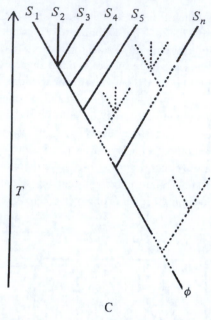

S_1 S_2 S_3 S_4 S_5 S_n

T

C

ϕ

FIG. 1.1 Three views of the genesis of organic forms. **A:** The 'Great Chain of Being',
created—fully formed—a few thousand years ago. The entire chain is
displaced forward by time, but each species, locked in its appointed place in
the chain, remains essentially unchanged in the displacement. **B:** Lamarck's
'transformism'. Time, already much extended, is intrinsic to the constitution
of the chain itself; every existing form represents a moment in a total
process of development initiated by spontaneous generation and moving
towards ever-greater complexity and perfection. **C:** Darwin's 'descent with
modification'. The chain is replaced by a branching tree, with just one point
of common origin. Existing forms have not occurred previously and will
not occur again. The time-scale has been extended even further, to cover
many millions of years, but time itself is an abstract frame, extrinsic to the
evolutionary process. A few further comments arise from this schematic
comparison. First, diagram A combines 'horizontal' (synchronic) continuity
with temporal discontinuity. In diagram B, the continuity of the 'chain of
being' is transferred from the horizontal to the vertical (temporal) axis, but is
mapped out in the distribution of forms in the present. In diagram C, there
is diachronic (genealogical) continuity, but synchronic *discontinuity*. The
sequential order of the past cannot be inferred from the contemporaneous
order of the present, but must be traced in the fossil record. Second, in
diagram B there are no extinctions; organisms of every species are in the
process of becoming those of the next species up the scale. In diagram
C most paths (indicated schematically by dashed lines) lead to eventual
extinction, whereas most new species originate through divergent radiation
(cladogenesis). Hence the appearance and disappearance of species present
quite different problems. S_{1-n}, species; T, time; ϕ, origin of life. Adapted,
with substantial modification, from Ruse (1979:10).

The idea that time, far from carrying forward the scale as a whole is rather intrinsic to its very constitution, as the movement by which its successive elements are revealed, is quite a different one. It was anticipated as long ago as 1693 by Leibniz, who nevertheless remained unaware of the challenge it posed to his own philosophical system (Lovejoy 1936:256–62). But it was that most maligned figure in the history of biology, Jean Baptiste Lamarck, who went the furthest in what Lovejoy has called 'temporalizing the great chain of being', by setting it in motion, replacing an essentially static picture of living nature with one of continuous flux. In Lamarck's conception, organisms could 'work their way up' the scale as if on a moving staircase. As fast as some reach the top of the scale, others are supposedly being created at the bottom—by 'spontaneous generation'—to ascend in their turn (see Fig. 1.1). Thus the chain is, strictly speaking, no longer one of being but one of becoming, defining not a series of fixed and unalterable positions but a trajectory of advance. However, superimposed on and complicating this linear movement is a 'lateral' process of adaptation to particular environments. Thus for Lamarck, the representatives of a species are undergoing constant transformation, both as they progress up the scale and as they encounter diverse physical conditions (Boesiger 1974:24–5). In his understanding of temporal variability and adaptive modification, Lamarck has perhaps as good a claim as Darwin to have founded the theory of evolution, as it is understood in contemporary biology (Mayr 1976; 1982:352–9). But when Lamarck's works were published, in the first two decades of the nineteenth century, 'evolution' still carried the connotation—from Bonnet—of preformation. And Bonnet was a staunch advocate of the fixity of species in the chain of being. That is why Lamarck chose a quite different concept—that of transformism—to characterize his theory.

The ideas of *continuity* and *temporality* are both crucial components of the Darwinian conception of evolution. Yet for Darwin they had connotations quite different from those they had for Lamarck and his predecessors. For the continuity of 'descent with modification' is not a *real* continuity of becoming but a *reconstituted* continuity of discrete objects in genealogical sequence, each of which differs minutely from what comes before and after. Thus the life of every individual is condensed into a single point; it is we who draw the connecting line between them, seeing each as a moment of a continuous process. And consequently, time is not intrinsic to evolution but is conceived as an *abstract dimension* in which these points are plotted; instead of an inner time that actively brings forth or reveals new forms in progressive succession, we have an outer time that provides a backcloth against which the whole parade of forms is to be projected. Gillespie is right to claim, in these respects, a complete hiatus between Lamarckian and Darwinian conceptions of the evolutionary process, for what Darwin did 'was to treat the whole range of nature which had been relegated to becoming, as a problem in being, an infinite set of objective situations reaching back through time' (Gillespie 1959:291). Of course, had it not been for Lamarck, the idea of the evolutionary transformation of species might have remained more or less inconceivable. However, Darwin's specific achievement was to have comprehended both the continuity and temporality of such transformation within a framework of being, according to which things exist only in and for themselves, and not as instants in the unfolding of a total system. This was made possible by the introduction of a new idea of *diversity,* one that worked 'upwards' from the level of the individual rather than 'downwards' from the level of the pre-established type.[3]

This is the third and most essential component of Darwin's conception of variability. It marked a radical departure from all previous evolutionary schemata, in so far as it implied a rejection not only of the fixity of forms in the chain, but also of the chain itself as a single line of progression (Fig. 1.1). Darwin replaced the image of the chain with that of the tree, thick with branches, twigs and buds (1872:97–8).[4] Variability, in short, implies not progression but *diversification.* As Mayr (1982:401) puts it, whereas Lamarck was concerned with the 'vertical' dimension of evolution, Darwin stressed its 'horizontal' dimension. Every individual is thus an incipient variety, every variety an incipient subspecies, every subspecies an incipient species, and every species an incipient genus: 'The several subordinate groups in any class cannot be ranked in a single file, but seem clustered round points, and these round other points, and so on in almost endless cycles' (Darwin 1872:97). As diversification can proceed indefinitely, so the number of possible forms is potentially infinite. In asserting that the world of living things presents a profusion of variants that can only arbitrarily be grouped into species, subspecies and varieties (1872:38–9), Darwin directly challenged the orthodoxy that supposed every organism to be a manifestation of the essential qualities of its kind, and to occupy a fixed place in a hierarchical God-given design. Yet variability for Darwin was also a source of some embarrassment, for although he could observe it wherever he chose to look, he was never able to achieve a satisfactory explanation of how it arose, or of how it was transmitted. It was left to modern genetics to provide the answer. The number of discrete genes carried by even a simple organism is so great that the possibilities for their combination and recombination are astronomical. 'For the more complex organisms, such as animals or plants, . . . the number of potential possibilities is much larger than the number of individuals which have existed on the earth in the past and at present' (Montalenti 1974:14). And although individual differences in genotype are discontinuous, they are in practice so fine as to give the impression of a continuous, multidimensional 'landscape' of variation.

The essential difference between the phenomena of the living and non-living worlds is beautifully portrayed in the closing sentence of *The origin of species.* Here, incidentally, Darwin uses the word 'evolved' for the first and last time, in the loose, vernacular sense of forms being laid out or unveiled (Gould 1980:36): 'There is grandeur in this view of life, with its several powers, having been originally breathed . . . into a few forms or into one; and that, whilst this planet has gone cycling on according to the fixed law of gravity, from so simple a beginning endless forms most beautiful and most wonderful have been, and are being evolved' (1872:403).[5] This, in a nutshell, is the contrast between a steady-state, Newtonian view of the universe as constituted by physical bodies whose cyclical motion is governed by 'laws', and the view of life as the revelation of an irreversible sequence of objects of ever-increasing diversity. It was in the presentation of this contrast that Darwin's argument ran counter to that of one of his greatest sources of inspiration, the geologist Sir Charles Lyell. Opposing the catastrophism of Cuvier, and pursuing ideas presented in 1795 by the Scottish geologist James Hutton, Lyell (1830–3) had attempted to reconstruct the history of the earth on the *uniformitarian* premiss that there is a constancy in the operation of natural laws, and therefore that processes going on in the present must also have been going on throughout the past and will persist indefinitely. Of these processes, Lyell considered the most important to be movements in the earth's crust, leading to the perpetual rise and fall of sea-levels and associated climatic fluctuations. Extending this view to the biological domain, he argued that although all the major groups of organisms had been present all along, particular species—appropriate to particular topographical and climatic conditions—would appear and disappear, only to reappear when the conditions were again right. Extinction would never be permanent; even the dinosaurs might once again walk the earth (Oldroyd 1980:45).

Darwin accepted Lyell's uniformitarianism and the perpetual, open-ended sense of time it entailed. As the closing passage of the *Origin* reveals, he thought life to have begun at some point in time but to end nowhere. The process, once started, may continue indefinitely, being carried on through a potentially infinite variety of forms. Moreover, natural selection has operated, and will continue to operate, so long as the necessary physical conditions exist for the support of life on this planet. But Lyell's view of endless *repetition* in the living world, as in the non-living, was categorically rejected. According to the theory of descent with modification,

> We can clearly understand why a species when once lost should never reappear, even if the very same conditions of life, organic and inorganic, should recur. For though the offspring of one species might be adapted . . . to fill the place of another species in the economy of nature, and thus supplant it; yet the two forms—the old and the new—would not be identically the same; for both would almost certainly inherit different characters from their distinct progenitors. (1872:274)

In short, Darwin was able to show how—in living nature—a constant mechanism, functioning uniformly through time, can generate sequences of forms that are strictly irreversible. This irreversibility, in turn, is predicated on the axiom of variability—that no individual organism is ever quite like another. It follows that individuality 'is the most important characteristic of life, the one which differentiates more substantially living from non-living things, physics from biology' (Montalenti 1974:11).

Let me elaborate on this theme, since it is of fundamental importance. The appearance of every organism constitutes a unique event in natural history. Each such event could be regarded as a kind of experiment, in which the organism is 'tested' for its effectiveness in both surviving and producing offspring in its particular environment. The environment, however, consists primarily of a large number of other organisms, each of which—in its own way—is likewise unique. Hence the series of experiments that add up to the history of life are *non-replicable,* a fact that has sometimes given rise to doubts as to the 'scientific' status of the theory of evolution by variation under natural selection (Popper 1957:108–9). The essential point, however, is that the theory is *retrodictive* rather than *predictive* (Scriven 1959) and consequently that natural selection must be treated as a *mechanism,* and not as a *law.* It does not allow us to make statements about the forms life might take in the future that could be checked against experience, in the same way that we might check, for example, the predicted trajectory of a planet (Hempel 1965:370). It only provides us with a way of accounting for why, *in the circumstances,* things turned out as they did. The complete explanation of any evolutionary sequence depends on the insertion of historically specific information regarding the pool of variability and the environmental context of adaptation (Winterhalder 1980:140–1).

But the mechanism of natural selection itself lies *outside* history, in that its operation can be specified without reference to any particular set of initial conditions (excepting, of course, the first appearance of entities that are both variable and capable of transmitting the components of variability through reproduction—that is, of *living* entities). As the nexus between particular historical conditions and particular historical results, natural selection may be presumed not only to have influenced the course of all sequences that have actually occurred in the evolution of life, but also to have a bearing on all those that could possibly occur—of which the former are but a minute sample (Hirst 1976:26). That is, it applies without exception to all living things (Reed 1981:67). Since there are potentially any number of ways of meeting the same adaptational challenge, the precise form of an organism will depend not only on the 'conditions of life' to which it is exposed, but also on the specific attributes received from forms preceding it in the direct line of descent. According to the premiss of variability, no two lines will ever be the same. We conclude that the course of evolution, in Darwin's sense of descent with modification, is not only irreversible but also *indeterminate* (Simpson 1953:310–12; Mayr 1982:57–9). This is not to say that it is random, for if it were, life would be a chaos of variation. It is rather that natural selection is constantly engaged in the ordered construction of novelty (Dobzhansky 1974a).

It is important to be clear that the irreversibility of evolution, conceived in Darwinian terms as a 'changeful sequence' (Lotka 1945:171), implies merely that particular events or chains of events in the sequence cannot be repeated: In other words it is *irrevocable* (Goudge 1961:174–5). There is no suggestion of directionality, let alone of progress. If the evolutionary clock, in Darwinian terms, cannot be put back, it also cannot be put forward. In a useful discussion of this point, Ayala (1974) has presented a hierarchically ordered series of distinctions, which can be summarized as follows: The concept of *direction* 'implies that a series of changes have occurred that can be arranged in a linear sequence such that elements in the

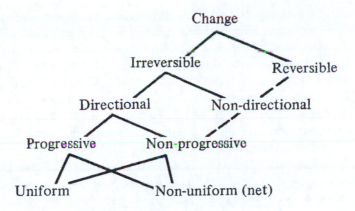

later part of the sequence are further apart from the early elements of the sequence than intermediate elements are, according to some property or feature under consideration' (Ayala 1974:340). But directional change is not necessarily *progressive*. For it to be so, the extension or enlargement of the property in question must be regarded, by some standard of evaluation, as an 'improvement or betterment' (Goudge 1961:182).

Consider a sequence of forms *A–B–C–D–E*. If each form represents a unique, non–recurrent configuration, the sequence must be irreversible in the specific sense already outlined. A directional trend may be (but need not be) manifested through from *A* to *E* in respect of one or more attributes: This may be uniform or non–uniform (net), depending on whether the same trend is apparent in every component step in the sequence. Even were such a trend apparent, we would still not be in a position to conclude that *E* is in some sense an 'advance' on A. Our criterion of advance could be absolute (such as some measure of overall complexity) or relative (adaptedness under present environmental circumstances). Natural selection necessarily generates improvement only in the latter sense. *E* might then be said to be 'better adapted' than A, but only if environmental conditions were to remain unchanged for the duration of the sequence. But the effective environment of an organism both depends on what it is organized to do and includes a range of other organisms that are simultaneously adapting (Monod 1972:120–1). It follows that the criteria of selection are liable to change as fast as the forms selected. In that case, *E* may be no better adapted to present conditions than A was to the conditions obtaining at the start of the sequence. It is therefore no 'further on' in any but a chronological sense. In Darwinian theory, although the path of evolution may be pointed by time's arrow (Blum 1955:210), it seeks an elusive target that recedes as it is approached.

Because it is still widely believed that Darwin discovered, in the guise of natural selection, a law of absolute or *general* organic progress (e.g. Harris 1968:117), it might be worth pausing to take a look at what he actually had to say on the matter in *The origin of species*. It obviously bothered him a good deal. The idea of progress was a pervasive one in the nineteenth century, and Darwin did not escape its influence (Mandelbaum 1971:80–5; Bock 1980:39). Yet in the world of nature there seemed to be no precise or objective criterion by which 'lower' forms could be distinguished from 'higher', and in the absence of such a criterion the idea of a generalized progression in the organization of life could be nothing but a 'vague yet ill-defined sentiment' (1950[1859]:292). Frustrated by this imprecision, he devoted only a single, highly inconclusive paragraph to the subject in the first edition of the *Origin* (1950[1859]:286). Even if a 'sort of progress' could be envisaged in theory, in that each successive form appearing under similar physical conditions must have beaten its immediate predecessor in the 'struggle for life', still there appeared to be no way of subjecting the idea to empirical test. However, in subsequent editions of the *Origin,* the original paragraph on 'the state of development of ancient forms' was revised and expanded, and an entirely new section entitled 'On the degree to which organisation tends to advance' was added to the crucial chapter on natural selection. It is this section that has perhaps fostered the popular impression of natural selection as the engineer of general evolutionary progress.

Although he still finds the subject shrouded by obscurity and imprecision, Darwin is at least able to come forward with an absolute criterion of organic advancement: 'The degree of differentiation and specialization of the parts of organic beings, when arrived at maturity, is the best standard, as yet suggested, of their degree of perfection or highness' (1872:288). Among vertebrates, advancement had to include that of the intellect, clearly culminating in human beings, whom Darwin unquestioningly placed at the summit of the organic scale. As regards the descent of man, which he made the subject of a separate work, he had no doubts whatsoever about the fact of progress, with primitive tribes at the bottom and European nations at the top (1874:217). But in this work, it was Darwin who was clearly borrowing from contemporary advocates of theories of social progress, rather than the other way around (Bock 1980:41). In its tenor and its arguments, *The descent of man* differs so much from *The origin of species* that it is better considered separately, as we do in the second part of Chapter 2. To return to the question of the advancement of life in general, one cannot avoid the impression that Darwin is trying to have it both ways:

> As the specialisation of parts is an advantage to each being, so natural selection will tend to render the organisation of each being more specialised and perfect, and in this sense higher; but not that it may leave many creatures with simple and unimproved structures fitted for simple conditions of life, and in some cases will even degrade or simplify the organisation. (1872:288)

If I read this correctly, Darwin is saying that, taking internal complexity as a measure of advance, natural selection might generate such advance, but on the other hand it might not. One cannot deny that the earth is swarming with 'lower forms', which show no signs of either advancing or becoming extinct. As Ayala points out, 'Today's bacteria are not more progressive . . . than their ancestors of one billion years ago' (1974:350). Therefore any theory of *necessary* progress or development must be invalid. But, writes Darwin, natural selection 'does not necessarily include progressive development—it only takes advantage of such variations as arise and are beneficial to each creature under its complex relations of life' (1872:92). After all, if you are an earthworm, what possible advantage could you derive from being more highly organized? Elsewhere Darwin is even more emphatic: 'There is no evidence of the existence of any law of necessary development' (1872:299).

That last remark should suffice to indicate just how far removed was Darwin's position from that of the progress theorists of his time—of whom the most prominent was of course Herbert Spencer (Freeman 1974). Like Spencer, Darwin found his criterion of evolutionary advance in the notion of increasing structural differentiation applied originally by von Baer to describe the course of embryonic development (compare Darwin 1872:91; Spencer 1972:39). But Spencer went on to model the evolution of life on the growth of the individual organism, viewing phylogeny simply as ontogeny writ large (Dobzhansky 1974a:309–10). The premisses of Darwin's theory were just the reverse. Descent with modification, he argued, depends on variability, and whatever the causes of that variability, it is manifested in the distortion or even the truncation of the 'normal' course of ontogeny in all kinds of quite unpredictable ways (Bock 1955:131–2). There is no plan in Darwinian evolution; the only plans are those contained in the hereditary materials of individual organisms, and evolution occurs because no two plans are quite alike. The idea of necessary progress, as Bury long ago pointed out, 'involves a synthesis of the past *and a prophecy for the future*' (Bury 1932:5; my emphasis). But when it comes to the future, natural selection is silent. It does not embody a design for tomorrow, adapting organisms only to today's conditions. Consequently progress is not inevitable but historically contingent. Or in Simpson's words, progress has occurred *within* evolution, but 'is not of its essence' (1949:261).

Nevertheless, a century after Darwin, one of the leading exponents of the modern 'evolutionary synthesis'—Julian Huxley—was continuing to insist that general progress *is* of the essence of evolution. In its cosmic dimensions, 'uniting nebulae and human emotions' (1957:100), Huxley's vision seems fundamentally at odds with that of Darwin, whereas it virtually 'out-Spencers' Spencer (Goudge 1961:159–60; Medawar 1967:40). 'The whole of phenomenal reality is a single process, which properly may be called evolution'—divisible into inorganic, organic, and 'psychosocial' phases. Moreover, evolution generates 'ever fresh novelty, greater variety, more complex organization, higher levels of awareness, and increasingly conscious mental activity' (Huxley 1956:3). Now Huxley was as much aware as Darwin that the earth is full of 'lower forms', and therefore that progress—conferring greater freedom from environmental control—cannot be 'compulsory and universal' (1942:546). It has to be seen as a rise in the *upper limit* of the envelope surrounding all those phylogenetic pathways that have actually occurred. If evolution 'generates' progress, this rise must be inevitable. To demonstrate this inevitability, Huxley resorts to the kind of reasoning epitomized in the statement: 'It happened that way because it could not have happened any other way' (see Blum 1955:203). Thus the path of progress, culminating in Homo *sapiens,* 'could apparently have pursued no other general course than that which it has historically followed' (Huxley 1942:569; see Williams 1966:21). This reasoning exemplifies what Mandelbaum calls 'the retrospective fallacy': the tendency to view earlier events as though they were controlled by their subsequent outcomes, when at the time of their occurrence any number of other outcomes might have been equally probable (Mandelbaum 1971:134–5). The appearance of mankind, as of any other species, was of course the precipitate of a long chain of evolutionary circumstances. Had the circumstances been significantly different, man would probably never have evolved. But there is no reason, instrinsic to the mechanism of variation under natural selection, why he ever *should* have evolved. And if the result was not inevitable, nor was the process leading up to it.

There remains the problem of whether there is any objective basis for the ranking of organisms into relatively 'higher' and 'lower' forms. Darwin felt that in principle there should be, and yet he despaired of applying it in practice: 'Who will decide whether a cuttlefish be higher than a bee?' (1872:290). The focus is usually on attributes such as complexity of internal organization, freedom from environmental control (or capacity to control the environment), powers of intellect, 'the ability to perceive the environment, and to integrate, co-ordinate and react flexibly to what is perceived' (Ayala 1974:352). These are all attributes in which, by common consent, human beings excel. It would seem, then, that the choice of our criteria of progress makes human eminence a foregone conclusion, reflecting an 'anthropocentric consideration of the data bearing on the history of life' (Williams 1966:35; see also Simpson 1974:48–9). Huxley anticipates this objection and seeks to counter it by what might be called 'the argument of the philosophical jellyfish'. Jellyfish can do some things that we cannot. If a philosophical jellyfish were to rewrite the history of evolution, would it not focus on the unique capabilities of its kind as an index of general advance, placing itself at the top of the scale and mankind somewhere near the bottom (see Midgley 1978:160)? Huxley answers with a resounding negative. The wretched jellyfish, contemplating man, would have to admit that it is indeed up a 'degenerate blind alley', from which there exists no possibility of escape (Huxley 1942:565). We, by contrast, hold the future of progressive evolution in our hands. This is all uncomfortably close to the kind of rhetoric put out a century ago by 'civilized men' about 'savages' (who, unlike the jellyfish, *are* able to philosophize and therefore have a right of reply). In any case, a jellyfish properly versed in Darwinian theory would certainly not be justified in coming to the conclusion Huxley attributes to it. Which of us is up a blind alley is something that can be judged only in evolutionary hindsight. In the present circumstances, a philosophical jellyfish would have good grounds for pessimism as regards the future of man.

Let us grant, for the moment, that there does exist a valid criterion by which all organisms may be ranked on a scale of general advance. Let us also assume that there are no 'leaps': Therefore to reach its current level an organism must—in the course of its evolutionary history—have passed through a continuous series of intermediary levels. We are forced then to the conclusion that progress *has* occurred. But it is quite another thing to conclude that progress *must* occur. The mechanism of natural selection, as we have shown, links particular historical circumstances to particular consequences. If, in certain lines, progress has taken place, *its cause must be found in the circumstances, not in the mechanism*. As Williams has remarked, 'There is nothing in the basic structure of the theory of natural selection that would suggest the idea of any kind of cumulative progress' (1966:34). I should like, however, to raise the possibility that evolution by natural selection incorporates a kind of ratchet mechanism. This possibility has been suggested by Stebbins in the form of a principle he calls the *conservation of organization* (Stebbins 1969:124–7). Though progressive modifications are certainly not inevitable, and are indeed conspicuous by their extreme rarity, Stebbins argues that once a certain level of organization is achieved in some particular line of descent, variants tending to preserve or raise this level may have a slight edge over those that tend to lower it. Hence what goes up is rather more likely to stay up than to come down. Whether this principle actually operates in organic evolution is an open question. Nevertheless Stebbins feels justified in extending his argument, in true Spencerian fashion, from the evolution of life to the evolution of human society (1969:131–44).

This might be the appropriate point to recall the closing paragraphs of Spencer's colossal *Principles of sociology,* the final volume of which appeared in 1896. The philosopher who, forty years previously, had confidently asserted the law of progress in all things, was now plagued by doubts about his theory and uncertainties for the future (Wiltshire 1978:105–10). 'Absolute optimism' has given way to 'relative optimism', the cosmic process 'brings about retrogression as well as progression', depending on the circumstances. In a remarkable passage as equivocal as Darwin's on the same theme, Spencer appears to renounce the very foundations of his original position:

> Evolution does not imply a latent tendency to improve, everywhere in operation. There is no uniform ascent from lower to higher, but only an occasional production of a form which, in virtue of greater fitness for more complex conditions, becomes capable of a longer life of a more varied kind. And while such higher type begins to dominate over lower types and to spread at their expense, the lower types survive in habitats or modes of life that are not usurped, or are thrust into inferior habitats or modes of life in which they retrogress.
>
> What thus holds with organic types must hold also with types of societies. (1972:261)

One suspects that, were Spencer alive today, he would have found the law of conservation of organization an attractive alternative to the law of progress, offering a way out of the old dilemma: How can progress be necessary if it has occurred with such rarity?

Underlying our entire discussion up to now has been a fundamental opposition between absolute advance 'stage by stage' and advance or adaptation relative to the circumstances, between necessary progress and contingent progress, or between determinate development and indeterminate ('unplanned') diversification. Another way of expressing this opposition would be in terms of the conventional dichotomy between *orthogenesis* and *phylogenesis*. Orthogenesis is congruent with the original meaning of evolution, either in the preformationist sense of a successive unpacking of immanent qualities, or in the epigenetic sense of emergent complexity. It is defined by Teilhard de Chardin as a 'law of controlled complication' (1959:120). Berg's *Nomogenesis, or evolution determined by law* (1926) and Osborn's (1934) theory of 'aristogenesis' are in the same genre. Their resemblance to Spencer's conception of evolutionary progress will at once be apparent. Darwinian evolution, by contrast, is phylogenetic, proceeding along any number of diverging lines, with no consistent direction or fixed target. Phylogenesis is, indeed, a logical corollary of variation under natural selection, necessarily leading to 'the improvement of each organic being in relation to its organic and inorganic conditions of life' (Darwin 1872:61), but not to any absolute standard. It follows that any truly orthogenetic movement in evolution must be established 'without reference to natural selection' (Simpson 1958a:24). If Darwinian theory is accepted, an orthogenetic account of the development of particular lines of descent is clearly out of the question.[6] But might it not still be possible to project the phylogenetic tree against the background of an orthogenetic picture of the evolution of life in general rather than of its particular lines? This possibility rests on one condition: that some force of overall advancement can be specified whose operation is explicable not as a *product* of natural selection, but as a necessary consequence of the same universal properties of life that *constitute* natural selection as a mechanism, that is of inherited variability and reproductive multiplication.

Sahlins (1960) believes he is onto such a force, and since it is invoked as a foundation for the construction of a theory of cultural as well as biological evolution, his ideas command our attention. Living things, he argues, have an inherent tendency to increase their 'thermodynamic accomplishment', in other words the rate at which they are able to capture energy and put it to use in the maintenance of organic structure: 'It is the amount [of energy] so trapped . . . and the degree to which it is raised to a higher state that would seem to be the way that a crab is superior to an amoeba, a goldfish to a crab, a mouse to a goldfish, a man to a mouse' (1960:21). This absolute measure of progress is taken as an index of what Sahlins calls *general* evolution, an overall movement of life from 'lower' to 'higher' forms. Superimposed on this grand (orthogenetic) advance is the *specific* (phylogenetic) evolution of Darwinian descent with modification, which 'is characteristically *relative*' (1960:14). The distinction is illustrated by a diagram, reproduced here as Fig. 1.2. The course of evolution is depicted as a vine whose branching represents divergence into separate phyletic lines but which, through time, has an inherent tendency to climb. A second glance at this diagram will reveal that it presents a most peculiar picture of the evolutionary process. For by the time the mammals had become established, the last protozoa would be about to disappear, whereas birds, reptiles, amphibians, fish and invertebrates would have been long extinct. True, the diagram *is* meant to be schematic. To make it a little less so, a lot of branches would have to be extended more or less horizontally from their existing tips to the time ordinate corresponding to the present. Once that is done, the appearance of the diagram is radically altered, for the propensity to climb would be limited to particular branches, whereas the majority are not moving up at all. Nor is it true that the most recently formed species are necessarily the most 'advanced'. Diversification is proceeding at all levels most of the time, whereas 'upward' movement is extraordinarily rare (Stebbins 1969:120). It is clear that Sahlins's diagram is an insidious piece of visual deception, for by obliterating all lines leading to contemporary 'lower' forms, evolution appears to have a *necessary* upward drift. Yet, as I have pointed out, the coexistence of higher and lower forms is precisely what led Darwin—and ultimately even Spencer—to reject any law of necessary development in evolution. The diagram should really be cast in three dimensions, the third being one of structural divergence, to avoid the erroneous impression that adaptive radiation or 'cladogenesis' necessarily involves differential rates of general 'advance'. Under most circumstances it does not. Such radiation should therefore be projected onto a plane perpendicular to the page, intersecting with it along the horizontal axis of time (Fig. 1.3).

There is, however, a grain of truth in Sahlins's argument. The evolution of life as a whole *is* characterized by a *net* increase in the rate at which energy is harnessed and used in organic maintenance (Lotka 1956[1924]:356–8). Sahlins's mistake is to suppose that such increase necessarily entails the serial replacement of 'lower' by 'higher' forms. This supposition in fact amounts to a special kind of reductionism. The complexity of a living organism cannot be judged by the mean internal complexity of the cells that constitute it, for that would be to ignore the very relationships that make the organism what it is—an *organized* system (Pittendrigh 1958:394). Likewise, recognizing that living nature includes an enormous number and variety of organisms, interacting with one another in highly complex ways, it would be absurd to reduce the level of organization of that living system *as a whole* to an average of the complexity of its individual components or 'forms'. We cannot expect, wrote Lotka, 'to express the basic directional principle of organic evolution in terms of the "organization" or any other property or assemblage of properties of individual species considered separately' (1945:194). And when he found such a principle in the form of an increase in 'the rate of energy flux through the system of organic nature', it was to the *total* system that he referred: 'Nature must be considered as a whole if she is to be understood in detail' (Lotka 1956[1924]:356). Life, in short, consists not only of organisms but also of the relations among them: Therefore if we are to assess its overall advancement, we must add the complexity of organisms in their internal relations to that of their external relations. A necessary advance in the sum of these two components of complexity is perfectly compatible with a contingent advance in either one. It may involve the appearance of 'higher' forms, but it could equally well entail the elaboration of relations between forms at existing levels of complexity, or both processes at once.

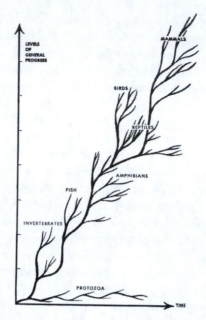

FIG. 1.2 Diversity and progress among major lineages of animal life (schematized). Reproduced, by permission, from Sahlins (1960:17) © University of Michigan Press.

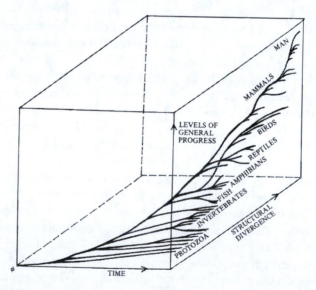

FIG. 1.3 General progress and adaptive radiation in the evolution of animal life. A schematic representation in three dimensions. For clarity, lines of descent leading to terminal extinction have been omitted. All lines indicated end where they intersect the right-hand vertical plane, representing the time transect corresponding to the present.

Ayala (1974:346) has suggested four criteria of general evolutionary advance, all connected to the 'tendency for life to expand' (Simpson 1949:243), or to 'augment itself' (White 1959b:36). Apart from increase in the total rate of energy flux, these are the increase in the total number of species, in the total number of individual organisms and in the total organic biomass. Simply, as more energy is harnessed, a greater amount and diversity of life are supported (Lotka 1945). This expansion can be related to the same properties of living things that underlie the operation of natural selection: their variability and their reproductive potential. The latter ensures that organisms are constantly competing for limited resources, and the former ensures that any opening, however narrow, will be 'snapped up' as it appears in the economy of nature. Together these properties account for the apparent 'opportunism' (Simpson 1949:160–86) of biological evolution. Living nature becomes ever more tightly packed, as though by 'ten thousand sharp wedges . . . driven inwards by incessant blows' (Darwin 1950[1859]:58). The concomitant diversification and multiplication of species generate increasingly complex sets of relations between the individual inhabitants of any particular natural domain or country. Thus the emergence, in the course of evolution, of 'higher' levels of organization is as inevitable as the adaptation of particular forms under natural selection. But this does *not* entail the displacement of simpler by more complex forms. The evolution of 'higher' forms could be regarded more appropriately as an *internalization* than as an augmentation of complexity, amounting to a convergent shift in the locus of control from the field of the organism's external relations to that of its internal relations (for a rather similar point, see Bateson 1973:332). Since the relative freedom from direct environmental control conferred by complex internal organization is balanced by a corresponding *simplification* in the field of external relations, the total organizational advance may be negligible or even zero.

As the description of a net progressive movement throughout organic nature *in toto,* Spencer's characterization of evolution—from incoherent homogeneity to coherent heterogeneity—may still have a lot going for it. Moreover, his understanding that this evolutionary movement consists in the sum of relations both *extrinsic* and *intrinsic* to the individual organisms (or 'superorganisms') undergoing adaptation is remarkably close to our own (Spencer 1972:121–2). It was in its extension from the organic to the inorganic domain that Spencer's evolutionary synthesis eventually fell apart, exploded by the second law of thermodynamics. For according to this law, already well established in Spencer's day, the evolution of the cosmos is proceeding towards states of increasing entropy, or degrees of disorganization. The process of life is able to run against this tide only by 'continually sucking orderliness from its environment' (Schrödinger 1944:75), so that on balance the cosmic trend continues relentlessly on the road to random disorder or—more graphically—total chaos.[7] But to remain with Spencer, I shall confine my attention to the organic world, the baseline from which he—and so many subsequently—have constructed propositions about the 'super–organic' or social domain of life. Having already set out the pre-misses of Darwinian theory, the distinctive aspects of Spencer's brand of evolutionism should be more clearly apparent.

Like Darwin, Spencer readily accepted the uniformitarianism of Lyell. In this he was quite explicit: 'True interpretations of all natural processes, organic and inorganic, that have gone on in past times habitually trace them to causes still in action. It is thus in Geology: it is thus in Biology: it is thus in Philology' (1874, III:122–3). And, as we would expect of Spencer, he claimed it to be thus in sociology too. Again, like Darwin but in opposition to Lyell, Spencer's uniformitarianism was combined with a commitment to the irreversibility of evolution. Yet this was irreversibility of a very different kind, and the implications of the difference are considerable. For Spencer, evolution describes a succession of internal states of a total system undergoing a process of development. Based on the 'law of progress', that 'every active force produces more than one change—every cause produces more than one effect' (Spencer 1972:47), this development takes the form of an indefinite, exponential multiplication—a kind of cascade. There is, in Spencer's words, 'an ever-growing complication of things'. And as the analogy with organic growth would suggest, the process of evolution is conceived to be essentially *eventless* (Bock 1980:39). In Darwin's conception, by contrast, every organism is regarded as a unique, isolated entity, and its appearance as a discrete event. Evolution then consists of an accumulating concatenation of such entities and events.[8] The semblance of continuity is created by running through the sequence on a time-scale that vastly exceeds the reproductive life-span of each individual, just as the continuous motion of figures on a film screen is achieved by projecting in rapid succession a very large number of separate images, each minutely different from those both preceding and following.

To generalize: Process is to event as continuity is to discontinuity, and change exists only in the opposition between the two. Either we start as did Spencer with process (as a property of the whole) and discover change by cutting it up into events, or we start as did Darwin with particulate events and discover change by aggregating them into process. To talk of 'events of change' or 'processes of change', as though change were *inherent* in either one or the other, is meaningless. The fundamental importance of this point will become apparent in the chapters that follow. I should like now to return for a moment to the significance of 'irreversibility'. In Darwinian terms, as I have shown, this could be rendered more precisely as irrevocability: connoting the *non-recurrence* of particular entities, or strings of entities, in the total sequence. But if we adopt the perspective of Spencer, irreversibility implies a developmental process that cannot be run backwards, any more than an organism can regress from maturity to infancy. In other words it is *unidirectional* or progressive. Obviously these latter concepts cannot characterize the irreversibility of a sequence that lacks consistent directionality; moreover Darwinian evolution admits the possibility of absolute retrogression as well as progression, and is therefore reversible in Spencerian terms. But conversely, the notion of non-recurrence makes no sense in the context of a focus on the continuity of process rather than the discontinuity of events. As Lotka has stated most forcefully, if we are to discover in evolution not merely a 'changeful sequence' but an overriding principle of directionality, we must cease to regard each component form as a separate entity, and instead attend to 'the evolving system as a whole' (1945:194). The crucial point is that for Spencer, irreversibility is a property of just such an 'evolving whole', inscribed in its developmental laws, whereas for Darwin it follows from a property of the parts, namely their individuality or uniqueness. The contrary meanings of irreversibility, and derivations of change, stem from a more fundamental opposition between holism and atomism.

Another problem is raised by the causal determinacy of Spencer's law of progress, which contrasts radically with the indeterminacy built into Darwin's principle of variation under natural selection. It is easy to see how a movement that is irreversible and indeterminate may go on indefinitely, just as a man lost in a fog can keep on walking without ever retracing his steps. But how can this open-ended view be applied to a movement that is assumed to be both determinate, directed and progressive? So long as the advance is conceived to be merely quantitative, the solution is simple. If we could attach a numerical value to an attribute such as complexity or orderliness, presumably it could increase towards infinity, under the guidance of constant laws. The problem arises as soon as we begin to think of evolutionary advance in *qualitative* terms, and especially if we attach to these terms a moral evaluation. In extending his principle of evolution to the social domain Spencer did both these things. The movement is traced from 'barbarous tribes' to industrial nations, and good conduct is distinguished from bad on the grounds of whether it is 'relatively less' or 'relatively more evolved' (Spencer 1907:19). The difficulty is that a qualitative series of evolutionary stages or levels must necessarily conform to a *finite plan* (Hirst 1976:25). To demonstrate the necessity of progress through these levels we have to know, or pretend to know, what the plan is. And this implies that any philosopher who thinks himself to be so positioned as to perceive the plan, as did Spencer, must also suppose that the course of evolution at that position is virtually complete, and that he and his contemporaries are 'on the point of opening the last envelope' (Burrow 1966:227). At most, there is but one more stage to come, the seeds of which are already implanted in the present.

Thus in shifting from a quantitative and physical to a qualitative and moral conception of absolute advance, the exponential trajectory of successive differentiations is replaced by one that levels off towards a plateau of perfection, or what Spencer called a state of 'equilibration', at which point human beings—the most advanced products of organic evolution—become completely adjusted to life in society (Spencer 1972:12–13). The adjustment was conceived in plainly utilitarian terms, such that every individual can fulfil his own interests without hindering the fulfilment of the interests of others. It was in this respect that Spencer's understanding of society was so very different from that of Comte, and subsequently Durkheim. The perfectly social state, for Spencer, implied the very *elimination* of that overbearing, institutional presence Comte and Durkheim identified as society, and to which they thought individual interests subordinate. This is a contrast of critical importance, to which we shall return (see Chapter 6). My present concern is to stress the incongruity between two very different ways of conceiving evolutionary progress, both of which Spencer appeared to hold simultaneously. One stressed ultimate, material causality, operating uniformly through all time to generate limitless directional change. The other, however, emphasized the final cause, the inevitable march of progress towards a morally desirable end-state that *at some time* (not too far distant) must be achieved. The existence of this contradiction in Spencer's thought allows one authority (Hirst 1976:31) to claim that he held a 'teleological conception of evolution', whilst another (Burrow 1966:206) can assert that 'to imagine Spencer as a teleological evolutionist, one would have to reverse the whole order of his ideas'. Burrow is correct in that it was Spencer's faith in ultimate causality that led him to formulate his evolutionary laws in the first place. But the appearance of teleology, of purposive direction in the workings of nature, was a logical corollary of the injection of morality into his scheme of progressive development (Wiltshire 1978:206–7). Since moral differences can only be in kind, the effect is to convert a quantitative scale into a qualitative rank order, and hence to conjure up the *telos* of an embodied plan or purpose. The contradictory appeal to both ultimate and final causality inevitably follows from any attempt to construct a system of ethics on a foundation of physical laws.

The Darwinian boast is once and for all to have banished teleology from natural history, opening the way for a purely mechanistic interpretation of living systems (Montalenti 1974). The two-stage process of variation and selection can account for the most characteristic property of organisms, that each is 'endowed with a purpose or project' (Monod 1972:20), without our having to suppose that this project existed as an idea (or 'entelechy'; see Dreisch 1914) prior to its material realization. Nor need it be supposed that the organism is fashioned expressly *in order that* its project might be executed—as a Creator might design forms to implement a divine plan, or as a human being might construct tools to do a job. Pittendrigh (1958) has suggested that the term 'teleonomic' be adopted to describe the inherent 'end-directedness' of living things, to avoid confusion between the recognition of this property and its (teleological) explanation in terms of final causes. The term has since received widespread acceptance (e.g. Williams 1966:258; Monod 1972:20; Montalenti 1974:10; Mayr 1982:48–9). Mayr goes on to make a further distinction between teleonomic and *teleomatic* processes, 'in which a definite end is reached strictly as a consequence of physical laws' (1982:49)—as when a stone falls to the ground in conformity with the law of gravity. It was precisely this kind of process that Spencer had in mind when he originally formulated his law of progress, and it led him explicitly to reject teleology in favour of an emphasis on the *mechanics* of evolution (1972:89). From this point of view, an evolving system is no more programmed to seek a target than is the falling stone.[9] Yet paradoxically, teleology is reintroduced 'by the back door' when the parallel is drawn between evolution and organic growth, and it becomes a pervasive part of an account that goes on to assume all evolution to be change for the better.

Spencer presented the world with a picture of evolution that was absolute and determinate, its laws underwritten by an 'Unknowable' or (more quaintly) 'Inscrutable Existence' (1972:216). Darwinian theory replaced the determinacy of the unknowable with the indeterminacy of revealed variability. Progress became relative, the future uncertain; beyond the known, observable world lay not a vital force but rather an existential void. No wonder it was deeply unsettling to those with serious religious convictions. It continues to trouble biologists, theologians and social philosophers. There have been many attempts to discover, in the evolutionary process, some objective principle of development by which mankind might judge its past progress, present conduct, and future prospects. 'We must accept the direction of evolution as good', Waddington assures us, 'simply because it *is* good' (1942:41). Julian Huxley is still more emphatic. The facts of evolution, pulsing through time from the swirling nebulae through the biosphere to the higher faculties of mind (or in an apt parody, 'from gas to genius'), speak out as commandments to fulfil our cosmic duty: '"Stand there", they say, "and do thus and thus"' (Huxley 1957:100). And in *The phenomenon of man* (1959), Teilhard de Chardin takes the same idea to its logical extreme in his fantastic (and parading as science, utterly outrageous) prophecy of a transcendent consciousness converging ineluctably on a final 'omega point'.

It would be wrong to regard the ponderous optimism of these statements as a symptom of supreme moral confidence. Those convinced of the overwhelming superiority of their world have no need to hope for better things to come. The promise of evolutionary optimism holds its greatest attraction for those struggling to regain a sense of destiny in a world that seems to be spiralling out of control; one might add, however, that to engage in such ethereal struggle is by and large the privilege of the affluent, who can afford to brood over the affairs of the cosmos whilst the rest of us get on with the urgent business of life. In the nineteenth century, Spencer's brand of evolutionism was a balm to 'the malaise of a society transforming itself by industrialization with a speed hitherto unprecedented in the history of the world' (Burrow 1966:99). And in modern times the experiences of two world wars, followed by the terrifying prospect of nuclear conflict, have bred a resurgence of evolutionary prophecy with a similarly auspicious message. As every advance in human knowledge appears to unleash a greater potential for destruction, we may expect to hear a lot more of the same. At least the prophets will not be proved wrong, for if they are, there will be no one left to tell them—except, perhaps, a surviving jellyfish.

2

MANKIND ASCENDING

The thesis which I venture to sustain, within limits, is simply this, that the savage state in some measure represents an early condition of mankind, out of which the higher culture has gradually been developed or evolved, by processes still in regular operation as of old, the result showing that, on the whole, progress has far prevailed over relapse.

Tylor, Primitive culture

Thus the grandfather of modern anthropology, in a work that launched the systematic study of human cultural forms. We have it on Tylor's own admission, in the preface to the second edition of his magisterial *Primitive culture,* that his ideas were conceived and developed independently of the work of both Darwin and Spencer. The direction of influence was rather in reverse: Darwin cited Tylor with approval in his *Descent of man* (1874:221), whereas Spencer was accused—by none other than Tylor himself—of having virtually plagiarized his ideas (Stocking 1968:95). My concern in the first part of this chapter will be to demonstrate the fundamentally non-Darwinian structure of Tylor's argument, and to lay to rest once and for all the belief that the evolutionary paradigm in anthropology rested on an improper extension to the domain of culture of biological principles derived from the *Origin of species.* Much of the responsibility for this misapprehension must lie with Franz Boas, whose reaction against orthodox doctrines of progressive evolution current in the late nineteenth century stamped the next fifty years of American anthropology. In an influential statement, he declared that the investigations of Tylor, Spencer and others were 'stimulated by the work of Darwin' and that their fundamental ideas could be understood 'only as an application of the theory of biological evolution to mental phenomena' (Boas 1911:175). The error of this statement has been amplified through its frequent repetition, for example by Lowie (1921:52), Lévi–Strauss (1968:3) and many others (see White 1959a:106–7).

Yet paradoxically it was Boas and his followers who were primarily responsible for the introduction of a genuinely Darwinian perspective into cultural anthropology (Harris 1968:295–6). That they did precisely what they falsely criticized their opponents for doing creates confusion enough. But this is compounded by the observation that Darwin himself, turning his attention from living nature in its entirety to consider specifically the evolution of his own kind, proceeded to endorse the progressive evolutionism of Tylor and Spencer almost to a fault. In the second part of this chapter I shall address the puzzling question of how he came to adopt a position on the descent of man so fundamentally at odds with the argument set out in *The origin of species*. There are, as a I shall show, two ways in which the theory of biological evolution can be applied to humanity and culture: by *extension* and by *analogy*. To adopt the former is to place mankind firmly alongside other animals and to treat culture as a product or offshoot of human nature, ultimately explicable in purely biological terms. This was Darwin's approach, and it led him to regard cultural ideas and practices as instrumental adjuncts of the human organism, as good for their purpose in the furtherance of life as the brain that produced them. Since the cultural thus complements the organic, so Tylor's project in *Primitive culture,* to delineate the stages of cultural progress, appeared to complement Darwin's project in *The descent of man,* to demonstrate a corresponding improvement in the innate faculties of mind, brought about through natural selection.

The attribution of cultural differences to hereditary variations in mental organization became the principal target of Boas's critical attack on the Darwinian legacy. What he found so improper about the extension of biological ideas to culture was the materialist premiss that ways of thinking could be reduced to the mechanism of the human brain. But in rejecting this premiss, and asserting the independence of culturally patterned behaviour from hereditary constraint, he unwittingly laid the foundations for the construction of a history of cultural forms *analogous* to the Darwinian picture of descent with modification in the domain of living nature. Thus the transference of the evolutionary paradigm of Darwin's *Origin* from species to cultures depended on the recognition of the autonomy of cultural phenomena from their material matrix in human organisms. This, in turn, entailed the adoption of a view of mind that ran counter to Darwin's. It ceases to be a producer and becomes a mere container of cultural ideas: The history of culture is inscribed in the human mind just as the history of species is inscribed in the materials of nature. The mind, in other words, is no longer agent but medium; culture is correspondingly elevated from the status of an instrument to that of a director of human purposes, substituting for natural dispositions rather than serving to put them into effect. This founding opposition is still with us, notably in some of the most recent attempts to 'biologize' culture: on the one hand by positing a cultural analogue of the gene, on the other by treating culture as a phenotypic expression of a genetically constructed biogram. And it is no surprise to find exponents of the latter view coming out with a theory of human evolution just as deterministic and progressive as Darwin's in *The descent of man*.

With that résumé of the general argument that follows, let us return to Tylor and to his *Primitive culture*.

Lines and stages

The idea that mankind is engaged in a more or less uniform ascent from bestial savagery to rational civilization has a long and distinguished pedigree. It was not because of any novelty that Tylor found it necessary to reassert this idea, in stridently polemical tones, but rather because it had come under sustained attack during the mid-nineteenth century from the advocates of degeneration.[1] Their thesis was that human beings originally had been installed, thanks to divine intervention, at some recognizable level of civilization, from which some groups had risen to their present pre-eminence and others fallen to a condition almost on a par with that of wild animals. Tylor's view, to the contrary, was that primitive society stood not at the end but at the beginning of civilization. He did not, of course, deny that many a civilization has declined and disintegrated, but to liken the state of its wretched survivors to the pristine condition of savagery was, he said, 'like comparing a ruined house to a builder's yard' (1871, I:38). Primitive men were taking the first steps in the construction of the edifice of culture, a construction, moreover, that was to proceed according to a prescribed plan. Thus the various 'grades' of culture were supposed to unfold in conformity with absolute developmental laws 'as definite as those which govern the motion of waves, the combination of acids and bases, and the growth of plants and animals' (1871, I:2). Looking around the world, one could observe the cultural edifice at various stages of completion, and by placing these stages in serial order, it would be possible to reconstruct the entire process by which it was built up.

It was as commonplace in Tylor's day as in our own to invoke biological principles as guides to the arrangement of cultural facts (e.g. Mason 1887:534). But they were the principles of a biology steeped in essentialist taxonomy and Lamarckian orthogenesis, still poised on the threshold of the Darwinian revolution. That this was so in Tylor's case is abundantly evident from the pages of *Primitive culture*. We need only reflect on the central position he accorded to what was known as the 'comparative method' and on the importance he attached to the evidence of 'survivals'. Returning to Fig. 1.1. B, which presents in schematic form the essentials of Lamarck's transformism, we recall that if populations of living things are conceived to be travelling—through the generations—along the same developmental trajectory, then the succession of forms assumed in the past will be translated into the diversity of forms apparent in the present. Substituting customs for species, we arrive at the proposition that if all human groups are similarly on the same path, towards what Tylor would call increasing 'degrees of culture', the contemporary customs of supposedly more primitive peoples may legitimately be compared—even identified—with those practised in the remote past by the ancient ancestors of the more 'civilized' peoples of today. Comparison could therefore provide a basis for the discovery of evolutionary laws (Tylor 1871, I:19–20).

There is, however, an important difference between this view and the standard Lamarckian picture. For if we suppose that all mankind shares a common origin, as well as a common developmental pathway, the differences observed among contemporary peoples must be due to variations in the *rate* of progress. 'Savages' are not the latest to step onto the moving staircase; *their* staircase is moving more slowly, if it has not ground to a halt (Lévi-Strauss 1953:18–19). Moreover, although Tylor is generally content to disregard variation between individuals or subgroups within a population, treating all who are on the same level of culture as essentially alike (1871, I:9–12), he does recognize that some exceptional individuals may be left behind on the road to progress, and that whole groups may—in their lighter moments—perform a mock replay of their past condition. The old woman who weaves with a hand-loom in the days of the flying shuttle is a 'case of survival'; so too is that part of the 'serious business of ancient society' that has sunk 'into the sport of later generations' (1871, I:15). Tylor uses the evidence of survivals, as a palaeontologist uses fossils, to reconstruct the sequence of forms *within* a line of descent, so as to provide independent confirmation for the existence of parallels *between* lines, which in turn was felt to justify the application of the comparative method.

This brings us to a point on which Tylor has often been misunderstood. A line of descent connects a population with its ancestors. Mankind, for Tylor, could be divided up into a large number of discrete populations, for which he used interchangeably the terms 'people', 'tribe', 'society' and 'nation'. Yet in his *Primitive culture,* he quite explicitly set out *not* to write a history of populations. His concern, in his own words, was with 'Culture, the history, not of tribes or nations, but of the condition of knowledge, religion, art, custom, and the like among them' (1871, I:5). I shall return in due course to Tylor's concept of culture. For the present I wish merely to note that whereas populations were viewed in the plural, culture always appears in the singular form (Stocking 1968:203). To trace the history of culture is like mapping the course of a road along which are marching successive cohorts (populations) of an advancing army (mankind), some in the vanguard, others lagging behind, with some individuals (cases of survival) falling by the wayside. At one point, Tylor defines his ethnographic project as the classification and arrangement of the phenomena of culture, 'stage by stage, in a probable order of evolution' (1871, I:3). This is like placing every cultural object in position on the road, so that the course resembles one of those board games in which each square contains a set of instructions that players must carry out before their pieces are able to move on. But many pages later, Tylor again sets out the task of ethnography, apparently in a quite different way. This time it is 'to work out as systematically as possible a scheme of the evolution of culture along its many lines' (1871, I:19). It might well be supposed that Tylor is here 'depicting the multi-linear character of cultural development' (White 1959a:119), as though each line represented a branch of a phylogenetic tree. This, however, would be a profound misunderstanding of Tylor's position. Let my try to show why.

The idea that the course of cultural evolution can be represented as a branching tree, bush or vine rests on a now very well worn analogy between human cultures (conceived in the plural) and the Darwinian conception of organic species. 'Cultures', wrote Boas in 1932, 'differ like so many species, or perhaps genera, of animals' (1948:254). I am not sure whether this was the first explicit statement of the culture–species analogy. At any rate it has been forcefully reiterated by Murdock (1945:136, 1959:131–2) and Childe (1951:171), and more recently by Sahlins and Service (1960). In the context of this analogy, the concepts of culture and population are indissolubly linked. For if a species consists of a population of organisms each bearing a particular combination of genetically transmitted traits drawn from a common pool, so by analogy a culture must consist of a population of human beings sharing a common heritage of learned attributes. Though it is common to refer to the heritage itself as 'a culture', it has no real existence except as the aggregate of elements actually carried by the individuals of a population at a particular time. 'The culture', as Lowie put it, 'is a living reality only as mirrored in its bearers; the two are inseparable' (1937:269). To pursue the analogy: Every culture, like every species, appears as a unique historical precipitate, from which it follows that the comparative method is an invalid basis for reconstructing the past (Boas 1948:270–80). It is as though, rather than marching at different rates along the same road, the cohorts of our human army had fanned out in all directions, each following no marked course but the line of least resistance. Therefore, the history of culture cannot be other than the meandrine routes actually taken by particular populations. Again in the words of Lowie: 'The singular order of events by which [our own civilization] has come into being provides no schedule for the itinerary of alien cultures' (1921:427). And if the latter left no trace of their devious journeys in the record of the past, we have no way of telling at what point they diverged from a supposedly common ancestral path.

Tylor's separation of the history of populations from cultural evolution, the fact that he never wrote of culture in the plural form, and his reliance on the comparative method should all lead us to suspect that by the evolution of culture 'along its many lines' he cannot have meant the divergent adaptations of culture-bearing populations. Whatever the line of culture may be, it cannot be equivalent to the line of descent. A vital clue to Tylor's meaning may be found in his own use of the organic analogy. For he sets out to compare the naturalist's species not with whole cultures but with separable *traits* of culture. Thus 'to the ethnographer, the bow and arrow is a species, the habit of flattening children's skulls is a species, the practice of reckoning numbers by tens is a species' (1871, I:7). And so a catalogue of 'all the items of the general life of a people' is analogous to the flora and fauna of a particular district. It is worth noting that, some seventy years later, A. L. Kroeber made precisely the same point. Indeed it underlay his attempt to establish and correlate 'natural' and 'cultural' areas, the former defined by local associations of organic species, the latter by local associations of traits. Kroeber's remarks are highly pertinent to our present discussion, since he sets up an explicit contrast between the two forms of the organic analogy:

A particular culture is not comparable to a species, even though the members of any one society are given, by their common culture, a certain likeness of behaviour somewhat comparable outwardly to the likeness of the members of one species. . . . Rather, it is ecological aggregates to which cultures can be compared: local associations of species of diverse origin. . . . The nearest counterpart of the organic species in the field of culture is perhaps the culture trait or trait cluster but not the culture entity or whole culture. It is the species that is repetitive in its individuals; the trait that is repetitive in its exemplars. (1952:93)

Notice that Kroeber employs 'culture' in its plural and relativistic sense, and not in Tylor's unitary, progressive sense. Notwithstanding this difference, the effect of the analogy that both Tylor and Kroeber propose is to disengage the evolution of culture from the lines of descent of its human bearers. Thus the lines of culture connect not populations with their ancestors but particular traits with their forerunners. Each line consists of a sequence of such 'ethnographic species' that have arisen one from another in a determinate order. Of the possibility of such linear development Tylor had no doubt, for 'it is recognized by our most familiar knowledge' (1871, I:13). But again, his view of development was Lamarckian rather than Darwinian.[2] Recall that, for Darwin, a species is a population of unique individuals, that each individual is the potential founder of a new variety, and each variety the potential source of a new species. On the Tylor–Kroeber analogy, the counterpart of the individual organism would be one particular exemplar of the trait: a certain bow and arrow, a flattened skull, a specimen of decimal counting. Although in the macabre 'species' of flattened skulls, no two may be quite alike, Tylor actually identifies the species with the practice or *habit;* in other words with a particular instruction or set of instructions that underlie each and every instance of behavioural expression. Likewise every bow and arrow is constructed on a template that includes certain preconceived and invariable elements, by which it may be recognized as a representative of its class, regardless of the identity of its maker.

In short, to compare traits with biological species is to adopt an essentialist concept of the species, whose rejection we owe primarily to Darwin. This point was recognized by Franz Boas as long ago as 1887, in an exchange of views with Otis T. Mason. It was wrong, Boas argued, to regard each 'ethnological specimen' as a manifestation of some essential type analogous to the Linnaean species or genus. Such classificatory divisions are mere abstractions; the reality with which we deal consists of individual objects. Referring explicitly to Darwinian teaching, Boas wrote:

It is only since the development of the evolutional theory that it became clear that the object of study is the individual, not abstractions from the individual under observation. We have to study each ethnological specimen individually in its history and in its medium. . . . In ethnology, all is individuality. (1974:62, 66)

Modern readers dismayed by Boas's reference to items of culture as ethnological specimens might bear in mind that his dispute with Mason was ostensibly about the best way to arrange display cases in a museum. Should each case contain a diversity of objects created by a single population, representative of its particular 'culture' (Boas), or should it contain examples of a particular type of object collected from diverse populations, representative of a *stage* of culture through which all were presumed to have passed (Mason)?[3]

This question neatly encapsulates the most fundamental difference between the Boasian concept of culture-history and the Tylorian view represented here by Mason. For Boas, the uniqueness of the object is ultimately derived from the individuality of the human being who made it, which in turn is a property of that person's entire constitution as the bearer of a particular culture (Lowie 1937:142; Stocking 1968:156). Therefore to comprehend an object 'in its history' is to place it on the line of descent connecting its maker with his predecessors; to comprehend it 'in its medium' is to regard it as just one expression of that integrated cluster or pattern of elements constituting the 'culture as a whole'. Again, the organic analogy may help to clarify the point. As we saw in the preceding chapter, the biological uniqueness of the individual lies in the fact that each carries a distinct combination of genetic instructions drawn from a pool of gradually changing composition common to the species. Similarly the individual 'culture-bearer' could be regarded as a unique assemblage of cultural instructions derived from a common repertoire. As Kroeber and Kluckhohn have remarked, 'The cultural heritage of each individual is unique, even though abstractly the total cultural heritage is available to all' (1952:184). The variability, whether genetic or cultural, among the individuals of a population depends on the multiplicity of ways in which large numbers of elementary instructions may be combined or constructed into complete, integrated templates. And this variability is a condition for the diversification of species or cultures, that is for the 'branchiness' of the Darwinian tree.

Returning to Tylor's conception of the 'ethnographic species': Since each corresponds to a single instruction, it follows that diversification on the Darwinian model is impossible. Individuals, as Kroeber pointed out, are here the exemplars rather than the bearers of cultural traits. Hence the appearance of every novel trait, far from introducing—like a genetic mutation—further potential for diversification *within* a species (of culture-bearers), brings into existence an entirely new species (of ethnological specimens). A 'line of culture' must therefore consist of a chainlike succession of such species, running the whole course of cultural evolution. Yet whilst it is conceivable that one kind of hunting weapon may be replaced by another more effective kind, that one form of myth, belief or rite may give way to another, or that one system of counting may be succeeded by another, it is also obvious that, for example, bows and arrows do not give rise to flattened skulls or concepts of number. Equally obvious is that no group of people can live solely by hunting, reciting myths and counting on their fingers. They need perhaps to call on these faculties, and surely on many more besides. There cannot, in consequence, be just *one* line of culture, analogous to Lamarck's temporalized chain of being. We should rather envisage a whole *bundle* of lines. Thus neither the chain nor the branching tree or vine constitutes an appropriate image of cultural evolution, as Tylor conceived it. What he had in mind was something more like a multistranded cable.

The picture is complicated to some extent by Tylor's recognition that his ethnographic species 'tend to run widely into varieties' (1871, I:13). For when it comes to the distinction between the species and the variety, his account becomes confused and contradictory; what appear as species in one context are said to be varieties in another. Moreover he fails to discriminate, as the logic of his argument requires, between 'syntagmatic' variation *along* a line and 'paradigmatic' differentiation *between* lines. As an example of the former we have the technological series from wheel-lock to flintlock to percussion-lock in the history of firearms; an example of the latter is the division of myths into those of sunrise and sunset, eclipse, earthquake and so on (1871, I:7, 13–14). As this second example reveals, what at first glance appears as one line or strand of culture, consisting of the successive forms of myth, may on closer inspection be seen to be composed of a number of fibres corresponding to the various and complementary types of myth. Each of these fibres, too, if examined in yet more detail, may resolve into a cluster of still finer threads. There are, in other words, lines within lines, and the process of discrimination can go on virtually without limit to reveal, in a cross-section of the entire cable, a hierarchy of classificatory orders (Fig. 2.1).[4] The crucial point, however, is that the lines of culture do not cleave or blend together. Each runs its own course, appearing here and there, in particular moments of its development, among particular peoples.

I mentioned in the preceding chapter the distinction Sahlins has drawn between 'general evolution' as an overall progressive movement, and 'specific evolution' as the divergence, through adaptive modification, of particular lines of descent. The distinction is supposed to apply equally in the domains of both biology and culture. With regard to the latter, Sahlins actually takes his cue from Tylor who—he says—'laid out the study of cultural evolution both "stage by stage" as well as "along its many lines"', and in so doing recognized 'the dual character of the evolutionary process' (Sahlins 1960:12). I hope to have made it clear that this interpretation is grossly in error. Not only does it set up a dichotomy that Tylor never intended through the juxtaposition of expressions that, in his text, are widely separated, but more fundamentally it rests on a confusion between lines of descent connecting successive populations of culture-bearing individuals and lines of culture connecting the exemplars of successive traits. Evolution 'along its many lines' does not stand in complementary opposition to evolution 'stage by stage', but is another way of expressing the *same thing*. Each stage is simply a segment of the cable made up by all the lines of culture, so that the ethnological method consists in placing every cultural art or institution 'at its proper stage in a line of evolution' (Tylor 1875:123). Equally erroneous, however, is the claim so often advanced by commentators blandly dismissive of nineteenth-century evolutionism that Tylor envisaged a universal sequence of *particular cultures* and that his view is therefore invalidated by the documented facts

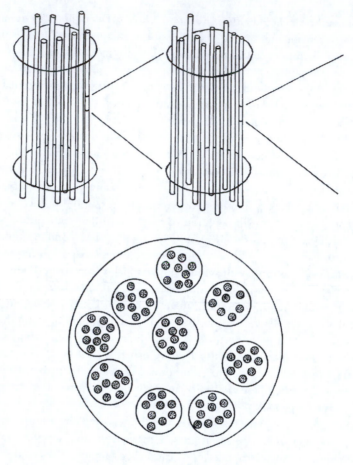

FIG. 2.1 The fibrous strands of culture: a schematic representation of Tylor's conception of ethnographic species. The *upper left-hand diagram* shows one segment of the cable, corresponding to a given stage of general cultural progress. Each vertical rod corresponds to one of the major lines of culture. When a segment of one of the rods is enlarged, it resolves likewise into a number of finer strands, as shown at the *top right,* each of which similarly resolves on further magnification into still finer threads. The *lower diagram* shows the cable as it might appear in cross-section.

of cultural diffusion (Steward 1955:14; Murdock 1959:127). We need only recall that Tylor's stage-by-stage arrangement was not of cultures but of 'the phenomena of Culture' (1871, I:3) and that it was his recognition of diffusion that led him—and subsequently Kroeber—to compare species with traits rather than peoples. Whether a certain trait happened to enter the cultural repertoire of a particular population through independent invention or diffusion was for Tylor an open question, to be answered in each case on the basis of available evidence (Lowie 1937:75), and did not in any way affect his conviction that mankind has advanced along the road to civilization (Bidney 1953:198–202). How else could he have written, with equal conviction, that 'civilization is a plant much oftener propagated than developed' (Tylor 1871, I:48)?

To grasp the essence of Tylor's project, it might be helpful to return to the image of the board game. For to reveal the evolution of culture is to ascertain the course, quite apart from the ways particular counters (peoples) may move along it—whether forwards, backwards or sideways. We have found that the course consists of an innumerable array of threads, all oriented in the direction of advance. Every human population, as it advances, hooks onto a particular combination of threads, weaving them into an intricate pattern that corresponds to the relativistic conception of its 'culture'. Invention and diffusion are properties not of the course but of the manner by which people arrive at particular points on it: whether by a gradual movement or by a short cut, whether by keeping along the same lines or by 'crossing over' (for to say that a people can switch from one line of culture to another is just another way of expressing the familiar idea of diffusion, that a trait can switch from one line of descent to another). Since the course is, in theory, already laid out, every invention is really only a discovery—the realization of an immanent possibility—and diffusion is merely discovery at second hand. 'The office of our thought', Tylor wrote, 'is to develop, to combine, and to derive, rather than to create' (1871, I:248). Hence the debate that dominated anthropology in the early part of this century, between diffusionists and evolutionists, rested on a misconceived identification of evolution with independent invention. As Bidney long ago pointed out, 'It is possible to arrange a series of culture traits, abstracted from diverse cultures and areas, in a hierarchical order, but this would not necessarily imply their actual realization in the culture history of any given society in that particular sequence' (1953:217–18). To lay out the course is not to prejudge the movements of the players, and Tylor never suggested that it was.

Where an analogy has been posited between organic and cultural evolution, on the Darwinian model of descent with modification, the qualification is invariably added that in the phylogenetic tree of human culture, branches grow together as well as diverge (Kroeber 1948:259–61; see Fig. 2.2). Thus in his explicit rejection of orthogenesis in favour of a phylogenetic account of cultural evolution, Boas noted that 'in place of a simple line of evolution there appears to be a multiplicity of converging and diverging lines' (1974:34). One staunch advocate of the Darwinian analogue was the archaeologist V. G. Childe. 'With certain modification', he argued, 'the Darwinian formula of "variation, heredity, adaptation and selection" can be transferred from organic to social [cultural] evolution, and is even more intelligible in the latter domain than in the former.' Yet for all that, 'in fine . . . the analogy between cultural evolution and organic evolution breaks down' (Childe 1951:171). Why? Because of the process of diffusion, which depends on the very criterion by which the cultural may be distinguished from the organic: its potential for transmission to others besides biological offspring. Individuals of one species cannot acquire genetic material from individuals of another, if each constitutes a reproductive isolate. But the boundary surrounding

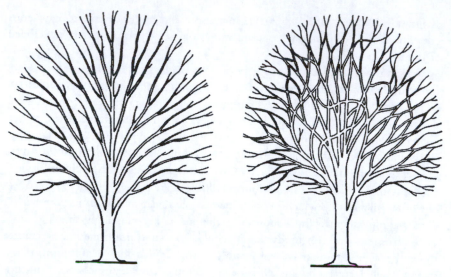

FIG. 2.2 'The tree of life and the tree of the knowledge of good and evil—that is, of human culture'. From *Anthropology,* new edition, revised, by A. L. Kroeber © the Kroeber estate.

the pool of attributes shared by individuals of a culture-bearing population is never wholly impermeable (Murdock 1959:132). Members of one population can pick up, and transmit to future generations, attributes derived or 'borrowed' from another. In this way the two sets of attributes represented in each population, if once discrete, overlap and perhaps eventually merge. It is important to notice that the concept of diffusion makes sense only in the context of a focus on the cultural repertoire of *populations*. Thus it has to do with the construction, in the history of specific populations, of diverse cultural elements into patterns, each of which is characteristic of what Tylor would call 'the general life of a people' (1871, I:8).

In Darwinian terms, the construction of patterns out of large numbers of discrete elements underlies the very process of evolution. Species evolve as the composition of the genotype undergoes successive modification, and by analogy, cultures evolve as traits are arranged and assembled in new combinations, shaping the lives of particular populations. But Tylor's version of the organic analogy presents us with an entirely different picture. Every cultural element or 'detail' is a species, evolution has to do with their appearance in linear sequence. As for 'the geographical distribution of these things, and their transmission from region to region, [they] have to be studied as the naturalist studies the geography of his botanical and zoological species' (1871, I:7). Quite simply, the construction of particular cultures corresponds not to the evolution of 'ethnographic species' but to their propagation and distribution, as well as their symbiotic association with other species. Let me recapitulate Kroeber's point, in the same vein, that 'it is ecological aggregates to which cultures can be compared: local associations of species of diverse origin' (1952:93). In short, what from a Darwinian perspective would be the very essence of cultural evolution was, for Tylor and Kroeber, not a matter of evolution at all, but of ecology. Nothing could demonstrate more clearly that, by the evolution of culture, Tylor was not in the least concerned (as was Boas) with the culture-history of populations. His 'lines of culture', as I have emphasized, are quite different from lines of descent, and whereas the latter may 'grow together' through a gradual merging of the attributes shared by formerly distinct populations, the attributes themselves do not blend, nor do the lines connecting them.

By excluding from his concept of evolution the diversity of ways in which the warp of culture is woven into the lives of peoples, Tylor also drained out of evolution all that appeared to him accidental or fortuitous. No law determined how a certain trait would come to be incorporated into the repertoire of a particular people, whether by invention or diffusion, or indeed whether it would be incorporated at all. But these were matters of an ethnographic ecology, not of evolution. The apparent determinacy of the evolutionary process was thereby left intact: For not only were all individual exemplars of an ethnographic species supposed to embody a common essence, but that essence was conceived to have been immanent in the course of evolution prior to its 'discovery', or realization at either first or second hand, in certain human societies. Again we are impressed by the basically Lamarckian structure of Tylor's argument. The course has been staked out in advance, the destiny of mankind is to follow it. The cultural landscape is so much scenery along the route, scenery that—in one slice of time—dominates the immediate experience of one group, lies in the fading memories of another, and in the undreamed-of future of yet a third.

Some remarks are in order at this juncture concerning the opposition between holism and atomism in evolutionary explanation. In Chapter 1 I contrasted the Spencerian and Darwinian paradigms of evolution in terms of this opposition, and one might inquire whether the same holds for the contrast between the Tylorian version of the evolution of culture and Boasian culture-history. I believe it does. On first glance, however, the position appears strangely contradictory. Boas, surely, was concerned with the assemblage of cultural elements into integrated patterns, into *whole cultures*. Tylor, to the contrary, was content to treat each element in isolation from its 'medium', as the exemplar of a taxonomic class. Likewise, in Mason's design for a museum, constructed on Tylorian principles, objects collected from a single people would be scattered in as many different cases, where each would be displayed alongside objects of similar type from as many different peoples, all laid out in their proper evolutionary sequence (Mason 1887; see Stocking 1974:4). In rejecting this design in favour of a 'tribal arrangement of ethnological collections' (1974:66), it would appear that Boas was proposing 'an empathetic *holistic* approach to tribal groups against the *fragmenting* comparativism of the evolutionists' (Stocking 1968:205; my emphases).

To equate holism with a focus on the construction and integration of 'wholes' is, in my view, fundamentally mistaken. Similarly it would be wrong to regard an atomistic approach as one that concerns itself exclusively with elements at the expense of their interrelations. The difference between atomism and holism really has to do with the direction of derivation, whether from parts to whole or vice versa. In an atomistic conception, the totality is seen to be constituted by the aggregation and interaction of discrete elements each of which exists as a static, independent entity prior to its incorporation. In a holistic conception, by contrast, elements have no existence apart from the total, continuous process of which they are but particular points or moments of emergence (Weiss 1969:5). We shall see in the following chapter how this contrast underlies the dichotomy between *individual* and *person*. For the time being we have only to remark that for Boas, as for Darwin, the world was composed of individuals, which are of course the units that constitute populations. The individual is an objective entity, a thing of parts, whose historical specificity depends on the combination of elements underlying its morphology and behaviour. Just as the biological individual is constructed according to a unique assemblage of genetic elements, so the performance of the individual 'culture-bearer' is an expression of a particular set of cultural instructions lodged in the unconscious levels of mind. It follows that the integration of cultural elements was, for Boas, 'a psychological integration . . . internal to the individual actor. Its obligatory character was not externally imposed, but based on unconsciously internalized categories' (Stocking 1974:8). In short the individual is *constituted* by its parts, not by its position in a wider system of relationships.[5]

The holism in Tylor's account of cultural evolution is evident from his very conception of culture, connoting not a cluster of elements but a *total process* embracing all mankind. The multifarious traits of culture, and their innumerable exemplars, are but so many manifestations of this unitary process, each one representing a determinate point in its unfolding. To write the history of culture was, for Tylor, to put every trait in its correct position in relation to the whole, to the evolving consciousness of humanity (Bidney 1953:184–5). This might be the appropriate point to take a closer look at what Tylor—and indeed many of his contemporaries—meant by 'culture', a concept that has since become the object of so much anthropological contention.[6] As we have already noted, nowhere in Tylor's writing does it appear in the plural form, whereas it frequently sports a capital C. This was quite consistent with the usage of the time, which regarded culture as an index of the 'cultivation' (refinement, development) of the intellectual potentialities—or the rationality—of mankind (Kroeber 1963:87–8). Thus when Tylor spoke of the culture of a particular people, 'he meant "the culture-*stage*" or the "*degree* of culture" of that group' (Stocking 1968:81), in other words, its rank on the scale of civilization. He would probably have accepted without reservation the more recent but anachronistic view of Ernst Cassirer that 'human culture taken as a whole may be defined as the process of man's progressive self-liberation' (1944:228; also Bidney 1953:143). In this sense, culture and civilization are synonymous.

Tylor states the synonymy at the very outset of *Primitive culture* where he introduces 'that complex whole', the celebrated blanket concept of anthropological lore: 'Culture or Civilization, taken in its widest ethnographic sense . . . includes knowledge, belief, art, morals, law, custom, and any other capabilities and habits acquired by man as a member of society' (1871, I:1). In different societies, Tylor continues, we may recognize the *same* components of culture, broadly defined, but in *various* grades of development corresponding to the unequal growth of human intellectual powers. The relativist perspective enshrined in Boasian culture-history is quite the reverse. It recognizes a plurality of discrete cultures, each a particular configuration of elements of diverse origin. These *various* cultural traditions impress themselves on the human mind, the basic organization and powers of which are supposed to be much the *same* amongst different peoples the world over. Boas himself provides an unusually succinct statement of the alternatives:

> It may be that the minds of different races show differences of organization; that is to say, the laws of mental activity may not be the same for all minds. But it may also be that the organization of mind is practically identical among all races of man; that mental activity follows the same laws every-where, but that its manifestations depend upon the character of individual experience that is subjected to the action of these laws. (1911:102)

Boas's adoption of the second alternative had important implications not only for the anthropological usage of culture but also for the way in which the observer is placed in relation to the observed.

If to belong to a culture is, as Boas maintained (1911:225–7), to bear the stamp of a tradition not of one's own making, to be imprisoned in one's thought and action within a framework of received categories that—remaining unconscious—cannot be transcended, and if this is the condition of all ordinary human beings, then anthropologists must consider themselves no ordinary humans. For they alone, having recognized 'the shackles that tradition has laid upon us', have managed to break them and therein have found enlightenment (Boas 1974:42). Although refusing to judge particular cultures or their elements according to any absolute standard, avowed relativists—in an attitude of neutral detachment—place them-selves in an ethereal, cultureless void. One culture may not be better or worse, more or less advanced, than another, but *they* are above culture. Compare this with Tylor's view, that the powers of intellect that enable us to engage in rational, scientific inquiry are an indication of our superior culture, and it becomes evident that the concept of culture has undergone a remarkable inversion in its reference. As Stocking has demonstrated so convincingly, what 'once connoted all that freed man from the blind weight of tradition [is] now identified with that very burden' (1968:227). The rational observer of the human condition, formerly the epitome of 'cultured man', has become cultureless; so-called primitives, once supposed to be all but devoid of culture, are now its principal bearers and custodians.

Even more remarkable is that this inversion went virtually unnoticed, so that a staunchly relativistic cultural anthropology could still credit Tylor with the estab-lishment of its subject–matter (Stocking 1968:72–3; see Kroeber and Kluckhohn 1952:9, 150–1). 'Culture' literally slid into its present meaning, dragging—notably in the early writings of Kroeber—'civilization' along with it. This slide, I believe, is readily explained. For basically, culture connotes an attitude of mind, characteristic of the liberal imagination, by which we distance ourselves as subjects from the alien peoples who form the objects of our attention. To seal their ways of life under the impress of an encompassing tradition is to confirm our superior position as privileged spectators, no longer in the vanguard of the cultural process—as the evolutionists conceived it—but altogether outside it. The change of perspective from Tylorian evolutionism to Boasian relativism may be compared to that of a climber who, having laboured up the slopes, glances back over his shoulder to perceive the world laid out like a two-dimensional mosaic far beneath his feet, its antlike inhabitants resembling so many flat-earthers unable to rise above the limitations of their existence. But whether we consider ourselves to be ascendant or transcendent, whether culture refers to the climb or the view from the summit, our own pre-eminence remains unchallenged. *We* relate to *them* as the enlightened to the custom-bound. Though the concept of culture has been transferred from subject to object, the relationship—and the attitude it contains—continues unchanged.

This is a matter to which I shall have frequent occasion to return. But to conclude my present discussion of Tylor's evolutionism, I should like to reiterate the discrepancy between what he intended to convey in his definition of culture, and the significance attached to this definition by an anthropology that styles itself as the study of 'other cultures'. We find a classic instance in the work of Lowie. Having presented his subject as a science that deals with 'cultures', he continues: 'By culture we understand the sum total of what an individual acquires from his society—those beliefs, customs, artistic norms, food-habits, and crafts which come to him not by his own creative activity but as a legacy from the past' (1937:3).[7] The apparent likeness of this definition to Tylor's wording is evidently intended, for Lowie goes on to remark that 'Tylor's classical definition of culture . . . is virtually our own' (1937:12). However, closer inspection reveals its import to be utterly different. For a start, Lowie's definition enumerates the items (particular beliefs, particular customs, etc.) that make up *a* culture, shared by the individuals of a given society—or in modern terms, a given population. Although concurring with Tylor that these items are acquired rather than inherited, Lowie introduces an alternative sense of acquisition, stating explicitly that it is not the result of a creative process but a 'legacy from the past'. Where Tylor's man actively acquires culture through the conscious exercise of will, Lowie's (like that of Boas) is but a passive receptacle for the cultural elements with which he happens to be infected, and which—by 'chance contact' (Lowie 1921:427)—he will in turn pass on to others. Strictly speaking, then, he does not *acquire* culture at all, but *absorbs* it (e.g. Goldenweiser 1933:59).

Tylor wrote of culture 'in its widest ethnographic sense'. If every component of culture were, as Lowie has it, a compendium of elements, culture taken in this sense could only be a disordered inventory including every single learned attribute to have appeared in the history of human populations. And this is precisely how it is construed by Lowie himself. 'Ethnology', he declares, 'is not merely the science of cultures but of culture—of every fragment of the universe pertaining to the social heritage of all human groups' (1937:358). It comes as no surprise, therefore, that whereas Tylor pedantically opens his *Primitive culture* with 'Culture or Civilization . . . that complex whole' (1871, I:1), Lowie exuberantly concludes his *Primitive society* with 'that planless hodgepodge called civilization' (1921:428). Tylor's monumental edifice has been reduced to rubble. To reconstruct it in the form Tylor intended, it is essential to recognize that his components of culture were not arbitrary assortments of elements but separable and complementary *strands* in which every element has its place in a total, logically ordered arrangement. Each strand represents a general capability of the human mind rather than its specific contents: That is why Tylor refers to belief, custom and art, and not to the aggregate of beliefs, customs and artistic norms. Moreover Tylor's man is not 'an individual', absorbing particular traits from a given tradition, but 'mankind', moving along universal channels from original savagery towards civilization. Culture, then, is the entire cable, the components of culture are its strands, and the traits of culture are points in their unraveling. Evidently the wording of Tylor's definition of culture could only have been taken to convey a 'thing of shreds and patches' (Lowie 1921:428) by an anthropology that had altogether abandoned his holistic vision of evolutionary advance, in favour of a fragmenting atomism.

Extension and analogy

It is now time to return to Darwin, and more specifically to *The descent of man*—a work that not only post-dated *The origin of species* by over a decade, but also presented a quite different facet of Darwin's intellectual personality. The wondering curiosity of the naturalist is still there, but it is thickly blended with the ponderous morality of the Victorian gentleman. Once he confronted the evolutionary position of his own kind, Darwin could no longer ignore those qualities of conscience that seem to raise human beings to their pre-eminence in the animal kingdom, qualities 'summed up in that short but imperious word *ought,* so full of high significance' (Darwin 1874:148). And his notorious conclusion was that this moral sense is incipient to some degree in all social animals, that it has an innate basis, and that its manifestation in human beings is the result of an intellectual development that facilitates an evaluation of the present and the future in terms of the past. 'The imperious word *ought* seems merely to imply the consciousness of the existence of a rule of conduct, however it may have originated' (1874:177). Take any being endowed with social instincts, bestow on it the capacity to reflect on its experience in the dimension of time, and it may be credited with a moral awareness. If man is unique in this regard, it is because he 'is distinguished from all other animals by his sense of past and future—that is to say, by his consciousness of time' (Whitrow 1975:35).[8]

Darwin was strongly committed to a view of the progressive enlightenment of mankind that was, for its time, thoroughly conventional. He had no qualms about comparing the various grades of general advancement to the stages of maturation of the human individual from infancy to adulthood (1874:194; compare Tylor 1871, 1:27). Siding with Tylor and others in their dispute with the advocates of degenerationism, he accepted quite uncritically the principal supposition of the comparative method, namely that existing 'savage' and 'barbarous' tribes represent the successive steps of a gradual and uniform ascent already trodden by the ancestors of 'civilized' nations (Darwin 1874:221–4; see Bock 1980:41–8). And yet, in *The origin of species,* Darwin had decisively rejected all notions of predetermined, orthogenetic advance in the world of nature. There could be no law of necessary development, no pursuit of perfection (Howard 1982:77). One can but wonder how, in composing *The descent of man,* he could bring himself so utterly to compromise the very principles he had set out with such conviction ten years earlier, to the extent of anticipating with confidence the triumph of virtue over base temptation (Darwin 1874:192). In the popular identification of Darwinism with mechanistic theories of biological and sociocultural progress, we are still living with the effects of this about turn in his approach, from a relativistic view of nature to a firm belief in man's rise towards moral and intellectual enlightenment.

There is a certain sense, we should admit, in which the compromise is more apparent than real. In the *Origin,* Darwin had touched only incidentally on man, yet *as a man,* he placed himself—the observing scientist—outside the spectacle of nature. His own absolute superiority (and by extension, that of his kind) vis-à-vis the rest of the animal kingdom was something he never thought to question. For the fact remains that no animal whose project is precisely inscribed in the materials of heredity could have written *The origin of species.* But conversely, an animal capable of performing this feat, or any other that involves conscious reflection on the material conditions of existence, must also be able to bend the course of evolution to its purpose. In writing *The descent of man,* Darwin relinquished his stand outside the world and took up a position right inside it, basing his understanding of the human condition as much on introspection as on the data of observation.[9] Consequently he could not avoid the questions of progress that were implicit in the ostensibly relativist programme of the *Origin.* Rather than taking for granted the pre-eminence of rational man (as a precondition for his engaging in scientific inquiry), the question became: How did he get there? Contrasting progressive evolutionism with cultural relativism in anthropology, I likened the change of perspective to the backward glance of a climber on reaching the mountain top. In precisely the same way, *The descent of man* is a reconstruction of the climb, *The origin of species* a view from the summit.

There is more to it, however, for besides the idea of progress, Darwin's thinking on human evolution contained two additional strands that were in some respects novel. One was his insistence that human beings evolved by the same mechanism of variation under selection whose operation throughout the rest of nature he had already attempted to demonstrate in the *Origin.* The other was a thoroughgoing philosophical materialism, based on the premiss that all mental activity can be explained as the functioning of a bodily apparatus, the brain (Gruber 1974:180; Gould 1980:24–7). 'By materialism', Darwin himself commented, 'I mean, merely the intimate connection of kind of thought with form of brain' (cited in Gruber 1974:201); indeed, in his notebooks he came to use the terms 'mind' and 'brain' almost interchangeably (Gruber 1974:316–17). In his own time it was this premiss, and its implications as regards the continuity between man and other animals, that occasioned all the controversy. On the other hand it was not until well into this century, boosted by the development of modern genetics, that the theory of variation under natural selection gained widespread acceptance amongst biologists—from whom it has subsequently found its way, in suitably modified form, into the human sciences. Just as the nineteenth-century followers and opponents of Darwin could debate the issues of materialism and man's descent from animals without reference to natural selection, so there are humanists today who advocate 'variation and selection' as a universal mechanism of historical change without for a moment supposing that the stuff on which this mechanism operates must consist of material rather than ideal entities or indeed that the selection is necessarily 'natural' at all (Campbell 1965; Jensen and Harré 1981).

In 1864 the co-discoverer of the principle of natural selection, A. R. Wallace, published his account of the bearing of this principle on the 'development of human races' (Wallace 1870:302–31). Wallace's paper met with Darwin's wholehearted approval and appears to have had a decisive impact on his thinking (George 1964:71). Having the advantage of a much greater familiarity and sympathy with the ways of 'primitive' men than Darwin ever had, Wallace was greatly impressed by the wealth and diversity of their cultural achievements. This led him to an explicit recognition, in strikingly modern terms, of the degree to which the ability to adapt to the environment through culture had freed human beings from the direct influence of natural selection on bodily form. Whereas other animals can adapt to changing environmental circumstances only through corresponding modifications in 'bodily structure and internal organization', man 'does this by means of his intellect alone, the variations of which enable him, with an unchanged body, still to keep in harmony with the changing universe' (Wallace 1870:313–15). So is there anything left for natural selection to work on? Certainly, Wallace continued, since 'from the moment that the form of [man's] body became stationary, his mind would become subject to those very influences from which his body had escaped'. Every slight improvement in 'mental and moral qualities' would give its holder an edge over his rivals in terms of reproductive success. Thus 'tribes in which such . . . qualities were predominant, would . . . have an advantage in the struggle for existence over other tribes in which they were less developed, would live and maintain their numbers, while the others would decrease and finally succumb' (1870:313, 317).

The implications of this position are far-reaching, and again we owe their explicit affirmation to Wallace. The only material variations to which natural selection had not become indifferent, he argued, were those having a bearing on the development of a generalized human faculty: the capacity to reason, to form judgements of right and wrong, and to respond constructively to novel environmental situations. It follows that there is but one standard of improvement for man, a standard, moreover, that has nothing to do with the immediate conditions of life for specific populations. The relatively more successful 'tribes' will be those that can better *transcend* their environmental circumstances. In short, whereas throughout most of the organic world, natural selection promotes divergent adaptation, in human beings it promotes the one-way development of adaptability. The latter, it appears, furnishes a criterion of fitness that is *absolute*. Now Wallace was well aware that natural selection, according to the argument set out in Darwin's *Origin,* 'has no power to produce absolute perfection but only relative perfection'—that is according to the needs of the present (Wallace 1870:334). But with man it is different. Whereas other animal species undergo constant, undirected modification, we remain—and forever will remain—unchanged in physical form, but in our 'mental constitution' we progress, slowly but surely, towards a condition of absolute perfection. We evolve, 'not by a *change* in body, but by an *advance* in mind' (1870:325; my emphases).

I have dwelt on Wallace's conclusions at some length, since they go a long way towards explaining why it was that when Darwin came to apply the theory of variation under natural selection to human evolution, he arrived at a view so precisely opposed to that outlined in *The origin of species.* Concurring with Wallace that, because of the human capacity for culture, natural selection operates only on 'the intellectual and moral faculties', Darwin was convinced that their improvement could be judged on an absolute scale, that natural selection would inevitably generate progress along this scale, and that this underlies a universal movement of mankind from savagery to civilization. There were, of course, some disagreements with Wallace, but by and large these concerned the explanation of variations in outward appearance among human populations. Wallace had explained such variations as the outcome of natural selection operating *prior* to the emergence of the capacity for culture. But as far as Darwin could see, none of the distinctive features such as head shape, hairiness and skin colour had any obvious advantages to their bearers that might have led to their establishment through natural selection. To account for racial differences in body form, Darwin proposed another mechanism, namely *sexual* selection. Each tribe, he suggested, recognizes its own marks of virility and feminine beauty, and since the most virile men would win the most beauteous women, and through them rear the largest number of offspring, these marks of male and female attractiveness would become reinforced and exaggerated (Darwin 1874:924–5).

The validity of this suggestion is not our concern here; what is more important is that in other respects, much of Darwin's argument—particularly in the crucial chapter 'On the development of the intellectual and moral faculties during primeval and civilised times' (1874:195–224)—is merely an elaboration of Wallace's theme. Thus, he asserts that although men depend on no specialized bodily apparatus for hunting and trapping, or for offence and defence, nevertheless 'individuals who were the most sagacious, who invented and used the best weapons and traps, and who were best able to defend themselves, would rear the greatest number of offspring'. And since 'the tribes, which included the largest number of men thus endowed, would increase in number and supplant other tribes', every increment of inherited intellectual ability would be preserved and accumulated (1874:196–7).

What goes for the intellect also goes for morality, though here the problem arises that a 'virtuous' man who sacrifices his own reproductive interests to those of another can hardly be expected to leave more numerous offspring. Darwin solves the problem in a move that anticipates more recent theories of group or inter-demic selection (Wilson 1980:298): the object is no longer the individual but the tribal population.[10] To capture the flavour of his reasoning, it is worth citing the relevant passage in full:

> It must not be forgotten that although a high standard of morality gives but a slight or no advantage to each individual man and his children over the other men of the same tribe, yet that an increase in the number of well-endowed men and an advancement in the standard of morality will certainly give an immense advantage to one tribe over another. A tribe including many members who, from possessing in high degree the spirit of patriot-ism, fidelity, obedience, courage and sympathy, were always ready to aid one another, and to sacrifice themselves for the common good, would be victorious over most other tribes; and this would be natural selection. At all times throughout the world tribes have supplanted other tribes; and as morality is one important element in their success, the standard of morality and the number of well-endowed men will thus everywhere tend to rise and increase. (1874:203–4)[11]

Notice how, with this emphasis on the tribe as the unit of selection, Darwin begins to invoke the language of direct competitive struggle, victory and conquest. Whereas in the *Origin,* he was at pains to stress the essentially metaphorical con-notation of the phrase 'struggle for existence' (1872:46), in *The descent of man* it acquires a literal, Hobbesian sense. 'Fidelity and courage', Darwin remarks, are 'all-important in the never-ceasing wars of savages' (1874:199).[12]

From the specification of absolute standards of intellectual and moral advance, it follows that if the hereditary differences between populations of human individuals—as judged by these standards—are sufficiently great as to warrant the division of man-kind into varieties ('races'), then such varieties *can* be 'ranked in a single file' despite Darwin's general assertion to the contrary in the *Origin* (1872:97). But are the dif-ferences that great? Darwin certainly thought they were. Yet he failed altogether to explain why some people should have progressed so much more rapidly than others (Bock 1980:55–7). The problem, he complained, 'is too difficult to be solved'. All we can say is that progress 'depends on the increase in the actual number of a popu-lation, on the number of men endowed with high intellectual and moral faculties, as well as on their standard of excellence' (1874:204–5, 216). But granted that the causes of favourable variations are unknown, why should Darwin not have assumed that they could occur in any population with equal probability, and therefore that—as they are everywhere notched up by natural selection—no population will advance significantly less rapidly than any other? Perhaps one partial answer is simply that he shared the prejudices of his day as regards the supposed inferiority of 'barbarians' and 'savages'. According to the premiss of materialism, this inferiority was presumed to have an innate basis. There is, however, another answer, contained in his oft-repeated statement that, throughout history, 'tribes have supplanted other tribes'—as even now 'civilized nations are everywhere supplanting barbarous nations'—the victorious groups always including a larger proportion of 'well-endowed men' (1874:197).[13] The existence of population differentials in hereditary mental endowment was, in Darwin's argument, a condition for the operation of natural selection. Adopting a literal interpretation of the struggle for existence between human groups, there had to be vanquished as well as victorious contestants. The lower races were introduced in order to play the role of losers in Darwin's evolutionary scenario.

Nowadays, though the innate component of intelligence remains the subject of angry controversy, the idea that there are significant differences in the average of hereditary mental endowment between entire populations has turned out to have no factual foundation whatsoever. And this brings us back to Boas, for it was he who pioneered the attack on nineteenth-century doctrines of racial formalism. As early as 1894 he could conclude, at least provisionally, that 'the average faculty of the white race is found to the same degree in a large proportion of individuals of all other races' (1974:242). At this stage of his career, Boas was still enough of a materialist to believe that mental function could be correlated directly with anatomical structure; however, he also held—with increasing scepticism—to the neo-Lamarckian idea that environmental circumstances could directly induce adaptive modifications in bodily form, which would be transmitted to future generations by inheritance (Stocking 1968:184–5, 191–2). Consequently any innate differences in mental function, distinguishing one 'race' from another, could be judged only in relation to the specific conditions of its environment. As regards the generalized faculties of intellect, there were no grounds for placing the races of mankind in separate grades of an overall hierarchy of rank. Subsequently as the doctrine of inheritance of acquired characteristics came to be discredited, the concept of culture was precisely substituted for that of racial temperament in Boas's argument. If the mode of thought of one people differs from that of another, it is because of their 'cultural heritage' rather than their 'racial heredity' (Stocking 1968:265–6). And the 'heritage' consists of an integrated pattern of ideal elements that are *lodged* in the brain, in place of a system of genetic instructions that materially *constitute* it. The organic structure of the human brain, Boas implied, is indifferent to the cultural forms that occupy it, and it is the latter—not the former—that direct an individual's thought and behaviour.[14]

Clearly this conclusion contradicts Darwin's materialist axiom, as he put it in one of his notebooks, that thought is but 'a secretion of brain' (in Gruber 1974:451). Darwin did not (contra Bock 1980:50) deny the facts of cultural variation—although he had little to say on the subject. We have seen how his recognition of the capacity to adapt to the environment through cultural means (Darwin's list included weapons and other tools, food-producing strategies, clothing and dwellings, fire and cooking, division of labour) led him, following Wallace, to concentrate exclusively on the advance, through natural selection, of the human *mind* (Darwin 1874:195–6). In other words, culture plays a crucial role in the argument of *The descent of man* by dint of its absence, for it allowed Darwin to relegate all the problems of *specific* adaptation to the ethnologist. Thus, where the exhaustive researches of Tylor and others could yield a classified inventory of the cultural items on which a people might draw for the conduct of their lives at each successive stage of moral and intellectual development, Darwin set out to demonstrate the 'ratchet-device' by which—in the long run—mental advance prevailed over retrogression. Between these two projects there was a certain complementarity, for each contained something the other lacked. If human populations were likened to the several hands of a clock, each moving at a different rate across the face, then Darwin's 'variation under natural selection' would constitute the mechanism and Tylor's 'culture' the dial (though in so far as we are dealing with a movement that is linear and progressive rather than cyclical, the analogy breaks down).

In view of this complementarity, we might note the irony that it was Boas's initial *failure* to recognize the implications of the human capacity for culture, his belief that adaptation involved environmentally induced and inherited bodily modification, that led him to adopt a *relativistic* theory of racial determinism—paving the way for an equally relativistic theory of cultural determinism. It would be incorrect, therefore, to claim that Boas recognized the facts of culture where Darwin did not and that herein lies their difference, for to begin with at least, the situation was quite the reverse—Boas attributed far more than Darwin to racial propensity. The real difference is that for Boas, culture came to replace race, rather than to complement it. This, in turn, entails a radically contrasting idea of what culture is, or does. Where Darwin regarded culture as an *instrument* through which the mind (equals brain) operates to practical effect, Boas conceived culture (as he had once conceived race) to be *directing* the mind in its operations. Darwin saw cultural 'arts' as 'products of the intellect' that man projects on the external world, whereas the thought of the Boasian individual reflects on an internalized cultural logic. For Darwin, organic form is related to cultural form as machine to product; for Boas, they are related as container to content. This latter view treats the human being as a temporary repository in which cultural elements, each with an ideal existence quite independent of its particular carriers, are fortuitously assembled, and from which they will eventually be transferred to others.

Evidently, the adoption of such a view entails a clean break with philosophical materialism. We cannot attribute to the functioning of individual brains ideas that bear as much relation to their material substratum as words have to the paper on which they are written.[15] The explicit recognition of this point was left to Kroeber, in his 'Eighteen professions' of 1915. The historian of culture, he declared, must assume 'the absolute equality and identity of all human races and strains as carriers of civilization' (1915:285). This is not to suppose that no hereditary differences exist between populations, for by all accounts that would be most improbable

(Dobzhansky 1962:75). Kroeber's thesis was rather that such differences as may be empirically established must be considered of no consequence at all for the functioning of individuals as culture-bearers. 'Man', Kroeber declared, is 'a tablet that is written upon' (1952:32), yet obviously the same words can be written on any kind of tablet. Although this position is necessarily idealist, it is also atomistic, and it is this latter aspect that links it to the evolutionary paradigm of *The origin of species*. The dichotomy between idealism and materialism is orthogonal to that between atomism and holism, which is why Darwin could present his argument in terms of an opposition between natural and supernatural (or spiritual) causation that apparently left no room for culture as a possible determinant of behaviour (Bock 1980:51). The kind of idealism to which he objected was one that postulated some form of supreme directing agency in evolution. To this holistic and teleological conception, the idea of evolution as the revelation of divine purpose, Boasian culture-history was equally opposed. The cultures of Boas, like the species of Darwin, lacked a spiritual author, and therein lay the basis of the analogy between them.

Two points should now be evident from our discussion. The first is that the Boasian concept of culture is totally incompatible with any form of biological reductionism, and hence with any attribution of culture difference to racial variation. Culture was conceived as a substitute for race, not as an appendage of it. But second, this severance of culture from innate, hereditary constraint is a precondition for the analogous application of the Darwinian explanatory paradigm, as set out in *The origin of species,* to the domain of cultural facts. To effect the break, it was necessary for anthropology to reject not only the 'forward' derivation of cultural behaviour from hereditary disposition, but also the reverse, 'backward' derivation implied by the Lamarckian notion of inheritance of acquired characteristics (which Darwin accepted, along with most of his contemporaries; see 1874:91). Thus in addressing the evolution of man and culture, it is quite essential to separate the two components of what often passes as 'Darwinism': on the one hand, the notion of descent with modification in populations of unique individuals and on the other, the premiss of philosophical materialism. So long as we can disregard cultural adaptation in the animal kingdom, and view all behaviour as the outcome of interaction between a genetically programmed object and its natural environment, these components are perfectly compatible, the one serving to uphold the other.

But when it comes to human beings, it seems we have two alternatives. Either we reject the materialist premiss and account for interpopulation differences in terms of an analogue of variation under selection operating in an autonomous domain of culture. Or we continue to seek the material foundations of human behaviour by concentrating our attention exclusively on the universal properties of the mind. In the first case we assert a dichotomy of substance between nature and culture, by virtue of which humanity is set apart from the organic world,[16] but an identity of historical process; in the second case we assert an identity of material substance, by which human beings become fully a part of nature, but a dichotomy of process—between divergent specialization and convergent generalization.

The former approach, working by *analogy, substitutes* the cultural for the natural, heritage for heredity; the latter, working by *extension,* treats the cultural as a *complement* of the natural, the acquired instrument of an innate reason. Because of the opposition between these two approaches, both of which have their roots in the Darwinian project, it was possible for Boasian cultural anthropology unknowingly to apply the relativist principles of Darwin's argument in the name of a rejection of its materialist premiss.

Let me now return to Tylor, to see how his understanding of human evolutionary advance differs, if at all, from Darwin's. On the idea of progress, they were of one mind. Both held that the mainsprings for the development of civilization lay in the evolution of consciousness, of the moral and intellectual faculties of mankind. That mental development had nothing to do with 'bodily configuration and the colour of . . . skin and hair' is again a matter on which they were agreed (Tylor 1871, I:7; compare Darwin 1874:307). Thus it is absurd to claim, as Opler has done, that 'the central place of the evolution of the mind in Tylor's theory stamps him as a philosophical idealist' (Opler 1964:143), for if this were so, we would have to regard Darwin as an idealist too. Darwin's materialism lay, as we have seen, in his assertion that mental functions could be reduced to the hereditary structure and organization of the brain. There are a number of indications in Tylor's later writings, post-dating the publication of *The descent of man,* that he thought likewise—though he refused to commit himself finally (Tylor 1875:107–10; 1881:60; see Voget 1967:144–5; Stocking 1968:102, 116; Schrempp 1983:98, 108 n. 9). However, his views on this matter had evidently changed from an earlier humanism more in keeping with the eighteenth-century doctrine of the 'psychic unity of mankind', originally the cornerstone of the comparative method (Leopold 1980:48). On the premise of innate mental uniformity, progress was regarded as the purposive cultivation of naturally given potentials and capabilities common to the human species. Yet even in his *Primitive culture,* Tylor was careful to stress the likeness of minds at the same *stage* of development, which did not preclude the possibility that advance depends on changes in cerebral structure akin to those accompanying the growth of the human individual, and hence that each stage corresponds to an innate condition of mind, rather than to a degree of cultivation (Harris 1968:139–40). It is remarkable that the movement in Tylor's thinking towards naturalism, reflecting a basic trend in the late nineteenth century, was to be precisely reversed by Boas's subsequent move towards humanism. For Boas concluded, where Tylor began, with the basic uniformity of the human psyche. In place of environmentally induced psychic diversity, Boas superimposed a diversity of cultural content on the common mind. Tylor went the other way, reducing cultural differentials once thought to be underwritten by a common psychic structure to hereditary differentials in the organization of the mind itself.

Tylor's starting-point had been the traditional eighteenth-century dualism of matter and spirit, by which the human brain is conceived as but the place of abode, within an essentially constant bodily form, for an incorporeal consciousness unique to mankind, with laws of development of its own. It was this idea that enabled earlier progress theorists such as Comte to reconcile their doctrine of mental advance with a belief in the fixity of organic species (Bidney 1953:86; Bock 1980:106). The difference between this and the alternative materialist view was, in Darwin's time, inseparable from the issue of whether or not there exists an evolutionary continuity between man and other animals. For if the progress of the mind can be correlated directly with an advance in the complexity of the brain, and if the human brain and those of other animals can be arranged in a single graded series, then the superiority of the European over the allegedly small-brained 'savage' must—it was thought—be similar to that of the latter over the ape, and of the ape over animals lower in the scale (Huxley 1894:107–11). Wallace, much to Darwin's disappointment, latterly veered away from this conclusion (George 1964:72–4). Although linking mental capacity to brain size, he felt that human beings had been created with a brain much larger than they needed for most practical purposes, especially whilst they remained in the state of savagery. 'Natural selection', Wallace wrote, 'could only have endowed savage man with a brain a little superior to that of an ape, whereas he actually possesses one very little inferior to that of a philosopher' (1870:356; for a recent expression of the same view, see Williams 1966:14–15). Progress towards civilization was simply a matter of the increasing utilization of an organ that happily had been prepared in advance for this very purpose, by none other than the 'superior intelligence' whose existence as an evolutionary agent Darwin had so strenuously denied (Wallace 1870:343, 359).[17]

Rather more congenial to Darwin's viewpoint were the unorthodox conclusions of that other great anthropological forefather, Lewis Henry Morgan, derived from his authoritative study of the American beaver. Morgan had suggested that the beaver could reason as intelligently as any savage; that in general the mental powers of man and animals were similar in kind, if not in degree of advancement. Yet Morgan was no materialist. He abhorred the reduction of thought to innate propensity, subscribing rather to the dualistic premiss that 'each individual [is] endowed with a mental or spiritual essence which is distinct from the body, but associated with it in a mysterious manner' (1868:249–50). But far from assuming such immaterial consciousness to be uniquely human, he considered what he called the 'mental' or 'thinking principle' to have been implanted as a 'Divine gift' in each separate species at the time of creation and subsequently to have progressed, at different rates for different species, within a framework of immutable physical forms. The explanation for man's pre-eminence lies 'in the progress he has made since his emergence from his primitive condition', but this is not to say that other animals have remained 'stationary in their knowledge from the commencement of their existence'. Within the time-span of human observation their mental advance may seem slight, but it is by no means negligible: Animals have history too (Morgan 1868:281–2). Thus although he concurred with Darwin that the human mind differed from that of other animals only in degree, Morgan was concerned to 'upgrade' animals, attributing to a 'free intelligence' what was conventionally put down to instinct (1868:275–6; see Resek 1960:100–2). Darwin, to the contrary, was more concerned to 'downgrade' man, attributing to instinct what previously had been taken as a manifestation of the human spirit. Though he knew of and respected Morgan's work, he naturally felt that the latter had gone 'too far in underrating the power of instinct' (Darwin 1874:114 n. 22). The contrasts between orthodox dualism, Morgan's less conventional view and Darwin's materialism, as regards the evolutionary status and progress of man and other animals, are illustrated schematically in Fig. 2.3.

It is worth our while to pursue Morgan's ideas, this time on man rather than the beaver. What little influence Morgan received from Darwin appears to have rested on a complete misunderstanding—replicated, incidentally, in Terray's recent and quite spurious attempt to demonstrate the possibility of a Darwinist reading of Morgan's work (Terray 1972:13–24). In Morgan's own words, his confrontation with Darwin's teaching forced him 'to adopt the conclusion that man commenced at the bottom of the scale from which he worked himself up to his present status' (cited in Resek 1960:99; see also Leacock 1963:liv). Darwin's scale was, in point of fact, virtually bottomless, extending far back into the animal kingdom, with even the 'lowest' human beings not far from the top. Besides, the idea of purposeful striving, of 'working up', permeates the writings of Morgan but is totally alien to the Darwinian conception of evolution. Though Morgan from time to time let slip such phrases as 'the struggle for existence' and 'the survival of the fittest', in his view 'the fittest led, they did not destroy the weak' (Resek 1960:103, 144). For Darwin, on the contrary, the distinctive property of natural selection was its impersonality: Progress was not the result of conscious striving, but of the cumulative orthoselection of chance variations. Luckily for human beings this orthoselection happened to be proceeding in the 'right' direction, securing for us a position of absolute dominance (Darwin 1874:72). As for Tylor, his view seems closer to Morgan's than to Darwin's: Thus 'history shows how development of the arts takes place by efforts of skill and insight' (Tylor 1875:121). But with his intellectualist leanings, Tylor's emphasis was on man's achieving civilization not so much by 'working himself up' as by 'thinking himself through' the stages of savagery and barbarism—just as a student must progress from the elementary and through the intermediate to reach the advanced level of a curriculum.

Morgan's greatest work, *Ancient society,* is full of paradox as regards the relation between brain, mind and civilization. In the preface he concedes to 'the uniformity of the operations of the human mind in similar conditions of society', and accordingly sets out the basic principles of the comparative method. Social evolution, he continues, follows a predetermined course, 'guided by a natural logic which formed an essential attribute of the brain itself' (1963[1877]:60). Are we then to understand that all human beings are endowed with brains of identical structure and that the various stages of evolutionary development represent different moments in its logical unfolding, the progressive realization of an immanent potential? One might think so, were it not for the following extraordinary statement: 'With the production of inventions and discoveries, and with the growth of institutions, the human mind necessarily grew and expanded; and we are led

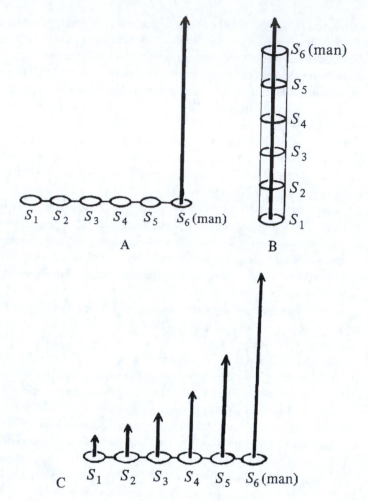

FIG. 2.3 Three views of the evolution of consciousness. **A:** Orthodox eighteenth-century dualism. All species are of immutable physical form, occupying successive positions along a chain of being culminating in man. But human beings are unique in their possession of mind, which undergoes a progressive advance within the framework of an unchanging body. **B:** Darwinian materialism. Mental advance is wholly contingent on the progressive evolution of bodily (more particularly cerebral) structure, from species 'lower' to those 'higher' in the scale, through apes to 'savages' and, ultimately, to 'civilized nations'. **C:** Morgan's view. Remaining committed to orthodox dualism, Morgan nevertheless agreed with Darwin that in their mental powers, humans differ from animals in degree rather than kind. He accordingly attributed mind not only to man but to all other animal species as well, supposing it to have advanced at different rates for the different species, without involving any change in their physical form. Rings, marked S_{1-6}, represent species ranked on a scale of nature; thick vertical arrows represent the progress of mind.

to recognize a gradual enlargement of the brain itself, particularly of the cerebral portion' (1963[1877]:36). Everything here seems back to front. The evolution of mind appears to correlate directly with changes in cerebral structure, which in turn are made out to be the consequences of the very process the brain was supposed to direct. Where Darwin had argued that the improvement of the brain would lead to an advance in mental function, which in turn would further the progress of civilization, Morgan put it precisely in reverse: The progress of civilization leads to an advance in mental function, which in turn leads to improvements in brain structure. Add to this Morgan's conviction that our present condition is the result of 'the struggles, the sufferings, the heroic exertions and the patient toil' of our ancestors (1963[1877]:563) and we arrive at the Lamarckian premiss that the human bodily form—including the brain—is the direct product of the labour of past generations (Stocking 1968:116–17). This readily struck a chord with Marx and Engels, both of whom were committed to the view that human nature is essentially man-made (Marx 1930 [1867]:169; Engels 1934:172).

This might be the appropriate point at which to expose the falsity of those numerous attempts, beginning in the work of Engels (1972[1884]:25–7), to read into Morgan a crude theory of the technological determination of culture. Comparing the evolution of 'inventions and discoveries' with that of 'institutions', Morgan had argued that 'the former stand to each other in progressive, and the latter in unfolding relations. While the former class have had a connection, more or less direct, the latter have been developed from a few primary germs of thought' (1963[1877]:4). He went on to use the successive steps of the ('progressive') technological sequence to calibrate the gradual process of institutional growth ('unfolding'), enabling him to mark off universally recognizable periods in the progress of mankind (1963[1877]:8–9). But it is absurd to construe Morgan's *identification* of 'epochs of human progress' with successive 'arts of subsistence' as a statement of the *determination* of the former by the latter. In one of the most recent interpretations of *Ancient society* in this genre, in which Morgan is heralded as the true precursor of Althusserian Marxism, Terray claims to find him expounding the decisive influence of the technological arts on the functional relations between different spheres of social life—family, government and property—within each epoch, determining in every instance which sphere will play the dominant role (Terray 1972:39–67). This, as Hirst (1976:32–48) has shown, is pure fabrication. Never did Morgan claim that successive inventions and discoveries would engender a corresponding series of social structural transformations. His view was that they were creations of the mind, which the historian could use as diagnostic indicators of a continuous mental development wrought by human effort, and by which that continuum could most conveniently be broken into more or less arbitrary and provisional divisions.

To revert to Tylor, and bearing in mind our demonstration in the earlier part of this chapter of the non-Darwinian structure of his argument, what are we to make of Opler's apparently contrary claim that it actually involved 'a transfer of Darwin's biological ideas to the cultural realm' (1964:142)? The evidence for this view is thin (Harris 1968:212; Stocking 1968:96–7) and boils down to just one sentence in *Primitive culture* that employs an unmistakenly Darwinian idiom: 'History within its proper field, and ethnography over a wider range, combine to show that the institutions which can best hold their own in the world gradually supersede the less fit ones, and that this incessant conflict determines the general resultant course of culture' (1871, I:62). This line of reasoning continues to attract philosophers who share Tylor's interest in intellectual progress. Thus Popper, writing a century later, has proposed that the growth of knowledge is the result of a quasi–Darwinian 'natural selection of hypotheses': 'Our knowledge consists, at every moment, of those hypotheses which have shown their (comparative) fitness by surviving so far in their struggle for existence; a competitive struggle which eliminates those hypotheses which are unfit' (1972:261). Now, if a 'fit' institution or hypothesis is merely one that 'survives' or 'holds its own', presumably by gaining plenty of adherents, there is nothing to stipulate that it will be more progressive in any absolute sense. As statements about progress, these propositions of Tylor and Popper can only be understood to mean that in culture as in life, less advanced forms necessarily pave the way for more advanced ones, which inevitably succeed in competition with their antecedents. In other words, an institution or hypothesis is not considered 'fitter' because it survives; rather it survives because it is, a priori, demonstrably superior: The institution is more effective, the hypothesis has greater explanatory power. As we saw in the preceding chapter, this is to comprehend the struggle for existence in Spencerian rather than Darwinian terms. The 'cultural Darwinism' that Opler claims to detect in the thought of Tylor bears about as little relation as does the analogous 'social Darwinism' to the argument of *The origin of species*. Both were applications, to the domains of culture and society respectively, of the doctrine of 'survival of the fittest' enunciated by Spencer in his *Principles of biology* of 1864.

Rather closer to the spirit of Darwin's teaching is the attempt by another contemporary philosopher, Stephen Toulmin, to view the history of ideas and institutions 'as the outcome of a dual process of conceptual variation and intellectual selection' (1972:139–42, 200). Likening 'populations of concepts' to populations of biological individuals, Toulmin shows that this analogue of natural selection is *not* a formula for absolute progress. Conceptual variants flourish that are adapted to their present intellectual milieu, others die out, and so intellectual disciplines undergo an evolution akin to that of organic species that is both irreversible and indeterminate. Notice that, 'cultural Darwinist' or no, these implications of the Darwinian paradigm flatly contradict Tylor's most basic working assumptions: that the course of culture is both determinate and progressive. Unfortunately Toulmin is himself profoundly muddled as regards the terms of his parallel between biological and intellectual history. For having compared concepts to individuals, he proceeds to set up an analogy between the discipline and the species that makes sense only if the constituent concepts of the discipline are likened not to the individuals of the species as a *population* but to the elementary traits making up the genetic *pool* common to that species (on this analogy, see

Ruyle [1973] and Hill [1978]). Toulmin's (1972:141–3) interchangeable use of the terms 'population' and 'pool' to denote conceptual plurality is indicative of his confusion. Taking the latter view, the 'individual' corresponds to a particular construction of the discipline, a unique configuration of concepts drawn from the common pool, and assembled in his mind, by an agent whom Toulmin introduces as 'the concept-user' (1972:139). With his appearance on the scene, we are confronted by the realization that any pseudo-Darwinian theory that treats ideas, hypotheses or institutional rules—rather than their carriers—as the objects of selection must admit that *somebody is doing the selecting*.

Darwin, of course, introduced the notion of natural selection by drawing a parallel with the kind of selection exercised by animal and plant breeders. It could be argued, moreover, that the breeder stands to variant strains much as Toulmin's concept-user stands to the diverse constructions of a discipline, as Popper's scientist stands to alternative hypotheses, or as Tylor's individual stands to the institutions of culture. Yet nature, as Gould has remarked, 'is not an animal breeder; no pre-ordained purpose regulates the history of life' (1980:42). Although Darwin often referred figuratively to Nature as a purposive agent, he was a great deal more careful than many latter-day Darwinians to emphasize the *difference* between natural and artificial selection in this respect. He begs his readers' indulgence for his personification of nature, but no such apology is necessary in the case of human beings who—quite literally—select in person (Darwin 1872:60; see Barnett 1983:38). 'Man', he continues in the same passage, 'selects only for his own good; Nature only for that of the being which she tends.' In other words, there is no plan in nature beyond those uniquely embodied in each and every one of the very objects of selection themselves. The limitations of the analogy between variation under domestication and under nature in no way invalidate the conclusions Darwin drew from it (Gould 1980:42), since from the point of view of the objects of selection it is immaterial whether the conditions that constitute their environment have arisen circumstantially or have been deliberately imposed by a selecting agent.

But with regard to the overall character of the evolutionary process the difference is all important. In the selection of ideas and institutions, as in the selection of domesticates, there lurks behind the 'conditions of life' of the objects, whether ideal or material, the will of a transcending subject, a guiding hand for whom each object is but a means towards the realization of its own, independently conceived ends. If one institutional or conceptual design displaces another, it is because it is considered, in the eyes of the subject, to be a more effective vehicle of moral or intellectual advance. To speak of an 'incessant conflict' between institutions (Tylor), or a 'struggle for existence' between hypotheses (Popper), is to understand conflict in the same sense as when we refer to the 'conflicting viewpoints' of a rational debate, where that side prevails that is consciously chosen and adopted by a majority as the more satisfactory alternative. Hence selection is synonymous with the exercise of reason, introducing 'teleology in the form of intentional agency . . . as a condition, and part-cause, of adaptive changes' (Bhaskar 1981:207). And yet, as Bhaskar recognizes, the major claim of Darwinian theory is that it has *undermined* the idea of teleology in nature (1981:196). This contrast brings us back to our earlier distinction between treating culture by extension as an instrumental complement of the natural, and treating it by analogy as a programmatic substitute for the natural. We might argue, with Darwin, that as human reason is the product of natural selection, human beings are in turn the rational selectors of their cultural forms (as of their domesticated species). But to construct a history of culture *analogous* to Darwin's 'descent with modification' in nature, we would have to envisage individuals in their capacity as bearers of culture, as selected rather than selectors, not choosing among the elements of culture but behaving under their combined impress. And for this view of things, we have to turn once more from Tylor to Boas.

I have mentioned already a number of the Darwinian aspects of Boas's thinking: the analogy between cultures—as integrated clusters of elements—and species, the concomitant emphasis on the history of individuals and populations, the substitution of nominalism for essentialism, indeterminate phylogenesis for determinate orthogenesis, atomism for holism, and relativism for the belief in absolute progress. And as we would expect, Boas's view of cultures and their history *embodies teleonomy but not teleology*. No conscious purpose is posited prior to cultural form; rather every individual comes into being as a unique and fortuitous assemblage of cultural elements, which subsequently orchestrate and direct his thought and action. Human beings, in this view, exist to execute a project, inscribed in a cultural analogue of the biogram. They are the instruments of cultural reproduction, serving to express, animate and transmit across generations a script that—by a chain of happy accidents—is constantly rewriting itself. It is an inescapable limitation of Boasian culture-history that it has nothing to say about the *agency* of consciousness. As the animator of a received historical tradition, Boasian man is basically a creature of habit, instructed by a cultural design of which he is largely unconscious, and searching for reasons after the event. 'The average man', Boas wrote, 'does not determine his actions by reasoning, but. . . . first acts, and then justifies or explains his acts by . . . secondary considerations' (1911:226). Thus consciousness is perceived to reflect on, but not to direct, what we do.

To highlight the contrast between this view and Tylor's, we can look again at their respective concepts of culture. For Tylor, as for Boas, culture is the project of mankind. Recall, however, that Tylor wrote of culture always in the singular form, as a continuous *process*. And so the *traits* of culture (barring 'survivals' that have outlived their usefulness) exist for a purpose, not for the sake of their own propagation, but as vehicles for this process—which is of course the elevation of the human mind. Far from being a passive medium, the mind—or consciousness—is an active agent, engaging its powers of reason in the selection of cultural objects and operating over the long course of history through the *instrumentality* of such objects.[18] Boas would naturally have rejected the teleological implications of this conception of the evolutionary process. Following the transferral of the attribute of culture, to which I have already alluded, from 'us' (enlightened, civilized) to 'them' (custombound), man came to be seen—by Boas and by many of his followers—'not as a *rational* so much as a *rationalizing* being' (Stocking 1968:232). Contrary to 'the impression . . . that the habits and opinions of primitive man had been formed by conscious reasoning' (as Tylor had supposed), Boas concluded explicitly that 'the origins of customs of primitive man must not be looked for in rational processes' (1911:227–8). The result of this change in perspective is a corresponding inversion of agent and instrument. People, instead of using the objective forms of culture as instruments for the conduct of their lives, become themselves mere vehicles for the conduct of culture. Where Tylor aimed to write a 'natural history of the human mind inscribed in . . . artifacts and institutions' (Voget 1967:134), for Boas the human mind is laid out as a blank slate on which is inscribed a history of cultural forms. In just the same way, Darwin saw nature not as the author of organic evolution but as the medium in which it is written. This history, whether of natural or cultural things, is full of patterns but devoid of purpose. When Boas wrote that 'in order to understand history, it is necessary to know not only how things are, but how they came to be' (1948:284), he did not mean to find the source of history in some creative force or conscious striving, but merely to locate the present as the precipitate of an antecedent sequence of singular events.

There is a fairly direct, if unfortunate, continuity between the line of reasoning established by Boas and some very recent attempts to bring cultural and organic evolution within the same conceptual framework by positing some cultural equivalent of the gene. Candidates for this distinction include the 'instructions' of Cloak (1975), the 'memes' of Dawkins (1976) and the 'culturgens' of Lumsden and Wilson (1981). Taking their cue from the idea that the organism is but a machine designed to promote the replication of its individual genes, these authors claim that human beings are no more than contrivances by means of which similarly objectified 'bits' of culture propagate themselves. In other words, '"Our" cultural instructions don't work for us organisms, we work for them' (Cloak 1975:172). But since the dissemination of culture can take place independently of biological reproduction, a particular instruction need not enhance the survival of its human carrier, so long as it makes him behave in ways that lead to its effective transmission to other potential carriers. A cultural instruction may therefore be likened, in Cloak's words, to 'an active parasite that controls some behaviour of its host' (1975:172). Or to return to the cancerous imagery of Dawkins: 'When you plant a fertile meme in in my mind you literally parasitize my brain, turning it into a vehicle for the meme's propagation in just the way that a virus may parasitize the genetic mechanism of a host cell' (1976:207). And so the hapless individual, his mind infested with an entire community of active, cerebral parasites, must respond mechanically to their commands—without heed to his own survival—and in so doing pass the infection on to others (just as the cold-sufferer, involuntarily sneezing, spreads his germ to all around). Jostling with each other for time and storage space in the medium that is the human mind, the 'bits' of culture are subjected to a process akin to natural selection, by which those with the most effective mechanisms of propagation will tend to displace the less effective ones (Cloak 1975:169; Dawkins 1976:211; 1982:109–10).

Most practising anthropologists would undoubtedly be inclined to write off this argument as an example of the bizarre aberrations of a scientific imagination that has long taken leave of the reality of human experience. I shall reserve more thorough discussion of the gene–culture analogue for the last chapter, and raise it now for two reasons only. First, it indicates the absurdities to which we may be led by pursuing, to its logical extreme, the atomistic conception of cultural determinism inaugurated by Boas. Second, it forces us to attend to the dichotomy between a view of mind as *agent* and as *medium*. Despite the gap of a century, there is some superficial similarity between Tylor's image of 'ethnographic species', associating in the life of a people, and the idea of Cloak and Dawkins that the traits of culture constitute a community of cerebral parasites. But the similarity ends there. For Tylor did *not* regard the mind as a vector for the propagation of traits, but installed it firmly in the director's seat, discovering, accepting and rejecting in conformity with its progressive purpose. To respond in the spirit of Tylor to the vulgarity of Cloak: 'We human beings do not work for our instructions; rather they work for us.' This observation accords well with the experience of common sense, and it underlies a good deal of what I shall have to say about the relationship between mind and culture in the remainder of this book.

If memes and culturgens are the bastard offspring of Boas's cultural elements, there is a still more peculiar connection between Darwin's *Descent of man* and the manifesto of that modern prophet of sociobiology, E. O. Wilson, *On human nature* (1978). Like most works that self-consciously announce the dawn of a totally new era of human understanding, this will probably be remembered by historians of the next century as a quaint curiosity whose principal interest lies in its uncritical reflection of many of the most deep-rooted ideas in the popular consciousness of the day. Nevertheless, we cannot pass over it entirely. For like Darwin, Wilson started off as an observer of other species rather than of other cultures and only subsequently turned his attention to humanity. And Wilson's view of man, like Darwin's, fairly reeks with the moral prejudices of the Western world, whilst it is similarly based on an astonishing ignorance of non-Western peoples, less permissible in an age when we know so much more about them. Again like Darwin, Wilson presents an equally deterministic picture of the evolution of society, as a process of 'growing up' from the natural condition of 'primitive hunter-gatherer bands' to the 'high culture of Western civilization' (Wilson 1978:87, 203). Most important of all, Wilson's argument incorporates two fundamental premisses of *The descent of man*: an arrant, mechanistic materialism and a view of culture as a kind of outgrowth of human nature rather than a substitute for it. On the first premiss, Wilson promises to explain the mind 'as an epiphenomenon of the neuronal machinery of the brain' (1978:195). The second is vividly expressed in his celebrated dictum 'The genes hold culture on a leash' (1978:167). Otherwise put, heredity stands to tradition in a relationship not of metaphor but of metonymy.

Granted the likeness of approach, we are naturally prompted to inquire whether Wilson has arrived at similar conclusions to Darwin's, for similar reasons. The answer is, Not quite. For Wilson is writing in an age when the assumption of substantial differences in average mental capacity between human populations is no longer scientifically credible. On the question of whether such differences exist at all, he is remarkably equivocal (Wilson 1978:48; see Bock 1980:119–21). 'Given that humankind is a biologial species', Wilson writes, 'it should come as no shock to find that populations are to some extent genetically diverse in the physical and mental properties underlying behavior' (1978:50). Yet he concedes that 'social evolution is obviously more cultural than genetic' and that only those dispositions 'powerfully manifested in virtually all human societies' can be 'considered to evolve through genes' (1978:153). Quite clearly there is no sense in trying to explain the movement of a society from hunter–gatherer band to advanced industrial nation in terms of the gradual improvement of innate properties of the mind when, as Wilson himself admits, the genetic endowment of the contemporary hunter–gatherer does not differ significantly from that of the modern European (1978:34).

If, however, we expand our temporal horizon to include the two or three million years of hominid evolution leading up to the appearance of *Homo sapiens* proper, we witness 'an unbroken advance in mental ability', latterly at the rate of one tablespoonful of cranial capacity every hundred thousand years (1978:87; see also Wilson 1980:272)! Wilson's explanation for this advance adds little to those of Wallace and Darwin, although he graces it with a new term—*autocatalysis*—that he has borrowed from chemistry. Simply, bigger-brained hominids produce superior artefacts, and as the latter confer a reproductive advantage on their possessors, natural selection will favour further improvement in the intellect, which in turn generates even more effective cultural equipment, and so on through mutual reinforcement (Wilson 1978:84–5). Eventually, though only in the last hundred thousand years or so, the evolution of culture 'took off' from its biological foundations, recently leading much of mankind (but inexplicably not all) to dizzying heights whilst human nature is left to plod along in the Stone Age. And so Wilson feels justified in assuming that 'the greater part of the changes that transpired in the interval from the hunter–gatherer life of forty thousand years ago to the first glimmerings of civilization in the Sumerian city-states, and virtually all the changes from Sumer to Europe, were created by cultural rather than genetic evolution'. His central problem is therefore to discover 'the extent to which the hereditary qualities of hunter–gatherer existence have influenced the course of subsequent cultural evolution' (1978:88).

At this point, Wilson's argument takes a rather peculiar turn. For he asserts that 'the key to the emergence of civilization is *hypertrophy*, the extreme growth of pre-existing structures'. All the institutions of modern society are to be understood as 'complex hypertrophic outgrowths of the simpler features of human nature', whose rudiments may be discovered in the repertoire of primitive hunter–gatherers. Moreover, the directions and outcomes of this developmental process are said to be 'constrained by the genetically influenced behavioral predispositions' common to the human species (1978:89, 95–6). The terms are strikingly reminiscent of Morgan's, in *Ancient society:* 'The principal institutions of mankind have been developed from a few primary germs of thought, [whose] course and manner of . . . development was predetermined, as well as restricted within narrow limits of divergence, by the natural logic of the human mind and the necessary limitations of its powers' (1963[1877]:18). For Morgan's idealized 'germs of thought' substitute Wilson's materialized 'genetic capital', and the formula is essentially the same. Note that Wilson's 'genes' have long since ceased to bear any resemblance to the particulate entities actually studied by geneticists. For now they lay down a plan not only for individual ontogeny but for cultural phylogeny. The latter is itself to be regarded as a kind of growth, predictable in all but details, of which the individual represents just a fleeting moment of epigenetic development.

This Spencerian vision of cultural evolution is confirmed when Wilson uses to describe it a metaphor derived from developmental biology. The metaphor is Waddington's (1957:29), and it likens the trajectory of individual ontogeny to that of a ball rolling down an inclined landscape furrowed by valleys, sometimes shallow, sometimes steep-sided. The landscape is shaped by the individual's genes, but at any point in its development environmental influences may push the ball into one valley rather than another, and hence into an alternative trajectory. But in Wilson's hands, the ball becomes society itself: 'The society undergoing cultural evolution can be said to be moving down the slope of a very long developmental landscape.' And although 'idiosyncratic features' may cause it to roll into one or another channel, the landscape itself is already laid out, ready for mankind to traverse (Wilson 1978:60–1, 114–15). It would appear from this metaphor that in switching track from biological to cultural evolution, human hereditary attributes have been elevated to the rank of 'supergenes', installed by natural selection, and combined to establish a developmental programme for a hypostatized culture that is deployed in advance of its realization in the individuals and populations it successively calls into being. Needless to say, the existence of such a supergenetic programme has not been demonstrated, nor is it ever likely to be. In effect, it has usurped the design of a transcendent consciousness, so that the precipitate of our biological past is construed as a template for our cultural future. For God, write natural selection.

It should come as no surprise, then, that Wilson proceeds to rediscover all the essential principles of the comparative method. The logic of the argument is extremely simple and should by now sound familiar. If it be supposed that all mankind shares a distinctive human biogram, traceable to our common origin as hunters and gatherers in the state of nature, and if it be further supposed that cultural forms are mechanically generated or 'printed out' by this biogram, the only way to account for cultural differences is to assume that they represent successive points of a universal developmental trajectory. Thus Wilson notes that 'the emergence of civilization has everywhere followed a definable sequence', on a scale of increasing complexity, from bands to tribes, tribes to chiefdoms, and chiefdoms to city-states. This parallelism is offered as evidence for the preponderant influence of the 'genetic capital' of the human species in directing the course of cultural development (1978:88–9). In startlingly similar terms, Morgan had drawn attention to the uniform channels of social progress as evidence for the primacy of his 'germs of thought' (1963[1877]:17–18). And since all societies traverse the same landscape, contemporary hunting and gathering or 'tribal' peoples may be held to represent earlier stages of our own advance to civilization. Hunters and gatherers, in particular, present us with the nearest approximations we have to the zero point of cultural development, furnishing a picture of human nature 'in the raw' (Wilson 1978:34, 82; 1980:292–3).

There is, however, one significant difference between Wilson's view of progress and that of the liberal enlightenment, vividly conveyed by his use of the term 'hypertrophy'. Culture, apparently, is not striving towards a target but—spurred by an autocatalytic momentum—has overshot the limits of its origin. Returning to the analogy of the ball in the landscape, it turns out that the ball is connected to its starting point by an elastic thread (the leash) that, as it lengthens, is becoming ever more taut. Moreover 'there is a limit', Wilson suggests, 'perhaps closer to the practices of contemporary societies than we have the wit to grasp, beyond which biological evolution will begin to pull cultural evolution back to itself' (1978:80). We live with the biological encumbrance of our primitive past that, though it has both its good and its bad sides, is increasingly at odds with the demands of modern civilization. In 'Hope', his concluding chapter, Wilson preaches that human salvation lies in the pursuit of rational self-knowledge, which might at least enable us to perceive and cultivate the better side of our nature. As Bock curtly remarks, 'It is startling to witness the acceptance by sociobiology of this classical form of the Christian philosophy of history. Saint Augustine might quibble about some of the phraseology' (1980:88).

It is all too evident that Wilson, although quite properly eschewing the virulent racism of the late nineteenth century, has unwittingly taken us back towards the eighteenth century (and beyond) rather than forwards to the twentieth. One is therefore disturbed by his readiness to write off much current thinking in the humanities and social sciences, which he finds to be 'devoid of the idioms of chemistry and biology' and reads 'as if most of basic science had halted during the nineteenth century' (1978:203). The evolutionary anthropology of a hundred years ago was, of course, replete with chemical and biological imagery: Recall Tylor's comparison of the laws of culture with those governing 'the combination of acids and bases, and the growth of plants and animals' (1871, I:2). That such language conforms to Wilson's vision of a future synthesis only underlies our impression of his own work, which reads as though most basic thinking about society had halted at least a century previously. If what he presents were really science (which it is not), modern anthropology could with good reason proclaim a post-scientific emancipation that promises to open up vast areas of human understanding that sociobiology has firmly closed off. These areas concern above all our knowledge of history, a subject on which sociobiology, though purporting to explain everything, explains nothing at all. A theory that claims to establish 'the main course of history's predictable trajectory' only to dismiss the whole affair as a product of 'accidental details' of 'cultural drift', superimposed on ultimate biological predispositions and current environmental requirements, can hardly be expected to provide much illumination (Wilson 1978:96, 116). Indeed, Wilson freely admits that 'the sociobiological hypothesis does not . . . account for differences among societies' (1978:153–4), sharing with orthodox Darwinism an inability to explain why one society has progressed where another has not. The proper comprehension of history requires an approach from quite another angle, that is from a position *within* the social process itself. Whilst separating the agency of consciousness from the instrumentality of culture, we must reject the reduction of human intentions to the action of organic machinery. Our immediate concern, in adopting an approach of this kind, is to clarify the dichotomy between history and evolution. Are these different words for the same thing, or do they stand in complementary opposition? This is the first major question to which we shall turn in the next chapter.

3
THE SUBSTANCE OF HISTORY

There are two conflicting concepts of the *modus operandi* of change: the 'historical' and the 'evolutionary'. Of these, the former assumes that changes are consequent upon 'events', the latter that changes are produced by slow, continuous modification of an eventless world.

Teggart, Theory and processes of history

The terms 'history' and 'historical' have crept into our discussion at a number of points in the last two chapters, sometimes as synonyms for 'evolution' and 'evolutionary', sometimes as antonyms, depending on the context. Our next concern is to look more closely at what we mean by historical change. I aim to show that, to the two senses of evolution identified in Chapter 1, there correspond two senses of history. Hence, whether we conceive of evolution in Spencerian or Darwinian terms, it is possible to find one kind of history to which it may be compared, and another to which it must be opposed. Underlying this double dichotomy is the same polarity of holism and atomism that divided the culture-history of Tylor from that of Boas. However, in order to establish the link between evolution as a total process, and the corresponding sense of history, it will prove necessary to substitute for the universal 'man' the particular 'social person' as the creative agent of change. By this route, we arrive at a fundamental distinction between a history of *persons* and a history of *populations,* the latter conceived as aggregates of objectified individuals. Much of this chapter is devoted to a discussion of the individual–person dichotomy and the different interpretations that can be placed on it. We shall find that to this dichotomy there correspond quite contrary forms of time, and this will provide our subject for Chapter 4.

Let me begin by presenting the two senses of history, around which my subsequent discussion will be constructed. According to the first, history consists of a concatenation of discrete and transitory entities or events, each unique in its particulars. This is obviously a conception as applicable to the world of nature, both inorganic and organic, as it is to the domain of human culture (White 1945a:243; Kroeber 1952:70; Trigger 1978:25). A geologist can speak of the history of the earth, and a biologist of the history of genera and species, in much the same way as a cultural anthropologist might speak of the history of artefacts, institutions and ideas. It is a sense that attributes a great deal to chance, contingency or 'happenstance', and little or nothing to purpose or design. History, a 'chapter of accidents'—or 'one damn thing after another', as Elton (1967:40) so eloquently puts it—is equated with all that is capricious or vagarious in the experienced world. It confounds our expectations, surprises us with its novelties and mocks our every attempt to confine it within the bounds of determinate 'laws'. Yet we ourselves have no hand in it; rather we stand apart as witnesses to chart its irregular course, treating the things of history as objects of positive knowledge.

The second view holds that history begins with consciousness, or to impose a further limitation, with self-consciousness. Most writers who take this view (e.g. Cassirer 1944:191; Collingwood 1946:215–17; Carr 1961:178; see Bidney 1953:281) assume that only human beings have history, though we shall have occasion to question the premises on which this assumption rests. History, they say, does not just happen, it is *made* through the intentional activity of conscious, purposive subjects—by people. But as historical agents, we act from within, as participants in our own creation: Collectively, 'man makes himself'. And although every individual agent has a transitory existence (as each of us, unconscious of the event, must make his entry and his exit), the history that we make, and that is made in us, transcends the bounds of our particular experience. It is, as I shall eventually show, nothing other than the *process of social life*. Moreover, this process cannot be apprehended as an accumulating series of discrete, empirical events. Our subjective life is not contained within events but is conducted through them: It is a continuous, creative movement, like a task that is never complete. And as all practising anthropologists know, to grasp this continuity one must join in the task of living, which means that we necessarily influence its direction. To stand aside is to lose sight of the connecting flow of consciousness, so that the continuum of life and mind appears to break into a myriad of minute, behavioural fragments.

We are presented, then, with a founding dichotomy, between a processual history of conscious subjects ('persons') and an eventful history of natural and cultural objects ('things'). This dichotomy has an important bearing on the vexed question of whether it is possible to divide history from science. Clearly if science is 'what scientists do', it makes sense to compare it with history only if the latter is understood as 'what historians do'. But opinions differ as to what defines the 'scientific' approach. Many choose to emphasize the importance scientists attach to objectivity, with the implication that observers must take up a position wholly external to the phenomena they are investigating. An approach of this kind would be incapable of yielding an understanding of what I have called the 'history of persons', since to appreciate the lived experience of historical agents is to enter subjectively into their social world rather than to remain a spectator on the sidelines (Collingwood 1946:214). On the other hand, the externalization of the object is a precondition for the establishment of a history of things, be they natural or cultural. In this sense geologists or palaeontologists are being thoroughly scientific, even though their concern is with the reconstruction of particular chronological sequences. The same goes for Boasian culture-history, which likewise rested on strict canons of objectivity. It was Boas's greatest disciple, Alfred Kroeber, who wrote of Darwin that 'he did more than anyone else to establish a historical approach as valid in science' (1963:181). More correctly, he should have praised Darwin for bringing a scientific approach to bear on natural history, just as Boas was to do for cultural history.

But here we encounter another common conception of what constitutes the essence of science. It is said that scientists are not interested in the unique and particular, nor in their chronological succession, but rather in the formulation of general laws valid for all places and times. This is frequently expressed as a contrast between 'idiographic' and 'nomothetic' approaches (Elton 1967:26–7). Thus palaeontology, a natural science by the criterion of objectivity, comes to be regarded as 'idiographic and historical' because of its reconstructionist aims (Trigger 1978:31). Radcliffe-Brown held a similar view of the ethnology of Boas, contrasting it with his vision of a mature social anthropology as a theoretically oriented, nomothetic, 'natural science of society' (1951:15, 22; 1952:1–3; 1957). Yet on another front, much closer to home, Boas found himself under attack from none other than Kroeber, for 'doing' science but not history (Kroeber 1952:63–5). Kroeber's argument is not easy to follow, and Boas found it frankly incomprehensible (Boas 1948:305–11). The gist of it was that a genuinely 'historical' approach is integrative and totalizing rather than analytic and atomizing. Whereas scientists confront the whole already broken into discrete fragments that can then be strung out in temporal succession to reconstitute process, historians aim to grasp the movement of the whole by a direct leap of intuition, by living it in their minds. History in that sense is like art, and the task of historians is to describe, translate and interpret, but not to dissolve into elements. This subjectivist approach, subsequently taken up by Evans-Pritchard (1950:122–3), may be opposed—as we have just seen—to a 'scientific' objectivism that reduces persons to things, or the flow of consciousness to the forms of its natural and cultural armature (Bidney 1953:250–61). Although Kroeber does not reserve his kind of history exclusively for man, he notes that it has worked best in the field of human societies, 'on the psychosociocultural level', and that its extension to the organic and inorganic domains meets with increasing difficulty (1952:63, 101). In the case of Kroeber's 'science', the direction of extension is precisely the reverse, as from Darwinian biology to Boasian ethnology.

For Kroeber, as for Radcliffe-Brown, historical knowledge was 'idiographic'. That the former could contrast such knowledge with that yielded by Boasian 'science', whereas the latter identified it with the fruits of Boasian 'history', shows that the notion of 'idiographic' is itself not free from ambiguity. Indeed this ambiguity has been present all along, from the moment when the dichotomy between nomothetic and idiographic was first coined by the German philosopher-historian

Windelband, in an address delivered in 1894 (see Collingwood 1946:166–7). As a prominent representative of the so-called neo-Kantian school, Windelband was concerned to separate the methods of science and history on the grounds that the latter, dealing in ideal values, requires a subjective or intuitive approach quite alien to the precepts of positive science. However, by expressing this intended contrast as one between the discovery of general laws and the description of singular events, Windelband's terms could readily be appropriated by positivism itself to denote not its opposition to subjectivist history, but the two successive stages of its own programme: first the assiduous collection of individual, empirical facts and second, the attempt to fit these facts into a framework of general principles. Moreover this appropriation was made all the easier by Windelband's rendering of history as idiographic *science*. It was left to Rickert to sort out some of these confusions and to show that there are distinct historical and scientific ways of attending to the particular (Collingwood 1946:168–9). Thus the axis particular–general is orthogonal to the axis subjective–objective (Fig. 3.1).

Kroeber, following in the neo-Kantian tradition, took his cue from Rickert (1952:123), whereas both Boas and Radcliffe-Brown remained firmly anchored in positivism, Boas with his feet on the ground of the first stage, Radcliffe-Brown with his head in the clouds of the second. That was why Kroeber could present anthropology as a kind of history that endeavours to provide a 'descriptive integration' of phenomena perceived 'in terms of their totality', a totality whose dissolution into elements would be the first task of objective, 'scientific' analysis (Kroeber 1952:63–4). And it was why Radcliffe-Brown, observing empirically a world already thus dissolved, could see a bifurcation of the discipline into two branches, one (idiographic) concerned with the reconstitution of history 'as an authentic account of the succession of events in a particular region over a particular period of time', the other (nomothetic) with the formulation and validation of 'laws of social statics' and 'laws of social dynamics' (Radcliffe-Brown 1951:22). The latter tasks represent an endeavour not at descriptive but at *theoretical* integration, which comes from the processing by induction of events as seen by an intellect that stands outside the world, rather than from the experiencing of events by an intuition installed within it. The opposition between these two ways of apprehending reality, which Bergson (1911:186) called the 'intellectual' and the 'intuitive', has been very well expressed by the biologist Paul Weiss: 'To me the Universe presents itself naively as an immense cohesive continuum'; however, 'we are used to looking at it as a patchwork of discrete fragments.' And moreover, something is lost in this fragmentation that cannot be recovered: 'The mere reversal of our prior analytic dissection of the Universe by putting the pieces together again . . . can yield no complete explanation of the behaviour of even the most elementary living system' (Weiss 1969:5, 7). A machine can be constructed from parts, but machines do not live: Thus *what is missing is the process of life itself*.

Let me approach this point in another way. It may be agreed that an idiographic account deals in particulars, but are we to conceive each particular as a moment or 'nexus' in the unfolding of a total process (as did Kroeber), or as an

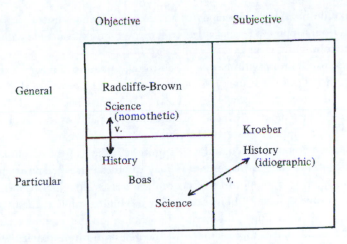

FIG. 3.1 Two ways of contrasting history and science. For Kroeber, the atomizing objectivism of Boas's approach marked it out as 'scientific', as opposed to his own, totalizing and idiographic ('historical') perspective. For Radcliffe-Brown, the concern with cultural particulars marked Boasian ethnology as idiographic and 'historical', as opposed to his own view of a generalizing or nomothetic, 'scientific' social anthropology.

isolable, empirical entity (as did Boas)? If we take the former view, our 'descriptive integration'—to use Kroeber's phrase—will be a partial depiction of the whole as seen from a particular vantage point in an unbounded, spatiotemporal continuum. To focus on the event is then to contemplate it as one would a crystal ball, whose outer surface appears to vanish as the eye penetrates ever further within. The whole world is there, in that event, if one can just see far enough. But place the ball somewhere else in space or time and the image will be different, like a photograph taken from another angle. To adopt terms recently suggested by the physicist David Bohm (1980:149), the order that unfolds in the total movement of history is 'enfolded or *implicate*' in every particular element we might abstract from it. Ultimately, therefore, 'one may say that everything is enfolded into everything'. Should we, to the contrary, confine our attention to the *explicate* order, we should see but a world of things each of which lies outside every other thing, and which are linked like the pieces of a jigsaw through external contact—whether spatial contiguity or temporal succession (Bohm 1980:177). Concentrating thus solely on the exteriority of events, and finding nothing of significance within, we could but proceed with the reconstruction of history through the painstaking recovery and enumeration of every single event we could find, putting each in its correct position in a particular sequence, and hoping thereby to end up with a reasonably complete picture. But even if we were to imagine our compilation of the facts to be exhaustive (which is, of course, a practical impossibility), the history we would have constructed would be a *dead* history; that is to say, an account of events that omits to mention the consciousness of those who lived through them. It would be rather like describing the biography of a person by giving a list of all his cast-off clothing, from nappies to funeral attire. In short, we would conclude with a history not of persons but of things.

To compare history with science is one thing, to compare it with evolution is quite another. For in the latter case our concern must be not with the historians' approach, nor with the knowledge it yields, but with what they take to be the substance of their inquiry (which will, of course, depend on the approach they adopt). Like evolution, however that term may be understood, history in this sense has been going on through the ages quite regardless of the combined efforts of scholars of manifold persuasions (who may call themselves scientists, historians, or both at once) to grasp portions of it from the real world and project them into the microcosmic domain of human knowledge. Unfortunately the issue has been clouded by the rendering of history as 'historicism' and of evolution as 'evolutionism'. Nobody seems to agree on what the first term means. After reviewing a wide range of highly disparate usages, Lee and Beck (1954) conclude that historicism implies an antipositivistic creed, which holds knowledge of the past to be a precondition for understanding the present. Stocking (1968:4) feels that it conveys a 'commitment to understanding the past for its own sake'. This relativistic connotation is denied by Popper (1957), who insists that historicism is an approach that aims at historical *prediction* (see Carr 1961:119–20 n.8). The term has since become a catch-all for virtually every theory of social or cultural progress, including those more usually known as evolutionary, whose stance is both positivist and antirelativistic. According to Mandelbaum (1971:42), a historicist interpretation of phenomena is one that gives each a place and a role to play 'within a process of development', as exemplified in the work of Comte, Tylor and Spencer.

But Spencer, for one, had no use for history. 'Until you have got a true theory of humanity', he remarked, 'you cannot interpret history; and when you have got a true theory of humanity *you do not want history*' (1972:83). We can see that Spencer is using 'history' here in two quite different senses. The first refers to the *reality* of change that, Spencer claimed, only he could interpret. But the kind of history he did not want was a particular *approach*, 'historicist' in the original sense of the term, marked by an exaggerated commitment to understanding events in the past for their own sake. To such historicism he opposed his own 'true theory', the theory of evolution. In fact, this was less a theory than a creed, for not only was it untestable, but its truth was—for its author—beyond question. It is rather ironic that Spencer's position, marked by its cantankerous repudiation of historical understanding, should latterly have itself come to be regarded as 'historicist'. Not much is to be gained from the continued use of a term that has moved from signifying one thing to its opposite, and it is best declared obsolete. Spencer's creed may, however, be fairly represented as evolutionism, if the suffix is taken to connote a shift from the phenomena of change to the doctrine of their inevitability.[1] But in the rash promulgation of the notion of evolutionism by Leslie White, that most valiant but erratic champion of evolutionary theory in post-Boasian anthropology, the significance of this shift was fatally obscured.

We are indeed indebted to White for rescuing the concept of evolution, in its original sense of progressive development, from the temporary oblivion into which it had passed following its appropriation in quite another guise by Darwinian biology, and its outright rejection by Boas and his followers. As part of this rescue operation, White was particularly concerned to highlight the contrast between evolution and history, which he held to represent processes of distinct kinds going on in the real world. He continued to define history in precisely the same terms as did Boas: 'a chronological sequence of unique events' (White 1945a:222; compare Boas 1948: 284). And he agreed that such history can be generalized across physical, biological and cultural sciences (1945:243). The same went for evolution: Thus natural or cultural scientists can study history, in so far as they are interested in the documentation of entities and events, and they can study evolution, if their concern is with the unfolding of total systems of relations between entities and events. This seems clear enough, but White starts to get into difficulties by what at first appears but a slip of the pen, namely the rendering of the process of evolution as the 'evolutionist process', and thence as 'evolutionism'. The slip, remaining unchecked, becomes a habit, until White is quite unable to discriminate between the process itself and the manner of its interpretation. This culminates in his preposterous assertion that 'evolutionism is a well–established fact' (White 1959a: 115).

It is no wonder that White's resuscitation of evolutionism fell foul of Kroeber's contemporaneous attempts to clarify (or obfuscate) the distinction between history and science. Where White's intention had been to show that both history and evolution could be legitimate subjects of scientific inquiry, Kroeber thought that he was trying to introduce a third approach—evolutionism—sandwiched between science and history. This approach, or so it seemed, purported to draw off from the former all that could be located in the dimension of time, and from the latter all that could be understood in terms of systemic process. The result would be to leave science with nothing but timeless abstractions, and history with the task merely of compiling the annals, providing evolutionists with fodder for their generalizations. 'It will not do', Kroeber protested, 'to gut history and leave its empty shell standing around; there might be the embarrassment of no-one's claiming it' (1952:96). To this, White could reply that Kroeber's reassertion of the history–science dichotomy constitutes 'a denial of evolution' (1959a:115). Of course it does not. For Kroeber's intention had been to establish a divergence of method, not of subject–matter. With the benefit of hindsight it is plain that much of the controversy rested on a mutual misunderstanding, brought on largely by White's cavalier disregard for conceptual precision, matched only by Kroeber's irrepressible verbosity. By a double confusion of the mode of interpretation with the reality to be interpreted, evolution was construed (by Kroeber paraphrasing White) as a method displacing history and science, and history and science (by White paraphrasing Kroeber) as processes displacing evolution. Science, of course, is a method (or the knowledge derived from its application), evolution is a process in the real world. 'History' is a term that can be used in both senses, as in our earlier citation from Spencer, and may be compared or contrasted with science in the first sense and with evolution in the second.

Having cleared up that particular source of confusion, we can look more closely at White's conception of the evolutionary process. As I have noted, this conception is essentially pre-Darwinian. 'The evolutionist process', as he was wont to call it, 'is concerned with the progression of forms through time. . . . One form grows out of, and into, another' (White 1945a:230). Echoing Spencer, he treats ontogeny—the growth of living beings—as an exemplification of this kind of process. As Kroeber remarked, the 'quality of predetermination, of spontaneous metamorphosis, of a teleological course, seems to be what is specifically characteristic of White's evolutionistic process' (1952:100). It consists of an 'unfolding of immanences'. White himself is explicit: 'We can predict the course of evolution, but not of history' (1949:230). There is an evolution of species that develop, one from another, in a definite order; and an analogous evolution of cultural institutions. These are contrasted with the histories of species and of institutions respectively (White 1945a:243). This view of the organic analogy is virtually identical to Tylor's, which we explored in the last chapter. Tylor, it will be recalled, excluded from his concept of cultural evolution the diversity of ways in which select traits and institutions are combined in the repertoire of particular peoples. Like the association of certain biological species in a particular geographic locale, this had to do with their propagation and distribution, not with their development, and was historically contingent rather than subject to general law. Similarly for White, the *history* of species tells where they made their appearance, where they flourished and whither they migrated, whereas history in culture is about the wanderings of isolable traits, whose several encounters and combinations in the formation of individuals are the 'actual events' out of which it is composed (White 1945a:235–6).

It follows from this that every individual of a species, as every expression of a trait, is the representative of a pre-established type and that each type takes its place as part of a systematic, evolutionary arrangement. Again White is explicit: 'In the evolutionist process we are not concerned with unique events, fixed in time and place, but with a *class* of events, without reference to specific times and places' (1945a:238). The order of evolution is an order of classes, not of individuals. But if the 'evolutionist process' has some counterpart in the real world, it must be possible to assign individuals to a class by virtue of a common essence. For were the essentialist assumption dropped, the delimitation of classes would become arbitrary and their evolutionary succession a figment of the imagination. This point, as has already been shown, lay at the heart of Boas's objections to the premises of Tylorian anthropology, but they apply with equal force to White's arguments. And by the same token, it should be clear that White's view of the evolution of organic forms, like Tylor's, is fundamentally at odds with the Darwinian paradigm, with its rejection of the essentialist concept of species and its substitution of indeterminate diversification for progressive development. White's failure to realize this was a fatal blunder that must have cost him the sympathy of those practising biologists who paid any heed to his work. 'Everyone is familiar with the evolutionist process', White blithely asserted, 'with the temporal sequence of forms from Eohippus to the modern horse' (1945a:235). Indeed, so confident was he that Darwin had an 'evolutionist approach' that he even chided Boas for having once characterized it as 'historical' (1945a:222–3).

Although Boas was himself somewhat confused about the relationship between Darwinian theory and the idea of progress in culture and society, he must be credited with having recognized Darwin's influence in bringing about an appreciation of 'the historical aspect of the phenomena of nature', through an approach in which 'chief interest centres in the event as an incident of the picture of the world' (Boas 1974:25–6). Descent with modification *is*, of course, a historical process, if history is understood as a temporal concatenation of empirical entities and events—which was the sense adopted by both Boas and White. Thus the 'evolution' of the Darwinian paradigm is formally analogous to the 'history' of the Boasian paradigm, representing the combination and recombination, in individuals and populations, of hereditary and acquired elements respectively (Murdock 1959:129–32). I have already dealt with the analogy at length and need not belabour it further here. There is a measure of convergence between Boas and White on the concept of culture-history, but none at all on the analogy between cultures and species. White's 'evolution of species' is Lamarckian, a temporalized Chain of Being, owing to Tylor its comparison to the 'evolution of culture as a whole', and to Spencer its characterization as a special case of a process equally apparent in the development of stars and galaxies, the growth of individuals, and the advance of social institutions. It follows that the opposition White draws between evolution and history is identical to the dichotomy that is already familiar to us through our comparison, in Chapter 1, of the evolution of Spencer and Darwin, and in Chapter 2, of the history of Tylor and Boas. Looking at culture piecemeal, in its elements, we get a history of invention, direct transmission and diffusion; looking at it as a developing, systemic whole, we get progressive evolution (White 1945b; 1959b:17–18, 29–30).

The same dichotomy reappears in a number of other anthropological contexts. Radcliffe-Brown, for example, regards history as a 'complex sequence of events' but gives virtually unqualified acceptance to the theory of social evolution as formulated by Spencer (1952:3, 7–8). For a time the followers of Radcliffe-Brown in Britain, and of Boas in America, constituted two divergent subdisciplines of anthropology—the 'social' and the 'cultural' respectively. The functionalism of the former and the historical particularism of the latter have both been interpreted as reactions against so-called evolutionism, but in fact both were fundamentally concerned with evolution—one taking it in the Spencerian sense the other in the Darwinian (see Stocking 1974:17). Kroeber's position, however, cannot readily be accommodated in the terms of this dichotomy. His conception of the substance of history appears to include most if not all of what White or Radcliffe-Brown would have regarded as evolution. He does not hesitate to describe the history of cultures or civilizations as a progressive development, analogous to that of organic growth, which is irreversible in that 'they cannot "disdevelop" or turn back' (1963:57). And he construes civilization as a *process* 'that works from a start of more or less randomness towards increasing coherence, and that moves from amorphousness towards definiteness, from fumbling trials to decision. Any civilization will tend to move in this direction on the way towards its culmination' (1963:23). Thus far, Kroeber appears to offer little more than a restatement of the Spencerian formula for evolution: 'from incoherent homogeneity to coherent heterogeneity'.

Where Kroeber differs quite fundamentally from orthodox social evolutionism is in his adoption of a pluralistic conception of civilization. Thus the process of development is by no means uniform for mankind as a whole; there is not one civilization but many, each discernible as a limited spurt or pulse of growth in a particular region of the spatiotemporal continuum. Once the peak of growth is past, it will rigidify or fall apart, contributing its pieces to the accumulating pool of fragments floating on the tide of history. Out of an amalgam of such fragments a new culture may be born and a new phase of growth initiated. Kroeber's hypostatization of culture as a superorganic being with a life history of its own, directed by an intrinsic 'master-plan', places his view a long way from the nominalism of Boas. The recognition of a plurality of cultures, each of which undergoes a cycle of growth and decay, evidently owes a good deal to Spengler and Toynbee, though Kroeber eschews the dogmatism of the former and the tendency of both to block off cultures or civilizations as discrete entities, thereby denying what he sees as 'the interconnectedness, in some degree, of *all* cultures' (Kroeber 1963: 79–84; see Kroeber and Kluckhohn 1952:175–6, n. 39). It is Kroeber's emphasis not on the laws of the total system, but on the shifting constellations or 'styles' that happen to form up out of diverse constituents, that seems to give his approach its stamp of historical particularism. Locating the cultural plan on a level intermediate between the individual and all mankind, Kroeber is able to combine the element of happenstance that goes into its formation with the determinacy of its subsequent unfolding.

Returning to White's dichotomization of evolution and history, Sahlins thinks he has settled the whole issue in his distinction between 'general' and 'specific' evolution. 'The historic development of particular cultural forms is specific evolution, phylogenetic transformation through adaptation. . . . The progression of *classes* of forms, or in other words, the succession of culture through stages of overall progress, is general evolution' (1960:43). The positive contribution of this reformulation was to sort out some of the aforementioned confusions engendered by shifts in the meaning of evolution. Both specific and general kinds of evolution, corresponding to White's 'history' and 'evolution' respectively, were extended across the separate domains of organic nature and human culture. In the course of this extension, Sahlins demonstrates, first, that the progressive evolutionism of Spencer and Tylor owed nothing to the Darwinian paradigm and second, that the latter epitomized what White should have regarded as organic *history* and not, as he thought, the process of evolution. That which White *did* regard as organic history, modern evolutionary biologists would relegate to the realm of descriptive ecology. But there is a great deal wrong with Sahlins's argument, not least in his misinterpretation of the 'lines' and 'stages' of Tylorian evolution, as explained in the last chapter. Like White, he seems not to realize that the stage-by-stage arrangement of cultural forms, marking out the course of *general* evolution, depends on an essentialist taxonomy whose rejection is necessary for the adoption of a *specific* evolutionary perspective. It is not so simple as Sahlins imagines to hold both perspectives at once.

The same problem can be illustrated by inspecting the principal criterion by which Sahlins claims to recognize general evolutionary advance. Drawing on White's energy theory of culture (White 1959b:33–57),[2] he proposes that 'in culture, as in life, thermodynamic accomplishment is fundamental to progress' (Sahlins 1960:33). Organisms generally, including human beings, 'harness and deliver energy' in the conduct of their lives—in other words, they eat and work. Likewise, or so Sahlins asserts, 'a culture harnesses and delivers energy' (1960:35), transforming it into people, goods, political systems, social customs, and so on. The cultural system, then, is being likened to a living organism. As we have seen, this was also Kroeber's view, and it underwrote his conception of the superorganic as an emergent level of organization (Kroeber 1952:22–51). It is easy to dismiss this view as an example of what Bidney (1953:137; following Whitehead 1938[1926]:66) calls 'the fallacy of misplaced concreteness', by which one comes 'to mistake a conceptual abstraction for an actual vital agent', overturning the relation between people and culture by regarding the former as vehicles for the life of the latter. However, Sahlins's presentation of the dichotomy between general and specific evolution entails a further contradiction, which in fact stems from an ambiguity in the meaning of the 'superorganic'.

I shall discuss this problem at greater length in Chapter 6, and I only touch on it at this stage. Briefly culture can be regarded as superorganic without being reified as an autonomous entity, a superorgan*ism*. Thus, if we draw an analogy between Darwinian descent with modification and Boasian culture–history, as Sahlins does in regarding both as instances of specific evolution, then the cultural system must be likened not to a living organism but to a set of instructions constituting a *design* for living, an ideal analogue of the genome. Such a system is superorganic in the sense that it transcends materiality, existing in the extrasomatic domain of ideas and symbols. But the bearers of culture, like the carriers of genes, are *individuals*: 'The culture by itself is an abstraction' (Lowie 1937:269). If cultures diversify like species, through adaptive modification, the reality must consist of populations of unique individuals. In short, the idea of specific evolution rests on a nominalist premise directly contravened by the hypostatization of culture as a living thing. Yet the latter is central to Sahlins's 'thermodynamic' conception of general evolutionary progress. Moving from the general to the specific, from development to diversification, Sahlins likens culture first to an organism, then to species, and in so doing slips from reification to abstraction. One can hardly regard as complementary, processes that rest on such logically incompatible premisses.

Is there any way, then, to reconcile the perspectives of the specific and the general, without risk of contradiction? Indeed there is, but we can reach it only by adopting a notion of general evolution rather different from that of Sahlins or White, one much closer to the original formula of Spencer than to the stage-by-stage arrangement of Tylor. It will be recalled that whereas Tylor's image of the evolution of culture was rather like a multistranded cable, Spencer's view was perfectly amenable to representation as a branching tree, diverging at every stage of its growth. 'Like other kinds of progress', Spencer wrote, 'social progress is not linear but divergent and re-divergent. . . . there have arisen genera and species of societies' (1972:133). These alternative models of the evolutionary process, though conceived independently, are not incompatible. The difference is simply that whereas Spencer was concerned with the trajectory of societies or peoples in their adaptation to diverse environments, Tylor set out to write a history *not* of peoples but of Culture as a whole, as distinct from its bearers (Tylor 1871, I:5). But with regard to Spencer, the question now arises as to how his concept of social progress is to be accommodated within the terms of the opposition between specific and general evolution. According to Sahlins himself, 'Specific evolution is the phylogenetic, adaptive, diversifying, specializing, ramifying aspect of total evolution. It is in this respect that evolution is often equated with *movement from homogeneity to heterogeneity*. But general evolution is another aspect. It is the emergence of higher forms of life' (1960:16; my emphasis). Can we regard Spencer, then, as a specific evolutionist? If so, how are we to comprehend the differences between the Spencerian and Darwinian paradigms?

To overcome this apparent impasse, it is vital to distinguish between two quite different ways of conceptualizing general evolutionary advance. One, broadly Lamarckian and adopted by Tylor, White and Sahlins, envisages the serial replacement of relatively primitive by relatively advanced forms (judged by some criterion of improvement), each engendered by the one preceding. The other, adopted by Spencer, posits a gradual process—analogous to organic growth—of structural differentiation, leading to ever-greater complexity. To recall our discussion of progress in organic nature (Chapter 1), it was shown that this is a corollary of the diversification of species and the resultant complexification of the relations between them and that it does not necessarily entail the appearance of forms of greater *internal* complexity. We are thus brought back to the fundamental distinction between tracing the specific history of each isolated branch and twig and depicting the evolution of the tree of life as a *total* system constituted by relations between the branches. This is what truly separates the evolutionary paradigms of Darwin and Spencer. The contrast Sahlins draws between general and specific evolution obscures the difference by virtue of its exclusive emphasis on forms at the expense of their interrelations. Thus what is important for Spencer is not merely the generation of heterogeneity—diversification—but the *coherence* of that heterogeneity, that is, its integration. Applied to the domain of culture, this means that we must be concerned with relations between as well as within societies of culture-bearing individuals. The image of the branching tree remains appropriate, whether our perspective be Darwinian or Spencerian, yet in the latter case the various branches appear not merely as a genealogical record of past events, but as channels for the conduct of a universal movement, of which every bud is an emergent growing-point.

Support for the Spencerian vision of general evolution comes from a most unexpected quarter, namely Lévi-Strauss, in his UNESCO pamphlet of 1953 entitled *Race and history*. Ostensibly this sets out to demolish the assumptions of progessive social evolutionism and to celebrate the boundless diversity of human cultures throughout the world. In the immediate post-war era, Lévi-Strauss has been among the most influential champions of the Boasian cause of cultural relativism. He is highly sceptical of the ideas of progress and civilization, at least as they have been conventionally understood in Western thought, and rejects out of hand the premisses of the comparative method. Such ideas underwrite what he calls a *false* evolutionism, as opposed to the *true* evolutionism of Darwinian biology. Recognizing that the former actually preceded the latter by a long way, and that both Spencer and Tylor worked out their evolutionary doctrines without having consulted *The origin of species,* Lévi-Strauss corrects (without ever acknowledging) the Boasian falsehood he himself had perpetrated only four years earlier, namely that 'the evolutionist interpretation in anthropology clearly derives from evolutionism in biology' (1968:3; compare 1953:14–6). These are, as he now admits, 'two very different things' (1953:15). Lévi-Strauss's own understanding of the history of culture, like Boas's, has a good deal in common with Darwin's conception of the natural history of species: notably the emphasis on diversification rather than development, on chance and contingency rather than purpose and design, and on the multiplicity and incommensurability of possible criteria of progress.

He goes on, however, to offer an intriguing contrast between 'stationary' and 'cumulative' history. Both presuppose that as carriers of culture, human populations have in fact followed a multitude of ever-divergent paths. But this multilinearity will be apparent only to the observer whose vision transcends history. From the perspective of an observer who, belonging to a certain culture, is positioned at the current extremity of one particular branch of the culture-historical tree, no other trajectory may be countenanced save that leading to the point where he perceives himself to stand—in splendid isolation. The history of every other culture will appear to him to have stopped short at the point at which its path diverged from that taken by his own. Hence the branches of the tree will seem lopped off, leaving but a sequence of knots, each the static image of a culture frozen in the past. 'Stationary history' evidently corresponds to this truncated vision of Sahlins's 'specific evolution', the product of an ethnocentric illusion. Yet for Lévi-Strauss it is crucial that cultures exist not in isolation but as the components of a wider system of interdependencies—a sort of global division of labour or 'coalition' in which each culture contributes its specific competence 'to the fullness of all the others' (1953:46; see Pace 1983:104–7). Thus 'we should not . . . be tempted to a piecemeal study of the diversity of human cultures, for that diversity depends less on the isolation of the various groups than on the relations between them' (1953:11–12).

Diversification, then, is a concomitant of the progressive evolution of a total system of intercultural relationships. And this evolution turns out to be none other than the Spencerian movement from homogeneity to heterogeneity. For example, Lévi-Strauss argues that since the cultures of pre-Columbian America were more homogeneous than those of Europe, having had fewer millennia in which to undergo differentiation, they readily succumbed to European conquest. Progress towards heterogeneity is 'cumulative history': not a prerogative of particular, supposedly more 'advanced' cultures, but rather a function of their collaboration. 'Cumulative history is the type of history characteristic of grouped societies—social superorganisms—while stationary history . . . would be the distinguishing feature of . . . the isolated society' (1953:40). In essence, this is the distinction between Spencerian and Darwinian evolutionary paradigms. Thus it would appear that Lévi-Strauss's defence of cultural diversity rests on the very premiss he claims to abhor—general evolutionary advance. In view of this, Pace's (1983:109) admission that in *Race and history* Lévi-Strauss 'seems to have contradicted himself a bit' on the subject of progress is a colossal understatement.

This is by no means the only context in which Lévi-Strauss has expounded on the substance of evolution and history, and we shall be returning to some of his other ideas in due course. Let me first pause to take stock of the position so far. We find in the writings of Boas, Radcliffe-Brown and White just one sense of history: It is a chronological sequence of empirical events, corresponding to what I have called the history of things. This kind of history is *opposed,* by both White and Radcliffe-Brown, to evolution in its Spencerian sense (corresponding to Lévi-Strauss's 'cumulative history'). It is *identified,* most explicitly by Murdock, with evolution in its Darwinian sense. Sahlins, for his part, identifies it with specific, as opposed to general, evolution. Clearly we can take our pick as to which meaning of evolution to adopt, and compare or contrast it with history accordingly. However, what all these authors share is a commitment to positivism. Consequently the substantial opposition between evolution and history, when drawn, may be mapped onto the methodological opposition between nomothetic and idiographic *science*. Thus White's 'evolutionist process' and Radcliffe-Brown's 'laws of social dynamics' may be apprehended through generalizing, nomothetic inquiry. But history consists of facts, which it is the tedious job of the idiographic scientist-cum-historian to collect. There is, however, another conception of the substance of history, neo-Kantian and antipositivistic, represented—though by no means consistently—in Kroeber's attacks both on Boas's idea of history and on White's idea of evolution. And this conception, too, may be either likened to, or contrasted with, the process of evolution, depending on the significance we attach to the latter. The next stage in my argument will be to examine the history–evolution dichotomy from this point of view, beginning with one of the most extreme exponents of historical subjectivism, R. G. Collingwood.

Reacting sharply against the view that history can be written across the disciplines of astronomy, geology and biology, as well as of the humanities, Collingwood argues that historians should approach their subjects from *within*

(1946:213–14). Their concern is with mind or consciousness, with the purposes and intentions of people in the past, and not with the objective manifestations of their activity. To grasp history in this inner aspect, historians must reconstitute in their mind's eye the subjects of their inquiry as living, thinking persons, and enter into a dialogue with them as though, like anthropologists transported in time rather than space, they were fellow-travellers in the same region of the total social process. In short, far from observing history as a spectacle, historians seek to invade the pitch of social action, becoming themselves part of the event. Yet life, seen from this angle, does not really consist of events at all. For events merely punctuate the flow of consciousness that, as a process in time, forever brings the past to bear on the future as it converts the future into the past. Regarded as a historical subject, man's being, in the memorable words of Ortega y Gasset, 'stretches the whole length of his past'; it is his life—'a relentless trajectory of experiences' (1941:216). In this trajectory, each event occupies but an instant of time, but the business of life goes on—and indeed *must* go on, else there would be no social relations, no consciousness and no purpose. In the real world, as opposed to the world of fiction, events are always overtaken by people, as continuity triumphs over discontinuity.

A history of persons, then, 'is not . . . a story of successive events or an account of change. Unlike the natural scientist, the historian is not concerned with events as such at all' (Collingwood 1946:217). For the history of natural things, which *is* constituted by a chronological sequence of events, Collingwood reserves the term 'evolution'—in its Darwinian sense (1946:321). People make their history, events in evolution simply happen: We confuse the two at our peril. It is clear from our preceding discussion that the same distinction separates the culture-history of Boas from history as Collingwood understands the term. Compare, for example, 'the archaeologist's interpretation of a stratified site and the geologist's interpretation of rock horizons with their associated fossils' (Collingwood 1946:212). Are they doing the same kind of thing? As long as archaeologists are content to use the material remains of human activity to reconstruct a phylogeny of cultural forms, adopting the proverbial attitude that 'the people, they're dead' (Sahlins 1972:81), there is not much difference in principle between the resulting picture and the palaeontologist's reconstruction of organic phylogeny on the basis of the fossil record. It is of course true that, as Lévi-Strauss remarks, 'an axe does not give birth to an axe in the physical sense that an animal gives birth to an animal' (1953:15); but although this is a fair objection to the species–trait analogy of Tylor and White (Tylor 1871, I: 13; White 1945a:237), it does not invalidate the parallel between culture-historical and palaeontological reconstruction. No more than axes, do bones give birth to other bones: Thus both historians of cultures and of species must read into the remains the individuals—or in aggregate, the populations—that carried those traits whose expression left a mark in the fossil or prehistoric record. Both are in the business of writing the history of populations, but *not* the history of persons. Only when they get a sense of people in the remote past not merely as the mechanical carriers, animators and transmitters of extinct cultural forms or projects, but as purposive agents acting *through* these forms in the creation and furtherance of their intersubjective life, do archaeologists begin to engage in what Collingwood regards as history. Whether such historical understanding is a practical possibility, in the absence of written records, is a moot point (Elton 1967:10; Renfrew 1982).

Perhaps it will be objected that to contrast the histories of Boas and Collingwood in these terms is to adopt a caricature of the former. If Collingwood sought to discover the 'processes of thought' behind events, surely Boas was just as concerned to 'get inside of other peoples' heads', probing beneath the outward manifestations of behaviour to discover underlying patterns of cultural meaning (Harris 1968:269; compare Collingwood 1946:213–17). This approach, which we would now call 'emic' as opposed to 'etic', has its roots in the neo-Kantian tradition to which Collingwood was also an heir; indeed it is well established that Boas's exposure to this tradition, prior to leaving his native Germany, had a decisive impact on the movement in his thought from naturalism to humanism. It appears that he was especially influenced by the philosophy of Wilhelm Dilthey, whose separation of *Geisteswissenschaften* and *Naturwissenschaften* provided a springboard for the subsequent declaration in Boasian anthropology of the autonomy of cultural facts (Harris 1968:268–70; Stocking 1968:152–4; Freeman 1970:53; Hatch 1973:42). In view of this influence, Bidney's judgement that Boas 'was no philosopher and had no understanding of neo-Kantian epistemology' (1953:253) seems harsh. In fact, as Stocking's researches have shown, Boas was an avid reader of philosophy in the early 1880s, even to the extent of taking a copy of Kant with him on his field trip among the Eskimos (Stocking 1968:143–4). So it cannot have been mere ignorance that motivated his incredulous response to Kroeber's assertion (discussed later in this chapter) that the dimension of time is inessential to history; and one can well surmise what his reaction might have been to Collingwood's aforementioned suggestion that historical inquiry neither deals in events nor renders an account of change. For without events, time or change, nothing remains of the history of culture as Boas conceived it.

There is here a divergence of approach of such fundamental significance that it cannot be glossed over by tracing each branch to a common philosophical root. Moreover it continues to pervade the discipline of anthropology to this day, underlying a series of antinomies in our understanding of what constitutes culture, meaning, consciousness and intentionality. We shall be dealing with some of these in subsequent chapters. At this point, however, I should like to highlight the ambiguity inherent in the idea, apparently shared by both Boas and Collingwood, of looking at the activity of people in the past 'from the inside'. The crucial question we have to ask is, Inside what? Let us answer, first, for Boas. From his point of view the social world is composed of a very large number of autonomous individuals each of which is the bearer of a unique pattern of cultural elements drawn from a common heritage. These elements, lodged within the individual's mind, direct thought and action. Therefore in order to discover what makes people behave the way they do, one must look not at the relations between them—which are simply the combined result of the behaviours of so many individuals—but into the *contents* of the mind of each one. Of these contents, individuals are supposed to remain largely unaware, for were this not the case, they would cease to be bound within the constraints of their cultural traditions. Hence it is the task of the anthropological-cum-historical observer to peel off the outer layers of secondary elaboration in order to reveal an inner programme, impressed upon the universal human psyche and expressed in culturally specific behaviour.

At first glance there seems to be something rather paradoxical about this pro-cedure. On the one hand, if the cultural project is apparent only to those who are not in the service of its execution, its discovery depends on the investigator's placing himself wholly *outside* the processes he is observing. On the other hand, from this detached standpoint he can know nothing of the subjective experience of the people themselves (which he dismisses anyway as a smoke-screen), remaining a mere witness of outward behaviour. From his observations he can construct a model that, though identified with the 'culture' of the people in question, remains an abstraction in his own mind. Thus we find Kluckhohn, for example, insisting on the distinction between *behaviour* and *culture*: 'Concrete behaviour or habits are part of the raw data from which we infer and abstract culture. . . . Culture, thus, is not something which is seen but an inferential construct.' Yet he promptly goes on to install this logical abstraction as a concrete reality within the minds of the people, from where—unbeknown to them—it controls their behaviour. Culture, though 'a logical construct', is nevertheless 'manifested either in men's acts or in the products of these acts' (Kluckhohn 1946:339).[3] This inversion receives an even more explicit statement in the commentary by Kroeber and Kluckhohn on psychological views of culture, where they address the problem of internality and externality only to dismiss it:

> There is no genuine problem as to the 'inwardness' or 'outwardness' of culture. It is 'outward' and 'impersonal' as an abstraction, a logical construct; it is very much 'inward' and affective as internalized in a particular individual. . . . It is highly convenient to construct an abstract conceptual model of a culture. But this does not mean that culture is a force like Newtonian gravity 'acting at a distance'. Culture is a precipitate of history but, as internalized in concrete organisms, very much active in the present. (1952:114)

It is clear from these remarks that the 'view from the inside' is obtained simply by implanting, into objectified individuals, the anthropologist's view from the out-side (Bourdieu 1977:96). As the relation between observer and observed is turned outside in, so the opposition between internal and external appears to dissolve. The little man within each of us emerges as none other than the anthropologist himself!

Collingwood is resolutely opposed to such objectivism. The reality he aims to grasp by 'penetrating to the inside of events' (1946:214) is that of lived experience, of consciousness, purpose and agency; and he grasps it through sharing in the expe-rience himself. As Bourdieu has recently put it, to renounce objectivist idealism 'it suffices to situate oneself *within* "real activity as such", i.e. in the practical relation to the world' (1977:96). But to do so is to adopt a quite different view of mind, as agent rather than medium. The difference is already familiar to us through our comparison, in Chapter 2, of the Tylorian and Boasian conceptions of 'culture'. If, like Boas, we treat the mind as a passive container or repository for cultural things, there being as many such containers as there are individuals, then to penetrate within is merely to open out its contents for inspection. Tylor, to the contrary, regarded the mind as an active and creative movement, endlessly borne along by generation after generation of individuals. Obviously to apprehend the mind in this sense is not a matter of climbing into individuals' heads, for there we would find but the instruments or templates for its conduct. Consciousness is not a property of individual objects but is an inter-subjective process, and to apprehend it is to become a part of that process—that is, to understand the purposes of other people by making them one's own (Ingold 1983a:6). To objectivists such a stance is inadmissible, for it implies that investigators allow themselves to become enmeshed in the skein of conscious rationalization people weave around their lives, becoming as blind as they are to the inward forms of culture that 'really' guide their conduct. One cannot, after all, grasp the contents of a bottle by becoming a part of the glass. To this, the subjectivist response is that things poured into glass bottles do not flow.

It might surprise the reader that Tylor, renowned for his view of culture-history as a natural science, should be credited with a view of mind not unlike that of Collingwood, equally renowned for his antiscientific, antipositivistic conception of historical inquiry. One should not, of course, underrate the differences; yet my impression is that to a great extent these are differences of idiom rather than substance. Positivism furnished the language of scholarship in Tylor's day, and both 'nature' and 'science' had connotations in the nineteenth century rather different from what they have in the twentieth. For us the crucial point is that Tylor, like other advocates of progressive evolution with humanist inclinations, regarded consciousness as an immense continuum, extending in space to embrace all mankind, and unfolding in time throughout the total course of human history. Though for the most part Tylor concentrated his attention on the objects through which this continuous movement was carried forward, the idea of such a movement lay at the very foundation of his entire evolutionary scheme, for without it culture would have broken up into Lowie's celebrated 'shreds and patches'. And so when Tylor wrote of primitive man, it was from a perspective located firmly *within* the evolutionary process: Both he and the savage were seen to be ascending the same slopes, if at different altitudes. These slopes might be envisaged as a surface in space-time, such that to move to regions remote in space is to take a trip back in time. A primitive society was thus the Victorian ethnographer's time-machine (Gellner 1964:18). And the essential attribute of a time-machine is that it enables its operator to perceive the *continuity* of the social process as it was experienced by people living in the past, which is lost in the mere record of events—however complete.

Now we find in the writings of Collingwood precisely the same emphasis on arriving at a knowledge of history through the re-enactment, in the present, of the continuity of past experience: not, however, by travelling to an exotic land to watch what people are doing there, but by the historian's rethinking the past in his own mind on the basis of available documentary material (1946:215). Given such material, one can dispense with the comparative method and the rather dubious assumptions it entails, whilst retaining the idea of history or evolution as a subjective process of mind. But we also find Collingwood explaining—very much in the spirit of Tylor—that as a living, thinking person, the historian is himself a part, or continuation into the present, of the very process whose trajectory in the past he has been trying to apprehend. Thus 'the historian's mind is heir to the past and has come to be what it is through the development of the past into the present, so that in him the past is living in the present' (Collingwood 1946:171). Moreover the idea of grasping life and consciousness directly, by thinking oneself into the situation of the people studied, together with the contrast in this respect with objectivist natural science, is exactly echoed in a remarkable passage from Tylor. Comparing the anthropologist with the astronomer or botanist, he writes that the former 'works a whole stage nearer to ultimate truth than do students who have more doubtfully to translate symptoms into inferences. Directer evidence of personal consciousness stands open to those who have to reason on the thoughts and acts of men like themselves, which might have been their own' (cited in Leopold 1980:48).[4] Exit Tylor the positivist!

Tylor's successor at Oxford, R. R. Marett, was still more emphatic about the need to breathe life into history by apprehending it from within: For 'unless what is outwardly perceived as a body of custom be likewise inwardly apprehended as a process of mind, the treatment is bound to be mechanical and correspondingly lifeless' (1920:1). Evidently influenced by the current of vitalism that held sway at the time, Marett advocated participation as a means to grasp the purpose that operates through the instrumentality of cultural forms. We have, he said, 'to project ourselves into the life of the peasant, and to arrive by intuition at the push of the life-force manifested therein' (1920:19). In a memorable passage he likens culture, 'a tissue of externalities', to a multicoloured suit of clothing adorning human life. Looking from the outside we may, by repeated observation, discover the pattern on which the suit has been cut, but of the wearer we would see only a dummy or model, whose purpose is merely to exhibit the style and further its propagation. The idea that people exist as instruments for the conduct of culture, central to Boasian objectivism, is dismissed by Marett as 'a doctrine . . . fit only for tailors', who of course need people in order that clothes should be worn. To be sure, 'a man naked of all culture would be no better than a forked radish', but to see of persons nothing but the culture they bear—to forget that they are also conscious, purposive agents—would lead us to a panorama of human history worthy of Madame Tussaud's (Marett 1920:11). The figures might be exquisitely realistic, they might even be contrived to move, but they do not *live*.

A more recent champion of historical understanding in social anthropology, profoundly influenced by the teachings of Collingwood, was E. E. Evans-Pritchard. Writing at a time when evolutionary thinking had been thoroughly eclipsed by synchronic functionalism, Evans-Pritchard's principal concern was to repudiate the vogue—inspired largely by Radcliffe-Brown—for presenting anthropology as an exclusively nomothetic discipline, emulating natural science in its search for laws. Social anthropology, he declared, 'is a kind of historiography, and therefore ultimately of philosophy or art, . . . it studies societies as moral systems and not as natural systems, . . . is interested in design rather than in process, . . . seeks patterns and not scientific laws, and interprets rather than explains' (Evans–Pritchard 1950:123; also 1951:62). The debt to Kroeber, and more generally to the neo-Kantian tradition, is obvious. Thus we find Evans–Pritchard agreeing with Kroeber that Boasian cultural anthropology, despite appearances, is 'fundamentally anti-historical in tendency' and that the essence of both historical and social anthropological method lies—or at least should lie—not in the collection of particulars, nor in the subsumption of the particular under the general, but in discovering 'the general in the particular' (Evans–Pritchard 1961:1–3; compare Kroeber 1952:63–5). He concludes by endorsing the celebrated dictum of the legal historian Maitland that 'anthropology must choose between being history and being nothing' (Evans–Pritchard 1950:123; 1961:20; see Maitland 1936:249).

There is something rather inconsistent about this conclusion. Maitland's pronouncement, made in 1899, was in fact delivered in the course of an attack on Spencer's evolutionary sociology, and on the premises of the comparative method as employed by Tylor and others. Maitland's approach to history, clearly paralleled in the work of Boas, 'was that of a positivist interested in the minute collection of fragmentary facts, but opposed to the sociological and anthropological assumption of "laws" of sociocultural history' (Bidney 1953:264; see Collingwood 1946:127). This is precisely the kind of history that Evans–Pritchard, following Collingwood, *rejects*. Bidney sets out the contrast with admirable clarity:

> Maitland's positivistic conception of history and [Evans–Pritchard's] own borrowed neo-Kantian, idealistic conception are antithetical. For the idealist, history . . . is a matter of interpretation and evaluation and hence is essentially subjective; for the positivist, history, like natural science, is an objective record of man's past yielding an organized body of established knowledge. (1953:264)

Was Evans–Pritchard's adoption of Maitland's motto simply an instance of mistaken identity? If so, he mistook Boas as well, for having disqualified the claim to historicity of Boasian anthropology, he cited with approval Boas's remark that 'in order to understand history, it is necessary to know not only how things are, but how they came to be' (Boas 1948:284; Evans–Pritchard 1961:6). This remark, like Maitland's, was made in the context of a critique of evolutionary law-mongering; thus, said Boas in the same passage, 'we do not hope to be able to solve an intricate historical problem by a formula'. The historian needs facts, not formulae. But as we saw in the preceding chapter, all Boas meant by knowing how things came to be was simply to have constructed a record of the antecedent sequence of events.

Whatever Evans–Pritchard's motives may have been in falsely identifying his vision of a historical anthropology with those of Boas and Maitland, the effect was to obscure a remarkable affinity between what he conceived as the substance of history and the Tylorian conception of evolution. The double opposition between the 'evolution' of Tylor and the 'history' of Boas, and between the latter and the 'history' of Evans-Pritchard, yields what is virtually an identity. Tylor's positivism, as we have seen, was only skin-deep, whereas Evans-Pritchard himself admits that—so long as the comparative method is applied with due caution—'we can return to the historical interests of the founders of our science' (1961:20). By these 'historical interests', he means of course their concern with continuity and progress, echoed in the more recent statement of Dumont—with which Evans-Pritchard fully concurs—that 'history is the movement by which a society reveals itself as what it is' (Dumont 1957:21; see Evans-Pritchard 1961:12). This amounts to saying that history is a kind of evolution, if the latter be understood in its original sense of a continuous unfolding, as directed movement rather than changeful sequence. Elsewhere, echoing Kroeber, Evans-Pritchard declared that 'history is not merely a succession of changes but . . . a growth. The past is contained in the present as the present is in the future' (1951:60). He could scarcely have been more explicit.

There is, moreover, an uncanny resemblance between Evans Pritchard's idea of historical generalization and White's of 'the evolutionist process'. To repeat the words of White:

> In the evolutionist process we are not concerned with unique events, fixed in time and place, but with a *class* of events, without reference to specific times and places. (1945a:238)

Now compare Evans-Pritchard:

> Events lose much, even all, of their meaning if they are not seen as having some degree of regularity and constancy, as belonging to a certain type of event, all instances of which have many features in common. . . . An historical fact thus shorn of its unique features escapes also temporality. It is no longer a passing incident, a sort of accident, but is, as it were, taken out of the flux of time. (1961:4)

We have, I think, a right to know how Evans-Pritchard's distinction between viewing events in their uniqueness, as accidental particulars, and viewing them as representatives of a determinate class, differs from White's separation of historical and evolutionary perspectives. Otherwise we may be fully justified in concluding, with Bidney, that between the approaches of Tylorian evolutionary ethnology and Evans-Pritchard's historical anthropology 'there appears to be no significant difference at all' (1953:265).

Where Evans-Pritchard is contradictory in his attitude to history, Lévi-Strauss is incoherent. In a well-known article, he offers the following alternatives: 'Either anthropology is focused on the diachronic dimension of phenomena, that is, on their temporal order, and thus is unable to trace their history; or anthropologists attempt to apply the method of the historian, and the time dimension escapes them' (1968:3). It is difficult to know what to make of this largely incomprehensible formulation. Perhaps Lévi-Strauss has in mind Kroeber's view that the essence of historical method lies in the immediate apprehension and depiction of the total sociocultural landscape from a particular point within it. Kroeber had gone so far as to suggest that the longitudinal projection of phenomena in time is incidental to historical understanding, since the historian's 'descriptive integration' could be cast just as well in space, as a synchronic 'cross-section'—most ethnographic accounts of peoples whose lived past is inaccessible being precisely of this latter kind (Kroeber 1952:102). Evans-Pritchard agreed: 'The fundamental characteristic of the historical method is not chronological relation of events but descriptive integration of them; and this characteristic historiography shares with social anthropology' (1950:122; see also 1951:61). Kroeber's characterization of a work of ethnography as 'a timeless piece of history' seems to be the prototype for Lévi-Strauss's image, in his second alternative, of the ethnographer as a historian who has lost touch with time. The first alternative would then correspond to Kroeber's 'science', which, dissolving the whole into empirical elements only to reconstruct it as a diachronically ordered series, fails to recover its specifically historical essence. Ethnology (or social anthropology) is accordingly presented as a science that has lost touch with history.

Elsewhere, though Lévi-Strauss registers his approval of Kroeber's point that history can make do without time, he blandly proceeds to contradict the very premises on which the point rests by identifying history (together with ethnography) and sociology (together with social anthropology) with the two steps of 'empirical observation' and 'model building' respectively (Lévi-Strauss 1968:285–6, 316 n. 15; see Barnes 1971:542). 'The historian', he explains, 'always studies individuals'; likewise 'ethnography consists of the observation and analysis of human groups considered as individual entities' (1968:2, 4). Indeed, Lévi-Strauss's atomistic conception of the substance of history owes more to Boas than to Kroeber or Evans-Pritchard; it is understood as an empirical 'succession of events' located in the diachronic dimension, in contradistinction to the 'synchronic' dimension of underlying structure (1968:21). That Lévi-Strauss could begin by associating a focus on diachronic sequence with an *inability* to comprehend history, as though one could locate in history itself the synchronic pattern behind the flux of events, only confirms his failure to grasp the differences on this point between Boas and Kroeber, and to apply his concepts consistently. These problems are compounded, as we shall see, by his attempts to accommodate history within a framework of categories (mechanical–statistical models, reversible–irreversible time) derived from Wiener's *Cybernetics,* which lead to the very identification of history with progressive evolution that Boas— and elsewhere Lévi-Strauss too—utterly *rejected.* To some extent, he manages to wriggle around this contradiction by recategorizing Boas as an ethnographer rather than a historian, dealing in mechanical and not statistical models. White is criticized for likewise using mechanical models, when his evolutionist approach properly requires the construction of models of a statistical type (Lévi-Strauss 1968:286–7). It is difficult to make much sense of this. A Boasian 'culture', as a specific assemblage of objectified elements, is not a model at all in Wiener's sense, whereas White's treatment of evolution—replete with thermodynamic imagery—was thoroughly 'statistical'.

This is a matter to which we shall return in the next chapter, when we consider the dichotomy between history and evolution in relation to the form of time. Let me first recapitulate the principal thrust of our argument to this point. Just as the Boasian conception of the substance of history as a succession of events may be likened to the Darwinian conception of evolution or descent with modification in the world of nature, so the latter may be opposed (as in Collingwood) to the idea of history as a process of mind. Given also the opposition, stressed by White, between Boasian history and evolution in its pre-Darwinian sense of unfolding or progressive development, we are left with the question of whether this whole set of correspondences and contrasts can be tied up by linking evolution in this latter sense to Collingwood's conception of history (Fig. 3.2). To claim a complete identity would be, at this stage, to stretch the point; however, we have found a number of indications of just such a link. Thus Tylor identified the history of culture with evolving human consciousness. Kroeber, adopting a neo-Kantian concept of history, could nevertheless write of the growth of culture in terms reminiscent of Spencer and was prepared to categorize many of White's examples of the 'evolutionist process' as 'merely large histories' (Kroeber 1952:102). Lévi-Strauss, when in the mood to follow Kroeber, asserts categorically that 'all history is cumulative' and admits that evolution—as White understands the term—may be equated with history in this sense (1953:36; 1968:286). And even Evans-Pritchard has come out with a view of historical generalization that appears to have remarkable affinities to the evolutionary ethnology of Tylor and White. Further evidence for the affinity is furnished by the sliding reference of 'historicism', mentioned earlier in this chapter, from neo-Kantian relativism to the Spencerian paradigm of progressive development.

What, then, are the common connotations of these paired concepts of history and evolution? There are four that can be mentioned right away. First, they both deal primarily with *process* rather than events. Compare, for example, Teggart's understanding of evolution—the 'slow, continuous modification of an eventless world'—with Collingwood's contention that 'the historian is not concerned with events as such at all' (Collingwood 1946:271; Teggart 1972:141). The second point follows from the first: Both start out from the premiss of the *continuity,* in both space and time, of real life: not the reconstructed continuity of the motion picture but continuity as it is immediately given in conscious experience. Third, and again as a corollary of our previous two observations, both connote a *holistic* or totalizing approach, absolutely opposed to the atomism of Darwinian evolution or

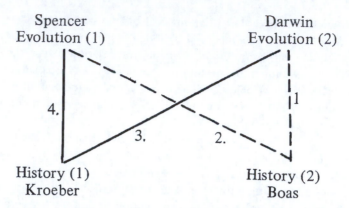

FIG. 3.2 Correspondences and contrasts between the two senses of history and evolution.

1. Darwinian *evolution* compared to Boasian culture *history:* Murdock, Sahlins (specific evolution), Lévi-Strauss (stationary history).
2. Progressive *evolution* contrasted to Boasian culture *history:* Radcliffe-Brown, White.
3. Darwinian *evolution* contrasted to *history* as a process of mind: Collingwood.
4. Progressive *evolution* compared to *history* as a process of mind: Kroeber, Lévi-Strauss (cumulative history), Evans-Pritchard, Bergson.

Boasian culture-history. If we are to speak of events at all, each is but a point on the spatiotemporal continuum, or a moment in its unfolding. And finally, both history and evolution, in the senses we are considering here, are given direction by the agency of consciousness: Far from 'just happening', they are made. In other words, they embody *teleology,* or purpose. Again, it is precisely the absence of teleology that characterizes the Darwinian and Boasian paradigms. For all these reasons, and there are more, I believe it is well justified to regard the history of persons as a kind of evolution that we may call social.

Indeed, I would argue that the notion of evolution is far better suited to this context than to that of Darwinian biology. Lamarck's 'transformism' and Darwin's 'descent with modification' convey much better than 'evolution' the specific character of organic adaptation, and biological science has performed a signal disservice in appropriating to itself a key term that so ill befits the interpretation that came to be placed on it. For were we to accept the biologist's inclination to dismiss any notion of evolution that does not conform to Darwinian principles, we would remain bereft of a concept to denote the continuous, directed and purposive movement to which the term originally and quite properly referred. Nowhere has the identity between this original sense of evolution and history, conceived as a flow of consciousness, been more explicitly drawn than in the work of the great French philosopher, Henri Bergson. I shall devote some attention to his ideas, since they provide an admirable foundation for the discussion of three major topics that will occupy us for much of what follows in this and the next two chapters. These are first, the dichotomy between individual and person; second, the nature of historical and evolutionary time; and third, the significance of chance, necessity and creativity. But before embarking on these subjects, two other issues remain to be sorted out. One has to do with the concept of relativism, the other with what we mean by events.

The difficulty with relativism is that the term may be used to characterize two approaches to both history and evolution that we have shown to be irreconcilably opposed. Just as, when inquiring into the import of viewing the past from the inside, we had to ask, Inside what?, so our understanding of relativism will depend on how we answer the question, Relative to what? Those who would push to its limits the pursuit of objectivity would say, Relative to *something*. They prescribe an austere ideal—practically unattainable for ordinary mortals, barring the likes of Lévi-Strauss (Pace 1983:118)—of absolute detachment, so that the thing can be recognized and appreciated for what it is, in itself. This is the kind of relativism implied in Darwin's theory of variation under natural selection, and it likewise informs the culture-history of Boas. The aim is to transcend our own (subjective) point of view and hence to combat 'centrism' in all its forms, whether the anthropocentric view of other species or the ethnocentric view of other cultures. Accordingly it rejects the idea of progress and celebrates diversity, regarding every species or culture as an object of intrinsic value. Needless to say, objectivist relativism is riddled with contradictions, which boil down to its inability to accommodate the fact of the observers' own existence in the real world (Bidney 1953:424; see Herskovits 1948:63–4). For example, in supposing the whole of humanity to be locked within the constraints of innumerable traditions, the cultural relativist not only places himself a cut above the common run of mankind, but also imagines the entire tapestry of 'ways of life' to be a pageant put on for his personal enjoyment. He alone purports to recognize 'other cultures' for what they really are, not the folk condemned to live incarcerated within them. Setting himself up, in Bidney's words, 'as the spectator of all time and culture', he 'establishes the facts of cultural ethnocentrism . . . and anticipates that somehow this enlightening information will liberate students of anthropology from the depressing limitations of their own cultural environment. Anthropologists, at least, will be free and enlightened souls, even if the rest of mankind is doomed to cultural bondage' (Bidney 1963b:5–6).

The advocates of progressive evolution, to their credit, do not confer on themselves a position of such absolute superiority, remaining ascendant in the world of humanity rather than transcendent as superhuman, superobjective spectators. It is vital to maintain the distinction between that kind of transcendence or 'decentration' entailed in the pursuit of total objectivity and the kind 'by which one enters imaginatively in other subjective points of view, and tries to see how things appear from other specific standpoints' (Nagel 1979:209). Whereas the former takes us outside the world, the latter enjoins us to remain *within* it but to take up a range of positions different from that in which we immediately find ourselves. 'Subjectivist' relativism, then, constitutes an affirmation rather than a denial of 'centrism', a recognition that—since to exist as a person is to have a point of view—there must be as many different centres, and hence as many prospects of the world, as there are persons in society. In other words, every prospect is relative to some*one* rather than some*thing;* what we see depends not on what we are looking *at* but on where we are looking *from*.[5] Moreover the imaginative exercise required by subjectivist relativism, the ability to transport oneself to another centre and to adopt the view of its occupant, depends on the notion that we are all fellow passengers in the same movement and hence that there is but one world (as opposed to the multiple worlds—corresponding to discrete cultures—of the objectivist, who sees all by virtue of belonging to none). Now this notion, appealing to our common humanity—perhaps even to our fellowship with animals—is the very underpinning of evolutionary thought in its classic pre-Darwinian mould. We need not be surprised, therefore, to find that most eminently reasonable of progressive evolutionists, Tylor, stressing the need to see things from the point of view of the primitive who is, after all, a rational agent and a human being like ourselves. 'The student of history must avoid that error which the proverb calls measuring other people's corn by one's own bushel. Not judging the customs of nations at other stages of culture by his own modern standard, he has to bring his knowledge to the help of his imagination, so as to see institutions where they belong and how they work' (Tylor 1881:410).

The same dichotomy between persons and things, and between subjective and objective, reappears when we come to the problem of how to define 'the event'. For although we might be inclined to regard events as particular moments in peoples' lives, these are *not* the constituent elements of Boasian culture-history. The 'actors' in such history, if we may so regard them, are not real people but the bits and pieces of culture that combine in the minds of individuals. Each event, therefore, is a meeting not of persons but of elementary traits or instructions. The analogy with Darwinian descent with modification is again revealing: Just as the appearance of every genetically programmed organism constitutes a unique event in natural history, so the formation of every habituated human being is a unique event in cultural history. Individuals *are* events; the life of each—played out and expended in the monotonous execution and transmission of a preformed behavioural project—is but the extension, in a motionless present, of a single instant in a succession of instants making up a particular historical sequence. This is not a history in which people do things, or in which things happen to people: Rather, as individuals, they are the things that happen. It follows that life, being collapsed within the instant of each event, is divorced from history, being their succession (see Fig. 3.3A). Here again, the Boasian conception of history contrasts with the subjectivist history of persons in precisely the same way that Darwinian evolution contrasts with evolution in its pre-Darwinian, developmental sense. Taking the latter sense in each contrast, both history and evolution are fundamentally concerned with the flow of life, not as a sequence of instants, but as a continuous, progressive movement analogous to organic growth (Fig. 3.3B). And this movement is not contained within events but is conducted through them: The role of the individual is to receive life and to pass it on, to act as a temporary vehicle for the projection of past into future. With this, we are brought back to Bergson's *Creative evolution* (1911).[6]

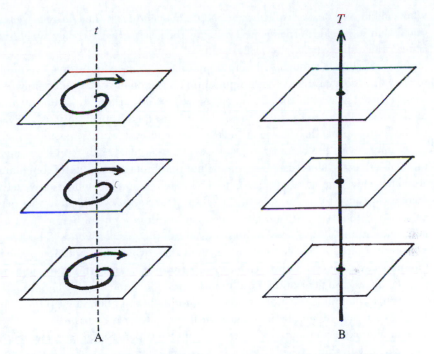

FIG. 3.3 Two views of the relation between evolution and the flow of life, or
between history and the flow of consciousness. **A:** Successive planes
represent individuals (events) in genealogical sequence, each occupying a
moment in abstract, chronological time (*t*), the life of each expended in the
revelation of preformed structure. **B:** Successive planes represent transects of
a continuous, progressive movement of life or consciousness in real time (*T*),
conducted *through* events.

Bergson regarded the substance of evolution, like that of history, as a continuous movement in real time, or what he calls 'duration'. This movement,
neither random nor predetermined but always creative, is equated with life and
consciousness. The individual organism is but an ephemeral vector of this creative
process: '*Life is like a current passing from germ to germ through the medium of a developed
organism*. . . . The essential thing is the *continuous progress* indefinitely pursued, an
invisible progress, on which each visible organism rides during the short interval
of time given it to live' (1911:28–9). By invisible, Bergson meant that it cannot
be apprehended retrospectively by the intellect, which forever dissects the flux of
experience into countless discrete and instantaneous states, only to reconstitute
them as an ordered sequence (1911:170–4). To discover the reality of life we must
abandon our stand outside the world, 'attaching ourselves to the inner becoming
of things' (1911:322). We must work, in other words, through intuition rather
than the intellect: 'It is to the very inwardness of life that *intuition* leads us', an
intuition 'that has become disinterested, self-conscious, capable of reflecting upon
its object' (1911:186). This intuitive perspective is also a holistic one: 'The real

whole might well be, we conceive, an indivisible continuity. The systems we cut out within it would, properly speaking, not then be *parts* at all; they would be *partial views* of the whole' (1911:32).

All this, naturally enough, led Bergson to oppose his view of organic evolution to Darwin's. To a great extent, this opposition hinged on the question of individuality. The uniqueness of the individual, as we saw in Chapter 1, is fundamental to the theory of variation under natural selection. Every organism is conceived in the terms of this theory as a singular entity, endowed with a specific project coterminous with the boundaries of its own existence. Its birth represents not a moment in a gradual process of becoming, but the abrupt appearance of something absolutely new. And what it passes on to the future is not its life (which, as we have seen, is expended in a static present) but a set of elementary instructions that may be recombined in the formation of other projects for other lives. Bergson, for his part, rejected the idea of absolute individuality in the organic world. 'The living being', he argued, 'is above all a thoroughfare', along which the impulsion of life is transmitted. And as each individual, like a relay runner, takes up this impulsion and passes it on, as each generation must lean over and touch the next, so how can we tell exactly where one individual ends and another begins (Bergson 1911:45, 90, 135)? As a bearer of life, the individual carries an entire past, a past that stretches back in unbroken continuity to its remotest ancestors and that is being constantly augmented with the passage of time. In this sense, the individual *is* its past, and as such its individuality overlaps that of all others with which it shares common descent and ultimately therefore with the totality of living beings (1911:45–6; for a similar view see Rensch 1972:6–8).

What has been said about the role of organisms in the evolution of life may also be said about the role of persons in the history of consciousness. Bergson himself is quite explicit about the analogy: 'The more we fix our attention on [the] continuity of life, the more we see that organic evolution resembles the evolution of a consciousness, in which the past presses against the present and causes the upspringing of a new form of consciousness' (1911:29). Life, as he elsewhere puts it, is 'consciousness launched into matter' (1911:191). The identity of the person, like that of the organism, lies in the entirety of his past carried forward into the present: In this sense both organism and person may be understood to have a history (1911:5, 16). And again, just as living things are thought to convey the impulsion of life, so is consciousness borne along by successive generations of mankind, in an endless creative movement. It follows that it is no more possible to ascribe absolute boundaries to persons, conceived as historical agents, than it is to organisms conceived as bearers of life. For if we identify persons with the trajectories of their past experience, that is with their particular cumulative biographies, we must admit first that no person can be quite the same from one moment to the next, and second that there is no obvious point at which we should begin. No complete biography would start with the birth of its subject, since the story of a life merely takes over from the story of other lives that have shaped it, and so on in infinite retrocession. The individual of Boasian culture-history, quite to the contrary, is clearly demarcated by the specific configuration of cultural elements in which his life is contained in the brief span from cradle to grave. To comprehend his behaviour we need know nothing of the past, but only of the present code of cultural practice.

Bergson's remarks on the concepts of person and personality are of such importance to our current theme that they deserve to be cited at length:

> What are we, in fact, what is our *character,* if not the condensation of the history that we have lived from our birth? . . . It is with our entire past . . . that we desire, will and act. . . . From this survival of the past it follows that consciousness cannot go through the same state twice. The circumstances may still be the same, but they will no longer act on the same person, since they find him at a new moment of his history. Our personality, which is being built up each instant with its accumulated experience, changes without ceasing. That is why our duration is irreversible. . . . Each of our states [may be] regarded as a moment in a history that is gradually unfolding . . . an original moment in a no less original history. . . . It is then right to say that what we do depends on what we are; but it is necessary to add also that we are, to a certain extent, what we do, and that we are creating ourselves endlessly. (1911:5–7)

Bergson might have done better to begin with 'Who are we?' rather than 'What are we?' For in answer to the latter question it might reasonably be asserted that we are but individuals, representatives of a particular species—*Homo sapiens*—and of some particular culture. But to 'Who are you?', the response 'a human being' might be less than helpful to any but an extraterrestrial observer. To answer *this* question at all completely, you would have to present a biographical account of yourself from your ancestry to the present, mentioning all the other people whose careers at one stage or another have impinged upon or run tangentially to your own. You would, in other words, present yourself as the predicate of an unfolding history of intersubjective (social) relationships.

With that qualification, we can recast the argument as follows. Consciousness is a movement in time, as a conscious agent *I* am therefore an accumulation of past experience. To say, then, that *I* do something, rather than that it is being done mechanically, is to imply that the whole weight of my past is brought to bear on the current action. (Conversely, to suppose that all the conditions for the performance of an action are contained within the present is to see the performance as undirected by conscious agency, that is as an instance of behaviour rather than action—a conceptual dichotomy we develop in a later chapter.) Yet even as the action proceeds, it is sinking into the past and thereby becoming part of the self that is acting. And so, as Bergson said, we continually create ourselves. Or in the words of Durkheim, 'In each of us, in varying proportions, there is part of yesterday's man; it is yesterday's man who inevitably predominates in us, since the present amounts to little compared with the long past in the course of which we were formed and from which we result' (1938:16; cited in Bourdieu 1977:79). But as Durkheim taught, the self is not simply home-made, nor does consciousness (*pace* Bergson 1911:103) explode like a cascade of fireworks, following innumerable and separate paths. Precisely because subjective life is never conducted in hermetic solitude, because 'human beings are not concocted like homunculi in retorts' (Schutz 1970:163), each one of us is constituted as a person by his social relations with others and may thus be represented as one point or vortex in a boundless field of such relationships. It was presumably this kind of field that Teilhard de Chardin envisaged in his notion of the 'noosphere', or sphere of mind, eloquently portrayed as an elastic membrane enveloping the earth (1959:226). Moreover, since consciousness implies temporal continuity, we must conclude that the person is essentially a locus of creative growth in the unfolding of this membrane along the dimension of time. By such unfolding, we mean the total process of social life. Thus, opposed to the self-sufficient individual conceived 'as a particular incarnation of abstract humanity', we posit the person, 'man as a social being, . . . a more or less autonomous point of emergence of a particular collective humanity' (Dumont 1972:39).

We find a view of the person remarkably similar to Bergson's in the writings of Ortega y Gasset. Like Bergson, he treats life as a continuous, progressive movement, an accumulation of experience. This does not imply a necessary acceptance of the absolute standards of earlier progress theorists, for our understanding of social evolution does not stand or fall on their judgement of moral superiority. The error of the classical doctrine of progress, as Ortega points out, 'lay in affirming that man progresses towards the better. . . . But that our life does possess a simply progressive character, that we can affirm *a priori*'. Thus, 'the European of today is not only different from what he was fifty years ago; his being now includes that of fifty years ago' (1941:218).[7] This is because lives overlap and are shaped by the past as they shape the future: Each of us takes up the story and carries it forwards. To one person's humanity is added the humanity of others, and so on in a cumulative process (1941:220). The progressive aspect of history rests, therefore, on the idea that social life as we experience it (though not as we think back on it) is an unbroken and directed flow. However, to freeze this flow in the instant of the present, and to reconstruct life as a succession of such instants, is to eliminate the agency of our subjective being. 'The past is I', writes Ortega y Gassett, 'by which I mean my life' (1941:223). Cut out the past, and I cease to exist. All that remains in the instantaneous present are the objective, thinglike attributes of my humanity, that is those attributes that have a given, fixed consistency and that can therefore be conceived to have an existence outside the flux of real time.

Now the sum of these fixed attributes constitutes what is often known as 'human nature'. And yet Ortega seems to go so far as to deny us even this: 'Man, in a word, has no nature, what he has is . . . history' (1941:217). This apparently forthright and unambiguous declaration needs to be interpreted rather carefully. It has often been understood as a radical manifesto for the more extreme versions of culture-historical determinism, for the primacy of nurture over nature, or the cultural over the organic. This is the sense in which it is taken up for criticism by Bidney (1953:154–5), who equates the dichotomy nature–history with the dichotomy nature–culture and urges the complementary recognition of both

terms of the polarity (see also Kluckhohn 1949:46). Dobzhansky likewise coun-
sels moderation, in the face of the equally radical (and thankfully now defunct)
counterassertion of C. D. Darlington that 'the materials of heredity contained in
the chromosomes are the solid stuff which ultimately determines the course of
history' (Darlington 1953:404).[8] For Dobzhansky, 'man has both a nature and a
"history". Human evolution has two components, the biological or organic and
the cultural or superorganic. . . . It is the interaction between biology and culture'
(Dobzhansky 1962:18). Bock, reporting on the debate in the context of a critique
of recent sociobiology, continues to represent Ortega as the passionate protagonist
of a humanism that ascribes ultimate priority to culture in the shaping of human
experience (Bock 1980:174–7). This is certainly not the place for a review of the
nature–nurture controversy. My concern is rather to show that those who have
harnessed Ortega to the cause of Boasian cultural determinism have completely
misunderstood what he meant by both man, nature and history. It is vital for us to
identify the sources of this misunderstanding.

Let me begin with the concept of nature. To describe the multiple meanings
of this concept, and the changes they have undergone, would take a book in itself.
For our present purpose, however, it suffices to distinguish just two. In one of these
senses, 'nature' connotes the material world as opposed to the world of ideas, the
inorganic and organic as opposed to the cultural. This is *not* the sense adopted by
Ortega y Gasset. For him, natural means 'thing-like'; the nature of the thing lies
in whatever constitutes the fixity of its being (1941:184–5). We can, in this sense,
talk equally well about the 'nature' of organic (natural in the other sense) and cultural things. In other words, Ortega's concept of nature *does not exclude* but rather
embraces culture. When, therefore, he tells us that 'man is not a thing, that it is false
to talk of human nature, that man has no nature', we must take him to mean that
the historical past—which 'is all he has'—is *not* a history of culture (1941:185, 230).
This leads us to the second source of misunderstanding: Ortega's history is a history
of persons, not of things, and as such is utterly opposed to the Boasian conception.
Man's past is his life, a life that is not given as a project ready-made, but which must
continually be built up by an exercise of will, each person taking over from where
others left off (1941:165, 220). 'The only thing that is given us and that *is* when
there is human life is *the having to make it*. . . . *Life is a task*' (1941:200). Nothing
could stand in clearer contrast to the idea of a life expended in acting out a programme already written for it in the materials of custom.

If the element of culture is a thing, so also is the individual human being—in so
far as his individuality is given by a unique assemblage of such elements. How, then,
can Ortega claim that 'man is not a thing'? This question leads to our third source
of misunderstanding, concerning what he means by man. For here he adopts a view
much narrower than that of his critics, going out of his way to separate life, consciousness and experience from the attributes through which it is conducted. 'Man
is not his body—which is a thing—nor his soul, psyche, conscience or spirit, which
is also a thing. Man is no thing, but a drama—his life' (1941:199). In short, far from
denying the organic and cultural components of our common humanity, Ortega

simply excludes them from his concept of man, which he limits to subjective being. Ortega's man is the answer to 'who we are', not 'what we are'; he is not an individual but a person. Thus where he writes 'Let us say, . . . not that man *is,* but that he *lives*' (1941:213), we would say that the individual *is,* the person *lives.*[9] Those such as Dobzhansky, who contrive to encapsulate the entirety of human evolution within the interaction of biological and cultural factors, leave out precisely what Ortega was above all concerned to stress, namely historical consciousness. As we maintain that consciousness is constituted by social relations (a point argued at greater length in subsequent chapters), it follows that we would translate his dichotomy between nature and history not as one between the biological and cultural (or 'sociocultural') but as one between the biological-cum-cultural constitution of the individual on the one hand and the social constitution of the person on the other. Viewed in this light, the burden of Ortega's argument—with which we fully concur—is that in the objective properties of human individuals lies not the source but the medium of our purposive, intersubjective life.

A few more words are necessary at this stage on the concept of man. For not only can it cover either or both of the subjective and objective aspects of human existence, it can also refer to the particular man as well as to mankind in general. Nothing can be more dangerous than to slip from one to the other, to suppose that because our particular person is the maker of history rather than the fortuitous precipitate of a sequence of events, so mankind is a kind of global agent subjecting the course of social evolution to a common purpose. The prophets of humanism have always been prone to this kind of exaggeration, nowhere better exemplified than in the writings of Julian Huxley. It is one thing to argue that as the person is his past, so his purposive action is a projection of the past into the future; it is quite another to claim, with Huxley, that collective man 'is nothing else than evolution become conscious of itself' and therefore that the future course of world history can be put down to the self-directing capabilities of an evolutionary super-consciousness (Huxley 1954:12–13). It is precisely on this point that our view of the history of persons must take leave of classical social evolutionism. One of the founding tenets of the latter is that the collective life of mankind is but the life of the particular man writ large, a passage from childhood to maturity. It was on this assumption that progress theorists could conceive human purposes to be under-written by the nature of the common man, as implied in the doctrine of psychic unity. We can now see that the trouble with social evolutionism lies not in the notion of evolution *per se,* but in an inadequate conception of the social.

Nor will the trouble go away simply by substituting society for mankind, and 'social structure' for 'human nature'. We must take strong exception to a persistent tendency in anthropological theory, largely attributable to the intellectual legacy of Durkheim, to impute purpose into history by ascribing efficacy to reified 'structures', acting in and through the individuals held in their grasp (see Bourdieu 1977:27, for a criticism of this tendency). One of the worst, and certainly one of the most influential, offenders in this regard is Lévi-Strauss, whose position is that the ultimate intentions of people in history are to be found deep in the unconscious levels of mind, where the individual merges with society—appearing as its particular incarnation. In support of this position, he presents a 'famous statement by Marx': '"Men make their own history, but they do not know that they are making it"' (Lévi-Strauss 1968:23). To the best of my knowledge Marx never said any such thing (Lévi-Strauss provides no reference), nor could he have done without compromising his entire philosophy of history. Probably the source of the alleged 'famous statement' is *The Eighteenth Brumaire*: 'Men make their own history, but they do not make it just as they please, they do not make it under circumstances chosen by themselves, but under circumstances directly encountered, given and transmitted from the past' (Marx 1963:15). For Marx, history is the result of the consciously directed, purposive action of human subjects (persons). His point here is that everyone acts within a social context or milieu that is formed through the previous actions of other people whose purposes, though not necessarily concordant with his own, will inevitably have a bearing on them.

We must agree with this point. For whether we like it or not, each of us enters the historical scene at a particular time and place, and must perforce carry on from there. Marx's words are echoed in this remarkable extract from the phenomeno-logical writings of Alfred Schutz:

> The unique biographical situation in which I find myself within the world at any moment of my existence is only to a very small extent of my own making. I find myself always within a historically given world which . . . had existed before my birth and which will continue to exist after my death. This means that this world is not only mine but also my fellow men's environment; moreover, these fellow men are elements of my own situation, as I am of theirs. Acting upon the others and acted upon by them, I know of this mutual relationship. (1970:163–4)

From this it follows that the person—as a historical agent—has no existence outside the spatiotemporal continuum of social relations and that his identity can be defined only as a position—or rather a biographical trajectory—on that continuum. Take away or bracket this domain of intersubjectivity and one is left only with a population of individuals, an association of things. This is precisely the import of Lévi-Strauss's distortion of Marx, which involves the substitution for 'circumstances unwilled by the actors' of 'structures of which they are unconscious'. By this move the context of purposive action has become a central directing agency; a tissue of relationships constitutive of persons has become a hidden operator with a teleology distinct from and subverting their intention, and to which they relinquish their responsibility for the conduct of life. Persons are thus reduced to the status of individuals in the service of structure.

In the dehumanized Marxism of Althusser, this reduction is taken to extraordinary extremes: What 'naïve anthropology' innocently took to be real people bound in relations of intersubjectivity turn out to be nothing more than 'supports' for impersonal structures, which are the 'true' subjects of history (Althusser and Balibar 1970:180).[10] Writing in this Althusserian vein, Terray remarks that given both the unconscious and determining nature of structure, 'history is opaque to the men who make it'; he goes on to note 'the structure's historical efficacy, its ability to shape and direct the course of events' (1977:299). We must reject such a mechanical view of history. By saying that the source of human intentions lies in the domain of the social we do *not* mean that people are the blind instruments of a history that is 'really' being made for them behind their backs by some underlying, ahistorical structure, but rather that the social is the field of our mutual self-determination *in* history. Persons do indeed make their own history, they know perfectly well that they are making it; yet that history is one of social relations through which, in effect, they progressively make one another. The only subjects of the social process, Marx wrote, are 'individuals in mutual relationships, which they equally reproduce and produce anew' (1973:712). We return to this point in Chapter 6; for now we must pursue the individual–person dichotomy.

We owe the first explicit statement of the dichotomy in social anthropology to Radcliffe-Brown:

> Every human being living in society is two things: he is an individual and also a person. As an individual, he is a biological organism, a collection of a vast number of molecules organized in a complex structure, within which, as long as it persists, there occur physiological and psychological actions and reactions, processes and changes. Human beings as individuals are objects of study for physiologists and psychologists. The human being as a person is a complex of social relationships. He is a citizen of England, a husband and a father, a bricklayer, a member of a particular Methodist congregation, a voter in a certain constituency, a member of his trade union, an adherent of the Labour Party, and so on. Note that each of these descriptions refers to a social relationship, or to a place in a social structure. Note also that a social personality is something that changes during the course of the life of a person. As a person, the human being is the object of study for the social anthropologist. We cannot study persons except in terms of social structure, nor can we study social structure except in terms of the persons who are the units of which it is composed. (1952:193–4)

We have here a clear statement of the autonomy of the social in the determination of who we are, as opposed to what we are. However, our view of the dichotomy differs from Radcliffe-Brown's in quite a number of ways. Let me indicate where these differences lie, with regard first to the person, and then to the individual.

It is instructive to compare Radcliffe-Brown's dictum 'The human being as a person is a complex of social relationships' with an apparently similar statement by Marx, in the sixth of his *Theses on Feuerbach*: 'The human essence is no abstraction inherent in each single individual. In its reality it is the ensemble of social relations' (Marx and Engels 1977:122). We take it that Marx is referring here to the substance of personhood (a term preferable to Radcliffe-Brown's 'personality' on account of the latter's unintended psychological connotations). Given the radical contrast between the respective attitudes of Marx and Radcliffe-Brown to history and social life, they can hardly be saying the same thing, even though they use almost the same words. The basic difference is this: Marx's person is a real historical agent, enmeshed in a fabric of intersubjective relations that unfolds in the course of his and others' purposive, creative action. Radcliffe-Brown's person is a puppet whose actions are entirely determined by rules; whatever is irregular or idiosyncratic is omitted from the specification of structure and hence cannot be put down to persons as its constituent units. In this conception, the person is nothing more than the part he plays, a place in a structure (notice, incidentally, the almost exactly similar view of Althusser, for whom apparent subjects are, in reality, only occupants of places or performers of functions; see Althusser and Balibar 1970:180). Now Radcliffe-Brown's usage is perfectly in accordance with the original meaning of the Latin *persona*, which specifically signified a *mask*, or more generally, an artificial role, a part in a play, or any kind of masquerade or imposture (Dahrendorf 1968:26–31, 63 n. 33). In a brilliant essay, Mauss has shown how the notion of person has since undergone a series of transformations, acquiring only within the last two centuries its present connotation as 'the *category of the self*, and hence as the locus of consciousness (Mauss 1979 [1950]:78–89). The distance covered in these transformations is precisely the difference that separates Radcliffe-Brown's 'person' from Marx's, and our own. What is crucial to our understanding is the criterion of *agency*, well brought out in another definition, proposed by Bidney (1953:342): 'A person may be defined as the socially recognized subject, or agent, of psychocultural interaction. . . . Only persons are the agents, or patients, of the cultural process.'

   Let me express this a little more concretely. It is a biographical truth that I *am* a citizen of England, a husband and a father, a voter in a certain constituency, a member of a trade union and an adherent of the Labour Party. Many others would fit the same description. Yet were *I* merely the summation of these roles, who would be the actor who plays them? As both the author and the actor of my part I am neither individual organism nor *persona*, yet it is precisely in this capacity, as myself, that I become involved in *real* social relations with other author-actors. Moreover, as we have already stressed, my personhood is a cumulative process in time: I am not the same person I was yesterday, nor will I be the same tomorrow. Radcliffe-Brown admittedly notes that social personhood changes in the course of a life; nevertheless the change for him is not continuous but punctual. I became a husband at a particular point in time, a father at another point a few years later. I remain to this day a husband and a father; these components of my person, in Radcliffe-Brown's sense, have not changed. But *I* have. And likewise the real relations between myself, my wife and my children (as opposed to the model relations 'husband–wife' and 'father–child') have undergone a continuous evolution as we have all grown older.[11] In short, our view of the person depends on the conception of the social as consisting not of relations between the component parts of a regular programme of practical conduct, but of the entwining of the lives that are being conducted. Elaboration of this conception must, however, await the chapters that follow. We turn now from the person to the individual.

The most obvious difference between our notion of the individual and Radcliffe-Brown's is that ours denotes not merely a natural object (using natural here to comprehend things physical) but one formed through the interaction of genetically and culturally transmitted elements. In other words, individual human beings are more than organisms, they are culture-bearing organisms (Ingold 1979:271). As such, they are objects of study, not only for physiologists and psychologists but also for ethnologists or cultural anthropologists. We may as well recall Boas's remark that 'in ethnology all is individuality' (1974:66) and Lowie's that culture is a reality 'only as mirrored in its bearers' (1937:269).[12] But another, and subtler, difference goes back to Bergson's critique of the notion of individuality implied by Darwinian theory. To recapitulate: Whereas in the Darwinian conception the individual is a unique configuration of fixed hereditary traits, suspended in the present, for Bergson it is identified with its past life. In the one sense it is a thing that may be said to have a 'nature', in the other it is the embodiment of a movement. 'It would therefore be wrong', Bergson continues, 'to compare [a living organism] to an *object*. . . . The organism which lives is a thing that *endures*. Its past, in its entirety, is prolonged into its present. . . .—in short, . . . it has a history' (1911:16). The same point is eloquently put by Cassirer:

> Organic life exists only so far as it evolves in time. It is not a thing but a process—a never resting stream of events. In this stream nothing ever recurs in the same identical shape. . . . The organism is never located in a single instant. In its life the three modes of time—the past, present and future—form a whole which cannot be split into individual elements. (1944:49)

What Bergson and Cassirer say about living organisms generally, Ortega y Gasset said of human beings: We are not things but dramas; we have no nature, only history; we *are* not, though we *live*. And all of this directly informs our view of the person as the locus of consciousness. In setting up the dichotomy between person and individual, we therefore conceive the latter in its Darwinian—or analogous Boasian—sense: a specific assemblage of elements, whose appearance represents a singular event in a history of things. This is not, however, the way Radcliffe-Brown sees it. His definition of the individual, in the statement cited earlier, envisages an evolving system of 'actions and reactions, processes and changes'. Thus in a complete inversion of our own position, Radcliffe-Brown ascribes life to individuals, whilst reducing persons to the status of things.

Individuality and personhood are, of course, complementary concepts; and I would not for one moment wish to suggest that the human being has *nothing but* one or the other. The difference lies entirely in the sorts of questions we ask about the human being, and the kinds of observations we make. For example, a philologist concerned to trace the history of a particular language might be content to

regard each speaker as a transmitter of utterances and to record each utterance simply as a sample of linguistic behaviour. Just what the speaker meant to say and why
would be irrelevant questions. The important point for our philologist would be
to show how minute variations in the style of language use between one individual
and another can, when compounded over the generations, add up to substantial
interpopulation differences, leading to the emergence of new dialects or even languages (analogous to the biologists' varieties and species respectively). But to know
or to have reconstructed the history of a language, or to have traced its genealogical connections with other languages, will not give us one iota of insight into the
intentions of those who have used it as their medium of thought and communication. The same limitation applies to the history of paralinguistic phenomena, or of
culture generally. It was a limitation that Boas himself recognized, if rather belat-
edly, even to the extent of regretting the overemphasis on historical reconstruction
(for which he bore some responsibility) as 'an error of modern anthropology' that
has drawn attention away from the attempt to understand the purposes of the people who live out their lives *through* culture (Boas 1948:269).

On the other hand, a history of persons would—on its own—be equally
incomplete. Telling us all about what people have said and done, and why, it
would turn a blind eye to the kaleidoscopic diversity of *ways* of saying and doing,
which is precisely where the richness of human culture lies. The same is true of
the Bergsonian conception of organic evolution as a flow of life. It is right to
emphasize what Darwinian biology tends to forget, namely that living things are
living as well as thinglike and that they differ in this respect from machines. But
this will not, by itself, take us anywhere in understanding the *adaptation* of forms
to diverse circumstances. Our point is that the evolution of life and consciousness
is precisely what is not recoverable from an evolution conceived exclusively as a
history of things. We cannot, for example, reconstruct the organism as a living
system from its genes: As Weiss has pointed out, genes can account only for *differences* in morphology and behaviour from one individual or species to another.
Strip away these differences and we are still left with a level of organization that
transcends the genetic system, a level that does not originate through 'spontaneous
generation' in each individual, but that 'has been ever present since the primordial
living systems, passed down in uninterrupted continuity . . . through the organic
matrix in which the genome is encased' (Weiss 1969:35–7). By this 'passing down'
Weiss means the evolution of life as opposed to the descent, with modification,
of its carriers. Likewise, we can put down variations in the behaviour of human
individuals or populations to different configurations of cultural elements, but that
still leaves us with consciousness as a higher-order system that imparts direction to
social life through the instrumentality of the cultural apparatus.

We have established that the individual is an event in the history of things.
Since a population is defined as an aggregate of individuals it follows that, viewed
on a large scale, the history of things is in fact a history of populations. Our contrast
between individuals and persons is therefore homologous to that between a history of this kind and the process of social life. We might recall in this connection

a key difference between the approaches of Tylor and Boas to the history of culture: The former resolved *not* to write a history of populations, whereas the latter did just this, introducing into anthropology the kind of 'population-thinking' that was also a hallmark of the Darwinian method in biology. Tylor's was a history of consciousness whose principal agent, however, was a collective mankind incarnated in autonomous individuals, rather than the particular person enmeshed in a web of social relations. For us the really crucial difference between a history of populations and a history of persons is that in the first, human beings bear no responsibility for their destiny. They provide merely the *material* for history. Thus we would have to say (as evolutionary biologists commonly do) that certain changes have taken place *in,* but have not been brought about *by,* populations of individuals. To return to the example of language: Our philologist might wish to trace changes in the dialect of a certain local population over a period of time; but he could hardly argue that the people *produced* these changes. Of course for there to be a history of language, there must have been successive generations of people to speak it; but their role in such a history is not as users of language but as vehicles for its replication. Similarly in the history of costume, people exist for the purpose of wearing clothes. To return to Marett's nice analogy, this is a history for tailors, not for wearers. Likewise to reduce the history of a people to a process of cultural adaptation analogous to organic adaptation under natural selection is to deny to those concerned any history of their own. As pawns in the service of culture, they live to execute and replicate a design not of their own making, trying out solutions to problems they cannot recognize, and expiring in the attempt. What 'survives' is not their life, but its trappings.

We are accustomed, as a kind of shorthand, to write about mankind as though it consisted of a multitude of discrete 'societies' or 'cultures'. A little reflection at once reveals the arbitrariness of these divisions. There are, however, two distinct ways in which we might arrive at them: by the aggregation of individuals into populations and by the division of a continuous field into subfields. The first, of course, has always been the procedure of Boasian anthropology, just as it has been of Darwinian biology. And in defining cultures, anthropologists have faced much the same problems as have confronted biologists in the definition of species. Darwin himself did not recognize absolute boundaries to species in the way most biologists do today, that is in terms of reproductive isolation (Howard 1982:28–9, 36). Instead he regarded the species as a population of genealogically related individuals, representing one particular lineage of the tree of life. But given that every lineage is both a segment of a higher-order one, and itself internally divided, the level of segmentation at which we recognize species rather than genera on the one hand, and varieties on the other, is more or less arbitrary: All three terms denote the same *kind* of entity, but at different *degrees* of inclusiveness on a continuous, hierarchical scale (Darwin 1872:38–9, 349; see Ghiselin 1969:93, 101). Thus when it came to the question of whether man is one species or many, Darwin had to admit that it is all a matter of definition. Without any accepted convention it is as hopeless to determine whether human races are separate species as it is 'to decide whether a certain number of houses should be called a village, town, or city' (Darwin 1874:272).

It is remarkable to find Lowie worrying about precisely this point in the context of a disagreement with Malinowski concerning the notion of the separate culture as an 'integrated whole'. Rejecting this notion, Lowie insists that 'a culture is invariably an artificial unit segregated for purposes of expediency' (1937:235). What we have in reality are *individuals,* each of which carries a unique configuration of elements. Thus if culture were an integrated whole, we would have to admit that there are as many such cultures as there are individuals. To suppose that all the individuals of a given population subscribe to a common culture whose constituent features can be independently specified is to lapse into a false essentialism, similar to that which underlay the Linnaean classification of species. There is no such thing as 'Trobriand culture':

> Social tradition varies demonstrably from village to village, even from family to family. Are we to treat as the bearers of such a closed system the chief's family in Omarakana, his village, the district of Kiriwina, the Island of Boyowa, the Trobriand archipelago, the North Massim province, New Guinea, or perchance Melanesia? The attempt to adhere rigorously to any of these demarcations precipitates absurdities. There is only one natural unit for the ethnologist—the culture of all humanity at all periods and all places. (Lowie 1937:235)

Like Darwin, Lowie is pointing to the arbitrariness of hierarchical taxonomic divisions, and attacking the idea that each class represents a distinct, unchanging and separately created entity. Against this he asserts the connectivity of all cultural traditions, an assertion also supported by Kroeber (1963:84). In this latter respect, the prospects for anthropologists who would strive to introduce some kind of order into the material of their inquiry are a good deal more daunting than those confronting biologists, for the degree of connectivity between the lines of the cultural 'tree' is vastly greater than in its biological counterpart (Kroeber 1948:261). This is because of the possibilities for diffusion, and hence for convergence as well as divergence in lines of descent, as we showed in the previous chapter. Another way of expressing this is to say that the connection and disconnection of lines is independent of the direction of time: whether we move backwards or forwards, some appear to split as others merge. The result is that there can be no neat, segmentary 'nesting' of taxonomic orders at successive levels of inclusiveness; we have to deal rather with any number of overlapping, polythetic sets.

The individual, then, can be considered as a point in a network through which he may ultimately be connected with each and every other individual that has ever existed, or may exist in the future (Lesser 1961). How does his position differ in this respect from that of the person? For the latter, as we have shown, may also be located in a field that can be stretched to include all mankind. And just as there is no essential line of demarcation for culture, so must we also admit to the arbitrariness with which one society is distinguished from another. Societies, it would appear, are changing all the time, though in the constancy of change lies a contradiction we will have to sort out in due course. 'Do we then', Evans-Pritchard asks, 'speak of a society at different points of time or do we speak of two different societies?' (1961:10). Or three or four, for that matter, depending on how many points we select? How much does a society have to change.before it ceases to be itself and becomes something else? The very absurdity of this latter question is highlighted in a recent remark by Rappaport, who contends that 'England as *a* system has survived from the fifth century until the present' (1977:81). The way to overcome such absurdities is to dispense with the idea of society as an enclosed, self-contained entity or functioning system, strictly analogous to the individual organism, for no such entity has ever existed except in the realms of imagination (Leach 1964[1954]:xii–xiii). For the life of society (*through* persons) we substitute the social life *of* persons; for an entity that *is* we substitute a process that is *going on,* moreover one that knows no boundaries either in time or space. The distinction we are drawing here ties in with our earlier discussion of the person, for it also involves the substitution of the player for his part.

Consider what happens when, as an anthropologist, I travel to a foreign land. It is convenient to say that I have gone to live in another society. To be sure, in doing so I have exchanged one part for another: For example once a citizen, my status is now that of an alien. Yet as the player of my part, I do not turn into someone else on crossing the Channel, and it is as myself that I become involved with the people I meet over there—who likewise are being themselves in their relations with me. That is to say, we participate as *consociates*. This very fact testifies to the continuity of the social landscape, a continuity that transcends the boundaries we have written across it. We might represent it schematically as a field constituted by the dimensions of space and time (Fig. 3.4A). Suppose I currently occupy point A on this field. The people with whom I go to live occupy point B (in reality they would, of course, occupy a cluster of points, but as our diagram is macroscopic, we may collapse them into one). Were I a historian, I might imagine myself a time-traveller at point C. Point D occupies that area where the interests of anthropology and history most naturally converge. It might be said, dividing the diagram into columns, that the historian studies the past of his own society; or dividing it into rows, that the anthropologist studies the society of his own time. But we can no more determine where *our* society ends than when *our* time begins. The spatiotemporal continuum depicted in Fig. 3.4A cannot properly be parcelled up into blocks. This was the gist of Collingwood's criticism of Toynbee's principles of history:

> He regards history itself, the historical process, as cut by sharp lines into mutually exclusive parts, and denies the continuity of the process in virtue of which every part overlaps and interpenetrates others. His distinction between societies or civilizations is really a distinction between focal points in the process: he has misunderstood it as a distinction between chunks or lumps of fact into which the process is divided. (1946:164)

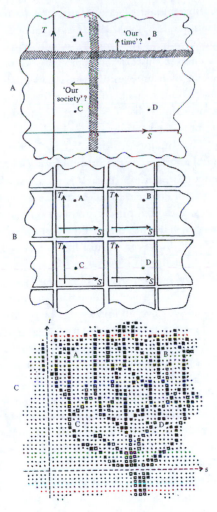

FIG. 3.4 The fragmentation of the spatiotemporal field. **A:** The points A, B, C and D represent different moments in the unfolding of the field. If we occupy point A, the boundaries of 'our society' and 'our time', separating us from the people at B, C and D, can be only vaguely and arbitrarily drawn. **B:** The field has been divided into parcels or blocks, each corresponding to a self-contained, societal entity with its own inherent time (*T*) and spatial extension (*S*), and which unfolds in a separate evolution. **C:** The fragmentation has proceeded so far that each block has shrunk into a single point, within which the extension of *real* time and space has been reduced to zero. The points are arranged relative to one another, in rows and columns, in terms of *abstract* time and space co-ordinates (*t*, **s**). The complete array of dots represents the total matrix of possible permutations of an invariant cerebral logic. Square dots indicate the small proportion of forms actually realized in the course of history, revealed in genealogical sequence. Blank squares correspond to past forms of which we have no historical record.

Dumont makes the same mistake. I cited earlier his premiss that 'history is the movement by which a society reveals itself as what it is', but we should take equal note of the inference he draws from it, which is that 'there are, in a sense, as many qualitatively different histories as there are societies' (Dumont 1957:21). Each, then, must have its own time and its own spatial extension, and since these constitute the substance of our social being, we can only conclude that it would be impossible—if Dumont is right—for a person to cross the Rubicon that separates his particular society from others, whilst remaining himself (see Fig. 3.4B).

In the writings of Lévi-Strauss, we discover the effects of this fragmentation when taken to its logical extreme. As the number of societies is multiplied by division, so the spatiotemporal extension of each is progressively attenuated until we are left only with an array of dots. Far from representing points within a field, these dots are all that remains of the field itself, smashed into smithereens. So what do we do with all the pieces? The first thing, Lévi-Strauss recommends, is 'to draw up a list of them'. The list, however, would have to be set out in rows and columns. 'Firstly, we have societies co-existing in space [he means time], some close together and some far apart but, on the whole, contemporary with one another.' We put them in rows. 'Secondly, we have social systems that have followed one another in time, of which we have no knowledge by direct experience.' They are arranged in columns (Lévi-Strauss 1953:9). The horizontal and vertical axes correspond, of course, to space and time, but certainly not to the kind of space or time with which we started. They are rather co-ordinates that are wholly *extrinsic* to our being, that which is intrinsic having been packed inside each point. Space and time in this sense are pure abstractions that, when compounded, describe an absolute void, an infinite extension of nothingness that is waiting to be filled. Doubtless in the filling, in the compilation of our list, we shall find many of the pieces missing and 'shall have, in such cases, to leave blank spaces, which will probably be far more numerous than the spaces in which we feel we can make some entry' (1953:10). If we lost all the pieces, we would still be left with space–time as one big blank (see Fig. 3.4C). And having already defined ourselves, the negligent keepers of a transcendental catalogue, outside the real world, this blank would correspond to none other than the domain of our own non-existence.

Lévi-Strauss returns to the theme of anthropology and history in the closing passages of *The savage mind* (1966a). Again he presents us with a human essence refracted in a myriad of discrete societies, and where the historian 'unfurls the range of human societies in time', the anthropologist unfurls them in space. Lévi-Strauss has nothing but contempt for the inward apprehension of history as continuous change. Just as we see (or rather, as an anthropologist, *he* sees) a diversity of social forms 'deployed in space' and presenting 'the appearance of a discontinuous system', so we ought to see a similar deployment in time. Thus time is not a privileged dimension that restores to us the continuity of things, but rather 'distribution in space and succession in time afford equivalent perspectives' (1966a:256).[13] With the equivalence of the spatial and the temporal we are in agreement; indeed we would go further to claim their inseparability: there can be no movement in time that is not also a movement in space, and vice versa (Giddens 1979:54). We would not, accordingly, elevate history over anthropology; nor, however, do we see any reasonable grounds for their complementary differentiation. This last contention is not trivial. From a comparison of Fig. 3.4A and C, it should be clear first that space and time mean to us something quite different than they do to Lévi-Strauss, and second, that neither in space nor in time do we perceive an array of discrete forms constituting a discontinuous system. We see only continuity, a continuity reflected in our own experience as persons.

As for the latter, Lévi-Strauss considers 'this supposed totalizing continuity of the self . . . to be an illusion sustained by the demands of social life' (1966a:256). The reality is that every episode in our life 'resolves itself into a multitude of individual psychic movements. Each of these movements is the translation of unconscious development, and these resolve themselves into cerebral, hormonal or nervous phenomena, which themselves have reference to the physical or chemical order' (1966a:257). Naturally, to entertain such a view of ourselves in the normal course of life would lead to a complete paralysis of will, which is why (so the savant tells us) we find it convenient to connive in delusions of holism. In our view, to the contrary, it is Lévi-Strauss himself who is deluded. The passage just cited attests to a blatant reductionism, by which one level of organization after another is peeled off to reveal nothing but a set of elementary building blocks awaiting assembly. But having dissolved the self in this way, there is no one there—no consciousness—to assemble them. Far from being inconvenient for social life, such a view denies the possibility of our ever having one. How can Lévi-Strauss allow himself to be taken in by so ridiculous a position? Evidently because of his commitment to an extreme view of scientific objectivism that I suspect few natural scientists today would accept without qualification.[14] 'If we place ourselves outside [the world in which we live]', he remarks, '—*as the man of science is bound to do*—what appeared as an experienced truth becomes confused and finally disappears altogether' (1966a:254; my emphasis). Exit historical consciousness, enter myth!

Now there is, as we shall later show, a curious and quite unexpected parallel between the construction of mythical projects in the human mind and the construction of organic projects (i.e. of individuals) in nature. And this, in turn, provides a clue to the answer of a question we posed earlier: How does the individual differ from the person when both can be represented as points in space–time? For the individual is, in effect, the residue or precipitate of the complete atomization of the social domain, and of the collapse of space and time as *lived* within the ambit of the particular event each one comes to represent. When, therefore, we rearrange these events to form a putative genealogical series, having a certain spatial 'span' and temporal 'depth', we must abandon the time that flows and the space that stretches out (both of which are now contained *in* events) for the abstract dimensions of a 'blank' container, to be loaded *with* events. In short, to the opposition between person and individual there correspond distinct conceptions of space and time, the one describing the movement that is the very substance of continuous (personal) existence, the other a null expanse in which are suspended motionless and discontinuous (individual) existents. We might note that this dichotomy is broadly congruent with the contrast we have already drawn between Spencerian and Darwinian constructions of the evolutionary tree: In one every point on the tree is a moment in a spatiotemporal process of growth; in the other it is an event in a genetic sequence located in abstract space-time. Darwin's tree is an inert trace left by things that have lived; Spencer's is tantamount to the process of life itself.

This last point re-establishes the connection between the individual–person dichotomy and the two conceptions of evolution with which our inquiry began. The individual is a thing, an object, assembled from countless elements part-genetic, part-cultural, its singularity resting on the fact that no two assemblages are ever quite alike—although it may be possible to define more or less clearly bounded populations of individuals drawing on the same pool of elements. The person is not a thing but a unique trajectory, stretching out and advancing within a continuum of real space and time. As Luckmann has put it, 'Personal identity is intersubjective and has a situational and biographical dimension. . . . Personal identities are not "things" but regulatory principles of the intentional structures of consciousness and of the intersubjective rather than instinctive organisation of social interaction' (1979:67). Thus the person is both the creator and the creation of what Collingwood and Ortega y Gasset would call *history,* which Luckmann *opposes* to evolution in its Darwinian sense (1979:65). Yet we could equally well reverse the terms of the distinction, regarding the mutual self-determination of persons as an evolutionary process (following Bergson), and the chronological succession of individuals or populations as a form of history (following Boas and White). Nothing is to be gained from an attempt to legislate on the proper use of these terms; but the least we can expect of any author is some degree of consistency.

Before proceeding to our next major theme, which is to examine the nature of historical and evolutionary time, I should make explicit a point that has been implicit in our argument up to now, but which will emerge as our principal concern in later chapters. It is that the distinction between pre- and post-Darwinian senses of evolution, between a history that is made and a history that just happens, and between personal and individual identities, is also a distinction between the *social* and the *cultural*. By social, we refer not to the interaction and association of individual objects (the sense usually adopted by students of animal behaviour) but to the relations constitutive of persons as intentional subjects. And by the cultural, we designate the range of objective, symbolically coded forms that serve as the vehicles of people's intersubjective life, translating their social purpose into practical effect. Our insistence on the distinction between the social and the cultural follows from the same premises on which we have separated the dichotomous meanings of evolution and of history. Thus to speak of 'sociocultural evolution' is not only to conflate agency and instrumentality, but also to confuse one sense of evolution with its opposite, the inner flow of life with the adaptation of the outer forms through which it is conducted. Social *life,* then, is to be counterposed to cultural *adaptation*. As Leach has written: 'Every real society is a process in time', whereas 'the cultural situation . . . is a product and accident of history' (1964[1954]:5, 16). But this is a far cry from the kind of history that historians usually study, for the latter is the very 'process in time' that is the reality of social life. It is rather ironic that in opposing its project to the study of history as understood by cultural anthropology, and in its concern with the continuity of process rather than the fortuity of events, social anthropology has come much closer than its cultural counterpart to ascribing to persons a history they could call their own. And conversely, nothing more effectively consigns the lives of supposedly 'primitive' folk to a monotonous present than the representation of their past as a history not of persons but of culture-bearing populations.

4

TIMES OF LIFE

Our duration is not merely one instant replacing another; if it were, there would never be anything but present—no prolonging of the past into the actual, no evolution, no concrete duration. Duration is the continuous progress of the past which gnaws into the future and which swells as it advances. . . .

Wherever anything lives, there is, open somewhere, a register in which time is being inscribed. . . .

We perceive duration as a stream against which we cannot go. It is the foundation of our being and, as we feel, the very substance of the world in which we live.

Bergson, Creative evolution

Our starting point for the discussion of time is again the philosophy of Bergson. For we find Bergson insisting on the distinction between *real* time (the duration of being) and *abstract* time (the eternity of non-being) in precisely the terms that we have had to adopt in order to pinpoint the essential contrast between our two paradigms of evolution. Real time is identified with the flowing movement of life and consciousness, and like the latter it is cumulative and progressive. Moreover, as our brief citations reveal, there is an indissoluble link between real time as duration and evolution as a process of life; without the one there could not be the other (Bergson 1911:24). What we intend to show now is that the time associated with Darwinian descent with modification is in fact abstract time, and therefore incompatible with evolution in Bergson's sense. The rudiments of our argument have already been set out: Briefly, as the duration of each individual organism is collapsed within the instantaneous present of the event it represents, the time occupied by a genealogical sequence or lineage of such events, far from constituting the foundation of life, is rendered lifeless—it is but a particular stretch of eternity. And as we shall see, the same argument applies to the culture history of Boas, to the diachronic linguistics of Saussure, and to just one of the kinds of history described by Lévi-Strauss. In the other kind, equated with progressive evolution, we recapture Bergsonian time and link it to Radcliffe-Brown's conception of reality as a continuous process of social life. Ultimately we find that, whereas time may be treated as concrete duration intrinsic to the thinker or as an abstract artefact of his thought, *consciousness* of time lies in the confrontation between the two, between the subjective world of persons and the objective world of things, or between Locke's sense of a 'perpetual perishing' and what Plato's Timaeus so memorably characterized as a 'moving image of eternity'.

We should perhaps begin by recalling that Darwin probably would never have conceived his theory of organic evolution, let alone had it accepted, were it not for the fact that since the latter part of the eighteenth century natural philosophers had begun to think in terms of spans of time of an entirely new order of magnitude. No longer could the biblical calculations of Archbishop Ussher, who around 1650 had dated the divine creation of the world to Sunday, 23 October, 4004 B.C., be taken seriously (Whitrow 1975:24). By adding officially another 160,000 years to the chronology of the earth (his unofficial estimate was nearer half a million), Buffon was the first to introduce the kind of time-scale necessary to render even remotely plausible any theory of the transmutation of species, in the face of their apparent constancy within the relatively short span of recorded history. Of course, Buffon's chronology, outrageous to the orthodoxy of his day, appears in retrospect absurdly short. Accustomed as we are to thinking in terms of millions, billions and trillions, it is hard for us to appreciate the innovative force of Buffon's vision. He was not, however, alone in his endeavours. For Immanuel Kant, in his *General history of nature and theory of the heavens* (1755), had advanced a theory of cosmic evolution that referred unhesitatingly to the flow of 'millions and whole myriads of millions of centuries' (cited in Toulmin and Goodfield 1965:132). Subsequently James Hutton, in his *Theory of the earth* of 1795, stretched time indefinitely, concluding that—as far as the history of our own planet is concerned—'we find no vestige of a beginning,—no prospect of an end'. Promulgated by Lyell under the rubric of his doctrine of uniformitarianism, Hutton's view of the indefinite extension of time formed an essential background to Darwin's thinking on organic evolution—as he himself was the first to admit (Darwin 1872:249–53; see also Reynolds 1981:7–8).

In the perspective of millions of years, the duration of our lived experience, of 'our time', appears utterly inconsequential. But though they shared this perspective, Kant's idea of natural history was quite different from Hutton's. The difference, which is crucial to our argument, hinges on their respective understandings of the Creation. For Kant the Creation was not a one-off event, but a directed, evolutionary process that is continually *going on*. It did indeed begin at one point, but it will never cease. The order of nature is forever *coming into existence,* but at no point can we stand back to contemplate its completion. Thus in the cosmos in general as in life in particular, time is the very essence of becoming. Hutton's view of the Creation, to the contrary, was strictly Newtonian. There was a moment, we know not how far remote as it left no trace, when everything was put in its place as part of an ordered, steady-state system. God set the planets in their orbits and set the geological forces of the earth to work. From that moment on, the order of nature—perfect and complete—has ticked over like a clock destined to run for all eternity. Since time, in such a mechanical system, can run just as well in one direction as in reverse, it is but a small step to dispense with the hypothetical Creation altogether, and to argue not merely (with Hutton) that there is no *vestige* of a beginning, but that there has never *been* a beginning; in other words, 'that past time was not merely indefinite but infinite' (Toulmin and Goodfield 1965:157–8).

It was this Newtonian conception of time that Darwin inherited from the uniformitarians. Indeed it can be shown that the reversibility of Newtonian time underwrites what we saw in Chapter 1 to be the peculiar character of irreversibility in organic evolution, namely that the sequence of consecutive forms is *undirected*. To appreciate this point, it is essential to bear in mind what most crucially distinguishes Darwin's 'descent with modification' from Lamarck's 'transformism'. According to the latter, the life of the individual is the gradual growing out of, or supersession, of its ancestor in the process of becoming its descendant. Thus individuals are the transitory carriers across the generations of a continuous, progressive movement, passing on to their successors the increment of advance achieved or acquired in the course of their maturation, together with the accumulated advance of their ancestors. Time, then, is the movement of the staircase on which every living being is travelling as it ascends the scale of nature. For Darwin, to the contrary, the individual's life is the realization of a project contained within the bounds of its own particular existence. Far from being built on the foundation of ground covered by previous generations, each life is constructed—as it where—'from scratch' on a template formed from the recombination of elements from past projects, and is in turn expended in the reproductive transmission of these elements to the future. They, and not the movement of life itself, are carried across the generations. Hence evolution, in the Darwinian paradigm, consists of a succession of templates or, as we would now say, of genotypes.

Let me suggest an admittedly rather crude analogy. Imagine I have a pile of cards on each of which is written one letter of the alphabet. Laying out the cards in a certain order, I can read off a unique sequence of letters that we could call a 'word'. If I repeatedly collect the cards, shuffle them and lay them out again, I can generate a succession of such 'words', each being a particular permutation of the constituent letters. Say that each 'word' represents a template and their succession an evolutionary line. It is obvious that this evolution is a sequence of states rather than a continuous movement, for one 'word' is certainly not in the process of becoming the next or ceasing to be the one preceding! It is also highly unlikely— we may say the probability is negligible—that precisely the same 'words' will ever recur. The sequence is therefore irreversible in this sense. However, there is no necessary reason why the 'words' should have appeared in sequence in the particular order they did; to suppose otherwise is to be deceived by the retrospective fallacy, namely the idea that because things happened in a certain way they could not have happened in any other way. A priori, the set of possible sequences that *could* occur includes both the sequence that *did* occur and its opposite. In short, the line of evolution that actually materializes is no less improbable than the same line run into reverse. And it is in precisely this respect that the reversibility of time is manifested in the Darwinian paradigm. That is to say: *Darwinian irreversibility is constituted by its relation to Newtonian reversibility.* Darwin himself said as much when, in the closing passages of *The origin of species,* he marvelled at the endless parade of organic forms that have made their appearance whilst the earth 'has gone cycling on according to the fixed laws of gravity' (1872:403).

Our conclusion might, at first glance, seem surprising, and it certainly contradicts the commonly held view that Darwin was partially instrumental in substituting for a steady–state picture of the world one of continuous flux. In reality he did no such thing (Gillespie 1959:290–1). Where Kant saw everywhere the creative hand of time bringing forth new forms and configurations in nature, for Darwin time was merely a backdrop against which things happened. In Kantian cosmology, as in Lamarckian transformism, time was immanent in the evolutionary process; in Darwinian descent with modification it was wholly extraneous to it.[1] The difference is of course related to Darwin's rejection of teleology in nature: Each individual is construed to exist only in and for the present, not as a moment in the purposive conveyance of past into future. If Darwin needed to invoke a Creator it was only (as for Newton and Hutton) to set the ball rolling, after which He could leave His Creation to look after itself. Time, in this view, is to be likened not to a riverine movement or flow but to a monotonous thread of infinite length, upon which each event (corresponding to the 'words' of our earlier analogy) is strung like a bead, occupying its allotted instant. To measure the lapse between successive instants, we can divide and subdivide the thread into segments, as we divide the length of a ruler into centimetres and millimetres. These identical chronological segments constitute, in Bergson's memorable image, the small change of eternity (Bergson 1911:335). Thus what is *of* time can only be the perpetual motion of bodies in a mechanical system subject to Newtonian laws, including of course the presumed motion of our own planet, which provides a basis for our common chronological reckoning of days and years. It follows that wherever in the world we find change or novelty, growth or decay, progression or retrogression, we can no longer regard it as the work of time, but only as the aggregate of discrete events strung out *in* time. The same argument applies in reverse: If all change is understood as the concatenation of events thus suspended, the continuous thread of time on which they are hung must be spun by a world machine whose motions are constant and perpetual.

Perhaps it will now be clear why it is fallacious to suppose that Darwinian evolution, being irreversible, entails a corresponding concept of irreversible time. For this would land us immediately into the contradictions of timeless time, non–processual process and eventless sequence. We cannot treat time as the substance of becoming and in the same breath dissolve the latter into a succession of events *in* time, without—as it were—turning time inside out, so that what was immanent in a real process is converted into an abstract container for events (see Whitrow 1975:136). If we *do* adopt (from Kant's cosmology) the idea of time as a unidirectional, creative movement, what in Darwinian eyes is an eventful sequence reappears as eventless process, and the medium in which the sequence is inscribed reappears not as time but as its very negation—for as Bergson wrote, time is *what is being inscribed*. Thus to the opposition between our two paradigms of evolution there correspond not only different kinds of irreversibility, but also different notions of time: one Newtonian, mechanical, eternal; the other Bergsonian, creative, cumulative. The Darwinian genealogical sequence, being a concatenation of non-recurrent entities and events, is suspended in the first kind of time; the second kind is intrinsic to the evolutionary movement conceived as a continuous unfolding or directed flow. This latter conception is shared by all those who claim to find some vital force or creative principle at work in evolution, including not only Bergson, with his *élan vital,* but also Spencer, whose cosmic movement towards increasingly coherent heterogeneity was underwritten by the hand of the Unknowable.[2]

Since up to now we have bracketed together the evolutionary philosophies of Bergson and Spencer, this might be the appropriate point to spell out the differences between them. Bergson in fact devotes the final section of his *Creative evolution* to a radical criticism of Spencer's views, from which it might appear that they had far less in common than they actually do. Yet for both, evolution was a cumulative building-up, involving the constant creation of new forms superseding the old. As regards the evolution of life, Spencer remained to the end of his days a committed Lamarckian; Bergson likewise described the individual organism rather quaintly as 'a bud that has sprouted on the combined body of both its parents', so that every generation is literally an outgrowth of the one preceding (Bergson 1911:45). So what was their point of contention? It was that, according to Bergson, Spencer had construed evolution as the consolidation of a world that his positivist imagination had already divided into a mass of little bits, whereas in reality all is movement (Bergson 1911:385–7). Bergson himself considered the material world to be 'an undivided flux', more like a continuous, elastic membrane than a vast collection of particles (1911:263). In short, the difference was between Spencer's 'statistical' view of the evolutionary process and Bergson's more 'topological' conception. It is a difference of far-reaching significance. I pointed out earlier that although the parallels between orthodox progressive evolutionism and the idea of history as a movement of consciousness are close, one could hardly claim a complete identity. We are now in a position to pin-point just where the identity breaks down. For positivism, theoretically reconstituting in externalized form a process initially apprehended from within, renders a topological movement in statistical terms. Yet despite this transformation, in the course of which intuited, historical experience is replaced by a covering of natural law, the form of time remains essentially unaffected.

This was convincingly demonstrated by Wiener in the first chapter of his *Cybernetics* (1961), a work that was to have a profound impact on both the natural and the social sciences. Here he links the dichotomy between Newtonian and Bergsonian time to one between 'mechanical' and 'statistical' systems.

The mechanical system is exemplified by the movements of celestial bodies under Newtonian laws, the statistical system by meteorological processes such as cloud formation. In the first instance, we encounter a small number of entities whose course is wholly predictable, given certain fixed parameters. As Bergson succinctly put it, 'The essence of mechanical explanation . . . is to regard the future and the past as calculable functions of the present, and thus to claim that *all is given*' (1911:39–40). Consequently, if we were to film a mechanical system in operation, and then run the film backwards, the result would not appear in the least strange or improbable, nor would it be contrary to physical law. That is why, 'in a Newtonian system, . . . time is perfectly reversible' (Wiener 1961:32–3). Cloud formation, by contrast, results from the aggregate interaction of 'a vast number of approximately equal particles', often closely coupled, and undergoing more or less random motion. Watching the cloud grow, we observe that nothing is quite the same from one moment to the next; there is, again in Bergson's terms, a 'continual elaboration of the absolutely new' (1911:11). Yet out of this flux there emerges a definite process, explicable in terms of Gibbsian statistical mechanics. Moreover, this process has an unmistakeable direction: To run a film of cloud formation in reverse would present us with a most unlikely picture, and one that certainly does not conform to physical law (Wiener 1961:32–3).

The irreversibility implied here is also that of Spencerian evolution, which was likewise tied—as we have seen—to a 'statistical' world-view and a Bergsonian conception of time. According to this view, irreversibility stems not from a property of the individual elements of the statistical system considered in isolation (namely their uniqueness), but is a property of the system itself considered as an evolving whole; thus the cloud grows, the organism matures, the thermodynamic system moves towards states of increasing entropy, the total system of living nature towards states of increasing complexity. Wiener, however, adopts his view of the evolution of life from Darwin rather than Spencer and regards Darwinian descent with modification as a movement in Bergsonian irreversible time. Here he is grievously in error. As we have already demonstrated, irreversibility in the Darwinian paradigm has a quite different connotation: the non-recurrence of events or entities in a linear sequence. As regards particular lines of descent, the record of palaeontology does *not*, as Wiener claims, indicate 'a definite long-term trend . . . from the simple to the complex'; nor did Darwin adduce, in his theory of variation under natural selection, 'a mechanism by means of which a fortuitous variability . . . is converted by a dynamical process into a pattern of development which reads in one direction' (Wiener 1961:36–7). It is the very absence of necessary directionality, of a progressive orientation, that is characteristic of the Darwinian conception of evolution. If any further confirmation of this point were needed, we would have only to apply the test that Wiener himself suggests: If we were to run in reverse the 'changeful sequence' of forms making up a line of descent, would the result appear contrary to natural law? The answer is no, though it would of course be contrary to what has actually happened. The time in which the sequence is suspended is therefore reversible. It is only when we view the movement of life as a whole, taking into account the facts of extinction, diversification and complexification, that a more fundamental irreversibility is revealed.

From Wiener's *Cybernetics* we move on, and back, to the structural anthropology of Lévi-Strauss. For it was from Wiener that Lévi-Strauss drew the idea of a dichotomy between 'mechanical' and 'statistical' models, and between the corresponding categories of reversible and irreversible time (Lévi-Strauss 1968:283–6; see Ardener 1971:233–5). Indeed, much of Lévi-Strauss's perfunctory discussion of these categories is lifted piecemeal and rather uncomprehendingly from Wiener's text, so that what appears clear and incisive in the latter reappears in the former in so garbled a form that scores of structuralist devotees—few of whom seem to have consulted Wiener—have been falling over one another in a hopeless attempt to discover what their master meant. Lévi-Strauss has even inherited Wiener's major mistake, which was to confuse the irreversibility of Spencerian with that of Darwinian evolution. Our present concern, however, is with Lévi-Strauss's understanding of history. Adopting Wiener's sense of the statistical, conjoined with the sense of irreversibility that Wiener had derived from Bergson, Lévi-Strauss writes that 'historical time is "statistical"; it always appears as an oriented and non-reversible process. An evolution which would take contemporary Italian society back to that of the Roman Republic is as impossible to conceive of as the reversibility of the processes belonging to the second law of thermodynamics' (1968:286). Notice the way that 'evolution' is slipped in here as a synonym for historical change, and the assumption that such change is necessarily *oriented* or progressive (Barnes 1971:541). History, as Lévi-Strauss understands it here, would have to be bracketed alongside such other examples of evolution in Bergsonian time as Kroeber's 'culture growth' and White's 'evolutionist process'. This need come as no surprise, for we have already noted the striking parallel between the 'cumulative history' of Lévi-Strauss and the Spencerian formula for evolution. What is odd in this context, however, is the strenuous effort Lévi-Strauss devotes to distancing his views about history from those of the proponents of progressive evolutionism.

Certainly Lévi-Strauss was not the first, nor the last, to view historical change in statistical terms. Tylor's depiction of the progressive march of human populations was quite explicitly statistical: Indeed he concludes a discussion on this very point with the remark that 'collective social action is the mere resultant of many individual actions' (1871, I:12). And a century later, Wilson presents his sociobiological interpretation of culture change—based on a very similar idea of human nature—'as the statistical product of the separate behavioural responses of large numbers of human beings who cope as best they can with social existence' (Wilson 1978:78). From this it would appear that culture 'bubbles up' (as the meteorologists say) rather like a thunder-cloud, though again like the cloud, it is characteristically fuzzy at the edges. But if we take this view, what becomes of the Boasian concept of culture-history, for which Lévi-Strauss professes to have so much sympathy? To answer this question, it is important to bear in mind that there are occasions when Lévi-Strauss opposes history to ethnography, and occasions when he endows them with a basic similarity of perspective. In contexts of the first kind, history is understood in the cumulative, statistical sense discussed earlier, whereas ethnography has to do with the recording and mapping of cultural particulars, both in space and time. The Boasian project is then characterized as ethnography *rather than* history, dealing in mechanical rather than statistical models, and hence in Newtonian reversible time rather than Bergsonian irreversible time. In contexts of the second kind, to which we have already referred, Boas reappears as a historian, 'unfurling' cultures in time where the ethnographer does so in space. This kind of history, then, is 'stationary' rather than 'cumulative' and is *opposed* to evolution as a progressive movement. Behind all this is the now familiar dichotomy between two senses of history, two senses of evolution and two senses of time. If history is placed on one side of the fence, alongside Bergsonian evolution, ethnography stands alone on the other; if history is joined with ethnography on the latter side, then it is evolution that stands alone.

The sense of evolution corresponding to Boasian history is, as we have so often stressed, Darwinian. Therefore, what we have said about the irreversibility of Darwinian natural history applies equally to the history of cultural things. Dealing in particular sequences rather than the growth and transformation of total systems, Boasian history is certainly not 'statistical', nor is it 'oriented'. Moreover, it is not consubstantial with time as in Bergson's conception of the duration that—to adopt one of his favourite metaphors—'gnaws on things, and leaves on them the mark of its tooth' (Bergson 1911:48). For Boas time does not flow, let alone gnaw on things; history, in consequence, is not the work *of* time but consists of things that happen *in* time and that, if cleared away, would leave nothing but motionless perpetuity. That Boas's notion of time was thoroughly mechanical is revealed in his frequent attribution to historical events of a 'chronological' referent: His time is of clocks rather than clouds (see Popper 1972:207–8). And in *The savage mind,* Lévi-Strauss concurs. Time eternal, spun by the uniform and perpetual revolutions of the earth, may be chopped into equal segments either of relatively low denomination, such as hours, days or years, or of relatively high denomination, such as centuries or millennia. Depending on the units (or the 'chronological code') we adopt, history can be either 'low-powered' or 'high-powered'; naturally enough, as we pass from one level of resolution to the next, so we move through a succession of different historical 'domains', each one in theory encompassing the totality of the past and future of humanity (Lévi-Strauss 1966a:258–61). Having chosen our unit of reckoning, we then assign to each segment a *date,* which denotes its position vis-à-vis other segments in a linear sequence. In the chronological encoding of history, events are attached to dated segments; some may be heavily loaded, some lightly, some may carry none at all. By means of this encoding, we can tell what came before and what after, which is the first requirement of historical knowledge. 'Without dates', Lévi-Strauss asserts, 'there is no history' (1966a:258)—though to this we might add the corollary: There can be dates without history, a time without events.

So long as we take the view of history as a succession of events, objectified and discrete, Lévi-Strauss's assertion is of course true, for unless there are dates on which to pin them, the whole sequence would fall apart. To give an example, imagine that we are presented with an assortment of undated photographic snap-shots, each of a different individual unique in physical features and cultural attire, and that we are asked to arrange them in the temporal order in which they were taken. Discounting any evidence not contained in the pictures themselves, or based on developments in photographic technique, we would be unable to do so. But now imagine that we are handed a similar assortment of snapshots, this time of the *same* individual taken at various moments in his life. We would then have little difficulty in putting them in order. The same would apply in the case of a growing cloud, a maturing organism or any other statistical system evolving in Bergsonian, irreversible time. Since in every such system, the present state encapsulates all pre-vious states through which it has passed, and is itself a moment in the projection of past into future,[3] we need appeal to no external chronological referent to appre-hend what Lévi-Strauss (1966a:258) calls 'the relation between *before* and *after*'. This relation is given in the very movement of becoming that we *read into* our snapshots and is enfolded in every instant we glimpse of it. It follows that to a his-tory that is statistical in Wiener's sense, and irreversible in Bergson's, *dates are quite superfluous.*[4] 'We do not *think* real time', Bergson writes, 'but we *live* it, because life transcends intellect' (1911:49). By the same token, we 'think' dates, but we do not 'live' them. Thus dates, far from constituting the foundation of history, are super-imposed on it by the intellect—we pin dates to history rather than history to dates. And so eternity, the sum of all possible dates, hovers over rather than underlies the real historical process (Bergson 1911:335).

Much of the more recent anthropological discussion of time has been couched in terms of a founding opposition between the 'synchronic' and the 'diachronic', and it is to this that we must now turn. Like all antinomies that are apparently simple and innocuous, this one harbours a morass of pitfalls and ambiguities. We cannot possibly explore them all. The principal point I intend to demonstrate is that a division of labour between a history concerned with diachronic facts and an anthropology concerned with synchronic facts will not suffice to grasp the con-tinuity and purpose of social life (see also Giddens 1979:7–8). To anticipate our conclusion, this is because both synchrony and diachrony, dealing in simultaneities and successions respectively, invoke a *chronological*—hence mechanical, eternal and abstract—sense of time, whereas social life is a process in real, Bergsonian time. The starting point of our discussion must be the lectures of Ferdinand de Saussure, reconstructed from the notebooks of his students as the *Course in general linguis-tics,* and in particular the chapter of the course entitled 'Static and evolutionary linguistics'. Let me then proceed directly to Saussure's original statement of the synchrony–diachrony dichotomy. We should always distinguish, he says,

> between (1) *the axis of simultaneities* (AB), which stands for the relations of coexisting things and from which the intervention of time is excluded; and (2) *the axis of successions* (CD), on which only one thing can be considered at a time but upon which are located all the things on the first axis together with their changes.

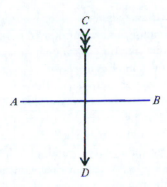

The first is the axis of synchrony, the second the axis of diachrony, one corresponding to the *state* of a language at a given time, the other to its *evolution* over a period of time (Saussure 1959:80–1).

Saussure uses the term 'evolution' often, apparently as a synonym for 'history'. And it is abundantly clear from his usage that this is not evolution (or history) as Bergson would have understood it. That is to say, it is not a movement, but a succession of states, each of which is momentarily fixed. The jump from one state to another is always brought about by an instantaneous event, which is purely fortuitous, wholly unintended by the speakers of the language (1959:85). In a famous, and highly inappropriate analogy, Saussure likens the functioning of language to a game of chess. At a particular moment, the state of the game may be comprehended as the totality of relations between the pieces, each of which occupies a certain position on the board. In the same way, a language state consists of a structure of relations between terms, in which each term 'derives its value from its opposition to all other terms' (1959:88). On the chessboard, only one piece is moved at a time, yet each move can radically alter the state of the game, affecting the relations even between those pieces not immediately involved. Again, a change affecting only one isolated element in a linguistic structure will have repercussions for every relationship in the structure. Moreover, Saussure continues, 'in chess, each move is absolutely distinct from the preceding and subsequent equilibrium. The change effected belongs to neither state: only states matter' (1959:89). This point is absolutely critical. For it implies that by analogy, the diachronic 'evolution' of language consists only of a concatenation of discontinuous states, separated by events. No more in language than in chess is the present structure a moment in the process of becoming the one following or ceasing to be the one preceding. An outsider, coming upon a game of chess in progress, could replace one of the players without being the slightest bit disadvantaged in relation to his opponent; likewise the speaker of a language can be fully competent whilst knowing nothing of its history.

Why is this analogy, apparently so powerful, also so inappropriate? The answer is that there cannot be a game of chess without players. Saussure himself admits this one crucial difference: 'The chessplayer *intends* to bring about a shift and thereby to exert an action on the system, whereas . . . the pieces of language are shifted—or rather modified—spontaneously and fortuitously. . . . In order to make the game of chess seem at every point like the functioning of language, we would have to imagine an unconscious or unintelligent player' (1959:89). But the consequences of this admission are a great deal more far-reaching than Saussure realizes. For it amounts to saying that there are really no players at all. Unknown, extraneous and possibly diverse forces are simply causing particular pieces, from time to time, to make quantum jumps from square to square. But in such a 'game', what is the counterpart of the language-speaker? His mind, or rather the collective mind of a population of language-speakers, is actually analogous to the *board* on which the game is played. A linguistic structure, Saussure tells us, is implanted in the mind of the speakers—who remain largely unconscious of it—and so a linguist must 'enter' the mind in order that it may be discovered and revealed (1959:72, 81). Our game becomes ever more curious. We must imagine now that the pieces hang upside down from the underside of the board, invisible to the spectator (the linguist). At the same time, the board is continually emitting signals of some kind, from which the spectator can infer the present position of the pieces. These signals are, of course, equivalent to acts of speech. Our inverted chessboard talks!

The analogy has now become so far-fetched that it is perhaps best left at this point. But before doing so I want to suggest that once we reintroduce the players and reinvert the board right side up, there is a certain parallel between a game of chess and the *process of social life,* regarded as a 'long conversation' going on between persons. For then we can see the succession of states of play as the visible record of an evolving relationship between the players, conceived as intentional agents. There is a sense in which real time is part and parcel of the game, as anyone who has played it knows. For, in the minds of the players, positions are not fixed but fluid, each move being not an instantaneous event but the culmination of a continuous process of conscious deliberation. Likewise, each line in a conversation is not an isolated utterance but grows out of the lines preceding as it conveys the conversation forwards. Thus the duration of the game, as of the conversation, corresponds to that movement or flow that is the thought or intentionality of the players, a flow conducted *through* states of play and of which every state is a transient moment. Caught up in this stream of consciousness[5] (compounded, if the analogy be taken literally, of two alternating streams), a given state gradually dissolves as the next takes shape in the mind of one player, only to be dissolved again as his opponent takes over and advances the game by a further step. To the extent that it is helpful to know an opponent, the outsider substituting for one of the players within a game *would* be at a disadvantage—just as would be a newcomer to a conversation—knowing nothing of the other's intentions as revealed in past moves. In short the game of chess, like the conversation that *is* social life, is creative, and what is created is a relationship of which each state of play is an index. The game as a whole represents a history that is made by those involved in it, rather than a chapter of accidents, whereas the board is but a vehicle for the conduct of life.

In Fig. 4.1A, I have tried to indicate this analogy diagrammatically. On each of the layered horizontal planes, we suppose, is projected a snapshot of a game (or conversation) in progress; running through them all is the irreversible duration of the players' (or speakers') consciousness. The snapshots, then, correspond to successive transects of the continuous movement of social life in Bergsonian time. Figure 4.1B presents, by way of contrast, the Saussurian analogy. Here each snapshot corresponds to a discrete, fixed state, suspended in abstract, mechanical time. The ordering of states is given by their attachment to dated chronological segments rather than by their position in a process of unfolding of the game as a whole. The little arrows in the diagram represent the signals emitted from the board, corresponding to instances of culturally coded behaviour by individuals who collectively carry a particular configuration of elements in their heads. At this point it is necessary to introduce another Saussurian dichotomy, between language (*la langue*) and speaking (*la parole*). The first is a structure imprinted in the mind, the second consists of observable, behavioural events, that is of particular acts of speech. To return to the analogy of Fig. 4.1B, language is the state of play on the underside of the board and speaking comprises the signals given off from the topside. It is important to realize (contra Lévi-Strauss 1968:212) that the synchrony–diachrony dichotomy is *not* congruent with that between language and speaking, nor does it correspond to the opposition between the system of associative or *paradigmatic* relations constitutive of language and the linear, *syntagmatic* sequences realized in discourse (Saussure 1959:123; see Ardener 1980:313). This point has often been obscured by a tendency to confuse the two analogies of Fig. 4.1. The identification of speech acts in a conversation with moves in chess is, as we have seen, precisely the opposite of what Saussure intended; for whereas he considered the former to be both 'wilful and intellectual', the latter—corresponding to the events of diachrony—were held to be motivated by neither purpose nor intelligence (Saussure 1959:14, 89).

Let us suppose, with Saussure, that a structure, once implanted in an individual's mind, remains more or less immutable. Passively acquired through a long childhood apprenticeship, it is—he argues—part of a common heritage or tradition inherently resistant to innovation (1959:73–4). Consequently, as Fig. 4.1B illustrates, language and speaking are but two sides of synchrony: the inner, cognitive side and the outer, executive side. We have therefore to distinguish between two kinds of event: on the one hand, events of speaking, motivated acts manifesting a stable structure and grouped on the plane of synchrony; on the other hand, unmotivated events of language change, by which one structure is supplanted by another in the dimension of diachrony. The life of the individual speaker, expended in the production of utterances (that is of events of the first kind), is therefore collapsed within the synchronic present, one of an undirected succession of such presents (events of the second kind) that add up to a diachronic sequence. It would appear that speaking, for Saussure, is rather like running on one spot. As the runner, after an indefinite number of paces, remains in the same place, so the speaker, however much he

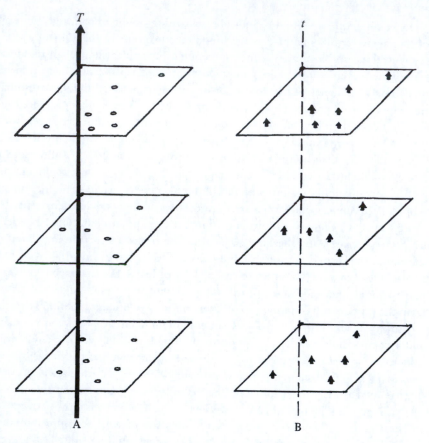

FIG. 4.1 The analogy between a game in progress and the history of a conversation **(A)** and of a language **(B)**.

talks, still occupies the same moment as when he started. From his first word to his last, time has not intervened. In this respect, the individual of Saussurian linguistics is closely akin to the individual of Boasian culture-history or of Darwinian evolutionary biology. In all three cases, as a singular instance of the self-assembly of discrete elements (linguistic, cultural, genetic) into structures, the individual is an object in a diachronic history of things, an object of which its every act is the expression of a particular facet.

One of the most conspicuous inadequacies of Saussure's linguistics, as Bourdieu has pointed out, lies 'in its inability to conceive of speech [i.e. speaking] and more generally of practice other than as *execution*' (1977:24). Whereas language, according to Saussure, pertains to the collectivity, speaking consists of individual acts that—though seemingly intentional—are yet 'accessory and more or less accidental' (1959:14). Each act appears as an isolated, momentary spark, lighting up first one, then another region of the linguistic structure. A little reflection will show the alleged intentionality of such acts to be illusory. As we have already argued, to suppose that all the conditions for an action are contained in the present state is to deny that it is motivated by consciousness, which is the projection of past into future. And this, precisely, is the implication of Saussure's relegation of speaking to the domain of synchrony. The individual, cut out from the flow of social life and thereby severed from his own past, is rendered *devoid* of purpose. Between language—'a system of signs that express ideas' (1959:16)—and the overt 'psychophysical' expression of particular ideas in speaking, there is no room for the intent of the speaker. One may as well envisage a robot equipped with a 'memory bank' of stored word-images and designed to turn out, at random, one string of words after another. By the 'wilfulness' of this machine we could but mean its inexhaustible capacity for aleatoric improvisation, or the indeterminacy built into its operation. Only by equating such indeterminacy with freedom, and by treating the latter as the essential attribute of will, can what is accidental be regarded as wilful. A similar argument would lead us to attribute consciousness to a one-armed bandit!

Language-users are not, of course, machines of this kind but social persons. Moreover, their utterances cannot be understood in isolation from one another, or from those of their fellows, but only in context as successive moments of that long conversation, social life. We owe to Malinowski the most eloquent affirmation of this point (1923:306–7). It may indeed be true, as Saussure claimed, that knowledge of the history of one's language is not a prerequisite for competent performance as a speaker. But to participate effectively in a conversation, Malinowski showed, it *is* essential to know something of its history, as any interloper—however proficient he may be in the language—would soon discover to his cost. It is in this sense that 'what is missing [from the Saussurian paradigm] is a theory of the competent speaker or language user' (Giddens 1979:17). Nor can this inadequacy be rectified within the terms of the synchrony-diachrony dichotomy. For to obtain a realistic picture of the speaker it is necessary to view the mechanism of language as a facility placed under the direction of practical consciousness. Like the chess players of Fig. 4.1A, the existence and activity of speakers cannot be wrapped up within the synchronic present, but must be seen to have an extension in real time—a Bergsonian 'duration'. Indeed the contrast between our two analogies, in Fig. 4.1A and B, may be taken as a summary of much of the argument of this and the last chapter. On the one hand we have a history of persons (speakers) and on the other we have a history of (language-bearing) populations.

In emphasizing with Malinowski that speaking is something that people do in the course of their lives, and not merely the mechanical articulation or execution of word-images, we also reverse the Saussurian priority of cognition over practice (Malinowski 1923:312–13). In our view it is language that is accessory to speaking, rather than vice versa (see also Hymes 1971:67). Although it is patently obvious that people could not speak without a language, we regard the latter as an instrument for the practical conduct of intersubjective life that—as a conversation—consists of people speaking. For Saussure, to the contrary, speaking is first and foremost the instrument of language, for it is through speaking that language is apprehended, reproduced and transmitted across the generations (1959:18–19). It matters not who is speaking or what is said, so long as *words are being spoken;* words that remain unspoken will eventually drop from the vocabulary, and if no words are spoken the language will die with the passing of the last generation of competent speakers. Now if the purpose of speaking were merely to promote the dissemination of language through imitative learning, then in theory (with apologies to language teachers, who know better in practice) our talking robot—introduced earlier—would do just as well. Likewise, to return to an earlier metaphor, the fashion designer who requires people to wear his costumes in order to popularize the style could get by with animated dummies, and indeed the 'dummification' of persons is precisely what is implied in the notion of 'modelling'. Speaking, for Saussure, is also a kind of modelling, though of a style that lacks a designer. The long conversation, throwing up countless exemplary utterances in the vernacular of a population, turns out to be not so much a process of life as an interminable language lesson.

By and large, linguistic signs are faithfully copied in the course of their intergenerational transmission. Saussure notes a number of factors that promote the immutability of the sign, of which he accords prime importance to the arbitrariness of the relation between signifier (sound-image) and signified (concept). Since there is no rational basis for preferring one image to another as the signifier of a given concept, we simply accept what is given: 'Because the sign is arbitrary, it follows no law other than that of tradition, and because it is based on tradition, it is arbitrary' (Saussure 1959:74). Nevertheless, in the very process of copying, signs are exposed to accidental alteration, leading to shifts in the signifier–signified relation. Had Saussure been teaching fifty years later he might well have turned to genetics for analogous illustration of the mutability of the sign. A genetic structure, like a linguistic structure, consists of a synchronic totality of relations between a large number of coexisting elements. And genes, like signs, are occasionally miscopied; that is to say, they undergo mutation. Each such mutation appears as a fortuitous and isolated incident whose cause, if it can be ascertained at all, lies wholly outside the structure itself, and which by the same token the structure is incapable of resisting. Yet every change rebounds throughout the structure, establishing a completely new state. Successive changes of state, in turn, add up to a process of evolution (Gerard, Kluckhohn and Rapoport 1956:15–25).

The genetic analogy, though imperfect, does help to clarify two points on which Saussure is obscure. One has to do with the role of time in the furtherance of change. Saussure admits his inability to give a satisfactory account of 'the causes of change in time'; it suffices for his argument that mutations do occur. Similarly, to justify his view of descent with modification, Darwin had only to point to the facts of variability for which, in his day, no explanation was available. Unfortunately, however, Saussure confuses the issue by promptly declaring that 'time changes all things; there is no reason why language should escape this universal law' (1959:77). This attribution of agency to time, however, flatly contradicts his idea of diachrony as the axis on which may be strung a changeful sequence of things. Darwin is much clearer on this point, recognizing that time does not *bring forth* modifications and that its passage is significant only to the extent that the greater the lapse of time, the more opportunities there are for variations to occur and to be accumulated (1872:76). Thus Saussure misleads by affixing the tip and tail of an arrow to diachrony, 'the axis of successions'. They should be replaced by symbols denoting its potentially infinite extension, for the time of diachrony is in fact reversible. This brings us to the second point of obscurity, namely the relation between diachrony and speaking. 'Everything diachronic in language', Saussure maintains, 'is diachronic only by virtue of speaking. It is in speaking that the germ of all change is found' (1959:98). This, and many similar statements, have led numerous commentators to suppose that for Saussure, language stands to speaking as synchrony stands to diachrony. Thus Giddens: '*Langue* can only be isolated by synchronic analysis; to study diachrony is to revert to the level of *parole*' (1979:17). Saussure's plan for a rational linguistics, reproduced here, lends no support to this interpretation (1959:98):

$$(\text{Human})\text{Speach} - \begin{cases} -\text{Language} - \begin{cases} \text{Synchrony} \\ \text{Diachrony} \end{cases} \\ -\text{Speaking} \end{cases}$$

Diachrony, here, is an aspect of language rather than speaking. Saussure's argument, as we have seen, was that apparently wilful acts of speaking, manifesting a synchronic structure, have as their unintended consequence the diachronic transmission of elements of that structure. In like vein, a contemporary sociobiologist might argue that behaviour we think to be purposive is unconsciously guided by a genetic system and ensures the representation of its components in the repertoire of subsequent generations. He would *not*, however, regard each successive behavioural act as a step in an evolutionary sequence, for the latter consists not of acts but of plans for acting, on the level of the genotype rather than its phenotypic expression. No more can we regard acts of speaking as events in diachrony. *Pace* Giddens, to study diachrony is to consider the *consequences* of *parole* on the level of *langue*, whereas to study synchrony is to consider the *manifestations* of *langue* in the form of *parole*. Language evolves, as Saussure explained, 'by virtue of speaking'; conversely, human beings speak thanks to language.

There is another reason why Saussure claims to find in speaking the germ of change, which has to do with its role in the origination rather than the dissemination of new elements. In the Darwinian evolution of species, every spontaneous mutation makes its first appearance in a particular individual, from which it may— under favourable circumstances—take root and spread throughout the population. Saussure likewise observes that in the evolution of language, innovations originate with individuals, and only as they gain wider acceptance do they enter the common repertoire of the community. Yet at the same time, he holds that language is a property not of individual minds but of an essential, collective mind, only partially realized in each individual brain: 'Language is not complete in any speaker; it exists perfectly only within the collectivity' and is constituted by 'the sum of word-images stored in the minds of all individuals' (1959:13–14). In that case, an image arising in the mind of only one or a handful of speakers would still be included in the complete language, from which we would have to suppose it had been drawn. Indeed we could come to no other conclusion than that the locus of linguistic mutation is the collective mind itself, and therefore that every innovation has a potential existence in all individual minds even though it is at first represented in only a few.

But this is as absurd as supposing that all genetic mutations are prefigured by changes in the ideal type of a species. To get around the problem, Saussure adopts another—and somewhat contradictory—tactic. The complete language now includes only those images common to every speaker. Whatever is idiosyncratic is defined *outside* language and relegated to the domain of speaking, a domain in which the mind of the individual, and not that of the collectivity, holds sway. From this he infers that every innovation originates historically with speaking (1959:18–19, 98). The implications, however, are no less absurd. Although an individual need never speak every word in his language, we might wonder how he can possibly speak, and thereby disseminate, what is *not* in his language. How can innovations ever become incorporated within language when at every stage they are categorically excluded from it? There is only one way to resolve these problems and that is to drop the essentialist assumption that an ideal language-state can be defined independently of the variety of states that actually exist imprinted in the minds of separate individuals. It is then easy to see that all the elements contained in the mind of a particular speaker belong to *his* language, regardless of the extent to which they are shared by others. Indeed, given the vast number of elements involved, we may reasonably expect the precise linguistic content of every mind to be unique, despite all the pressures towards standardization. We have therefore to introduce into diachronic linguistics the kind of 'population thinking' characteristic of Darwinian evolutionary biology. And this leads us to recognize that language, like culture in general, though an instrument of social discourse and the heritage of human populations, is basically a property of individuals.[6]

Contrarily, we have already demonstrated that speaking, as something people do, is essentially social. So we leave Saussure with a complete inversion of his position. Where he regarded language as social, speaking as individual, we have found language to pertain to populations of individuals, speaking to the social life of persons. In reaching this conclusion, we are not of course ruling out the culture-history of populations in favour of an exclusive focus on social process. The two kinds of history (or evolution) represented in Fig. 4.1 are, as we have already shown, both distinct and complementary. The Saussurian paradigm, stripped of its unwarranted essentialism, is quite appropriate as a framework for the history of things, each defined synchronically as a fortuitous combination of elements, and following one another in a diachronic sequence. Within this framework, the opposition between *langue* and *parole* is homologous to that between culture and behaviour, and between genotype and phenotype. Kluckhohn, for example, whilst distinguishing between covert cultural rules and overt behavioural practice, goes on to assert—in terms that anticipate one of the major trends of contemporary anthropological thought—that every culture design 'is a structure [in which] . . . the full significance of any single element . . . will be seen only when that element is viewed in the total matrix of its relationship to other elements' (1949:32–5). What we do, however, consider to be a retrograde step was the subsequent attempt by the alleged founder of anthropological structuralism, Lévi-Strauss, to apply the conceptual apparatus of Saussure's linguistics to *social life* by rewriting the conventional dichotomy between culture and behaviour as one between *social structure* and *social relations* (1968:279). The former appears as a kind of code, a synchronic system located in the collective unconscious and suspended in reversible time; the latter, far from unfolding in the course of consciously directed practice, are reduced to executions, signals or messages sporadically 'sparked off' rather than action continually 'carried on'. It is difficult to see how such executions can be regarded as social, in any sense of the word, let alone as relations. In Saussurian terms, they would not be social at all, but individual, whatever relations there are being present in the structure itself rather than its emissions. In our terms, the implied objectivism amounts to a *denial* of social relations—of intersubjectivity, personhood and consciousness as we understand it. And what all these have in common is that they are not things but movements in real time.

The loss of this sense of time in Lévi-Strauss's structuralism, and the consequent representation of history as a chain of discrete particulars suspended in the boundless void of eternity, is well expressed in this critical comment by Althusser: 'Diachrony is reduced to the sequence of events, and to the effects of this sequence of events on the structure of the synchronic: the historical then becomes the unexpected, the accidental, the factually unique, arising or falling in the empty continuum of time, for purely contingent reasons' (in Althusser and Balibar 1970:108). However, not all anthropologists have remained so faithful to the spirit of Saussure in their use of terms such as synchrony and diachrony. A case in point is Kroeber, whose view of a work of ethnography as providing a 'descriptive cross-section' of a society, at once 'synchronic' and 'historical', so confounded Boas. It will be immediately apparent that Kroeber's 'synchrony' conforms with the sense of neither Saussure nor Lévi-Strauss. It does, however, conform with the idea of a transect or snapshot of a continuous process, as presented in Fig. 4.1A. Such a snapshot is historical in that it enfolds the movement of its becoming. But this movement has of course to be 'read into' the snapshot, just as we would interpret a still photograph of people we know. And in our interpretation, we would not say that those people occupy the same frame because they happened to converge at a particular chronological instant, but rather that they are pictured together because they were, at that moment, mutually involved in *doing* something. That is to say, there was a communion of real time intrinsic to their intersubjective life. It would seem important to introduce a clear conceptual distinction between this sense of shared, inner time, and the notion of chronological contemporaneity—of outer time commonly occupied but not lived. Following Fabian (1983:31), I suggest we apply the term 'coeval'

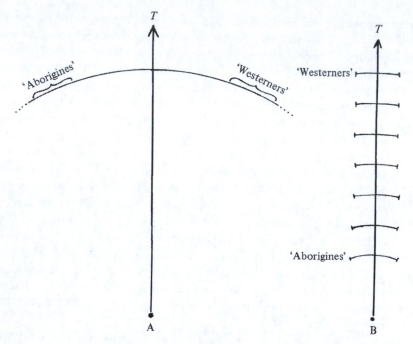

FIG. 4.2 Two views of human progress. **A:** Mankind as a whole, advancing on a continuous front; **B:** discrete societies following each other in lockstep.

to persons sharing lived time, and 'synchronous' to things or events co-occurring in segments of abstract time. The difference between the horizontal planes in Fig. 4.1A and B is then that they express coevalness and synchrony respectively.

The anthropological field-worker, participating in person with the people among whom he is studying, is coeval with them; though regarded as individuals, he and they are merely all synchronous. This at once rules out the kind of time-travel envisaged in the application of the comparative method, where it is supposed that to move outwards from a spatial centre is, *ipso facto,* to move backwards in time from a centrally located present, so that distant contemporaries are assimilated to proximate predecessors. *We* cannot move back in real time since, as Bergson recognized, 'our duration is irreversible' (1911:6). Yet if the Other is automatically defined as a predecessor, we would have to be able to do just that in order to participate with him. The fact that we can, nevertheless, participate with people wherever they may live, serves once again to demonstrate that mankind is advancing on a continuous front, rather like the crest of a spherical wave, and is not divided into ever so many discrete societies each following behind the other in lockstep (Fig. 4.2). Coevalness, we could say, characterizes the relation between any two persons, separate in space, who are potential consociates, as between any two points on a continuous surface unfolding through time. Those who are *not* our potential consociates are persons who have already lived and who have yet to live—'predecessors' and 'successors' in Schutz's terms (1962:15–16). The distance

that separates us from the former, and that will separate the latter from us, is a distance covered by real time. Adopting the Bergsonian notion of duration to denote
the temporal flow of social life, we can conclude that coevalness stands to duration
in the world as lived, in the same way that synchrony stands to diachrony in the
world as thought about. To emphasize the point, let us set up a formulation comparable to Saussure's. We have (1) *the axis of coevalness* (AB), which stands for the
world of persons not separated by the flow of time; and (2) *the axis of duration* (CD),
which represents the flow that both separates and connects the world of predecessors and the world of successors. Combined, these axes describe not an empty void
to be filled with things but a continuous field intrinsic to life and consciousness.
And in this case we, unlike Saussure, are entirely justified in affixing the tip and tail
of an arrow to the vertical axis.

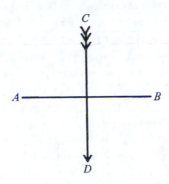

Now we have found that Bergsonian time inheres in evolution or history,
conceived as a continuous, oriented and progressive movement, regardless of
whether this movement is understood in 'topological' or 'statistical' terms. We
have also found that the concept of diachrony summons up a form of time that is
abstract and reversible, totally opposed to time as duration. It is therefore necessary to reject, once and for all, the commonly encountered notion that history as
an irreversible flux or 'stream of events' is essentially diachronic, as opposed to the
underlying domain of synchronic structure. The source of this notion, as ever,
lies with Lévi-Strauss, for whom the historical consciousness of 'hot' societies
(those that see in history 'the moving power of their development') is indicative of the ascendancy of diachrony in its allegorical 'struggle' with synchrony
(Lévi-Strauss 1966a:231–4). The victory is rather of a vision compounded on
the axes of coevalness and duration over one embracing the perspectives of both
synchrony and diachrony. Lévi-Strauss's error, which leads him to equate with
progressive evolutionism a history otherwise opposed to it, apparently rests on
the mistaken identification of the components of a statistical process, elementary
behavioural interactions conceptually equivalent to Saussure's *parole,* with the
non-recurrent events of a diachronic sequence. Much confusion has been caused
by a failure to discriminate between two classes of event: those that in aggregate

constitute a life-process and those that mark changes in the objective structures channeling this process. We are already familiar with the dichotomy from our discussion of Saussure's linguistics, in which we had to separate events of speaking (constituting a conversation) from events of language change. Biologists have to operate with much the same distinction: Thus in physiology one is concerned with the innumerable molecular reactions that add up to the life of the organism, whereas in the study of evolution (conceived not as ontogeny writ large but in Darwinian terms as descent with modification) the significant events are those involving changes of genotype as between one individual and another. Seen from this latter, strictly diachronic perspective, reactions of the first kind do not appear to add up to a process at all, but are ranged in synchrony.

This brings us to the heart of the differences between Lévi-Strauss and Radcliffe-Brown as regards their respective approaches to history and social life. Both start from the perception of events as discrete snippets of behaviour analogous to the Saussurian speech act. Sometimes Radcliffe-Brown brings such behavioural interactions under the rubric of 'social relations', despite their individual (or at most dyadic) and contingent nature, and this appears to be the source of Lévi-Strauss's rather peculiar usage, to which we have already alluded (Lévi-Strauss 1968:303–4). But whereas Lévi-Strauss goes on to treat these 'social relations' as so many manifestations of a particular structure, one of a diachronic series in which every event is a structural transmutation, Radcliffe-Brown adds them up into what he sees as a continuous, quasi-physiological process of social life. His conception of social life is quite clearly a 'statistical' one, for it 'consists of an immense multitude of actions and interactions of human beings, acting as individuals or in combinations' (Radcliffe-Brown 1952:4). In this flux of events, nothing ever recurs. Indeed, Radcliffe-Brown appeals for his idea of reality to the celebrated vision of Heraclitus, of a world in which all is motion and nothing fixed, and in which it is no more possible to recapture a passing moment than it is to step twice into the same waters of a flowing river (Radcliffe-Brown 1957:12). As Stanner has justly remarked, Radcliffe-Brown's Heraclitean view of the substance of social life, with its emphasis on continuity through change, is of a fundamentally historical character (Stanner 1968:287; see also Barnes 1971:549). But it envisages, of course, a history that is *processual,* utterly opposed to the Lévi-Straussian history of structural entities 'unfurled' in time.

This reading of Radcliffe-Brown may surprise those who are accustomed to accusing him, along with Durkheim, of the reification of society (see for example, Evans-Pritchard 1961). As the advocate of a functional theory whose explanatory power rests on the assumption of constancy and equilibrium in social forms, his reputation rests largely on his attempts to collect and classify societies as though they were *things* comparable—in his own words—to sea shells or, in the words of a critic, to butterflies (Radcliffe-Brown 1953:109; Leach 1961:2–3). Yet for all that, he never ceased to insist that the reality with which we deal 'is not any sort of entity but a process' (1952:4; also Gluckman 1968:221). Let us return to the analogy between society and organism, which was so central to Radcliffe-Brown's presentation. The crucial point to bear in mind is that an organism can be regarded in two different ways: either as an individual entity, a specific configuration of elements; or as the embodiment of a life-process that consists, as Cassirer put it, of 'a never resting stream of events' (Cassirer 1944:49; see also von Bertalanffy 1952:124). There is certainly a parallel between societies as Lévi-Strauss understands them and organisms conceived in the first of the aforementioned senses, that is as things. Indeed, Lévi-Strauss's plan for drawing up an inventory of societies, with a view to establishing their complementarities and differences, is the nearest thing to butterfly-collecting yet encountered in the annals of anthropology. Radcliffe-Brown, for his part, went out of his way to play down this aspect of the organic analogy, stressing that whereas organic forms can be isolated as discrete, self-contained entities ('a pig does not become a hippopotamus'), the same *cannot* be said of social forms, which can only arbitrarily be cut out from what is in reality a continuous field of relations (1952:181; also Evans-Pritchard 1961:10). This did not escape the attention of Lévi-Strauss, who notes with regret Radcliffe-Brown's 'reluctance toward the isolation of social structures' and his commitment to 'a philosophy of continuity, not of discontinuity' (1968:304).

That Radcliffe-Brown adopts the *second* sense of organism will be recalled from our earlier discussion of his conception of individuality. In the organic as in the social domain, he maintains, life consists of a continuous process constituted by 'a vast number of actions and reactions', though in the former case these are between molecules rather than human beings. Thus the analogy is not between organism and society as things, but between organic *life* and social *life* considered as movements (Radcliffe-Brown 1952:178–9, 193–4).[7] This amounts to saying that both organic and social forms *endure,* in the sense that real (Bergsonian) time enters their very constitution. Yet it was from Spencer, and not Bergson, that Radcliffe-Brown drew his theory of process. Starkly positivist, it was linked directly to Spencer's 'statistical' paradigm of evolutionary development. For his theory of epistemology, on the other hand, Radcliffe-Brown turned to Durkheim (Stanner 1968:286), an appeal that was to land him in contradictions from which he was never fully able to extricate himself. For Durkheim's was a philosophy of discontinuity, in which societies are externally presented to us for observation as so many 'distinct individualities', whose succession 'resembles a tree whose branches grow in divergent directions'. The progressive movement of mankind, he maintained, is 'a wholly subjective idea'; what exist in reality 'are particular societies which are born, develop and die independently of one another' (Durkheim 1982[1895]:64). Indeed there is no way in which Durkheim's first rule of sociological method, to *consider social facts as things,* can be squared with Radcliffe-Brown's conception of reality as irreversible process.

The contradiction could, however, be conveniently hidden by exploiting an ambiguity inherent in the notion of 'social life', one to which we have already had occasion to refer, between the social life of persons and the 'personal' life of society. Quite clearly, Durkheim had in mind the latter: the birth, maturation and death of a superorganic entity. Radcliffe-Brown equivocates. At one moment he tells us that the reality we observe consists of a network of particular relations built up and carried on by particular persons as *actors,* from which we derive social form as an abstraction. Yet at another moment, this form acquires substance as a reality, consisting of a working system of enduring relations between generic persons as *parts,* through which is conducted the purposive life of society. Stripped of intentionality, the occupants of these parts are then reduced to the status of biological organisms, yielding the individual–person dichotomy as Radcliffe-Brown presents it (1952:190–4). It is precisely by rewriting social life as the life of society that Radcliffe-Brown arrives at another pervasive dichotomy: that between *persistence* and *change.* A society exists as a definable entity only in so far as it persists in a stationary state; change then involves the abrupt substitution of one state for another. Thus nothing can change where nothing persists; nor, as Gluckman has forcefully argued, can we know *what* has changed except in the context of an assumed equilibrium (Gluckman 1968:231).

That is why, to return to an issue raised but not resolved earlier in our inquiry, it is contradictory to say that a society—or any other kind of entity—is *constantly* changing. And for the same reason, we must conclude that the opposition between persistence and change is not congruent to that between continuity and discontinuity. It is a fatal error, born of the tendency to conceive a world already parcelled up into discrete blocks, to equate continuity with the persistence of form. We can only define the continuous, as did William James, 'as that which is without breach, crack or division' (1890, I:237). Such, James argued, is the uninterrupted current of our thought, in which no state—once gone—can ever recur. If we grant that the reality of social life (of persons) is a progressive movement, through which the present forever grows beyond and encapsulates the past, we may likewise say that its duration is continuous. The antinomies of persistence and change are then the result of a dissection of this continuous movement into discontinuous steps. Each step corresponds to the 'life' of a distinct societal entity, whose characteristic rhythms are dictated by what Gluckman (1968:221) calls the 'structural duration' of its constituent institutions. To analyse an institution, Gluckman explains, 'we have to "throw it" . . . into its structural duration', that is to project it as a component of an equilibrium system. Notice that duration here connotes permanence rather than movement, that it is a property of institutionalized roles and role relations rather than of the intersubjective life of the people who play them (hence of persons as parts and not as actors), and that it pertains to the static, Durkheimian world of things as opposed to a Bergsonian world of flux (Gluckman 1968:221–3, 231). In each of these contrasts, the first term stands to the second as persistence stands to continuity, as the life of society to social life.

To return to Radcliffe-Brown, it was this same analytic procedure that has led him to introduce yet another dichotomy, between *synchronic* and *diachronic* problems. Although the terms apparently are borrowed from Saussure, Radcliffe-Brown's use of them is a far cry from that of Lévi-Strauss, or of Saussure himself (Evans-Pritchard 1961:17; Barnes 1971:542). In a synchronic account, he says, we treat a society *as though* it were persisting in a steady state, ignoring any changes that are taking place in its features. In a diachronic account, we are concerned with showing 'how societies change their type' over a period (Radcliffe-Brown 1952:4; 1957:88–9). The effect is similar to that of representing an undivided landscape by a model built up from contoured layers. However, as the recurrent phrase 'as though' indicates, synchrony and diachrony are not for Radcliffe-Brown to be taken as co-ordinates of the real world, but rather are to be applied in social analysis for resolving conceptually the flux of experience into relatively constant and relatively variable components. Far from apprehending change by putting together into sequence what are really discontinuous entities (living societies), as Durkheim or indeed Lévi-Strauss would have us do, Radcliffe-Brown proceeds by cutting into segments what is really a continuous flow (the social life of persons). The result is a punctuated series of equilibria in what Vaihinger (1924:xlvii) called the unreal world of 'As if' (Leach 1964[1954]:ix, 285; Gluckman 1968:221).

Synchrony stands to diachrony, then, as persistence stands to change: the former to the horizontal, the latter to the vertical components of a stepwise progression. The smaller and more frequent the steps, the closer the approximation to reality. Once it is admitted that this reality is but flowing movement, like the river of Heraclitus, we can but concur with Bergson 'that there is no essential difference between passing from one state to another and persisting in the same state' (Bergson 1911:2). In other words, as we approach reality, the distinction between synchrony and diachrony (in Radcliffe-Brown's usage) simply dissolves to yield duration, just as the distinction between persistence and change dissolves to yield continuous process. Bergson, though writing of psychic rather than social life, describes with admirable clarity the way in which the analytic imagination works by arbitrarily cutting up the flow into a changeful sequence of persistent states:

> If the state which 'remains the same' is more varied than we think, on the other hand the passing from one state to another resembles, more than we imagine, a single state being prolonged; the transition is continuous. But, just because we close our eyes to the unceasing variation of every psychical state, we are obliged, when the change has become so considerable as to force itself on our attention, to speak as if a new state were placed alongside the previous one. Of this new state we assume that it remains unvarying in its turn, and so on endlessly. The apparent discontinuity of the psychical life is then due to our attention being fixed on it by a series of separate acts: actually there is only a gentle slope; but in following the broken line of our acts of attention, we think we perceive separate steps. (1911:2–3)

To the extent that it is possible to summarize our argument diagrammatically, we have attempted to do so in Fig. 4.3.[8]

One of the commonest objections to the so-called structural–functional paradigm in social anthropology, as propounded by Radcliffe Brown, is that, in the words of one critic, it 'neither permits nor promotes the study of change'

(Smith 1962:77). Yet a glance at Fig. 4.3 reveals, quite to the contrary, that 'social change'—as a subject of study distinct from that of normal social life—is actually *constituted* by its complementary opposition to a functionalist conception of persistence as the life of society, having to do with the death or 'disintegration' of one social order and the birth or 'emergence' of the next. Combining both terms of the polarity yields what Gellner approvingly calls a 'neo-episodic' rather than continuous theory of progress; a view of history 'as a succession of plateaux, interrupted by steep, near perpendicular cliffs'. The sociology of each cliff, he goes on, 'must be concerned primarily with *change;* but the sociology of the societies on the intervening plateau may tend to be "functionalist" and be concerned primarily with the manner in which they maintained themselves in relative stability' (Gellner 1964:43; for a comparable argument see Gluckman 1968:223–4). The trouble with this view is that it cannot accommodate the life-process of those whose fate it is to scale the cliffs. Like initiates in a rite of passage, people undergoing social change are depicted in a state of limbo, perilously suspended between two different worlds and two different times, to which—more often than not—are affixed the labels 'traditional' and 'modern' respectively. The break from plateau to cliff-face is then signalled by an abrupt switch from an 'ethnographic present' that never recedes to a narrative past that never arrives (Gluckman 1968:224). The first is a time, though not our own, in which life is indefinitely prolonged through the repetition of events; the second, though connecting our world and theirs, is a time saturated with those unique and particular events that interrupt and sever the flow of life. In other words, it is the connecting thread of narrative that also maintains the perceived disjunction between one lived present and another.

It is worth pursuing the analogy, suggested a moment ago, between social change and rites of passage. Figure 4.3 could just as well represent the career of a particular person through a succession of parts or positions (e.g. boy, youth, elder) within a single institutional order, as the movement of social life through a developmental series of such orders. The distinction between the continuous, curved line and the discontinuous, horizontal lines again corresponds to that between two concepts of the person: as conscious subject, or agent, and as a summation of parts within a fixed institutional arrangement. Rites of passage, as is well known, serve to mark the division of a person's life into distinct stages or states, in each of which he can assume a different range of parts, and to 'lift' him from one stage to the next (van Gennep 1960[1909]). In one sense he is of course the same person all along, if by personhood we mean the unbroken trajectory of experience that *is* his life. But in the other sense, with each rite he literally ceases to be one person and reappears, following a symbolic death and rebirth, as quite another. During the intervening, liminal period he is outside both 'structural' time and space. It might be said that, having been stripped of all relationships formerly constitutive of his person, and still to be instated in new ones, he plays no part in the life of society. Yet in this 'naked' condition, as Turner puts it, 'people can "be themselves", . . . free to develop interpersonal relationships as they will. They confront one another, as it were, integrally and not in compartmentalized

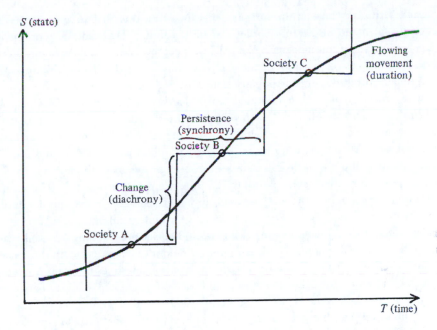

FIG. 4.3 Persistence, change and continuity. The continuous curved line represents the social life of persons, each of the discontinuous horizontal levels represents the life of a society (A, B, C) *through* persons. The intersections between curved and horizontal lines, marked by small circles, correspond to points of attention.

fashion as actors of roles' (1967:101). Indeed, neophytes who are 'fellow passengers' in the same ritual process often form deep and lasting attachments. But these relationships are not between parts in an instituted structure. They are real relations between persons as pure subjects or consociates, a binding together of lives in a shared experiential movement. And this intersubjective movement, we hold, is the very essence of the process of social life.

A focus on the liminal period in rites of passage thus serves to highlight the opposition between discrepant and commonly confused notions of personhood and social relations. The neophyte, though perhaps more a patient than an agent, is a self without a position, a person without a *persona*, living socially yet excluded from the life of society, and having a duration that is real, continuous and progressive rather than structural, persistent and repetitive. There has been a tendency in anthropological analysis, however, to equate all that is social with the latter term of each of these contrasts, with the result that the neophyte—devoid of the substance of social being—is conceived as but an organic individual, part of the formless and undifferentiated biological substratum upon which the edifice of society is to be built. It follows that the only thread connecting successive social states is the continuity of the organic life of the individuals on whom they are impressed. This thread, then, is equated with the flow of real time, a flow that is artificially broken up into segments in such a way that an appearance of constancy in the institutional order can be sustained. For example, writing of age organization among certain East African peoples, Baxter and Almagor assert that 'the process of aging is a visible physical record of the irrevocable passage of time', corresponding to the curved line of Fig. 4.3. Age-systems, however, 'endeavour to make aging a cultural rather than a physical process' (Baxter and Almagor 1978:24). All such systems 'seek to arrest time for a period, so that it moves forward in jerks. The periods between sets (or generations or grades) which are marked by transition rites are periods of liminality, or moments out of time, which allow time to catch up with events or events with time' (1978:7). This jerky movement corresponds to the stepwise graph of Fig. 4.3. The point I wish to stress here is the way the opposition between continuity and disconti-nuity is rendered as one between the *physical* (or biological) and the *cultural*. No clear distinction is made between cultural and social orders; thus it is said that 'the biological facts of birth and death must slide out of alignment with the social order with which they should conform'. Yet only a few lines later this discrep-ancy between biological reality and social order is represented as a 'gap between the cognitive order and the social reality' (1978:5–6).

This slip is extremely revealing. For it is perfectly true that growing old is not merely a biological process and that we experience the irreversible flow of real time because it is intrinsic to our lives, not only as organic individuals, but also as social persons. It is also true that the opposition between persistence in structural time and transition out of time, which age-systems apparently establish, is based on the attempt to accommodate a moving reality within a fixed framework of cognitive categories. We might reasonably conclude that the problem age-systems are intended to resolve is bringing the social into line with the cultural, or rec-onciling the world as lived with the world as thought about. The conventional view, however, is that age-systems—with their associated rites of passage—serve to impress a *social* discontinuity on the *biological* continuity of growing old, as though the process of maturation—'the insensible, infinitely graduated, continu-ance of the change of form' (Bergson 1911:20)—pertained to body but not mind. It is surprising how often, not only in the specialized language of anthropology but also in our own everyday discourse, the duration or passage of time intrinsic to life and consciousness is represented in exclusively physical terms. For example, we refer to a person's experienced past as his *biog*raphy, even though we intend to convey a history of social relations in which the person figures as conscious subject rather than physical object. Strictly speaking, we should adopt some such term as 'sociography' for a trajectory of this kind, with the qualification that it is meant to connote not the life of society (analogous to the literally biographical trajectory of the individual organism), but the intersubjective life of the person in his capacity as a social agent. Such a sociography, as we have previously remarked, does not begin with the physical birth of its subject, nor does it end with his death, for his life is built on and prolongs that of his predecessors just as it is pro-longed in the life of his successors.

Our propensity to 'biologize' human life-history may in part be due to a rather fundamental tendency in Western thought to locate the mainsprings of social behaviour in the inherent nature of autonomous individuals. Against this kind of reductionism, anthropologists have time and again drawn attention to the disjunction between social and biological facts, one instance of which is the frequent observation that individuals at very different stages of physical maturation may be treated as being of the same 'social' age, and expected to behave accordingly. The bedrock on which such counterarguments rest is Durkheim's conception of the duality of man, in whom 'there are two beings . . . an individual being which has its foundations in the organism, . . . and a social being which represents . . . society' (1976[1915]:16; also 1960[1914]:337]). Any explanation of social phenomena in terms of the biological or psychological properties of individuals was presumptively declared false (1982[1895]:129). And yet, in terms of the Durkheimian paradigm, a sociographical account of the life of the person remains utterly inconceivable. To adopt the particular man as subject would perforce be to frame the account in biological terms, since as a social being he is not a living subject at all. For Durkheim *society itself* is the 'particular subject', with 'its own personal physiognomy and idiosyncrasies', which lives *through* the persons who represent it (1976[1915]:444). In short, the imputation of agency to society, and consequent reduction of persons to their parts, leaves us with just as biological a view of the continuity of human life as that of the philosophical materialists whom Durkheim so vehemently opposed.

As we have seen, Radcliffe-Brown inherited this problem from the Durkheimian legacy. In supposing that an exhaustive account of the 'human being living in society' may be obtained by superimposing the parts constitutive of his social *persona* on his individuality conceived as a process of organic life, there could be no possibility of comprehending his career save as a chronological record of positions held. Socially man's being would be contained in a disjoint succession of presents, and only as a biological organism would the movement of his life be manifest as a projection of past into future. This is tantamount to a denial of intersubjectivity, of our mutual and creative involvement in the unfolding course of each others' lives. Shorn of the usual trappings of social position, as during a rite of passage, we could confront one another only as discrete, organic individuals, synchronous but not coeval, joined not by a community of inner time but only by our common exclusion from the 'time' of society. Durkheim, in his conclusion to *The elementary forms of the religious life,* offers a revealing comment in this connection that appears to be aimed directly at Bergson. 'The concrete duration which I feel passing within me', he says, 'expresses only the rhythm of my individual life'; it is a matter of private experience and does not suffice to constitute 'the idea of time in general'. This latter 'should correspond to the rhythm of a life which is not that of any individual in particular, but in which all participate' (1976[1915]:441). Durkheim is referring, of course, to the life of society, and by its 'rhythms' he clearly anticipates the notion of structural duration that Gluckman was to formulate half a century later.

Moreover, the time that is founded in collective life is not a real movement, not a commemoration of the past in the present, but 'an abstract and impersonal frame . . . like an endless chart, where all duration is spread out before the mind, and upon which all possible events can be located in relation to fixed and determined guide lines'. And these guide-lines, which provide us with the familiar calendrical divisions into days, weeks, months and years, 'correspond to the periodical recurrence of rites, feasts, and public ceremonies' (Durkheim 1976[1915]:10). The import of Durkheim's argument is that the opposition between concrete, Bergsonian duration and abstract, chronological time is congruent to that between the individual and the social components of man's being. It implies that for the social person, duration could be but one identical moment succeeding another. Remembering Bergson's words, 'there would never be anything but present—no prolonging of the past into the actual' (1911:4). Our contention, to the contrary, is that this kind of 'prolongation' characterizes not only the organic life of individuals but also the social life of persons, understood as an intersubjective process. It follows that real time stands to the conscious self as abstract time stands to the *persona* in which it is enclosed. The same intellectual operation that takes us from an experienced duration that flows to an abstract and divisible void to be filled with events (Durkheim's 'endless chart') also takes us from the person as a locus of consciousness to a division of parts within a perpetual order, to be filled with objectified individuals.

This theme of the relationship between personhood and temporality is central to an influential paper by Geertz, ostensibly about the interpretation of certain aspects of Balinese culture. His basic thesis is that the Balinese link a 'depersonalizing conception of personhood' with a 'detemporalizing conception of time' (Geertz 1975:391). To make sense of such a paradoxical statement, we have to recognize that Geertz is alternately invoking the two contradictory senses of person and time on which we have just elaborated. A 'depersonalized person' is a position without a subject;[9] 'detemporalized time' refers to an abstract ever-present from which the duration intrinsic to the flow of consciousness has been extracted. In reality, Balinese people, like the rest of us, are caught up as subjects in a movement by which the past is forever projected into the future: 'Of course, people in Bali *are* directly, and sometimes deeply, involved in one another's lives, they *do* feel their world to have been shaped by the actions of those who came before and orient their actions toward shaping the world of those who will come after them' (1975:390). But in Balinese thought, the experience of personhood as a unique sociographical trajectory, and of social life as an irreversible 'stream of historical events', is apparently played down in favour of an emphasis on 'social placement', or the notion of the person as connoting a 'particular location within a persisting, indeed an eternal, metaphysical order' (Geertz 1975:390).

If this is indeed the way the Balinese think, it bears an uncanny resemblance to the thought of a Durkheim or a Radcliffe-Brown. There is the same denial of intersubjectivity, the same identification of persons with their parts. Nor do the parallels end there. We find the same contrast between the individual being, undergoing a gradual process of physical maturation, and the social being as a component of a persistent, instituted order. One of the most important ways by which human beings are made aware of the passage of time, Geertz explains, is through their recognition 'of the process of *biological* aging, the appearance, maturation, decay and disappearance of *concrete individuals*' (1975:389; my emphases). Yet although 'physically men come and go as the ephemerae they are, . . . socially the *dramatis personae* remain eternally the same' (1975:371–2). Still more striking is the similarity between Durkheimian and Balinese treatments of time. The Balinese calendar, establishing an elaborate and endlessly repetitive chronology, charts a time that neither advances nor recedes, of which every division is a segment of eternity. Application of the calendar, Geertz argues, 'blunts the sense of dissolving days and evaporating years' associated with the history of persons, 'by pulverizing the flow of time into disconnected, dimensionless, motionless particles'. What Geertz claims for the Balinese, Durkheim claims for mankind: 'We cannot conceive of time, except on condition of distinguishing its different moments' (1976[1915]:10). And for both Durkheim and the Balinese the reason is the same: an inability (or disinclination) to comprehend personhood other than as a position in an absolute present. As Bloch has noted, the conjunction of depersonalized personhood with detemporalized time, allegedly symptomatic of Balinese conceptions, neatly epitomizes the classical theory of social structure as it has come down to us from Durkheim through Radcliffe-Brown (Bloch 1977:286).

Armed, then, with a peculiarly Balinese logic, anthropology has by and large settled for the recognition of two kinds of time: one linear and progressive, associated with what is mundane, pragmatic and natural; the other cyclical and repetitive, associated with what is ritualized, expressive and cultural (Bloch 1977:282). They correspond, of course, to the 'two beings' in Durkheim's man, individual and social. One celebrated statement of the dichotomy is to be found in a pair of essays by Leach on 'the symbolic representation of time' (1961:124–36). Our notion of time, Leach argues, embraces 'two different kinds of experience which are logically distinct and even contradictory'. The first is the experience of repetition: 'Whenever we think about measuring time we concern ourselves with some kind of metronome; it may be the ticking of a clock or a pulse beat or the recurrence of days or moons or annual seasons, but always there is something which repeats.' The second is the experience of linearity or non-repetition: 'We are aware that all living things are born, grow old and die, and that this is an irreversible process' (Leach 1961:125). We can immediately recognize this as the distinction between Newtonian and Bergsonian time, or in Wiener's terms between the time of mechanical and statistical systems respectively. The contradiction between them can be simply stated as follows: Were time considered intrinsic to the life-process, the moments spun by a Newtonian machine would be but segments of a timeless eternity; if on the other hand, time is regarded as an eternal thread, the life process would dissolve into a multitude of events suspended *in* time.

It is one thing to admit that time can take these alternative senses but quite another to claim, as Leach does, that they correspond to different kinds of experience. Consider, for example, the 'experience of repetition'. Clearly this requires both some*one* who experiences and some*thing* that repeats. Let us follow William James in supposing that in the stream of consciousness, 'no state once gone can recur and be identical with what was before' (1890, I:230). Whatever repeats must therefore lie outside the consciousness of the experiencing subject; a mechanical system, lacking consciousness, cannot experience its own repetition. Conversely a consciousness whose duration is cumulative and irreversible can never repeat itself. As a conscious subject, I become aware of repetition in the objective world of things only because I feel myself to be 'further on' from when those things were last in the same position. In terms of my own experience, the time that has elapsed, as Bergson wrote, 'coincides with my impatience, . . . with a certain portion of my own duration' (1911:10). It follows that repetition is perceived through the superimposition of a mechanical chronology, establishing a system of fixed intervals, upon the duration of consciousness. That is to say, the experience to which Leach refers corresponds not to one kind of time rather than another, but to the confrontation between the two—between the time intrinsic to the life of the subject and that given by the mechanical universe he inhabits or has constructed for himself. Moreover, it is precisely this confrontation that is implied when we speak of human *consciousness of time*. One kind of time inheres in the consciousness that apprehends, the other in what is apprehended. The former, taken on its own, would give us consciousness, but not a reflexive consciousness *of*; the latter alone would give us a time without consciousness—eternity or 'every when', to use the evocative term by which Stanner characterizes the mythical Dreamtime of the Australian Aborigines (Stanner 1965:159).

The same conclusion emerges if we reflect on what is meant by 'cyclical time', a recurrent notion in the anthropology of time-reckoning. This is often said to be manifested in those systems of kinship where there is an alternation of terms applied to successive generations along a single line of descent. As a case in point, Lévi-Strauss cites the terminology of the Hopi, among whom persons in a man's mother's line are alternately called 'sibling' and 'nephew': This, he claims, attests to 'an undulating, cyclical, reversible time' (1968:74, 301–2). But as Barnes has rightly remarked, the opposition between reversible and irreversible is not identical to that between cyclical and non-cyclical. Cycles 'run always in the same direction, in the same temporal sequence of generations, and cannot be reversed' (Barnes 1971:541). Surely what gives these cycles their direction is the flow of life across the generations. In reality, children do not beget their parents; it is for this reason that we can speak of descent lines as connoting an oriented movement. To arrive at true reversibility we would have to abstract away this movement, by which each generation grows out of and supersedes the one preceding, to leave but pure geometrical lines of the kind we draw on genealogical charts, which can be read in any direction. But then, this would not only eradicate the component of cyclicity, but would be tantamount to removing the people themselves.

It would be quite wrong, therefore, to distinguish the 'cyclical' as a special mode of human time-awareness, opposed to our own, allegedly 'linear' mode. There are not two ways of articulating the passage of time but just one: that is by impressing a scheme of metronomic intervals (described by a reversible mechanical system such as a pendulum or the rotating earth, or by a comparable 'mechanical model' of kinship and social organization) on the irreversible movement of life and consciousness. Let me return to Leach. 'We talk of measuring time as if time were a concrete thing waiting to be measured; but in fact we *create time* by creating intervals in social life. Until we have done this there is no time to be measured' (Leach 1961:135). If this were literally true, we would be put in a peculiar quandary. How can we measure intervals of measurement? Do we analogously create length by dividing a tape measure into feet and inches, or create heat by calibrating a thermometer? Of course not. Duration, like the spatial extension and heat of physical bodies, *is* an immanent property of the real world waiting to be measured—more than that, it is a constitutive property of ourselves, the measurers. So what is this time that we create, as distinct from that which creates us? It is nothing more than an *idea,* which stands to the reality of our duration in the same way that temperature stands to heat. For the notion of temperature, like the idea of time, is a product of the intellect and connotes a system of divisions on an abstract scale. What it gives us, then, is not heat but a set of categories for talking about it. Likewise, by creating intervals in social life, we establish time as an object of discourse.

The awareness of time is generally, and with good reason, thought to be uniquely human. It was, as we saw in Chapter 2, central to Darwin's conception of humans as moral beings. Durkheim, too, pointed out that animals have no *representation* of time (1976[1915]:11 n. 1). Yet if we follow Bergson, wherever anything lives, real time is flowing, a flow identified with the evolution of consciousness. Time must therefore be distinguished from *awareness* of time just as consciousness should be distinguished from self-consciousness: the former being intrinsic to life, the latter distinctive of *human* life (Harré 1979:291). To reflect on his self, and on the passage of time intrinsic to his being, the person must be able to 'cut out' past states from the stream of his consciousness and 'hold them over' for re-presentation as objects of attention in the here and now. And this excision and retention is effected precisely through the imposition of a system of chronological categories on the flow of life. Durkheim's point was that these categories are instilled in us by virtue of our active participation in the life of that collective entity he called 'society'. That is why he felt it so important to distinguish between time, as a socially defined category, and concrete duration 'such as the individual consciousness can feel' (1976[1915]:441 n. 1). Granted the necessity of separating consciousness from the cognitive categories through which it receives outward expression, we hold that the former is not a property of isolated individuals but is constituted by *social* relations, whereas the latter are components of a design carried by *individuals* in their capacity as culture-bearers. Hence we reach the fundamental conclusion that *awareness of time lies in the mapping of a repetitive, culturally coded routine on the linear continuity of the social life of persons.* Or even more generally, it is a function of the dialectical confrontation between subjects and objects, persons and things, what lives and what is.

Consider further the life of the person. Let us imagine that he is a hunter, enmeshed in a skein of intersubjective relations with other hunters associating together in what is commonly known as the 'band'. As he goes through life, he performs a great number of every day acts—for example slaughtering a beast, making a tool, building a dwelling—each of which has a definite starting-point and finishing-point. What runs through or informs these acts is the purpose or intentionality of their subject. The intentional content of action derives, in turn, from the context of social relations in which the hunter is located as an agent of production. If this social component is conceptually removed, we are left with nothing more than the physical movements corresponding to each act, together with their lasting environmental impressions. Thus hunting, as consciously motivated activity, is reduced to predation—the killing and consumption of prey. This, of course, is equivalent to Saussure's reduction of speaking to execution, the mere utterance of words. Figure 4.4 shows, in a highly schematic way, what happens when acts are separated from the intentionality of those who perform them, and their environmental impressions laid one upon the other in a cumulative series. Each of the small vertical lines represents one 'bit' of behaviour, that is a directed sequence of physical movements that lead from the initiation of an act to its completion. The broad horizontal band in Fig. 4.4A represents the intentionality of the subject who is 'moving through' these acts, each of which constitutes an instrumental phase in the realization of an ongoing purpose. Unlike the vertical lines, this band is continuous, just as the life of the subject is continuous. When it is subtracted, as in Fig. 4.4B, action fragments into extremely numerous, unconnected bits, of which we may suppose only a few leave any durable environmental impression. In Fig. 4.4C, we can see how these impressions are recombined in sequence through the slow process of natural deposition, yielding, for instance, the record of a prehistoric site. The horizontal band here represents the environment, and each 'bump' on the band represents one impression (bracketed bits yield no impression).

In purely chronological terms, Fig. 4.4C combines a very short time-perspective with a very long one. An individual act may take seconds, minutes or hours; the formation of a record out of the impressions left by these acts takes millennia. This represents a difference in order of magnitude of some 10^7. It appears that the longer the blocks of time with which prehistorians deal, the more their attention becomes focused on the minutiae of behaviour, rather as explorers of the cosmos focus on the behaviour of subatomic particles. The temporal perspective of the anthropologist, working 'forwards' from a knowledge of people's intentions rather than 'backwards' from an environmental record, is rather closer to ordinary human experience. If a person's present intention lies at the tip of an arrow (Fig. 4.4A) whose movement corresponds to the duration of his consciousness, it is also true that the arrow has a characteristic length that is relatively independent of the total distance covered—measured chronologically. This length, the yardstick of 'anthropological' time, is a function of the total system of relations that constitutes the person as a social agent, judged for example by the genealogical depth of a maximal lineage or clan (Evans-Pritchard 1940:106–7). Its approximate constancy

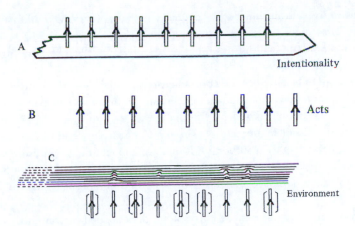

A   Intentionality

B   Acts

C   Environment

FIG. 4.4 A schematic representation of the relations between acts, intentionality and environmental formation. Reproduced from Ingold (1984:10).

rests on the premiss that, even as consciousness is sucking present states back into the past, so past states are dropping out of consciousness. In Fig. 4.4A and C, the 'band of intention' is as continuous as the 'band of environment'; the processes of social life and environmental formation are going on concurrently. The former, however, bends a *certain length* of past to face the future in an active advance, whereas the latter is the passive sedimentation of a past that—turning its back on the future—recedes indefinitely. This, of course, is the difference between a dead and a living past: As we conceive subjective life, in Whitehead's phrase, as a 'creative advance into novelty', so the environment contains an accumulation of all that has fallen away from, or is placed outside, living subjects. On it is inscribed a history of lifeless objects, things.

To the threefold distinction between acts, intentions and environments there correspond, then, three conceptions of the scale, or 'term' of time. Acts are consummated in microtime, the intentions integrating and directing these acts endure in mesotime and the environments that bear their imprint build up in macrotime. This trichotomy is virtually equivalent to Braudel's (1972:20–1) division of historical time into *individual* time ('the history of events'), *social* time ('the history of groups and groupings') and *geographical* time ('the perspective of the very long term' evident in man's relation to his environment). If the middle term were omitted we would be left with a pseudo-Darwinian view of culture change: the gradual accumulation, over countless generations, of minute individual differences within a slowly changing environment. Consciousness and social life would have no place in such a view; indeed some prehistorians (the palaeoeconomic school in particular) have appealed to the very long term as grounds for relegating social phenomena to the category of ephemeral 'noise' in an evolutionary process conceived entirely on Darwinian lines (Higgs and Jarman 1975:4–5; see Ingold 1980a:92; Bailey 1981:98–100). Others have written of the evolution of consciousness as though the life of early man were conducted in ponderous slow motion, thereafter speeding up on a logarithmic scale, so that what takes us a day would have occupied our most ancient ancestors a millennium or more.

This kind of temporal distortion has been rightly criticized by Lévi-Strauss:

> It is not only fallacious but contradictory to conceive of the historical process as a continuous development, beginning with prehistory coded in tens or hundreds of millenia, then adopting the scale of millenia when it gets to the 4th or 3rd millenium, and continuing as history in centuries interlarded, at the pleasure of each author, with slices of annual history within the century, day to day history within the year or even hourly history within a day. All these dates do not form a series: they are of different species. (1966a:260)

For Lévi-Strauss, history may be chronologically encoded on a number of different time-scales or wavelengths, all running concurrently and without beginning or end, to each of which we must 'tune in' separately. Events discernible on one channel, or at one frequency, will vanish at another, either because they expand to occupy the entire field of vision, or because they are reduced to insignificance. The same is true of the codification of space. Something that shows up as a distinct entity under the microscope, at a low power of magnification, may be virtually invisible to the naked eye, whereas at a higher power of magnification it appears as an ill-defined back ground on which are inscribed a class of things of another order of minuteness. At each power, a different world is revealed to the observing eye, yet one that is coextensive with every other, in theory encompassing the infinitude of space.

Not only will differing time-scales bring into focus different kinds of event, they may also require us to adopt different principles of causality. That is to say, we have to introduce into our explanatory constructs a certain 'time perspectivism' (Bailey 1981:103; also 1983). To my knowledge this was a point first made by Haldane in an important paper entitled 'Time in biology' (Haldane 1956a). He distinguishes between five levels at which biological processes may be examined, to each of which there corresponds a particular range of time intervals. They are the molecular (10^{-5} to one second), the physiological (10^{-2} seconds to one hour), the developmental (up to a lifetime), the historical (covering many generations, but not enough for significant modification through variation under natural selection), and the evolutionary (from about 10,000 years upwards). In this list the largest interval is over 10^{22} times the smallest, a colossal difference in order of magnitude. Haldane goes on to suggest that the different time-scales correspond to different levels of organization, so that in the reduction of processes on one level to those operating on the level below (e.g. the developmental to the physiological, or the physiological to the molecular) we dissolve each process into a very great number of smaller and much more rapid steps. The lower the level of organization, and the shorter the time-scale, the more we are inclined towards a starkly mechanistic materialism, epitomized by molecular biology. Conversely, as we move towards higher levels of organization and longer time-scales we are much more inclined to seek teleological explanations for what we observe (1956a:386–8, 398–400).

There is a strange flaw in Haldane's argument. As a staunch Darwinian, he should have known that the highest level of organization in his list of five is in fact the middle one—the developmental or ontogenetic. It is here that the end-directedness of biological processes is most apparent. To follow through a reductionist programme is in fact to move from the middle term (the time of life) simultaneously in two contrary directions: towards the very short term of molecular biology and towards the very long term of evolutionary 'descent with modification'. Both are associated with an atomizing materialism and with the banishment of final causes.[10] And it is from molecular biology that many of the discoveries have come that have filled crucial lacunae in our understanding of how variation under natural selection actually works, the most obvious and striking example being the deciphering of DNA. To push the reduction further, stripping away the molecular level of organization, would take us altogether out of biology into particle physics. This, the 'hardest' of the sciences, has also introduced us to both the shortest and the longest time-scales yet conceived. Alternatively, taking leave of biology in the opposite, totalizing direction, we could move 'up' to the highest level of organization of all, namely consciousness. Here, in the realm of historical anthropology, the short term and the long term converge in the mesotime of Fig. 4.4, the time of social life corresponding to our own existence as subjects, where teleology reigns supreme.

There are two ways out of history, Lévi-Strauss asserts, either down through the bottom or up through the top. One leads 'from the consideration of groups to that of individuals' and thence to 'an infra-historical domain in the realms of psychology and physiology' ultimately reducible to the behaviour of atoms and molecules. The other is 'to put history back into prehistory and the latter into the general evolution of organised beings, which is itself explicable only in terms of biology, geology and finally cosmology' (Lévi-Strauss 1966a:262). Our argument is that these are not alternative routes. They are the product of a single movement of objectification, a progressive analytic fragmentation of the phenomenal world, which takes us from an anthropology conceived as a study of the expressions of consciousness, through the various levels of biology (from developmental to molecular) to chemistry and physics. At each stage in the reduction, the short term of elementary events and interactions becomes still shorter, the long term that they occupy still longer; the approach towards zero in the former is also an approach towards the infinite in the latter. In Fig. 4.5, we show this bifurcation of time schematically. At some point, as we descend the vertical scale, the limits of finality are breached and teleology gives way to pure mechanism. Here, at once in the very short term of neural interactions and in the very long term of cerebral evolution, in the world of microseconds and millennia, we discover the ends of purpose. Yet however far we may, in thought, pursue existence to its temporal extremes, for the mortal thinker there can be no escape from history. Were he the bundle of elements, suspended in a boundless universe, to which he would reduce all others, he could not think the thoughts

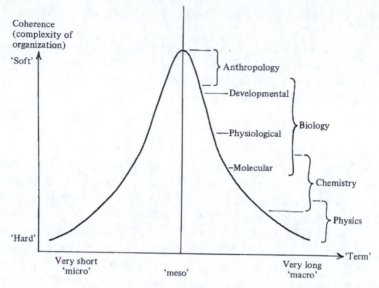

FIG. 4.5 The bifurcation of time-scales in the progressive reduction from 'soft' organicism to 'hard' mechanism.

he does. For in so doing, he mobilizes the very highest levels of consciousness in a purposive, creative movement. Even as he contemplates the ultimate and the eternal, his subjective life passes, and history is being made. Indeed it is largely in the attempt to think themselves out of history, and to evade the implications of the passage of time, that human beings have created a history of thought. And it is to the significance of creativity that we must now turn.

5

CHANCE, NECESSITY AND CREATIVITY

There are two sides to the machinery involved in the development of nature. On one side, there is a given environment with organisms adapting to it [through natural selection]. . . . The other side of the evolutionary machinery, the neglected side, is expressed by the word *creativeness*.

Whitehead, Science and the modern world

Evolution creates new living systems to occupy the ecological niches that are available. . . . It is not on the level of mutation, but rather on that of natural selection and other genetic processes that take place in living populations, that the creativity of evolution manifests itself.

Dobzhansky, 'Chance and creativity in evolution' ©
1974 by the Regents of the University of California.
Published by the University of California Press.

Here are two leading exponents of the principle of creativity in evolution, whose positions could, nevertheless, hardly be more different. Dobzhansky, one of the major architects of the evolutionary synthesis of neo-Darwinian biology, finds the principle at work in the adaptation of organic forms to diverse environments under pressures of natural selection. Whitehead, influenced more by Bergson than by Darwin, locates creativity in the very movement of becoming that Darwinian biology, with its atomizing materialism, *leaves out*. His term for this movement is 'concrescence', a kind of cumulative building-up or advance of organization in which nature forever surpasses itself. Dobzhansky, for his part, explicitly rejects the Bergsonian conception of creative evolution, though in apparent agreement with Whitehead, he regards the essence of creativity as the production of patterned novelty (Whitehead 1929:28; Dobzhansky 1974a:329). It is clear from this initial contrast that there must be at least two ways of understanding the generation of the absolutely new and moreover that these correspond to the opposed senses of evolution, history and time on which we have elaborated in previous chapters. And our argument would lead us to expect them to be linked, likewise, to what we have called respectively the cultural adaptation of populations and the social life of persons. Up to now, we have reserved the notion of creativity for the latter, treating the former as something that 'just happens' through a mixture of pure chance and mechanical necessity. We must therefore begin by looking rather critically at the reasoning that causes Dobzhansky and others to attribute something more than chance and necessity to the history of organic species, and then consider whether it applies analogously to the history of human cultures. This will enable us to pinpoint more exactly the special meaning of creativity that, we believe, characterizes the process of social life.

It is well to recall, first, the principal steps of the argument by which Darwinian theory, amplified in the light of modern population genetics, claims to refute teleology in organic evolution. It starts from the recognition of variability in populations of genealogically related individuals, each of which is assembled on a template consisting of a unique combination of discrete units of heredity (genes). The ultimate source of variation lies in those errors in reproductive transcription of the hereditary material known as genetic mutations. Whatever may be the causes of particular mutations (if not purely spontaneous), they are believed to be wholly unrelated to the current needs and functioning of the organisms in which they occur, or to the nature of their environments. In this sense alone, each may be regarded as a chance event, an accident. Probably the vast majority are either neutral or deleterious in their effects. However, compared with the number of faithful transcriptions of genetic material, mutations are very rare indeed. That is to say, an outstanding characteristic of genetic copying is its accuracy; but for this very reason, those errors that do occur will be automatically replicated with equal fidelity. Bearing in mind the large number of genes that constitute the template of even a relatively simple organism, as well as the number of cellular generations in the life of a single individual, there are ample opportunities for mutations to occur, and hence to be accumulated over the generations. In sexually reproducing populations, the production of variation is enormously enhanced by the random recombination of parental genes in each generation of progeny. Although the representation of genetic variants in future generations depends on the reproduction of the organisms whose assembly they direct, in a finite environment there are limits to the numerical size of the population that can be supported. Therefore genes that either singly, or more often in combination, confer a reproductive advantage on the individuals bearing them will have their representation in the population proportionally increased, whereas those whose consequences for reproduction are relatively deleterious will be gradually eliminated. Through this mechanism of natural selection, working retroactively on populations of unique individuals, and not through the implementation of a transcendental design, the challenges presented to life by an ever-changing environment have been—and continue to be—met through adaptations as diverse as they are ingenious.

From this summary review, it is quite clear that the element of chance plays a central role in the Darwinian account of evolutionary adaptation, parodied by one of its last leading detractors as a theory 'which explained how by throwing stones one could build houses of a typical style' (Driesch 1914:137). No one was more troubled by this than Darwin himself: Shortly after publication of *The origin of species,* he confessed in a letter to Asa Gray of his inability to 'think that the world as we see it is the result of chance; and yet I cannot look at each separate thing as the result of Design. . . . I am, and shall ever remain, in a hopeless muddle' (in F. Darwin 1888:378). We are no less muddled today. The deep divisions that continue to plague the philosophy of biology on the issue of 'chance and necessity' were especially highlighted by the recent publication of a little book on the subject by the distinguished biochemist, Jacques Monod, and by the controversy that ensued.[1] Monod's position, based on a postulate of absolute 'scientific' objectivity, is radically reductionist, utterly opposed to all holistic, subjectivist or vitalist views that claim to discern in evolution a purposive, creative movement. Treating every living organism as a self-constructing 'chemical machine', Monod finds nothing in its development that is not already contained in its molecular constituents—hence epigenesis 'is not a *creation;* it is a *revelation*' (Monod 1972:51–2, 87). As such, it is fundamentally opposed to evolutionary emergence, 'which, owing to the fact that it arises from the essentially unforeseeable, is the creator of *absolute* newness' (1972:113). Were it not for the intervention of chance in the transmission of hereditary elements, evolution could not occur. The core of Monod's thesis is contained in the following, characteristically outspoken passage:

> We say that these events [of mutation] are accidental, due to chance. And since they constitute the *only* possible source of modifications in the genetic text, itself the *sole* repository of the organism's hereditary structures, it necessarily follows that chance *alone* is at the source of every innovation, of all creation in the biosphere. Pure chance, absolutely free but blind, at the very root of the stupendous edifice of evolution: this central concept of biology . . . is today the *sole* conceivable hypothesis, the only one compatible with observed and tested fact. And nothing warrants the supposition (or the hope) that conceptions about this should, or ever could, be revised. (1972:110)

This last remark, quite unbecoming of a scientist, effectively converts hypothesis into dogma. Fortunately most practising biologists seem no more inclined to accept it than was Darwin.

Broadly speaking, opposition to Monod's views has taken two forms. On the one hand, there is the opposition he anticipates from those who remain committed to the antireductionist cause (e.g. Koestler and Smythies 1969). On the other hand, there are neo-Darwinians who agree that variation under natural selection, and nothing more, accounts for organic evolution, but who consider that the operation of natural selection cannot be comprehended within the terms of the antinomy between chance and necessity (Wright 1967:117; Mayr 1982:520). This is Dobzhansky's position. He refers to natural selection as 'the antichance factor in evolution', generating order out of the building blocks of heredity without imposing a necessary determinism. In evolution, chance (variation) and antichance (selection) are blended in a creative process (Dobzhansky 1974a:318; 1974b:132–6). Central to Dobzhansky's argument is his rejection of the 'sieve' model of natural selection. According to this model, selection is merely a weeding-out of deleterious genetic variants and a retention of those that are favourable. Barring the case of micro-organisms, the model is far too simple, for it ignores the fact that in real situations, genes are tested by selection not singly but in specific *combinations*. Any mutant that is not a dominant lethal (which would, of course, be eliminated in the same generation as it arises) will enter into a great many different combinations in different individuals: In some its effects may prove beneficial, in others harmful, and again in others of no consequence at all. The overall effect of selection will then be to adjust the relative incidence of different genes in a population in such a way as to increase the probability of appearance of certain favourable (though never exactly identical) genetic combinations. In that sense, Dobzhansky continues, natural selection is engaged in a job of construction rather than mere censorship:

> The statement that the process required a supply of 'chance' mutations is true but trivial. What is far more interesting is that these genetic variants were not simply caught in a sieve, but were gradually compounded and arranged into adaptively coherent patterns, which went through millions of years and of generations of responses to the challenges of the environments. Viewed in the perspective of time, the process cannot meaningfully be attributed to the play of chance. (1974a:323)

On these grounds, Dobzhansky feels it is legitimate to regard selection as a kind of *engineer,* admittedly one that is 'blind and dumb', devoid of foresight, such that every act of construction is itself a decision about what is to be constructed (1974a:331).

We shall return later to the question of whether the engineering metaphor is appropriate. I want first to compare the ways in which Monod and Dobzhansky employ the concept of creativity. One might imagine that the concept would have no place in Monod's exclusively mechanistic evolutionary scenario. But he does in fact use it on a number of occasions, two of which we have cited. 'Blind chance', responsible for 'evolutionary emergence', is the 'creator of absolute newness', the source 'of all creation in the biosphere' (Monod 1972:110, 113). There are two facets to the meaning of creativity, as it is commonly understood. The first is the implication of subjective *agency:* To create is to cause to exist, to make or produce. The second, which for Monod distinguishes (evolutionary) creation from (epigenetic) revelation, is that what is brought into being is *novel*. There is no creativity in the mechanical execution and replication of a preformed project; evolution involves the successive creation of new projects rather than the unfolding of existing ones.[2] However, in Monod's view of the natural world, there is no room for the creative subject, whose existence and activity is excluded by virtue of the postulate of objectivity. Instead, in place of the subject, there stands the figure of chance. But chance alone is not an agent; rather we use the word 'chance' to fill the blank in the sentence that would otherwise be occupied by the name of the agent, if one existed. Through such substitution, chance deputizes as creative subject, whilst actually signalling its absence. Thus we interpret 'chance creates novelty' to mean that 'novelty is not created, it just comes about'. And so, too, we must conclude that Monod's position is tantamount to a denial of creativity in evolution – though not, of course, a denial of novelty. To suppose otherwise is to be deceived by an animistic figure of speech.

The natural world of Dobzhansky, like that of Monod, is populated exclusively by objective things. Yet as we have seen, Dobzhansky locates evolutionary creativity not in the chance events of genetic mutation and recombination, but in the cumulative action of natural selection in adjusting the relative frequencies of different genes and thereby building the raw materials of heredity into coherent patterns. Is this usage any less deceptive than Monod's? The first point to note is that in Dobzhansky's terms, what is created is not merely novelty but *structured* novelty. And in the place of the agent, there stands not chance but *antichance*. Now the notion of antichance, just like that of chance, serves a deputizing function, standing in for a nonexistent subject. As Dobzhansky is perfectly well aware, the prime significance of Darwinian teaching lies in its demonstration of how the formation of adaptive or teleonomic structures is possible in the *absence* of a creative designer. Therefore the statement 'Natural selection, or antichance, creates structured novelty' should be read as follows: 'The structure of novelty is not created, but takes shape of its own accord, by virtue of the differential preservation of variant elements tested in diverse combinations and under diverse environmental conditions.' It would seem that, so long as we insist that the implication of agency is essential to our conception of creativity, we would have to deny the operation of a creative principle in Darwinian evolution, despite our recognition that organic forms possess a coherence or design that is not merely the result of 'one-time lucky', chance combinations.

Not content with regarding living things as highly complex machines, Dobzhansky—along with other leading neo-Darwinians—insists that they possess the essential qualities of works of art. Thus natural selection, substituting for the artist, has been compared (as Gould reports) 'to a composer by Dobzhansky; to a poet by Simpson; to a sculptor by Mayr; and to, of all people, Mr. Shakespeare by Julian Huxley' (Gould 1980:44). Here is just one instance of the comparison, emphasizing the 'censorship' role of selection: 'Just as a sculptor creates a statue by removing chips from an amorphous block of marble, so natural selection creates new systems of adaptation to the environment by eliminating all but the favourable gene combinations out of the enormous diversity of random variants which could otherwise exist' (Stebbins 1950:104). Continuing in much the same vein, Goudge suggests that in its 'construction' role, 'determining what gene combinations will survive and how they will be built into organised wholes, natural selection can be regarded as similar in its operation to the activity of a poet who determines what words in which particular combinations will produce the aesthetic whole he desires to create' (Goudge 1961:120–1). Both analogies are highly misleading. Take the sculptor first. What in the organic world, we might ask, corresponds to the slab of raw stone and to the finished statue? As the latter is a 'new system of adaptation' so the former must be an old one, and both must be represented by innumerable copies, each minutely different, corresponding to the individuals of a population. Moreover these copies must, at every stage, be regarded both as products of the metaphorical sculptor's work and as raw material for the next one, for it is the population that evolves under natural selection. In other words, new forms are assembled out of the bits of old ones. We must imagine our sculptor not removing chips from the raw block, but discarding a large part of his finished output in order to retain what may come in handy for future work. When it comes to the positive assembly of these bits and pieces, we move from the analogy of sculpture to that of poetry. The poet, it is said, puts together words and phrases—the fragments of old poems—into that whole 'he desires to create'. But that is precisely what natural selection does not do. No desire or intention precedes the assembly of living things, unless we reinstate that of a metaphysical Creator. If there is pattern in the assembly, it is purely a consequence of differential discard.

Consider further the properties of an object of art. Customarily, we call this object a 'work', but only on account of the movement of attentive thought and action—the *work* of the artist—invested in its composition and of which it is a kind of crystallization. The distinction between these two senses of work corresponds to Wieman's (1946:68–9) between 'created goods' and 'creative good', the one consisting of objective ideas and things, the other denoting a process of subjective (or intersubjective) life (Birch and Cobb 1981:178–80). But the category of created goods includes both mechanical contrivances and artistic compositions. Perhaps it is idle to draw a dividing line between them, for there is a sense in which any precision instrument may be regarded as a work of art (Kubler 1962:1). We might, for example, so designate a well-formed flint implement recovered from an archaeological site. What is it that distinguishes this flint among the heap of other flints in which it was found? It strikes us first by its novel, even unique, appearance. Of course every stone is a little bit different, as a result of accidents of wear and tear, but this one seems to have a pattern, coherence or structure about it that others lack. Indeed it may appear to us as a thing of considerable aesthetic beauty—a beauty, however, that resides not just in its abstract, geometrical form but in its elegance as a solution to the particular practical problem for which it was evidently designed (Steadman 1979:10–11). All these properties of the flint—its novelty, design and beauty—are seen to inhere in the thing itself, given to us as an object of contemplation in the immediate present. But when it comes to the life of the person who made and used it, the stone is silent: That life belonged to the past and is in no way contained in the object that it brought into being and that once served as its conductor.

It happens that the very properties that would incline us to designate the flint implement as a work of art may also be readily attributed to living things. Contemplating their 'endlessly diverse structures and ways of life', as Dobzhansky puts it, the observer of nature cannot fail to be impressed by the novelty of each and every one, by the elegance of their design, and by their extraordinary beauty. Do we not then have as good a reason to include living things alongside mechanical devices in the category of created goods? According to Dobzhansky, 'Every new form of life that appears in evolution can, with only moderate semantic license, be regarded as an artistic embodiment of a new conception of living' (1974a:329). We are to suppose that they are like so many designs in an exhibition, at which the naturalist is a fortunate spectator. He is, of course, himself a living thing, and by rights should hang beside the others, were it not for the liberation of his spirit, which—transcending materiality—is free to wander, surveying the panorama of evolution as from a pinnacle. And it is in his mind alone that there forms a conception, or model, of which the particular organism is regarded as an embodiment. Certainly there is no suggestion that the organism itself has any conception of its mode of life: It exists, in this view, merely to execute and replicate the mode. And Darwinian theory rules out the possibility that such a conception could originate in the plan of a Creator. We can only conclude that living things, though sharing the intrinsic qualities of created goods, are fundamentally opposed to them in this respect: that the former embody conceptions that follow rather than precede their material realization, in the mind of the spectator rather than the artist or inventor. This difference surely is no mere semantic quibble. It amounts to saying that organic forms, however singular, coherent and pleasing to behold, are not *works*. Perhaps this is what ultimately distinguishes organic from inorganic bodies: The latter, unless worked upon by a life, cannot be endowed with both novelty and design (a crystal has design but is not novel, a naturally eroded stone is novel but lacks design).

Goudge (1961:119–20) has isolated three senses in which the term 'creative' may be applied to processes that result in the production of things. The first is creation *ex nihilo*, as in the divine act by which, according to traditional Christian theology, the universe was brought into being. We are not now concerned with creation of this kind, though it is well to remember that the theory of evolutionary descent with modification does not in itself rule out the possibility of a creator having, as it were, set the stage and fired the starting shot, placing the earth in its revolutions and 'breathing life'—as Darwin wrote—into the very first organisms. The second sense of creation is to bring something into existence 'by rearranging bits of material already there', as when we build a model out of the parts of a construction kit. Goudge calls this *mechanistic* creation. As such it is contrasted with the third kind, *organic* creation, which results in total systems that are more than mere mechanical aggregations of interacting parts and that cannot be analysed into their components without irrecoverable loss. A work of art, Goudge maintains, is a creation in this sense. Invoking the analogy between natural selection and the sculptor or poet, he suggests the same may be true of living things. We have no need to repeat our criticism of this analogy; our present concern is rather with the dichotomy between mechanism and organism.

Notice first that, in Goudge's terms, the mechanical contrivance and the artistic composition, though both created goods, are fundamentally distinct, involving different kinds of creation. How then are we to tell apart, say, an exquisitely shaped flint implement and a masterpiece of sculpture? The most obvious answer would be to observe that the former has a practical, instrumental function whereas the latter is purely expressive. More subtly, perhaps, they are expressive in different ways. The tool manifests a particular project, its meaning lies in what it can do rather than in who made it; we regard it, then, not so much as a work than as a *thing that works*. The sculpture, on the other hand, enfolds the consciousness of its maker, and it is here that its significance resides. In other words, the meaning of the sculpture *is* the very life-process that was also the process of its creation; it is thus the sedimentation of a trajectory of past subjective experience. And as this trajectory defines the identity of the sculptor, so there is an identity between the sculptor and his work. A record of all his works would, in effect, be tantamount to a personal biography: In them, we can read his life. But in the record of his implements we could read nothing but technique, the *way* in which he went about his task. The flint-tipped spear of the ancient hunter is therefore comparable to the sculptor's tools, whereas sculpture itself must be compared to a life of hunting. In general terms, the work of art stands to the mechanical instrument as the flow of life stands to the manner of its conduct.

We would be the first to agree that living organisms are not just machines, for the very reason that they are alive (von Bertalanffy 1952:16–17). Likewise, what makes poetry or sculpture (as distinct from a vocabulary or toolkit) is their enfolding of a portion of lived, subjective experience. Machines serve to conduct the movement of life, but do not enfold it. In the machine, as Bohm explains, 'each part is formed independently of the others, and interacts with the other parts only through some kind of external contact. By contrast, in a living organism . . . each part grows in the context of the whole, so that it does not exist independently, nor can it be said that it merely "interacts" with the others, without itself being essentially affected in this relationship' (Bohm 1980:173). If we grant this distinction, however, it must also be admitted that the conception of the organism in neo-Darwinian theory is essentially mechanistic. For that reason, it is far more appropriate to see natural selection as deputizing for an engineer, in Dobzhansky's image, than for a sculptor or poet. The assembly of a genotype through successive combinations and recombinations of elementary units of heredity *is* a matter of 'rearranging bits of material already there', and hence accords with Goudge's criterion of mechanism. If there is no more to evolution than variation under natural selection, there can be nothing in the life of the organism that is not prefigured in the conjunction of its genetic constituents.

In treating natural selection as an organically creative agent, Goudge is therefore doubly at fault. First, as we have shown, selection does not really create at all but stands in for a creator. Second, it can be held to account only for the construction of living *things* as mechanical objects.[3]

On further inspection, everything Dobzhansky says about organic forms as works of art appears to apply to precision instruments as distinct from sculpture, poetry or music. That is to say, so long as organism is equated with mechanism—or so long as we remain committed to what von Bertalanffy (1952:16–19) calls a 'machine-theoretical biology'—the analogy between organisms and works of art can be sustained only if the latter are identified with, and not opposed to, the products of mechanistic creativity (Steadman 1979:16). Let me return to Dobzhansky's statement that every novel organic form can be regarded as 'the embodiment of a new way of living' (1974a:330). So too, in their time, did the bicycle, the microscope and the telephone embody new ways of moving, seeing and communicating. We can of course refer to these inventions as works of art if we wish, but then it is important to be clear about just how they are *not* the products of what Goudge would call organic creativity. For what each embodies is a 'conception' (i.e. a thought or idea) that has lodged itself in the inventor's mind. The organically created work, by contrast, embodies the process of thinking rather than the detached thought, a consciousness rather than a conception, life itself rather than a way of living. And for the same reason, its meaning can be grasped only by an intuition that relives the experience that brought it into being, rather than an intellect that contemplates the finished product from a disinterested, external standpoint. If the organism is to be compared in these terms to a work of art, we have to see it no longer as a unique configuration of elements but as an embodiment of the movement of life, as a thing that endures. And that, of course, takes us from Darwin to Bergson.

An artist, Bergson tells us, does not simply transfer onto the canvas a conception that springs ready-made to his mind. That is to say, he does not live to execute thoughts that think themselves in him. Rather, his picture evolves as he works on it, so that 'the time taken up by the invention is one with the invention itself'. Thus the duration of the artist's consciousness is built into his creation, becoming 'part and parcel of his work' (Bergson 1911:359). The same, Bergson continues, is true of the works of nature. Their novelty enfolds the progessive impetus of life, just as the novelty of the painting enfolds an irreversible movement of consciousness (1911:360). And so it is to this inner impetus that we should look in order to discover the creativity of evolution. Implied here is the notion that the creative principle is consubstantial with, and not detached from, the created work. Or in Bohm's (1980:149) terms, it pertains to the *implicate* rather than the *explicate* order. Each work, then, is one moment in a sequence of moments through which is unfolded a total, creative movement. Reality, for Bergson, 'appears as a ceaseless upspringing of something new, which has no sooner arisen to make the present than it has already fallen back into the past' (1911:49). This is the sense of Whitehead's vision of the cosmos as 'a creative advance into novelty', and it is echoed by Bohm, who writes of the movement of the undivided whole as 'a creative inception of new content' (Whitehead 1929:314; Bohm 1980:212). When it comes to the evolution of life, Bohm argues, 'we should say that various successive living forms unfold creatively and in the sense that later members are not completely derivable from what came earlier, through a process in which effect arises [mechanically] out of cause' (1980:212).

To understand creativity in this sense means having to reject the conventional, transitive usage of the verb 'to create'—as when we say that a particular subject A creates a particular object B. To speak thus implies that every creation is a separate act, beginning with a novel conception in the mind of A and ending with its materialization as B. Life and consciousness, however, are continuous processes, punctuated but not terminated by the objective forms they successively bring into being and that serve as vehicles for their conduct. They are not, in other words, encompassed within the execution of specific projects. We refer, by these processes, to the reflexive self-creation of the subject, an idea better conveyed by such intransitive verbs as 'to live,' to grow' and 'to work' than by the transitive 'to make or produce.' To say that A lives is to affirm that, as an agent, he is creating himself; likewise social life refers to a process of mutual self-creation. Therefore, in place of the object B we must write the subject A one moment or increment further on. Whitehead (1929:39) calls it the 'superject'. To this contrast between object and superject there correspond alternative conceptions of novelty, which can be derived logically from the two senses of irreversibility discussed in previous chapters. Thus in the formula 'A makes B', every B is a novel entity, a thing of fixed consistency, detached from the A who made it and lying *outside* all preceding and subsequent entities. The succession of objects B_1, B_2, B_3 . . . constitutes a changeful sequence, irreversible in the sense that its elements are non–recurrent. They are like so many separate beads of different colours suspended on a thread that is the subject (A)—'a formless *ego,* indifferent and unchangeable' (Bergson 1911:3). But in the formula 'A lives', every new state *encapsulates* all preceding states and is in turn a moment in the coming–into–being of what follows. Hence the succession of states A_1, A_2, A_3 . . . yields so many snapshots of that movement that is the life of the subject, irreversible in the sense that it is progressive and directed (see Fig. 5.1).

Darwinian 'descent with modification', as we have already demonstrated, connotes a changeful sequence of the form B_1, B_2, B_3, . . . where A is replaced by chance (variation) and antichance (selection). Dobzhansky regrettably employs the term 'evolution' both for the *mechanism* of variation under natural selection and for the *outcome* of descent with modification, which is why he can speak simultaneously of the appearance of novel forms *in* evolution, and of evolution as a force that creates or brings novelties into being (1974a:329–30). The essential point for us to grasp, however, is that in neither sense can evolution be equated with the flow of life. We cannot say that the organism evolves, even as it lives, since in the Darwinian paradigm it can be countenanced only as an evolved object, one of a sequence of such objects. This is a point explicitly recognized by Monod, where

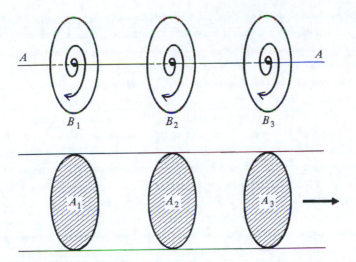

FIG. 5.1   A schematic representation of the contrast between the formulae 'A makes
B' and 'A lives' (compare Fig. 3.3). The spiral arrows in the *upper diagram*
indicate the movements by which successive objects B_1, B_2, B_3, ... are
revealed. The arrow in the *lower diagram* denotes the *creative* movement that is
the life of the subject, of which A_1, A_2, A_3 ... are successive transects.

he compares his own mechanistic view of the 'evolutionary emergence of absolute
newness' with the vitalism of Bergson:

> Where Bergson saw the clearest proof that the 'principle of life' is evo-
> lution itself, modern biology recognizes, instead, that all the properties of
> living beings are based on *a fundamental mechanism of molecular invariance*. For
> modern theory, *evolution is not a property of living beings,* since it stems from
> the very *imperfections* of the conserving mechanism which indeed constitutes
> their unique privilege. (Monod 1972:113)

Life, in this view, is revelatory rather than creative, being the manifestation in
an extended present of any one invariant structure in an undirected succession of
structures. Whereas Monod thus denies creativity to life, Bergson would deny it
to the mechanical construction of the genotype. 'Fabrication', he writes, 'works
on models which it sets out to reproduce; and even when it invents, it proceeds . . . by a new arrangement of elements already known' (1911:48). Likewise,
in the quotation that begins this chapter, Whitehead ascribes the creativity of
organic evolution to something *other* than adaptation under natural selection.
Compare his view that 'the primary meaning of "life" is the *origination* of conceptual novelty' (Whitehead 1929:142) to Dobzhansky's that the organism lives
to *execute* the novel conception of which it is an embodiment and whose origination must therefore lie outside life (1974a:329–30). Returning to Fig. 5.1,
neo–Darwinism would inscribe life on each of the synchronic planes B_1, B_2, B_3 in

a diachronic line of descent, whereas for both Bergson and Whitehead, each plane (A_1, A_2, A_3) represents a coeval transect of the flow of life in real time. A glance back at Fig. 3.3, which shows exactly the same contrast, will connect our present discussion to the ground already covered.

No cosmology that affirms the movement of organic creativity in evolution can escape the problem of its point of origin. Do we begin with the most elementary stuff of a lifeless universe or with the first appearance of life on that little corner of the universe we call earth or with consciousness as a specific quality of life supremely manifested in our thinking selves? Broadly speaking, three kinds of answers have been proposed to this question, contained in the doctrines of panpsychism, vitalism and evolutionary emergence. The first, as Nagel succinctly puts it, is 'the view that the basic physical constituents of the universe have mental properties, whether or not they are parts of living organisms' (1979:181). The continued attraction of this manifestly implausible view perhaps lies in the eminent plausibility of the assumptions on which it rests. For if it is supposed that evolution works smoothly, without leaps or interruptions, does it not follow—as William James remarked—'that consciousness in some shape must have been present at the very origin of things' (1890, I:149)? Short of denying the consciousness we experience in ourselves, or our involvement in the real world, are we not forced to postulate the existence of some 'primordial mind–dust'? Foremost among the mind–dust theorists of a century ago was Herbert Spencer, who, in his *Principles of psychology*, had this to say about it:

> There may be a single primordial element of consciousness, and the countless kinds of consciousness may be produced by the compounding of this element with itself and the recompounding of its compounds with one another in higher and higher degrees: so producing increased multiplicity, variety, and complexity. (1870, I:150)

James, a tireless critic of everything Spencer wrote on the subject of psychology, recast this 'gas to genius' argument in a somewhat more intelligible form:

> Each atom of the nebula . . . must have had an aboriginal atom of consciousness linked with it; and, just as the material atoms have formed bodies and brains by massing themselves together, so the mental atoms, by an analogous process of aggregation, have fused into those larger consciousnesses which we know in ourselves and suppose to exist in our fellow–animals. (1890, 1:149)

Against this view, James declared that 'atoms of feeling cannot compose higher feelings, any more than atoms of matter can compose physical things!' (1890, I:161).

In the philosophy of recent and contemporary biology, panpsychism has found both its eccentric and its distinguished advocates. The most prominent of the former is Teilhard de Chardin, who always insisted that the stuff of which the universe is made has a double aspect: 'Coextensive with their Without, there is a Within of things.' And before the dawn of life this Within, a kind of protoconsciousness from which all mental phenomena are derived through a continuous process of intensification and complexification, assumed the same granular, atomic form as matter itself. Thus every atom has an inside and an outside, manifesting psychical (or 'radial') and physical (or 'tangential') energy, the first being the source of the progressive, forward momentum of evolution (Teilhard de Chardin 1959:58–70). Although the credibility, both philosophical and scientific, of Teilhard de Chardin's views remains suspect, we find no less a biologist than Sewall Wright (1964) asserting that if mind cannot appear from nowhere, it must be present 'not only in all organisms and in their cells, but in molecules, atoms and elementary particles'. Likewise Bernhard Rensch believes 'that all "matter" is protopsychical in character' and that the phenomena of consciousness originate as the particles of this 'matter' are arranged in ever more complex structures (1971:298; 1972:96–8; 1974:250). A very similar view is taken by Birch who, along with Wright, acknowledges a particular debt to Whitehead's philosophy of organism. 'If subjectivity is present everywhere, consciousness is an elaborated form of something germane to the primordial stuff of the universe. It does not necessarily have to have survival value. It is there, period' (Birch 1974:231–2).

One desire that appears to be shared by all panpsychists, from Spencer onwards, is to have their materialism and eat it too. For the vision from which they set out, of an original fragmentation of the universe into ever so many elementary grains of matter, is itself a *product* of the withdrawal of mind from nature, and its confrontation of the world as an external, objective reality. But like a man who, having left his house, would fain find someone within, the panpsychist wishes to recover the process of his own thought in a picture of the world from which it has already been excluded. He does so by ascribing mentality to atoms and electrons that, according to Birch, can have subjective experiences or points of view, and even engage in 'social' (intersubjective) relations just as people do (Birch 1974:234)! Anthropologists, whose business it is to study social relations, may be excused for finding this position somewhat bizarre. It can quite easily be shown to be fallacious. For the atoms that compose my brain are identical to those that compose the brains of other persons, and indeed other creatures, whose subjective experiences are quite unlike my own. They must therefore be wholly indifferent as regards the subjectivity of their carriers (Nagel 1979:194). It follows that the arrangement of atomic particles into complex neural structures, although constituting a mechanical foundation for consciousness, cannot constitute the flow of consciousness itself. That is to say that neither the structures nor their constituents can be credited with anything more than purely physical properties. The idea of an 'atom of mind' is, indeed, a veritable contradiction in terms, for the fragmentation of nature is tantamount to the elimination of mind. Consciousness is not a property of things *in vacuo*, but of the field from which those things have been arbitrarily cut out. Hence it cannot be reconstituted through their statistical compounding, but only by replacing each in its proper position as one point in the unfolding of a continuous spatiotemporal surface. That continuum is mind and every position on it is a 'point of view'.

This, as we saw in the previous chapter, was the essence of Bergson's critique of Spencerian evolutionism, which entailed the substitution of a topological conception for a statistical one. And in place of Spencer's panpsychism, Bergson proposed a form of vitalism to account for creative evolution. The *élan vital* is certainly the weak point of Bergson's philosophy. Advocates of Darwinian theory, on the one hand, could readily rebut the argument by which Bergson attributes to this impetus the creation of novel *structures*. On the other hand, those who felt there was more to life than the replication of structure could still question the absoluteness of the divide between living and non-living, and by implication the idea of the *élan* as an alien influx added to, or launched into, matter, imparting a progressive momentum. It was on these latter grounds that vitalism was rejected by the leading advocate of the doctrine of evolutionary emergence, C. Lloyd Morgan. To the question 'what is new at successive stages of evolutionary advance?', Morgan's answer was 'always some new *mode of substantial relatedness* which entails new units of stuff' (1933:33; my emphasis). One such mode, which entails the appearance of units at a 'supermolecular' level, may properly be called the vital; yet it is but one emergent level in a pyramidal series of levels, each inclusive of those preceding and characterized by relations of higher complexity. Thus, Morgan argued, we have to deal with at least three kinds of natural systems: 'mind–life–matter systems; life–matter systems; and matter systems. At the top level there are modes of effective relatedness which are not present at the mid-level; at the mid-level there are modes of relatedness which are not present at the bottom level' (1923:22). Yet we are not to think of first life, and then mind, as having been inserted into the world of matter from without. 'All qualities', Morgan insisted, 'are emergent *within the pyramid.*' By this he did not mean that we could, for example, deduce the properties of living organisms by algebraically compounding the properties of their physico–chemical constituents. Such would be the approach of mechanism, against which 'emergent evolution rises in protest'. Morgan's point, to the contrary, was that the qualities he called vital are not 'resultants' but 'emergents', whose source lies in a mode of relatedness that, at a purely physico–chemical level, simply does not exist (1923:2–8, 13).

The doctrine of emergence, then, is incompatible with both mechanism and vitalism. It is also incompatible with panpsychism. For the latter, as we have already shown, rests like mechanism on the premiss that all properties of complex systems, including life and consciousness, can be derived as resultants from the compounding of the properties of their elementary constituents, though of course it differs in ascribing to these elements a protopsychic quality (Nagel 1979:182). This logical contradiction between panpsychism and emergence did not prevent Teilhard de Chardin, for one, from adhering to both doctrines at once! Where Morgan proposed a three-tiered pyramid (though with a number of intermediate levels in each tier), Teilhard de Chardin envisaged a similarly trichotomous series of concentric spherical layers, with a *noosphere* (of mind) superposed on a *biosphere* (of life), in turn superposed on the *lithosphere* (of inorganic matter). First biogenesis, and then noogenesis, are understood as evolutionary leaps onto new and previously non-existent planes, each adding a higher, more complex and also more concentrated domain of being to what had gone before. Like Morgan, Teilhard de Chardin regarded the emergent step not as bridging an interruption or hiatus, but as the continuous passage through a critical point, as when water brought to the boil turns to steam (Teilhard de Chardin 1959:186–7; compare Morgan 1923:5).

Teilhard de Chardin's views struck a chord of sympathy with those of Julian Huxley, whose vision of evolution as a cosmic process, generating ever-fresh novelty and complexity, was similarly characterized by the conventional trichotomy of matter, life and mind, yielding 'cosmological', 'biological' and 'psycho–social' phases respectively (Huxley 1956:3; 1960:19). Even such a hardened Darwinian as Dobzhansky has come out in favour of a doctrine of what he calls 'evolutionary transcendence', preferring it to the alternatives of panpsychism and vitalism. 'There is no doubt', he writes, 'that life transcends the ordinary limits of inanimate matter, and that human mental abilities transcend those of any other animal'; and again, 'life arose from lifeless matter and mind from life lacking self-awareness. Evolution has shown itself capable of bringing about radical novelties' (1974a:333–6). It is hardly necessary to repeat that this celebration of evolution as the originator of life and mind is altogether at odds with Darwinian theory, which conspicuously fails to account for the origination of either, dealing only with the construction of objective mechanisms for their conduct. Indeed to understand the creativity of evolution in this sense it is necessary to identify the creative principle successively with the concrescence of matter, the flow of life and the movement of consciousness, treating each as a phase in a grand evolutionary process that, in Huxley's phrase, is 'self-transcending' (Huxley 1956:3). Perhaps this accounts for the affinity Dobzhansky feels for Teilhard de Chardin's depiction of evolution under natural selection as a kind of 'groping' (Dobzhansky 1974a:312; Teilhard de Chardin 1959:121). But it is no excuse for confusing, under the single rubric of evolution, the forward propulsion of life with the endless tinkering of those manifold mechanical contrivances by which it is enabled to feel its way into every nook and cranny of the habitable world (Jacob 1977).

The doctrine of emergence has had its adherents in anthropology too. Indeed it underlies the claim that the study of man, though concerning itself 'with just one segment of the world of living things, a particular species product of evolution', nevertheless embraces within its field of inquiry 'a distinctive domain of life, variously conceived by such curiously hybrid terms as superorganic, psycho–social, extra-somatic and sociocultural, all intended to convey its irreducibility to the physical or biological conditions of existence' (Ingold 1983a:1). This domain, it is said, *emerged* as the trajectory leading to modern humanity passed through one or a series of critical thresholds (Geertz 1975:62–3). Undoubtedly the most celebrated anthropological statement of the doctrine is Kroeber's paper of 1917 entitled 'The superorganic':

The dawn of the social is not a link in a chain, not a step in a path, but a leap to another plane. It may be likened to the first occurrence of life in the hitherto lifeless universe, the hour when that one of infinite chemical combinations took place which put the organic into existence, and made it that from this moment there should be two worlds in place of one. (1952:49)

Kroeber's imagination, just like Teilhard de Chardin's, was caught by the metaphor of boiling water, one that inspires both to lyrical excess. Thus Kroeber, watching the heating kettle, observed at length that

steam is produced: the rate of enlargement of volume is increased a thousand fold; and in place of a glistening, percolating fluid, a volatile gas diffuses invisibly. . . . The slow transitions that accumulated from zero to one hundred have been transcended in an instant, and a condition of substance with new properties and new possibilities of effect is in existence.

Such, in some manner, must have been the result of the appearance of this new thing, civilization. (1952:50)

Nothing can match the exuberance of Teilhard de Chardin, whose kettle contains a seething liquid of protohuman life:

When the anthropoid had been brought 'mentally' to boiling point some further calories were added. . . . Consciousness was now leaping and boiling in a space of super-sensory relationships and representations. (1959:187)

We might do best to leave Teilhard de Chardin to wallow in his fantastic imagery, though it is only fair to note that his idea of an 'effervescence' of consciousness had long before been propounded by that other convinced superorganicist, Émile Durkheim (1976[1915]:216–19). We shall, in the next chapter, show how both Durkheim and Kroeber were led by their acceptance of the doctrine of emergence to formulate a conception of the superorganic in radical contrast to that of Spencer, who first coined the term to denote a complex resultant. At this point, however, I want to return to the alleged creativity of organic adaptation under natural selection, to see in what respects it finds its analogue in the history of cultural things.

Our point of departure lies, as before, in the anthropology of Boas. It is clear that the element of chance is as central to the Boasian conception of culture history as it is to Darwinian descent with modification. The most striking fact about human behaviour, Boas maintained, is the extent to which it is moulded by custom and tradition. The individual, being a creature of habit, devotes his life to the execution of a project engraved upon his mind, whose components he has absorbed from the heritage of his population and which he, in turn, will pass on to succeeding generations. Unable to stand back to survey his own accomplishments, he is neither deliberately inventive nor rationally selective. Therefore the only possible source of all innovation, and hence of historical change, lies in the occasional, arbitrary and apparently unmotivated 'miscopying' of elements of tradition in the process of intergenerational transcription. And just because, by and large, the transcription of elements is so accurate, because culture is so intensely conservative, every innovation will be faithfully preserved and replicated. There is, in consequence, a cumulative buildup of variation. This variation, in turn, furnishes the raw materials for an endless diversification of cultural forms, brought about through the fortuitous combination and recombination of variant traits in individuals and populations. Every individual, manifesting a unique configuration of traits, is a novel entity; every cultural tradition exists only as represented in the population of individuals regarded as its bearers. By invoking the agency of chance, Boas could reconcile the ubiquity of cultural change with the 'iron hold' of tradition. In other words, innovation stands to tradition as chance to necessity. With the simple substitution of the cultural for the genetic (DNA) structure, the following words of Monod might almost have been written by Boas—though perhaps in rather less forthright terms: 'Once incorporated in the DNA structure, the accident—essentially unpredictable because always singular—will be mechanically and faithfully replicated and translated. . . . Drawn from the realm of pure chance, the accident enters into that of necessity, of the most implacable certainties' (Monod 1972:114). For accident, replace genetic mutation by cultural innovation; for necessity, replace heredity by tradition.

For Boas, a culture is more than a conglomerate of fortuitously assembled traits, however. For the assemblage exhibits the properties of design, that is a certain patterning and coherence. On the rare occasions when Boas refers to 'creative factors' influencing culture, they are credited with the generation not of novel elements and permutations but with the construction of pattern. That is to say, they play a role analogous to that of 'antichance' in Dobzhansky's conception of evolutionary creativity. Indeed, contemplating the diversity of cultural forms, we may discern in each—as Dobzhansky discerns in biological species—'the embodiment of a new way of living', at once singular, coherent, and for the observer, a source of aesthetic satisfaction. However, the precise nature of the creative impulse remains enigmatic in Boas's writings. It does not issue from the natural environment, for this is only a limiting factor: 'Environmental conditions may stimulate existing cultural activities, but they have no creative force' (Boas 1948:266; see also Hatch 1973:64). Nor can it be an emanation of consciousness, since in Boas's view people are not the authors but the executors of the cultural design, and their conscious life, to adopt Monod's distinction, is revelatory rather than creative. And yet he wrote of the adaptation and reinterpretation of acquired traits to accord with their context within an integrated totality—a totality that corresponded to what he called 'the genius of the people' (Stocking 1968:214). Ideas are 'evolved or accepted' in conformity with 'laws governing the activities of the human mind', which operate in the same way for all men (Boas 1974:155; 1911:122). Some form of internal selection seems to be implied, working on an unconscious level of mental functioning, yet what it is we cannot definitely say.

For amplification, we can turn to the work of two of Boas's great disciples, Benedict and Kroeber, both of whom had a good deal more to say about creativity—though in the latter case only through a marked departure from Boasian orthodoxy. Benedict, if anything, was more forthright in her assertion of the cultural determination of behaviour than was her mentor. Like Boas she stressed the uniqueness and diversity of cultural patterns, each one a fortuitous integration of elements combined, interpreted and elaborated in a particular way. Those patterns revealed in the ethnographic record form but a tiny sample of the range of possibilities, for 'the diversity of the possible combinations [of traits] is endless, and adequate social orders can be built indiscriminately upon a great variety of these foundations' (Benedict 1935:31). Wherein, then, lies the creative principle that imparts integration and coherence to cultural novelty, and how does it operate? Benedict's answer to the first question is 'in the unconscious mind', and to the second 'through selection'. Without selection, she asserts, 'no culture could even achieve intelligibility', in other words it would lack any kind of integration (1935:171). Like a particular art form, a culture 'has used [its] elements to its own purpose. This purpose selects from among the possible traits in the surrounding regions those which it can use, and discards those which it cannot. Other traits it recasts into conformity with its demands' (1935:33). There are a number of peculiarities about this argument. One is its personification of culture as a selecting agent, endowed with specific purposes. Elsewhere it is suggested that the culture selects the very purposes it makes its own, which does indicate a certain confusion between the criteria of selection and the objects selected.[4] Yet the very next moment, Benedict explains that though we write as though there were choice and purpose, these are in fact illusory products of an animistic linguistic idiom that requires us to insert a creative subject even where none exists. In reality, 'there was no conscious choice, and no purpose'. Darwin, of course, had to introduce a very similar qualification when he wrote that 'Nature selects'. Benedict's solution, however, is to appeal to a teleology of the *unconscious*. All the miscellaneous traits constitutive of a culture, she claims, are 'made over into consistent patterns in accordance with unconscious canons of choice that develop within the culture' (1935:34).

Before proceeding, a few more words are necessary about the notion of internal selection, which Boas hints at and to which Benedict gives explicit recognition. In the Darwinian paradigm, selection is of course *external,* being a function of the interaction between populations of organisms and the conditions of their environment. As such, it operates on the mature phenotype, whose relative reproductive proficiency determines the representation of its genes in future generations. By and large, biologists have been reluctant to recognize that this may be preceded by an internal selection in which particular genetic variants are tested for their mutual compatibility in jointly co-ordinating the initial and highly complex process of epigenetic development in the individual organism, even before it is significantly exposed to external conditions. The idea was not formally proposed until twenty years ago, and then by a non-biologist (Whyte 1965). Every genotype, Whyte argues, has to satisfy certain *co-ordinative conditions* (CC), if the organism whose development it controls is to pass the first test of internal selection and subsequently enter the external selective arena. Those that do not are either eliminated, as a failure of co-ordination among their mutant components leads to lethal ontogenetic irregularities, or they are modified to conform with the CC by back-mutation or else by what Whyte calls 'reformation'—an adjustment of initially arbitrary mutations to fit in with the total system of which they are parts, under pressure from the whole (1965:23–6).

Although the validity of these ideas for biology remains contentious, one cannot fail to be struck by their resemblance to the Boasian view, formulated so much earlier and quite independently, of selection in culture. Here too it is supposed that novel elements or traits are selected for their compatibility within an integrated totality that is conceived to orchestrate the life-process of the individual; thus the culture sets up its own conditions of selection, compared with which external environmental conditions are held to be relatively permissive and inconsequential. Benedict's notion, cited earlier, of the 'recasting' of traits to conform with the demands of the cultural system has its exact parallel in Whyte's concept of genetic reformation. And finally, the laws of operation of the human mind are accorded just the same role, in imparting coherence to specific configurations of cultural elements, that Whyte accords to his coordinative conditions in the composition of the genotype. Indeed, Whyte anticipates the discovery of a single set of CC, constituting a unified and generalized 'bio-logic' as yet unknown but in principle amenable to mathematical formulation, of which every possible organic form may eventually be regarded as a particular and discrete solution (1965:71–2). As we shall see, a precisely similar expectation underwrites Levi–Strauss's search for a universal logic of the unconscious mind, governing every instance of cultural patterning through the operation of a unitary set of transformational rules.

The most recent elaboration of the idea that the creative principle behind the history of culture is a mechanism of internal selection is to be found in Gregory Bateson's *Mind and nature*. Here the biological parallel is quite explicitly drawn. There is a formal resemblance, Bateson argues, between the 'intracranial' selection of randomly induced thoughts in the process of learning and the intra–organismic selection of random genetic mutations in the course of epigenesis. Thoughts are tested for their logical consistency as genes are tested for their mutual compatibility, and so 'in the process of thought, *rigour* is the analogue of *internal coherence* in evolution' (1980:201). The sequence of novel thought patterns is stochastic in that it is generated by the play of variation and selection, or chance and antichance. Thus, '*creative* thought must always contain a random component. The exploratory processes—the endless *trial and error* of mental progress—can achieve the *new* only by embarking on pathways randomly presented, some of which when tried are somehow selected for something like survival' (Bateson 1980:200). The implication of this view is that consciousness, far from being a movement from which thoughts are recursively detached, is but a logical working-out of thoughts that have already installed themselves in the thinker's mind, and is in that sense analogous to the epigenetic revelation of structure as opposed to the evolutionary creation of novelty (on the similarity of this position to Monod's, see the earlier discussion and n. 2, this chapter). For that very reason, Bateson's understanding of creativity is thoroughly mechanistic: 'The genesis of new notions is almost totally. . . dependent upon reshuffling and recombining ideas that we already have' (1980:201). A computer could do this just as well.

Bateson, though something of a maverick both inside and outside anthropology, was very much a part of the same intellectual current as was Benedict. And Kroeber, too, shared a concern with creativity and cultural patterning, or what he called 'style'. Yet in his view, it is the very working-out or growth of the style itself that is creative. As long as there are potentialities to be explored, the civilization in which the style is manifested goes on living, but when these potentialities are exhausted it undergoes at least a figurative 'death' (Kroeber 1963:57). Creativity, then, is equivalent to a potential for growth. According to Kroeber,

> Every cultural growth involves first of all the acceptance, by traditional inheritance or diffusion from elsewhere, of a body of cultural content; second, an adequate adjustment to problems of environment as well as social structuring; and third a release of so-called creative energies more or less subject to shaping by the factor of style. (1963:85)

It was in the third of these conditions that Kroeber's ideas marked a significant departure from Boasian anthropology (yet at the same time a return to its neo-Kantian forbears). Style and creativity are linked in that style 'is the manner in which creativity expresses itself', or in other words, 'creativity necessarily presupposes and produces a style' (Kroeber 1963:68). Quite clearly, the kind of creativity that Kroeber has in mind is organic rather than mechanistic, a process of life or growth in which style figures as both subject and superject. This is quite different from the view that would treat each cultural pattern as a created object, the product of a stochastic mechanism of variation and selective retention. Moreover, as a consequence of his heresy, Kroeber was forced to compromise his earlier pronouncements—squarely in line with Boas's teaching—as regards the determination of behaviour by habit and custom. If there is to be creativity in place of mere replication in the unfolding of style, we must suppose a consciousness capable of transcending its limitations, one that can work with it and on it, and thereby carry it forward (Hatch 1973:110). We must, that is, conceive of people in society as composers as well as performers, actively shaping the future as they have been shaped by the past. Thus, in his introduction to *The nature of culture,* Kroeber admitted that his theory of 'deterministic' pattern realization and exhaustion 'contains a concealed factor of striving and will, in the individuals through whom the realization is achieved. A creative urge and spark must be accorded them, and potentialities of the same to all men, no matter how much the concept of creativity has in the past been abused and vulgarized' (1952:9). In what this abuse and vulgarity consists, Kroeber does not say, but we have at least demonstrated that the concept is fundamentally ambiguous.

The Boasian emphasis on the diversity of cultures as created objects, and the location of the creative factors that impart to them their pattern and coherence in the unconscious workings of the mind, finds its modern counterpart in the structural anthropology of Lévi-Strauss—above all in his analysis of the structure of myth. This is not the place for an elaborate discussion of Lévi-Straussian 'mythologic'; more than enough has been written on the subject already. There are just two points on which I wish to focus. The first concerns the way in which Lévi-Strauss, very much in the spirit of Boas, treats people for the most part as vehicles for the replication of cultural structures of which they are largely unaware. The second concerns the mode of mental functioning that Lévi-Strauss calls *bricolage*. I shall show (following Jacob 1977) that it bears a striking resemblance to the operation of natural selection and indeed that many of the more misleading connotations of Dobzhansky's characterization of natural selection as an 'engineer' would disappear if we were to regard it instead as a *bricoleur*, working in the organic rather than the cultural domain. This will fulfill our promise, entered in Chapter 3, to demonstrate the parallel between the construction of mythical or ideational projects in the human mind, and the construction of organic projects in the world of nature.

We might begin with a remark by Levi–Strauss that is at once autobiographical and yet intended as a general comment on the human condition:

> I never had, and still do not have, the perception of feeling my personal identity. I appear to myself as the place where something is going on, but there is no 'I', no 'me'. Each of us is a kind of crossroads where things happen. The crossroads is purely passive, something happens there. A different thing, equally valid, happens elsewhere. There is no choice, it is just a matter of chance. (1978:3–4)

As an anthropologist's self-confession, this is patently absurd, for a passive locus simply could not have this kind of perception about itself. But it is symptomatic of the dilemma of objectivism that the observing subject, having taken up a position outside the world, is unable to countenance the reality of its own worldly existence. Lévi-Strauss's remark must be interpreted as a justification for his treatment of the rest of humanity as so many loci for the combination and assembly of diverse cultural elements. In this respect, the distance separating his position from that of Boas is negligible. The world, it seems, is populated not by persons but by individuals, and humankind is but the medium in which is inscribed a history of things. Each individual is a repository or meeting-place for bits and pieces of culture that, in their wanderings, chance to converge there. Welded into a coherent structure by the universal human psyche, they direct the individual's performance, by means of which they are replicated and transmitted. Going their separate ways, they meet in other individuals in other combinations. The task of the anthropologist, starting from primary ethnographic material, is one of setting up 'an inventory of mental enclosures, of reducing apparently arbitrary data to order, of reaching a level where necessity reveals itself as immanent in the illusions of freedom' (Levi-Strauss 1966b:53).

This last remark serves to demonstrate the extent to which the structuralist programme is rooted in a paradigmatic opposition between chance and necessity. Levi–Strauss, however, goes one step further than Monod, for even the play of chance appears to him revelatory rather than creative of *absolute* novelty, disclosing now one permutation, now another, from the total (perhaps infinite) set of permutations that can be generated by an invariant cerebral logic (Webster and Goodwin 1982:45). As for ourselves, whom we fondly imagine to be free and creative agents, in reality—says Lévi-Strauss—'we act and think according to habit, and the extraordinary resistance offered to even minimal departures from custom is due more to inertia than to any conscious desire to maintain usages which have a clear function' (1968:19). This again is no more than a restatement of the Boasian position, as is Lévi-Strauss's frequent appeal to the 'unconscious finality of mind'. Chance furnishes the materials out of which novel structures are built, each one a template (or 'mental enclosure') whose dictates the individual is bound to follow. As consciousness is the revelation of structure, so the origination of structure must lie in a mechanism external to consciousness. What Boas said of cultural projects generally, Lévi-Strauss says of myths: They 'have no author' and 'exist only as they are incarnated in a tradition' (1966b:64).

When it comes to the question of whether myths can be regarded as works of art, precisely the same considerations apply as in our earlier discussion of Dobzhansky's conception of the artistic quality of organic forms. To the discerning observer a finely flaked flint implement, a sea shell and a myth all appear as objects that are both novel, endowed with structure or design, and of great aesthetic appeal. Yet if we follow the logic of Lévi-Strauss, the bearers of the mythical tradition would be no more aware of these properties than is the shell-bearing mollusc. If the tradition embodies a conception of a way of life, it is not *their* conception, for they are but slaves to its disclosure. As Lévi-Strauss famously remarked, men do not think in their myths; rather it is the myths that 'think themselves out' through the medium of men's minds and without their knowledge (1966b:56).[5] Thus the locus of the conceptions myths embody must be in the transcendent mind of the spectator, who is of course the bearer of 'models which are built up *after*' empirical reality (Lévi-Strauss 1968:279). In this respect the myth contrasts just as does the sea shell with the flint implement; for the latter is the artefactual embodiment of a conception that *preceded* its materialization, in the mind of the practitioner rather than the spectator. In other words, unlike the implement, neither shell nor myth is a *work*.

As regards mythology, there is again a precedent for this view in the writings of Boas. And for its antithesis we can turn to Tylor, who held that myths and beliefs were the outcomes of peoples' deliberate attempts to explain the world around them, and hence that they were as eligible for inclusion in the category of created goods, actively acquired, as technological equipment designed expressly to operate on the environment.[6] Against this Boas saw in human deliberations not the origination but the execution of a preformed cultural project, passively absorbed, aspects of which we denote by such terms as 'mythology', 'theology' and 'philosophy'. These, he argued, refer to 'the same influences which shape the current of human thought, and which determine the attempts of man to explain the phenomena of nature' (1911:204). We are left with the problem of accounting for the origination of this intellectual scaffolding. To this crucial question, Lévi-Strauss provides somewhat contradictory answers. He repeatedly emphasizes the intellectual creativity of 'primitive' men, only to dismiss it all as an illusion (Glucksmann 1974:88–9). Thus 'human societies, like individual human beings, . . . never create *absolutely:* all they can do is to choose certain combinations from a repertory of ideas which it should be possible to reconstitute' (Lévi-Strauss 1961:160). Evidently the constructor of novelty is not the person but the mechanism of his brain, which arranges into patterns the ideas it happens to receive from the heritage of tradition, patterns that subsequently work themselves out in the processes of his thought. And it is this organizing activity of the universal brain, what might be called the antichance factor in the origination of cultural novelty, that Lévi-Strauss compares to *bricolage.*

The *bricoleur,* in practice, is a person who delights in making novel contraptions out of the bits and pieces of old ones. His structures do not long endure but fall apart in the course of time, yet he throws little or nothing away. The pieces may always come in handy for making something else. It follows that as far as the *bricoleur* is concerned, the elements out of which his structures are composed bear no prior relation to one another, but are brought into relations through his own creative imagination. They may be of the most diverse origin, having previously served time in quite different structures, similarly the products of *bricolage.* And likewise, any element may be used to effect in all kinds of ways, in the context of different projects. As Levi–Strauss explains, the content of the stock of tools and materials the *bricoleur* has on hand 'bears no relation to the current project, or indeed to any particular project, but is the contingent result of all the occasions there have been to renew or enrich the stock or to maintain it with the remains of previous constructions or destructions' (1966a:17). Now compare the *bricoleur* with the engineer. The latter sets out with tools and materials specifically fashioned for the job at hand, and already related in the form of a plan, in order to create something concrete. Or in more general terms, he starts with a structure and ends with its eventuation as a material entity. The *bricoleur* begins where the works of the engineer find their ultimate repose: in the scrapyard. Starting from a stock of material entities, or rather their indestructible remains, he ends with a structure, only to have it knocked down again to provide the materials for the next project—having nothing else at his disposal with which to work. Crudely, we find the engineer 'creating events (changing the world) by means of structures and the bricoleur creating structures by means of events' (Lévi-Strauss 1966a:22).

Now *bricolage* is to engineering, in the realm of practice, as myth is to science in the realm of thought. That, at least, is Lévi-Strauss's contention, and again it finds its precedent in a remark by Boas: 'It would seem', he observed, 'that mythological worlds have been built up, only to be shattered again, and that new worlds were built from the fragments' (1898:18; cited in Lévi-Strauss 1968:206, and 1966a:21). The scientist designs concepts according to the requirements of the theoretical project, so that a necessary relation obtains both between project and concepts, and among the concepts themselves. But the elements that are combined in myths come ready-made, from anywhere; and as Boas himself noted, the sheer contingency of their association in so many different combinations, constituting such diverse patterns, militates against the interpretation of myths as pseudo-scientific attempts to explain the phenomena of nature (Boas 1974:140). They should rather be understood to 'determine' such attempts, that is to provide a paradigmatic framework within which they can be made. But this means that to compare 'mythical' and 'scientific' thinking is not quite to compare like with like. For whereas in the latter case the 'thinker' is the scientist in person, designing concepts and building theories as the engineer designs and builds a mechanical apparatus, in the former case the construction of the myth is no less than the construction of the thinker. And for Boas, as indeed for Lévi-Strauss, the assembly of myth 'provided a model for the development of culture in general' (Stocking 1974:130). The real products of *bricolage* are thus individuals, each conceived as an animated assemblage of cultural elements. So who is the *bricoleur?* He can be neither you nor I, nor the 'native' in his mythological world, for we are all but the exemplars and executors of his work. He is instead an undercover agent whom Lévi-Strauss addressed as 'this uninvited guest', who always sits among us and accompanies us wherever we go, *'the human mind'* (1968:71). He was referring, of course, to the brain, which no longer figures as a passive repository but rather as an active compositor of cultural content.

If we now revert from the construction of mythical or cultural projects to that of individual organisms, the likeness is at once apparent. An essential component of Darwin's attack on the argument from design, the idea that every organism appears as the material embodiment of a prior conception, was his observation that the various parts from which any adaptive mechanism is built are to be found in other ancestral or related forms, in different combinations and serving quite different purposes; thus 'evolution makes a wing from a leg or a part of an ear from a piece of jaw' (Jacob 1977:1164). Hence not a single part could have been fashioned with a particular end in view. This was a major theme of one of Darwin's lesser-known works, *On the various contrivances by which British and foreign orchids are fertilized by insects,* originally published in 1862. In this work he attempted to show that to facilitate the transfer of pollen, the orchid utilizes whatever parts happen to be available, parts that may have originated as adaptations to quite different functions (Ghiselin 1969:136–7; Gould 1983:20–5). Indeed it has no other stock on which to draw than that which it receives by inheritance. To emphasize the point, Darwin introduced a metaphorical figure whose resemblance to the Lévi-Straussian *bricoleur* is almost uncanny:

> Although an organ may not have been originally formed for some special purpose, if it now serves for this end, we are justified in saying that it is specially contrived for it. On the same principle if a man were to make a machine for some special purpose, but were to use old wheels, springs and pulleys, only slightly altered, the whole machine, with all its parts, might

be said to be specially contrived for that purpose. Thus throughout nature almost every part of each living being has probably served, in a slightly modified condition, for diverse purposes, and has acted in the living machinery of many ancient and distinct specific forms. (1862:348)

Ghiselin expresses this idea of organic *bricolage* perfectly when he likens the products of evolution to *contraptions* rather than contrivances, or still more vividly, to 'Rube Goldberg devices' (1969:134, 215). Thus 'organic mechanisms may be shown . . . to have been haphazardly thrown together, out of whatever materials the moment happened to supply. . . . New structures are invariably elaborated out of preexisting components which, by coincidence, already happened to possess useful physical or chemical properties' (Ghiselin 1969:153). Likewise, Pittendrigh regards the organism as 'a patchwork of makeshifts pieced together, as it were, from what was available when opportunity knocked' (1958:400). Gould and Vrba have recently formalized the same idea in their notion of the evolutionary *co-optation* (as opposed to construction) of characters that, although 'apt' for their current purpose, were not especially built for it and are therefore better defined as 'exaptations' than as 'adaptations' (Gould and Vrba 1982).

Equipped with the distinctions between contrivance and contraption, adaptation and co-optation, we can return to Dobzhansky's conception of natural selection as an 'engineer'. Engineers, as a rule, impose designs already construed in the imagination on a mass of amorphous raw material. Even if they use the remains of old things, such as scrap metal, rags or empty bottles, they first melt or pulverize them, destroying all vestiges of form. This has no analogue in the sphere of organic evolution. Indeed we have already noted, in criticizing the idea of selection as a sculptor chipping away at a slab of stone, that there is nothing in nature analogous to the raw block. The only materials selection can use, in the construction of new forms, are the bits of old ones. Hence the appearance of a form is bound to depend on the kinds of bits that happened to be available. Whereas engineers, starting with ideal structures and formless matter, end with concrete entities, natural selection proceeds by fitting and refitting the remains of concrete entities into structures. A celestial Designer, if one existed, would create events (individual organisms) by means of structures; in evolution under natural selection, however, structures are created out of the pieces of events. The most indestructible pieces are of course the genes that, just like the components of myth, serve alternately as elements of a finished product and as materials for others that have yet to appear. As between science and *bricolage,* so between engineering and natural selection the priority of structure over event is inverted (Lévi–Strauss 1966a:22, 33). In short, and contra Dobzhansky, natural selection is not an engineer but a *bricoleur,* whose products are not contrivances but contraptions (Jacob 1977:1163–4).[7]

Our concern, in these last few pages, has been with the mode of creativity that governs the construction of novel entities, be they organic or cultural, adding up historically to a changeful sequence whose elements are non–recurrent. And however we construe the creative agent, whether as engineer or *bricoleur,* whether operating through internal or external selection, the creativity implied is essentially mechanistic in that it proceeds through a combination of random innovation and the reshuffling of pre-existing items. It is now time to return to that *other* kind of creativity, expressed in the formula '*A* lives' as opposed to '*A* makes *B*'. One of the most cogent statements of this opposition that I have found is by the theologian H. N. Wieman. It is necessary, he writes, to 'distinguish carefully between two kinds of creativity, which is to say two meanings of this word. . . . One is a characteristic doing of the human person. The other is what personality undergoes but cannot do'. A human being is creative in the first sense 'when he constructs something according to a new design which has already come within the reach of his imagination. . . . The second kind of creativity is *what progressively creates personality in community*' (Wieman 1961:63–6; my emphasis). The latter, we hold, pertains to the intersubjective process of social life, a process in which the person is forever becoming with the perishing of time.

It is appropriate at this stage to refer back to our distinction, in the previous chapter, between the social life *of* persons and the life of society *through* persons. The second of these alternatives, it will be recalled, depends on an analogy between society and organism conceived as functioning entities, and a conception of the person as a position or part in a regular programme of practical conduct, whose incumbent is the biological individual. By eliminating the agency of the subject, or the person as self, this view of things also excludes any recognition of the creativity of intersubjective life. All action is resolved into two components: that which is constant, rule bound and repetitive; and that which is variable, contingent and idiosyncratic. The former, attributed to persons, is socially determined; the latter, attributed to individuals, is held to be free or undetermined. That is to say, one obeys a kind of necessity, the other is a matter of chance. As Radcliffe-Brown explained, in studying society synchronically one ignores the component of variability, treating it as though it were a persistent, steady-state system. Yet it is precisely in this component that we find the deviations that add up to longterm, diachronic change (Radcliffe-Brown 1952:4; 1957:88–9). It follows that to the paired oppositions between change and persistence, and between diachrony and synchrony, there also corresponds the opposition between chance and necessity. And just as the first two resolve, as we approach reality, into the continuity of process and the duration of consciousness, so the last resolves into the creativity of the social life of persons. Or to put it the other way round, the result of our analytic dissection of the flux of experience, and its reconstitution as a succession of states, is to decompose duration into synchrony and diachrony, movement into persistence and change, creativity into necessity and chance. We reproduce as Fig. 5.2 an earlier diagram (Fig. 4.3) with the latter triad of terms substituted for the former two. The elimination of duration and movement is tantamount, of course, to the elimination of consciousness as the locus of creativity. Being the projection of past into future, it is no more contained in a diachronic infinitude of moments than in the present synchronic instant.

Consider further what is meant by 'necessity'. This can imply a doctrine of either radical mechanism or equally radical finalism. As Bergson showed, there is

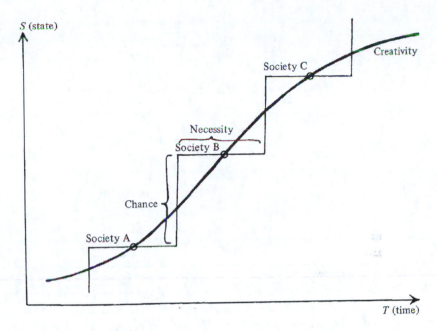

FIG. 5.2   Chance, necessity and creativity (compare Fig. 4.3).

little to choose between the two. Both suppose that, from the outset, *all is given* (Bergson 1911:41–2; see also Bourdieu 1977:72–3). The finalist asserts that all things come to be as parts of a pre-arranged programme, and therefore that their appearance amounts only to a revelation. The mechanist, too, reduces all performance to a programme, but it is one that came into being with the machine, rather than prior to its realization in the mind of a Creator, and that consequently remains to be discovered and comprehended by the human intellect. Either way, to say that something 'necessarily' follows is to affirm that it reveals or replicates what already *is,* and therefore that its appearance attests to the *persistence* of a particular state of affairs. If, in the event, something else quite unexpected comes to pass, the mechanist would be led to conclude that—by chance—a novel state has come into being, of which the unexpected is a necessary consequence. Thus we find again that persistence is to change as necessity is to chance. But what if the reality is not a succession of states but a continuous process? Then, as nothing persists, we cannot say of anything that it is necessary. Nor can it be put down to chance, as the latter is constituted by its opposition to necessity. This is precisely the dilemma into which we are led by our rewriting the life of society as the social life of persons.

Radical finalism, though it dismisses chance, can offer no solution to the dilemma. If every state is to be traced to an antecedent intention, we have still to account for the origination of that intention. The prototype for this kind of finalism is the image of a person purposefully constructing an artefact according to a template that exists ready-formed in his mind. So whence came the template?

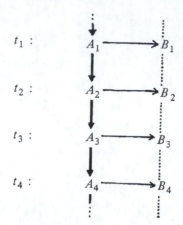

FIG. 5.3 Intentionality and conduct.

Returning to Wieman's two kinds of creativity, the execution of a plan is the 'doing of the person', as when A makes B. Yet its origination lies in what the person undergoes, namely the *life of* A. Even as a man makes, so he lives: Thus no sooner has he embarked on a plan than he has moved beyond the original intention. There is something in the action that was not given in its initial conditions, and of which neither mechanism for finalism can render any account whatever. On this point, Bergson deserves to be cited in full:

> For each of our acts we shall easily find antecedents of which it may in some sort be said to be the mechanical resultant. And it may equally well be said that each action is the realization of an intention. In this sense mechanism is everywhere, and finality everywhere, in the evolution of our conduct. But if our action be one that involves the whole of our person and is truly ours, it could not have been foreseen, even though its antecedents explain it when once it has been accomplished. And though it be the realizing of an intention, it differs, as a present and *new* reality, from the intention, which can never aim at anything but recommencing or rearranging the past. (1911:49–50)

Let us recast this argument in the form of a diagram (Fig. 5.3). Looking back over a stretch of a person's life, however short, we might isolate any number of separate intentions, sequentially ordered, realized in a corresponding series of acts. Every intention is a state of consciousness of the subject (A), every act a component of his conduct (B). The 'doing of the person' then resolves into a succession of episodic steps: $A_1 \rightarrow B_1$, $A_2 \rightarrow B_2$, $A_3 \rightarrow B_3$, ... Within each of these steps, nothing new is added: Thus B_1 'necessarily follows' from A_1, B_2 from A_2, B_3 from A_3. Yet in the experience of the living subject, A_1, A_2 and A_3 are but moments in a continuous flow of consciousness—each of which, as Bergson remarks, 'has no sooner arisen to make the present than it has already fallen back into the past' (1911:49). The transformation that the subject effects on the external world as he executes one intention ($A_1 \rightarrow B_1$) is also an internal transformation of the subject by which a new intention grows out of, and encapsulates, the old ($A_1 \rightarrow A_2$). And just as the latter comes to govern conduct ($A_2 \rightarrow B_2$), so again there forms a novel intention (A_3) that is no more contained in the relation A_2–B_2 than A_2 was contained in the relation A_1–B_1.

From Fig. 5.3, it can be seen that the difference between the two kinds of creativity depends on whether we read the diagram horizontally (*A* makes *B*) or vertically (the life of *A*). Mechanism and finalism share an exclusively horizontal reading, though for mechanism the direction of the arrows should in principle be reversed ($B_1 \rightarrow O_1$, $B_2 \rightarrow O_2$, $B_3 \rightarrow O_3$, where *O* is the observer in whose mind there develop successive conceptions of the behavioural programme embodied in the machine). The person, in this view, is the carrier and executor of a design that, for the mechanist, has arisen purely by chance or that, for the finalist, is constituted on the instant by a spontaneous free will (Bourdieu 1977:73). This notion of freedom is one to which we must return; suffice it to say now that it leads us to speak of acts and intentions 'as if these were distinct unities or elements in some way aggregated or strung together in action' (Giddens 1979:55). Thus we begin with a string of intentions and end with their translation into a string of performances:

$$\left\{ \begin{array}{l} A_1 \rightarrow B_1 \\ A_2 \rightarrow B_2 \\ A_3 \rightarrow B_3 \end{array} \right\}$$

If Fig. 5.3 is read vertically, intentionality appears as a continuous stream to which, by the argument presented in the previous paragraph, there must correspond a parallel, continuous stream of conduct:

$$\ldots \rightarrow A_1 \rightarrow A_2 \rightarrow A_3 - \ldots$$
$$\ldots --B_1----B_2----B_3-- \ldots$$

This view, as Giddens points out, leads to an emphasis on 'intentionality' *as a process* (1979:56–7). More explicitly, 'The intentional character of human actions is: (a) not to be seen as an articulation of discrete and separate "intentions", but a continuous flow of intentionality in time; and (b) not to be treated as a set of conscious states that in some way "accompany" action' (Giddens 1979:40). The isolation of conscious states, and the articulation of separate intentions, is rather a product of what Giddens calls 'the reflexive monitoring of action', that is when the subject turns his attention back upon himself in order to render an account of his conduct in response to the queries of both himself and others (1979:40–2, 56–9). In other words, acts and intentions are constituted retroactively by the intellect 'whose eyes', as Bergson remarked 'are ever turned to the rear' (1911:49). Artificially carved out of the duration of consciousness, they are linked into a chain of antecedents that, following an infinite regress, can never wholly exhaust the real experience of the living, creative subject.

The two parallel streams, of intentionality and conduct, correspond to the movements of consciousness and social relations respectively. And the connection between them is one of enfolding and unfolding: Consciousness enfolds social relations and unfolds *in* social relations. Together they represent two distinct aspects of a single trajectory that is the life of the person, seen 'from the inside looking "outwards", and from the outside looking "inwards"' (Ingold 1983a:9). Hence, in this view, the person no longer appears as a thread on which is hung a series of discrete acts and intentions, but rather as a locus of creative growth within a total field of intersubjective relations. Hence also, in the life of the person we find the origination and not merely the execution of novelty—a contrast that precisely parallels the differences between the conclusions of Whitehead and Dobzhansky on the question of organic creativity. For further illustration of the point, consider the use of language in the production of texts. Referring back to Fig. 5.3, a horizontal reading would portray the author as the bearer of a 'bundle of intentions' (A_1, A_2, A_3) that are revealed in the assemblage of phrases B_1, B_2, B_3. Drawing an organic analogy, we might say (as does Kristeva 1969:278–89) that the two sides are related as 'geno-text' and 'pheno-text' respectively, the work of the author being to translate *en bloc* from one to the other, from covert plan to overt expression. But with a vertical reading, the text appears not as a complete, self-contained, bounded object, but as something undergoing continuous and cumulative growth, such that with every new phrase—engendered by what came before—there comes into being a totality that supersedes and encapsulates the old. Moreover the production of the text $(B_1 \ldots B_2 \ldots B_3)$ is also the evolution of its author $(A_1 \rightarrow A_2 \rightarrow A_3)$; as he writes, and as his text advances, so he continually overtakes himself. This view is expressed clearly by Giddens, who contends that 'the author is not simply "subject" and the text "object"; the "author" helps constitute him- or herself through the text, via the very process of production of that text' (1979:43–4). With that, we come back to Bergson's conception of art as an enfolding of the consciousness of the artist, in whose works we can read his life (Bergson 1911:359–60). This, it will be recalled, is just what *cannot* be discerned in the works of the mechanic, engineer or *bricoleur*, which provide but a conduit through which the life of the fabricator slips and vanishes into the past. In the same way, the social life of persons slips through the mesh of culture. Yet the former differs in two ways from the production of texts or works of art. First, it is a process by which people constitute not only themselves but, mutually, one another. And second, we can never stand back to contemplate the finished article. Real life is always in the nature of work in progress.

Whilst on the subject of language and texts, it is important for us to bring out the contrast between the kind of creativity we are attributing to an author and what Chomsky calls 'the creative aspect of language use'. The latter rests on the observations, first, that any competent speaker can and does, in the normal course of things, produce sentences that have never been heard or written before; second, that these novel constructions do not arise as responses to external stimuli but appear to be entirely voluntary and spontaneous; and third, that they are nevertheless appropriate and coherent, hence understandable to a listener or reader (Chomsky 1968:10–11). Grammar, for Chomsky, comprises a set of rules—part universal, part culturally specific—that *enable* human beings both 'to express new thoughts and to understand entirely new expressions of thought' (1968:6). Each thought, then, corresponds to a novel state of the subject, each expression to a unique linguistic object (a sentence). Clearly, Chomsky's notion of 'rule-governed creativity' (1964:22–3) can be accommodated within an exclusively 'horizontal' reading of Fig. 5.3, for the rules serve simply to translate thoughts (A_1, A_2, A_3) into expressions (B_1, B_2, B_3), or vice versa. Both thoughts and expressions add up to a changeful sequence, irreversible in the sense of the uniqueness or non-recurrence of its elements, each of which lies *outside* those preceding and succeeding. By the same token, Chomskian linguistics can render no account of the sense of *flow* that we discern in a conversation or a text, the way in which every statement seems both to grow out of what was said and anticipate what will be said. Nor can it account for the creative self-constitution of the speaking subject, which is reflected in this flow. In short, the creative principle that Chomsky discovers in the human use of language characterizes not the life or consciousness of persons but the production of things, what we do rather than what we undergo.

We can no longer postpone some discussion of the contentious notion of 'free will'. Chomsky, for one, associates creativity with freedom of thought and its wilful expression. And despite the very considerable gulf that separates his views from those of Saussure, the idea remains that freedom lies in the capability of the individual speaker to generate an infinite variety of expressions, using only finite means.[8] The difficulty rests, with Chomsky as with Saussure, in the identification of such freedom with the exercise of will. It is one thing to have an infinite generative capacity and quite another to be able to put it to purposive use in the practical business of life (Hymes 1971:58; Bourdieu 1977:25). Clearly, freedom, like creativity, means different things to different people. The principal point I wish to establish is that so long as the concept of freedom is constituted by its opposition to determinism, a free creativity must, as Bateson argued, 'feed on the random' (1980:57) and cannot properly be said to be wilful or purposive. Conversely, if we are to associate creativity with the exercise of will, or the movement of practical consciousness, then it can be neither free nor 'rule-governed'. The argument is, in effect, an extension of that which we have already presented in connection with Fig. 5.2. The opposition between the free and the determined (or rule-bound) is simply mapped onto that between chance and necessity. Just as creativity transcends the latter dichotomy, so purpose transcends the former. Or to summarize:

Persistence	:	Change	→	Movement
Synchrony	:	Diachrony	→	Duration
Necessity	:	Chance	→	Creativity
Determinism	:	Freedom	→	Purpose

In each case, the first pair of terms resolves on approach to reality into the third.

The idea of free will is of course closely bound up with a Cartesian view of isolated human subjects who, as intelligent beings, are supposed invariably to think before they act. The same rationalism informs Chomsky's *Cartesian linguistics,* which purports to account for the spontaneous generation, and expression, of new thoughts (Chomsky 1966). What is implied is that the subject first *considers,* from a potentially infinite range of appropriate propositions, which to adopt and then *executes* what the selected propositions enjoin. In other words, to act wilfully 'is to do a bit of theory and then to do a bit of practice' (Ryle 1949:30). As practice is here reduced to the mechanical execution of a predetermined plan, so the freedom that makes an act wilful rather than automatic lies in the consideration of alternatives. So deep-rooted is this idea, in contemporary Western thought, that many of the terms we have to denote intentionality (such as 'wilful', 'deliberate') extend simultaneously to formal decision-making or rational choice ('volition', 'deliberation'). And for the same reason, we find it difficult to comprehend the intentionality of action by other animals that, rightly or wrongly, are thought not to possess the intellectual faculty of reason (Ingold 1983a:17 n.4). Yet animals are surely conscious, and in so far as their actions are directed by consciousness, they can be said to embody intent or purpose. What perhaps they cannot do, lacking the distinctively human linguistic capabilities that Chomsky has rightly emphasized, is to subject their conduct to reflexive monitoring and to articulate their intentions in discourse (Chomsky 1966:3–5; Giddens 1979:56–7).

The essential difference between the Cartesian position and our own can be stated as follows: Whereas for the rationalist, wilful conduct is predicated on the prior operation of the intellect in generating novel thoughts, we hold that intentionality resides in the very movement of consciousness of which 'thoughts' are an inessential by-product, recursively constituted by the intellect. What rationalism gives us, then, is a *reconstruction* of conduct, aggregated from a very large number of steps, each of which consists of a 'free' act of choice followed by its 'determined' execution. In this reconstruction, as Bergson puts it, the will appears bent on imitating the mechanism of the intellect. Whereas, he continues, 'a conduct that is truly our own . . . is that of a will which does not try to counterfeit intellect, and which, remaining itself—that is to say, evolving—ripens gradually into acts which the intellect will be able to resolve indefinitely into intelligible elements without ever reaching its goal' (Bergson 1911:50). Such a will, we claim, although creative, is not free—so long as freedom is seen to lie in the negation of causal necessity (Bidney 1963a:29).[9] That is because, having its locus in the self, in the person as one point of unfolding of an intersubjective field, it must be continuous with the trajectory of his past life. Or to put it another way: I cannot at this instant be other than the person I currently am, with the purposes I currently hold; yet even as I am responsible for my present conduct, so I am the creator of myself—both subject and superject.

Consider for a moment the reverse proposition. Imagine that I am free to put into practice whatever ideas come to mind: To what extent can I be held responsible for my actions? Quite clearly, a roulette wheel is not responsible for 'choosing' the number at which it eventually settles. Nor is there anything less capricious about the free choice by an impartial witness of a card from a pack proffered by the conjurer. In neither case could the choice, or the action possibly predicated on it (if the number or card contained an instruction), reasonably be regarded as purposive. In other words, these are examples of freedom without will, a kind of freedom that leaves the individual with no more control over his activity than have subatomic particles, whose movements have a random component (Harré 1979:255; Ingold 1983a:5). It is quite different with the choice of moves, say, in a game of chess; the difference is that, here, alternative options are judged for their appropriateness in the pursuit of a paramount objective—winning the game. It follows that there can be wilful freedom only in the execution of purpose, not in its origination, and that every intention that is the product of rational 'deliberation', as well as the course of action it entails, must be part of a strategy for the implementation of some yet more fundamental goal. If we suppose that all our actions are deliberate in this sense, we must also assume our deliberations ultimately to be underwritten or motivated by a set of desires that are 'natural' in the sense of being constant, universal and absolute. But that is an argument for removing the responsibility for conduct from the particular social person and transferring it onto an external and generalized human nature. Knowing the ends of Everyman, and the means available to him, the rational course of action could, in principle, be calculated. Hence, unless two or more courses were equally appropriate, or unless a statistically 'mixed' strategy were recommended (in which case the choice would again be based on caprice rather than reason), the freedom of the individual amounts to no more than the freedom to err, to make mistaken judgements and—more positively—to progress, according to Popper's view of scientific advance or Tylor's of institutional reform, by trial and error. Yet here too, it is chance that furnishes alternative variants, simultaneously presented to an ego—our universal individual—who stands outside and above them all. In this situation the will, such as it is, *selects* but does not create. That is to say, creativity is not wilful but the result of a stochastic process with a built-in random factor.

We can no more grasp the purposive creativity of social life by treating it as a game in which every act is a separate move than by likening it to a drama in which everyone plays a predetermined role. Though the former analogy allows an element of choice that the latter denies (Barth 1966:4–5), both suppose the life of persons to be wrapped up within the execution of a specific project—game or drama—whose finalities or 'values' are forever given. In this fantasy world, everything anyone does is a means to an end whose very realization is the end of the world. Once you win the game, it is finished; once all the lines have been spoken, the curtain falls. Social life, to the contrary, *must continue*. Therefore, all 'ends' are but means to the furtherance of life, every destination but a transit point in an everlasting journey. As, in this journey, we constantly overtake our prior purposes—even in their execution—so our best-laid plans are necessarily engulfed in the very process we seek to direct. We confront here the essential limitations of the analogy, drawn in the preceding chapter, between social life and the game of chess. In the latter there is an overriding purpose, concordant with the game's objective, that governs the choice of each successive move; in the former, every act, or increment of conduct, is also an increment of advance in the evolution of purpose in the acting self. The will, as Bidney has stressed, 'is not absolute but relative to the nature of the self and its powers of action', and therefore unfolds—as the conscious self unfolds—in social practice (Bidney 1963a:18).

There is consequently no basis in reality for the distinction, which the game analogy suggests, between the execution of moves within a game and moves from one game to another. It is, of course, just this kind of logic that leads to the counterposition of individual freedom and social change. On the one hand there is the motivated pursuit of value–goals presumed common to all members of a society, governed by rules of procedure that are either constricting (as they were for Saussure) or enabling (as they are for Chomsky). On the other hand, there is the unmotivated substitution of one set of goals for another, held to mark the abrupt transition to a new social state. The first subjects freedom to the determination of a collective will; the second subjects such determinism to an unwilled freedom. A glance back at Fig. 5.2 will reveal the correspondence between these alternatives and the plateaux and cliffs of that diagram. To both, we oppose our view of social life as constituted through the creative conduct of persons. Such creativity is not to be attributed to the free play of private minds encased within the bodies of autonomous individuals, nor is it manifested in the ascendancy of rationality over social conditioning, or of the exception over the rule—hallmarks of the entrepreneurial model of social change (Bourdieu 1977:26; see Barth 1966:17–18). No more are we to construe the social as an external discipline, setting up what Dorothy Lee, characterizing the Western concept of society, called 'a fence around the formless area of freedom' (Lee 1959:57). Dahrendorf speaks in this vein of society as a 'vexatious fact', a system of all-pervading constraints that stands between ourselves and our desires with all the concreteness of a brick wall, leaving freedom as 'a residual range of choice that escapes calculation and control' (1968:58). But to imagine the walled-in individual detached from his social milieu, from the history of mutual involvement that made him who he is, is to alienate him from the very source of his purpose. His much-vaunted freedom, far from being wilfully creative, becomes nothing more than an aimless vibration within the bounds of a persistent, determining structure (Levine and Levine 1975:176). By contrast the freedom of the *person*—the conscious, wilful subject of social relations—can be no better comprehended through its opposition to determinism than can his creativity as an escape from blind conformity to social conditions. This kind of freedom, as Bourdieu explains, 'is as remote from a creation of unpredictable novelty as it is from a simple mechanical reproduction of the initial conditionings' (1977:95). The essential quality of life and consciousness is to transcend this dichotomy.[10]

A few more words are necessary to relate the idea of creativity developed here to our discussion of time in the previous chapter. Referring back to Fig. 5.3, the point I wish to make is simply that with a vertical reading, real time or duration is intrinsic to the flow of both intentionality and conduct, consciousness and social relations. With a horizontal reading, on the other hand, every intention and its corresponding execution occupies an instant in the chronological succession of instants that is abstract time. By running them in quick succession, we can generate the appearance of continuity, just as a film projector translates a series of discrete images into a moving picture. According to Bergson, this is precisely the way in which the movement of life, recursively dissected by the observing intellect, is replayed in thought. When we shoot a film, the experiential movement of the subject cannot be captured, since the camera can only record a succession of states separated by minute intervals. And when the film is subsequently projected, continuity is effected by compounding these states with the movement of the apparatus. Thus an extrinsic, mechanical time comes to substitute for the intrinsic duration of lived experience. 'Such', wrote Bergson, 'is the contrivance of the cinematograph. And such is also that of our knowledge. Instead of attaching ourselves to the inner becoming of things, we place ourselves outside them in order to recompose their becoming artificially' (1911:322).

Where, as in the 'horizontal' formula 'A makes B', conduct is understood as the execution of a design that exists preformed in the imagination, and to which nothing new is added, time does not intervene. That is to say, the passage of time is wholly incidental to the realization of the project. Again, Bergson furnishes us with a nice analogy when he compares the child assembling a jigsaw puzzle with the artist at work on a picture. The child who practises can complete the puzzle more and more quickly:

> The operation, therefore, does not require a definite time, and indeed, theo-
> retically, it does not require any time. That is because the result is given. It is
> because the picture is already created, and because to obtain it requires only a
> work of recomposing and rearranging—a work that can be supposed going
> faster and faster, and even infinitely fast, up to the point of being instantaneous.
> (1911:359)

The artist's picture, to the contrary, is not preformed but evolves or 'ripens' in harmony with the flow of consciousness of its creator. Here, 'time is no longer an accessory; it is not an interval that may be lengthened or shortened without the content being altered'. It is, rather, an integral part of the work itself. Thus the difference between the child's puzzle-solving and the artist's composition corresponds, once more, to that between the horizontal and vertical readings of Fig. 5.3. So, in a sense, does the contrast between the performance of a piece of music and its original composition. Although music, unlike painting, requires a temporal dimension for its revelation, the performance appears to suspend the passage of time in an extended present, or in effect to deny that time is passing at all. As Lévi-Strauss remarks, music 'transmutes the segment of that time which is devoted to listening into a totality which is synchronic and enclosed in itself' (1966b:61). The same, he argues, goes for the revelation of myth that, unlike music, was never consciously composed; and indeed the point could be extended to cover the execution of any kind of 'score', whether it be written in notes, words, customs or genes. The immortality we gain when listening to music has its counterpart in the timeless 'ethnographic present' of the traditional culture-bearer.

Returning to Bergson's comparison of puzzle-solving with artistic composition, we should note another important difference. Suppose the child picks up, and solves, one puzzle after another. At any one time, his activity is completely encompassed by the project in hand. The past, therefore, is inert, a repository or storehouse into which every puzzle is discarded once it has been amply solved (and anyone with children will know that the example is not entirely fictional). The artist, on the other hand, in so far as he is the true author of his work, rather than accessory to its resolution, brings to bear on it the entirety of his past. Indeed he *is* the course of his past life, and therefore to say that his work involves the whole of his person is to attribute to the past a creative efficacy. Thus consciousness, as we saw in the previous chapter, bends the past into an active advance on the future. Likewise, as Giddens remarks, although 'every process of [social] action is a production of something new, a fresh act; . . . at the same time all action exists in continuity with the past, which supplies the means of its initiation' (1979:70). This, again, requires us to adopt a vertical reading of Fig. 5.3 for the comprehension of social life. The difference between a 'dead' past and a 'living' one, or between the sedimentation of created things or works and the creative work of persons, clearly relates to our earlier discussion of the nature of freedom. If, with Sartre, we take every novel project to be constituted in the present instant by a spontaneous and unfettered imagination, the past becomes (like the earth) a platform for human activities, an accumulating deposit—formed of the material residue of previous projects—on the surface of which the individual subject leads a solitary and narcissistic dance. Once we breathe life back into history, the person can no longer be free in this sense; nor, however, is he wholly imprisoned, as Braudel would have it, in a destiny fixed by the immutable constraints of the long term—which 'always wins in the end' (Braudel 1972:1244). Human destiny is, by and large, man-made.

These conclusions invite some reflections on the relation between history and tradition. Adherence to tradition is something we ascribe far more readily to others than to ourselves. Those others may be contemporary 'natives' or our own ancestors. How far we have to travel outwards in space or backwards in time before we encounter tradition will depend on just how tightly, in a particular context, we draw the boundaries around 'people like us'. But whether our concern is with natives or ancestors, to view their lives as the enactment of tradition is to adopt the position of an external spectator. If we take history in its sense as the history of persons, which we have already identified with the process of social life, what for *them* is history becomes for *us* a tradition—that is, a kind of scenic background or landscape against which *our* history unfolds. Likewise the history we are currently making will, in the retrospective vision of our descendants, appear thoroughly traditional. People living under the sway of tradition are held to be subject to the dictates of a *necessary* routine, relieved only by an 'eventful' element of *random* idiosyncrasy or innovation. Hence the point where history becomes tradition coincides with the death of the past, beyond which *creative* social action—no longer enlivened by consciousness—reverts to mere culturally *determined* behaviour. Tradition, in other words, is an exoskeleton of objective forms drained of the life that once pulsed through them: history without duration. For this reason, 'traditional' people are supposed to live in a perpetual present nevertheless disjoined from our own. And by the same token, history stands to tradition as action stands to value. For what standard ethnographic parlance denotes as 'cultural values' are the dimensions of the project to the fulfilment of which traditional culture-bearers are conceived to devote their entire lives. Yet in reality, human purposes are not thus constrained. As traditions are the residue of history, so values are the durable products of past social action—'created goods' in Wieman's terms. And as such they provide a context, but not a strait-jacket, for social life. If people can render an account of their actions in terms of the fulfilment of values, it is only because the former forever overtakes the latter; hence the account can never be complete. History is always one step ahead of tradition.

These arguments make us profoundly sceptical of the idea, still commonly entertained in anthropology, that people in so-called primitive societies are really more encased by tradition than we are and conversely that the dominance of historical consciousness is a characteristically Western phenomenon. It seems that traditionalism is very largely a by-product of the anthropological construction of 'other cultures' and that, like the universality of the incest taboo, it has entered the literature as an established truth about the people of such cultures long before anyone bothered to subject it to any kind of verification. It may well be that the supposedly 'cold' societies, frozen by objectivist structuralism into an assumed posture of pure timelessness, will eventually reveal to us the essential creativity of intersubjective life that we in the West, trapped by the oppositions of freedom and determinism, diachrony and synchrony, event and structure, find so hard to grasp. And once we extend the field of history to embrace not just ourselves but all mankind, why stop there? It is noteworthy that Whitehead applies precisely the same logic to distinguish the organic life-process from physical inheritance that we have applied in distinguishing social life from cultural tradition. To appeal to either heritage or heredity is merely to affirm the necessity of what *is*, rather than to explore the potentialities of becoming. But life, Whitehead argues 'is the name for originality, and not for tradition'. And again: 'An organism is "alive" when in some measure its reactions are inexplicable by *any* tradition of pure physical inheritance' (1929:145–6). Naturally, to extend the argument in this fashion leads us to pose one further question, consideration of which is long overdue. Do animals other than human beings have history? I shall devote the final pages of this chapter to suggesting some possible answers.

There is one obvious sense in which the life of every individual animal manifests an event in the history of its species. But this is a natural history of *populations,* equivalent to Darwinian evolution, and does not take us beyond the view of life as the revelation of tradition that Whitehead explicitly rejects. We have already explored this sense of history in Chapter 3, and it need not detain us now. It is also perfectly legitimate to inquire to what extent animals execute and transmit instructions that are learned as well as innate. There is plenty of evidence that they do,[11] though the question raises certain issues about the relation between genetic and cultural inheritance whose consideration we shall have to postpone to a later chapter. Perhaps it may then be said that some species of animals (primarily vertebrates) have 'culture-histories', formed through the differential preservation of innovations in tradition, rather than of mutations in the materials of heredity (Bock 1980:148). Although an advocate of the view 'that humans are the only animals that have histories' because of 'the varieties of sociocultural life that are simultaneously displayed within the species', Bock for one admits 'that species other than man might have had *something like* histories' (1980:158, 225 n. 8). But this is still to understand history in its Boasian sense, opposed to Darwinian evolution only in so far as it deals with cultural rather than natural things, and takes us no nearer to anything in animals comparable to the history of persons.

Unlike Bock, Haldane is in no doubt that animals *do* have histories, but at least until recently they have had very few historians. 'The first history of a wild animal species', Haldane claims, 'was published in 1952. This is James Fisher's *The fulmar*' (Haldane 1956a:395). This book describes the spread of the Atlantic fulmar southwards from the Arctic, to colonize first Iceland, thence St. Kilda, Orkney and Shetland, the Scottish mainland, and eventually southern England. That is precisely the kind of history, of migration and colonization, that White had in mind when he applied his distinction between history and evolution to the field of biology. Like Tylor, it will be recalled, White had compared cultural traits to species. So the analogue of Boasian culture-history, dealing as it did with the wanderings and encounters of isolable traits in human populations, was not Darwinian evolution but a kind of ecological history concerned with the dispersal and association of species. As a historian, 'the biologist wants to know where a certain genus or species appeared, where it migrated, where it flourished or perished, etc.' (White 1945a:235). As we saw in Chapter 3, this view of biological history led White to the erroneous conclusion that the *evolution* of species (as opposed to their history), by variation under natural selection, is a determinate unfolding akin to organic growth. Once it is recognized that Darwinian evolution is properly analogous to Boasian history, what White or Haldane would call history in animals—exemplified by Fisher's fulmar study—turns out to be analogous to a kind of human ecology.

Conversely, anything akin to a history of persons in animals would be analogous to the organically creative movement that White called evolution. Perhaps the first to credit animals with this kind of history was Morgan, in his work on the American beaver. Morgan was fully prepared to accept that all animals were wilful, purposive subjects and as such were the authors of their own progressive advance, within a set of bodily frames that had remained unchanged since the day of Creation. Thus for every animal species, including man, evolution was conceived as a movement of mind or consciousness (see Chapter 2 and Fig. 2.3). Moreover this movement was identified by Morgan with the principle of life: All there is of life is the life of the mind—the 'spiritual essence', as he called it.

'It is I—the spirit—which lives, and not the body, which is material' (Morgan 1868:256). Bergson likewise treats consciousness as a principle that breathes life into the body it animates, and he is emphatic that anything that lives in this sense 'has a history' (1911:16, 284–5). It would be quite wrong, however, to conclude that Morgan and Bergson were arguing along the same lines. For Morgan, mind equals intellect, a thoroughly Cartesian 'thinking principle' inhabiting every animal body, yet distinct from it. Like the rational human being, the animal is supposed first to choose freely from amongst alternative courses of action, and then to act accordingly: It 'sets the body in motion to execute a resolution previously reached by a process of reasoning' (Morgan 1868:271). Its actions are wilful because they are predicated on the operation of the intellect. The beaver, for example, when he 'stands for a moment and looks upon his work, . . . shows himself capable of holding his thoughts before his beaver mind; in other words he is conscious of his own mental processes' (1868:256). But if he knows what he thinks, why can he not express it? Only, thought Morgan, because he lacks the necessary bodily (vocal or gestural) speech-apparatus. That is why he referred to animals as 'mutes'. Put the beaver mind into a human body, and it would tell all.

Our current knowledge of animal awareness undoubtedly weighs against Morgan (though see Griffin 1976). Most would probably agree with Bock that whereas, say, the construction of a Gothic vault can be explained 'by reference to the doings of persons', the same could not be said of the architecture of spiders, bees or for that matter of beavers (Bock 1980:182–4; also Marx 1930 [1867]:169–70). Thus Morgan was guilty of imputing to the beaver a prior conception of the latter's work that in fact originated a posteriori in his *own* mind, formed on the basis of wonderfully accurate observation. With this, we return to the alternatives of mechanism and finalism, or of chance mutation and free intelligence in the construction of novelty. But the upshot of our earlier discussion of these alternatives was that neither of them can embrace the life of the subject. The beaver's life does not end with the completion of his lodge; the lodge, rather, is accessory to his life. The same goes for the Gothic architect. And the life of the person, as that of the animal, corresponds to Bergson's sense of history. Whether or not the acting subject, human or animal, can reflect on its own state of mind (i.e. whether it is self-conscious or merely conscious) is incidental to the fact that, unlike the machine, it *lives*. This then is the key to the difference between Morgan and Bergson on animal history: For Bergson subjective life is not founded on the workings of the intellect. The beaver has a history because it is alive and conscious, because it acts on the world, even though it may never represent to itself—and in that sense 'know'—anything of what it is doing. 'The further removed men are from animals', Engels wrote, 'the more their effect on nature assumes the character of premeditated, planned action directed towards definite preconceived ends' (1934:178; see Ingold 1979:282). To the extent that animals participate in history, this occurs without their knowledge. Thus human history differs from animal history, again in the words of Engels, 'as the evolutionary process of *self-conscious* organisms' (1934:34, 237).

Some of the most interesting speculations on the differences between human and animal history are to be found in the early writings of Marx, notably *The economic and philosophic manuscripts of 1844*. He points out that for the non–human animal, there is but one single stream of life:

> The animal is immediately one with its life activity. It does not distinguish itself from it. It is *its life activity*. Man makes his life activity itself the object of his will and of his consciousness. It is not a determination with which he directly merges. Conscious life activity distinguishes man immediately from animal life activity. (Marx 1964a:113)

To be conscious of life-activity is, by Marx's own logic, to be conscious of the self: Thus, strictly speaking, self-consciousness is the distinguishing mark of humanity. What I take Marx to mean, then, is that whereas the animal's activity is one with its consciousness, in human beings there is a bifurcation into two opposed yet complementary streams—of intentionality and conduct—that mutually condition each other. This opposition is, in turn, a precondition for the alienation of man's subjective being from the objective constituents of his activity, that is for the estrangement of labour (which was Marx's principal concern in the passage from which we have just cited). We distinguished the two streams in Fig. 5.3, and we have argued that intentionality stands to conduct as consciousness stands to social relations. It follows from our argument that the disjunction between consciousness and social relations is also the constitution of the acting self, whose boundaries are set at the interface. This is what defines the nature of the person as a social being, or as Marx sometimes calls him, 'a species being'.[12] Thus, man is 'a being that treats the species as its own essential being, or that treats itself as a species being' (1964a:113). Or, in less awkward language, he sees himself in the mirror of his relations with others, even as he sees others as they are reflected in himself. Whereas the animal, whose consciousness is inextricable from its activity in the world, 'does not enter into *"relations"* with anything, it does not enter into any relation at all' (Marx and Engels 1977:51). It is this difference that makes human history more than just a process of life. It is a process of *social* life.

These remarks should help us to understand at least part of the meaning of Marx's assertion that 'history itself is a *real* part of *natural history*—of nature developing into man' (1964a:143). This is absolutely *not* an assertion to the effect that all human history can ultimately be regarded as an extension or outgrowth of human biological evolution. Nor, to the contrary, does it justify E. O. Wilson's bizarre claim that 'Marxism is sociobiology without biology', marred by 'its tendency to conceive of human nature as relatively unstructured and largely or wholly the product of external socio-economic forces' (Wilson 1978:191; Lumsden and Wilson 1981:355). Human history was not, for Marx, a history of biologically preconstituted or environmentally conditioned objects, tacked onto the end of a prehuman natural history culminating in the emergence of man. Rather, natural history can be countenanced, in Marxian terms, only in the context of a human history made by conscious subjects (Schmidt 1971:46).[13] That is to say, human and natural history complement each other, as do the streams of intentionality and conduct, as two sides of a perpetual encounter between subjective and objective—or social and physical—domains of reality. Marx's concern, therefore, was above all with the 'human history of nature' rather than the 'natural history of man' (Moscovici 1976:x; also Schmidt 1971:76–8, 191). Thus conceived, nature is extrinsic to man's social being though intimately involved with it; it is *'the objectification of man's species [social] life'* (Marx 1964a:114). Through its appropriation or engagement in social relations, its 'humanization', nature *acquires* a past, and hence a history, consisting of the progressive embodiment of man's creative conduct, work or production, in the external world. Just as we can read the life of the artist in his works, or of the author in his text, so is human history enfolded in the world of nature. Man, Marx wrote, 'contemplates himself in a [natural] world that he has created' (1964a:114). And in this contemplation, made possible through the detachment of consciousness from conduct, lies the process of our own self-creation. In short, we continually constitute ourselves as historical subjects through our dialectical confrontation with objective nature in the work of production.

To take these issues further at this stage would be to trespass on the themes of the next two chapters. There we shall look more closely into the varieties of consciousness, discursive and practical, into the question of intentionality in animals and human beings, and into the dichotomy between action and behaviour. We shall have to return, too, to the distinction between culture and social life, relating it to the different senses of evolution, history, time and creativity outlined in this and previous chapters. But before tackling any of these problems, it is necessary to address a question rarely addressed in anthropology, perhaps because it is so central to the present constitution of the discipline that it is better left alone. Yet it is vitally important to have an answer, if only to resolve the persistent differences and misunderstandings between the practitioners of history and biological science, both of whom have from time to time laid exclusive claim to the field of social anthropology. To subsume the study of the social under the study of man is to suppose not just that we are inherently social animals but further that no other animals are social in quite the way we are. What, then *is* a social relationship?

6

WHAT IS A SOCIAL RELATIONSHIP?

There are three ways of regarding a human being. Let us say he is an individual, a thing with certain fixed attributes, like one marble in a bag. Yet unlike the marble, silent and transparent, he is the source of a veritable effusion of signals that seem to throw a smoke-screen around his inner being. Put him together with a number of other such individuals and the result is an incessant buzz, as we might experience in a crowded room where we understand not a word of what anyone is saying. Is this social life? Some would suppose so, arguing that it is a process compounded out of ever so many dyadic interactions: between speakers and listeners in a room, buyers and sellers in the marketplace, workers on the factory floor, or for that matter bees in the hive. Each interaction, they say, is a social relationship, one that is over in the instant it is begun. Others would hold that there is more to social life than the aggregate of interactions. A man, they contend, is the incumbent of a position, a player of his part. These positions, systematically ordered, constitute another, superior kind of thing, one that regulates and controls human conduct. This thing is known as society, though it is often called culture, and even more often it is called culture and society interchangeably. And like the individuals it dominates, it also is supposed to have a life of its own—that is, social life: the life of society. A social relationship, say the advocates of this view, is no mere will-o'-the-wisp, a fleeting interaction, but an enduring connection between positions in a systemic structure. But then there is a third view: The human being is after all himself, a conscious subject, whose life is a trajectory as entwined with those of others around him as the lives of the latter are with his. Does not social life exist in the entwining? If it does, if social life is the process by which we constitute one another as persons, then social relationships, too, must be understood as movements rather than as the persistent properties or momentary emissions of things.

Now we have introduced the three senses of the social—the interactive, the regulative and the constitutive—around which the whole of our discussion in the present chapter is to be constructed. We shall eventually opt for the constitutive sense, tying the contrast with the interactive to one between social and material relations, and the contrast with the regulative to the fundamental distinction between social relations and culture. The argument is rather long and involved, and for that reason is broken down into three major sections. The first is devoted to the concept of the superorganic and its elaboration in the work of some of the founders of the discipline of anthropology. We also introduce here the question of whether, or in what sense, non–human animals are social. The second part, which draws much of its inspiration from some of the writings of Marx, is a development of the notion of constitutive relations, and of the social–material and social–cultural distinctions. In the third and final part, we illustrate the different senses of sociality with reference to the phenomenon of gift exchange, introduce a further distinction between communication and communion, and unpack a key term in all discussions of social behaviour in animals and man—namely 'altruism'. We conclude with a word on the nature of moral conduct.

The superorganic

It was Spencer who coined the term 'superorganic' to denote such phenomena as constitute the subject–matter of sociology. Since that time, in 1876, when the first volume of his massive *Principles of sociology* appeared in print, the superorganic has become a banner of convenience under which have paraded anthropological and sociological philosophies of the most diverse kinds, some of them openly antagonistic to the Spencerian project. This fact alone attests to the multiple and contradictory ways in which the term can be read, and although its currency is nowadays much reduced—having given way to such concoctions as 'sociocultural'—the inherent ambiguities remain very much with us. I shall begin (somewhat following Bidney 1953:34–9, 329–33) by outlining three alternative senses of the superorganic, associated respectively with the sociological traditions established by Spencer in England and Durkheim in France, and the American tradition of cultural anthropology, which claims Boas as its founder. Of course these traditions admit of no absolute separation, and the positions adopted by such leading anthropological exponents of the superorganic as Kroeber and Radcliffe-Brown were decidedly ambivalent. Nevertheless this very ambivalence offers some vital clues to the shifting conceptions of the social, as well as high–lighting the central question of how society is to be demarcated from culture.

For Spencer, society was a super*organism*. That is to say, it was conceived not only to possess the attributes of evolving organization, such as internal heterogeneity and coherence, but also to be consubstantial with the elements—individual organisms—from which it was compounded. The 'super', then, denotes not a transcendence of the organic by an emergent domain of reality but an extension of organization beyond the boundaries of the individual. Spencer's society was a resultant, not an emergent, containing nothing that was not already prefigured in the properties of its original constituents. For that reason, he was perfectly prepared to admit to the rank of superorganic entities the 'societies' of ants and bees, birds, and a range of mammalian species (1876, I:4–8). But by the same token, he had frankly to recognize one cardinal difference between the individual organism and the superorganism. The former, though admittedly 'a nation of units' formed through the compounding of cells, is governed by some kind of central directing agency with a purpose of its own. The units, therefore, are subservient to the ends of the whole as a corporate body. But if, in the statistical aggregation not of cells into organisms but of organisms into superorganisms, nothing new comes into being, there can be no social purpose over and above the separate purposes of the individuals that make it up.

Hence, Spencer writes, 'the claims of the body politic are nothing in themselves, and become something only insofar as they embody the claims of its component individuals' (1876, 1:480). Here he follows a well-established tradition of liberal social philosophy, according to which society is rationally constituted as an instrumental adjunct to the satisfaction of extrasocial and purely hedonistic ends, namely the pursuit of happiness and the avoidance of misery. Observing that the capacity for feeling pleasure and pain is something everyone possesses in approximately equal degree, Spencer concludes that quite unlike the organism, 'the society exists for the benefit of its members; not its members for the benefit of society' (1876, 1:479). Thus conceived, the essence of sociality lies in the association, interaction and co-operation of numerous, discrete individuals, each equipped with a set of purposes in advance of their entry into mutual relations, purposes that must therefore be a property of their constitution as organic things (and in that sense, of their 'nature'). Whether our concern is with insects, birds or human beings, the rationale for social co-operation is to be found in the net advantages it brings to each and every one of the contracting individuals. As we shall see, this Spencerian conception underwrites much of the most recent ethological and sociobiological discussion of social behaviour in animals and man. Indeed there are good grounds for arguing that Spencer, and not Darwin, was the first sociobiologist. Conversely the roots of the contemporary anthropological critique of sociobiology are to be found in the anti-Spencerian superorganicism of Durkheim, Boas and Kroeber.

Spencer almost never used the term 'culture' (Carneiro 1967: xxxiii). He does, however, refer to 'that accumulation of super-organic products which we commonly distinguish as artificial', including language, science and technology, custom and law, myth and religion, and both fine and applied arts (1876, I:14; see Radcliffe-Brown 1947:80). Though this cluster of human achievements may readily be identified with Tylor's 'Culture or Civilization', an identification that Kroeber (1952:56) makes quite explicitly, by their designation as 'superorganic products' Spencer did not for one moment mean to imply their separate categorization in a domain apart from the natural or biophysical. They were to be understood, rather, as the products of social superorganisms (as distinct from those of individual organisms), embracing—in Spencer's own definition—everything where by virtue of 'the co-ordinated actions of many individuals', results are achieved 'exceeding in extent and complexity those achievable by individual actions' (1876, I:4). Thus the category of superorganic products would include not only what we would otherwise call culture, but also the collective works of social animals, including for example the impressive architecture of certain insect species, constructed on a plan that may be presumed to be entirely innate rather than grounded in an acquired tradition. Kroeber is therefore fully justified when he chides Spencer for failing to 'conceive of human society as holding a specific content that is non-organic' (1952:38; see also Bidney 1953:34–5). And Carneiro misses the point of Kroeber's criticism when he suggests that the superorganic meant, for Spencer, 'something beyond the purely biological' (1967:xxxii). The supraindividual is not equivalent to the suprabiological.

Behind Spencer's conflation of the innate and the acquired lies an issue of fundamental significance. For Spencer was a staunch and lifelong advocate of the so-called Lamarckian doctrine that the characteristics an individual acquires during its lifetime would be automatically transmitted to its offspring through direct physical inheritance (Freeman 1974). I say 'so-called' because although explicitly formulated by Lamarck at the close of the eighteenth century, the doctrine was certainly not original with him, nor can it have been entirely central to his evolutionary theory since it was shared by many of his nineteenth-century opponents—most notably Charles Darwin, whose notion of 'pangenesis' was specifically designed to account for the inheritance of acquired capabilities (Zirkle 1946). Another allegedly Lamarckian thesis to which Spencer subscribed, but which in fact was no more held by Lamarck than by Darwin, is the belief that characters are passively acquired by an organism through the direct, 'moulding' impress of its environment (Mayr 1982:356). What Lamarck *did* argue was that alterations in the environmental conditions of life of an animal lead to the perception of new 'needs', to which it actively responds by initiating appropriate behavioural changes, leading in turn to adaptive modifications in structure that are then transmitted to offspring (Boesiger 1974:26; Howard 1982:18). Again, Darwin's was also a theory of adaptation, and like Lamarck he believed that variation was stimulated by environmental change. But although admitting that characters could be strengthened or diminished through the inherited effects of use and disuse, Darwin attributed the origination of novel traits to chance rather than an exercise of will on the part of those individuals in which they occur. From a supply of variations in no way oriented to current needs, appropriate modifications could be established only through the 'second stage' of selection. This is the difference usually implied when 'Darwinian' and 'Lamarckian' mechanisms of adaptation are compared (we shall have more to say about the comparison in the next chapter, as it is one key to the difference between organic and cultural adaptation). However, the real crux of Lamarck's transformist paradigm, of which his ideas about specific adaptation were really but a secondary elaboration, was the premiss that all living things are subject to a law of increasing complexification or progressive development. This, likewise, was the centre-piece of Spencer's general theory of evolution, but was consistently rejected by Darwin (Gruber 1974:193).

We discussed this final contrast at length in Chapter 1. The question for us now is why Spencer should have adhered so doggedly to the doctrine of inherit-ance of acquired characteristics, even to the extent of engaging in his last years in a somewhat vitriolic argument on the issue with August Weismann, who was the first to subject the doctrine to convincing empirical refutation (Carneiro 1967:xlvi). Evidently he considered it to be a corner-stone of the philosophical synthesis to which he had devoted a lifetime's work, so much so that the ulti-mate collapse of his system, were that corner-stone removed, appeared a foregone conclusion. The reason lay in Spencer's commitment to a vision of cosmic unity according to which the several kinds of evolution—inorganic, organic and super-organic—were conceived not as analogous processes going on in separate domains of reality, but as distinct phases in the integration of a single reality. There are not, he wrote, many evolutions but just 'one Evolution going on everywhere after the same manner' (1972:72). It was only by invoking the Lamarckian doctrine that the supreme achievement of cosmic evolution, human civilization, could be comprehended as part and parcel of the same process otherwise manifested in the evolution of the human organism, and by extension in the progressive evolution of life in general (which in turn is a further phase in the integration of inorganic matter). As Peel has pointed out, Spencer *had* to resort to Lamarckism 'because it alone permitted a plausible unity to be claimed between the subject matters of sociology and natural science' (1972:xxiii). Not only that, however, for it also allowed him to make the identification, crucial to his evolutionary synthe-sis, between ontogenesis and phylogenesis. The development of the individual, building on the inherited achievement of its antecedents and similarly prolonged in its descendants, could be conceived as an integral part of a total evolution-ary movement likewise understood as a creative process of life. We showed, in Chapter 4, the significance of the Lamarckian principle in this regard, and the point need not detain us further.

Quite unlike Spencer's super*organism,* society as envisaged by Durkheim was a *super*organism—an emergent rather than a resultant, suprabiological because supraindividual (1933[1893]:349). To be sure, individuals are but organisms when taken in isolation; however, 'by aggregating together, by interpenetrating, by fusing together, individuals give birth to a being, psychical if you will, but one which constitutes a psychical individuality of a new kind' (1982[1895]:129). The whole, as Durkheim repeatedly insists, is more than the sum of its parts. Society is to be identified with the emergent component that would remain were we, in thought, to subtract the totality of individuals. The social, then, denotes a domain of reality over and above the organic, so that social facts *'have a different substratum'* (1982[1895]:40). And simply because Durkheim places the organic and the social on *different* levels, he is able to *deny* the difference Spencer has to draw between organism and society in consequence of his placing them on the *same* level. Thus the irreducibility of the social to the biological provides Durkheim with an epistemological foundation for his analogy between soci-ety and organism, the former surpassing the resultant of its organic elements as the latter surpasses that of its inorganic elements (Hirst 1973:9–10). If, as both Spencer and Durkheim would agree, in the individual organism the lives of its parts subserve the corporate life of the whole, so in Durkheim's view does the 'interpenetration' of individuals give rise to a corporate consciousness, with an individuality of its own, to which the lives of its constituents are similarly subservient. Durkheim develops his ideas on this point quite explicitly in opposition to those of Spencer. In moving from organism to superorganism, he argues, there is no inversion of means and ends as between parts and whole: The society imposes an external constraint on its individual members, overruling and subverting their separate interests to an original purpose—essentially moral rather than psychological—in no way derivable from the general properties of human nature (Durkheim 1982[1895]:125–30).

Moreover, social life, the proper subject of sociology, is for Durkheim uniquely human. We may speak of animal societies, but only in the Spencerian sense of an aggregation of discrete, self-contained individuals whose association is governed by innate predisposition. With human beings we are concerned with phenomena of an entirely different kind, with no counterpart in the animal world. As Durkheim wrote:

> The great difference between animal societies and human societies is that in the former, the individual creature is governed exclusively from *within itself,* by the instincts. . . . On the other hand human societies present a new phenomenon of a special nature, which consists in the fact that certain ways of acting are imposed, or at least suggested *from outside* the individual and are added on to his own nature: such is the character of [social] 'institutions'. (1982[1917]:248)

In fact, in comparing animal and human societies, Durkheim is juxtaposing totally discrepant notions of sociality. Had he adhered consistently to his conception of society as a systematic arrangement of regulative institutions, rather than a spontaneous pattern of association, he could only have concluded that the difference between men and other animals is that the former, besides enjoying an individual, organic life are also vehicles for the life of society. Humans, it would appear, are social beings; animals are not, however much it may be in their individual interests to co-operate.

The contrast between these two senses of sociality, interactive and regulative, is particularly clear from Durkheim's polemical critique of Spencer in *The division of labour in society* (especially Book One, Chapter 7). Spencer had argued that as a society advances in internal coherence and heterogeneity, the less its constituent members are required to submit to the authority of the group, vested in its institutions of central government. At first, in societies of a primitive type, the interests of the individual—being more or less coincidental with those of his fellows, and in that sense 'public'—are simply surrendered to a despotism of the collectivity, whose will to self-preservation is no more than that of the individual compounded to a higher degree, and whose organization is predominantly milita-ristic, geared towards survival and conquest in an intergroup struggle for existence (Spencer 1882, II:568–75). Progressive differentiation leads to the gradual decline of militarism in favour of peaceful coexistence, the consequent emancipation of the individual from collective coercion, and the rise of a form of solidarity that Spencer calls industrial. In an advanced industrial order, every man can best pursue his now 'private' interests by entering spontaneously into contractual agreements with specific others, each of whom likewise stands to gain from the transaction. 'The typical social relation', as Durkheim puts it, paraphrasing Spencer, 'would be economic, stripped of all regulation and resulting from the entirely free initiative of the parties' (1933[1893]:203). Industrial society, then, would consist of a complex network of such relations (Spencer 1882, II:606–15).

To this, Durkheim's principal objection was that no society, constituted on this basis, could possibly endure unless every contract were underwrit-ten and regulated by a code of conduct that, since it does not derive from the free consent of the associating parties, is essentially non–contractual in nature. Moreover, as the scope of contractual relations increases, alongside the division of labour, so also does the 'volume' of this *non*-contractual component. More numerous and extensive contracts require more complex regulative institutions, all of them eventually brought under the central direction of a higher-level agency that we call the State—'the cerebro-spinal system of the social organism' (1933[1893]:219). Thus whereas Spencer had deduced an inverse correlation between the powers of the State and the division of labour, Durkheim argued that both developed hand in hand. Though agreed on the point that the ambit of individual action increases with social differentiation, for Durkheim there was no contradiction between the emergence of individualism and the elaboration of regulative structures of social control (1933[1893]:193–4). Now it is precisely the latter, and not the co-operative interactions they regulate, that Durkheim places in the realm of social facts. Products not of the external contact of dis-crete, individual consciences but of their internal fusion and interpenetration, they correspond to the emergent, non–contractual component by which the whole exceeds and transcends the resultant sum of its parts. Hence that unreal-ized state of social perfection towards which Spencer thought all superorganic evolution to be striving, a state in which the individual would be completely free from institutional regulation to pursue his desires rationally, without hindrance to or from others (Spencer 1907:14), would if translated into Durkheim's terms appear perfectly asocial, as well as being a theoretical impossibility. In short, from Durkheim's point of view, Spencer was proposing a programme for the *elimina-tion* of society. Yet for Spencer, the sphere of social relations would have been entirely encompassed in the residue.

Turning now from Spencer and Durkheim to Boas, we encounter a figure profoundly different both by intellectual background and temperament. Boas's implacable hostility towards Spencerian evolutionism was combined with a gen-eral antipathy towards abstract philosophical speculation of any kind. And yet, for all the contrasts of method and idiom, Boas was drawn to conclusions that bore a remarkable affinity to those of Durkheim. These affinities have been admirably set out by Hatch (1973:208–13), and I shall merely recapitulate them here. First, both Boas and Durkheim held that people absorb characteristic ways of feeling, thinking and acting from the social or cultural milieu in which they are brought up; thus Boas's remarks on the habituation of the culture-bearing individual have their counterpart in Durkheim's views about education as a process through which 'the social being has been fashioned historically' (1982[1895]:54). Second, just as Durkheim rejected Spencer's instrumentalist conception of society, so Boas rejected Tylor's equally instrumentalist conception of culture. For one society, for the other culture, was seen not as an artefact of rational deliberation, subservient to universal human interests, but as something that, having taken shape of its own accord (*sui generis,* as Durkheim was wont to say), imposed its own finalities on the minds of human beings, orchestrating their thought and conduct. Third, for Boas as for Durkheim, people's commitment to social or cultural norms is underpinned by emotion rather than reason. Durkheim's man, like Boas's, is a rationalizing but not a rational being. And finally, both Durkheim and Boas were sceptical of the idea that societies or cultures could be arranged along a single continuum of advance, preferring to adopt a relativistic notion of diversification on the Darwinian model of the branching tree.[1]

Plainly, Boas and Durkheim were in accord over their rejection of biopsychological reductionism and in their consequent assertion of the autonomy of ideas in the determination of human behaviour. And for both, this break with philosophical materialism was a precondition for their indulgence in analogies between the social or cultural and the biological. Yet the analogies were formulated rather differently in each case, and these differences turn out to be of crucial significance. Quite simply: Durkheim's 'society' was a real entity analogous to the individual organism; Boas's 'culture' was a nominal entity analogous to a biological species. It is true that Durkheim also spoke of 'social species', but the constituent individuals of his species were not particular human beings but whole societies. Moreover, Durkheim's conception of species, whether biological or social, was thoroughly essentialist. Though species differ from one another, each 'is the same everywhere for all the individuals who comprise it' (1982[1895]:109). Because every society is a structured combination of parts, and because these parts can combine only in a finite number of possible ways, it is possible in theory to construct a table of essential social types *prior* to seeking out their empirical manifestations in the form of individual societies. Even a single representative would suffice to establish the existence of the type. 'Thus', Durkheim concludes, 'there are social species for the same reason as there are biological ones. The latter are due to the fact that the organisms are only varied combinations of the same anatomical unity' (1982[1895]:116). Durkheim is here alluding to the biology not of Darwin or Lamarck, but of Cuvier, whose powerful influence did so much to eclipse the development of evolutionary thinking in nineteenth-century France. A firm believer in the fixity of species,

Cuvier had proposed—according to his famous principle of the 'correlation of parts'—that each and every naturally existing organism manifests one of the total set of logically possible working combinations of basic organs. Discontinuities between species were explained on the grounds that intermediate forms would represent functionally incoherent or unworkable combinations, and therefore could not exist (Steadman 1979:37–8).

Boas's insistence on the uniqueness of every culture, and his views on the unprofitability of grand generalization, set him on a course firmly opposed to Durkheim's comparative taxonomic enterprise, whereas the nominalism inherent in his conception of the history of cultures links his project to the biology of Darwin rather than that of Cuvier. We have already discussed (Chapter 2) the analogy between Darwinian 'species' and Boasian 'cultures'; what concerns us now are its implications for the distinction between the latter and Durkheimian 'societies', a distinction fundamental to the divergence between the traditions of cultural and social anthropology. Pursuing the Darwinian analogue, there is no design in culture apart from those established by unique configurations of elements lodged in the minds of discrete human beings. Hence, although superorganic in the sense that its elements (unlike genes) are ideal or extrasomatic, and can vary quite independently of hereditary constraint, culture does not encompass the individual within a higher-order system of relationships. To the contrary, culture in the Boasian perspective is itself encompassed or contained as a property of its individual bearers. No more to a culture than to a species does there correspond a supraindividual substance or 'essence'. It follows that the transcendence of the cultural over the organic is in no way analogous to that of the organic over the inorganic. Whereas the latter indicates the emergent properties of an organized whole by which it surpasses the resultant of its parts, the former points to a dichotomy of substance—between material and ideal—in the constitution of the parts themselves (individuals) that together make up a society. In other words, unlike Durkheim's 'society', Boas's 'culture' is not a product of the fusion of individual minds into a larger entity, directing their operation from without, but is separately installed *within* each one prior to their association. We cannot, in consequence, speak of cultural life as Durkheim spoke of the life of society, as a mode of being over and above the life of individuals. In short, there may be a domain of cultural reality that can be called the superorganic, but there is no such thing as a cultural superorganism.

Doubtless it was for reasons such as these that Boas himself preferred not to use the concept of the superorganic in reference to cultural systems. It was left to Kroeber, in his famous essay of 1917, to introduce the concept into the mainstream of American cultural anthropology. To a great extent, this essay represented a polemical reaffirmation of the principles on which the historical science of culture that Boas had established staked its claim to disciplinary autonomy. Much of it is devoted to a demonstration of the independence of race and culture, or heredity and tradition. Kroeber rejects both the 'forward' derivation of culture from race, inspired by Darwin's teaching in *The descent of man,* and the 'backward' derivation of race from culture based on a popular belief in the 'Lamarckian' inheritance of acquired characteristics, a belief that long outlasted its scientific refutation by Weismann in the 1880s. Looking back on his essay, some thirty-five years after its publication, Kroeber identifies these themes as its principal thrust: 'What the essay really protests is the blind and bland shuttling back and forth between an equivocal "race" and an equivocal "civilization" '(1952:22). Spencer, as we have seen, could not abandon his commitment to the Lamarckian doctrine without blowing apart his conception of the unity of the evolutionary process, and by implication that of the subject-matters of biological and social science. Kroeber, conversely, was among the first to recognize the full significance of the refutation of Lamarckism for the absolute separation of cultural and organic phenomena, thenceforth setting cultural anthropology and evolutionary biology on mutually independent courses (Stocking 1968:265–6). Thus although he acknowledges a debt to Spencer for the title of his essay, 'The superorganic', Kroeber employs it in a fundamentally different sense. His super-organic is 'civilization', and although this includes much of what Spencer would have placed in his category of 'super-organic products', the criterion for inclusion is not that an item be produced through the co-ordinated action of many individuals, but that it should manifest a design inscribed on their minds by force of tradition—rather than one indelibly 'pricked in' by the materials of heredity.[2] The human organism, Kroeber declares, is a vessel into which all manner of superorganic content may be poured (1952:32, 37–8, 56).

All this is perfectly consistent with the Boasian position. And yet many of Boas's most committed followers reacted to Kroeber's paper with considerable unease, among them Sapir, who suggested that 'the superorganic' is a concept we could better do without (Sapir 1917:447). For Kroeber had, in fact, read into the concept a good deal more than Boas would have allowed; indeed there are parts of his argument that approach the superorganicism of Durkheim. Consider the following passage: 'The social or cultural . . . is in its essence nonindividual. Civilization, as such, begins only where the individual ends; and whoever does not in some measure perceive this fact . . . can find no meaning in civilization, and history for him must be only a wearying jumble, or an opportunity for the exercise of art' (1952:40). The superorganic, Kroeber maintains, is not only suprabiological but also supraindividual. Outside society, the individual is no more than a biological organism. Although civilization comes into being through the combination of individuals, it cannot be understood as a resultant—'the sum total of [their] psychic operations'—but only as 'an entity beyond them', that is as an emergent. This 'superpsychic' entity is conceived to have a life of its own, analogous to the life of the individual organism, but unfolding on a higher plane of reality. Where the process of organic life gives us biography, the process of superorganic life gives us culture-history (Kroeber 1952:41, 49, 53–4).

Clearly this is to construe history in a sense radically different from the Boasian 'history' of culture-bearing populations. Finding a meaning in history, for Kroeber, meant seeing it not as an undirected, chronological sequence of non-recurrent entities and events, but as a determined process of growth (Bidney 1953:52). We have already discussed the difference at length in Chapter 3 and need not pursue it here. However, it is important to stress how Kroeber was led by his view of the superorganic to posit a dualism between humans as organic individuals and as cultural beings entirely in accord with Durkheim's thinking on the subject. 'Man', he wrote, 'comprises two aspects: he is an organic substance . . . and he is also a tablet that is written upon'. But the source of the message is *extrinsic* to every one of the individuals that bear it, 'imposed on them, external to them' (1952:32). For Boas man's cultural being was an aspect of his very individuality. Naturally it was Kroeber's detachment of culture from the individual, and the attribution to the former of a purpose transcending the residually innate dispositions of the individuals subject to its dominion, that most worried his fellow Boasians. As Goldenweiser insisted in a response to Kroeber, the biography of the 'concrete individual' manifests a unique psyche constituted not only by those attributes he has received by heredity, but also by a selection of elements passed on and absorbed from the cultural heritage of those around him. Hence 'the civilizational stream is not merely carried but is also unrelentingly fed by its component individuals' (Goldenweiser 1917:449). They are the inscribers as well as the inscribed.

How could Kroeber simultaneously uphold two such contradictory positions, maintaining (with Boas) that culture is entirely contained within the minds of individuals, and yet (with Durkheim) that it comes to them from an outside source in a transcendent, supraindividual level of reality? The answer seems to lie in the fact that, at the time of writing, no clear convention existed to regulate the use of the key terms, 'social' and 'cultural', nor were they yet differentiated.[3] Rather confusingly, Kroeber presents his argument in terms of an opposition between the 'individually mental' and the 'culturally social' (1952:41). Two quite separate dichotomies are implied here: on the one hand between the individual and the collectivity; on the other, between the innate and the acquired. Collective life is, of course, a condition for the intergenerational transmission of an acquired cultural tradition, that is for the transfer of ideational content from one individual mind to another. Thus culture might be said to be 'social' in its mode of reproduction. But by a consistent substitution of 'social' for 'cultural', it was all too easy to slip into the belief that tradition is essentially social in its mode of *existence*—hence that its locus lies in a supraindividual consciousness. That is why Kroeber imagined that to demonstrate the autonomy of tradition from hereditary constraint was, *ipso facto,* to assert its character as a supraindividual emergent. Years later, he recanted most of his views about superpsychic essences, significantly enough in the context of a clarification of the social–cultural distinction (1952:22–3, 112). It is vital for us to take a closer look at how this distinction came to be made.

The problem arose initially over the question of whether ants are social. With his characteristic flair for conceptual inconsistency, Kroeber had stated in the same breath that the ant is both social and antisocial: 'Social the ant is, in the sense that she associates; but she is so far from being social in the sense of possessing civilization, of being influenced by nonorganic forces, that she would better be known as the anti–social animal' (1952:31). The first sense of social, here, is entirely in line with Spencer's use of the term. Thus ant society is super*organic*. What ants lack, presumably, is *super*organic culture. One of the earliest attempts to articulate this contrast was by Bernhard Stern. 'The distinction between the social and the cultural', he argued, 'is predicated on the distinction between the organic and the superorganic, the biological and the cultural' (1929:264). A society is constituted by the association and interaction of individual organisms; the cultureless animal can enjoy a social life, but the converse does not hold. Since association is a condition for the reproduction of culture through teaching and learning, an asocial animal could not possibly bear a cultural tradition (see also Hallowell 1960b:329; Bonner 1980:76). Kroeber latterly accepted Stern's argument. In an auto–critique of his earlier contrast between 'the cultural society of man and the cultureless pseudo–society of the ants', Kroeber admits that 'today we might rather say that ant society is a genuine society but manifests a pseudo–culture' (1952:52, 56). Elsewhere he accepts as a 'truism' that social and cultural dimensions 'are distinguishable in principle because societies occur among many subhuman species of animals unaccompanied by any tangible culture'. The existence of complex societies among insects proves that 'developmentally, evolutionistically, society far antedates and thus underlies culture' (Kroeber 1963:122, 176; see also 1948:7–10).

What is particularly noteworthy here is that once having abandoned the notion that the essence of culture is superpsychic, Kroeber was prepared to accept a thoroughly Spencerian definition of society. The same was true of those Boasians who, all along, had insisted that the locus of culture was the individual mind, acting as a store of elements received from other such minds and in turn to be passed on (e.g. Goldenweiser 1933:59). If culture does not emerge through the interpenetration of minds on a higher level, but is separately contained in each one, and if the cultural contents direct the thought and conduct of those whose minds they occupy, it follows logically that society can be nothing but the resultant of their interactions. In other words, it is the product of the external contact of discrete, self-contained individuals, the manner of whose association is entirely predictable from the properties constitutive of their 'nature'. The only difference between this and the orthodox, Spencerian position is that 'nature' must be read to include not only the genetically transmitted but also the culturally acquired components of individuality. Either way, society is conceived in purely instrumental terms as an adjunct to the execution of extrasocial ends, written into the genetic or cultural constitution of its component individuals. In this sense the apparently antithetical arguments of cultural anthropology and sociobiology, harking back to Boas and Spencer respectively, are remarkably similar: 'For one the social is the instrument of culture; for the other it is the instrument of [biogenetic] nature' (Ingold 1983a:16). The irreconcilability of these alternative positions stems from their very likeness: Opposing natural to cultural determination, they leave us with no option but to choose between one or the other.

Kluckhohn offers a most succinct statement of the society–culture dichotomy, very much in keeping with the Boasian tradition, which will serve to exemplify the points we have just made.

> Since culture is an abstraction, it is important not to confuse culture with society. A 'society' refers to a group of people who interact more with each other than they do with other individuals—who co-operate with each other for the attainment of certain ends. You can see and indeed count the individuals who make up a society. A 'culture' refers to the distinctive ways of life of such a group of people. (Kluckhohn 1949:24; see also Kroeber and Kluckhohn 1952:135–6, where the social is rendered as the 'interactive')

For Kluckhohn, as for Spencer, society is a network of interactions between co-operating individuals, but the ends they seek are culturally defined and hence specific to a given tradition rather than universal. It is revealing to compare Kluckhohn's view that any society is constituted by a certain number of individuals with Kroeber's remarks on the same theme, written in 1917 when he was still an advocate of superpsychism: 'All biology necessarily has this direct reference to the individual. . . . The Darwinian doctrine relates, it is true, to race: but the race, except as an abstraction, is only a collection of individuals. . . . But a thousand individuals do not make up a society' (1952:40–1). Thirty-five years later, Kroeber was prepared to admit, with Kluckhohn, that a number of individuals *do* make a society, that cultural anthropology—like biology—makes direct reference to the individual, and that the notion of culture is an abstraction in just the same way as the notion of race.

Let us now turn from Kroeber to his great contemporary and founder of the British tradition of social anthropology, Radcliffe-Brown. Though none too clear on the concept of culture, Radcliffe-Brown was in no doubt that his concern—as Spencer's—was with the evolution of *society* (1952:4–8). Indeed he insisted that the anti-evolutionary arguments of Boas and his followers, since their reference was to cultural phenomena, 'have no bearing at all on the theory of social evolution'. That theory, again, was Spencer's (Radcliffe-Brown 1947:80). So was his 'preliminary definition of social phenomena':

> What we have to deal with are relations of association between individual organisms. In a hive of bees there are the relations of association of the queen, the workers and the drones. There is the association of animals in a herd, of a mother-cat and her kittens. . . . In social anthropology, as I define it, what we have to investigate are the forms of association to be found amongst human beings. (1952:189)

These forms of human association, Radcliffe-Brown implied, are no more to be regarded as phenomena of culture than are the relations of bees in the hive, all of which exemplify the superorganic of Spencer (1947:79 n.1). The complex network of interactions amongst an aggregate of individual human beings is what

Radcliffe-Brown calls the 'social structure'. He goes on to suggest that, just as the individual organism is formed through the compounding of cells, and cells from the compounding of molecules, so the social superorganism is formed from the compounding of its constituent individuals (1952:190).

At this stage of his argument, having taken his cue from Spencer, Radcliffe-Brown switches abruptly into the Durkheimian mode. In the society, as in the organism, the lives of the parts are subservient to the corporate life of the whole; thus 'the social phenomena which we observe in any human society are not the immediate result of the nature of individual human beings, but are the result of the social structure by which they are united' (1952:190–1). With this, structure promptly ceases to be an interactional network and reappears as an arrangement of regulative institutions, an emergent property of the fusion of individuals into a collective entity. It is true that Radcliffe-Brown is aware of this shift and does his best to retain the distinction between the two senses of the social by differentiating social structure from what he calls 'structural form'—the latter denoting an abstraction derived from the mass of empirically observed instances. Yet this abstraction soon hardens into concrete reality, and as it does so structural form becomes conflated with the notion of social structure itself. Indeed the distinction between structure and form has been dropped by most of Radcliffe-Brown's followers who, preferring to pursue the Durkheimian rather than the Spencerian strand in the master's thought, are content to regard social structure as a kind of normative framework, or a system of rules (Fortes 1949:56). The effects of this shift of emphasis in the conception of sociality, from the interactional to the regulative, are profound. We have already noted some of them in Chapter 4. Regarding the reality as 'an immense multitude of actions and interactions of human beings', social life appears as a continuous *process,* of which any social structure is a transect taken 'at a given moment of time' (Radcliffe-Brown 1952:4, 192). But once the reality comes to be seen as an 'ordered arrangement of parts of components', we seem to be dealing with a discrete *entity* rather than a process, social life becomes the life of society, and continuity is replaced by the dichotomization of structural persistence and structural change (1952:9–11).

Like Durkheim, Radcliffe-Brown maintains that man is double: He is an individual and a person, an organism and a social being. Beginning with social structure as a Spencerian superorganism, an association of *individuals,* he ends—only five pages later—with social structure as a Durkheimian superorganism, an ordering of *persons,* which has a life of its own imposed on the lives of its organic, individual constituents. Radcliffe-Brown's notion of the person will be recalled from Chapter 3; it refers to a part or position in a regulative order. 'We cannot study persons except in terms of social structure, nor can we study social structure except in terms of the persons who are the units of which it is composed' (1952:194). But if that is so, what are we to make of the 'society' of the beehive? Every bee is surely an individual organism, but is equally surely *not* a person as well. If society is constituted as a system of relations between persons, in Radcliffe-Brown's sense, then bees cannot be social. Indeed we would have good reason to restrict sociality to beings capable of projecting and externalizing their shared subjective experience on the level of ideas, hence of forming collective representations. Such, as Durkheim argued, are *human* beings: Bees associate as individuals, but man alone lives socially. But if we pursue this line of argument, the distinction between culture and society, on which Radcliffe-Brown is so insistent, begins to look decidedly thin.

Consider again the grounds for this distinction. The associations of bees in the hive, of deer in the herd and so on are, as Radcliffe-Brown contends, 'social phenomena; I do not suppose that anyone will call them cultural phenomena' (1952:189). If the beehive is a society, and granting that bees lack culture, the social and the cultural must be separable. That was Stern's argument also, and latterly Kroeber's. But it holds only in so far as social life is understood as the resultant of individual interactions. When it comes to humans, who by all accounts do *not* lack culture, the argument implies that the locus of culture must be in the several minds of the interacting individuals. Now Kroeber, as we have seen, originally drew culture off from the individual, relocating it on an emergent, supraindividual level of consciousness. Radcliffe-Brown, meanwhile, by separating the organism from the social person, transferred the concept of society from the biological domain of material things to the suprabiological domain of ideas. Together they converge on an imaginary, vital essence that is both supraindividual and suprabiological, an essence that nowadays (apparently following Sorokin) goes under the name of the 'sociocultural system'. Whenever the terms 'society' and 'culture' are used interchangeably, as they very often are even in contemporary literature, this is a sure sign that some such essence is implied. All we need say about it is that the belief in its existence is a straightforward consequence of the fallacy of misplaced concreteness, the reification of what is at best a convenient abstraction.[4]

Our argument is summarized in Fig. 6.1. Box A is occupied by the organism, the biological individual. The other three boxes are occupied by the three senses of the superorganic: the Spencerian (box B), the Boasian (box C) and the Durkheimian (box D). It remains for us to show that, had Radcliffe-Brown adhered consistently

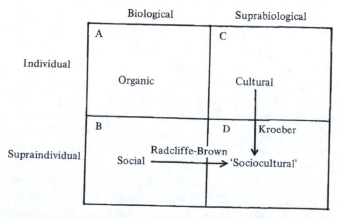

FIG. 6.1   Spencer, Durkheim, Boas and the superorganic.

to the Spencerian conception of society, and to the separation of the social from the cultural, he would have had to conclude that the constituent units of human society are not persons as parts in a Durkheimian regulative order, but Boasian culture-bearing individuals. The difference between viewing social structure as an arrangement of persons and as an interaction of individuals, in the senses just adduced, is illustrated schematically in Fig. 6.2. In the upper diagram, X and Y are individuals who, in Radcliffe-Brown's terms, happen to be the incumbents of the institutionalized positions—let us say—of brother and sister, terms that denote components of personhood. The social relation here is the generic sibling bond 'brother–sister', consisting of a set of rules regulating the mutual behaviour of the incumbents and defining their respective rights and obligations. But where do these rules reside? The Boasian answer is: in the minds of individuals. They form part of a cultural system that is internal to each actor, in the same way that the genetic system is internal to each organism. They are shared because those actors have partaken in a common heritage, just as shared genes indicate common descent, and *not* because they manifest a common essence of superpsychic individuality. Thus, as we show in the lower diagram of Fig. 6.2, the formal relation of siblinghood is ascribed

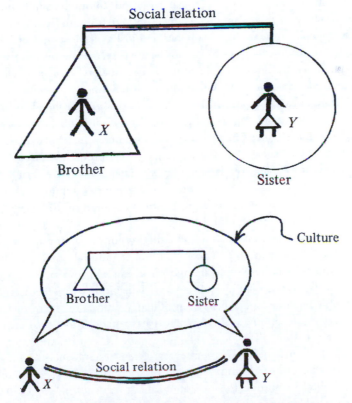

FIG. 6.2   The 'social relation' as an arrangement of parts in a regulative order (*above*) and as an interaction between culture-bearing individuals (*below*).

to culture rather than society, and as such is contained within the individuals X and Y, rather than containing them. It is a relation between parts in a programme that is internalized in both, whereas the *social* relation exists directly between X and Y as actors. Social life, then, is constituted by the aggregate of interactive associations of the type $X–Y$, occurring spontaneously in a population of individuals. This of course takes us right back to Radcliffe-Brown's initial understanding of social structure as 'a complex network of actually existing relations [amongst] a certain number of individual human beings' (1952:190). Nor is this sense of the social in any way altered if we revert from human beings to supposedly cultureless bees. X could be a queen bee, and Y a worker or a drone. Although the 'queen–worker' or 'queen–drone' relation would be inscribed in the common genetic constitution of the individuals concerned, the social relation would still be the interaction $X–Y$ between particular bees.

In view of Radcliffe-Brown's frequent allusions to the social life of bees, and Kroeber's to that of ants, this might be the appropriate point to consider what students of insect behaviour—and indeed ethologists and sociobiologists generally—actually mean when they speak of 'societies' of non-human animals. Lorenz presents us with an extreme case. He considers the most 'primitive' form of society, the absolute baseline of social evolution, to be 'the anonymous flock', such as the shoal of fish, inside which 'there is no structure of any kind . . . but just a huge collection of like elements' (1966:123). Most authors, however, would agree with Spencer's century-old dictate that 'the mere gathering of individuals into a group does not constitute them a society'. *Co-operation,* Spencer always insisted, 'is at once that which cannot exist without a society, and that for which a society exists' (1882, II:244). We find this view echoed in the definition of a leading sociobiologist: '*Society:* A group of individuals belonging to the same species and organized in a co-operative manner. The principal criterion for applying the term "society" is the existence of reciprocal communication of a co-operative nature that extends beyond mere sexual activity' (Wilson 1978:222). According to Dobzhansky, again, 'Society is a complex of individuals bound by co-operative interactions that serve to maintain a common life' (1962:58). For Alexander, 'sociality means group living' (1974:326). Finally, Emerson defines society as 'a group that manifests systematic division of labour among adults of the same sex'. He goes on to point out that human cultural systems are functionally analogous to genetic systems in cultureless animals, insofar as they generate specific patterns of association. 'Most social behaviour of insects is genetically determined, while most social behaviour of man is culturally determined through symbolic communication . . . [but] symbols have many functional attributes of genes' (Emerson 1958:331).

These definitions speak for themselves. Their resemblance to the original Spencerian conception is astonishing, and their continued appeal has much the same basis.[5] For purporting to be as applicable to insect colonies as to human communities, they offer the prospect of a unified theory of social evolution (Ingold 1983a:5). The resemblances stretch even to the various criteria adduced to determine the placement of any society on a universal scale of evolving sociability. Here are Spencer's criteria:

> Like evolving aggregates in general, societies show *integration,* both by simple increase of mass and by coalescence and re-coalescence of masses. The change from *homogeneity* to *heterogeneity* is multitudinously exemplified. . . . With progressing integration and heterogeneity goes increasing *definiteness.* . . . Thus in all respects is fulfilled the formula of evolution, as a progress towards greater size, coherence, multiformity and definiteness. (1876, I:617–18)

Thompson, comparing the social groups of insects and humans, lists five dimensions of sociality: size and density, cohesiveness, syntality (the degree to which group members can act as a co-ordinated unit), stability (the fixity of interactions over time), and permeability (the degree to which the group permits intrusions by strange individuals). These criteria, barring the last, are essentially Spencer's (Thompson 1958:298–308). Wilson presents a more comprehensive list of ten 'qualities of sociality', most of which can likewise be derived from the Spencerian formula (Wilson 1980:12–14). The first, *group size,* requires no further comment. *Cohesiveness* and *amount and pattern of connectedness* are varieties of Spencer's criterion of 'coherence', based on the modern distinction between density and reachability in the analysis of social networks (see Mitchell 1969:15–20). *'Permeability',* as Wilson defines it, is equivalent to Spencer's 'coalescence of masses', since it has to do not with the intrusion of individual strangers but with the fusion of whole groups. As such, it is an aspect of what Spencer calls 'integration', whereas Wilson's quality of *compartmentalization* corresponds to Spencer's 'definiteness'. The *differentiation of roles* and *integration of behaviour* clearly reflect the notion of an evolving division of labour that Spencer denotes by the change 'from homogeneity to heterogeneity'. Only three of Wilson's criteria cannot be accommodated within the Spencerian paradigm. These are the *demographic distribution* of individuals in the society, the amount of *information flow* between them, and finally the *fraction of time devoted to social behaviour.* We shall return shortly to consider the last of these criteria.

There is a certain circularity in the sociobiological argument that, having conceived the order of nature in the image of civil society, proclaims the latter to rest on a natural foundation (Sahlins 1976a:101–7; Ingold 1983a:5). This was apparent over a century ago to Marx and Engels, who both made much of the way Darwin's choice of metaphors—taken all too literally by Spencer and those of his followers who styled themselves 'Darwinists'—reflected the contemporary view of society as constituted by the interplay of a multitude of discrete and competing interests. 'In Darwin', Marx wrote, 'the animal kingdom figures as civil society.' A few years later, Engels followed up this lead in a letter to Lavrov:

> The whole Darwinist teaching of the struggle for existence is simply a transference from society to living nature of Hobbes's doctrine of "bellum omnium contra omnes" and of the bourgeois-economic doctrine

> of competition together with Malthus's theory of population. When this conjurer's trick has been performed, . . . the same theories are transferred back again from organic nature into history and it is now claimed that their validity as eternal laws of human society has been proved. (Engels [1875]; see also Marx [1862]; both citations in Schmidt 1971:46–7)

In fairness to Darwin, it should be emphasized that his use of metaphorical expressions remained just that, nor was he ever too happy with them. The 'Darwinist teaching' to which Engels referred was in fact Spencer's, for it was after all he who added a Hobbesian twist to the 'struggle for existence' by recasting it as the 'survival of the fittest' (see Chapter 1). As we have seen, the prototype for the sociobiological conception of animal society is also to be found in Spencer rather than Darwin. It is therefore hardly surprising that when sociobiologists argue by extension from animals to human beings, the result is Spencerian 'industrial solidarity', reconstituted in all its essentials.

But to describe the circularity as an oscillation 'between the culturalization of nature and the naturalization of culture', as Sahlins does (1976a:105), only confuses the issue. Sahlins's real and legitimate objections to sociobiology do not differ all that substantially from those that Kroeber, sixty years previously, had levelled at Spencer, concerning the 'shuttling back and forth' between the innate and the acquired. Nowadays this shuttling takes the form of positing hypothetical genes underwriting cultural dispositions and proceeding to derive the latter from the former, replacing the discredited 'Lamarckian' inheritance of acquired characteristics with a mechanism of genetic assimilation that simulates its effects (Lumsden and Wilson 1981:21–2). However, our concern here, as that of Marx and Engels, is with the 'naturalization' not of culture but of *society*. And this is something for which both sociobiology and the cultural anthropology of which Sahlins is an advocate can be held equally responsible. For the transference from mankind to animals of the Spencerian notion of society as an aggregate of co-operative interactions has been followed by a reverse transference from the genetically based societies of animals to the culturally based societies of specific human groups, without in the least affecting the fundamental premiss that social life is a derivative of the extrasocial 'nature' of autonomous individuals.[6] The result of this double transference, as Bidney has pointed out, is merely to substitute one (cultural) fatalism for the equally objectionable (genetic) fatalism it opposes (Bidney 1953:136; see also Midgley 1980:29). Indeed neither of the two senses of sociality so far encountered, the interactive and the regulative, enables us to comprehend social life as a creative process whereby human beings relate to one another as the authors as well as the players of their parts. For this we must adduce a third sense, altogether different from both previous ones.

The constitution of persons

Consider the alternatives. According to the view of social life as an interactive process, culture is opposed to society as preconstituted project to the summated effects of its execution by the population of individuals in whose separate minds the project is contained. According to the view of society as a normative system for the positive regulation of practical conduct, social structure merges with culture as a project to be executed, located on a superpsychic level. Either way, the particular individual, living in society, apparently exists only to perform a programme he had no hand in writing; in this respect it is immaterial whether 'social relations' are conceived to link parts of the programme or the individuals who are executing it (see Fig. 6.2). To arrive at our third sense of social life, which we have already introduced in previous chapters, we must take something from both of the other alternatives and add something else that is included in neither—namely a concept of the person as conscious, subjective agent. What we take from the interactive view is the notion of social life as a *process* going on between particular human beings. We consider this process, however, not in statistical terms as the resultant of a mass of associations between atomic individuals, but in topological terms as the unfolding of a continuous field of intersubjective relations in which persons do not so much interact with as *constitute* one another through the history of their mutual involvement. Interaction, after all, can occur only between objects that arrive on the scene, so to speak, 'ready-made' and therefore has to be radically distinguished from the process by which we, as subjects, make ourselves. That process we call the social life of persons. From the view of society as a regulative entity we take the idea that the intentions and purposes of persons are given not in advance of their entry into social relations but in fact have their *source* in the social domain. Thus we reject the utilitarian premiss that the content of social relations is exclusively instrumental, providing a set of means for the satisfaction of the naturally or culturally defined ends of individuals. On the other hand, we do not accept the attribution of purpose to a separate superpsychic entity called 'society', empowered to act as a central directing agency. The locus of purpose, we hold, is the person himself, yet the former (what he intends) just like the latter (who he is) is constituted by his relations with others.

Now it is precisely this 'constitutive' view of the social that informs the early writings of Marx. The following passage, from the 1844 manuscripts, is definitive: 'Above all we must avoid postulating "Society" again as an abstraction *vis-à-vis* the individual. The individual *is the social being*. His life, even if it may not appear in the direct form of a *communal* life in association with others, is therefore an expression and confirmation of *social life*' (1964a:137–8). By the 'individual' Marx means the particular subject who, far from being a mere vehicle for the life of a hypostatized 'society', as in the Durkheimian conception, is constituted as a vital agent by his involvement in social relations. It is as an actor, not as a part, that man is a social being. When we speak of the life of the subject, and of social life, we are concerned with identical and not with analogous processes, for the life of the subject *is* social. This passage gives the lie to those 'structuralist' interpretations of Marx that convert social structural abstractions into active historical agents, riding on the backs of real people who are conceived to live *for* society rather than to live socially. But it also flies in the face of 'technicist' readings that imagine social relations to consist of

patterns of co-operative association appropriate to the deployment of certain tech-
nologies under given environmental conditions. That, in Avineri's words, would
be to render the sphere of the social 'devoid of any content that is not instrumental'
(1968:88). As Marx states, the mutual constitution of persons as social beings, their
endowment with identity and purpose, has nothing directly to do with whether,
or to what extent, they associate in the practical pursuit of their respective goals.
Thus the 'constitutive' view of social relations must be distinguished from both the
'interactive' and the 'regulative'.

These remarks should help us to make sense of one of the most contested of
Marx's pronouncements, in his preface to *A contribution to the critique of political
economy,* that 'in the social production of their existence, men inevitably enter
into definite relations, which are independent of their will'.[7] He goes on to spell
out the distinction between economic infrastructure and legal-political superstructure, concluding with his celebrated dictum that 'it is not the consciousness of
men that determines their existence, but their social existence that determines
their consciousness' (1970 [1859]:20–1). Marx's point, as I have stated elsewhere,
was simply that 'social relations *constitute* the conscious, wilful subject and are not
wilfully designed by subjects whose consciousness is somehow given in advance,
as though individuals had an independent, subjective existence outside of and
opposed to society' (Ingold 1983a:9). This was also his point in the sixth of the
Theses on Feuerbach, where he insists that we cannot take the subject of social relations to be the 'abstract—*isolated*—human individual', for every subject exists only
as an 'ensemble of the social relations' that constitute his consciousness (Marx and
Engels 1977:122; see also our discussion of personhood in Chapter 3). In short,
Marx was objecting to the view that would treat society as an artefact of rational
deliberation, or as a compact voluntarily entered into by autonomous individuals
for the satisfaction of their natural desires. It is a view that still has plenty of adherents. For example, Bidney speaks of the regulations and organizations of society as
'socifacts' that, along with material 'artifacts' and conceptual 'mentifacts', are all to
be regarded as 'instruments invented by man for the better satisfaction of his needs
and wants' (1953:130). Still more recently, Harré has argued that the biological
make-up of man engenders a set of problems whose solution has taxed human
ingenuity, 'and one of the cleverest devices we have invented to deal with them
was society' (1979:36). History would then appear to be the result of a process in
which human beings have conjured up in their imaginations, and proceeded to
execute, one social plan after another. It becomes a catalogue of inventions (see
also Reynolds 1976:65).

This view of society as an artefact or contrivance was, of course, one Durkheim
equally abhorred. It is not, he argued, to be conceived as a Hobbesian machine
'wholly constructed by the hands of men and which, like all products of this kind,
is only what it is because men have willed it so' (1982 [1895]:142). It was in opposition to the artificial that Durkheim characterized society as a *natural* system, in
the sense that it has arisen *sui generis* rather than under voluntary human authorship. Beyond this, however, the positions of Marx and Durkheim could not have

been more different. The crux of the difference lies in the question of agency. Durkheim, as we have seen, does not endow the particular man *qua* social being with a will of his own; his destiny is to convey the transcendent will of society. But when Marx writes that the relations into which persons enter are 'independent of their will', he means not to deny the agency of the socially constituted person, but to affirm the social constitution of the agent. Human beings *are,* for Marx, the authors of their social relations; there is no superior purpose that subverts their intentions (which is not to say, of course, that the purposes of the more powerful may not override those of the relatively powerless). It might appear paradoxical, at first glance, to hold this view in conjunction with one that rejects the voluntary basis of society. The paradox, however, persists only so long as society is conceived as an objective entity or structure, and social life as the revelation of structure. There is a problem, as Durkheim well recognized, in treating as an artefact of the human will a design that, no sooner created, turns its erstwhile creators into slaves to its execution. That problem goes back to Rousseau.

But for Marx, social life is a creative rather than a merely revelatory process: namely, human beings' production of their existence'. As we shall see in the next chapter, Marx uses the term 'production' here in a special, intransitive sense: To produce is to live, and the relation between producer and product is one between subject and superject—our subject a little further on. To return to the theme of the preceding chapter, social life is not something the person does but rather what the person undergoes, not the performance of a programme but the very process of composition. Men do not make societies but, living socially, make themselves. Recalling Wieman's distinction, 'social' connotes the creative good, not created goods; it is an attribute of process rather than of things. Hence social relations, like the persons they constitute, must likewise be understood in processual terms, and not as the components of a fixed, structural framework. Real time, Bergsonian duration, inheres in social relations, thus conceived, just as it does in the flow of consciousness. That which is independent of human will, in the present instant, is no less than the past that has made us who we are, a past of mutual involvement with others and of which our future existence is necessarily a projection (Marx 1963 [1869]:15). To suppose, contrary to Marx, that the person could constitute his relations in the immediate present by an act of spontaneous free will would be tantamount to a denial of the evolution of purpose in the acting self, and to an ascription of conduct to a generalized and timeless human nature, external to the subject, which would impose a determination of its own on human affairs. Freedom would thus be secured at the expense of creativity.

It is abundantly clear that, for Marx, the movements of consciousness and of social life are two sides of the same coin. 'Consciousness', he wrote in *The German ideology,* 'can never be anything else than conscious existence, and the existence of men is their actual life-process' (Marx and Engels 1977:47). There is, admittedly, something rather tautological about Marx's assertion that it is men's 'social existence that determines their consciousness'. For as social life is equivalent to purposive action (production), so that action presupposes consciousness

(Avineri 1968:75–6). Thus the connection between consciousness and social relations, as we showed in Chapter 5, might better be understood as one of enfolding and unfolding respectively. Those, however, who appeal to the authority of Marx to justify a search for invisible, deep structures of social life that, unbeknown to their human bearers, are supposed to underlie conscious experience (Lévi-Strauss 1968:23; Godelier 1972:xix, 260) have entirely misconstrued his meaning. Reading the 'determination' of consciousness by social existence as a relation between cause and effect, rather than between the total process and its moments (Giddens 1979:160), the 'unwilled' is replaced by the 'unconscious', and that which—having been—is unalterable becomes that which—masked by consciousness—is unknowable. The intersubjective past that is active within us gives way to a timeless, synchronic structure, internal to each subject, whose elements are linked by hidden and determinate 'social relations' and whose mere mechanical replication is the object of production. This is to reduce production to nothing more than execution, from which practical consciousness has been withdrawn—only to be appended as a contemplative afterthought: Structure directs, consciousness reflects. Such a reduction can in no way be reconciled with Marx's recognition of both consciousness and social relations as complementary strands of a single life-process, nor with his identification of that life-process as production itself—not the enactment of plans but the unfolding of consciousness in *'sensuous human activity, practice'* (Marx and Engels 1977:121).

Armed with this constitutive view of the social as an intersubjective process, we have now to proceed by asking: What is *not* a social relationship? And as before, this is a question best approached by considering whether, in the terms we have just outlined, animals other than humans enjoy a social life. Marx's answer was considered briefly towards the close of the previous chapter, and we return to it here. 'For the animal', he wrote, 'its relation to others does not exist as a relation.' The paradox of this statement lies in the double meaning of the term 'relation'. No one denies that animals relate as individual objects. But to have a *social* relation there must be a subject whose own consciousness is at least to some extent disengaged from its life in the world, sufficiently so that it can assume the point of view of another that can do likewise (Habermas 1979:136–7). 'Where there exists a relationship', as Marx declared in the aforementioned passage, 'it exists for me.' The animal that lacks consciousness of self, that cannot tell 'I' from 'you', 'does not enter into any relation at all' (Marx and Engels 1977:51). Only when the flow of consciousness begins to run along a channel distinct from, though parallel to, the flow of conduct, does the latter appear as action directed by a self towards others, that is as social action. In short, what Marx called the 'emancipation' of consciousness from the world is a condition for the emergence of inter- (rather than trans-) subjectivity, and hence for conduct to appear as the evolution of a continuous field of social relations.

If it is granted that the intersubjective domain of social being is irreducible to the association and interaction of objectively defined individuals, it must follow, as I have elsewhere stated, that 'there is no evolutionary continuity between what biologists generally regard as social behaviour in animals, and those systems of social relations identified by anthropologists, within which subjects are located as conscious agents' (Ingold 1983a:6; see Bock 1980:149). The origins of social-ity, in the latter sense, must be sought in the evolution of consciousness, not in the associational characteristics of organisms such as insects or even corals whose behaviour, as everyone seems to agree, is entirely pre-programmed and reflexive, and is not governed by conscious intent. The bees of Radcliffe-Brown's hive, for example, though amply fulfilling each of Wilson's ten 'qualities of sociality' could not be said to enjoy a social life in the anthropological sense of the term. This is not to deny that human beings associate as individuals in the conduct of their activities and that the resultant patterns of association bear comparison with those of insects, birds, non-human primates, or whatever. But it *is* to deny that such patterns can be called social. And it is also to deny the possibility of a purely biological or even 'culturological' understanding of social life. If, then, interactive relations are deemed to be non-social, how are they to be characterized?

Let us see how Marx approaches the issue. We find in *The German ideology* an initial formulation of a dualism that pervades the entire corpus of Marx's writings on the human condition, between *material* and *social* relations (Cohen 1978:92–3). 'The production of life', he writes, 'appears as a double relationship: on the one hand as a natural, on the other as a social relationship.' He goes on, however, to offer a definition of the social that sounds thoroughly Spencerian: 'By social we understand the co-operation of several individuals, no matter under what condi-tions, in what matter and to what end' (Marx and Engels 1977:50). Taking this definition at face value, it would serve merely to separate intraspecific, communi-cative interaction from interspecific, exploitative interaction, the former involving exchanges of information, the latter involving transfers of materials and energy that would nowadays be regarded as components of the ecosystem. There is nothing in these that is specifically human: Bees, after all, communicate with other bees and frequent nectar-secreting flowers. Surely, even though the dance of the bees may be reckoned as 'social' behaviour, it is none the less 'natural' for that. And, indeed, Marx himself proceeds to characterize co-operation as a 'productive force', subsequently including in the same category the sum of the attributes of man as a natural being, that is as an individual, confronting nature 'as one of her own forces' (1930 [1867]:169). Furthermore, in the development of the Marxian paradigm, productive *forces* came to be systematically opposed to productive *relations*: the former having to do with the practical arrangements by which particular tasks are implemented, with *how* they are done; the latter constituting the persons *who* are carrying them out, and directing their purposes (Ingold 1983a:7).

This opposition, as Cohen has pointed out (1978:98), is just another aspect of the ubiquitous dichotomy between nature and society, or between material and social relations. Co-operation, originally the definitive criterion of sociality, now reappears on the material side, *counterposed* to social relations that constitute the co-operators.[8] Or to put it another way, co-operative relations obtain not between *persons who* co-operate in the production of their existence, but between *things that* are instrumentally *co-operated* in the labour process. And these things are none other than the faculties and powers—'arms and legs, head and hands' (Marx 1930 [1867]:196)—constitutive of objective human nature, augmented of course by culturally acquired attributes including knowledge and skills. Under capitalism, as Marx showed, these faculties and powers are surrendered by the workers to an employer. Hence it cannot be said that the former co-operate *qua* subjects in the labour process; rather it is the employer alone who 'cooperates' the labour-power of the producers (Marx 1930 [1867]:349; Ingold 1983b:135). Moreover what goes for the co-operation of individual natures estranged from the subjectivity of their bearers, where—in Marx's words—producers 'have already ceased to belong to themselves' (1930 [1867]:349), also goes for the co-operation of individuals presumed devoid of subjectivity in the first place. Relations between bees in the hive are material rather than social, in the same sense as are relations between detail workers on the factory floor, because they obtain in both cases between objects and not subjects, though the latter differ from the former in so far as the blueprint for co-operation is imposed by the capitalist rather than being the outcome of natural selection (or, as in 'traditional' human communities, of its cultural analogue), and therefore serves *his* interests and not those of the co-operating individuals (Marx 1930 [1867]:347). It follows that those patterns of human interaction comprised by the organization of work, the ways in which given natural and cultural capacities of individuals are co-operated to practical effect, have their counterpart in what biologists regard as the 'social organization' of insect communities. In terms of the distinction we have drawn here, both would be characterized as material. Evidently the contrast between the material and the social corresponds to that between the interactive and the constitutive, and to a whole series of derived contrasts: between individuality and personhood, objectivity and subjectivity, co-operation and consciousness, instrument and purpose.

Just as intersubjectivity, the locus of conscious intent, cannot be reduced to the instrumental association of objects, so from a knowledge of the material or 'work relations' (Cohen 1978:111–12) binding individuals it is impossible to deduce the form of the social relations constitutive of producers as persons, or indeed whether such relations exist at all (we presume they do not with bees). As a further illustration of this point, consider the organization of the hunting band. This is commonly conceived as a loose assemblage of individuals or families, free to come and go more or less as they please, whose organizational characteristics arise out of the practical exigencies of foraging under particular environmental conditions. Some kinds of foraging entail more or less extensive and complex cooperation, others do not; likewise the size and permanence of local bands will depend to a considerable degree on factors of environment and technology. In Steward's classic application of the method of cultural ecology to 'band societies', the various organizational forms are presented as resultant 'behaviour patterns' arising from the conjoint exploitative strategies of enculturated individuals (Steward 1955:40–1).[9] To equate such patterns with 'social organization' is clearly to adopt an interactive view of the social, for Steward's concern was essentially 'with the process of work, its organization, its cycles and rhythms and its situational modalities' (Murphy 1970:155; also 1977:22). Co-operative arrangements, just like knowledge, tools and the skills to apply them, form part of a purely instrumental, adaptive apparatus (Ingold 1979:278–9). Hence in Marxian terms, they pertain to the productive forces or material relations, as *opposed* to the social relations of production. In other words, relations constitutive of the band are not to be regarded as social at all, even though they exist between human beings, for as Cohen notes, 'not all relations between men are social' (1978:93). Meillassoux calls them 'relations of adhesion', noting that if band members are differentiated at all, the terms used are 'likely to refer to the demarcation of age, sex and functional categories connected with participation in productive activities' (1981:17).

To identify the character of *social* relations among hunters, we would have to attend to the perception of person and self *vis-à-vis* others in the community. What is most striking in this respect is that the person of the hunter absorbs, incorporates and merges with those around him to an extent unknown in societies where persons are confined to the occupancy of specific positions in a regulative order. Through the widespread sharing of food and other produce, hunters are directly and deeply involved with one another in the mutual production of their existence, quite irrespective of whether the conduct of their exploitative activity is solitary or co-operatively organized. Even should a man hunt alone, he confronts nature as a subject of social relations, and just as his life is produced through the activity of others, so the products of his activity are as much theirs as his. Thus every act of hunting is but a moment in a total process by which social life is carried on through men's collective encounter with nature (Ingold 1980b:79). Considered in isolation from this productive process, practices reduce to executions, and hunting—as we saw in Chapter 4—reduces to predation. It is as a predator that man 'confronts nature as one of her own forces', *interacting* with her other forces as an individual (Marx 1930 [1867]:169). Such interactions between predator and prey, or more generally between organisms and their environment, pertain exclusively to the domain of *ecological* relations. Hunting, however, is *social* action, directed *on* the physical world rather than going on *within* it (Ingold 1983a:10). As a hunter, man confronts nature *in person;* the confrontation is *dialectical* rather than interactive and pertains to the human history of nature rather than the natural history of man (on the latter distinction, see the penul-timate paragraph of Chapter 5). Hence the reduction of hunting to predation parallels that from the social to the material. It is nonsense to speak, with Habermas, of the 'co-operative hunt' as the 'first mode of production' (1979:135). For co-operative relations—linking objects—characterize a mode of predation, they are an aspect of the labour process; hunting is purposive activity, an aspect of the productive practice of socially constituted subjects. And the autonomy of the subject, manifested in the free association of the band, derives not from its total isolation or self-contained privacy, but from its total congruence with a generalized and unbounded collectivity. Each is not exclusive but inclusive of every other; the word for the person is mankind (Woodburn 1982:448; Ingold 1983a:17–18 n. 5).

The fact that hunting is a form of social action even though, considered in its material aspect as predation, it may be solitary rather than co-operative, raises a further point of contrast between constitutive and interactive relations. This has to do with Wilson's tenth 'quality of sociality': the fraction of time devoted to social behaviour. According to the interactive view, individuals are social when they act in consort but cease to be so when acting alone. Hence their time may be divided into social and non-social episodes, so that in principle the proportions of time devoted to each may be estimated. Adopting this idea, some observers of primate behaviour have attempted to measure the sociality of various species by the percentage of time devoted to 'social interaction', as opposed to solitary pursuits (Davis et al. 1968; Teleki 1981:310–11). Likewise Humphrey, for whom 'a social interaction is typically a transaction between social partners', remarks that animals that use up a lot of time in unproductive social activity 'must inevitably have less time to spare for basic subsistence activities', that is for solitary foraging (Humphrey 1976:309–11). But if we accept a constitutive view of social relations, such attempts to quantify sociality, or to confine social life to limited periods in a regular schedule of activity, are manifestly absurd. Whatever a person does as a socially constituted subject, including the procurement of subsistence, must qualify as social action, irrespective of whether it is conducted in isolation or in association with others (Ingold 1983a:7). A herdsman, for example, may spend weeks at a stretch alone with his flock in remote pastures. Yet he remains *someone,* and if we were to inquire into who he is, we might reasonably expect an answer couched in terms of a history of interpersonal relationships. And we should be able, once this history is filled out in sufficient depth, to discover from it the reasons why he is where he is, at that particular time, tending the animals of that particular owner. In short, the source of both his personal identity and his current purpose lies in the social domain.

This is the appropriate point at which to raise another issue touching on the comparison between the sociality of man and other animals. It has become commonplace, in biological descriptions of animal 'societies', to apply concepts derived from the realm of human experience (Sahlins 1976a:6–7). These include hierarchy and despotism, caste and class, worker, soldier and slave, queens (more often than kings), and in relation to physical space, ownership and tenure (for examples, see Wilson 1980:128, 137, 146–54). In more popular accounts, the beehive or termite colony appears as a veritable archaic state. Wondering whether such a term as slavery is as applicable to ants as to human beings, Bonner thinks that it is, for 'in both ant and human slavery individuals forcibly *capture* members of their own species or related species and *cause* their captives to *do work* for the benefit of the captors' (1980:11). But this statement is far from what Bonner thinks it to be, namely 'a simple description of conditions'. For the words used (which we have italicized) convey conscious intentionality on the part of both captors and captives, of a kind that ants are presumed to lack altogether. Human slavery is a relationship of domination between subjects, such that the will of one—the slave—is wholly appropriated by, and subservient to, the will of another—the master (Marx 1964b:102). When the slave works he does so as an agent of production, not as a mechanical instrument; and when the master causes his slave to work this is not as he might cause a machine to 'work' by operating the controls (for then he himself would be the producer) but by exerting his domination, through capture and coercion, over the *person* of the slave. The causation, in other words, is intersubjective. On the Cartesian assumption that non-human animals are mindless automata, beings without will, Marx relegated the domestic animals of man to the category of instruments of labour and hence denied that the man-animal relation in such instances is akin to slavery. Domestic animals, he wrote, 'may indeed render services, but their owner is not thereby lord and master' (1964b:102; see also 1930 [1867]:172). In the case of higher animals this is a difficult view to sustain, and I have argued elsewhere that the relation of taming, like that of slavery, is essentially social (Ingold 1980a:88). However, Marx's conclusion follows quite logically from the Cartesian premiss. And if the animal-machine cannot be regarded as the slave of a human master, then most emphatically, it cannot be enslaved by other animal-machines.

Yet this is precisely the sense in which sociobiologists claim that ants are the slaves of other ants. When the latter 'cause' the former to 'do work', the work done consists not in purposive action but merely in the exertion of mechanical force, and the causative relation exists between objects rather than between subjects. It is a relation, in Wilson's words, of 'impersonal intimacy' (1980:179), which might well be contrasted with the highly personal inimicality of human slavery. The colony of ants is envisaged as an immensely large and complex mechanical system, composed of relatively autonomous working parts (individuals), whose structure is genetically encoded in each individual and whose functioning is represented as 'social life'. To describe the hierarchy of control by which certain parts either govern or are governed by certain other parts, it would be better to draw on the language of the systems engineer, not the social historian. Or to return to our earlier discussion, the hierarchy is constituted by relations that are not social but material. Co-operative organization amongst human beings may have its counterpart in the insect world, but class relations do not. Consider the detail worker of capitalist manufacture, programmed to execute repeatedly but one operation and whose individual nature—as Marx says—is converted into 'the automatic specialised instrument of that operation'. An aggregate of such workers, with complementary specializations, constitutes what Marx calls 'the *living mechanism* of manufacture' (1930 [1867]:356; my emphases).[10] Likewise, the aggregate of ants constitutes the living mechanism of the colony. Within both such mechanisms, individual parts may be linked by control hierarchies. But the capitalist's domination over his work-force is of an entirely different kind, resting as it does on the former's appropriation of control over the mechanism itself and on his consequent ability to put it to use for his own purposes.

Once this fundamental distinction is made, separating material relations between parts of a productive apparatus from social relations between agents in respect of its control and use, what Wilson regards as the 'paradox' of social evolution simply dissolves. Comparing the colonial invertebrates, the social insects, the non-human mammals and man, he asserts that the progression from 'more primitive and older forms of life to more advanced and recent ones' is accompanied by a retrogression in the 'key properties of social existence', by which he means the scale, cohesiveness and complexity of interactive organization. Yet humans are unique in having reversed this 'downward trend' in social evolution, a fact that, for Wilson, represents 'the culminating mystery of all biology' (1980:179–82). The mystery can readily be explained as follows. At one end of the scale we are dealing with material relations between organisms that may reasonably be regarded as virtual automata (Midgley 1978:146–7). The 'downward trend' is associated with the evolution of consciousness (i.e. of a control system internal to the organism) by virtue of which individuals are progressively better able to make their own adjustments to external conditions. To recapitulate a point made in Chapter 1, the evolution of 'higher forms' involves an internalization of complexity that tends to be balanced by a measure of simplification in the field of the organisms' external relations. Only with the development of a conscious awareness of self, and hence of intersubjectivity, are the preconditions for a reversal of this trend established. Co-operation on a scale resembling or exceeding that of the lower animals depends on the emergence of relations of intersubjective dominance, such that agents are required to surrender their self-control to an alien will that imposes a design of its own on their activities. In short, the foundation for complex co-operation in human societies lies not in the absence of will but in its subordination to a dominant purpose—in the differentiation of *social power,* ultimately in class exploitation (Ingold 1983a:7–8). This is a mystery to sociobiology only because class relations, existing between persons in respect of things, cannot be comprehended within a reductionist paradigm in which only things are held to exist.

Our primary concern, in the preceding paragraphs, has been to distinguish constitutive from interactive relations and to map this distinction onto another between the social and the material. But it is equally important to contrast constitutive with *regulative* relations. I shall now attempt to show that this contrast corresponds to the essential distinction between the social and the cultural. We may as well begin again with the question of slavery. Comparing the forms of 'slavery' amongst ants and men, Kroeber concluded that despite the apparent resemblances, they rested on quite different foundations: 'The actual mechanism of ant slavery . . . would presumably be a directly organic, congenital, instinctual one, in distinction from the suprahereditary, devised and learning-transmitted human institutions' (1948:36). Yet were we to accept this view, human slavery would appear no less a 'mechanism' than that of the ant, though one that is culturally instituted rather than genetically encoded. 'Master' and 'slave' would be given as positions in a complete regulative order, contained in the minds of the several individuals making up a population and transmitted from generation to generation as a learned tradition. The population would then be conceived as a 'society', and social relations as interactions between its members (see Fig. 6.2). Now consider what Marx has to say:

> Society does not consist of individuals, but expresses the sum of interrelations, the relations within which these individuals stand. As if someone were to say: seen from the perspective of society, there are no slaves and no citizens: both are human beings. Rather, they are that outside society. To be a slave, to be a citizen, are social characteristics, relations between human beings A and B. Human being A, as such, is not a slave. He is a slave in and through society. (1973:265)

Marx is here opting once more for a constitutive view of the social. *A,* the slave, is constituted as such by his involvement with *B,* the citizen. *A* and *B,* moreover, are conceived as real historical subjects, so that the 'relations' of which Marx speaks exist not between institutionalized parts or statuses, to be filled by asocial individuals, but between *lives,* each of which participates in the movement of the other.

Confusion arises because the word 'slave', just like 'person', can be used in two quite separate senses. If the person is defined in jural terms, then slavery denotes the negation of a bundle of rights constitutive of citizenship. But if we take personhood as a category of the self, slavery denotes the negation of control over the self by another who is the master. The relation between citizen or master and slave is regulative in the first sense and constitutive in the second. The former pertains to culture, a suprabiological and learning-transmitted programme; the latter pertains to the actual process of social life. Throughout this work, we have argued that social life is not contained in the execution of a cultural programme, but that culture is a vehicle for the conduct of social life. Against Kroeber, we hold that a human being does not blindly submit to being a master, let alone to being a slave, in fulfilment of a set of imperatives bequeathed by cultural tradition—as the ants are impelled by their instincts. Life is not like a play in which you and I, cast by culture in the roles of master and slave, perform as dominator and dominated. It is rather a process in which subjects impinge directly on one another, through the *instrumentality* of culture. The rules and regulations of which culture consists, far from directing action as though mechanically, add up in reality to an *enabling* device (Salzman 1981:243), by means of which certain forms of action are made possible or facilitated. Thus the codification, in customary law, of the abilities and disabilities of 'masters' and 'slaves' provides a mechanism that may be used to effect by certain persons in imposing their will on certain other persons. That is to say, the regulative relation 'master–slave', a relation between *statuses,* is part of an objective instrument of intersubjective domination, or for the exercise of *power.* Another such instrument, technological rather than ideological, is furnished by the apparatus of physical coercion: Indeed neither can function effectively without the other.

If the system of regulative relations exists for this purpose of domination, the question arises as to whether there can be such a thing as an 'egalitarian society'. Dahrendorf thinks not and dismisses the claims of anthropologists to have discovered such societies as fantasies that belong 'only in the sphere of poetic imagination'. Society, Dahrendorf argues, '*means* that norms regulate human conduct. . . . Because there are norms and because sanctions are necessary to enforce conformity of human conduct, there has to be inequality of rank among men' (1968:172–6). In other words, some persons must be in a position to impose the sanctions and therefore to exercise power over those who are sanctioned. Hence 'for modern social science', as Levine and Levine put it, *'society is domination'* (1975:177). But now let us put the argument in reverse. Where persons do not dominate other persons, where there is no differentiation of power, conformity to norms of conduct cannot be enforced, so that society as Dahrendorf conceives it—a *compulsory* regulative order equivalent to 'the law in its broadest sense' (1968:167–9)—cannot exist. Is there, however, any necessary reason why such an order *should* exist? In those 'assertively egalitarian' societies identified by Woodburn (1982:431–2) amongst certain hunting and gathering peoples, an order of this kind, of regulative relations between fixed and binding status positions, is indeed conspicuous by its absence. Apparently devoid of structure, these would not qualify in Dahrendorf's terms as 'societies' at all (see Bloch 1977:288). And yet a group of hunters and gatherers is no mere aggregate of individuals. Assuredly they enjoy a social life, relating to one another directly, 'face-to-face', rather than indirectly as the incumbents of parts. Not only, therefore, is social life without domination theoretically conceivable, it is here demonstrably realized in practice. Our contention, moreover, is that the differentiation of power, which Dahrendorf holds to be a prerequisite for the existence of society, itself presupposes the establishment of social (intersubjective) relations. It follows that the egalitarian condition must be considered both ontologically and developmentally *prior* to the emergence of power differentials. And the latter, far from being 'called forth' to meet the demands of the regulative order, are rather served by its elaboration. The volume of 'social structure' grows with the intensity of domination, and the one—conferring legitimacy and stability—is accessory to the other (Bloch 1977:289). The correlate of entrenched oppression is structural hypertrophy.

Durkheim, as we observed earlier in this chapter, was also concerned with the elaboration of the regulative order, which he correlated positively with the power of the State. Let us now proceed to contrast our view of sociality with his. We have noted previously that what Durkheim called 'society' is an objective entity constituted by regulative relations and that as such it is virtually indistinguishable from 'culture', as originally conceived by Kroeber. We have found, moreover, that to ascribe to this entity a supraindividual mode of existence is simply to be deceived by the fallacy of misplaced concreteness; or rather to confuse the mode of existence of culture with its mode of transmission. I shall return to this confusion shortly, as it has an important bearing on the concept of socialization. Our conclusion at this point is that Durkheim's 'social facts' are really facts of culture and that as such, they have no other foundation than the separate minds of individuals. But conversely, what Durkheim held to be essentially individual, namely the consciousness of the particular subject, we have found to be constituted by social relations. In Chapter 4, we reached similar conclusions regarding the linguistics of Saussure. Where Saussure held the mode of existence of language to be social, we found it to be individual; where he held speaking to be the execution of the individual will, we found it to be social action *par excellence*. Saussure, of course, was strongly influenced by Durkheim, and both can be faulted on the same grounds: first, for an unwarranted essentialism that led to the positing of an ideal state—of language or culture—with an existence independent of, and antecedent to, its realization in particular individuals; and second, for an assumption that subjectivity is an attribute of the individual *in vacuo* rather than the social person, with the implication that action initiated by the subject cannot be social. It is the second of these assumptions that I wish to examine now.

Recall Durkheim's assertion that man is double. 'There are in him two classes or states of consciousness that differ from each other in origin and nature, and in the ends towards which they aim.' One class is intimately linked with individual organic life and is wholly encompassed within the framework of the bodily machine whose workings it expresses. The other class comes to man from an external source in society and has its reference in the collectivity rather than the particular person. States of consciousness in this class 'transfer society into us and connect us with something that surpasses us' (Durkheim 1960[1914]:337). From this dualism, there follows the corollary that direct contact between individual consciousnesses is impossible—they are, 'by nature, closed to each other'. Communication from one to another is possible only by way of the collective consciousness; to reach you both you and I must go outside ourselves, where we meet as fellow representatives of society. It is true that Durkheim elsewhere speaks of the interpenetration and fusion of individuals, yet his point is that the area of interpenetration—where consciousnesses overlap—at once ceases to belong to any of them, constituting rather a consciousness of a new kind (1982[1895]:129). Hence what remains of the consciousness of the particular subject is only the part that is exclusive to himself. His own sphere of awareness is essentially private. By this logic, the opposition between subjectivity and objectivity is mapped onto another between private and public. My conscious experience, it would appear, is strictly my own affair, it is not something in which you can participate. Your knowledge of my experience depends on an exercise of encoding and decoding: I have first to articulate it in the form of concepts that form part of a common repertoire; you have then to perform the same operation in reverse so that you can relive the experience in your own private world. As Durkheim puts it, 'It is only by expressing their feelings, by translating them into signs, by symbolizing them externally, that the individual consciousnesses . . . can feel that they are communicating and are in unison' (1960[1914]:336). Language and collective representations, being public, objective and social, act as a bridge between consciousnesses that are private, subjective and individual, holding them apart as much as furnishing a channel of intercourse.

We have reached conclusions precisely opposed to these. On the one hand, we hold that the objective forms of culture have their locus in discrete individuals and are private in the sense of being wholly contained as a property of each. On the other hand, we deny the possibility of a consciousness exclusive to the individual. There can be no consciousness of self outside the milieu of social relations. 'The world of my daily life', as Schutz wrote, 'is by no means my private world but is from the outset an intersubjective one, shared with my fellow men, experienced and interpreted by others; in brief, it is a world common to all of us' (1970:163). Indeed there could be no more pithy definition of the intersubjective view of the social that we adopt here than that offered by Schutz: 'Sociality is constituted by communicative acts in which the I turns to the others, apprehending them as persons who turn to him, and both know of this fact.' This differs radically from the Durkheimian, regulative view in that the relations are between persons as agents, not as parts; and equally clearly from the interactive view in that persons 'are given to one another not as objects but as counter-subjects, as consociates in a societal community of persons' (Schutz 1970:165). Now let us return for a moment to Saussure and to his distinction, introduced in Chapter 4, between language and speaking. It should be evident that this is homologous to the distinction between the regulative and the interactive. Treating social structure as an ordered arrangement of parts, we are, as Fortes famously remarked, 'in the realm of grammar and syntax, not of the spoken word' (1949:56). And the events that structure regulates are conceived as spontaneous and wilful executions by self-contained, private individuals precisely analogous to the Saussurian speech act. These are what Lévi-Strauss, and also Radcliffe-Brown in his Spencerian vein, designate as 'social relations', that is, elementary behavioural interactions. Our constitutive view of the social, then, corresponds exactly to that which the opposition between *langue* and *parole,* in Saussure's terms, *leaves out:* namely practical consciousness. In short, the three senses of the social that we have identified—regulative, constitutive and interactive—are equivalent to cultural form, conscious intentionality and behavioural execution respectively.

Once this correspondence is recognized, our present discussion can readily be connected with the elaboration in previous chapters of distinct kinds of evolution and history, of the dichotomy between individual and person, of real and abstract forms of time, and of the notions of freedom and creativity. Throughout, we have opposed the process of social life in which persons are constituted as intentional agents to the history of cultural forms that serve as vehicles for this process, and their behavioural manifestations. Ignoring the duration of consciousness as a creative movement, only the latter remains, so that the distinction between the cultural and the social—if drawn at all—can only be one between covert rules and overt interactions. This, for example, was how Kluckhohn saw it (1949:32). A similar logic underlies biologists' identification of 'social behaviour' amongst cultureless animals as the phenotypic expression of genetic structure. But to comprehend social relations as constitutive of persons, rather than as interactions between pre-constituted things, is to adopt a distinction between the social and the cultural of far more fundamental significance. The cultural attributes that make up the individuality of the particular human being, we hold, conduct the flow of consciousness just as the genetically constructed individuality of the particular organism conducts the flow of life. If consciousness is not recoverable from the dissection of the flow into a series of synchronic instants, so likewise, the social component of action is eliminated through the fragmentation of the flow of conduct and its reconstruction as an aggregate of behavioural executions. Culture, manifested in behaviour, *translates a social purpose into practical effectiveness* (Ingold 1983a:14). Where interactive behaviour is subservient to the reproduction of culture, the latter is in turn subservient to the social production of life.

Taking this view of culture and social life, we might ask what becomes of the concept of socialization. In its usual sense, this implies the *inscription* of a Durkheimian regulative order on the 'raw material' of humanity—immature individuals. It is the process by which an external entity, 'society', moulds those individuals into parts of itself, so that each has a part to play (Levine and Levine 1975:188). As such, socialization (the acquisition of parts) must be distinguished from social life (their enactment). Only when his socialization is more or less complete does the particular subject begin to partake of the life of society. Now as we have already shown, the idea that rules of conduct are derived from a supraindividual, 'social' source is based on a very simple confusion between their mode of transmission or reproduction and their mode of existence. This confusion is so common, and so pernicious in its effects, that it is worth our while to expose it by means of an example. According to Habermas, 'The intersubjectively shared knowledge that is passed on is part of the social system and not the property of isolated individuals; for they have become individuals only in the process of socialization' (1979:171). Let us call this knowledge culture. Habermas's point can then be rephrased as follows: Because individuals acquire culture by virtue of their association, the mode of existence of culture is social rather than individual. This reasoning is as shoddy as if a biologist were to argue that because the existence of the individual organism depends on the reproduction of the species, each acquires its nature from a common species essence that existed before it was conceived. No one denies that culture is transmitted by teaching and learning, by precept and example, and that this depends on the mutual involvement of individuals. Thus when Linton referred to culture as 'social heredity', or when Lowie called it 'social tradition', they were putting the emphasis 'on how culture is acquired rather than on what it consists of' (Kroeber 1948:253). They were not for one moment supposing that culture is social *in essence*. In the Boasian tradition that Lowie represents, culture is seen as a property of discrete individuals and society as an aggregate of interacting culture-bearers. Hence Lowie's corruption of the Tylorian definition of culture, consisting of 'what an individual acquires from his society' (1937:3), must be interpreted to signify what a unique individual acquires from other unique individuals of the same population in consequence of their interaction. The process of acquisition itself is conveyed much more accurately by the the term 'enculturation' than by the notion of socialization, with its inappropriate essentialist connotations.

Although enculturation has to do with the constitution of individuals as things, a case could be made for regarding as socialization the process by which persons are constituted as agents. But if we are to do this, as Giddens (1979:129) has shown, a number of common connotations of the term have to be dropped. First, 'we cannot speak of *the* process of socialisation', as though it were the same for everyone. For as each person follows a unique 'sociographical' trajectory, the process undergone will appear differently in every case. Second, 'socialisation does not just stop at some particular point in the life of the individual, when he or she becomes a mature member of society. . . . [It] should really be understood as referring to the whole life-cycle of the individual'. Quite simply, the constitution of persons is a process that is continuous and that cannot therefore be regarded as the working up of a raw material into a finished, 'moulded' product. Third, and most crucial of all, the person undergoing 'socialization' is by no means passive but throughout an active, creative agent. Giddens affirms what every parent knows: 'Children "create parents" as well as parents creating children.' From early infancy onwards, the child participates in the lives of those around him, just as the latter participate in the life of the child; they are all, in Schutz's words, 'growing older together' (1962:16–17). Or as Giddens puts it: *'The unfolding of childhood is not time elapsing just for the child:* it is time elapsing for its parental figures, and for all other members of society. . . . Socialisation is thus most appropriately regarded not as the "incorporation of the child into society", but as the *succession of the generations'* (1979:130). However, to understand socialization in this sense is to render it identical to the process of social life itself, rather than as something that must be completed *prior* to the person's involvement in the life of society. We conclude that the term is not only redundant but positively misleading, on account of its implication (common to all concepts of '-ization') of moving from an initial to a final state. It is best dropped altogether.

Gifting and altruism

In many ways, a paradigmatic instance of the social relationship is furnished by the exchange of gifts. To exemplify the distinctions we have drawn between regulative, interactive and constitutive relations, it is instructive to review some alternative anthropological interpretations of gift exchange, beginning, of course, with the classic essay by Mauss (1954[1925]). The paramount importance of this work is precisely that it directs our attention to the very heart of the question of the nature of sociality. For as Mauss himself observed, the giving and receiving of gifts (unlike the exchange of commodities in the market) is a 'total social phenomenon' in that it 'contains all the threads of which the social fabric is composed'—not only economic but also religious, political, legal, moral and aesthetic. Moreover in speaking of gifts we are not narrowly concerned with wealth in the form of useful goods and real property, but with 'courtesies, entertainments, ritual, military assistance, women, children, dances and feasts . . .'; indeed the list could be extended indefinitely (1954[1925]:1–3). The key problem in understanding gift exchange, which Mauss poses on the very first page of his essay, is this: *'What force is there in the thing given which compels the recipient to make a return?'* In tackling this problem, Mauss's point of departure appears at first glance to be resonant with that of his principal mentor, Durkheim. The return, superficially spontaneous, is in fact a matter of obligation whose basis lies in a non-contractual, instituted order. Continuing in a Durkheimian vein, we should have to say that the force that compels the return

emanates from the collectivity; it is the moral force of society to which the individual feels bound as the incumbent of a position within a regulative structure. Thus
the gift would signify a relation between positions, and every exchange of gifts, in
so far as it serves to reproduce and perpetuate that relation, could be regarded as a
moment in the life of society. Mauss seems to endorse this view when he asserts
that the gift form of exchange 'is nothing less than the division of labour itself', and
that the parties to the exchange are *moral persons* including 'clans, tribes and families', the latter defined as corporations aggregate each of which is a jurally defined
person represented by a plurality of individuals. It is a view, furthermore, that
underlies a second sense in which he uses the term 'total', namely to characterize
prestations not between individuals but between clans, or between the holders of
chiefly office (Mauss 1954[1925]:1, 3–4).[11]

For a more recent development of the Maussian concept of total prestation,
denoting a back-and-forth movement between structurally constituted groups,
we can turn to the economic substantivism of Polanyi and his followers (notably
Sahlins), where it reappears under the rubric of *reciprocity*. Setting out from a conception of society as a complete and perfectly coherent institutional order, Polanyi
holds that the economy consists of that aspect of the functioning of the social order
involving the flow of material means. If this order comprises a number of discrete
segments, such as clans or lineages, which are symmetrically disposed *vis-à-vis* one
another as equal and opposite, then reciprocity will figure as the dominant form
of integration of the economy, establishing an artificial interdependence between
otherwise autonomous segments, binding them in a network of alliance and thereby
creating an organic solidarity (Polanyi 1957:251–2). Hence reciprocity, like the
total prestation, expresses the relations between fixed components of a persistent
structure; the flow and counterflow of material means attests to the operation of the
structure. 'A material transaction', Sahlins writes, 'is usually a momentary episode
in a continuous social relation. The social relation exerts governance: the flow of
goods is constrained by, is part of, a status etiquette' (1972:185–6). This is clearly to
adopt the regulative sense of the social: Material flows are *governed by* social relations;
it is these relations that oblige the incumbents of the statuses they define to give,
receive and repay. If this obligation appears to reside in the things given, its source
lies not in the individual subjects who are but executors of the social programme,
but in that supraorganic and supraindividual agent, 'culture' alias 'society', directing
operations from above and subjecting the doings of its individual constituents to its
own purposes. It comes as no surprise, therefore, to find Sahlins resorting to a blatant superorganicism in his conception of the economy as *'a component of culture'* and
(echoing Polanyi) as 'the material life process of society' (1972:186 n. 1).

If we return to Mauss's text, however, we find that the burden of his argument
points in a direction quite contrary to its initial Durkheimian premisses. For it rests
on the recognition of reciprocal transactions as successive moments *not* in the life
of society but in the social life of persons. And this, as we have seen in previous
chapters, depends on an invocation of the idea of personhood as a *category of the
self* rather than as a part in a structure (usages that Mauss himself was to distinguish

in his essay of 1938, 'The notion of person' [in Mauss 1979 (1950)]). The argument concerns the inseparability of persons and things. Mauss repeatedly insists that in the context of gift exchange, the thing given is indissolubly linked to the person of the giver (1954[1925]:62). Therefore the bond created in the exchange 'is in fact a bond between persons, since the thing itself is a person or pertains to a person. Hence it follows that to give something is to give a part of oneself' (1954[1925]:10). And again, in giving respects and courtesies, 'a man gives himself, and he does so because he owes himself—himself and his possessions—to others' (1954:44–5). Were we to retain the notion that the donor and recipient of gifts is the moral person, the Durkheimian social being, this argument would be incomprehensible. For such a being, pertaining to the external and objective order of society, is no part of the self. Indeed there are indications in Mauss's analysis that the giving of gifts is a part of the process by which the boundaries of the moral person are *constructed,* and conversely that a failure to reciprocate can lead to their dissolution. A man, by withholding his self, risks losing his part—colloquially, he 'loses face'. In gift exchange, Mauss remarks, 'it is the veritable *persona* which is at stake, and it can be lost in the potlatch just as it can be lost in the game of gift-giving, in war, or through some error in ritual' (1954[1925]:38).

These observations point undeniably to one conclusion: The statuses constitutive of the regulative order, 'social structure', far from confining their incumbents in hermetic solitude, each in his private world, in fact serve as vehicles for their mutual involvement, and as such are subject to the effects of use and disuse. The exchange of gifts is not mere role-play, nor are the relations it establishes just between *dramatis personae.* If in a play, character A is instructed to offer a gift to character B, and if I play A and you play B, then I would give nothing of myself to you, for we would meet only outside ourselves, in our parts. Yet Mauss is saying quite unequivocally that you and I, alternately donor and recipient (agent and patient), become parts of *one another* and in that sense enter actively into each other's constitution. Hence the relationship between us is intersubjective, of a kind whose possibility is categorically denied within the Durkheimian theoretical framework. For that part of me that becomes a part of you, the zone of subjective interpenetration embodied in my gift, would by Durkheim's argument cease immediately to belong to either of us, becoming rather a part of an alien presence wedged between us—society. And hence the obligation attached to the gift would represent the 'hold' not of myself over yourself, but of society over both of us. Mauss's view is quite different. The 'spirit' of the gift, by virtue of which it is more than an inert object, derives not from a personified 'society' but from the person of the giver, corresponding to his intentionality. It is *he* who, as Mauss puts it, 'has a hold over the recipient', for the gift 'even when abandoned by the giver . . . still forms a part of him' (1954[1925]:9). Mauss is here demonstrating the practicability of *exchange without alienation,* which by definition distinguishes gifts from commodities. The commodity is a thing that 'changes hands', by becoming wholly detached from one person and subsequently attached to another, quite unrelated person. The exchange of commodities creates

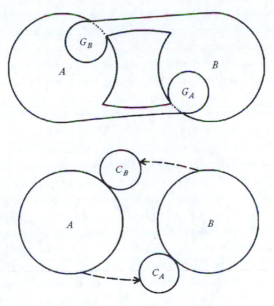

FIG. 6.3 Gift exchange and commodity exchange. *A* and *B* are persons. Through A's gift (G_A), A becomes a part of B; reciprocally through B's gift (G_B), B becomes a part of *A*. In commodity exchange, the object *CA* is entirely detached from *A* and externally attached to B, and vice versa for *CB*

a *quantitative* relation between objects, expressible as a 'price' of one in terms of the other. No such relation is established by the exchange of gifts; rather what is set up is a *qualitative relation between subjects* (Gregory 1983:104–7). The difference is indicated schematically in Fig. 6.3; as I shall show presently, it underlies a very important distinction in modes of communication.

Mauss's remarks on the personification of things can be generalized to cover the entire relation between social life and culture. The objective forms of culture—technological, institutional and ideational—are by themselves as passive as the things that may be given as gifts, if the latter are considered in isolation from the social context of exchange. Indeed it is from the repertoire of cultural forms that items for exchange are selected, for example a tool, a ceremony or a figure of speech. 'Cultural objects *per se*', as Bidney has pointed out, 'whether artifacts, socifacts, or mentifacts, are but inert, static matériel, or capital, for cultural [social] life and . . . of themselves exert no efficient creative power' (1953:137). Only persons can act as vital agents; one should not attribute efficient causality to symbolic forms. The speaker can use words to convey meaning, and the hunter can use spears to kill game, but words no more direct the utterances of the speaker than the spear directs a man to hunt. As I have stated elsewhere, 'Culture, *divorced from social purpose, is practically inert*. To be activated, it must bear the intent of the hunter of game or the speaker of language, and the source of intent (as opposed to referential significance) lies in the domain of the social' (Ingold 1983a:14). Likewise Mauss could write of the gift that 'the thing given is not inert', because it carries, and is vitalized by, the intent of the socially constituted subject (Mauss 1954[1925]:10). Thus do the things of culture convey the social life of persons.

To regard social life as the mere *revelation* of cultural structure, on the other hand, is to turn this proposition on its head, converting individual subjects into vehicles for the 'life' of culture. In just the same way, the power over persons imputed to things by virtue of what Marx called the 'fetishistic character' of commodities is the very obverse of the power Mauss attributes to gifts over their recipients, which is of persons over other persons through the *medium* of things. Like commodity fetishism, cultural determinism breathes an imaginary life into the alienated products of human hands and minds, artefacts and 'mentifacts' that return to haunt their makers as if the latter were beings possessed, mere vectors for the replication of a system of relations between things (Marx 1930[1867]:45–6).[12] The difference between this view, and one consonant with the Maussian position, may be illustrated by means of Fig. 6.4. The outer pentagon comprises social relations between persons (*P*) mediated by things—or symbols—that are items of culture (*C*). Together these items constitute a structure (middle pentagon) whose relations are mediated by individuals (*I*) *qua* culture-bearers. The material relations between these individuals form the inner pentagon. Disregarding the latter, culture appears as a vehicle for social life, that is for the establishment of intersubjectivity (as in the exchange of gifts). Disregarding the outer pentagon, social life—now conceived as a pattern of interactions—appears to be a vehicle for the reproduction of culture, establishing (as in the exchange of commodities) an interrelation of objects.[13] Indeed the difference between the relations *I–I, C–C* and *P–P* is precisely that between the interactive, the regulative and the constitutive, and the diagram describes a hierarchy of means and ends. Moreover, what goes for cultural also goes for natural things. Taking the inner two figures alone, we have the sociobiological view of interactive behaviour serving the reproduction of genetic structure; adding the outer figure, the latter itself appears as a mechanism subservient to the conduct of life.

We must now go on to consider the factor of time, which plays no part in the exchange of commodities but which—in the giving and receiving of gifts—is of the essence. One does not make immediate recompense but rather always allows a certain period to elapse, else the relationship with the original donor is deemed terminated. Besides, 'the period interposed', as Bourdieu observes, 'is quite the opposite of the inert gap of time', which, being incidental to the realization of a preformed project, could in theory be extended indefinitely or compressed into an instant (Bourdieu 1977:6). We have seen that relations of intersubjectivity, like the persons they constitute, have their existence only in the current of real time. As the material embodiment of a constitutive process the gift is likewise imbued with duration, carrying with it a history of relations among those through whose hands it has passed, and by bearing the intent of the giver, projecting these relations into the future. The spirit of the gift, its vital force or subjective load, corresponds exactly to this durational content. In that sense the gift is like a work

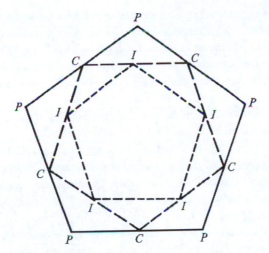

FIG. 6.4 Interactive (*I–I*), regulative (*C–C*) and constitutive (*P–P*) relations.

of art: As the latter enfolds the consciousness of the creative subject, so the former enfolds the movement of intersubjective life. The cultural object *acquires* a past through its engagement in social relations, in the same way as does the natural world—including the land and all that grows on it. Thus in the history of the gift we have the cultural counterpart of the human history of nature, a human history of culture as distinct from a culture-history of man. It follows that the time that separates the receipt of a gift and its handing on becomes consubstantial with the gift itself, and the greater the delay, the more the object is weighted with the condensed experience—that is with the person—of its temporary holder. Divorced from the flux of real time, 'detemporalized', the gift would revert to its original condition as an inert object, just as persons are reduced to things, and as nature loses its human past. This is why gift exchange has to be conceived as a *directed* process, rather than as a sequence of isolable events or executions strung out in a time that is extraneous, abstract and chronological. Like a line uttered in a conversation, a particular prestation picks up the flow of social life and conveys it forward, and its meaning can be understood only in the context of a history of previous exchanges of which it is but a singular moment.

In his critical commentary on Mauss's text, Lévi-Strauss comes to conclusions precisely opposed to ours. Mauss, it will be recalled, sought to discover a force that would connect the giving and receipt of a gift to its subsequent repayment: that force, the spirit of the gift, is identified with the consciousness of the original donor. Lévi-Strauss considers that in according such primacy to consciousness, Mauss was simply deceived by indigenous theory, by the secondary elaborations people weave around their lives in order to rationalize their conduct. In reality, he holds, what Mauss identified as separable components of the exchange—the obligations to give, receive and repay—are all underwritten by a single synchronic structure, or mechanical model, existing simultaneously in the unconscious minds of every one of the several individuals making up a society. Only in the revelation of this structure, in the course of social life, does it appear dissolved into its elements. 'It is the exchange that constitutes the fundamental phenomenon, and not the discrete operations into which it is decomposed by social life' (Lévi-Strauss 1950:xxxviii). Mauss, starting from a unity already thus fragmented, had to invoke a 'spirit' or 'force' to recompose the whole. Once the underlying structure is recognized, Lévi-Strauss maintains, we can dispense with such subjective notions, for the apparently antithetical principles of giving and receiving are so in experience only; at base they are but two aspects of the same thing and may even be denoted by the same linguistic term (1950:xl). A person repaying a gift is not moved (as he himself may claim to be) by the spirit of the gift previously received, but by the 'unconscious necessity' of structure.

In eliminating the agency of consciousness, Lévi-Strauss reduces prestations to elementary executions, devoid of intent, precisely analogous to Saussurian *parole*. The exchange structure itself figures as a primary code (analogous, again, to Saussure's *langue*), manifested in a series of discrete emissions that succeed one another in no particular order. Each emission involves a communicative interaction between the sender and recipient of the encoded signal, and for Lévi-Strauss this interaction is a social relation. In the image of Fig. 6.4, Lévi-Strauss discards the outer pentagon and concerns himself only with the inner two, *C–C* and *I–I*, which in his terms correspond to social structure and social relations respectively. In fact, he deals with regulative and interactive relations on three distinct levels, having to do respectively with kinship, the economy and language. Thus 'the rules of kinship and marriage serve to insure the circulation of women between groups, just as economic rules serve to insure the circulation of goods and services, and linguistic rules the circulation of messages' (Lévi-Strauss 1968:83). Consistent with this approach, women and messages are treated, like goods and services, as *commodities,* that is as objects detached from the persons amongst whom they circulate. This is linked, as we shall see, to a particular understanding of the nature of communication. But it is also linked to a *denial of temporality* in exchange, and this is our immediate concern. The lapse of time is significant, as it is in the marketplace, only in so far as it increases the number of opportunities for exchanges to occur. However, these exchanges, regarded as the output of a single mechanical structure, are not compounded statistically but are arranged synchronically in an extended present.

The effect of this procedure is to extract what for Mauss is the very essence of the gift as a 'total social phenomenon', namely its irreversibility, evident in that one could not run a series of prestations in reverse without destroying their meaning (just as a conversation would become meaningless if the order of lines were reversed or randomized). As Giddens points out, 'The removal of the temporal components of the gift, in Lévi-Strauss's analysis, represses the fact that, for the gift exchange to occur, the counter-gift must be given at a later time, and must be different from the initial gift' (1979:25–6; see Bourdieu 1977:4–5). A totalizing apprehension of the structure of exchange thus leads Lévi-Strauss, perhaps

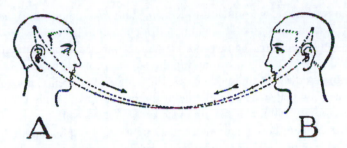

FIG. 6.5 Saussure's diagram of a conversation. Reproduced from Saussure (1959:11).

paradoxically, to *atomize* the process of social life. Far from taking to its logical conclusion Mauss's recommendation that we should be concerned 'with "wholes", with systems in their entirety', Lévi-Strauss moves in quite the opposite direction. For Mauss, apprehending the whole meant focusing on a concrete, lived reality that is all movement, flux and process, not on abstract structures. 'In society', he wrote, 'there are not merely ideas and rules, but also men and groups and their behaviours. We see them in motion as an engineer sees masses and systems, or as we observe octopuses and anemones in the sea' (1954[1925]:78). What more potent image of flux could one choose than the writhing octopus! Mauss evidently shares with Radcliffe-Brown a basically Heraclitean view of social life as an irreversible, statistical process; to treat the gift in the context of the whole is '*to catch the fleeting moment* when the society and its members take emotional stock of themselves and their situation as regards others' (1954[1925]:77–8; my emphasis). That moment, pregnant with the past, will never recur.

I referred earlier to a distinction in modes of communication, parallel to that between gift and commodity exchange, and this is a matter to which we must now return. In one mode, speaker and listener are private, individual subjects, 'closed to each other' as Durkheim put it (1960[1914]:336). They communicate by means of messages, each of which has first to be detached from one party in order to be attached to the other; thus the message belongs to the world of objective things or created goods, separate from one another and from their makers. It is, in other words, like a commodity, and the sender and recipient are like seller and buyer respectively (compare Fig. 6.3). As with commodities, the exchange establishes a relation not directly between subjects, but between the objects transacted, in this case between the symbolic representations in terms of which the experience of the subjects is outwardly expressed. This was the view of communication presented by Saussure in a celebrated diagram (Fig. 6.5).

The conversing subjects here are individuals A and B, and the diagram purports to represent a simple exchange of words between them. The exchange comprises two separate acts: In the first A speaks and B listens; in the second it is the other way round. Notice that this is to understand speaking and listening in a special, transitive sense; they are 'doings of the person' analogous to making and observing. Thus in the first act, A executes an utterance, which is immediately severed from A himself, as it is from all his preceding and succeeding utterances. B, the observer, hears it. The process of audition that goes on in B's head when he listens is, according to Saussure, the precise reverse of the process of phonation that is A's speaking (Saussure 1959:12). Moreover the attention of the listener as observer, just like the intellect of the speaker himself, is always directed rearward, capable of grasping only that which, in the life of the speaker, has already fallen into the past (Bergson 1911:49). For the complete utterance available for monitoring by the listener contains nothing more than the intention corresponding to the state of consciousness of the speaker at the moment when the utterance was initiated, and leaves out the increment by which his consciousness has advanced in the very act of execution. The listener is therefore, of necessity, one step behind the speaker. As Fabian points out, models of communication based on distinctions between sender, message and receiver 'project, between sender and receiver, a temporal distance (or slope). Otherwise communication could not be conceptualized as the *transfer* of information' (1983:31).

There is, however, another kind of listening, familiar to anyone who has played chamber music—but equally (if less obviously) characteristic of everyday life—that corresponds not to observation but rather to silent participation. To listen in this way, as Schutz has argued, is to join immediately in the speaker's stream of consciousness (1970:166). Thus when I listen to the speech of a conso-ciate, I am not so much decoding a message as entering into the very process of its production. I am, so to say, 'with him' in his project and understand because, hav-ing linked my train of thought to his (though remaining mute), I have made his purposes my own. This is to envisage a relation between speaker and listener that exists, in Bourdieu's phrase, 'on the hither side of words and concepts' (1977:2), one of direct intersubjective involvement. In this relation the listener does not fall behind the speaker but is right up with him in what Schutz calls his 'vivid present'; together they describe a common trajectory and share a communion of inner time. Both listening and speaking have now to be understood intransitively, as aspects of a conversation considered not as a changeful sequence of discrete executions but as a continuous process of life, *essentially relating the participants rather than the things they say*. Moreover, we can no longer regard listening as the reverse of speaking: Both are oriented in the same direction by the movement of consciousness. To convert listening into speaking requires only that this move-ment be harnessed to the phonic apparatus, just as when the violinist, after a few bars' rest, reapplies the bow. In the conversation between A and B, each carries on alternately from where the other left off, to yield an endless flow of conduct. This Schutzian view of the conversation is compared with the Saussurian view in Fig. 6.6, and the comparison clearly relates to our contrast between 'vertical' and 'horizontal' readings of Fig. 5.3.

The mode of communication to which we have been referring is precisely what Malinowski (1923:315) called *phatic communion*: 'a type of speech in which ties of union are created by a mere exchange of words'. Malinowski deliber-ately draws on the imagery of gift exchange to describe this phenomenon, for

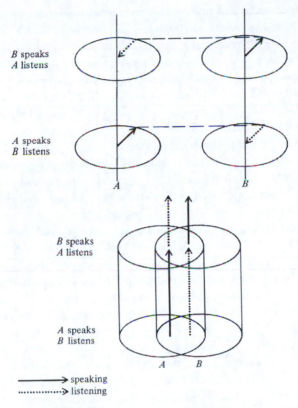

B speaks
A listens

A speaks
B listens

A   *B*

B speaks
A listens

A speaks
B listens

A   *B*

———→ speaking
·············▸ listening

FIG. 6.6 Saussurian (*above*) and Schutzian (*below*) views of the conversation compared.

the two are indeed alike. As gifts break tension so words break the awkward silence that precedes the opening of a new relationship; not to listen is, like the refusal of a gift, a declaration of hostility. As the donor has a hold on the recipient, so the speaker 'holds' his listeners until they have their turn to reciprocate. What counts above all in the exchange is not the ideas or thoughts the words express, but the relation set up between the parties. That is to say, the value of the words lies not in their referential significance, which may be trivial, but in their embodiment of the speaker's intent. In exchanging apparently meaningless verbal courtesies (which Mauss included in his list of possible gift items), people participate in each other's lives. Writing of his beloved Trobriand Islanders, Malinowski famously remarked that '*the whole of tribal life is permeated by a constant give and take;* . . . *every ceremony, every legal and customary act is done to the accompaniment of material gift and counter-gift*' (1922:167). It is no accident, then, that he writes in like vein of 'the give and take of utterances which make up ordinary gossip' (1923:315). The speaking that, for Malinowski, is the stuff of everyday life (amongst ourselves as much as amongst Trobrianders) is essentially directed by practical consciousness, it is 'an indispensable element of concerted human action'. It is *not*, primarily, a medium for the replication of a system of ideas or for the communication of information; indeed in phatic communion, 'there need not or perhaps there must not be anything to communicate' (1923:316).

It is worth emphasizing the implied distinction between *communion* and *communication,* as it is particularly apt to describe the contrast we have been drawing here. Rather than speaking, as we have up to now, of two modes of communication, it may be advisable to reserve the latter term specifically for interactions involving the exchange of 'bits' of information, encoded in signals, between individuals who confront each other as entirely separate entities (Cherry 1957:8–9). This is precisely the sense in which it is used by sociobiologists such as Wilson (1980:7, 14) who consider reciprocal communication to be the essential criterion of sociality in both non-human animals and human beings. Bastian has gone so far as to claim a basic identity between interactive behaviour (the 'partial, and usually reciprocal, determination of an individual animal's actions by one or more other animals' actions') and social communication (1968:576). The identification of the communicative with the interactive is clearly apparent in another biologist's definition of society as 'an aggregation of socially intercommunicating, con-specific individuals that is bounded by frontiers of far less frequent communication' (Altmann 1965:519). This view is exactly replicated by Lévi-Strauss, who regards society as an entity that 'consists of individuals and groups which communicate with one another' much more than with those across its borders (1968:296).

Although communication, in this sense, clearly has adaptive consequences for the communicators, it does not imply any intentionality on their part. Thus Burghardt is fatally confused in singling out *intent* as the fundamental property of all communication, including that of lower organisms, when he means to refer only to its end-directedness (1970:12). This error, so pervasive in the literature on animal behaviour, leads him into the absurd position of having to distinguish what *he* takes to be intentional (whatever is of adaptive significance) from what *we* take to be intentional (action directed by consciousness). Langer goes to the other extreme. Defining communication as 'the intentional transmission of ideas from one individual to one or more others', she comes to the extraordinary and quite unnecessary conclusion that non-human animals do not communicate at all, thus writing off at a stroke one of the most interesting and productive fields of ethological inquiry (Langer 1972:202). What she means is that animals do not *converse,* in the sense of engaging their ideas in discourse. So what is the nature of the bond between them? Significantly enough, Langer calls it *communion,* a kind of empathy or unity of feeling, unmediated by signs or symbols, 'having no propositional contents', and in human beings 'progressively weakened by the growing tendency to individuation' that goes with the development of the intellect (1972:202, 312–13).

We would not go along with Langer in attributing empathy and communion even to the 'social life' of ants and bees (1972:204–6). Because of her refusal to countenance the possibility of animal communication, she has no alternative but to extend the notion of communion to cover relations established between objective individuals through external, physical contact. This results in considerable obscurity. To us, communion suggests the interpenetration or merging of conscious *subjects,* as opposed to their individuation, which we take to be a precondition for communicative interaction. Thus ants and bees communicate, though they do not do so intentionally, let alone converse. Human beings converse, because they can articulate their ideas by means of language, but the intentional component of communication is derived from their intersubjective communion and is not a property of communication *per se*. In short, communion stands to communication as conscious intentionality stands to behavioural execution, and hence as constitutive relations stand to interactive relations. Where persons are joined in communion, they are separated as individuals in communication. To anthropologists, the distinction will be familiar from the many discussions of sacrifice, where it has often been shown that aspects of both communion and communication may be present simultaneously, expressing respectively the conjunction and disjunction of man and God (Beattie 1980:38–40). If the sacrifice is conceived as a gift, then human beings and God are united in the thing given; if it is conceived as a contract, they are separated by it. Hence again, communion and communication are opposed as gift and contract.

To end our review of the foundations of sociality, I should like to consider the significance of a concept that remains a keyword in many contemporary discussions of the subject, namely *altruism*. The word was coined by Auguste Comte, who held it to be a principle of moral conduct based on regard for others and hence the opposite of egotism (Hawthorn 1976:78). The paired notions of altruism and egotism figured prominently in the writings of both Spencer, notably in *The data of ethics* (1907[1879]), and Durkheim, first in *The division of labour in society* (1933[1893]) and subsequently in *Suicide* (1952[1897]), in which 'altruistic' and 'egotistic' came to denote two of the basic types of self-destruction. My aim now is to show that Spencer and Durkheim understood altruism in fundamentally distinct senses, that this distinction is based on the opposition between society as an aggregate of interactions and as a supraindividual regulative order, and that it continues to be a source of much misunderstanding in the confrontation of biological and anthropological arguments concerning the conditions of social life. Ultimately, we shall argue, both senses of altruism are predicated on a certain notion of the subject, or *ego,* as a discrete individual. It is only because we view our everyday life through an atomizing ideological glass that presupposes the isolation of the subject that the common experience of intersubjectivity is rendered, in distorted form, as the ascendance of altruism over egotism. For that reason, no theory purporting to explain the prevalence of altruism in human behaviour can suffice to account for the evolution of social life as we understand it. And this, we hold, seriously weakens the claims of contemporary sociobiology to have provided such an account.

According to Spencer, action is altruistic if it benefits others instead of the self. 'Whatever action, unconscious or conscious, involves expenditure of individual life to the end of increasing life in other individuals, is unquestionably altruistic' (1907[1879]:173). Three important points need to be made about this definition.

First, altruism is seen to characterize transactions *between individuals* in which one party is prepared to accept a negative balance of cost and benefit. It does not, therefore, express the subordination of the interests of the parts (individuals) to that of the whole (society), for in Spencer's conception of the social superorganism there is no purpose in society over and above those of its several constituents. Second, altruistic behaviour need not, in Spencer's definition, be consciously motivated. It may indeed be purely instinctive. This qualification enabled him to extend his discussion of altruism right across the animal kingdom, seeing in human beings only its most elevated and evolved form. Third, and as a corollary of the preceding, the concept of altruism must attach to the physical consequences of behaviour for affected individuals, and not to the subjective intention that informed it. For were altruism held to be a property of conscious intentionality rather than behavioural execution, it could hardly be ascribed to animals (such as the lowly insects) whose behaviour is presumed to be entirely undirected by consciousness. With regard to human beings, whose conduct *is* intentional, Spencer took it as axiomatic that every individual is engaged in the rational pursuit of personal happiness or satisfaction. In the absence of any supraindividual purpose, it would follow that all action voluntarily initiated must be egotistic *in intent*. Granted that the individual derives an immediate sensual gratification from the fulfilment of desires constitutive of his nature, and that this nature includes an evolved predisposition to dispense benefits to specific others (offspring, kin, and possibly unrelated individuals), then intentionally egotistic action would be altruistic in its effects. A perverted world full of intentionally altruistic individuals, forgoing all opportunities to derive pleasure from giving by remaining obstinately on the receiving end of benefits, that is by *behaving* in a thoroughly egotistic manner, would—Spencer imagined—be a miserable place indeed.

As a paradigmatic instance of altruism, Spencer dwelt at length, and in surprisingly modern terms, on the phenomenon of parental care, positing an essential continuity 'through infinitesimal gradations' from the automatic sacrifices on behalf of its progeny made by the lower organism that has not the slightest knowledge of what it is doing, to the love consciously extended by human parents towards their children (1907[1879]:174). He noted that altruistic traits that enhance the prospects for survival and reproduction amongst offspring will, being inherited by those offspring, tend to become established and spread in the course of evolution, whereas 'such defect of altruistic acts as causes death of offspring or inadequate development of them, involves disappearance from future generations of the nature that is not altruistic enough' (1907[1879]:175). In other words, traits expressed in a diminution of the level of parental care will tend to be eliminated by natural selection, as fewer progeny will survive to reproduce. And so the 'average egoism' of a population, as Spencer called it, will decrease, though not of course to the extent that reproduction itself is impaired. He goes on to suggest, moreover, that as there is a continuum from unconscious to conscious expressions of parental altruism, so also a direct connection exists between altruism in its parental, 'familial' and 'social' forms (1907[1879]:176). The altruism displayed in an insect colony is familial, since it is a function of the biological kinship of the constituent individuals. True social altruism is found only where there exists 'a union among like individuals substantially independent of one another in parentage', most notably in human societies (Spencer 1876, I:6). Though Spencer wrote, of course, in ignorance of modern genetics, it would not be too much to claim that he had already identified the major kinds of altruism—'nepotistic' and 'reciprocal' (discussed later)—almost a century in advance of their formalization as central components of contemporary sociobiological theory.

Turning from Spencer to Durkheim, we find the terms 'egotism' and 'altruism' being employed to characterize not the interactions between individuals as members of a social aggregate, but the condition of the relationship between the individual and society, the latter conceived as a higher-level, inclusive entity. 'Conduct is egotistical', Durkheim wrote in *The division of labour*, 'in the measure that it is determined by sentiments and representations which are exclusively personal'—in other words, to the extent that it issues from the individual rather than the social component of man's being. Conversely, conduct is altruistic in so far as it is an execution of the will of society. Pure egotism and pure altruism are both hypothetical limiting cases, never realized in practice, for the individual subject can no more exist entirely outside society than can society exist without a substratum of individuals. 'Wherever there are societies, there is altruism'; likewise wherever there are individuals there is egotism. Just as a man is both an individual and a social being, so egotism and altruism are always found combined, 'the one relating to the individual alone and the other relating to the things which are not personal to him' (Durkheim 1933[1893]:197–8). But the balance between them can tip too far in either direction, and in *Suicide* Durkheim argued that both egotism and altruism, if taken to excess, can trigger a response of self-destruction. Rampant egotists, insufficiently incorporated into society, abandon life because—short of the unattainable infinite—it is for them without purpose; they feel there is nothing to live and to suffer *for*. 'If life is not worth the trouble of being lived, everything becomes a pretext to rid ourselves of it' (1952[1897]:213). Altruists, to the contrary, are as passionately committed to the goals of their society as egotists are apathetic; it is the social being that dominates within them. But carried too far they are apt to lose their sense of self entirely, ultimately laying down their lives for the sake of the life of the group. Egotism, then, is the state 'in which the individual ego asserts itself to excess in the face of the social ego and at its expense'; altruism 'expresses the opposite state, where the ego is not its own property, where it is blended with something not itself, where the goal of conduct is exterior to itself, that is, in one of the groups in which it participates' (Durkheim 1952[1897]:209, 221). Returning to the opposition in *Moral education*, Durkheim observed that what differentiates altruism and egotism is the direction followed by the activity in the two cases. 'When it is egotistical, it does not go beyond the acting subject; it is centripetal. When it is altruistic, it overflows from its subject. The centers around which it gravitates are outside of him; it is centrifugal' (1961 [1925]:214).

Recall that as a supraindividual and supraorganic emergent, society was for Durkheim uniquely human. Therefore, altruism, the surrender of self to society, must equally be a phenomenon unique to mankind. Behaviour grounded in instinct, since it issues from the organic individual, can in Durkheim's terms be regarded only as egotistic (see also Langer 1972:124). The same would apply to all intentional action whose goal is the pleasurable satisfaction of innate or naturally given desires, including a great deal that Spencer would have classed as altruistic. If it is in the nature of a man, for example, to lavish affection on his child, then his love would remain egotistic however much the child materially benefits. But to the extent that the father cares for his child *because society expects him to do so,* it being part of his jural responsibility as the incumbent of the social position of *pater,* he would be acting altruistically. Even punishment, meted out in painful fulfilment of moral obligation, would be an altruistic act, and the overzealous father, taking altruism to excess, loses all trace of affect. The balance between the affective (or domestic) and moral (or jural) aspects of parental care, a recurrent theme of social anthropological analysis, corresponds to the Durkheimian balance between egotism and altruism. And this brings us to the crux of the difference between Spencer's and Durkheim's conceptions of altruistic action. For according to Durkheim such action, far from being voluntary and spontaneous, is essentially carried out under obligation, or *performed as a duty.* This would include even altruistic suicide, which is typically obligatory (Durkheim 1952[1897]:221). Altruism is not the *expression* of dispositions inhering in the nature of individuals but the *suppression* of these dispositions by a higher purpose. So when I offer you a gift, my action is altruistic, not because I have willingly relinquished some good on your behalf, but because I have suffered myself to be ruled by a moral code that obliges me, as the incumbent of a certain position, to make the requisite prestation. That code is society, for as Durkheim elsewhere declared, 'the domain of the moral begins where the domain of the social begins' (1961[1925]:60). In short, altruism attests to the regulation of the individual by society, or the subordination of the psychological to the social, and is conditional on the governance of conduct by rules emanating from an external, supraindividual source.

The notion of altruistic behaviour was introduced into biology by Haldane (1932; see Barnett 1983:41) to denote interactions involving a net transfer of benefit from one individual to another, genetically different, with positive consequences for the reproduction of the latter. Such interactions are generally considered by students of animal behaviour to constitute the foundation for living in groups, that is for sociality as envisaged in most biological definitions of the term. For those who would attempt to account for social behaviour as the outcome of a process of variation under natural selection, this has posed a fundamental problem. How could a mechanism that, in theory, favours the establishment only of traits that would enhance the relative reproductive success of individuals, in practice promote genetically based predispositions that cause individuals to forgo their immediate reproductive advantage for the sake of conspecific, genetic competitors (Williams 1966:194)? It is widely believed that the biological explanation of society hangs on the solution to this problem. Many since Darwin have sought an answer in the notion of group selection, whose principal advocate in recent years has been Wynne-Edwards (1963). If selection operates concurrently not only on individuals but also on self-perpetuating local populations, then altruistic traits injurious to the individual may nevertheless be preserved if they enhance the continuity of the population of which the individual forms a part. Continuity is secured through the maintenance of numbers around an optimum determined by the sustainable yield of the environment, and the function of altruism would be to restrict the fertility of individuals so that the optimum is not exceeded (or, if it has been temporarily exceeded, to bring numbers down). The argument goes that if we have two populations of the same species, one of individuals relatively well adapted in terms of reproductive fitness and another of individuals amongst whom are strongly represented certain traits causing them to forgo opportunities for reproduction (and whose fitness is concomitantly lower), the latter is better adapted *as a population* than the population of better-adapted individuals (see Williams 1966:108). Whereas the one is liable to collapse through uncontrolled numerical expansion and resultant overexploitation of its resource base, the other will go through to the next round, as it were, of the selection process.

This is not the place for a detailed critique of the theory of group selection. We need only note one crippling defect shared by all versions of the theory, which is that they fail to account for how an altruistic genetic variant, which originally must have made its appearance in a single individual, can possibly have spread within the population in the first place, to reach such a frequency as to give the population as a whole a selective advantage over other populations in which the variant is not represented (Williams 1966:113). The contemporary sociobiological interpretation of altruism rests on a far more austere application of Darwinian principles, in which everything hinges on the reproductive success not of individuals but of the particular genes they carry. The technicalities of the arguments, presented principally by Hamilton (1964) and Trivers (1971), need not concern us here; they have already given rise to a vast body of literature that it is beyond our competence to review. All of them invoke the notion that altruism is part of a phenotypic behavioural mechanism selected for its efficiency as a vehicle for the replication of basically 'egotistic' genes (Dawkins 1976:4–7). Or as Alexander puts it, 'Such altruism . . . may be described as phenotypically (or self-) sacrificing but genotypically selfish' (1979:46).

What Hamilton presented was a theory of 'kin selection' (Maynard Smith 1964) based on the concept of inclusive fitness. This is obtained for a particular individual by adding to his fitness expressed in production of adult offspring (disregarding the effects on this production of the harmful or beneficial actions of his neighbours) 'certain fractions of the quantities of harm and benefit which the individual himself causes to the fitness of his neighbours' (Hamilton 1964:8). These fractions express expectations of the proportions of the individual's genes that also will be carried by each of the neighbours he affects, and depend on the closeness of their genealogical relationship: one half for full siblings, one quarter for half-siblings, one eighth for full first cousins, one sixteenth for half first cousins, and so on. If, by an altruistic transfer of benefit to his kin, the loss of fitness to the individual can be compensated by an equivalent gain in the fitness of at least two full siblings, four half-siblings, or eight first cousins (or correspondingly greater multiples of more distant relatives), then his contribution to the representation of his genes in future generations will be greater than it would be were no such transfer effected. That is to say, his inclusive fitness will be enhanced, and traits conferring a tendency towards altruism will be preserved in the course of natural selection, at the expense of those prescribing more egotistic behaviour.

Where Hamilton's theory applies only to altruism between kin, or 'nepotism', Trivers has devised a model of reciprocal altruism that purports to account for the evolution of behaviour by which an individual contributes at its own expense to the fitness of another so distantly related, in genealogical terms, that kin selection can be ruled out. The argument is simply that if the cost to the altruist is less than the benefit to the recipient, and if at a future date the situations of benefactor and beneficiary are liable to be reversed, reciprocal altruism pays off for both, providing each with an additional increment of fitness (Trivers 1971:36). Again, it is supposed that natural selection will preserve traits that direct behaviour in the appropriate manner, since the bearers of these traits will make relatively greater contributions to the gene pool of subsequent generations. But this argument, compared with Hamilton's, is markedly less convincing and has been trenchantly criticized by Sahlins (amongst others). The objection is that reciprocal altruism secures an equal benefit to all involved, so that it confers no *differential* advantage on the altruistic individual as against unrelated genetic competitors. It is true that reciprocators, *as a group,* may have a reproductive edge over non-reciprocators; but the lone reciprocator in a population of unrelated individuals that do not share the altruistic trait would initially be at a marked disadvantage. Consequently the theory suffers from precisely the same defect as that of group selection: It fails to explain how an altruistic variant can have become sufficiently widely established to be positively selected. Indeed, as Sahlins notes, Trivers's model *is* one of group selection, 'or as it might better be called, "social selection"' (1976a:87).

Without going further into these objections at this stage (see Alexander 1979:52–3), I should like to emphasize the striking resemblance between the sociobiological treatment of altruism and Spencer's discussion of the same theme. In both cases, altruism is defined as an imbalanced transfer of utility from one individual to another, reducing the fitness (or what Spencer called the 'life') of the former to the end of increasing the fitness of the latter (compare Trivers 1971:35; Wilson 1980:55). In both cases, too, altruism is seen to be programmed into the nature of individuals and emerges as the spontaneous expression of that nature. 'The deep structure of altruistic behaviour', as Wilson puts it, 'is rigid and universal' (1978:162–3). By no means unique to human beings, such behaviour is found in an enormous range of species, from the 'lowest' to the 'highest'. Again for the sociobiologists as for Spencer, the conscious motivations that may accompany an action are quite irrelevant to its characterization as either egotistic or altruistic. It is no less altruistic for being instinctive, for what counts is not the intentional component of the act but its consequences in terms of reproductive success (Barash 1977:77; Clark 1982:56). So long as individuals are conceived to be following the dictates of their natures, every action must be assumed to be egotistic in *intent,* that is in so far as it has any intentional content at all. Most remarkable, perhaps, was Spencer's anticipation of the distinction between nepo-tistic and reciprocal altruism, the former (familial) directed towards biological kin, the latter (social) directed towards genealogically unrelated individuals. As we have seen, Spencer was well aware of the connection between nepotism and parental care, and of the argument that altruistic behaviour on behalf of those who share a part of one's own heritable nature, by contributing to the represen-tation of that nature in future generations, will *ipso facto* establish the nature that is altruistic. Wilson calls this kind of altruism, oriented to close relatives, 'hard-core', as opposed to the 'soft-core' altruism that does not depend on genetic kinship (but which does imply the expectation of a future return), noting—just as Spencer did—that it is above all in human societies where soft-core altruism is carried to the most elaborate extremes (Wilson 1978:155–9).

It comes as no surprise, then, to find anthropologists steeped in a sociocul-tural superorganicism reacting to sociobiology very much as Durkheim reacted to Spencer's sociology. Nowhere is the opposition more vividly expressed than in the last work of the greatest exponent of the Durkheimian tradition in British social anthropology, Meyer Fortes. 'Human acts of altruism', he writes, 'are cultur-ally defined, rule-governed, intentionally exercised, perceived as moral obligations without expectations of reward or reproductive benefit, and this is what distin-guishes them critically from the presumably automatic, genetically determined acts of altruism reported for nonhuman primates and other species' (1983:29). Let us consider each of Fortes's points in turn. First, altruistic acts pertain to the execution of a cultural rather than a genetic programme. This point could be accepted without implying any rejection of other aspects of the biological par-adigm. We could suppose, in other words, that altruism takes the form of an imbalanced interaction between autonomous culture-bearing individuals, that it is the spontaneous expression of cultural instructions unconsciously and automati-cally followed, and that it serves to promote the transmission and replication of these instructions across the generations. Such a view would be broadly in accord-ance with the Boasian understanding of culture and social behaviour, and with much of cultural anthropology since. Fortes's subsequent points, however, clearly follow Durkheim rather than Boas. The essence of altruism, he insists, is that it is *rule governed.* Thus the 'axiom of amity', which in all societies informs the rela-tions between kin (Fortes 1969:232), is not part of the nature (innate or acquired) of individuals, but belongs to a supraindividual moral order that is imposed on them. It is a rule of *prescriptive* altruism, to which people become subject by virtue of their incumbency of particular statuses related together in a kinship structure. Consequently, and this is Fortes's third point, human altruistic action is not spon-taneous but obligatory.[14] Otherwise put, it is altruistic because it conveys the moral purpose of society, not because it has beneficial consequences for the reproduction of affected individuals. Unlike the 'blind, genetically based altruism imputed to individual animals by sociobiology', whose aim is to promote the inclusive fitness of the individual, 'the institutionalized, rule-governed prescriptive altruism binding among humans . . . works to maintain the mutual trust that underlies ongoing social relationships' (Fortes 1983:32). Without rules, Fortes argues, there can be no such relationships and indeed no such thing as society; nor can society exist in the absence of the specifically human capacity for culture (1983:34). And if society conceived as a culturally encoded, regulative order is uniquely human, so is the prescriptive form of altruism that implies the social subjection of individuals to a higher purpose.

As a further illustration of the divergence between sociobiological and anthropological understandings of altruism, we might return to the substantivist model of exchange proposed by Sahlins. This model envisages a continuum of reciprocities, from the altruistic extreme at which one gives without thought or expectation of return to the egotistic extreme at which one takes what one can without any consideration of recompense. Between the extremes, of 'generalized' and 'negative' reciprocity respectively, is a midpoint of 'balanced' reciprocity, one of mutuality, where strict equivalence is maintained in the flow and counterflow of prestations (Sahlins 1972:193–6). Having set up the continuum, Sahlins suggests that the 'sidedness' of reciprocity may be correlated directly with the social distance—or more specifically, the kinship distance—separating the parties to exchange. Thus 'reciprocity is inclined toward the generalized pole by close kinship, toward the negative extreme in proportion to kinship distance' (1972:196). Regarding the 'plan' of a primitive society, from a particular point within it, as a series of ever-widening and more inclusive sectors (household, lineage, village, tribal, pan-tribal etc.), it is supposed that generalized reciprocity prevails in the narrowest sectors, balanced reciprocity in the intermediate sectors, and negative reciprocity in the widest sectors. Hence in the model, the sectoral plan is superimposed on the reciprocity continuum, as depicted by Sahlins and reproduced here as Fig. 6.7.

It will be recalled that, adopting the premises of economic substantivism, Sahlins treats exchange as an aspect of the functioning of an instituted, regulative order, involving the flow of material means. Thus the pressure to give, in exchanges towards the generalized end of the continuum, has its source in society; it is a moral obligation imposed on the individual by virtue of his situational incumbency of a particular (kinship) status relative to that occupied by the recipient. Sahlins contends that the intensity of this moral obligation, which is in the nature of a stipulation or expectation, varies inversely with social distance. Fading out altogether at the extremities of society, no restriction remains on the free play of private self-interest that is manifested as negative reciprocity. Not only society, then, but also morality is sectorally structured, and 'the structure is that of kinship-tribal groupings' (Sahlins 1972:200). From this it follows that the continuum from generalized to negative reciprocity is formally analogous to Durkheim's from altruism to egotism. Where the altruism of generalized reciprocity reflects the surrender

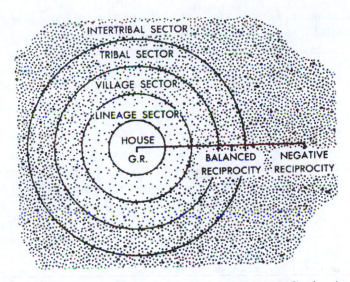

FIG. 6.7 Reciprocity and kinship residential sectors. G.R., generalized reciprocity.
Reproduced from Sahlins (1972:199) © Taylor and Francis.

of the individual to a solidary group, and the maximal subordination of private
desires to public goals, the egotism of negative reciprocity reflects the isolation
of the individual from social constraint in contexts where collective pressures are
weak or non-existent. In short, the sidedness of reciprocity is a function of the balance between moral obligation and individual interest in particular social situations.

Sahlins's model, however, has since been seized on by sociobiologists as offering convincing proof of their expectations concerning the evolution of social
behaviour. The first to do so was Alexander, who continues to claim that the
model 'is an uncanny match for that of the evolutionary biologist' (1979:200;
see also Alexander 1975). Others such as Crook (1980:173–6) and Durham
(1976:110–11) have followed Alexander's example, whereas Barash, in a recent
sociobiological textbook, asserts unequivocally that Sahlins's findings 'coincide
exactly with the prediction that behaviour will tend to maximize inclusive fitness', remaining oblivious to the protestations of Sahlins himself to the contrary
(Barash 1977:315–16; Sahlins 1976a:122 n. 7). Much of the argument concerning
the relevance of the model for sociobiological theory hinges on the question of
the degree of 'fit' between biological and cultural kin-relatedness. Every anthropologist knows that in any particular society, the set of people whom a man treats
as his close kin may include a substantial number who bear little or no genetic
relationship with him. 'No system of human kinship relations', Sahlins writes,
'is organized in accord with the genetic coefficients of relationship as known to
sociobiologists' (1976a:57). Yet as Alexander counters, it is preposterous to deny
that there is any correlation at all between genetic and cultural coefficients; by and
large people in the same family, or lineage, are more closely related genetically
than people in different families or lineages (Alexander 1979:201–2). And if the

suckling of infants, as Sahlins himself suggests (1972:194), is the logical extreme of generalized reciprocity, it is surely the case that in all societies, most mothers suckle their own offspring and not other people's.

I do not intend to prolong this argument, which not only seems unprofitable, but also obscures a much more fundamental source of sociobiological misunderstanding concerning the very definition of altruism. For the stipulation of generalized reciprocity between close kin is a facet of the Fortesian 'axiom of amity', and the prescriptive altruism entailed in both is a Durkheimian surrender of self to society, or to what Fortes calls 'the sovereignty of the rule' (1983:34). A kinship relation, for Sahlins as for Fortes, exists between positions in a regulative order which is uniquely human; this order is both supraindividual and suprabiological, and organizes the biological individuals on which it is imposed according to a scheme of its own (Sahlins 1976a:58–9). Sociobiology, currently recapitulating the arguments of Spencer, finds kinship relations in all sexually reproducing species, existing between *individual organisms* by virtue of their common parentage. Far from having their locus outside individuals, in culture or society, such relations are an expression of their constitution as genetically assembled things. Kinship altruism therefore appears no longer as the suppression of the extrasocial, naturally given interests of the individual in conformity with the social demands of his kinship office, but rather as the spontaneous execution of innate nepotistic dispositions established through countless generations of kin selection. From the anthropological point of view, of course, the genetic relatedness of the incumbents of kinship statuses is simply irrelevant: Even if it were shown that the coefficients of genetic relationship are high, this would not alter the fact that altruism involves an appeal to rules that transcend the natures of individuals. Thus for Sahlins, altruistic acts are supposed to promote the reproduction not of human beings *per se,* 'but the system of social groups, categories, and relations in which they live' (1976a:60). As with the giving of gifts, each act is conceived to be a moment in the life of society.

Returning to Fig. 6.7, it is evident that where in the original, the plane on which it is drawn corresponds to a *moral* space, in its sociobiological re-presentation (as in Alexander 1979:57) that plane corresponds to an *interactive* space. In the one, every point designates a social alter relative to a social ego at the centre; in the other ego and alter are not social persons but individuals. In the one, reciprocity is an expectation that attaches to a structural relation between positions; in the other, it is a feature of spontaneous interaction between individuals. Thus the 'norms' of reciprocity are moral or jural in the first case, and statistical in the second. And finally in the one *moral intensity,* whereas in the other *interactive frequency,* grades off towards the periphery. In order to translate from the former version of the diagram to the latter, it would be necessary first to compress the entire moral scheme within the confines of the individual, to provide it with an underpinning in his genetic make-up, and then to reconstitute it as the aggregate outcome of his interactions. It could be said that the effect of this procedure is to convert what in the first view is the moral basis of reciprocity into an exchangeable commodity. Consider, for example, the colloquial expression of altruism in the formula 'love your neighbour'. What happens to 'love' in the transformation we have described? Initially it appears as a quality inherent in the relation of neighbourhood, understood as a relation between parts, and to love is to adopt the part of the good neighbour, to conform to a status etiquette. Finally, it reappears as a kind of benefit that can be alienated and appropriated, such that what is an absolute gain to the recipient is an absolute loss to the donor. To love is to accept a negative balance in an exchange of commodities and is thus akin to sacrifice in its contractual sense. The good neighbour is one who, by nature, indulges in the spontaneous dispensation of favours.

Both views are almost pathological distortions of our real experience of social living, generated by an ideologically conditioned refusal to countenance the possibility of intersubjectivity. We are, in our everyday world, continually and often intensely involved in each other's lives; but believing firmly that we are not, that every ego is the private inhabitant of his body (or even *nothing but* his body), the part of ego that is also a part of alter is represented as something external to both. Thus the love that ego and alter bear for each other becomes a thing (a commodity), or an aspect of a thing (society), that comes between them and keeps them separate. By playing the part of the loving neighbour, or by dispensing goods that belong to the part, a person may keep others at arm's length. *Truly* to love one's neighbour is surely the very opposite. It is to see things from the neighbour's point of view, to align one's purpose to his own. If this involves sacrifice, then what is sacrificed must be in the nature of a gift rather than a commodity; it must embody the *person* of the giver. Perhaps we may call this altruism, but then it is to understand the term in neither of the two senses that we have reviewed and that permeate the languages of biological and social science. It is to say that persons are united in their amity, not divided by it. We should, then, cease to regard altruism as a process of alienation and bring it under the same terms by which we understand the exchange of gifts, namely as a form of communion. No longer a property of individual, communicative interactions, nor an expression of the dominance of a supraindividual, regulative order, altruism would come to characterize the mutual constitution of persons. And as such every act of altruism, far from diminishing the self by subtraction from a fixed essence, would—as it expands the sphere of the person's involvement with others—contribute to its progressive augmentation.

To inquire into the conditions of altruism is also to raise quite fundamental questions about the nature of moral conduct. I should like to conclude this chapter with a few remarks on the implications of the contrasting senses of altruism adduced earlier, corresponding to the interactive, regulative and constitutive conceptions of sociality, for our understanding of morality. It is not my intention to pontificate on the criteria of good and evil, but rather to discover what it is about human action that renders it open to evaluation of this kind in the first place. That is to say, we are required to distinguish the moral not from the *immoral* but from the *amoral*. And the thesis I wish to propose is that conduct is moral to the extent that it is *complete,* and concomitantly that any theory that presents us with a one-sided picture of human activities will inevitably fail to grasp their moral aspect. Shall we then say, with Spencer and with contemporary sociobiology, that the roots of moral conduct lie in the evolution of our innate dispositions? Or, with Darwin, that morality implies the *consciousness* of rules that have themselves become established through variation under natural selection (1874:177)? This would be to attribute to consciousness, at most, the capacity to monitor behaviours that spring from our hereditary nature, according to criteria that have their foundation in the very same source (Lorenz 1966:219). For sociobiology, an act (such as an instance of nepotistic altruism) would appear moral to the extent that it is subjected to retrospective evaluation by an intellect that, whatever its overt rationality, covertly has an eye to the maximization of inclusive fitness. Now approving, now disapproving, the scrutiny of the moral conscience mimics the scrutiny of natural selection in assessing behaviour for its effects on reproductive success (Alexander 1979:278).

With Durkheim we are at the other extreme. For the moral conscience is here no longer judge but governor, and its seat resides outside the individual. 'Morality', he wrote, 'consists of a system of rules of action that predetermine conduct' (1961[1925]:24). These rules are refractory to change and derive their binding force from the subordination of the individual to the social group. Far from entering society fully equipped with all the essential rudiments of morality, the individual outside society is totally amoral. His conduct, entirely without regulation, is liable to shoot off in all directions towards ends that, being indefinite, forever elude satisfaction. Thus morality for Durkheim is a barrier, and if weakened at any point, 'human forces—until now restrained—pour tumultuously through the open breach; once loosed, they find no limits where they can and must stop' (1961[1925]:42). These are the forces unleashed in egotistic action, expressing the biopsychological impulses constitutive of human nature. A man acts morally, Durkheim tells us, only when he places himself in the service of society— in other words, when he acts altruistically. Amoral egotism and moral altruism strain in contrary directions, the one centripetal, the other centrifugal: Hence moral conduct is fundamentally *unnatural* (1961[1925]:58–60, 214). As Reynolds has pointed out, Durkheim's was a theory 'strongly at variance with both a naturalistic approach to human society and a modern conception of instinct' (1981:20–1).

There is surely something grossly inadequate about both conceptions, naturalistic and sociologistic, of moral conduct. On the one hand, it seems undeniable that human performance, and arguably that of other animals, is channelled by learning-transmitted tradition, that is by customs or *mores*. In that sense, the words 'moral' and 'cultural', expressing *ways* of living, are all but synonymous. On the other hand, we cannot accept that moral rules, as such, have their locus anywhere else than in the minds of separate individuals, or that conduct is any the less moral for being animated by dispositions and feelings that are deeply embedded in human nature. Customary regulation and natural inclination cannot strain in opposite directions but must rather be mutually complementary; indeed in real life the two are so intimately interlocked that it would be a fruitless endeavour even to attempt to separate them. Moreover the complete altruist, in the Durkheimian scenario, would be as much a moral cripple as the nepotist of sociobiology who is the puppet of his genes. A robot could be programmed to perform precisely according to a set of social rules; unlike the human being, its life would not be complicated or perturbed by any primordial sentiment issuing from within. Yet we would hardly regard the machine as a moral creature, for the simple reason that its action is devoid of feeling—in a word, it is inhuman.[15] Natural man, to the contrary, is a sensuous being, and as Marx emphasized, to feel is also to suffer. Because we feel what we suffer, we are also passionate beings—this passion is, in Marx's words, 'the essential force of man energetically bent on its object' (1964a:182). Thus, as I have argued elsewhere, 'the emotional energy that imparts a moral charge to social action has a foundation in human nature; that is to say it rests on certain innate potentialities which are of course open, in that they can be realized in any number of ways, depending on the cultural context' (1983a:8). In short, where Durkheim held that the forces of human nature—or the tumult of passions—detract from the morality of conduct, we hold that they complete it. Emotions and feelings, to adopt Midgley's image, form the 'power house' that sustains our life as moral beings (Midgley 1983:35).

Yet there is still something more, for we have said nothing of the responsibility for conduct. An action is moral not only because it conforms to customary regulation, not only because it is animated by deep-seated sentiments and feelings, but also because it is directed by the conscious purpose of a knowing subject. Both naturalism and sociologism offload the responsibility for conduct from persons onto things—whether these things are internal or external to the individual, genes or societies. A truly moral purpose is one formed by a subject who acts with regard to the purposes of others as they act with regard to his, and who is therefore accountable for what he does. This is the meaning of altruism in its constitutive sense, implying the personal involvement of the self in the other. But purposes are nothing if they are not translated into practice, and it is precisely in the translation that the other essential components of morality come into play, namely the cultural rules that serve as vehicles for their implementation, and the primordial sentiments and motivations that (like the physical powers of the individual) energize the whole process. Morality, we conclude, does not reside exclusively in the rules of culture nor in the forces of nature nor in the consciousness of the socially constituted person. It resides, rather, in the way these three components of human conduct are welded into an integrated totality. To grasp the morality of social life is to apprehend it in its completeness: We find ourselves once more, with Mauss, in the realm of total social phenomena.

7

CULTURE AND CONSCIOUSNESS

We began this inquiry with a contrast between two ways of understanding evolution in the organic domain: either as the progressive movement or advance of life in general, representing just one phase in a cosmic process, or as the adaptive modification of particular forms along divergent lines of descent, making up a phylogenetic tree. And we promised that this contrast, initially linked to the theories of Spencer and Darwin respectively, would ultimately be found also to underlie the difference between social evolution and cultural adaptation. In the last chapter we established the grounds for our distinction between social life and culture, linking this distinction to alternative conceptions of history, time and creativity. We saw that to regard the human being simply as an *individual* culture-bearer is to reduce his social life to an aggregate of overt behavioural interactions, which serve to reproduce the elements of culture just as the phenotypic behaviour of an organism results in the reproduction of elements of the genotype. But if he is regarded as a *person,* that is as a locus of consciousness, then social life appears as the temporal unfolding of consciousness through the *instrumentality* of cultural forms. Whereas the individual is a vehicle for culture, his mind a *container* for cultural content, the conscious life of the person is a *movement* that adopts culture as its vehicle. Thus culture stands, in a sense, between the person and the individual; worked by one, it works the other.

In the present chapter we complete the argument in three major stages. First, we look more closely at the meanings of consciousness (and the unconscious), distinguishing its *practical* from its *discursive* sense, a distinction that can be mapped onto that, just noted, between mind as movement and as container. This leads us to an extended discussion of the relation between consciousness, language and thought, and to the nature of conscious awareness in non-human animals. Second, we show that the practical and discursive correspond to two kinds of intentionality or 'subjective meaning': one pertaining to the socially constituted consciousness that presents action; the other to the prior conception or conscious model that represents it—a model constructed out of the elements of culture. Focusing on the question of whether non-human animals produce, we link this contrast to alternative notions of production—intransitive (as in 'A lives') and transitive (as in 'A makes B')—bringing us ultimately to the central distinction between social action as a continuous flow of conduct and cultural behaviour as a series of discrete emissions. In the third and final part of the chapter, our concern is specifically with the nature of cultural things, and we return to the question first raised in Chapter 2 as to whether, or to what extent, culture is artificial or 'man-made'. The problem of setting up criteria to delimit the class of artefacts leads to a re-examination both of the notion of culture as 'extrasomatic' and of the opposition of tool-using and tool-making. The distinction between 'innate' and 'artificial' culture (or convention and invention) is shown to rest on the presence or absence of a prior conception of the object and is related to alternative modes of transmission, by observational learning and formal tuition respectively. Eventually we shall find the distinction to hinge on two ways of representing the 'cultural analogue' of natural selection: either as the internal selection of cultural attributes, or as a process of artificial selection of conceptual variants. The contrast takes us back to the contrary schemata of culture change, Darwinian and Lamarckian, with which our whole inquiry began, and in so doing, brings our project to its logical conclusion.

The practical and the discursive

Nothing is more intrinsic to our experience than consciousness, yet so it transpires, nothing more completely eludes our grasp. Popper candidly admits that the problems of the emergence of consciousness in the animal kingdom, and of the specifically human consciousness of self, are 'most likely insoluble' (1974:273). And when it comes to the governance exercised by consciousness over neuronal processes in the brain, apparently involved in every normal occurrence of wilful action, Eccles confesses that it is completely beyond his understanding (1974:98). There are good grounds for believing that consciousness embraces precisely what can never be fully known about ourselves, since without it there can be no knowing of anything. Thus Hume's attempts to find it ended in failure, leading him to doubt the very existence of the conscious self, which of course had all along been doing the seeking. Taking a look at myself I find no one at home, no 'ego', for the simple reason that I have gone outside in order to look in. All I see is the shadow I left behind, a rapidly fading image (Smythies 1969:234). Indeed to expect any *objective* account of consciousness is rather like expecting my own reflection to look back at me, just as I look at it. Only the blind have no subjective experience of seeing, and yet that experience is precisely what we ourselves cannot see. 'The self as a pure centre of consciousness', Harré explains, 'cannot be the . . . object of any kind of consciousness'; it is not something that I can say I am 'aware of' or 'attending to', since it *is* the awareness that attends (Harré 1979:291).

However, to proceed from this evident impossibility to a categorical denial of subjective and intersubjective awareness would be palpably absurd. Were the subjective merely another word for the illusory, where would *we* be? And what cause would we have to take seriously the statements of those who make such claims, statements that, if true, would be devoid of intent? For creatures that lack consciousness cannot *claim* anything at all (Clark 1982:14). It is a curious quirk of the human condition that we are inclined to spend much time, and write an exorbitant number of learned volumes, debating the possible non-existence of that without which such debate could not go on at all. Instead of trying to understand the familiar, human reality that we know from first-hand experience, modern Western science has largely devoted its attention to the characterization and dismissal of that reality as a fantasy bred of ignorance, and to the conversion of its own fantasy world—one strange and alien to our experience—into an inhuman reality destined to take the place of the old. Thus the mind is to be 'torn down' and rebuilt as the circuitry of neurons (Wilson 1980:300–1).[1] If, and when, the reconstruction is complete—should the millennium of 'total knowledge' ever arrive as Wilson for one has prophesied, a century from today—there will be no room in the new world for us.

I do not believe it is profitable to pursue the self-mockery of scepticism with regard to the existence of mind, or to submit to the tyranny of the reductionist's 'nothing but'. That philosophical staple, the mind-body problem, cannot be resolved so simply as by doubting one or the other term of the opposition (Popper 1974:273–5). We should rather look to the possibility of its transcendence. The method of natural science hinges, of course, on the postulate that an objectified 'nature' constitutes the final arbiter of true knowledge (Ingold 1983a:3–4). And that, in turn, presupposes the isolation of the disembodied, pure subject, to whom the world of nature is revealed as a spectacle. Hence the Cartesian separation of matter and mind, 'two sorts of independent substances', as Whitehead put it, 'each qualified by their appropriate passions' (1938:178). Hence also, the dichotomy between the material and the ideal, the identification of the latter with that which pertains to mind, and the consequent portrayal as 'idealist' of any theory that ascribes primacy to consciousness in the conduct of life. One such theory, as we saw in the last chapter, was that of Marx. Yet subsequent generations of advocates, concerned above all else to preserve its claim to be a form of materialism, have confused the distinction between base (infrastructure) and superstructure with one between 'matter' and 'spirit', relegating consciousness to an entirely epiphenomenal, reflective or masking role (Avineri 1968:76).

Our view, broadly following Whitehead's philosophy of organism, is that consciousness is neither material nor ideal; it is no kind of substance but a movement or process. It is not idealist to ascribe efficacy to consciousness working *within* the real world, since the ideal is constructed, in opposition to the material, only by virtue of the withdrawal of consciousness *from* the world. As mind is essentially a process of coherence, its withdrawal amounts to the dissolution of that coherence, yielding the category of matter comprising all the constituent particles of the universe. The ideal, recovered in the image of the material, retains like an image an aura of unreality. Indeed it is as common to oppose the ideal to the real as to the material, so that the appearance of ideal realities—such as Durkheimian collective representations—seems like a contradiction in terms (see Durkheim 1976[1915]:422). It is not my intention to unpack the concept of idealism, a concept simultaneously embroiled in so many different but overlapping philosophical arguments that it 'needs the closest scrutiny whenever it is used' (Williams 1976:125–6). I merely wish to register the point that the material–ideal dichotomy is the product of an atomizing objectivism and that it promptly disappears once consciousness is restored to its rightful place in the real world. For this reason, we must reject the thesis of 'psychophysical parallelism' between mental and bodily states. Mind and body are not two different processes, simultaneously running along separate lines; they are different ways of looking at the *same* process: holistically (from within) and atomistically (from without). It is equally unsatisfactory to postulate the mind as an independent object, somehow interacting with the body of its possessor (Popper 1974:275–6); this is as hopeless as attributing the power of vision to my reflection and imagining then that we can inspect each other. Since the body is constructed as an object of contemplation by the exclusion of mind, there can be no interaction of body and mind save in the nowhere world behind the looking-glass.

To add to the confusion, the notion of consciousness is as commonly adopted to refer to a region or level of the mind (usually in opposition to 'the unconscious') in which certain ideas are to be found, as it is to denote the wilful act of grasping them. Thus we may say of a person that he is conscious, meaning that—subjectively—he knows, and of an idea that it is conscious, meaning that it is objectively known. In the one case we speak of the person's consciousness *of,* in the other of the idea's locus *in* consciousness. Popper has attempted to maintain the disjunction between the body of objective knowledge and the subjective experience of knowing by placing them in different 'worlds'. There is the 'world of mental states' (World 2), and the 'world of the contents of thought' (World 3), corresponding to 'subjective' and 'objective' senses of knowledge respectively (in Popper and Eccles 1977:38, 122). Both are to be distinguished from World 1, 'the universe of physical entities'. The three worlds are unified in a total vision of emergent or creative evolution on the cosmic scale, their successive appearance supposedly marking off major stages in a continuous process (1977:16–17). But whilst purporting to locate the phenomena of consciousness within this process, Popper in fact does the very opposite. The material World 1 and the ideal World 3, corresponding very roughly to what most anthropologists would call nature and culture, are constituted by the *emancipation* of consciousness from evolution. To such a free-floating mind, World 1 appears as a macrocosmic container, whose contents are all the physical things of the universe (including living organisms, hence also human bodies and brains). World 3 is the microcosm into which these contents are projected; it is the world of images 'inside the subject's head', including his theories about the physical universe and how it works. World 2, then, appears to be none other than the projector, perhaps better regarded as a kind of gatekeeper, actively transmuting from World 1 to World 3 and back again. 'I am inclined to approach the psychological World 2', Popper writes, 'mainly from the point of view of its . . . function in relating World 3 to World 1' (1977:106). Yet he is equally inclined to refer to World 2, in the same vein as in reference to Worlds 1 and 3, as a container whose contents are 'World 2 objects'—including thoughts, discoveries, memories and other isolable mental states (1977:41). How such a collection of objects, recursively detached from the flow of consciousness, can be identified with the experience of the living subject is not entirely clear.

This multiplication of worlds—Popper has even suggested adding Worlds 4 and 5, or more according to taste (1974:275)—obscures the real nature of the distinction we wish to draw between subjective consciousness and the objective forms of culture (Ingold 1983a:16). The fundamental premises of an evolutionary cosmology are that there is but one world, that this world is not a collection of inert things but a continuous and creative movement, and that as conscious subjects, we human beings are a part of it. Consciousness must, therefore, be understood as an active force within the world, rather than as its projection into an other-worldly microcosm. We can only return to Wieman's dichotomy, central to our argument in Chapter 5, between created goods and the creative good. Popper's World 3 is a world of created goods or works, or rather of plans for their execution, and the relating of World 3 to World 1 involves the materialization of a prior conception in the mind of the fabricator, just as, conversely, the relating of World 1 to World 3 involves the conceptualization in the mind of the observer of an already existing material entity. Consciousness, however, is not another world of things but a process, a creative good, which works through a whole series of fabrications and observations in the course of its unfolding. It cannot, therefore, be reconstructed as an aggregate of mental states accompanying instantaneous events of execution and discovery. Nor can it be regarded as something that, in the words of Eccles, 'each of us has privately for himself' (1974:87). The image of the solitary consciousness, sitting in resplendent isolation astride the world, may serve to legitimize the scientific enterprise as the pursuit of objective knowledge, but it cannot conceivably accord with reality. For such a consciousness could not enjoy a social life; moreover it is precisely because we do live socially, because our purposes are shaped by the milieu that makes us who we are, that total objectivity remains a chimera.

Perhaps the whole question of the mind–body relation, which we are inclined to see as a by-product of the dominant scientific attitude, would be better left to professional philosophers and psychologists, for after centuries of argument the waters are now so muddied and treacherous that the rest of us can no longer expect to navigate with any assurance. But in order to add some precision to the specific sense of consciousness that we adopt in this work, it may help to expose certain areas of ambiguity that have resulted from the intrusion of the contrastive term—'the unconscious' (notice, however, that it is rare to hear of 'unconsciousness'). No one has better expressed our intuitive understanding of consciousness than David Bohm: It is, he writes, 'a coherent whole, which is never static or complete, but which is an unending process of movement and unfoldment' (1980:ix). The question of how to relate this to the unconscious has been quite explicitly formulated by Ricoeur: 'What is the meaning of the unconscious for a being whose task is consciousness? . . . What is consciousness as a task for a being who is somehow bound to those factors, such as repetition and even regression, which the unconscious represents for the most part?' (1974:108–9). For Ricoeur as for us, consciousness is essentially a forward movement, one 'which continually annihilates its starting point' (1974:113). The unconscious, to the contrary, forever pulls us back to where we began, to 'the order of the pri- mordial'. Thus he concludes, 'consciousness and the unconscious will answer to two inverse interpretations, progressive and regressive. We might say that consciousness is history, while the unconscious is fate' (1974:118). Or to adopt a mechanical analogy, the unconscious in Ricoeur's conception could be likened to a spring, fixed at one end, the other end pulled by a consciousness whose task is continuously to strive to overcome its tensile force.

Lévi-Strauss both addresses and resolves the problem of the relation between consciousness and the unconscious in quite a different way. For in his view the task that cultural human beings live to execute is itself inscribed in the unconscious. So Ricoeur's question would have to be rephrased as follows: 'What is the meaning of consciousness for a being who is somehow bound to a task that is already repre- sented at the unconscious level?' Part of the answer emerged from our discussion, in the previous chapter, of Lévi-Strauss's analysis of gift exchange. Although the plan of exchange exists in its totality as a synchronic structure, it is revealed piece- meal, in a succession of disconnected, momentary episodes. Consciousness is the plane on which these episodes are put together in a linear reconstruction or model of the whole. Or alternatively (and this is never quite clear), it is the agent of recon- struction, the explorer or model-builder. Evidently for Lévi-Strauss, consciousness can only be a reflexive consciousness *of*, which intrudes but intermittently in the ordinary conduct of life. Thus 'any speaker who consciously applies phonological and grammatical laws in his speech . . . would not be able to pursue the line of his argument for very long', and the same applies—Lévi-Strauss suggests—to the successful narration of myth, which requires that its structural properties remain hidden to the narrator (1966b:55).

Clearly we do many things in the course of everyday life without having to represent to ourselves in the form of conscious models or blueprints the rules and procedures by which they are performed. Anyone who has learned to speak a foreign language or to ride a bicycle knows that in the former case, complete flu- ency comes when the application of syntactical rules becomes as automatic as for a native speaker, and that in the latter case, a perfect balance is achieved only when one ceases to deliberate on the correct way to go about it. So much of our learn- ing, as Medawar has compellingly argued, consists of 'learning *not* to think about operations that once needed to be thought about' (1957:138). The hyperreflective subject, too concerned to put theory before practice, is liable to end up in the predicament of Koestler's allegorical centipede who, when asked in which order he moved his hundred legs, 'became paralyzed and starved to death because he had never thought of it before and had left his legs to look after themselves' (Koestler 1969:205). The fate of the centipede underlines Ryle's point that to do something skilfully or intelligently does *not* require of a person to consider what he is doing while doing it, or to put the point more generally, that 'efficient practice precedes the theory of it' (Ryle 1949:30–1). To know *how,* in Ryle's terms, is not necessarily to know *that;* the competent practitioner can be a poor theoretician, and vice versa (Ingold 1983a:12).

Seemingly on the basis of an assumption that action, to qualify as purposive or consciously directed, *must* involve the application of overt, theoretical 'knowledge *that'*, Lévi-Strauss arrives at the extraordinary conclusion that most of what we say and do, since it does *not* involve any deliberate application of known theoretical principles, cannot be directed by consciousness. This extremely limited view of the role of consciousness stems directly from the way in which it is set up in *opposition* to a particular conception of the unconscious. For so long as the latter is understood not as a movement or force but as a particular region of the mind, in which the structures regulating conduct are thought to be contained, then consciousness implies the opening of this region and its contents for inspection, in such a way that they can be formulated by the intellect with a view to subsequent application. In other words, the opposition conscious–unconscious yields a sense of consciousness that is *discursive,* whose products include the entire gamut of 'home-made models' by which people interpret (or misinterpret) their behaviour (Lévi-Strauss 1968:282). There is, however, another sense of consciousness, *practical* rather than discursive, which is not opposed to the unconscious as defined earlier but actually complements it (Giddens 1979:25). This corresponds to the agency of mind, working *through* the various levels of structure—from the wholly unconscious to the more or less conscious—in the implementation of purpose. Consider again the example of speaking. Supposing the speaker to be wholly unaware of the structural properties of his language, is speaking conscious or unconscious? For Lévi-Strauss, the unconscious linguistic structure 'continues to mould discourse beyond the consciousness of the individual' (1968:19). And yet, as we argued in Chapter 4, language does not tell anyone what to say, nor is the speaker a machine geared to the aleatoric improvisation of utterances. He is, rather, an intentional agent, for whom the linguistic structure—though not discursively available—is in essence a facility placed under the direction of practical consciousness. Remove that component of consciousness, divorce the speaker from the field of constitutive social relations, and speaking *would* dissolve into a series of random emissions, like the output of a machine left to 'tick over' in the temporary absence of its operator.

To recapitulate: Two senses of consciousness, practical and discursive, are constituted by their respective opposition to two corresponding senses of the unconscious. Regarded as a progressive projection of past into future, practical consciousness can only be opposed to an unconscious viewed, as it is by Ricoeur, as a regressive retraction of the future into the past. But if the unconscious is taken to be the locus of structure, then consciousness will appear as its discursive revelation. Or to put it another way, the meaning of consciousness for a being who experiences the unconscious as a force of resistance will be the practical task of counteracting it, whereas for a being whose task is written in the unconscious the meaning of consciousness will be discursive. This fundamental distinction corresponds to a whole series of contrasts, many of which have been developed in previous chapters. For example, whereas practical consciousness implies the notion of mind as the enfolding of an intersubjective process, discursive consciousness is a mapping of the regions of the mind as though it were a container, private to each individual. The first is an essential component of action, whereas the second pertains to cognition. Referring back to the key terms of our argument in Chapter 5, practical consciousness is creative whereas discursive consciousness is revelatory—merely laying bare the structures that are already there. Again, real time—Bergsonian duration—inheres in practical consciousness, which is one reason why this form of consciousness cannot be comprehended within the structuralist paradigm, constructed as it is on the abstract axes of synchrony and diachrony. Discursive consciousness, revelatory of synchronic structure, is played out in a motionless, extended present and has no essential time component. And following from all these contrasts comes the most basic of all: Discursive is to practical consciousness as culture is to social life. If, with Lévi-Strauss, we hold that cultural forms 'think themselves out' through the medium of consciousness, that consciousness is discursive (Lévi-Strauss 1966b:56). But the consciousness that unfolds in and enfolds social relations is practical.

Such has been the tendency to associate consciousness with cognition rather than practical action that the term has, in many anthropological discussions, become virtually synonymous with culture. There is, of course, a precedent for this in the work of Durkheim, whose notion of a consciousness of the collectivity came to be identified with a common system of ideal representations. A recent advocate of the same view is Peacock, for whom consciousness is likewise a system 'which unites a plurality of symbolic forms into a single structure' and 'tends towards a mode of integration which has been termed "logico-meaningful"', otherwise known as cultural (Peacock 1975:4, 12 n. 6; see Geertz 1975:145). As regards the unconscious, Peacock suggests that the term 'consciousness' be interpreted sufficiently liberally to encompass 'both the lucidly conscious and the murkily unconscious thoughts, feelings, sensations, motives, beliefs and memories which are expressed through symbolic forms' (1975:6). The justification for this extended usage is somewhat odd, namely that a good part of what is unconscious is partially conscious, lying within the field of the person's awareness, whereas what is not can simply be forgotten about, being 'of no concern to the student of symbols'. Peacock seems not to encompass but to carve up the unconscious, appropriating what he can to the conscious and discarding the rest. When it comes to practical action (as distinct from symbolic expression), residually defined as 'techno-social', consciousness appears to play no significant role whatever. Indeed Peacock finds no difference in principle between the relationships established amongst humans and amongst ants; the former could just as well be replaced by mechanical robots making up, like the latter, 'a society without consciousness'. Thus 'techno–social relations need not involve consciousness, whereas logico–meaningful relations, by definition, must' (1975:7). Our conclusion from the last chapter, quite to the contrary, is that although 'techno–' (i.e. material or interactive) relations are external to consciousness, the latter is *constituted* by social relations, whereas 'logico–meaningful' relations constitute the objective forms of culture through which it is conducted.

The peculiar anthropological identification of consciousness with the domain of overt symbolic structures or cultural forms may go some way in explaining the persistent misunderstanding, to which we alluded in Chapter 6, of Marx's notion of the 'determination' of consciousness by social relations. Once more we note that the Marxian sense of consciousness, like our own, is practical. Consider, however, the implications of substituting for this practical sense a discursive one. The first would be to take consciousness out of production, which would consequently appear as the mechanical replication of a given structure, to what extent technologically determined depending on the opinion of the author. Second, that which Marx held to be unwilled in production, namely the social relations in which the producers momentarily find themselves, would seem so not because practically unintended but because discursively unavailable. Hence the non–intentional is replaced by the unconscious, an inner recess of the individual mind within which are supposed to be concealed the regulative structures production is presumed to replicate. And finally, consciousness would reappear not as an enfolding but as an epiphenomenon of these 'invisible' social relations, alternately the constructor of, and a repository for, an assemblage of symbolic representations, normative or ideological models, constituting a 'logico–meaningful' pattern of culture. What was the reality of consciousness becomes, by this substitution, a partial and distorted reflection of an unconscious reality (Ingold 1983a:9).

It may be agreed that a first requirement for discursive consciousness, that is for the intellectual construction of theoretical models or plans for implementation equivalent to Ryle's 'knowledge *that*' or a Popperian World 3, is the distinctively human capacity for symbolic thought. This, in turn, appears to be predicated on certain specific properties of human language. However, the definition and elucidation of these properties have proved difficult and contentious. Whether there exists an absolute difference in kind between the linguistic capabilities of human beings and other animals, which admits of no intermediate stages (Lenneberg 1960:886), remains a legitimate subject of speculation (Griffin 1977:29). An enormous amount of recent research has been devoted to this question and it would be beyond my competence to review it in any depth, nor does space permit (see especially the collections edited by Hinde 1972, and Sebeok 1977). One approach, adopted in a series of papers by Hockett (1959, 1960, 1963; also Hockett and Altmann 1968; Thorpe 1972), is to enumerate the various 'design features' of human language, regarded as a system of communication, and to find out which of these features are or are not shared by the communication systems of other animals. That Hockett has found it necessary to increase the number of features from the seven originally proposed (1959) to thirteen (1960), and subsequently to sixteen (1963), is symptomatic of the difficulties involved in locating the uniquely human. Thus two capacities commonly credited to ourselves alone are 'productivity' and 'displacement', denoting respectively our ability to produce totally novel yet comprehensible utterances and to refer to objects *in absentia,* that is outside the temporal and spatial context of utterance. Yet both these features are also exemplified in the celebrated waggle-dance of the honey-bees, by which they can signal the exact location of distant feeding-sites (von Frisch 1950; see Griffin 1976:36). Two features added to Hockett's latest list, however, seem to separate human speech unequivocally from the dancing of bees. These are 'prevarication' and 'reflexiveness'. Quite simply, bees cannot lie about the location of sites (any mistakes can be due only to random interference, faulty mechanism or tampering by human experimenters); nor, as Hockett puts it, can they 'dance about dancing' (1963:10). A human hunter could, by contrast, lie if he wished about the whereabouts of game; he could also explain—perhaps to a visiting anthropologist—that this is what he was talking about.

We can do these things, which bees cannot, because our language consists of words that function for the most part as symbols rather than signs. That is why Cassirer chooses to define a human being as an *animal symbolicum* (1944:26). Symbols, he insists, 'cannot be reduced to mere signals', for they belong to an entirely different domain: 'A signal is a part of the physical world of being; a symbol is a part of the human world of meaning. Signals are "operators"; symbols are "designators"' (1944:32). The same contrast has been elaborated by Langer. A sign, she explains, is directly or indirectly 'called up' by an object in the natural environment whose presence it indicates and evokes a behavioural response—more or less automatic—oriented towards that object. The verbal symbol, on the other hand, does not *announce* an object but rather leads the subject to *conceive* it; its reference is therefore not to a thing but to a conception of a thing, and what it evokes is an orientation of attention towards that conception. This orientation is what we commonly mean by the process of thinking. In short, to borrow Langer's succinct statement of the dichotomy, 'The sign is something to act upon, or a means to command action; the symbol is an instrument of thought' (1942:63). Thus when the hunter describes a sighting of prey, his words convey an image of what he saw, enabling his listeners to recreate a conception of the sighting for themselves. Although this conception may constitute a plan for action, it is not the words themselves that trigger a predatory response towards an absent prey. They merely make such a response literally *conceivable.*

With the honey-bees it is quite otherwise. We have no reason to believe, Langer remarks, 'that a "dancing" bee sends out other foragers with factual information and instructions where to go and what to look for' (1972:204). Bees cannot conceive a plan of campaign, but those that have been in physical contact with the dancer will automatically replicate the latter's excursion. Every dance, then, sets off a fresh cycle in a total foraging act 'that is handed over from one highly sensitive semi-individual to others' (Langer 1972:205). However, in his polemical essay,

The question of animal awareness, Griffin steadfastly denies that the communicative actions of honeybees and humans differ in the absolute fashion suggested by Langer and others, whose arguments we follow here. Not only is he convinced that the bee's dance is genuinely symbolic, but he is also inclined to believe that the dancer consciously and intentionally proffers information and advice, just like the human forager in our example (Griffin 1976:33, 99). This seems far-fetched, although it would be difficult to disprove. Part of the problem lies in Griffin's definition of the symbolic, derived from Morris, according to which any sign provided by an internal state of the organism, which *substitutes* for another sign having direct reference to an environmental object, is to be regarded as a symbol (Morris 1946:25–6). In this sense the waggle–dance does indeed qualify as symbolic, for the orientation of the dance with respect to the vertical substitutes for a direct pointing to the food source (Griffin 1976:24–5). But nothing here entails reference to a concept, and if *that* is our criterion, no amount of substitution will convert a sign into a symbol. Thus the position (P) of the food source relative to the hive may induce modifications in the internal bodily state (S) of the bee that flies between them, which in turn induces the bee to dance with a certain orientation (O). We may say that O is a symptom of S, which is a symptom of P. Although the relation between O and P is certainly indirect, it differs from properly symbolic denotation in that the mediating term S is not a concept that O could be said to connote, nor could it be brought to bear in the absence of the object P that called it up. It is, of course, entirely specious to claim that the bee is capable of conceptual thought because of evidence of so-called symbolic behaviour, when the behaviour can be classed as such only by adopting a special definition of the symbolic that does not require that experience be mediated by concepts at all (Langer 1972:138).

Precisely because the symbol retains its conceptual connotation regardless of the presence or absence, or even of the real existence, of the object it denotes, the kind of 'displacement' characteristic of human language-use is quite different from that involved in the dancing of bees (von Glasersfeld 1976:222). The latter, resting as it does on the substitution of an internally induced sign for an externally induced one, can only indicate something that is actually (rather than hypothetically) *there*. Fundamental to true linguistic displacement, however, is the detachment of concept from object, or the separation of connotation and denotation, marking off the 'inner world' of representations from the 'outer world' of physical things (corresponding to Popper's Worlds 3 and 1 respectively). It enables human beings to think and talk not only about things remote in space and time, but also about things that have never occurred, that could never occur, or that might be construed to occur in the future. These capabilities lie at the root of the distinctively human propensities to fantasize, to speculate, to argue and to deceive. Clearly the opposition between truth and falsehood, and the concomitant need to criticize, can only be relevant to a being capable of envisaging and describing a situation that has never existed. On these grounds, Popper has concluded that the most characteristic aspects of human language are its *descriptive* and *argumentative* functions (in Popper and Eccles 1977:58–9, 456).

With the reflexive facility of language, human beings are able systematically to explore, in thought, the percepts acquired in the course of their practical exploration of the real world, isolating from the flow of their subjective experience particular moments on which to concentrate attention and converting those moments into objects of reflection (Cassirer 1944:39–40). Moreover, through the logical manipulation or juggling of symbols it is possible to generate novel conceptions that correspond to no already existing object but that, once crystallized in the mind, the designer may strive to implement. In this way, thought may come to anticipate and shape practice, rather than merely accompanying and expressing it: We have the ability to envisage and plan, to construct projects for action and to create intellectual models of the human life-process (Reynolds 1976:182; Crook 1980:140). In Crook's words, 'Language enables the logic of a strategy to be stated, examined and developed' (1980:143). It is important to add, too, that human beings can reflect not only on their own practices but also on those observed elsewhere in the animal kingdom, finding 'ready-made' in nature the solution to many technical problems of design in the construction of cultural artefacts. 'An animal', as Marx noted long ago, 'forms things in accordance with the standards and need of the species to which it belongs, whilst man knows how to produce in accordance with the standard of every species' (1964a:113–14). By studying and applying these standards, perfected over many millennia of adaptation under natural selection, man could, so to speak, 'short-cut' the painful and time-consuming process of blind trial-and-error experimentation, which had already been done for him in nature, enjoying the benefits of evolutionary specialization whilst suffering none of the costs (Steadman 1979:159). Not that the imitative transferral of animal design has been without its disasters, as is evidenced by the sad history of earlier attempts to fly on the model of birds (Ingold 1983a:13).

The difference between the animal form and the construction modelled on it—between, say, the wings of the bird and those of the hopeful human flier—is essentially that between the natural and the artificial. By definition we take an artefact to be a *work* in the sense outlined in Chapter 5, that is the realization of a prior conception in the mind of its author. Although such a conception *followed* the appearance of the bird, it *preceded* the appearance of the flying machine: the latter is an artefact, the former is not. Now if it be supposed that all culture is artificial, and in *that* sense opposed to the natural, then certain corollaries follow that touch centrally on the comparison between the evolution of natural and cultural things. First, cultural evolution could not begin until the symbolic faculty had reached a certain level of development attendant on the emergence of specific properties of human language. If our hominid ancestors once spoke a language that lacked these properties, they must also have lacked discursive consciousness and hence the ability to construct conceptual designs in advance of their realization as artefacts. Second, the genesis of novel conceptions implies an awareness of alternatives, of other possible ways of doing things, allowing the subject to stand back and judge rationally amongst them. Man thereby becomes the agent rather than the object of selection, a designer rather than a bearer of culture, adopting and rejecting in accordance with his purposes. As we saw in Chapter 2, the idea of an intentional selecting agent, with its implications of teleology, is quite foreign to the Darwinian theory of evolution by natural selection. Hence one cannot, at one and the same time, equate the cultural with the artificial *and* maintain that a strict analogy obtains between the processes of organic and cultural adaptation. The analogy would be rather with the artificial selection of domesticates. Third, if a prerequisite for culture is the articulation of conceptual forms in language, it must be transmissible by teaching as well as learning; conversely, any tradition that can be learned but not taught cannot qualify as culture.

These are important issues to which we shall return later in this chapter, and I bring them up here simply to point out the implications of treating culture as the sum of the products of discursive consciousness, and the evolution of culture as a kind of World 3 history (Popper and Eccles 1977:458). I wish now to turn to the difficult question of how we are to regard the consciousness of non-human animals. Granted that they lack the highly developed symbolic faculty of human beings, are we to conclude that they are without consciousness altogether? That, of course, was the position of Descartes, and he has had many followers (Walker 1983:5–20). It will be recalled that Morgan, in his work on the American beaver, retained a Cartesian conception of mind as a thinking principle that he neverthe-less supposed to inhabit the bodies of animals of every species. Thus the beaver has thoughts, just as we do, but being mute he cannot tell us about them. Those today who would credit animals with consciousness, yet who cannot conceive that this would take any other form than rational deliberation and reflective self-awareness, are bound to arrive at similar conclusions. One of the most outspoken recent proponents of this view, still something of a heresy in the fields of ethology and psychology, is Donald Griffin. He puts the question about animal consciousness in the following way: 'Do animals have any sort of mental awareness of probable future events, and do they make conscious choices with the intent to produce certain results?' (1977:31). Griffin suspects that they do, but admits that there is no way of knowing for sure unless a mode of communication can be devised that would allow the animal to deliver an introspective report on its experiences to a human investigator. Hence the need to experiment with alternative channels (using, for example, manual gestures rather than vocal sounds) until an appropriate medium can be found for two-way communication, providing us with a 'window' into the animal's mind. Advocating what he calls a 'participatory approach', Griffin likens the problem faced by the ethologist in establishing a dialogue across spe-cies boundaries with that faced by anthropologists in making contact with human beings of other cultures, and he suggests that anthropological methods could well be extended to the study of other species (1976:87–90).

This idea rests on a fundamental misconception about the nature of language, according to which it is but a means for the outward expression or broadcasting of thoughts that would otherwise remain private, known only to the subject. The non-human animal has its thoughts, it is supposed, as does the human native of another culture; in both cases, to discover what these thoughts are, we have only to teach them our way of communicating, or preferably to learn theirs. But language is not just a system for *transmitting* ready-made thoughts; it is, first and foremost, an essential instrument for their very production, without which there could be no deliberate thinking at all (though for a contrary view, see Walker 1983:112–14). The native differs from the animal in this crucial respect: The former possesses a language—albeit different from ours though no less sophisticated—that enables him to think; the latter does not. Even if we could acquire a perfect knowledge of the animal's communicatory mode, we should still not be able to establish a true dialogue in the sense of an exchange of ideas. Suppose I pretended to be a bee as Griffin in all seriousness suggests (1976:92–3): By manipulating a model that could execute on my instruction a faultless waggle–dance, and succeeding in getting other bees to respond in an appropriate fashion, I should still be doing something no bee has ever done, namely dancing out an idea. Nor could any bee grasp the idea, as I can 'read' the meaning of the dance. I think, in my language, That means the food is over there; the bee simply flies off and finds it. In short, man and animal are not interchangeable partners in the 'conversation' between them, so that participation in the full anthropological sense is out of the question.

The point that animals are not muted thinkers may be illustrated in another way. A person who is deaf and dumb nevertheless is endowed with the faculty of reason and can perfectly well express his thoughts if an alternative medium can be devised to overcome the physical impediment. The normal animal is not like that at all. Throughout its waking life it continually emits and receives a veritable profusion of signals, but without a reflexive linguistic facility it cannot isolate thoughts as objects of attention (Reynolds 1976:29–30). That is to say, rather than thinking without communicating, it communicates without thinking, so that the signals it transmits correspond to bodily states and not to concepts. No amount of searching for alternative channels of communication, or attempts to inculcate humanlike communicative modes in animals, will reveal thoughts that simply are not there.[2] Lest this view should seem too anthropocentric, it should be recalled that for the most part, we do not stop to consider before we act, any more than do animals. Indeed, ordinary life would be impossible if we did—remember the fate of Koestler's centipede. Both non–human animals and human beings know *how;* they can perform consummately without having to apply any conscious prescriptions. Such performances are not unintelligent, however close they may come to being instinctive, in so far as they are finely attuned as solutions to the demands of the moment (Langer 1972:31; also Humphrey 1976:304; Clark 1982:20). Animals and humans thus share what Cassirer calls 'a practical imagination and intelligence', but only humans (he goes on) have *'a symbolic imagination and intelligence'* (1944:33).

The essential point to grasp is that the symbolic imagination, though it sets us apart (or as some would say, above) in the animal kingdom, is by no means continually engaged in the guidance of human conduct. We might like to think that fully articulate, propositional language, such as is printed in books, is the norm of human communication, and that all the rest—including all non–verbal communication—adds up to no more than a residue of exceptions left over from our animal heritage. This, as Midgley has trenchantly argued, is to commit a gross error of proportion; for the reality is that the sphere of non-verbal communication has in no way contracted with the transition to humanity and that articulate speech is like the tip of an iceberg in comparison (Midgley 1983:88). Yet however much our executions and utterances are spontaneous, impulsive and unpremeditated, we still feel ourselves to be conscious agents. It is rather ironic that we should expect of an animal, as a condition of its being considered conscious, that it display in all its activities the reasoning abilities of a philosopher, abilities we exercise but seldom in the course of practical, everyday life. To say that the animal is not conscious because (lacking language) it does not think before it acts, whilst admitting that we are conscious even though (despite language) we usually act before we think, is surely to apply double standards. To be consistent, we should either equate consciousness with the rational intellect, and in so doing exclude it not only from the life of animals but from most human life as well, or we should admit that what reason offers is a *reconstruction* of the movement of consciousness intrinsic to the lived experience of humans and animals alike.

Recognizing the distinction between discursive and practical consciousness, the issue is readily resolved. For Griffin, consciousness involves the construction of mental images of desired future states, that is the articulation of prior intentions, as a guide for conduct (1976:5). In denying that animals without language do this, we deny them discursive consciousness. But we do *not* deny that their action is intentional in the sense that it is directed by practical consciousness, just as is similarly habitual action by human beings. Such a denial may be appropriate in the case of honey-bees and other 'social' insects, but it is scarcely reasonable with regard to higher animals, which—as Marx wrote of men—are demonstrably sensuous and therefore *suffering* beings (see Marx 1964a:181–2). Lorenz has remarked, with ample justification, that in view of the similarities in nervous processes of human beings and higher animals, it would be extraordinary if they did not 'have subjective experiences which are qualitatively different but in essence akin to our own' (1966:180). Although such animals do not converse, philosophize or engage in propositional disputation, there seems little doubt that they engage with one another (or if tame, with human partners) in some kind of communion (Langer 1972:202; Midgley 1983:115). However, without the emergence of a sense of self this must take the form of trans-rather than intersubjectivity, analogous perhaps to the communion of a human mother and her infant before the latter has developed an identity of its own (see Harré 1979:331). As we saw in Chapter 6, a great deal of the human use of language is practical rather than discursive in that it serves likewise to relate persons rather than ideas and concepts—as in Malinowskian 'phatic communion'.

Let us grant, then, that non-human animals are purposive agents, but that they do not impose a conceptual grid on the flow of experience and hence do not encode that experience in symbolic forms. Since the self that one can be conscious *of,* as an object of reflection, can only be an abstraction based on the discursive reconstruction of its activities, the animal must lack consciousness of self (Harré 1981b:158). For the same reason, as we saw in Chapter 4, it must lack an awareness of time. Its consciousness, and the duration intrinsic to its being, is not detached from, but effectively consubstantial with, its life in the world. 'Just as animal life', Langer writes, 'is lived "here", "there" and en route from one place to another, but not in a geometric space, so its "time" is a present always heading into a future, but not a homogenous temporal dimension in which earlier and later events are ranged' (1972:337). Time and space as *dimensions,* infinite and undirected, are, like the self whose activities may be plotted in them, elementary abstractions dependent for their appearance on symbolic presentation. But most crucially, the animal's conduct is characterized by intentionality, even though it does *not,* as Griffin claims, picture itself as a participant in imagined future events and make a choice as to which image of the future it will try to bring to reality (Griffin 1976:5). The general question this raises about the nature of intentionality will serve to introduce our next theme: In what sense can action be regarded as intentional when it is not the execution of an intent previously arrived at by a process of rational deliberation, and therefore already present as a thought that may be articulated in discourse? The answer to this question hinges on a vital distinction, due to Searle (1979), between *prior intention* and *intention in action*. In what follows I shall show how this distinction relates to the senses of consciousness already outlined, to different understandings of the meaning of production and ultimately to the dichotomy of social action and cultural behaviour.

Intentionality, conception and behaviour

Consider first the connection between seeing some object in the environment, say a flower, and our memory of that object. The latter is an image, by which the flower may be *re*presented as an object of attention at some future time. But I see many things that leave no such image, and the memory of the object is not essential to visual perception. On the other hand, the very phrase 'I see' implies the experiencing self as a centre of consciousness. A camera can record images for posterity but does not actively *see;* a person sees but does not necessarily retain an image for future reference. Now the relation between intention in action and prior intention is exactly that between seeing and memory, except with the direction of causation reversed (mind to world, instead of world to mind). A prior intention is an imaginative *re*presentation of a future state that it is desired to bring about, and differs from memory only in that it precedes rather than succeeds the objective realization of that state. This is also to say, of course, that states conditional on the articulation of prior intentions are necessarily artificial. The intention in action, by contrast, corresponds to the experience of actually doing; in that sense it is *presentational* rather than *re*presentational. And just as we can see without retaining an image in memory, so analogously, we can act without necessarily holding before our mind a picture of the intended state (Searle 1979:267–8). Thus prior intention is not an essential component of action, whereas the intention in action is precisely that without which we could not speak of action at all.

As the camera records but does not see, so a mechanical robot can execute the prior intention of its programmer, but does not purposively *act*.

If it were argued, to the contrary, that a necessary and sufficient condition for intentional action is the conceptual representation of an intended state prior to its implementation, we would soon be at a logical impasse. For we would have to ask, Whence came the prior intention? Behind it must lie another prior intention, of which the former is a realization, behind that another and so on *ad infinitum*. Likewise if seeing were dependent on memory alone, to see would be to have a memory, of a memory, of a memory, . . . But there is, as we saw in Chapter 5, something *more* to intentional action than the mechanical execution of prior conceptions, describable in terms of the formula 'A makes B'. This corresponds to the creative movement of consciousness epitomized by the formula 'A lives', in other words to the flow of intentionality *in* action, by which the person advances beyond the prior intention even in the course of its execution. In this movement lies the origination of conceptual novelty; thus prior intentions are, like memories, but inessential snapshots artificially cut out from experience by the operation of the intellect and held up to view, in the rationalist reconstruction of conduct, as a series of discrete antecedents. This is just another way of saying that prior intentions are the products of discursive consciousness, whereas intention in action corresponds, of course, to what we have called practical consciousness. And returning to the question of consciousness in animals, we may answer it by saying that animal conduct may be intentional in its *presentation,* and may therefore qualify as action, regardless of the fact that the animal cannot *represent* it as the revelation of its prior intentions. A dog chasing a ball, to use Searle's example (1979:271), is acting intentionally although it cannot describe itself as doing it.

Now consider the following passage from Schutz, which represents a very widely held view. He is concerned here to distinguish conscious action from unconscious behaviour:

> An action is conscious in the sense that, before we carry it out, we have a picture in our mind of what we are going to do. This is the 'projected act'. Then, as we do proceed to action, we are either continuously holding the picture before our inner eye (retention), or we are from time to time recalling it to mind (reproduction). . . . This 'map-consulting' is what we are referring to when we call the action conscious. Behavior without the map or picture is unconscious. (1970:129)

We can immediately recognize the mental picture as a prior intention and the procedure of map consultation as a reflexive monitoring of conduct. Our own view, following Searle, is radically different. What makes for conscious action rather than unconscious behaviour is not the existence of a plan, but the presentational intention of the actor who experiences the action as something *he* does. There may be no plan at all, and even where one exists it is unlikely to be more than a partial representation of what is actually, and intentionally, accomplished. For all that is not covered by the plan, there is intention in action, but no prior intention (Searle 1979:259). Schutz's error, surely, is to have confused the intentionality of the planning and consultation process with that of the plan's execution. The fact that I see a photograph does not mean that the camera consciously saw the object depicted. Conversely, the fact that I programme a machine to follow certain directions, and regularly check up on its operations, does not mean that the machine consciously did what it was told. On the contrary, the machine is genuinely unconscious, since there is nothing in its operation not contained in its initial conditions. Hence what it does, in unintentionally executing a prior intention, can only be described as behaviour. Were we to accept that intentionality resides in the consultation of a plan rather than its mechanical execution, we would still—if Schutz's logic were followed—have to posit the existence of a plan for the consultation of plans, leading again to the problem of infinite regress. As soon as we recognize, however, that prior intentions are *not* preconditions for intentional action, the problem simply evaporates. To say that I *do,* wilfully and purposively, I need have no map to read, let alone a map for map-reading.

There is a delightful passage in Morgan's book on the American beaver in which he pictures the mental processes of this remarkable animal at work.

> A beaver seeing a birch-tree full of spreading branches, which to his longing eyes seem quite desirable, may be supposed to say within himself: 'If I cut this tree through with my teeth it will fall, and then I can secure its limbs for my winter subsistence.' But it is necessary that he should carry his thinking beyond this stage, and ascertain whether it is sufficiently near to his pond, or to some canal connected therewith, to enable him to transport the limbs, when cut into lengths, to the vicinity of his lodge. (1868:262)

Morgan regarded the beaver as a consummate engineer, capable of representing in its imagination a complex series of operations *in advance* of their execution. Fifty years later, Kroeber poured scorn on this idea. Complex the beaver's achievements may be, but they are dictated by instinct, not reason.

> The beaver is a better architect than many a savage tribe. He fells larger trees, he drags them farther, he builds a closer house. . . . But the essential point is not that after all a man can do more than a beaver, or a beaver as much as a man; it is that what a beaver accomplishes he does by one means, and a man by another. . . . Who would be so rash as to affirm that ten thousand generations of example would convert the beaver from what he is into a carpenter or a bricklayer,—or, allowing for his physical deficiency in the lack of hands, into a planning engineer? (1952:31)

Morgan undoubtedly exaggerated the beaver's intellectual capabilities, and we may agree with Kroeber that it does not and cannot construct an imaginary blueprint of its future accommodation, something of which even the most 'savage' human is capable. This means that unlike the human house, the beaver lodge cannot be regarded as an artefact or work, since it is not the realization of a prior conception in the mind of the builder, any more than is the shell of a snail. But we have no reason whatsoever to deny that the beaver is acting intentionally, for as we have just seen, the existence of a plan is not a necessary condition for the intentionality of action. Indeed such a denial would relegate a great deal of spontaneous human conduct, too, to the category of unconscious behaviour, in direct contravention of our own experience of acting as wilful, purposive agents (Ingold 1983a:12).

Kroeber's remarks on the uniqueness of human works were anticipated by Marx in his celebrated comparison of the architect and the bee, where his concern was to establish a form of labour 'peculiar to the human species':

> A spider carries on operations resembling those of the weaver, and many a human architect is put to shame by the skill with which a bee constructs her cell. But what from the very first distinguishes the most incompetent architect from the best of bees, is that the architect has built a cell in his head before he constructs it in wax. (Marx 1930[1867]:169–70)

Thus the architect, who here stands for cultural man, carries a blueprint of the task to be performed, prior to its performance, whereas the animal does not. 'The labour process ends', Marx continues, 'in the creation of something which, when the process began, already existed in the worker's imagination, already existed in an ideal form.' Is there, then, nothing more to production than the execution of a prior intention, the revelation of a cultural design? Apparently something is still missing, for 'apart from the exertion of [the producer's] bodily organs, his *purposive will,* manifesting itself as attention, must be operative *throughout the whole duration* of the labour' (1930[1867]:170; my emphases). In other words, production—as opposed to the purely instinctive behaviour of bees—must be informed by *intention in action.* It is extremely important to recognize that two quite separate issues are being confounded here. There is, on the one hand, the question of whether activity is purposive, in the sense of being directed by *practical consciousness;* on the other hand there is the question of whether, or to what extent, it follows the dictates of a *conscious model.* If we accept that practical consciousness is a necessary condition for production, then perhaps bees do not produce but beavers surely do; we do not know at what point consciousness emerges in the animal kingdom, but the line definitely does not lie between mankind and the rest. The construction of conscious models, depending as it does on the symbolic function, may be characteristically human, but it is not essential to production, just as prior intentions are inessential to the intentionality of action. It seems, however, as though Marx's eagerness to discount the work of animals led him to emphasize as a condition of production a criterion that, taken on its own, would take intentionality *out* of the work process itself, and lead us to treat all human conduct as subordinated to the determination of cultural ideas, or to the realization of objectives that are symbolically constituted. And this apparently compromises the materialist thrust of the entire Marxian thesis, as we shall see later in this section.

Engels also worried about the question of whether animals produce, apparently without being able to make up his mind. At one juncture he accepts that they do, but that only man 'has succeeded in impressing his stamp on nature', in the sense of creating an *artificial* world fashioned on the basis of a design constructed in advance of its realization. 'The more that human beings become removed from animals', Engels writes, the more accurately do the material consequences of their actions 'correspond to the aim laid down in advance' (1934:34). Yet having remarked on man's capacity to work towards definite, preconceived ends, he promptly went on to admit that animals, too, 'act in a planned, premeditated fashion' and that their ability to do so is 'proportional to the development of the nervous system', attaining amongst mammals a fairly high level (1934:178–9). Apparently, then, Engels assumes that production is conditional on the formulation of prior intentions, but he is far more prepared than Marx to credit animals with the ability to envisage and plan. Unfortunately, however, Engels demolishes the credibility of his own case by confusing, under the rubric of the 'planned mode of action', the end–directedness or teleonomy of animal behaviour with its alleged teleological conformity to a preconceived idea. So it appears that even plants lay plans: 'There is something of the planned action in the way insect-eating plants capture their prey, although they do it quite unconsciously.' Quite how the plant can unconsciously premeditate is not entirely clear! Nor does Engels draw the line there, for he is quite prepared to attribute embryonic planning to the lowest forms of life, 'wherever protoplasm, living albumen, exists and reacts' (1934:179).

Let me return for a moment to the human architect. Is it in fact the case that, unlike the beaver or the bee, he has constructed his house in the imagination before setting out to build it? Perhaps this is true of the professional architect of modern Western society, who by the logical manipulation of structural elements is free to design and build houses of new and different kinds. But what of the 'traditional' society in which every individual is his own housebuilder? Here what has to be explained is not the speed of change but the extraordinary persistence of architectural style, often over immense spans of time. In his *Notes on the synthesis of form*, Alexander expresses the difference in terms of a rough-and-ready contrast between 'unselfconscious' and 'selfconscious' cultures: 'I shall call a culture unselfconscious if its form-making is learned informally, through imitation and correction. And I shall call a culture selfconscious if its form-making is taught academically, according to explicit rules' (1964:36). Thus unselfconscious architects know *how* but not *that;* their skill and competence lie in the fact that they have learned not to think. They do not knowingly impose designs of their own but faithfully replicate forms sanctified by the weight of tradition. Their actions are governed by habit, their decisions guided by custom (Alexander 1964:34). Self-conscious architects, to the contrary, know *that* but may not know *how;* they have been taught to think but lack practical competence. They are the authors of their own designs, each of which is rationally selected from a range of alternatives as a novel solution to a perceived environmental problem. But untried and untested, these designs are very likely not to work, as we know from bitter experience (Ingold 1983a:12).

For our present argument, the importance of this distinction is that it rests on precisely the same criterion by which Marx separated human practices from those of other animals, here transposed in such a way as to separate out different kinds of human practices. What distinguishes the *most incompetent* self-conscious architects from the *best* of unselfconscious architects is that the former have put their theories first, however inept their practices. Working from symbolic blueprints, they are the constructors of an *artificial* environment, whereas the buildings of unselfconscious architects are no more artificial than the beaver's lodge. By self-consciousness, Alexander is of course referring to the construction of a mental picture, both of the intended object and of the context in which it is supposed to fit. And one of the hazards of self-conscious design, he argues, is that the representation is bound to be incomplete or incorrect: 'In the unselfconscious process there is no possibility of misconstruing the situation: nobody makes a picture of the context, so the picture cannot be wrong. But the selfconscious designer works entirely from the picture in his mind, and this picture is almost always wrong' (Alexander 1964:77; see also Steadman 1979:169–85). In short, unselfconscious culture-*bearers* are the executors of solutions to problems they cannot see; self-conscious culture-*designers* see problems they usually fail to solve, on account of the inadequacy of their models. The inadequacy stems, apparently, from an inability to comprehend more than one part of a total situation at a time. The interjection of reflective thought into complex, innate or learned action sequences breaks them into discrete fragments, so that the self-conscious actor, rather than following unhesitatingly a familiar course, finds himself in an unknown terrain where any number of paths could be followed at every turn. Langer notes that animals, without concepts and symbols, can often operate more effectively than humans can in similar situations, because their instinctive acts—adapted through countless generations of phylogenetic history—are 'unconfused by any awareness of merely possible exigencies, possible errors, or thoughts of other possible acts' (1972:77; see also Cassirer 1944:223). But the same could be said of the habitual acts of human beings, in cases where procedures are not discursively represented in consciousness.

Take such a commonplace act as eating, in which we use in intimate conjunction both an innate apparatus (the jaws and teeth) and a complex of culturally fashioned implements (knives and forks, plates and bowls). To operate this equipment we do not need to carry an instruction manual in the imagination, although in theory we would be capable of constructing one (Ingold 1983a:11). But if eating is, by and large, unselfconscious, it is certainly not unconscious. It is something we do very much on purpose, which is to say that it carries a component of intentionality. Take away this component and eating would reduce to a series of physical movements and their consequences in terms of the ingestion of food. It would be no more something we could claim to be *doing,* in person, than the subsequent bodily process of digestion—where indeed 'intentionality lapses' (Cohen 1978:55).

In general, then, a complete action must contain two components: the intention in action that corresponds to our experience of doing, and the actual physical execution that accompanies it. Remove the latter and we have an action unfulfilled; remove the former and we have no action at all, but merely behaviour (Searle 1979:274). Another illustration of the same point, familiar from previous chapters, concerns the distinction between hunting and predation. A person whose intention to hunt is not complemented by the requisite executive capability, and who therefore kills no game, is not a predator but a failed hunter. An animal that kills without intent, say an insect, is a predator but does not hunt. Or consider speaking. Where for Malinowski speaking is something we *do* in the practical conduct of life, for Saussure it consists merely of 'psychophysical' utterances. The one view focuses on the intentional content of speaking, the second takes no cognizance of intentionality, reducing speaking to a sequence of executions.

To these two components of action, the intentional and the executive, may be added a third component, strictly speaking extrinsic to the action itself, consisting of the representation in the imagination of the intended performance. The elements out of which this representation is constructed are drawn from a cultural (or linguistic) code. In our example of eating we would include in the conscious model the rules of etiquette, which—as Schutz would have said—constitute a map that we consult from time to time as we proceed through a meal. But this map is, of course, part of a much larger pattern of 'logico-meaningful' relationships imprinted in the mind (qua container) of the enculturated individual, and constituting a complete regulative order. Supposing now that we were to disregard the intentional component of action whilst retaining the map, we would then be left with the classic opposition between culture and behaviour, or between rules and executions. Each execution is a discrete item of behaviour, or—as in Saussurian *parole*—an elementary interaction between one individual and another. And just as the physical utterance of words is necessary for the transmission and perpetuation of language, so—to recapitulate a point from Chapter 6—social life, if understood as an aggregate of interactions, serves the reproduction of culture.

Consider once more the architect, depicted in Fig. 7.1A, who sets out with a plan already lodged in his mind (and corresponding to a prior intention) and finishes with the completed house of which the plan is an exact representation. The entire operation could presumably be broken down into any number of constituent steps, each preceded by the appropriate mental instruction and contributing *in toto* to the finished good. But from beginning to end, the activity of the architect is wholly contained in the execution of the preformed cultural project: He *exists* to put the plan into effect, just as the fashion model exists to manifest the style. Of course, there could be no architecture without people to build the houses, no costume without people to wear the clothes, no language without people to speak the words, and no culture without people to exhibit it in their interactive behaviour or communication. Yet as we have insistently argued throughout this work, human beings are *not* simply instruments for the replication of culture; rather they *use* their culture (including architecture, costume and language) as a vehicle for living, for the mutual creation of themselves. In order to arrive at this view, it is necessary to replace what has deliberately been omitted from Fig. 7.1A, namely the intentional content of action that, as we have shown, corresponds to the movement of consciousness by which the person advances beyond a particular act, and into the next, in the very course of its execution. Figure 7.1B, then, gives us the complete picture, indicating the relationships between intention-in-action (informing the life of the subject), prior intention (the plan in his imagination) and execution (the construction of the object). Where prior intentions, executions and objects are discrete and particulate,

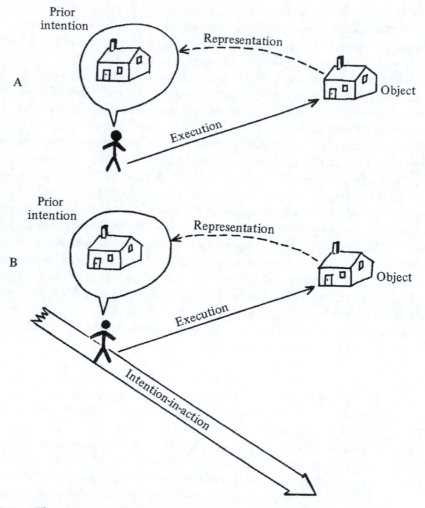

FIG. 7.1 The architect and his house. **A:** The activity of the individual is encompassed in the execution of an object discursively represented as a prior intention. **B:** The translation of image into object reappears as one moment in the life of the person, where the arrow of intention-in-action corresponds to the movement of practical consciousness.

linked by the mechanical necessity of cause and effect, intention-in-action is continuous and creative.

This at once enables us to link our present discussion of intentionality with the central theme of the previous chapter, in which we distinguished between constitutive, regulative and interactive relations. There it was shown that these distinctions could be mapped onto the trichotomy of practical consciousness, cultural form and behavioural execution. The congruence between this trichotomy and the aforementioned components of action should now be obvious. As the person does not live in isolation, his intention-in-action enfolds constitutive social relations, whereas his prior intentions reveal different regions of the cultural map from which he derives his uniqueness as an individual. Subtract both kinds of intention and only the events of individual interaction remain. Such events ensure the transmission and perpetuation of the regulative order whose dictates they follow, but this order is in turn a vehicle for the inter-subjective life of persons. In a nutshell, prior intention is to intention-in-action as culture is to social life; disregarding the intentional content of action is tantamount to the reduction of persons to individuals, and of social relations to material relations. The consequence of this reduction is to invert the relation between man and culture, so that far from the latter being the instrument of man, it appears that man himself is the instrument of culture.

Let me turn now to the implications of these conclusions as regards the meaning of production. If we were to take Marx at his word, in his comparison of the architect and the bee, the totality of production would of necessity comprise numerous separate acts, each with a definite starting-point in the form of a conscious representation, and an end-point in the form of the corresponding object. Since everything about the object is already prefigured in the image, nothing new would come into being in the course of the act of production itself, which would therefore be revelatory rather than creative. For the same reason, the passage of time would be incidental to production; each act could in theory be compressed into an instant, so that a series of acts would occupy but a succession of such instants, arranged chronologically. But now suppose that we adopt Marx's *other* lead, arguing that what is crucial about production is not so much that the producer holds an image before his mind of the task to be performed, but that his action throughout is informed by 'purposive will'. This, of course, is to take the existence of intention-in-action, rather than of prior intentions, as a necessary criterion for production. In that case, production—like the intentionality that informs it—becomes *continuous*. It does not begin or end anywhere but like a stream is carried on, as life is carried on, *through* the entire succession of images and objects that punctuate its progress. To produce, in this sense, is consciously to live, rather than to make things; thus production has to 'be understood *intransitively,* not as a transitive relation of image to object' (Ingold 1983a:15). As in the formula '*A* lives', it refers to the reflexive self-creation of the subject and not, as in '*A* makes *B*', to the construction of objects. Producing their life, human beings in effect produce themselves. And as a creative advance into novelty, real Bergsonian time must inhere in production, just as it inheres in practical consciousness.

This is the sense of production that Ortega y Gasset had in mind when he wrote of human life that it 'is not given us ready-made', that it is not the realization of a project written for us in advance, but rather that 'we must make it for ourselves, each one his own. *Life is a task*' (1941:165). And since, for Ortega y Gasset, man's subjective being is consubstantial with his life, the end of production could only be the end of the producer. As long as there is life and consciousness, production must be going on. This view is echoed by Ricoeur, in a passage cited earlier in this chapter: 'Consciousness is not given but a task. . . . What is the meaning of the unconscious for a being whose task is consciousness?' (1974:108–9). Likewise Cassirer equates production with the creation of human history, rather than the revelation of human beings' natural or cultural attributes, when he asserts that 'man's outstanding characteristic, his distinguishing mark, is not his metaphysical or physical nature—but his work' (1944:68). Marx, too, was concerned to isolate the specifically human quality of production, but particularly in his earlier writings, this was conceived to be most fundamentally not of pre-represented things but of life itself. There is a well-known passage in *The German ideology* where he claims that men 'begin to distinguish themselves from animals as soon as they begin to *produce* their means of subsistence, a step which is conditioned by their physical organiza-tion. By producing their means of subsistence men are indirectly producing their actual material life' (Marx and Engels 1977:42). A mode of production is thus a '*mode of life*'. Furthermore, 'as individuals express their life, so they are. What they are, therefore, coincides with their production' (1977:42). As a producer, I am my life, both subject and superject of production.

The difference between this sense of production, signifying the life of the sub-ject, and the one Marx subsequently adopted, signifying the translation of images into objects, is illustrated schematically in Fig. 7.2. Here the broad horizontal arrow denotes the flow of intentional action, whereas each of the short vertical arrows denotes the execution of a prior intention. If to produce is to live, as a conscious (but not necessarily self-conscious) agent, then—unlike Marx—we find no good reason to doubt that many higher animals other than ourselves engage in production as well. If, on the other hand, to produce is to implement a conscious model, then production encompasses but a small part of human conduct. Either we allow that the unselfconscious architect produces as he constructs his houses, in which case the beaver does also, or in denying that beavers produce, we admit only the houses of the self-conscious architect as products. Be that as it may, it was with the latter view of production in mind that Marx addressed the question of how production relates to consumption. In a notebook posthumously published as an introduction to the *Grundrisse,* Marx holds that consumption establishes the prior conception, subsequently realized in production: 'If it is clear that production offers consumption its external object, it is therefore equally clear that consumption *ideally posits* the object of production as an internal image, as a need, as drive and as purpose. It creates the objects of production in a still subjective form' (1973:91–2; see also Schmidt 1971:100). In somewhat less tangled language, the representation in the imagination of an object to be produced is constituted by expectations about

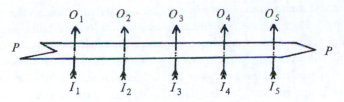

FIG. 7.2   Production and execution. The broad horizontal arrow signifies production
(*P*) as a process of life; short vertical arrows are separate executions,
translating a succession of images (*I*) into corresponding objects (*O*).

how that object, once made, will be consumed. But if this representation, furnished by consumption, 'is active in production as its determinant aim' (1973:91),
is this not an argument for the absolute priority of consumption over production,
and by implication for the cultural determination of conduct?

Indeed it is, so long as production is viewed, as Marx views it here, as the
execution of a prior intention, subject to the symbolic teleology of consumption.
However, Marx himself would have it otherwise, and he presents an extraordinarily tortuous and ultimately circular argument in an attempt to demonstrate that
production and consumption are 'moments of one process, in which *production is
the real point of departure* and hence also the predominant moment' (1973:94; my
emphasis). To prove this, he has to show that somewhere along the line, products
miraculously appear that 'present' to the consumer the need that subsequently
motivates their production (see Sahlins 1976b:153–5). The endeavour by which,
as Sahlins puts it, 'Marx transforms the pre-existent image of production into its
objective consequence' (1976b:153) must be deemed to have failed. The illogical-
ity of the argument is precisely analogous to that of Saussure's claim that new words
enter a language by virtue of first having been spoken (see Chapter 4). If language
is a condition of speaking, how can one utter words not already in one's language?
Likewise, if the image furnished by consumption is a condition of production,
how can one produce objects not already represented symbolically in the cultural
plan? These difficulties, highly inconvenient for Marx, are most convenient for
Sahlins, who is out to show that all human conduct is governed by an independent
cultural logic, and that human beings exist as the instruments through which this
logic works itself out in practice. 'The general determinations of praxis', Sahlins
contends, 'are subject to the specific formulations of culture; that is, of an order
that enjoys, by its own properties as a symbolic system, a fundamental autonomy'
(1976b:57). Marx's admission that human wants are posited symbolically prior to
their satisfaction through the production of useful things (or 'use–values') surely
only proves Sahlins's point. One has but to add that the value of the thing, like
the meaning of a word, derives from its relations to other things within the total
cultural structure, as one constituent element of a 'way of life'. Production, then,
appears subservient to the reproduction of culture.

Suppose, however, we were to adopt the *alternative* view of production, not
as the objective materialization of a way of life, but as the process of life itself.

That is to say, suppose that what is produced consists not of successive utterances manifesting a language but of a directed conversation; not of kills demonstrating a technique of predation but of the communal life of the hunters; not of houses exhibiting an architectural style but of the domestic life of their inhabitants. This, of course, is precisely what is ignored by cultural determinists who seem to think that there is nothing more to life than the way of living it. Now if we accept such a view of production, then clearly it stands to consumption as the horizontal arrow stands to the vertical arrows in Fig. 7.2. Consumption, as Marx himself admitted, establishes a transitive relation between image and object. Production, on the other hand, is action directed by practical consciousness whose 'product', at any particular moment, is the consumer in person. Thus production presents, consumption represents; the one is characterized by intention-in-action, the other is the source of prior intentions. Looked at from this angle, consumption is unquestionably accessory to production, and not the other way round. This is but another way of expressing the subordination of culture to social life, where the latter is understood as the process of mutual constitution of persons, rather than as the sum of interactions. Similarly language is accessory to speaking, so long as speaking is regarded *not* as a series of discrete, individual behaviours but rather as socially directed action. The point can be most readily appreciated by referring back to Fig. 6.4. To translate this figure into the terms of our present discussion, we need only read the interactions I–I as *executions,* reproducing a system of representations (C–C) posited by *consumption,* which in turn serves as a vehicle for the social *production* of, and by, persons in mutual relationships (P–P). Production envelops consumption as social life envelops cultural form, but with the withdrawal of its intentional component, production reduces to execution and so comes to be enveloped *within* the given finalities of consumption, just as interactive relations are contained by the regulative order they express.

Figure 7.2 could in fact be taken as a model for a number of other familiar Marxian dichotomies. We have already mentioned that between social relations and material relations, corresponding respectively to the life of persons and the interaction of individuals. It could similarly be argued that the horizontal arrow represents social labour as distinct from its particular technical forms, which are defined by the manner of its execution. The tailor, to cite one of Marx's favourite examples, follows a different set of instructions in making a coat than the weaver does in making linen; the difference lies in the *ways* each of them work, but the same man may tailor one day and weave the next (Marx 1930[1867]:10–13). If these specific and impersonal features of representation and execution are disregarded, we arrive at the notion of social labour as a trajectory of intentional conduct, which may be in tailoring, weaving, or whatever. And again, whereas technical labour yields particular useful objects, *use-values,* social labour yields real *value.* The use-value of the object, the manner in which it is consumed, depends on its position in the cultural system; its value resides in its enfolding of a certain stretch of the life of the producer, who is of course a socially constituted agent. In considering a work as a use-value, we are concerned with its objective properties and potential application irrespective of who made it; in considering its real value we see the work as an embodiment or crystallization of the intentional activity of its maker, irrespective of what it may be used for. Thus value relates to use-value, we might argue, in the same way as, in Fig. 7.2, production relates to consumption, or consciousness to models *in* consciousness. In effect, the distinction is identical to Wieman's between the creative good (subjective life) and created goods (objective things).

However, in *Capital*, Marx writes of social labour and value not as personal realities, but as impersonal abstractions. This is because his prime concern is with the production of commodities by workers whose own executive capacity (labour-power) has become estranged from their subjective intentionality. From the point of view of the capitalist, they *do* exist merely to execute a plan (just as do human culture-bearers generally, from the alien perspective of Western anthropologists). They cannot produce, any more than they can co-operate, *in person,* since 'in the labour process they have already ceased to belong to themselves' (Marx 1930[1867]:349). On the factory floor, production can only be execution, and the producer only a cog in 'the great labour machine' (Mumford 1967:191). In a remarkable passage in *Creative evolution,* Bergson describes how thought artificially reconstitutes the flow of life from a succession of discrete states or events. Imagine, he writes, that you want to portray on a cinema screen a marching regiment.

> The process then consists in extracting from all the movements peculiar to all the figures an impersonal movement abstract and simple, *movement in general,* so to speak: we put this into the [cinematographic] apparatus, and we reconstitute the individuality of each particular movement by combining this nameless movement with the personal attitudes [captured on each frame of the film]. (Bergson 1911:322)

This is as good a description as any of how Marx arrives at his concept of abstract social labour, which is combined with the technical particularities of each execution to yield a complete account of the labour process. But it is an account that starts from an original fragmentation into discrete episodes, already divorced from the intentionality of the subject who plays them, just as the cinematographic projection starts with a frame-by-frame record of the bodily attitudes of the marching men, minus the intentional component of action that corresponds to the soldiers' experience.

In other words, what is captured on film is no more, and no less, than what is captured in the capitalist's appropriation of the labour-power of the workers, namely the component of behavioural execution. Hence in the reconstruction of conduct, the duration of practical consciousness is replaced by a time that is abstract and mechanical. For the intrinsic movement denoted by the horizontal arrow in Fig. 7.2 we substitute a pure geometrical line divided into fixed intervals—a time *dimension.* Each vertical arrow represents an instruction and its execution, or, in the case of the film, an image and its projection. And the extrinsic movement of the projector, in Bergson's analogy, corresponds to the movement of the *clock,* which, as Mumford has argued, was the archetype for all subsequent machines (1967:286). That is why abstract social labour can be quantified in chronological units: days, hours, and minutes. Consequently, abstract value, as the congelation of abstract labour in commodities, is determined by the number of such units required for their manufacture (Marx 1930[1867]:7). But since the dimension of chronological time, like that of geometric space, describes a boundless void, it is difficult to see how the accumulation of any amount of abstract social labour can add up to anything *real* or *substantial* at all. To return to reality, it is necessary to reintroduce intentionality into production, to revert from what the camera records or what the capitalist appropriates to what *we* see and do.

Imagine the horizontal band in Fig. 7.2 as a uniform strip of film, the images (I_{1-5}) as successive frames, and the objects (O_{1-5}) as their projection on the screen, and it will be clear that Bergson's notion of the 'cinematographical method' furnishes an excellent metaphor for the 'bitty' view of production entailed in Boasian cultural determinism. There are, in this view, only pre-existent ideas and corresponding executions, each occupying an instant in abstract time. Nothing in production is not prefigured in culture; the former is but the revelation of an intellectual or cognitive order that is fundamentally *discontinuous*. Yet as Bergson insisted, 'There is *more* in a movement than the successive positions attributed to the moving object, *more* in becoming than the forms passed through the turn', or as we would add, *more* in production than the execution of ideas one after another (see Bergson 1911:333). For production, far from being encompassed within the finalities of consumption, forever overtakes them in the very process of their implementation. And it does so by virtue of its direction by the agency of consciousness as a movement in real time, a projection of past into future, which as we have shown is essentially *continuous*. The opposition between continuity and discontinuity is perhaps the most fundamental of all and underlies the entire constellation of derived oppositions we have been exploring in these pages. It may be convenient at this stage to summarize them:

Continuity	Discontinuity
Consciousness	Conscious models
Intention-in-action	Prior intentions
Production	Consumption
Presentation	Representation
Social life	Culture

The cultural grid, then, imposes discontinuity on the continuity of social life, much as the intellect decomposes subjective experience in its construction of an abstract 'self', or as production is segmented by the successive 'ends' of consumption.

The parallel that we have noted between the capitalist's appropriation of the executive capacity of the producers, and the construction and appropriation by an objectivist anthropology of 'other cultures', is by no means accidental. Both involve a kind of alienation, by which practices are divorced from the intentionality of those who carry them out. The anthropologist, like the capitalist, is an 'alien will' (Marx 1930[1867]:347) who, so long as he remains a spectator rather than engaging as a participant, can grasp by observation only the plan and its execution. For both, people are construed to exist as instruments for the enactment of the plan, although—unlike the capitalist—the anthropologist is not (or at least claims not to be) the *author* of the plan, which is supposed to have arisen *sui generis*. As those powers and skills that constitute the nature of the worker are placed under the command of the capitalist, so the particular competences of the culture-bearer are harnessed to the will of the anthropologist, for whom the objects of culture are goods that can be turned to account in his own pursuit of rational enlightenment. Ways of life, removed from the life they conduct, contribute to the anthropological accumulation of culture in the sense of civilization, just as means of production, severed from the life of the producers, contribute to the capitalist accumulation of wealth. And if the capitalist is interested in people only in so far as they can be employed in the operation of productive means, the anthropologist of similar bent would treat them merely as the animators of their way of life, putting on a performance for his own personal benefit and enjoyment. As capitalism inverts the relation between man and machine, turning the one into the slave of the other, anthropological objectivism inverts the relation between man and culture. Only the anthropologist remains 'above' culture (claiming thus to be 'cultured'); only the capitalist remains 'above' production (appropriating thus the wealth that is produced). Finally, as relations between workers on the factory floor, in the course of the labour-process, are limited to material relations of co-operation, likewise in the enactment of culture only interactive relations are admissible. Persons do not co-operate by means of culture; rather as individuals, they are *co-operated* by culture.

The comparison is summarized in Fig. 7.3, though I should emphasize at once that my criticisms are directed not against the concept of culture *per se,* nor against all of anthropology, but only against a particular anthropological *usage* of the culture concept. This usage is, however, deeply rooted and pervasive, stemming as it does from the way in which the concept was originally introduced into anthropology as a synonym for civilization, and subsequently transferred from the observers to the observed. Far from challenging the assumed superiority of the former over the latter, the effect of this transferral was, as we saw in Chapter 2, to convert an explicit relative superiority into an implicit, absolute one, or ascendance into transcendence. It was for this reason that culture came to denote not just an acquired tradition, but a fatalistic bondage to tradition diametrically opposed to the liberty of the rational observer. Where the epitome of the 'civilized man' is the self-contained, free-floating individual, surveying the many worlds of culture as though from outer space (or more realistically, spending his life in transit between international airports), the 'man in a culture' is conceived as a prisoner condemned to the monotonous replication of his heritage, and without hope of reprieve. As the

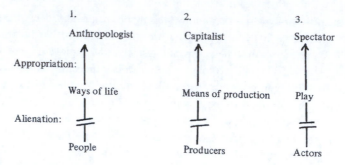

FIG. 7.3 The appropriation of culture.

1. People exist to enact ways of life for the benefit of the anthropological observer; social relations are reduced to interactive behaviour.
2. Producers exist to operate means of production for the benefit of the capitalist; production is reduced to execution, social relations of production to material relations of co-operation.
3. Actors exist to perform for the benefit of the spectators; 'real-life' action is reduced to action in the dramaturgical sense.

former gazes on the infinitude of a boundless universe, the latter is confined to the occupancy of a fixed point in an abstract, spatiotemporal continuum. Drained of the movement that in reality flows through them, cultural forms are, so to speak, framed and hung, side by side along the galleries and corridors of space and time, just like the objects of art with which they are so often bracketed. Or if they cannot be exhibited as such, they may be packaged as scripts or scores to be performed. This commodification of culture for external consumption is, I believe, the source of what is surely one of the most pernicious metaphors of social science: the idea that life is but the enactment of a drama in which people exist only as the parts they play, as *dramatis personae*.[3] We have come across this metaphor on several occasions already, and I intend to elaborate on it only briefly at this point.

What is it that makes an actor's performance on stage different from the action we think of as 'real life'? For one thing, the script he is to follow, and all the details of his movements, are already worked out (Harré 1979:192). Barring accident or extemporary improvisation, everything happens in conformity with a series of prior intentions, with a plan. And for another thing, his performance consists in 'going through the motions', without actually *doing* what those motions suggest. Suppose the script requires him to act out a fight. It is very realistically done, so that the bodily movements and the accompaniment of expostulations are identical to what one might expect in real life. If it *were* real life, we would say the actor was fighting, but because it unfolds on the stage, we say he is *not* fighting but only acting. In other words, the dramaturgical sense of the verb 'to act' is 'to perform the motions required by a set of pre-existent instructions without a corresponding intention-in-action'. The 'real-life' sense, by contrast, is intentionally to *do,* which implies, as we have already shown, the existence of intention-in-action, but not necessarily of any prior intention. This difference, between practical action in the world and the bodily execution of an abstract, choreographic design, is what Bourdieu is getting at when he cautions that gymnastics or dancing can be regarded as geometry 'so long as we do not mean to say that the gymnast and the dancer are geometers' (1977:118). It is because they are not that they can experience the exercise as something they do, as agents rather than operators.

Of course we do not deny that the stage actor is an intentional agent, that he is—subjectively—a person like the rest of us. What he *does,* in real life, whilst performing on stage, is to *interpret* the script, which is to say that the intentionality of his acting resides in the equivalent of what Schutz called 'map-consulting'. But if this interpretative action were itself understood as acting in the dramaturgical sense (such that he performs the role of 'actor' when on the stage and the role of 'family man' when he goes home to relax with his wife and children), we would have a play within a play, in which the person of the actor is doubly masked. That is, he would be playing the part of an actor playing a part. From this it follows logically that if *all* action were conceived dramaturgically, we would be led once again into the abyss of infinite regress. And this is tantamount to the ultimate dissolution of the person. For we could peel off one mask after another, without ever finding the subject within. As every action refers us back to a prior intention, of which it is supposed to be the execution, we could never reach the intention-in-action that corresponds to the consciousness of the agent. However, the sociologist, armed with the concepts of status and role, and fortified by the immortal lines of Shakespeare in *As You Like It*—'All the world's a stage / And all the men and women merely players' (II, vii)—is apt to conclude that there is no such thing as practical consciousness anyway. Unmindful of the limitations of the dramatic metaphor, he forgets that 'behind all roles, personas, and masks the actor remains a real being, a person in no way affected by the parts he plays' (Dahrendorf 1968:27). So when I experience my action, say fighting, as *something I do,* he tells me I have got it wrong. 'Since the world you inhabit', he says, 'is indeed a stage, you are not fighting but acting a fight. Your action is only a performance, the execution of a role concomitant with your occupancy of a position in the regulative order of culture or society.' Nor does he offer me any hope of escape, for the end of the play—my last exit—is the end of me, or as Shakespeare so eloquently wrote, 'mere oblivion, sans teeth, sans eyes, sans taste, sans everything'. If people literally exist to play their parts, then when the parts are played, they have no further business to exist.

The consequence of the dramatic metaphor, therefore, is to take the intentionality out of action, leaving only prior intentions and executions, status and role, norms and behaviour. Man is thus reduced to a mere figment of his true self. Where once stood the person of real life, now stands an artificial construct whom Dahrendorf has christened *Homo sociologus:* 'the alienated persona of the individual, . . . a shadow that has escaped the man to return as his master' (1968:44). For sociology, as Dahrendorf fully recognizes, this poses 'the moral and philosophical problem of how the artificial man of its theoretical analysis relates to the real man of our everyday experience' (1968:25). This is, of course, the relation between person and part, or self and *persona*. The dramaturgical model of action contrives to dismiss the whole problem simply by denying the existence of the former. This denial, we contend, is the result of the very process by which hypostatized 'societies' or 'cultures' are held up as objects for external contemplation. The spectacle of the *theatrum mundi,* of the world as a stage, is one available only to beings who do not have to live on it: It is a 'sovereign point of view', in Bourdieu's words, 'one afforded by high positions in the social structure' (1977:96). From such a privileged position, overlooking a society, it is easy to imagine that as people go about their business, scurrying this way and that, they are simply giving expression to a symbolically constituted, regulative order. No sooner do they make their entrance on the cultural scene, or so it appears, than they step out of themselves, executing a plan for which they bear no responsibility. Likewise under capitalism, the producers cease to belong to themselves at the very moment when the labour process begins, and hence can no longer be said to produce in person. But in reality, we argue, the world is *not* a stage, and the business of human beings is not to enact a plan but to produce their lives by means of it. This takes us back to the 'real–life' sense of action, which thus stands to the dramaturgical sense in the same way that the sense of production corresponding to the conscious self-creation of the subject stands to the sense corresponding to the 'architectonic' realization of preformed conceptual structures. Naturally enough, to adopt the latter view of human work is also to treat all action as dramatic performance (Harré 1979:6).

In what follows, the concept of action will be retained, as throughout this work, in its real–life sense. For the other sense, we reserve the concept of *behaviour*. It is now high time to consider the dichotomy between action and behaviour in somewhat greater depth than heretofore, as it is of the utmost importance; moreover our understanding of the dichotomy differs in certain rather crucial respects from social scientific orthodoxy. The classic statement on which this orthodoxy rests was made by Max Weber, in his *Wirtschaft und Gesellschaft,* where he presents a formal definition of social action:

> In 'action' is included all human behaviour when and in so far as the acting individual attaches a subjective meaning to it. . . . Action is social in so far as, by virtue of the subjective meaning attached to it by the acting individual (or individuals), it takes account of the behaviour of others and is thereby oriented in its course. (1947:88)

Behaviour, conversely, consists of bodily movements considered apart from subjective meaning, or executed in the absence of such meaning (Levine and Levine 1975:165). According to Weber, to grasp the meaning the subject attaches to his action is to expose his state of mind, which requires a process of observation and interpretation Weber called *Verstehen,* a word usually translated as 'understanding'. Although *Verstehen* is primarily applicable to the context of human affairs, Weber did not rule out the possibility of gaining such understanding even of the mental states of non-human animals, both domestic and wild. If animals react to humans in ways not purely instinctive but in some sense consciously meaningful, then— so Weber thought—it would in theory be possible to formulate a sociology of their mutual relations. Indeed he went so far as to suggest that the understanding we may gain of animals is every bit as great as that which we may gain of primitive human beings, a view that says much for his sympathy towards animals but little for his appreciation of so-called primitive peoples. As Parsons points out, Weber fails to take account of the fact that 'no non-human species has even a primitive form of language; whereas no human group is known without a "fully-developed" one'. If language is a condition for the articulation of subjective phenomena, the same degree of understanding must be possible for human beings of every other culture, and equally impossible for animals of every other species (Weber 1947:104 and n. 27).

The question of whether we can 'understand' animals, in the technical sense Weber had in mind, highlights a critical ambiguity in the notion of subjective meaning. This ambiguity was already present in the writings of the neo-Kantian philosopher, Wilhelm Dilthey, who was for Weber a major source of inspiration (Hodges 1944:21). Dilthey began by defining understanding as the process of inward apprehension by which we find enfolded within every event the total movement of consciousness of which it is a moment. 'In understanding', he wrote, 'we start from the system of the whole, which is given to us as a living reality, to make the particular intelligible to ourselves in terms of it. It is the fact that we live in the consciousness of the system of the whole which enables us to understand a particular statement, a particular gesture, or a particular action.' Subsequently, however, we find Dilthey defining the term in quite another way, as 'our name for the process in which mental life comes to be known through expressions of it which are given to the senses' (cited in Hodges 1944:20–1). The difference between these two modes of understanding, by participation and observation respectively, corresponds to an equally important and indeed commonplace distinction between what an actor *means* to say or do, and the *meaning* of his utterance or performance (Schutz 1970:173; Giddens 1979:85). The former sense of meaning is *intransitive* and denotes the intentional content of action, or in other words the responsibility of the agent for what is carried out. Clearly one can grasp this kind of meaning only by viewing acts and intentions as moments in a total process of life, in relation to what comes before and after. To take an obvious and familiar example, it is by following and participating in a conversation that one can understand what a particular speaker meant by what he said on a particular occasion. Yet an interloper, competent in the same language, would have no difficulty in understanding the meaning of the words spoken—that is, their referential significance. This latter sense of meaning is *transitive* and in the present context establishes a relation between a concrete behavioural execution and a conceptual image (the content of a subjective state), of which it is taken to be the realization. For example, we come to know the plan that the self-conscious architect has constructed in his imagination by the external observation—through our sense of sight—of the house he builds. That, of course, is Dilthey's *other* sense of understanding. But it leaves us no wiser as to *why* he built it.

It should be quite evident that the transitive and intransitive senses of meaning, as outlined here, correspond respectively to production as the discrete execution of a prior intention, and production as a continuous process of intentional conduct. And referring back to the earlier part of this chapter, it is plain that although we may 'understand' the conduct of non-human animals as governed by conscious intentionality, we cannot hope to discover amongst them prior intentions whose discursive articulation depends on the symbolic facility of language. Whereas it is not entirely clear from Weber's account whether 'subjective meaning' refers to the component of intention-in-action or to the prior intention realized in practice, Talcott Parsons, in his subsequent development of the Weberian theory of action, leaves us in no doubt that the latter is what is implied (see Levine and Levine 1975:166). Action resolves into elementary 'unit acts', atoms of conduct, each specified by an *end* that 'exists' only ideally, in the private mind of the actor, and that is accessible to the observer solely by virtue of its ensuing realization. 'The end must in the mind of the actor be contemporaneous with the situation and must precede the "employment of means". And the latter must, in turn, precede the outcome' (Parsons 1937:731–3). These relate as initial image (start), execution and final object (stop). Thus the 'unit act' is depicted by each of the short, vertical arrows in Fig. 7.2. This view of action envisages the mind not as a movement but as a *container* whose contents ('subjective meanings') are in fact symbolic representations. Popper would doubtless have called them 'World 3 objects'; so that in his terms the 'unit act' would be an event of translation from World 3 to World 1.

In short, the orthodox definition of action that has come down to us from Weber, through Parsons, embraces all instances of behaviour *explicitly* grounded in a framework of cognitive categories, that is in a cultural system. And if human beings are uniquely distinguished by their symbolic faculty, it would follow that they alone can act, whereas other animals can only behave (Parsons 1977:25–6). Another way of making the same point would be to say that action depends on discursive consciousness, on the precedence of the conscious model over practice. This raises a certain problem concerning conduct that is of a routine, habitual or 'traditional' nature, where no such model is consciously formulated. Does the unselfconscious architect act or behave as he builds his house? Logically, in so far as he does *not* carry an advance picture of the work in his mind, we would have to admit that his building is mere *behaviour,* and conversely, that the outcome of *action,* strictly speaking, can only be artificial. Apparently it is considerations such as these that lead Bock to adopt what at first glance seems a rather eccentric view of the action–behaviour distinction, according to which human beings normally behaving under the impress of fixed routine are pressed into action whenever faced with unfamiliar circumstances that demand a novel response. Traditions and customs, Bock asserts, are powerful shapers of habitual behavior. When, for any reason, the hold of tradition on a people is loosened, human activity becomes possible. Activity thus means the doing of something new and different, and it is responsible for sociocultural differences and for historical changes such as the appearance of what we call civilizations. . . . The contrast between activity and behavior is strikingly brought out when we notice the extremely rare and limited signs of activity in other animals. (1980:185)

In this view, then, behaviour switches over into action (or activity) at the point when theory overtakes and guides practice rather than lagging behind it, that is, when the conscious model precedes rather than follows the execution. Action yields works, behaviour does not. But no sooner has the novelty worn off and the execution become habitual than the model sinks back into the unconscious, and activity reverts to behaviour.[4]

There is something very odd about this conclusion. Why should my conduct in building my first house be classified differently from that involved in building my hundredth, by which time I can 'do it without thinking', when both are executions of the same design, beginning with the same 'end'? In neither case does anything inhere in the conduct itself that is not already present in its identical initial conditions. There is of course the thinking that, in the first case, accompanies the doing, but that is a separate matter. Or to take another example, how does a fight carried out on stage by an actor performing the part for the first time differ from one performed by an actor so accustomed to it that he can go through the motions without a single fault whilst thinking about something entirely unconnected? Surely we would not say that the first is actually fighting whereas the second is not. If we ask what the former is doing, the answer must be that he is *acquiring* or *mastering* a part, a process that is not necessarily shaped by any consciously held plan. And if *that* is where the action lies, it follows that it cannot be identified in contradistinction to behaviour by the presence of such a plan. In general, the problem with defining action as the execution of discursively articulated ends or prior intentions is simply that it seeks to characterize conduct in terms of a property that, though externally *attached,* can no more *inhere* in that conduct than can an image inhere in the object of which it is a reflection. As the object is unaffected by the removal of the mirror, so conduct is indifferent to the subsidence of prior intentions through habituation. On the other hand, it is most decidedly affected by the withdrawal of that kind of intentionality that is presentational, and by virtue of which it can be assigned to a responsible agent.

Our position is that conduct is to be regarded as action whenever it is practically presented by an agent, irrespective of whether it is discursively represented as an 'end' in his mind. Returning to the Weberian definition, this implies that 'subjective meaning' is to be understood intransitively as intention-in-action, rather than transitively as a prior intention. Conduct devoid of intention-in-action is behaviour, even when a prior intention is attached. Now, inasmuch as practical consciousness has its source in the social relations it enfolds, the latter may be said to invest action with intentionality, and in that sense give it meaning (Crook 1980:270–1). But it is a great mistake to imagine that as the mainspring of subjective meaning, social relations must constitute a system that 'is *itself symbolic*' (Sahlins 1976b:139). By subsuming both the transitive meaning of reference and the intransitive one of intent under the general notion of the symbolic, Sahlins contrives to dissolve the distinction between culture and social relations. In our view, culture alone is symbolic in that it represents conduct, furnishing a set of ideal 'meanings' to which this conduct may be referred. Social life, to the contrary, is the intentional presentation of that which is represented in culture. Constituting consciousness rather than models in consciousness, social relations generate meaning not 'in the sense of referring symbolically to another reality; they *are* the reality' (Ingold 1983a:15). Hence we arrive at the absolutely crucial distinction between social action and cultural behaviour, the one issuing from an agent whose purpose is given by his position within an unfolding field of intersubjective relations, the other revealing a plan lodged in the mind of the enculturated individual.[5] A glance back at Fig. 7.2 will show that the distinction corresponds to that between the horizontal and vertical arrows of the diagram. Action thus is essentially continuous and originates with the person rather than the conception. Disregard the agency of consciousness, and action dissolves into an endlessly repetitive series of individual performances, or 'bits' of cultural behaviour (analogous to successive frames on the strip of film, in Bergson's metaphor of the cinematograph). Life becomes a conveyor-belt.

It will be apparent that our view of action entails a notion of the subject quite different from the one implied by Parsons when he speaks of the subjectivity of 'ends'. The latter usage, as already noted, envisages the subject as a detached individual whose mind is a container, the contents of which are 'meanings'. Subjective and objective therefore contrast as ideal image and material execution, or to adopt current jargon, as 'emic' and 'etic' (terms derived from 'phonemic' and 'phonetic' in linguistics, which likewise denote the constituents of symbolic meaning and physical utterance respectively). For us this opposition between the ideal and the material is itself the product of an objectivism that reconstructs the subject by a kind of double inversion, projecting back 'into the actor's head' the reflection of his activity cast in the mind of the external observer. This way of knowing the mind by *inference* from 'expressions of it which are given to the senses' (to recall the words of Dilthey) contrasts, then, with a subjectivism that apprehends it *directly*, not as a passive repository for ideas, already detached from the world, but as a movement or process active within it. Such apprehension requires a totalizing perspective, an understanding gained by entering into a living reality, or—again in Dilthey's phrase—'in the consciousness of the system as a whole'. This is to view the subject as a 'real-life' person rather than as an individual performer of parts, whose identity is constituted not by a unique integration of ideal elements, but by a past history of social relations. The difference between these two ways of grasping the life of the mind 'from the inside', by double inversion and immediate intuition, is already familiar to us from our comparison, in Chapter 3, of the historical approaches of Boas and Collingwood, both of whom derived much of their inspiration from the neo-Kantian tradition Dilthey represented. We can now appreciate how, departing from the same source, they arrived at such contrary destinations.

The distinction we have drawn between action and behaviour may be summarized as follows. Action is equivalent to production as a continuous process of self-creation by a socially constituted, conscious agent (the person); the intransitive 'subjective meaning' of action lies in the intentionality that practically presents it, which can be apprehended only through participatory understanding. Behaviour is equivalent to execution as a sequence of discrete events or performances, revelatory of a symbolically constituted design (culture) whose medium is the mind of the individual; the transitive 'subjective meaning' of behaviour lies in the prior intention that discursively represents it, which can be inferred only through observational understanding. Action is *carried on* by persons in mutual relationships; behaviour is *emitted* by interacting individuals. Where behaviour reproduces the finalities of culture, the latter serves as a vehicle for social action, that is for intersubjective life. The notion of behaviour need not, of course, be reserved for culturally encoded emissions: The determination that it follows (if indeed it is determined at all and not purely random) may just as well be genetic as cultural, innate as acquired, or more reasonably, some combination of the two. No serious cultural anthropologist has ever denied that human behaviour has a genetically determined component (despite frequent accusations to this effect), nor do any but the most rampant sociobiologists really believe it is under complete genetic control, even though in their less guarded moments they are inclined to say as much. But whatever their differences, they are unanimous in excluding consciousness from conduct, such that the latter can never be anything *else* than behaviour, empirically observable physical movements that 'must by definition exist outside of consciousness' (Levine and Levine 1975:167).

So defined, behaviour may be observed throughout the natural world, both living and non-living, wherever there is matter and motion. Indeed the present 'scientific' usage of the term is based on an extension from the inanimate world of physico–chemical reactions to the animate world of beasts, and ultimately to that of humans (Ingold 1983a:5).[6] With action the direction of extension is the other way round, from the domain of human affairs to the conduct of nonhuman animals. We may, with Bock (1980:184), abhor the tendency of sociobiologists to treat all human conduct as if it were nothing but behaviour, and their consequent inability to grasp the properly historical dimension of social life (see also Reynolds 1976:230). It is only fair to point out, however, that those who, like Bock, define action as behaviour *plus* a prior intention, are open to precisely the same criticism. For the prior intention, representing conduct, is necessarily external to it, so that all that remains *in* conduct is behaviour. Although this view of the action–behaviour dichotomy signals a division between two branches of the history of things, dealing respectively with cultural artefacts and natural objects, it fails altogether to comprehend the process of social life as a history of persons. Recognizing that the essence of action lies not in the representation of conduct but in its attribution to a responsible agent, we insist that *the first requirement for action is not culture but practical consciousness.* This carries the further implication that action, like production, is by no means unique to human beings. To be sure, the human agent may have acquired a relatively inclusive—though far from complete—knowledge of the physical operations activated by his purpose, whereas the animal probably has no such knowledge. But this does not, in itself, render the animal's conduct any less purposive. In short, the characterization of conduct as action is indifferent to the balance of innate and symbolic components of intelligence, or of convention and invention, underwriting its expression.

We have finally to relate the key distinction between action and behaviour to the form of time. To recapitulate, and slightly to rephrase, a major conclusion from the discussion in Chapter 4, our point is that awareness of time lies in the imposition of repetitive, culturally determined behaviour on the irreversible continuity of social action. What follows is merely an elaboration of this point. Consider, first, what happens if time is conceived in its abstract, chronological sense, as an infinite and directionless thread spun by a perfectly mechanical system. The perpetual recurrence of the internal states of the system provides a basis for the division of the thread into equal segments, numbered in sequence as dates. Whatever does not recur then goes into history, regarded as a sequence of unique entities or events suspended *in* time, each assigned to the appropriate date. The resulting relation between history and time has been very well expressed by Kubler:

> Our actual perception of time depends upon regularly recurrent events, unlike our awareness of history, which depends upon unforeseeable change and variety. Without change there is no history; without regularity there is no time. Time and history are related as rule and variation: time is the regular setting for the vagaries of history. (1962:71–2)

He goes on to suggest that the same relation obtains between the conventional products of routine performance (replicas) and the novel products of self-conscious design (inventions); thus 'the replica relates to regularity and to time; the invention relates to variation and to history' (1962:77). This corresponds precisely to Bock's distinction between behaviour and action, the former dictated by heredity or custom, the latter 'the doing of something new and different' (1980:185). Hence we might conclude that history stands to time as action stands to behaviour, and that every novel act is a historical event.

This conclusion leads us, in fact, into the very same difficulties that attend attempts to define the character of conduct on the basis of the presence or absence of a property necessarily extrinsic to it. My first house, apparently, is a historical object, but my hundredth has already faded into the backdrop of time against which a succession of other novelties may make an appearance in history, only to recede in their turn upon subsequent replication. Why, of two identical houses, built in exactly the same way, should one be accorded a place in history and the other not? Following exactly the same reasoning as before, we argue that the historicity of an object lies not in the existence of its ideal representation (positing the object as a use–value), but in its enfolding of the consciousness of its maker (i.e. in its real social value). Therefore, if the reduction of history to time is analogous to the reduction of action to behaviour, we must understand that history as one of persons rather than of artefacts. But as has already been shown, the essence of such history is the movement of real time. And so we can conclude that action is to behaviour as real time is to abstract time. In Chapter 4, we attempted to demonstrate that time aware-ness depends on the confrontation of these two kinds of time: the one intrinsic to the consciousness of the experiencing subject, the other contained in the objective order of culture. In subjective life, as William James insisted, nothing ever recurs; rather 'what is got twice is the same *object*' (1890, I:230–1). Taking the former on its own, we would have 'a duration without measures of any sort, without entities, without properties, without events' (Kubler 1962:71)—a time of experience but no experience of time. Taking the latter on its own, we would have the regular repeti-tion of culturally prescribed behaviour, establishing a system of fixed intervals, but no consciousness to apprehend their passage.

Elementary behavioural executions, the little arrows of Fig. 7.2, can be likened to the ticking of a clock, punctuating the flow of action much as every tick marks off a moment in the onward march of real time that we feel as our impatience. The situation of the historical agent, in this analogy, is like that of a man in a room watching a clock, except that the design of the clock is 'inside his head', and its movements are those of his own body, responding to the promptings of culture. Disregarding consciousness is like removing the man from the room, leaving only the clock. As the executor of a traditional, cultural design, the individual is no more *aware* of the passage of time than is the mechanism of the clock, even though both— in a sense—'create' the time in terms of which a non–repeating consciousness can order its experience. Translating the analogy into a Durkheimian idiom, the clock corresponds to the system of regulative relations known as society, whose execu-tive arm is the social being. Functioning in every respect like a machine, whose operation is predictable and repetitive, society generates an *idea* of time through the regular rhythm of prescribed conduct, just as the repetition of the clock yields an abstract chronology. But for this very reason, because of the recurrence of its internal states, society *cannot* correspond to a higher centre of consciousness and is therefore unable to apprehend time as the recurrence of the behaviour it regulates. The consciousness that actually *experiences* the passage of time, measured by the intervals between recurrent behavioural events, can be none other than that of the social person, in his capacity as an agent rather than as the player of a part. Without behaviour we could not measure time, but without action there would be no time to measure. And the time that is measured inheres in the measurer, not in the instru-ment of measurement, in the consciousness of the actor rather than the mechanism of culture. To impute consciousness to culture is to imagine that the clock, in our analogy, is watching the man.

If every culture is a clock, regulating the behaviour of its bearers, then the history of culture must be a chronological sequence of clocks. For the historian, inhabiting a cultural void, the appearance of every novel design is an event, datable according to a universal, astronomically based standard. Yet in that one event, occupying but an instant in the observer's scale of time, are compressed not only the first expression of the design but also all subsequent replicas fashioned on the same model. Together their regular repetition furnishes a specific chronology by which the individual *inhabitant* of culture can order the non-recurrent events of his life. In other words, what is a historical event for the spectator *constitutes for the performer the dimension of time itself.* Within the former's zero is packed the latter's infinitude. That is why objectivism construes the life of the individual to be played out in a single moment of history, an ever-present, which nevertheless opens out, from the inside, into an endless sequence of moments, each of which is marked by a discrete behavioural execution. We would not say, then, that the first execution of a novel design belongs to history, and the hundredth to time. Rather for the observer both belong to the same event of history, located on a common *axis of simultaneity,* whereas for the performer both are part and parcel of the same time, constituting an *axis of successions.* From the very first the execution is built into the mechanism of the clock, whose eventuation marks a point in time for the one, but marks time for the other. But of course in the history of clocks, what is left out is the duration of consciousness that is measured by them, which is also the real time that both separates and connects the recurrent events of life.

The innate and the artificial

I should like to conclude by returning to a leading question that has been begging for attention throughout: How, if at all, is the cultural to be distinguished from the natural, and in what way does the answer we give affect our understanding of the relation between biological and cultural evolution? We should begin by noting that the concept of nature can be interpreted in at least three different senses. In one sense, we may refer to the nature of a thing as that which constitutes the fixity of its being. This, as will be recalled from Chapter 3, is the sense adduced by Ortega y Gasset when he declared 'that man is not a thing, . . . that man has no nature' (1941:185). His concern was to exclude all that is static and thinglike, both bodily and spiritual (or material and ideal) from the concept of man, restricting the latter to the process of subjective life. Nature, in this sense, *includes* culture; so that if we were to speak of the 'nature' of an individual, we would be referring to the sum of both innate and acquired attributes conferring on that individual a specific identity. 'These are the elements', we might say, 'of which it consists: This is its nature.' However, a second sense of the natural, and without doubt the most common in anthropological parlance, *opposes* the cultural, as material to ideal. It is important to recognize how the contrast between this view of what is *not* natural, and the first, ties in with the different notions of subjectivity compared earlier in our discussion of the distinction between action and behaviour. For here the consciousness of the subject is conceived not as a movement (hence opposed to what has a static 'nature') but as a container for ideas (as opposed to their material manifestation). But there is still a third sense of the natural, introduced earlier in this chapter, by which what is innate or conventional is distinguished from the *artificial* products of deliberate invention (Wagner 1975:51). In this case it is a question not of separating the idea from its materialization, but rather of indicating the precedence of one over the other. In the production of artefacts, the conscious conception comes before the object, whereas with natural things this order is reversed. Clearly not all culture is artificial according to this definition, the most obvious example of the non-artificial or conventional in culture being what are commonly called 'natural languages'. If we are to believe Lévi-Strauss, myth would fall into the same category, and much else besides. And Durkheim was making the same point about the naturalness of culture when he insisted that, although in essence supraorganic or ideal, the order of regulative relations ('society') is in no way an artefact or contrivance of the human will, but fully 'a part of nature, and indeed its highest representation' (1976[1915]:18, 422; see also 1982[1895]:143). In what follows, the relation between the cultural and the artificial will be the focus of our concern.

Very commonly the two are simply identified or confused, as evidenced by the selection of citations in Kroeber and Kluckhohn's review of definitions of culture, all of which emphasize the notion of culture 'as a product or artifact' (1952:64–5; see also Geertz 1975:50–1). One of the most explicit, which will serve as an example, comes from Folsom: 'Culture is the sum total of all that is *artificial*. It is the complete outfit of tools, and habits of living, which are *invented* by man and then passed on from one generation to another' (1928:15; my emphases). In a similar vein, Herskovits refers to culture as 'the man-made part of the environment' (1948:17), equating it thus with the category of created goods. For Bidney, culture—or the 'social heritage'—consists of 'the sum total of artifacts, socifacts and mentifacts'. Included in socifacts are norms, 'which serve to regulate the conduct of the individual within society', and in mentifacts such things as scientific theories, as well as the whole gamut of 'language, traditions, literature, and moral, aesthetic, and religious ideals' (1953:130). All of these, according to Bidney, are cultural products, *authored* by man and turned to account in the process of man's 'cultivation' of himself, the development of his own innate potentialities. This view of human beings as the active originators of their cultural forms, employed as instruments for the advance of life and consciousness, goes back, as shown in Chapter 2, to Tylor, whose notion of intellectual progress is one to which Bidney is also committed.[7] And it stands in absolute contrast to the Boasian conception of man as the *executor* of cultural forms, of which he is no more the author than the organism is of its genes. Human beings may be unique in their possession of culture, but this cannot be taken to imply that it is all an invention. Indeed the essential difference between scientific theories and myths, or between mathematics and language, is that only the former are man-made.

Between what is genetically inscribed ('natural' as opposed to cultural) and what is rationally designed (artificial as opposed to 'innate') there lies, then, a third source of human values, as Hayek puts it, 'a tradition of learnt rules

of conduct which have never been "invented" and whose functions the acting individuals do not understand' (1978:5). Virtually reiterating the Boasian
position, Hayek pictures the mind not as an agent but as a medium for this
traditional, regulative order, which it passively absorbs. This leads him to reject
the argument by extension, which holds that as reason is the product of human
organic evolution, so cultural evolution followed as the product of human reason (see Chapter 2). One can no more claim, Hayek declares, *'that thinking
man has created his culture than that culture created his reason'* (1978:6). Men have
not consciously built their institutions, as Tylor held and as we are inclined to
believe on account of our tendency to equate the cultural with the artificial (or
concomitantly, to identify the instinctive with the non-rational). The bearers
of culture do not select, but are themselves selected, through a process vaguely
analogous to natural selection:

> The structures formed by traditional human practices are neither natural
> in the sense of being genetically determined, nor artificial in the sense
> of being the product of intelligent design, but the result of a process of
> winnowing and sifting, determined by the differential advantages gained
> by groups from practices adopted for some unknown and perhaps purely
> accidental reasons. (Hayek 1978:6)

I shall not pursue Hayek's arguments further, as they rapidly degenerate into a
bizarre, offensive and unscholarly diatribe against everything apparently connected
with what he sees as the new savagery of socialism (including even sociology). We
shall return, however, to the evolutionary implications of the distinction between
'natural' and 'artificial' culture, as these are of fundamental importance. But before
doing so, the notion of the artificial needs to be elaborated.

On the face of it, the difference between artificial and natural objects seems
rather obvious. But in fact the matter is anything but simple, as Monod has shown
by asking us to imagine how a computer constructed by the intelligent inhabitants of another planet should be programmed in order to detect evidence of
artefact-producing activity on Earth (Monod 1972:15–21). If it were instructed
to take into account only the macroscopic, structural properties of the objects it
encountered, it might well be capable of distinguishing a cave from an architect-
designed house, but it would certainly be unable to distinguish the latter from,
say, an example of 'traditional' architecture, or for that matter from a beehive
or a snail shell. All of these have a certain geometrical regularity, showing some
kind of formal symmetry or repetition of elements, which the cave—wrought
by geological forces—presumably lacks. Suppose, then, that we programme our
machine to attend to the functional properties of objects. Again it would fail
conspicuously to isolate the artificial, consistently lumping the executive armature
of animals and plants, built to genetic specifications, with works of human engineering imitating animal and plant models. The eye functions like the camera, the
wing of a bird functions in some respects like that of an aeroplane, and—to take

a classic example from the work of D'Arcy Thompson—the skeleton functions like the cantilever (Thompson 1961 [1917]:241–58). Indeed it would seem that the simple examination of finished objects, whilst indicating their form and function, could not possibly suffice to decide on their status as artefacts. To do that, Monod concludes, the computer would have to be programmed to inspect not just the complete object but also its genesis and construction. It would then note that, amongst all those objects endowed with structure and design, there is a class of objects whose properties result from the application to their constituent materials of forces *exterior* to the objects themselves. These, and these alone, would be counted as artefacts (Monod 1972:21).

This latter criterion does indeed enable us to recognize the distinctiveness of living things, which is Monod's prime concern. For whereas the inanimate artefact arises from the imposition of a pre-existent design on formless raw material, the organic project originates with—and is internal to—the organism itself. But if our imaginary computer correctly identified the bee as a natural thing rather than a purpose-built machine, what would it make of the beehive? Surely the forces that shape the hive are external to it, so is it to be classed with the house as an artefact? There is a real ambiguity here, which reflects not so much on the inadequacy of the computer as on a certain confusion amongst ourselves, the programmers. The problem lies in deciding where we are to draw the boundaries of the phenotype. It may seem obvious that the hive is external to the bee, but not nearly so obvious that the shell is external to the snail. Let us admit that the shell 'just grows', as part of an autonomous and spontaneous morphogenetic process, the products of which are, as Monod himself insists, 'entirely distinct from artifacts' (1972:21). The shell, then, is a phenotypic effect of the gasteropodous genotype. But is it really any different with the beehive? In other words, is there a sense in which the hive is 'bee-made'? Assuming that behaviour may be just as much under genetic control as morphology, the answer must be negative. As the outcome of the constructive behaviour of bees, the hive is—just like the snail's shell—a phenotypic effect of a particular set of genes. Of course it is an indirect effect, but granted that even those effects that are internal to the body of the organism (e.g. wing pattern) are linked to the genotype through a long and devious chain of causal connections, the difference between internal and external effects can only be a minor one in the *degree* of indirectness. Thus, when we consider the phenotype *as a whole,* the boundary of the organism—or the living body—appears to dissolve. On these grounds, Dawkins (1982) has defined the sum of the expressions of a genotype that happen to be situated *outside* the body of the organism as the *extended phenotype*, including in this category all so-called animal artefacts that result from genetically programmed behaviour. The beaver phenotype, for example, includes not only the animal itself, but also its lodge, dam and the lake that forms behind, which is no less than 'a huge extended phenotype'. In the case of the beehive, it is necessary to add the proviso that the extended phenotype can be built under the joint influence of genes in not one but a great many individual bodies (Dawkins 1982:198–200). The crucial point for our argument, however, is this: If the hive is an inanimate, 'extended' part of the same objective phenotype that includes the living bee, then the former can be no more 'artificial' than the latter.

Evidently some other notion of exteriority is required, to delimit the class of artefacts, than one based on the boundary of the organism. Perhaps one way of approaching the problem is to ask not what distinguishes artefacts from organisms, but under what conditions organisms can become artefacts. Consider another example. The human body is itself in some respects an artefact, an originally 'raw' object that has been operated on, most often for ritual or decorative purposes—as in coiffure and manicure, tattooing, scarification and circumcision (P. J. Wilson 1980:104). And in its 'natural' state, it provides us with the basic apparatus to do these things, and all else besides. The body, as Mauss once remarked, 'is man's first and most natural instrument', and all his technical operations have an essential bodily component (1979 [1950]:104). Instrument and product are here both 'packaged' within the individual human being (Moscovici 1976:30). And so Monod's imaginary computer, looking for external forces impinging on the object as grounds for its classification as an artefact, would find none. But we humans recognize something that the computer does not, namely the *conceptual plan* that is expressed in body decoration. And although internal to the individual, this plan is external to the body, regarded as a material or organic entity. We therefore conclude that the body is an artefact to the extent that its 'phenotypic' appearance is the result of behaviour serving to execute the plan. Generalizing from this conclusion, any object that results from the imposition of prior conceptual form on material substance, whether that object lies within or beyond the body of the individual concept-holder, must be counted as artificial. And conversely, objects formed in the absence of their prior representation in a conscious model cannot be artefacts, even if they are external to the individual of whose behaviour they are products. Another way of putting the same point is to say that end-directed or teleonomic performances yield artefacts only when teleologically motivated by a set of prior intentions, which are open to discursive formulation. It follows that only humans, being possessed of discursive consciousness, can make artefacts; but more than that, only humans can recognize them for what they are. Thus we can understand why Monod's computer must necessarily fail to isolate the artificial, for to succeed it would have to be equipped with a symbolic facility such that, to all intents and purposes, it would become a human being itself.

It was Lotka who introduced the term 'exosomatic' to refer to the artificial products of human knowledge (1945:188). The subsequent history of the term reflects the ambiguity that we have been concerned to expose. Medawar (1957:139) uses it to distinguish instrumental 'organs that are made' from the 'endosomatic instruments . . . that we are born with'. Thus the axe is exosomatic, the hand that holds it is endosomatic. The former category includes all instruments that, although anatomically separate from the body, can be seen as its functional extensions— 'constituting a kind of shell or skin around man's body, interposed by him between his naked self and the environment around' (Steadman 1979:124). Medawar specifically has in mind the products of human industry, expressing a learning-transmitted tradition, and simply dismisses as odd exceptions the use of tools by non-human animals, whilst ignoring the entire class of tools whose function is to provide accommodation or shelter. Once this omission, which is extraordinary for so eminent a biologist, is rectified, it is at once apparent that Medawar's 'exosomatic instruments' correspond to Dawkins's 'extended phenotype', and may just as well comprise the expressions of a genetic as of a cultural template. Of course we are not literally 'born with' any endosomatic instruments, rather they grow; but as we have shown, the construction of exosomatic instruments under genetic control does not differ in principle. It makes no more, and no less, sense to say that the bee is born with the hive than to say that it is born with its wings.

Lotka's terms, however, were also adopted (with slight modification) by White, who defines human culture as 'an extrasomatic tradition' (1959b:39 and n. 18). Moreover he explicitly equates the extrasomatic with the *suprabiological* domain of ideas and symbols (1959b:12). The somatic, then, designates the sum of bodily movements entailed in symbolically determined behaviour, resulting in 'things and events'. The beehive can be understood in a somatic context, by looking at the constructive behaviour of bees, but not in an extrasomatic context, because it has no correlate on the level of ideas. Human body decoration, though its results are internal to the soma, *can* be understood extrasomatically, by looking for the 'subjective meanings' it transitively expresses. Or again, the extrasomatic aspect of the axe lies not in its anatomical separation from the body, but in the 'conception of its nature and use' without which it would be devoid of significance. One sees the axe, then, in its extrasomatic context, not as an extrasomatic product. Thus whereas for Medawar, the artefact is an exosomatic extension—beyond the individual—of an endosomatic project (albeit learned and traditional), for White it results from the somatic, behavioural execution of an extrasomatic, ideal project. What is 'exteriorized', in the second case, *is not the product but the plan.*[8] And since, in White's view, 'extrasomatic' signifies the ideal in contrast to the material aspect of things, and not what lies outside rather than inside the individual, he finds no contradiction in the observation that extrasomatic phenomena are *internal* to individuals (1959b:15; 1959c:235–6).

One important implication of our argument is that not all tools are artefacts. Whether or not Benjamin Franklin was right, when in 1778 he pronounced man as the 'tool-making animal', has been the subject of a protracted debate that we have not the space to review here. But I do wish to sort out some of the ambiguities surrounding the all-important contrast between tool-*making* and tool-*using*, or more accurately, between making tools for future use, and using tools that have not been made. For as Hallowell has remarked, with ample justification, we cannot hope to pin down what is special or unique about hominid tool-making until we are clear about what constitutes tool-using (1960b:322). There is, first, a sense in which the latter implies the mobilization of objects that happen adventitiously to be available at the time, and that cannot be considered as tools outside the context of their use (Moscovici 1976:53). Thus Bartholomew and Birdsell suggest that the larger arboreal primates are 'tool users in their locomotion. As they move through the maze of the tree tops, their use of branches anticipates the use of tools in that they routinely employ levers and angular momentum' (1953:482). This may seem a slightly tenuous example, but plenty of others may be adduced from all branches of the animal kingdom (see Beck 1980). Consider the history of an ordinary stone, just like any other, lying on the ground. At one moment it has been used by a thrush as an anvil on which to crack open a shell, at another it becomes a means of defence or refuge for a tiny lizard that hides beneath it, and at yet another moment it may be picked up by a man as an offensive weapon to hurl at his adversary. We may say that the stone is particularly *apt* for all three purposes, but it is *ad*apted to none of them. Recalling terms suggested by Gould and Vrba (1982), such tools are not constructed but *co-opted* by their users, harnessed to a project but not made for it. They may perchance have been constructed as adaptations to some other purpose, but are co-opted as *exaptations* for the present one—as when we use a knife for want of a screwdriver, or our teeth for carrying when our hands are full.

Contrasted to this improvisory sense of tool-use, the making of tools implies a transformation of raw material into objects endowed with specific functions, in other words their constructive adaptation. Here it is not the use of an object that makes it a tool, but the make of the tool that gives it a use. There can of course be degrees of adaptive modification, and one can sympathize with Moscovici's point that 'the distinction between fabricated and improvised tools is not an easy one to make, especially when the archaeological data are inconclusive' (1976:54). The difficulty goes deeper, however, for even if we restrict our attention to the class of adapted objects, excluding the virtually unlimited range of things that can be co-opted for one purpose or another, we would still have to agree, with Pumphrey, that 'the web of a garden-spider and the nest of a chaffinch are highly fabricated implements quite as difficult to explain away as any product of lower Palaeolithic man' (1953:233). On the strength of the objects alone, we would have no more valid reason for assigning intellect to the human being than to the spider. The construction of tools, Popper admits, effectively 'goes back to the very beginning of life' (in Popper and Eccles 1977:451–2); for as we saw in Chapter 5, natural selection allows us to account for phenotypic adaptations (both internal and external to the organism) in the absence of a designer. How then, to pursue Popper's question, are we to distinguish the production of enzymes by a gene from the production of tools by a human brain, both of which involve the imposition of form and function on raw material?

The answer normally given is that the brain, or rather the intellect, begins by constructing not the tool itself but a mental image of the tool. A quite different sense of 'making' is then invoked that hinges not on the adaptation of the product but on the priority of the plan (Hallowell 1960b:323–4), designating all manufacture initiated by a mental image—as in the familiar formula '*A* makes *B*'. That image, constituting the object as an *artefact*, is itself constituted by an expectation of how it will be used or consumed; that is, it posits the tool as a use-value. Engels had this view in mind when he asserted that 'labour begins with the making of tools'

(1934:176), for by labour he meant the planned activity of self-conscious (human) organisms in the construction of an artificial environment (Venable 1945:68–9, 148). Yet he recognized a sense in which non-human animals also have tools, citing the ant, the bee and the beaver. However, their tools, in use, mediate an interaction in nature, but not a transforming reaction *on* nature (Engels 1934:34). They are not artefacts, nor are they used to make artefacts. Another proponent of the definition of man as a toolmaker, *Homo faber,* was Bergson, who likewise dwelt on the comparison between human and animal tools—in terms, however, that sound rather strange to modern ears. Human instruments, Bergson claimed, are 'unorganized', whereas animal instruments are 'organized'. Both kinds of instrument are constructed, the latter by the non-reflective faculty of instinct, the former by the reflective faculty of intellect. Animal instruments are organized because they extend 'the organizing work of living matter'; human instruments—or at least those that can be regarded as artificial products of the intellect—are unorganized because the principle of their organization is imposed from outside, it is not intrinsic to the material. Tool-making, then, consists in the transference of form and function onto matter that, from the point of view of the maker, is inherently disorganized and therefore malleable to any purpose. 'Intelligence', Bergson concluded, '*is the faculty of manufacturing artificial objects, especially tools to make tools, and of indefinitely varying their manufacture*' (1911:146). Nowadays we write intelligence as the capacity for symbolic thought, which is as much a foundation for speaking as for tool-making. In stressing the manufacture of tools to make tools, Bergson foresaw the reflexiveness of tool-making that, as I shall show very shortly, is a property it shares with language.

   Homo faber has found his modern advocate in Kenneth Oakley. In a series of publications (1950, 1951, 1954, 1957), Oakley has argued that the power of conceptual thought—and the related capacities to invent and transmit by teaching—are fundamental to the regular manufacture of tools. Man, he asserts, is basically an artist in the Aristotelian sense of art, which 'consists in the conception of the result to be produced before its realization in the material'. Among non-human primates, conception 'is no more than nascent', although 'there is, of course, the possibility of gradation between these two extremes, perceptual thought in apes, conceptual thought in man' (1954:14). Now these extremes correspond to the opposition of tool-using and tool-making; no longer one between the co-optation and construction of objects, but (to adopt Alexander's terms) between unselfconscious and self-conscious construction. To be sure, the animal makes its tools, in one sense, in so far as 'they are the result of an effort and the transformation of raw material' (Moscovici 1976:53). But tool-making, for Oakley as indeed for Bergson, implies not just the implementation but the *invention* or authorship of designs. 'Invention becomes complete', Bergson wrote, 'when it is materialized in a manufactured instrument' (1911:145). In unselfconscious construction, to the contrary, the constructor 'need not himself be able to invent forms at all' (Alexander 1964:58).

   By combining both senses of the using–making dichotomy, one focusing on the properties of material objects (whether or not functionally adapted), the other signalling the presence or absence of an ideal plan, it is possible to generate four classes of tool:

1. Unselfconsciously co-opted (as the stone used by the thrush for shell-breaking, the branch used by the monkey as a lever for locomotion);
2. Self-consciously co-opted (stones earmarked by man for future use, and perhaps transported from their site of natural occurrence, say for grinding or pounding, or for making other tools, but which are not modified for the purpose);
3. Unselfconsciously constructed (such tools may be internal to the body, or external to it; compare the beaver's teeth, used for felling trees, and the dam that it builds with the trees. External tools in this category may be genetically determined, like the beehive and the spider's web, but also included are the products of conditioned, habitual behaviour amongst both animals and humans);
4. Self-consciously constructed (many human tools, originally invented, and whose construction is subject to explicit, taught rules rather than learned by example and imitation. Instances of such tools internal to the body could perhaps be adduced from modern surgical practice).

Class 1 tools are unequivocally *used;* class 4 tools are just as definitely *made.* The problem lies with classes 2 and 3, which are both used in one sense and made in another. Thus it is often said that human beings do not just make tools, they use tools to make tools. If using is to making as co-optation to construction, we would have to admit that the beaver does the same, and many other animals besides. If, on the other hand, making means the *self-conscious* execution of design, then all manufacture must necessarily involve the use of other tools (minimally including the executive instruments of the body; class 3). What is special, of course, in the human use of tools to make tools is the self-conscious co-optation of objects (which therefore fall in class 2). But taking self-conscious planning as the criterion of making, we would have to say that the co-opted object is, in a sense, 'made' as well.

Concentrating for the present only on classes 3 and 4, we can say that tools in class 4 are artefacts and those in class 3 are not; the former are 'made' to be used, the latter used but not made. It is tempting to imagine that tool-making, in this sense, is something that during human evolution gradually replaced tool-using, leaving the latter as a residual category. But the consequences of such a view are absurd. Suppose we observe a man sharpening a stick with a stone. If he has no conscious idea of the final product, nor of its future use, we could only say that he is 'using' a stone tool. But now if he conceives his product in advance, we can equally well say that he is 'making' a spear. Yet his actual performance in manipulating the stone is not in the least changed by the addition of the mental image. It would be patently nonsensical to claim that because he is now making a spear, he is no longer using a stone. Thus we must conclude that all tool-making is also tool-using, though not vice versa. We could say that tool-using is also tool-making in so far as the user attaches an image of the end-product. From our choice of words, it is immediately apparent that the dichotomy is identical to Weber's between action and behaviour. The notion of tool-making is apt to mislead, just as is the Weberian concept of action, because it labels conduct in terms of a property that is strictly extrinsic to it, and to whose presence or absence the conduct is itself indifferent. Behaviour remains behaviour, even when a prior intention is added; tool-using remains tool-using, even when initiated by a conception of a tool to be made.

Granted that tools become artefacts by virtue of their relation to a set of ideas governing their construction and use, located in the makers' consciousness, the totality of these ideas constitutes what we commonly call a *technology*. As Sahlins has rightly stated, 'A technology is not comprehended by its physical properties alone' (1972:79). It is, first and foremost, a *corpus of knowledge,* transmitted by instruction (Ingold 1979:278). A collection of instruments, taken on their own, do not make a technology; rather they express a technology, only in so far as they are brought into relation to their makers. And since manufacture is the application of technological knowledge, it is clear that *Homo faber* (man the tool-maker) and *Homo sapiens* (man the knower) are one and the same (Kitahara-Frisch 1980:221). It might be said that the latter is a bearer of models *of* (representations of reality) and the former a bearer of models *for* (instructions for action), to adopt the distinction suggested by Geertz (1975:93–4). But of course a model *of* becomes a model *for* at the very moment when its bearer is brought into a practical relation with the material world, the same relation that—supplying objects with an image—converts them into artefacts. Now it is no accident that attempts to demonstrate the distinctiveness of human beings as tool-makers have run parallel to, and to some extent converged with, the search for unique properties of human language and symbolism. For if our argument in the earlier part of this chapter is valid, namely that language is an instrument not merely for the dissemination of thoughts but for their very production, then possession of language must be a prerequisite for the origination of the image whose self-conscious execution terminates with the appearance of the artefact. Thus Oakley holds not only that conceptual thought is essential to tool-making, but also that language is the essential tool of conception: 'It is extraordinarily difficult, if not impossible, to think effectively, to plan, or to invent, without the use of words or equivalent symbols. Most of our constructive thinking is done in unsounded words' (1954:18). Words, then, are used, but are they made? Carried away by his view of the artificiality of *all* cultural practices and products, Oakley goes so far as to claim that verbal language is itself 'a tool that had to be invented' (1954:18). It is certainly difficult to see how folk could invent, either piecemeal or *in toto,* that without which invention is impossible. Language is surely one component of culture that, as a constituent of thought, cannot be regarded as its man-made product. Indeed the arbitrariness of linguistic signification, which Saussure was so concerned to stress, attests to its foundation in convention rather than invention, and is an important factor in accounting for its stability.

Just as we draw on the conventions of language in the creation of novel utterances, so perhaps there may exist a similarly conventional 'grammar' and 'vocabulary' of motor operations—analogous to Saussurian *langue*—that may be combined and recombined in the invention of dissimilar tools (Holloway 1969:402–3; Montagu 1976:269). Thus the analogue of the tool is the complete utterance, not the spoken word. In the first part of this chapter I discussed three features of human language that all depend on the fact that it deals in symbols rather than signs. These were reflexivity, prevarication, and a particular kind of displacement predicated on the separation of denotation and connotation. Precisely analogous features can be identified in human tool-making (Holloway 1969:402; Kitahara-Frisch 1980:217–18). In language, an utterance is 'called up' by a conception in the mind of the speaker, denoting an object that may be remote from his immediate experience, or that may not exist at all. Likewise in self-conscious design, an artefact is called up by a conception of its future use, which may be held independently of the environmental context for which it is intended. Both are examples of the symbolic operation of displacement, by which people can produce words to denote, or make tools to act in, environments other than those that surround them, which perhaps have yet to be encountered or may never be encountered. The construction of tools for use in contexts that are non-existent, even fabulous, is the equivalent of linguistic prevarication. Such tools are quite familiar—we usually call them toys. A toy is like a lie in that it depends for its effectiveness on pretence and illusion. The strict analogue of linguistic reflexivity, talking about speech, is making tools for use in the context of tool-making (e.g. the manufacture of a stone implement for sharpening a wooden point). But it can be generalized to include all self-conscious manufacture of instruments that will be employed in the planned transformation of the natural environment. This is apparently the sense of reflexivity implied by P. J. Wilson when he writes that

> tools indicate that knowing one's ability to change the environment is accompanied by the idea of modification in a certain manner; that is, a tool reveals a technique that reveals an idea of what the technique will produce, which in turn indicates a knowledge by the individual that he is capable of carrying out the technique and realizing the idea. (1980:31)

Thus a man may not only envision an environment utterly transformed from the one in which he now stands (a cultivated field, say, instead of a patch of forest), but he may also conceive the tools (axes and digging-sticks) to effect the transformation, and bring forth these tools—according to his conception—as means to set about his task. But with this kind of reflexivity, by which one can both explore in thought or describe an imagined state not yet in being and design the tools by which it can be brought about, comes a sense of separation from the environment, a detachment of consciousness from the material world. 'The raw materials of nature', as Wilson puts it, 'come to stand not only as objects but as things in some sort of opposition to the toolmaker' (1980:31).

If the similar cognitive operations involved in tool-making and speaking manifest a single, fundamental capacity for symbolic thought, it is entirely plausible that they should have emerged together, marking some kind of threshold in the course of human evolution (Kitahara-Frisch 1980:218–19).[9] Current evidence dates this threshold to the Middle Pleistocene, an era that began (about 1.5 million years ago) with the first appearance of tools involving the imposition of arbitrary design rules, and ended (about 200,000 years ago) with a sharp upward turn in the degree of functional and regional differentiation of tool types, contrasting markedly with the extraordinary uniformity and stability of hominid tools throughout all preceding periods (Isaac 1976:283). Popper is probably quite right to believe that 'human tool-making *presupposes language*' and is on an altogether higher level from 'the kind of tool-making which does not presuppose language' (in Popper and Eccles 1977:453). For the latter, though an instance of constructive behaviour, is not a self-conscious process and does not result in artefacts in our sense of the term. It cannot be denied that Plio-Pleistocene hominids were already setting tools in stone a good million years before the threshold of tool-making proper was reached, and that the technique of doing so, although it could have had some instinctive component, was largely passed on through imitative learning. We can credit them, then, with a tool *tradition*, or a material *culture*, but the same goes for many contemporary non-human primates whose constructive behaviour has a substantial learned component (McGrew and Tutin 1978). Indeed our earliest ancestors may have been habitually *executing* tools 'for any length of time before they began to design them in their minds' (Ingold 1983a:13; see Haldane 1956b:9). The threshold came at the point when, with a critical degree of development of the symbolic faculty, the representation of technique in the imagination was no longer constrained to follow, but could actually move ahead of, and *lead*, the operations represented, shaping them to an imagined plan. 'From that point on, practice follows one step behind technology, rather than the other way around' (Ingold 1983a:13). The result was a stepwise increase in the tempo of cultural adaptation.

This reversal in the relative priority of technique and technology, practice and theory, or (in Ryle's terms) knowing *how* and knowing *that*, hinges on the ability to transmit culture, as a system of rules, independently of its material embodiment. It requires of the novice that he first learn not by experience, imitation and reinforcement, from others who have done likewise, subjecting his performance only retrospectively—if at all—to the scrutiny of the rational intellect, but rather that he learn in advance the abstract principles by which he can generate artefacts of his own, in the light of a critical evaluation of the efforts of his predecessors. This is the difference between the passive absorption and active acquisition of knowledge, which as we saw in Chapter 2, distinguishes the Boasian and Tylorian understandings of cultural transmission. It is also, and most fundamentally, the difference between learning by example and learning by *teaching*. It is worth recalling that Alexander picks on this difference as a diagnostic criterion for separating unselfconscious and self-conscious processes (1964:34–6). For example, we learn to ride bicycles by practice reinforced by the informal rewards of success and the evident penalties of failure. If we stop to think we are liable to topple. But we are taught to stop to think before crossing the road, as part of a positive, explicit code designed to ensure safety in any one of an indefinite number of conceivable situations. Should we fail we are liable to get run over. Teaching, as P. J. Wilson has put it, 'is an activity that rests on forms without reality beyond themselves and prepares the learner without requiring him to experience the object taught'. It involves the deliberate articulation of conscious models or 'maker's knowledge', entailing 'some form of analytical instruction . . . by reference to rules and possibly symbols' (1980:32, 145). There is experimental evidence to suggest that the more complex tools, such as those that made their appearance in the critical transitional phase of the Middle Pleistocene, could not be constructed by novices without the aid of such instruction (Washburn and Moore 1974:123). And it could not, of course, have taken place without the facility of language. Artificial culture, therefore, is taught culture. If, then, we follow Wilson in amending the cliché that culture is learned behaviour to 'culture is taught behaviour', we could only reach the conclusion that all culture is artificial (1980:146).

This conclusion is surely unacceptable without some qualification, for language— at least—is transmitted within a population of native speakers without overt reference to rules at all. The same goes for much traditional craft production: the skilled wheelwright or shipwright, according to Steadman, 'knows how to make the object, he follows the traditional procedure . . . but in many respects he literally *does not know what he is doing*'. Here he stands opposed to the engineer, who 'works from principle rather than precedent' (1979:233–6). So why should we be embarrassed by the observation that a significant part of culture is learned but not taught, and in that sense 'innate' rather than artificial? The reason is that, on a broad interpretation of learning, culture could no longer be reserved for human beings, nor even for our closest primate cousins, and hence would be lost as the special province of anthropology. As Voegelin has observed, unless 'additional conditions' are invoked before granting learned behaviour the status of culture, we would have to admit 'that infra-human animals' have culture as well (1951:370). Nor is there any obvious point on the scale of progressive evolution where learning begins. According to Harlow, 'There is no scientific evidence of a break in learning capabilities between primate and nonprimate forms' (1958:288). No less a figure than Darwin devoted a great deal of attention to the apparent learning capabilities of earthworms, which are considerable, challenging us either to recognize that we are not so exalted as we are inclined to think, or to be a bit more precise about what it is that actually raises us above the more lowly products of natural selection (Ghiselin 1969:202–3; see Darwin 1881). And a century later, Bonner is looking for the rudiments of culture among the inhabitants of a Petri dish. 'Bacteria are not capable of culture themselves', he admits, a trifle reluctantly, 'but . . . they do have the basic response system' (1980:56). The invention of such terms as 'protoculture' and 'euculture', to distinguish the learned component of non-human and human behaviour respectively, will not in itself help without further specification of just where the difference lies (Hallowell 1960b:337 n. 90; Lurnsden and Wilson 1981:3).

To clarify the issue, a first requirement is that the opposition nature–culture be disentangled from another with which it has become unwittingly caught up, that between organism and environment. Every organism, of course, lives and grows in an environment, and it is well known that at any stage of epigenesis, environmental impacts can 'elect' from a number of possible developmental pathways—already prefigured in its genetic structure—the one that is actually followed (Medawar 1960:92; see also Waddington 1957:29). Hence all phenotypic effects, whether morphological or behavioural, must be the outcome of the interplay of genetic characters and environmental influences. This at once gives the lie to arguments on the one hand that organisms are totally preformed and that what we see are pure expressions of their 'nature', and on the other hand that, having no nature, they are entirely moulded by environmental pressures, thus expressing their 'nurture'. The so-called nature–nurture controversy, formulated in these terms over a century ago by Francis Galton (1874), no longer deserves serious consideration; but it has left a legacy of confusion behind it, largely due to the unfortunate identification of 'nurture' with 'culture'. To make matters worse, when it comes to behaviour nature was identified with the 'instinctive' and nurture with the 'learned', with the result that learning became a matter of environmental conditioning, and conditioned behaviours a matter of culture. A great deal of effort has since had to be expended in showing that instinct and learning, so defined, are not either/or alternatives, that one cannot speak of the one *versus* the other, since the behaviour we observe is the expression of an innate potential brought out in a certain way by virtue of environmental experience (Simpson 1958b:529). Meanwhile, anthropologists who continue to insist on the independence of cultural variation from genetic constraint are still branded (e.g. by E. O. Wilson 1980:274) as the upholders of an extreme environmentalism that accords no place to innate predispositions in the determination of behaviour. Cultural differences, it is said, since they are a function of differential environmental impact on the developing organism, are *purely phenotypic*. Following from this is a view of culture as a kind of exosomatic shell surrounding the organism, protecting it from the environment, but at the same time providing it with the essential means to live, or to satisfy its primordial needs (a classic exposition of this view is Malinowski 1944).

The implications of the position bequeathed by Boasian cultural anthropology, pursued to their logical conclusion, are entirely different. Far from being a process of environmental conditioning of the organic phenotype, the acquisition of culture is held to be integral to the very constitution of the underlying behavioural project whose phenotypic expression may then be subject to external, environmental impacts. Learning, from this point of view, is a *mechanism of inheritance,* by which a set of non-genetic instructions may be transmitted, down the generations, from individual to individual. To adopt Medawar's terms (1960:90–4), it is not elective but instructive, not a matter of steering phenotypic development along one of a number of possible paths, but of mapping out sections of the epigenetic landscape that would otherwise remain blank. In other words, it involves the acquisition of parts of a programme without which normal development could not take place at all (Geertz 1975:46–9).

We may refer to these parts, not already written into the genotype but which have to be 'filled in' to complete the programme, as the constituents of a *tradition*. It may be supposed that the organism's genes instruct it, at certain critical junctures, to *seek further instructions,* essentially by observing the execution of these instructions by conspecifics (Cloak 1975:167). Once 'wired in' to the nervous system, instructions direct the behaviour by which they may be similarly passed on to yet other individuals in the population. In short, the transmission of tradition entails a kind of observational learning fundamentally different both from environmental conditioning (which applies to organisms whose behavioural programme includes no traditional component at all) and from formal teaching or tuition (which depends on the prior transmission of a linguistic tradition and is unique to human beings).

In no other species than man does observational learning play such an important role in development. However, it is unique neither to humans nor to primates generally. Thus individuals of certain avian species, though it is in their nature to sing a particular kind of song, cannot if reared in isolation deliver more than an impoverished and incomplete version. Those elements of the song whose acquisition depends on the imitation of conspecifics add up to a tradition, even though genetic instructions so tightly constrain what may be acquired that only one species-specific song is admissible (Reynolds 1981:22). This is what Lumsden and Wilson mean by a 'pure genetic culture', consisting of behaviours all of which are learned, but which are all that *can* be learned under existing genetic rules governing acquisition (1981:9). Less extreme are cases where a variety of song components are learnable, with roughly equal ease. Accidents of miscopying will then provide the material for a historical diversification of traditions, in different localities. At the opposite pole, where learning is most 'open', we have the acquisition of culture by human beings. For example, no one any more supposes that genes have any influence at all on what particular language a child learns, and the number of possible languages is effectively infinite. Yet it is still the case that human children are genetically 'programmed' to acquire linguistic competence at a particular age and that they automatically 'lock into' the particular languages to which they are then exposed. Deprived of contact with other speakers during the crucial period of acquisition, the child is unable to utter coherent speech, and his cognitive development is radically impaired. Thus with both birds and humans, the formation of a complete behavioural programme depends on a complex interlocking of genetically inherited and learning-transmitted instructions; the difference lies in the extraordinary extent to which human beings are 'programmed to learn' (Pulliam and Dunford 1980), and in the degree of genetic indifference to what is learned. We can therefore concur with Reynolds that culture is 'a generic name for the traditional information component of innate-learning interlockings' (1981:33), recognizing, however, that with man this component is uncommonly large.

Granting the integration of genetic and cultural components in the total programme, it remains the case that overt behaviour will partly depend on the specific environmental conditions under which the programme is practically implemented.

That is why it is so essential to distinguish 'learning' as the acquisition and transmission of traditional information, from 'learning' as a property of organism–environment interaction in epigenesis. Moreover it is precisely this distinction, between the observational learning of instructions and the environmental conditioning of development, that is overruled by the confusion of culture with nurture. Figure 7.4 will help to clarify the point. It shows three individuals, linked in an 'ancestor–descendant sequence' (Hull 1981:29). The inner circle, for each, contains a set of inherited instructions that, following Hull, may be called *replicators* (R). For simple organisms, they consist only of genes. These are realized in the phenotype, which is the entity that actually interacts with the environment (E). Thus we call this entity an *interactor* (I), noting that its appearance will depend on environmental circumstances (Hull 1981:33). Hence to specify the exact form of I we need a knowledge of both R and E. In the language of the conventional nature–nurture opposition, R is nature, E nurture, and I the result of their combination. And the horizontal arrows $R \rightarrow I$ and $E \leftrightarrow I$ correspond to 'instinct' and 'learning' respectively. Thus learning, in this view, is wholly contained in the organism–environment relationship, a continuous process of adjustment manifested, according to Thorpe's classic definition, *'by adaptive change in individual behaviour as the result of experience'* (Thorpe: 1956:66). Judging the balance of instinct and learning is then a question of assessing the relative magnitudes of genetic and environmental components in the variance of observed, phenotypic traits (Dobzhansky 1962:56).

Suppose we are dealing with complex, culture-bearing organisms such as human beings. The inner circle will, in this case, include not only genes but non-genetic replicators. Considering the latter alone, we find culture, as what is 'learned', right inside the individual rather than stamped on its outer surface in the manifest properties of the phenotype. That is to say, culture is first and foremost lodged in replicators, and only derivatively in interactors—these corresponding to covert rules and overt practices respectively (Harré 1979:371–2). Moreover learning (the mode of intergenerational transmission of cultural information) is denoted in our diagram by the *vertical* arrows $R_1 \rightarrow R_2$ and $R_2 \rightarrow R_3$; it is thus (to retain Hull's terms) a process of replication rather than interaction. And the balance of instinct and learning is now determined by the relative control of genetic and cultural replicators on phenotypic behaviour, quite apart from any possible environmental influences. In this connection, it is worth pointing out the relation between the alternative conceptions of learning, $E \leftrightarrow I$ and $R \rightarrow R$, and the corresponding notions of *adaptation,* which Toulmin (1981:179) has called 'developmental' and 'populational' (see also Pittendrigh 1958). The former refers to the ongoing accommodation of the individual organism to the variable conditions of the environment in the unfolding of its own life; this is the sense in which Thorpe, in the definition just cited, considers adaptation to be the essence of learning. The latter sense of adaptation is the classic Darwinian one: the successive modification of heritable traits in a population of individuals linked by ancestor–descendant relations in an evolving lineage.[10] If learning is understood as a mechanism for the vertical propagation of cultural replicators, then—returning to Figure 7.4—the arrows

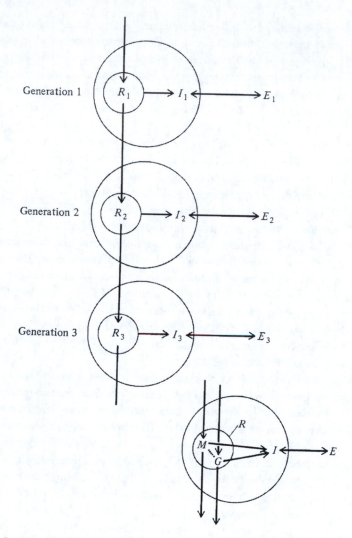

FIG. 7.4   Intergenerational transmission and organism–environment interaction.
R, replicators; *I*, interactors; *E*, environments. The *lower diagram* illustrates
the more complex situation where replicators include both memes (M) and
genes (G). Adapted from Diener et al. (1980:12).

$R \rightarrow I$ stand for the cultural component in the determination of behavioural practice, which is *contrasted* with the environmental component $E \leftrightarrow I$. Hence the
phenotype is actually a product of the combination of culture and nurture, and can
be specified only if we know *both* what has been learned by instructive transmission
from other individuals ($R \rightarrow R$) *and* what has been acquired in terms of the elective
steering of development by environmental forces ($E \leftrightarrow I$). Finally, by admitting
learning *only* in the former sense, we would—reverting to the simple acultural
organism—have to admit that it does *not* learn and that its behaviour, having no

traditional component, is essentially instinctive. This is not to deny the obvious fact that manifest behaviour is subject to environmental influence, but merely to recognize that such influence is better not regarded as a learning process.

This approach cries out for the recognition of some cultural analogue of the gene, extrasomatic in the sense of being the elementary unit of an ideal structure, though endosomatic in the sense of having its locus inside the individual. And indeed such analogues have been repeatedly posited in the literature, going under a variety of names. Perhaps the earliest was in a paper by Gerard, Kluckhohn and Rapoport, who speak of 'implicit culture'—the inferred cultural structure—as the 'cultural genotype' (1956:10). Blum (1963) calls it the 'mnemotype'. Murray (see Hoagland 1964) has christened the analogue of the gene as the 'idene'; Cavalli-Sforza (1971) prefers the simple term 'idea', whereas Hill renders it as the 'concept' (1978:379). For Emerson (1965:58) it is the 'symbol'. Swanson (1973) introduces the rather awkward term 'sociogene', Cloak (1975) speaks of 'instructions' and Dawkins (1976, 1982) of 'memes'. Finally, Lumsden and Wilson suggest that we use the word 'culturgen', going so far as to recommend how it should be pronounced (1981:7). What they all have in common is a similar abode (in the brain rather than in the chromosomes), a similar mode of conservative transmission (observational or imitative learning rather than sexual reproduction) and a similar vulnerability to occasional miscopying in the transmission process. But once the analogy is posited, a new problem arises concerning the relation between genetic and cultural instructions, or between genes and memes. Our initial reading of Fig. 7.4 was somewhat oversimplified, in so far as we considered only the latter and ignored the former. If memes exist, then genes must also, so that in reality genetic and cultural transmission must be going on concurrently, and any item of behaviour is liable to come under the joint control of both kinds of replicator. Hence in place of the single line of transmission $R_1 \rightarrow R_2 \rightarrow R_3$ we should write two parallel lines: $M_1 \rightarrow M_2 \rightarrow M_3$ (for memes) and $G_1 \rightarrow G_2 \rightarrow G_3$ (for genes). Each of the inner circles would include a set of memes (M) and a set of genes (G). And both M and G would be expressed in the phenotype I, whose actual appearance would again respond to variations in specific environmental conditions (E) to which the interactor is exposed during development. This point, that I depends on M, G and E, has been put quite clearly by Richerson and Boyd, who state that 'to predict the phenotype of a cultural organism one must know its genotype, its environment and its "culture-type", the cultural message that the organism received from other individuals of the same species' (1978:128).

Perhaps the simplest approach to dealing with the relation between genetic and cultural instructions is to deny that any such relation exists, and to assume that the replication of genes and of memes presents us with two parallel but unconnected processes, both of which happen to use as vehicles the same organisms. This is an approach taken by Cloak (1975), and latterly by Dawkins (1982:109–10). Thus Cloak distinguishes between what he calls *i-culture*, consisting of 'the set of cultural instructions [individuals] carry in their central nervous systems', and *m-culture*, consisting of the set of manifest behaviours, and their outcomes, which

these instructions control. Just as genes are the minimal units of physical heredity, so are we to regard instructions as '"corpuscles of culture" . . . transmitted
and acquired with fidelity and ease' (1975:168).[11] Similarly, Dawkins distinguishes
between 'memes' (replicators) and 'meme-products' (their phenotypic effects).
The meme, like Cloak's instruction, is a 'unit of information residing in a brain',
whereas meme-products consist of the consequences of these units in the outside
world, 'the outward and visible (audible, etc.) manifestation of the memes within
the brain'. As i-culture is to m-culture, so memes are to their phenotypic effects.
And according to both authors, as we recall from Chapter 2, culturally determined behaviour is simply a means by which memes or instructions make copies of
themselves, using 'the apparatus of inter-individual communication and imitation'
(Dawkins 1982:109). Memes, like genes, are subject to selection, which automatically favours those that generate behaviour most conducive to their replication. As
for the relation between genes and memes, Dawkins simply asserts that there is 'no
reason why success in a meme should have any connection with genetic success'
(1982:110). A meme may be highly disadvantageous with regard to the replication
of the genes of its carriers, but it can still 'catch on' and spread at the expense of
other more benign variants (Cloak 1975:172).

The total independence of genetic and cultural transmission is difficult to accept,
if only because the capacity to acquire cultural information is genetically encoded,
but not vice versa (Bonner 1980:18). There can be instinct without tradition, but
no tradition without instinct, even though the latter may consist of no more than
a set of instructions for its acquisition. This fact has spurred the elaboration of a
number of formal models of so-called gene–culture coevolution, designed to show
how the selective retention of variant cultural instructions depends on their relative contribution to the genetic fitness of their carriers, and conversely how this
contribution in turn affects the natural selection of genetic variants. The principal
contributions in this field are those of Durham (1976, 1979), Richerson and Boyd
(1978), Cavalli-Sforza and Feldman (1981), and Lumsden and Wilson (1981).[12]
Not much can be said for these models in their present state of development; the
assumptions on which they rest are either so remote from reality or so utterly trivial
that they do not so much advance our understanding of evolutionary processes
as provide an excuse for the exercise of mathematical ingenuity. Durham's argument is perhaps the most straightforward. His premiss is that, by and large, cultural
attributes will be positively selected to the extent that they permit the individuals
carrying them 'to survive and reproduce and thereby contribute genes to later generations of the population of which they are members' (1979:46–7). Thus, unlike
Cloak and Dawkins, Durham assumes that the propagation of a meme *does* depend
on its contribution to the genetic fitness of carriers, if for no other reason than that
human individuals usually enculturate their own children (or those of close genetic
kin), so that the representation of their memes in future generations roughly coincides with that of their genes. As Cloak prosaically remarks, 'A cultural instruction
whose behaviour helps its human carrier-enactor (or his/her relatives) to acquire
more children thereby has more little heads to get copied into' (1977:50).

A rather more sophisticated argument is presented by Richerson and Boyd (1978). They recognize that phenotypic behaviour is the outcome of compound determination by the individual's genotype and its 'culture-type', the latter defined by the informational content of the message acquired from other individuals through the learning-based transmission of tradition. It can happen, then, that behaviour that is optimal for the reproduction of cultural traits may be less than optimal for genetic replication, and vice versa. For example, if there exists a patrilineal bias in the transmission of tradition, a cultural trait instructing its carrier to extend nepotistic altruism preferentially to close agnates should have a selective advantage over one that makes no distinction between agnatic and uterine kin. With a genetic trait, the balance of advantage will be the other way round. Given that optimal phenotypes for genes and memes may be different, Richerson and Boyd envisage the actual phenotype (which is likely to be somewhere between the two optima) as the outcome of a metaphorical game in which the two sets of instructions, genetic and cultural, compete to control the behaviour of the individual they inhabit (1978:129). But the contest is not seen as an equal one, since the 'capacity for culture' is itself under genetic control and must have evolved as a trait contributing to genetic fitness. This point is crucial for Lumsden and Wilson, whose argument hinges on the supposition that the capacity for culture does not rest on a single set of 'promethean genes' common to all mankind, and that individuals and populations vary with respect to the genetically prescribed rules directing the acquisition of what they call culturgens. These rules, they hold, are bound to introduce innate tendencies or biases towards the adoption of certain culturgens rather than others. Hence if a new culturgen appears that enhances the genetic fitness of its holder, we can expect natural selection to promote any modifications in the epigenetic rules that would increase the likelihood of the culturgen's acquisition and transmission. This is the process of 'genetic assimilation' (see Waddington 1969:373–4) by which genes are said to 'track culture and bias the epigenetic rules to favour the most successful forms of culturally transmitted behaviour'. Gene–culture coevolution is then defined as change in epigenetic rules due to shifts in gene frequency, and the changes in culturgen frequency that result. 'No sharp line', Lumsden and Wilson conclude, 'can be drawn between genetic and cultural evolution' (1981:11–13, 21–2, 296, 343).

These are controversial conclusions, currently unsupported by solid evidence, and I do not intend to dwell on them further. I do, however, wish to indicate the general problem of positing analogies between processes of variation and selective retention operating in the respective worlds of material and ideal things, especially in the light of the crucial distinction between 'innate' and 'artificial' culture. Briefly, the problem is this: Only when culture is understood in the former sense, as a passively learned tradition not open to discursive formulation, can a strict analogue of the Darwinian process be applied; yet only when it is understood in the latter sense, as a series of inventions based on explicit, taught rules, can we posit an adequate principle of selection. In seeking this principle in rational human deliberations, we destroy the very foundations of the argument by analogy. It is worth stressing that neither the analogy, nor the problem it raises, is a new one, as some of its recent rediscoverers seem to believe. In fact it is almost as old as Darwin's theory itself. One of the earliest writers to have suggested it was William James, in an essay dating from 1880:

> The new conceptions, emotions and active tendencies which evolve are originally produced in the shape of random images, fancies, accidental out-births of spontaneous variation in the functional activity of the excessively unstable human brain, which the outer environment simply confirms or refutes, adopts or rejects, preserves or destroys—selects, in short, just as it selects morphological and social variations due to molecular accidents of an analogous sort. (1898:247)

James must have been content with the analogy, since it reappeared ten years later in his *Principles of psychology,* this time as a model for the advance of science, in which novel conceptions are selected by surviving the test of experimental ver-ification—a test in which the vast majority 'perish through their worthlessness' (1890, II:636). The idea that knowledge progresses through the systematic testing of wild speculations re-emerged, not always in such an explicitly Darwinian form, in the writings of a number of other scholars of the same period, including Jevons, Souriau, Mach, Boltzmann and Poincaré (Campbell 1974:155–8). Indeed, as Campbell has documented, it had already been formulated, in advance of Darwin's teaching, by Alexander Bain and Michael Faraday, in 1855 and 1859 respectively (1974:154). And as we saw in Chapter 2, the same idea has found its modern advo-cates in Popper and Toulmin, amongst others.

When it comes to the evolution of cultural forms, the analogy with organic adaptation under natural selection is again an old one, which has been reasserted on countless occasions in the literature of biology and anthropology.[13] As a repre-sentative instance, I shall consider just one statement of the analogy, by Murdock (1971[1956]), which has the virtue of being unusually clear and explicit. Murdock's approach is firmly grounded in the Boasian tradition in that he considers culture to consist in the first place of *habits* common to the individuals of a population, heritable through imitative learning. The first requirement for culture change is that there be a source of innovations akin to mutation, and Murdock outlines three ways in which this can happen in culture, by 'variation', 'invention' and 'tenta-tion'. Variations arise through the simple miscopying of elements in the transmission process, and are thus strictly analogous to genetic mutations. Inventions, however, are rather different, since they assign an active role to individuals in the *origination* of novel syntheses. As for tentation, this involves an element of deliberate planning that is entirely absent from the literal Darwinian interpretation of organic adapta-tion. However, passing over these problems for the moment, we come to the next stage in the process of culture change, analogous to selection, which Murdock actu-ally divides into three separate processes: 'social acceptance', 'selective innovation' and 'integration'. The first is a kind of preliminary screening, cutting out variants that are demonstrably unsuitable. Those that remain subsequently enter 'a competition for survival': 'So long as it proves more rewarding than its alternatives a cultural habit will endure, but when it ceases to bring comparable satisfactions it dwindles and eventually disappears. . . . By and large, the cultural elements that are eliminated are the less adaptive ones' (1971[1956]:330). Finally there is a process of 'integration', by which habits that have passed the test of selection are internally adjusted to one another, though Murdock admits that the integration is never perfect.

Returning to the question of innovation, we must ask whether it is possible to admit 'variation' and 'invention' as alternative components of the same model of cultural adaptation. Strictly speaking, the answer must be negative, since the only way in which the alternatives can be separated is by presupposing, in the case of invention, the existence of a designer (the inventor) whose disappearance, in the case of variation, renders it effectively 'blind'. Invention, as we have shown, yields artefacts, which are classed as such by the priority of the conception in the mind of the subject over the realized object. The Darwinian analogue, on the other hand, rests on a principle of 'blind-variation-and-selective-retention' (Campbell 1975:1105) that purports to account for the teleonomy of performances *without* the invocation of teleology, amongst individuals presumed to be *unable* to conceptualize solutions to problems of adaptation in advance of their realization. Such individuals learn but do not teach (nor are they taught); they *execute* received instructions—sometimes incorrectly—but do not invent at all. Hence the only possible source of innovation is chance miscopying. The distance that separates variation and invention, in Murdock's terms, also separates unselfconscious and self-conscious construction, tool–using and tool–making, the innate and the artificial. It is also, and this is the really crucial point, the distance that separates 'Darwinian' and 'Lamarckian' models of culture change. For the essential difference between them, as we saw in the previous chapter, lies in the attribution by the latter of the origination of novel traits not to the play of chance and antichance but to an exercise of will on the part of individuals in actively responding to perceived needs, which they do by initiating constructive adaptations that are subsequently transmissible to offspring. It follows that blind variation and invention can be comprehended only within the same model of change if that model is a general one that admits 'Darwinian' and 'Lamarckian' processes as two poles on a continuous spectrum of possible schemata.

Such a model has been recently formulated by Harré (1979:364–6; 1981a:167). The key variable is the *degree of coupling* between what Harré calls 'M-conditions' and 'S-conditions', where M stands for mutation and S for selection. The Darwinian schema can then be defined as the special case in which the degree of coupling between M and S is reduced to zero. This is usually, if somewhat loosely, described as the 'random' character of mutation, meaning not that mutations are wholly undetermined but that whatever forces induce them bear no relation at all to the environmental conditions of their subsequent selection. At the other end of the spectrum is the Lamarckian schema, in which M and S are completely coupled—with the implication that mutations are initiated by a conception of the environmental need they will subsequently fulfil. In natural history we generally deal with decoupled situations, in cultural or intellectual history with more or less fully coupled ones (Toulmin 1972:338–9). 'Most of the sources of cultural "mutations"', as Alexander admits, 'are at least potentially related to the reasons for their survival or failure' (1979:74). The apparently Lamarckian nature of cultural adaptation has often been pointed out (e.g. by Medawar 1960:98; and Gould 1983:70–1), and Steadman has gone so far as to suggest that the error of Lamarck's conception of organic evolution may have lain in the fact 'that he was working by analogy: drawing analogies *from* culture *to* nature, and projecting an essentially cultural conception onto the natural world' (1979:129). One might add that many contemporary neo-Darwinians have fallen into exactly the reverse error, projecting a naturalistic conception onto the entirety of culture.

However, to draw the line between Darwinian and Lamarckian schemata at the boundary between nature and culture is to make a false identification of the cultural with the artificial. So long as individuals are but passive repositories for cultural elements and have no hand in their origination, a Darwinian schema is perfectly applicable, despite the fact that inherited characteristics are acquired by learning and form part of a tradition. Only when the plans and procedures governing behaviour begin to become available for discursive formulation, allowing the individual to build on his own creative efforts and on the teachings of his predecessors, does the schema of culture change approach the Lamarckian pole. 'This means', as Harré recognizes, 'that we should expect people to conceive innovations, not merely by random reshuffling of their knowledge, beliefs, rules of conduct, habits, social practices and customs, but by deliberate design in the light of the conditions that [they] anticipate will occur' (1979:365). Harré links weak and strong M–S coupling, in an evolutionary scenario, to 'early human' and 'later human social conditions': In our terms these represent stages in the crucial transition by which theory came to overtake practice, or by which man became the self-conscious designer—literally the *inventor*—of his cultural forms. However, complete coupling, we would hold, *never* applies over the entire field of culture (just as not all culture is artificial), nor is the movement from weak to strong coupling necessarily irreversible. Procedures once purpose-built for a situation may through repeated execution become habitual, part of the 'cultural baggage' that individuals unwittingly take with them into environments of selection far removed from those for which they were originally designed.

The major difficulty with the Darwinian schema of cultural adaptation comes when we turn from considering the first stage of variation to the second stage of selection. No one has yet come up with a convincing statement of how the selection of cultural traits occurs, which does not compromise the premises of the analogy with the natural selection of genetically determined characters. Murdock's previously cited view is a typical one; competitive selection, ostensibly analogous to the Darwinian selection of genotypes, brings variant traits before the bar of 'satisfaction'. We have then to ask, Satisfaction for whom? Not, of course, for the traits themselves, but for their *users*. At the very moment when the concept of satisfaction is introduced, we must cease to regard individuals as vehicles for the replication of the traits they carry, and turn them instead into rational selectors—'economic men', harnessing culture to the fulfilment of natural, hedonistic desires. This, as we saw in Chapter 2, is to invoke an analogue not of natural but of *artificial* selection: artificial, because it is underwritten by a prior conception of a desired future state in the mind of a selecting agent. Consider again the nature of invention. We have argued that invention differs from blind variation in the relatively close coupling of the former to the environmental conditions of selection, but we have not explained exactly how such coupling comes about. For to be sure, every invention may start its life, as William James so vividly described, as one of a plethora of accidental events of spontaneous variation in the human mind, which are subsequently subjected to a selective process of trial-and-error. This is the process that Murdock called 'tentation'. But it is crucial to recognize that the conditions of selection, for these variations, are not simply embodied in the 'outer environment'. For the inventor already *knows* the adaptive problem he sets out to solve, and in this knowledge lie the conditions of its solution.

Even in the case of natural selection, of course, the criteria according to which variants are selected 'are not given by the environment alone but depend upon what members of the subject population are seeking to do in it' (Ingold 1983a:14). Different organisms interact with components of their environment in different ways, and consequently sustain different kinds of pressure. There is therefore a sense in which an organism can be said to 'elect', through its own teleonomic performance, the conditions that constitute its *effective* environment of selection (Monod 1972:120–1; see also Waddington 1960:399–401; Beurton 1981). But what the (non-human) organism does *not* do is to represent to itself these conditions of selection, by visualizing in advance both its objectives and the possible environments under which they might be realized (Sahlins 1976b:208). And it is precisely this *internal representation* that constitutes the effective environment of selection for the variant images that furnish the raw material for invention. This is shown in Fig. 7.5, where S denotes the conditions determined by actual performance in the material world, and S' the conditions determined by projected performance in an imagined world. $M_1 \ldots n$ is a range of mutations *preselected* by S', yielding M_s as the chosen solution. In so far as S corresponds to S', the coupling of the invention (M_s) with the outer conditions of selection (S) is explained. This may be compared with the situation depicted in Fig. 7.5B, where there is no internal representation of the conditions of selection, hence no preselection of variants, and no coupling of novel traits to the conditions of their practical deployment. Summarizing the contrast, it could be said that Lamarckian, 'directed' variation occurs to the extent that the operation of the rational intellect in selecting amongst initial variants according to a prior conception of need *pre-empts* their retroactive selection under external environmental conditions. Conversely, only in so far as the work of reason is denied can we invoke a pure Darwinian schema in the field of culture change.

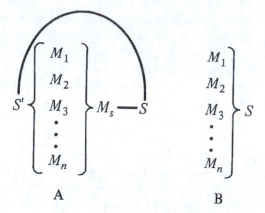

FIG. 7.5 Preselection and retroactive selection of conceptual variants.

This is the point at which to take stock of a crucial ambiguity in the notion of 'cultural selection', which relates directly to the non-congruence of the oppositions innate–artificial and nature–culture. Darwin, in *The origin of species,* presented a theory of adaptation by *natural* selection operating on what we now call *genetic* traits. This may be contrasted, on the one hand, with *artificial* selection and on the other hand with the natural selection of *cultural* traits. The former, transposed onto the world of ideas, corresponds as we have seen to a theory of rational choice, with the agent as selector, purposefully fitting his chosen concepts into structures for subsequent realization as cultural artefacts. The latter treats individuals as no more than the carriers of traditions of which they are barely conscious: Their cultural forms are therefore innate rather than artificial, revealed in human conduct but not manmade. Advocates of a cultural analogue of natural selection have sometimes gone for one view, sometimes for the other, though more often than not they have—like Murdock—landed themselves in the position of proposing both simultaneously.[14] A recent example of the same confusion lies in Durham's attempts to demonstrate the coevolutionary complementarity of natural selection and 'cultural selection'. Apparently adopting a literal Darwinian schema, Durham argues that cultural selection works by the differential retention of variants according to their relative contribution to the inclusive fitness of individuals. Now this, of course, *is* natural selection, so that strictly speaking, Durham should have compared not natural and cultural selection, but the *natural* selection of *genetic* and *cultural* instructions, or of genes and memes (Cloak 1977:50). But if we make this substitution, the difficulty arises that since the transmission of cultural instructions does not depend on the biological reproduction of carriers, there is no *necessary* reason why memes should be selected that enhance genetic fitness. That they often are 'is merely an accidental truth, an empirical generalization of no theoretical import', for as Cloak goes on to remark, selection should just as well promote cultural traits leading carriers to *adopt* children, to whom those traits may be transmitted, even though, if anything, this would enhance the genetic fitness only of the children's natural parents (1977:50).

To counteract this objection, Durham enumerates a number of factors that, in his opinion, *do* bias selection in favour of traits that enhance the ability of individuals to survive and reproduce in a given environment, apart from the fact that parents often play a major part in the enculturation of their natural offspring. These rest on the rather obvious considerations that human beings *desire* to survive and reproduce, that they usually have a fair idea of what is good for them in this regard, and that good things tend to be selected on the grounds of the satisfaction they confer (Durham 1979:45). Elsewhere Durham states his belief that 'people do show a remarkable amount of conscious concern for the welfare of their children and relatives, and do readily recognize the parameters of their own well-being' (1976:98). This is a statement of common sense with which few would wish to quarrel. But what Durham fails to realize is that by invoking the criterion of personal satisfaction, by recognizing that 'human beings are not just passively receptive to cultural innovations but . . . have and develop a number of selective biases' (1979:48), and by suggesting that much cultural variability, unlike genetic variability, 'is a response to perceived needs' (1976:100), he has totally abandoned the Darwinian paradigm of natural selection for a form of artificial selection that is in no way comparable. The argument no longer proceeds by analogy but by extension: As natural selection has established innate, generalized desires consonant with the needs to survive and reproduce, so individuals—motivated by these desires—seek out and select the cultural forms that will lead to their satisfaction. One advocate of this extensionist thesis is Ruyle, who holds that the individual, in seeking to satisfy genetically based drives, 'is himself the motive force and primary selective mechanism of cultural evolution' (1973:203). And he legitimately takes Durham to task for attempting to shackle a process in which people 'create ideas in order to satisfy their own needs' to a mechanistic schema of blind variation and selective retention derived from Darwinian biology (1977:55). The problem, simply, is that Durham tries to have it both ways. He wants to bring organic and cultural adaptation within the same paradigm of Selection (with a capital S, to cover both varieties of the process, dealing with physically inherited and learning-transmitted characters respectively). But in the absence of any clear-cut selection criteria for cultural traits, he has to fall back on the biological criterion of differential reproductive success. Hence he has individuals deliberately selecting amongst variant traits according to innate preference criteria, or in a word *designing* their cultural forms, a process that has no analogue in the natural world.

The logical consequences of adopting a strictly Darwinian schema for the interpretation of culture change are quite the reverse. They have been admirably set out by Steadman, and I can do no better than to restate his conclusions:

> The first result, curiously, is that the individual designer or craftsman tends to fade away, and even disappears altogether. Certainly his conscious and deliberate contribution to the creation of designs is seriously underestimated and undervalued. . . . [His] only role . . . is that of copying and making small accidental or 'blind' changes as he does so. . . .

> The craftsman, in the evolutionary analogy, becomes merely a kind of mid-wife, his purpose to assist at the rebirth of the inherited design. The real, effective 'designer', in this view, is the 'selective' process which is constituted by the testing of the object in practical terms when it is put into use. The craftsman has only an error-correcting function; . . what is not imagined is that he anticipates in any conscious way the results of [induced] changes, or that he intentionally makes alterations to the design which are meant to produce specific effects.
>
> Just as Darwin inverted the argument from design, and 'stole away' God as designer, to replace Him with natural selection, so the Darwinian analogy in technical evolution removes the human designer and replaces him with the 'selective forces' in the 'functional environment' of the designed object. (Steadman 1979:188–9)

Moreover if the designer disappears, his intentions and purposes disappear with him, so that it no longer makes sense to speak of the fitness of objects in terms of their appropriateness for the fulfilment of preconceived ends, or for an intended purpose. As Steadman observes, with some justification, 'The concept of an intended purpose without a human agent having the intentions or the purposes is perfectly absurd' (1979:190).

However, he takes these conclusions further, to argue that the direct comparison of organic and cultural evolution constitutes no less than a *denial of tradition,* and indeed of 'the very fact of culture'. The phenomenon, in short, disappears along with its human designer (1979:216). But according to the argument we have developed in these pages, this is true only in so far as the cultural is identified with the artificial. Steadman himself makes just this identification when, drawing on Popper's categories, he equates culture with 'the whole World Three body of traditional knowledge and *the historical accumulation of man-made products'* (1979:216; my emphasis). These products consist, of course, of World 3 concepts embodied in World 1 artefacts. Yet there is absolutely no reason why the entirety of culture should have been designed in this sense: Languages certainly were not, and curiously enough Steadman goes on to suggest that the same may have been true of traditional craft procedures, thus contradicting the premises of his own thesis. One of his examples (an imaginary one) is drawn from the history of cooking. It is supposed that in a traditional culture, recipes are passed down from generation to generation, so that the cooks of every generation, making each dish 'like mother used to make it', have no more than to copy the recipe, possibly with some accidental variation. Moreover the recipe is presumed not to *represent* the dish but to consist merely of 'a set of instructions by which to make it' (Steadman 1979:232). Whatever the merits of the example, it demonstrates rather clearly how the existence and replication of tradition may be reconciled with the elimination of intentional design. A Darwinian schema of cultural evolution, far from implying a denial of tradition, simply affirms its foundation in convention rather than invention.

In Chapter 5 I argued that the designs of cultural forms, to the extent that they could not be put down to prior conceptions in the minds of agents, result from the operation of a mechanism of *internal* rather than external selection. There is no need to rehearse the argument, except to mention the correspondence of internal selection with the process Murdock called 'integration'. It is our contention that this mechanism allows us to account both for the *patterns* of culture, and for the essential *arbitrariness* of these patterns considered in relation to external environmental conditions. Many of the difficulties that surround the application of a Darwinian analogue to the history of culture, particularly as regards the specification of adequate selection criteria, would disappear if the distinction between internal and external mechanisms were duly recognized. In the field of organic adaptation, the latter have been amply demonstrated, whereas the applicability of the former remains problematic. But in the field of culture change, the situation is precisely reversed: The demonstration of internal selection dates back to the early writings of Boas, whereas external criteria continue to elude us. We also saw in Chapter 5 how the external (natural) selection of physical traits, just like the internal selection of cultural traits, yielded products that could best be regarded as items of *bricolage*. By contrast, the products of artificial selection, or of deliberate, rational design, are items of *engineering*. It follows that the distinction between *bricolage* and engineering exactly reflects that between 'innate' and 'artificial' culture, and between the two ways of reading the notion of 'cultural selection'—as the natural selection of elements of tradition or as the rational selection of instrumental artefacts. Again, with *bricolage* the individual is an unselfconscious *executor* of design (as in the narration of myth); with engineering he is a self-conscious *originator* of design (as in the construction of scientific hypotheses). And of course the same contrast is there in the distinction between learning through informal imitation and learning through formal tuition, or the passive absorption and active acquisition of knowledge.

Given such a pervasive dichotomy, with its contrary implications of tradition and civilization, diversification and progress, it is scarcely surprising that evolutionary analogues have been adduced to support utterly divergent moral and philosophical positions. Some, such as Hayek (1978) and Campbell (1975), have been led by their adoption of a Darwinian schema of human history to stress the cardinal importance of unreflective loyalty, obedience to established rules and conformity to custom. In their view the accumulated but largely unconscious wisdom of countless generations, enshrined in traditions that have survived the test of time, provides a far better foundation for the security of future humanity than anything a rational intelligence could devise and should not be lightly jettisoned. As Cohen recognizes, not without some apprehension, 'Evolutionary theory applied to human affairs leads to conservatism' (1981:207). Others, however, have found in evolutionary theory the rationale for a programme of reform, based on the liberal doctrine of progressive enlightenment. This is what it meant for Tylor, and what it means for Popper, who sees in variation and selection the twin principles of inspired conjecture and reasoned criticism that have propelled the advance of civilization. Likewise according to Huxley, cultural or 'psychosocial' selection is always directed towards the satisfaction of felt needs, involving conscious purpose or the awareness of an aim. Whereas natural selection operates blindly, pushing life on from behind, psycho-social selection 'pulls man onwards from in front' (Huxley 1960:20).

Faced with these alternatives, we seem to be caught once again in the dilemmas of freedom and determinism, chance and necessity. Yet it has been a guiding principle of this work that these dilemmas can be transcended in the recognition that there is more to evolution than the adaptation of organic and cultural forms, namely the movements of subjective life and consciousness. And it is here that we find the true creativity of the evolutionary process. This point underlies the distinction we have made throughout between culture and social life, and we can only concur with Radcliffe-Brown that 'a theory of the evolution of culture cannot be the same thing as a theory of social evolution' (1947:82). For the latter is above all a process of *life,* conducted through the objective forms of culture. We cannot afford to maintain the illusion that we stand, like gods, aloof from the world, as immortal spectators on the panoply of natural and cultural things. To admit both ourselves and others (not only human others) as equal participants in a total evolutionary process is to acknowledge not only our fellowship with all that lives, but more important, the full measure of our moral responsibility in the real world—a responsibility that must transcend the bounds of culture and species. We do not know how far consciousness extends in the animal kingdom, we do not even know what consciousness is, but short of denying our own subjectivity we cannot deny that other living organisms, as Birch and Cobb put it, 'are subjects experiencing their world as well as objects of human experience', and that if this is so, 'the most important story of evolution has not yet been written' (1981:134). A first requirement, before proceeding to write this story, is to clear out some of the accumulated conceptual debris of a century of evolutionary and social theorizing. That, no more and no less, is what I have attempted in this book. How far I have succeeded is for others to judge. At this particular moment, it is the best I can do.

NOTES

Chapter 1

1 See, for example, Sahlins (1960:40), Kroeber (1963:179–99), Burrow (1966), Voget (1967:133), Stocking (1968), Mandelbaum (1971:77–111), Teggart (1972:110–11), Toulmin (1972:321–36), Freeman (1974), Hirst (1976), Bock (1955, 1980) and Reynolds (1981:10).

2 For an excellent account of the history of this term, far more detailed than can be attempted here, see Bowler (1975).

3 This idea was actually foreshadowed in the *Histoire naturelle* of Buffon, a century earlier, and constituted the basis for his rebuttal of the essentialist taxonomy of Linnaeus (Oldroyd 1980:14–26). 'In reality', Buffon wrote in 1749, 'individuals alone exist in nature, while genera, orders, classes exist only in the imagination' (cited in Lovejoy 1959:90). Later, however, he completely reversed his thinking on this point.

4 The image of the tree, though vivid, is not altogether appropriate, for a tree not only grows upwards, suggesting necessary progress, but also has a trunk that might be taken to represent a 'main line' of development. A better analogy would be a dense bush, or even a spreading strawberry plant (Midgley 1978:158). Mandelbaum suggests as a simile 'the spread of ground cover from a single original plant, which had sent shoots in all directions, some of the shoots having taken new root, others having withered and died, and others barely surviving' (Mandelbaum 1971:84). That Darwin chose the image of the tree may indicate that he could not entirely shake off the traditional idea that life proceeds by ascent, even though the idea received no support from his theory. See also Reynolds (1981:13).

5 The omitted words after 'breathed' are 'by the Creator'. They appear only in later editions of *The origin of species* and were presumably intended to appease the consciences of Darwin's readers, and perhaps his own as well (Gruber 1974:209).

6 This does not, of course, exclude the possibility of 'orthoselection' in circumstances where an environment remains stable over an extended period of time. In such circumstances, we may expect that increasing adaptation to the environment would yield a uniformly directed or 'rectilinear' trend. We can account for limited trends of this kind without having to posit an orthogenetic principle of preplanned development operating independently of environmental circumstances (Goudge 1961:83–4).

7 Although Schrödinger's view is widely accepted, there is in fact some disagreement on this point. For 'orderliness' in the thermodynamic sense may not correspond precisely to

what we mean by 'organizational complexity' in the organic world. The components of a complex molecule may be regarded as more 'mixed up' than they were prior to its formation, so that entropy may correlate positively with organization (Needham 1943:226–7; Medawar 1967:54–5). However, it is beyond my competence, and our present concerns, to delve further into this controversy.

8 For an illuminating discussion of the distinction between history as a succession of events and as a process of development (presupposing some totality that is developing), see Mandelbaum (1971:45–6).

9 In *The study of sociology*, Spencer inveighs against Canon Kingsley for supposing that there might be anything less automatic about the trajectory of human society (1972:93–4). Kingsley had pointed out that a dropped stone would not necessarily hit the ground if someone decided to catch it. And if we imagine moving stones to be living people, endowed with as much will as their jugglers, anything might happen.

Chapter 2

1 Amongst the most prominent of the degenerationists was Richard Whately, Archbishop of Dublin, whose views were set out in a lecture, delivered in 1854, 'On the origin of civilization'. See Tylor (1871, I:34) and Stocking (1968:75–6).

2 For a recent expression of the same idea, see Harris (1968:232). 'No group of men', he writes, 'can will into existence whenever and wherever they choose, the apparatus of production, . . . *except in a definite order of progression.*' Offering a textbook exemplification of the retrospective fallacy, he continues: 'That order of progression corresponds precisely to what the combined efforts of archaeologists and ethnographers have revealed it to be.' Tylor would, no doubt, have agreed, but what makes Harris's assertion so bizarre is that it is made in the context of an argument that purports to apply a Darwinian paradigm to 'the realm of sociocultural phenomena' (1968:4). For the feature that specifically differentiates this paradigm from the Lamarckian conception of evolution is that is entails *no* definite order of progression.

3 Mason's order of priorities was clearly set out in the following passage: 'The explorer who goes among a people to study their entire creed and activity will do his work better by having in mind the determination to bring each industry into comparison with the same activities in other times and places' (1887:534). In the same article, he advocates an approach to culture based on 'the methods of the biologist', drawing precisely the same analogy between traits and species that had been proposed by Tylor. 'Inventions of both customs and things spring from prior inventions, just as life springs from life.'

4 The most explicit statement of this view that I have found is by Kubler, who, like Tylor, is concerned to discover pattern and sequence in the history of things. Kubler defines a formal sequence as 'a historical network of gradually altered repetitions of the same trait. . . . In cross section let us say that it shows a network, a mesh, or a cluster of subordinate traits; and in long section that it has a fiber-like structure of temporal stages, all recognizably similar, yet altering their mesh from beginning to end' (1962:37–8). Later in the same work, Kubler speaks of the flow of time 'as assuming the shapes of fibrous bundles, with each fiber corresponding to a need upon a particular theater of action, and the lengths of the fibers varying as to the duration of each need and the solution to its problems' (1962:122).

5 It involves no concession to holism to recognize that the expression of any one cultural element will be conditioned by the total pattern of elements into which it happens to be inserted, since the outward performance of the individual is the resultant of the simultaneous and conjoint operation of all its components. Hence the paradoxical antimony that Stocking (1968:213–14) finds in Boas's work between the 'perception of wholes' and 'the approach to culture in terms of its elements' is largely illusory. The apparent influence of the whole on its parts boils down to the combined influence of the parts on the appearance of the whole.

6 Leopold (1980:67–115) provides a much more detailed account of the use of 'culture' by Tylor and his contemporaries than can be attempted here. See also Kroeber and Kluckhohn (1952), Bidney (1953:23–53) and Stocking (1968:69–90).

7 Lest this be thought an isolated instance, I would refer to the compilation by Kroeber and Kluckhohn (1952:43–4) of definitions of culture directly influenced by, and in some cases plagiarizing, Tylor's original formulation. Here is another revealing example: 'To paraphrase Tylor, culture includes all the capabilities and habits acquired by an individual as a member of a particular society' (Klineberg 1935:225). Notice especially the substitution of 'an individual' for 'man', and the insertion of 'a particular' before 'society'.

8 Compare this statement, by a contemporary author, with one by Darwin (1874:170): 'A moral being is one who is capable of comparing his past and future actions or motives.' We shall return to the crucial problem of the relationship between time and consciousness in chapter 4.

9 Reflecting on his encounter with the natives of Tierra del Fuego during his voyage on the *Beagle,* Darwin commented: 'Viewing such men, one can hardly make oneself believe that they are fellow-creatures, and inhabitants of the same world' (1889:154). Yet it was precisely because of this sense that they *were* of the same world that his reaction was tinged with disgust rather than humility. Conversely the respect for 'primitive' people on which relativism prides itself is secured at the expense of sealing their lives within *other* worlds.

10 The same point was reasserted by Sir Arthur Keith, in his Presidential Address of 1916 to the Royal Anthropological Institute. 'The evolutionary human unit in the past', he declared, 'has been the primitive tribe, the world was covered with a mosaic of them' (1916:33). The most prominent recent advocate of the theory of group selection, also with reference to human evolution, is Wynne-Edwards. Reviving an argument originally propounded by Carr-Saunders (1922:223), he contends that if not all cultures are 'equally promising and viable' they will be 'subject to natural selection. The more successful ones survive and spread'. Moreover 'the yardstick of fitness between one culture and another applies to each cultural group as a whole, and ignores the personal differences in fitness that exist among the individuals that comprise each group' (Wynne-Edwards 1971:277). His claim that the natural selection of cultures would promote altruistic, 'public-spirited' behaviour, thus 'protecting the stock against the sabotage of short-term individual advantage', merely rehearses that advanced by Darwin exactly a century before, and which we cite here.

11 One of the first to recognize the full import of Darwin's remarks, in *The descent of man,* on the evolutionary significance of those 'social qualities' that lead primitive people to give and receive aid from their fellows (1874:167), was Prince Kropotkin. In savage society, he argued, the life of the individual is totally subservient to the life of the tribe, such that 'within the tribe the rule of "each for all" is supreme'. Yet relations between tribes are in a state of chronic, amoral conflict in which antagonists may inflict on one another 'the most revolting cruelties' (Kropotkin 1902:111–13). Kropotkin's *Mutual aid* was amongst the earliest studies of co-operation in animals and humans. Many others have followed his lead (see citations in Crook 1971:255). The whole question of the supposed hereditary basis of altruism has been reopened by recent developments in sociobiology, and a flood of publications has appeared on the subject. We shall defer discussion of this question to Chapter 6.

12 These inconsistencies between Darwin's two major works indicate the pitfalls encountered by both eulogists and critics who have insisted on treating the entire Darwinian corpus as all of a piece, often citing indiscriminately from here and there. The discussion of 'group selection' provides a case in point. Its advocates can find chapter and verse, as we have done, in *The descent of man:* Tribes in whose members an altruistic trait is relatively strongly represented would supplant other tribes, *'and this would be natural selection'* (1874:203; my emphasis). Yet, as Ghiselin rightly points out, the focus on individuals as the units of selection is the logical underpinning for Darwin's entire argument in *The origin of species.* On these grounds he asserts that group selectionists are 'grievously in error', or at least that the mechanism they propose 'is not the same as the type of natural selection discovered by Darwin' (Ghiselin 1969:57–8). What he fails to note is that first

and foremost amongst those who have thus misrepresented the argument of the *Origin* was its author.

13 The increasing superiority of these 'well-endowed men' over their female counterparts was, for Darwin, a foregone conclusion (1874:857–61).

14 This account of the transition in Boas's thinking from racial to cultural determinism is offered with some caution and relies heavily on the authority of Stocking (1968). It was typical of Boas that his more general works were composed by stitching together fragments of articles written at quite different times, in no particular order, and with little regard for internal consistency. It is therefore extremely hard to make out the direction of his thought. Thus, from *The mind of primitive man* (1911), assembled out of pieces written over a formative period of almost twenty years, one can find statements in support of two quite distinct and contradictory positions, which I take to be 'early' and 'later' respectively.

Position 1: The condition of an individual's body (including the organization of his brain) depends on the particular milieu to which he is exposed; his mode of thought reflects the material structure of his brain.

> If we grant . . . the plasticity of human types we are necessarily led to grant also a great plasticity of the mental make-up of human types. . . . We must conclude that the fundamental traits of the mind, which are closely correlated with the physical condition of the body . . . are the more subject to far-reaching changes. (1911:64–5)

> Environment has an important effect upon the anatomical structure and physiological functions of man. . . . If we consider mental condition as dependent upon . . . the structure of the body, particularly the brain, . . . very large differences in individual disposition may be expected. (1911:75, 93)

> It does not seem probable that the minds of races which show variations in their anatomical structure should act in exactly the same manner. . . . As we found evidence of difference in structure between the races, so we must anticipate that differences in mental characteristics will be found. (1911:114–15)

Position 2: The organization of the brain is basically the same for all mankind, though inherited bodily form varies between populations. An individual's mode of thought reflects the ideal contents of his brain, and these depend on the particular milieu to which he is exposed:

> 'There can be no doubt that in the main the mental characteristics of man are the same all over the world', but on this unity is imposed 'the diversity produced by the variety of contents of the mind as found in various social and geographical environments'. (1911:104)

> The mental activities . . . of the human mind are common to the whole of humanity. (1911:122)

> 'Mythology', 'theology', and 'philosophy' . . . denote influences which shape the current of human thought. (1911:204)

> The variations in cultural development can be as well explained by . . . the general course of historical events as by material differences of mental faculty in different races. (1911:29)

15 As will be obvious from our choice of metaphor, there is a direct link between the cultural determinism of Boasian anthropology and the celebrated dictum of John Locke, that the human mind is, at first, a 'yet empty cabinet' that subsequently comes to be filled with all manner of ideas. 'Let us suppose the mind to be, as we say, white paper, void of all characters, without any ideas:—How comes it to be furnished? Whence comes it by that vast store which the busy and boundless fancy of man has painted on it with an almost endless variety? . . . To this I answer, in one word, from EXPERIENCE. In that all our

knowledge is founded' (Locke 1894[1690], I:48, 121–2). On the continuity from Locke, through Turgot, to Boas, see Harris (1968:10–16).

16 Thus Kroeber again, in his 'eighteen professions': 'All men are totally civilized. All animals are totally uncivilized because they are totally uncivilizable' (1915:286). One could scarcely be more blunt. Kroeber, of course, was using civilization to mean heritage or tradition.

17 Old ideas die hard. Reproduced here is a diagram presented in all seriousness to a conference of distinguished psychologists and biologists, held in 1968. It depicts what is called the 'conceptual homunculus'. According to its originator, J. B. Calhoun, 'The body of man has remained his earlier biological self, but the degree to which he has effectively utilized his cortex has continually increased.' This is indicated by the increasing size of the head, representing its 'conceptual target diameter'. The dates, marking off a series of 'revolutionary' thresholds, have been calculated according to a mathematical formula. The next revolution, due shortly, has been brought forward by four years in deference to Orwell. See Calhoun (1971:372–4).

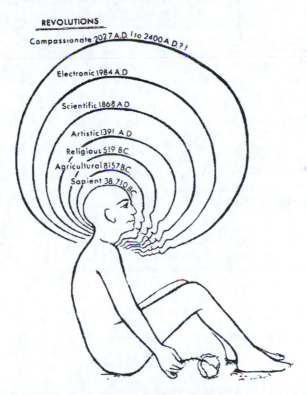

18 A recent advocate of this view is David Bidney. Reverting to an eighteenth-century view of progress, Bidney understands cultural evolution as 'the unfolding or activating of the potentialities of human nature through a process of self-conditioning and education in relation to a given environment'. This 'self-cultivation', as he elsewhere calls it, is 'contingent upon human effort and rational selection'. We are the active originators of our cultural forms, not just passive vehicles or carriers, and these forms are instrumental 'in promoting the psychocultural evolution of man in the interests of human welfare' (Bidney 1953:82–4, 126). The apparent anachronism of this view, in the context of postwar American anthropology, may account for the remarkable contemporary neglect into which Bidney's important study has fallen.

Chapter 3

1 As a curiosity that conveys much about the intellectual climate of the time, we might note an early paper by one of Spencer's most powerful critics—William James—entitled 'Great men and their environment' and originally published in 1880. Here James attempts to refute the Spencerian doctrine of historical inevitability and to re-enthrone the idea that history is shaped by the genius of exceptional individuals, by appeal to an analogue of Darwinian variation under natural selection: 'The relation of the visible environment to the great man is in the main exactly what it is to the "variation" in the Darwinian philosophy. It chiefly adopts or rejects, preserves or destroys, in short *selects* him' (1898:226). But his appearance is a mere accident.

   James's argument is, of course, based on a serious misunderstanding of Darwinian theory in that it supposes selection to operate not on populations of unique individuals but on occasional, hopeful mutants appearing by saltation in otherwise homogeneous communities.

2 We shall not enter here into a full discussion of this eccentric episode in the theory of cultural evolution. White's argument is summed up in the following statement: 'Since culture, as an extrasomatic tradition, may be treated logically as a distinct and autonomous kind of system, we may interpret the evolution of culture in terms of the same principles of thermodynamics that are applicable to biological systems' (White 1959b:39). Hence, the more complex the system of cultural ideas, the more energy must be harnessed and expended in its maintenance and reproduction. As an example, White cites with approval the work of a certain David Burns, who 'reports on experiments in which the amounts of energy required to give lectures were measured' (1959b:38 n. 14). Presumably, the more elaborate and sophisticated the content of the lecture, the more calories the lecturer was expected to use up in delivering it. One could, of course, expend a good deal more energy in the explosive enunciation of gibberish than in the dispassionate presentation of a complex idea. Anyone inclined, like White, to reduce the production of culture to the operation of physical laws would do well to bear in mind one of the more penetrating remarks of Teilhard de Chardin on the question of mind–matter dualism: 'To think we must eat. But what a variety of thoughts we get out of one slice of bread!' (1959:69).

3 Precisely the same ambiguity afflicts the 'structures' of Lévi-Strauss. Like Kluckhohn's 'culture', the term 'social structure', for Lévi-Strauss, 'has nothing to do with empirical reality but with models which are built up after it'. And just as Kluckhohn distinguishes culture from behaviour, so Lévi-Strauss separates 'social structure' from the 'social relations' that according to the English original, 'consist of the raw materials *out of which the models making up the social structure are built*' (1968:279). Now consider the French wording of the passage I have emphasized: 'qui rendent manifeste la structure sociale elle-même' (1957:306). Apparently, Lévi-Strauss meant to say that the social structure *is manifested* in social relations. Again, notice the similarity with Kluckhohn's wording: Culture is manifested in behaviour. Indeed, anyone who supposes that Lévi-Strauss introduced anything novel in his distinction between social structure and social relations has simply been blinded by a superficial change of terms. Nor can one blame the translator for an apparent distortion of Lévi-Strauss's text, for it results merely from his attempts to be consistent where the author is not. We may wonder (as indeed the translator must have wondered) how structural models that 'are built up after' empirical reality in the mind of the investigator can elsewhere be presented as structures more 'real' than the reality we see, located in the minds of the people studied, in a Boasian 'unconscious', and manifested in their behaviour. For that amounts to saying that they are not models at all, but things whose existence does not in the least depend on there being an anthropologist on the scene to observe their effects.

4 This statement is a virtual reiteration of the principal thesis of Giambattista Vico, in his *New science* of 1725, that human beings can only fully understand that which owes its origination to the human mind; for 'what men have made, other men, because their

minds are those of men, can always, in principle, "enter into'" (Berlin 1976:27). Vico's thesis is summed up in a famous passage, which is worth citing in full: 'In the night of thick darkness enveloping the earliest antiquities, so remote from ourselves, there shines the eternal and never failing light of a truth beyond all question: that the world of civil society has certainly been made by men, and that its principles are, therefore, to be found within the modifications of our own human mind. Whoever reflects on this cannot but marvel that the philosophers should have bent all their energies to the study of the world of nature, which, since God made it, He alone knows: and that they should have neglected the study of the world of nations or civil world, which since men had made it, men could come to know' (Vico 1948[1744]:331).

5 Another way of expressing the difference between a view relative to the subject and one relative to the object is, following Fabian, to contrast *'reflexion* qua subjective activity carried out by and revealing the ethnographer, and *reflection* as a sort of objective reflex (like the image in a mirror) which hides the observer by axiomatically eliminating subjectivity' (Fabian 1983:90).

6 Of this work, Oldroyd remarks that it 'is now a dusty occupant of the lumber-room of speculative philosophy' and that 'we, with our contemporary Olympian vision, may be inclined to regard it as a philosophical aberration' (1980:278). Certainly the copy I consulted had accumulated plenty of dust. But since in a whole range of fields, from physics to sociology, the received atomism of twentieth-century Western thought is now at last being questioned, it is perhaps time to retrieve *Creative evolution* from the shelves. On rereading, this 'aberration' will be found to contain most of the ideas towards which we are currently groping, expressed with an eloquence sadly lacking in the ponderous and convoluted philosophical language of today.

7 For a similar view, see Kroeber (1963:83–6). Despite his avowed relativism, Kroeber felt that the 'trend toward progress' in human culture must be accepted as a fact. 'Such progress is manifest in the total quantity of culture controlled by societies, and making therefore for mastery of the environment; in the size of the cohesive social unit, internal and external; and in recognition of reality. Many anthropologists are still shy of admitting any sort of cultural progress; but this is an outdated position. In naive days there was indeed much ethnocentric assumption of progress that was false; but these are no longer naive days. We can fully accept cultural relativism, and yet not make of it a curtain that obliterates all deeper inquiry into values' (1963:84).

8 Darlington's scenario is set out in a massive work entitled *The evolution of man and society* (1969). The general idea is that humans as hunter-gatherers first split up into a number of isolated breeding populations, leading to the formation of distinct races. Then, with the formation of class-based, agricultural civilizations, the better-endowed of these races came to establish their hegemony over others. Hence racial boundaries no longer lie between spatially segregated societies but within societies between classes. The ranking of classes corresponds to inherited intellectual ability and should be preserved in the interests of civilization. Thus 'we [upper class folk] may still be able to get the message of the Athenian painter or playwright or the Hebrew poet as though he were living among us today. But, alas, it is a message we cannot expect to pass on to the butcher or the baker at our door' (Darlington 1972:114). It is hard to believe that such preposterous views, wholly lacking in substantiation, could have been printed by a reputable academic publisher barely more than a decade ago.

9 And of course, so long as there is life, there is movement. It is a universal fact of our existence, Fernandez remarks, 'that all humans are disposed to movement, recognize the need for it, are interested in joining it or observing it when it occurs'. In short, 'we move, are moved, or we die' (Fernandez 1979:61).

10 As Glucksmann has pointed out, this is a matter on which Lévi-Strauss and Althusser, despite their otherwise considerable differences, are more or less in accord: '[The] antihumanism [which] is one of the most distinctive aspects of Althusserian Marxism . . . has many similarities with Lévi-Strauss's anti-subjectivism. For both of them, relations and structures are the unit for analysis, rather than man's lived and subjective experience,

and these are to be explained by impersonal structural forces (play without an author)' (Glucksmann 1974:113). Commenting on the similarity, Giddens (1979:160) notes that Althusser proceeds by substituting for the total social process existing in its particular moments the idea of a 'structure existing in its effects'. Purposive action by human agents is thus rendered as the epiphenomenon of a structural cause. There are also parallels between Althusserian Marxism and the sociology of Parsons: 'Each reaches a position in which subject is controlled by object' (Giddens 1979:52, 112).

11 This is to say that I and the members of my immediate family are, in Schutz's terms, 'consociates': 'Sharing a community of [inner] time . . . implies that each partner participates in the on-rolling life of the other. . . . They may thus share one another's anticipations of the future as plans, or hopes or anxieties. In brief, *consociates are mutually involved in one another's biography; they are growing older together;* they live, as we may call it, in a pure We-relationship' (Schutz 1962:16–17; my emphasis).

12 The Boasian 'culture-bearing individual' corresponds neither to the individual (qua organism) nor to the person of Radcliffe-Brown. As regards the latter, the lack of correspondence is evident from Radcliffe-Brown's criticism of Kroeber's treatment of the phenomenon of classificatory kinship. In an article written in 1909 and directed principally against the rather fanciful sociological reconstructions of Radcliffe-Brown's mentor, W. H. R. Rivers, Kroeber had concluded that 'terms of relationship reflect psychology, not sociology. They are determined primarily by language and can be utilised for sociological inferences only with extreme caution' (1952:181; see Rivers 1968[1914]). By psychology, Kroeber did not mean to refer to the universal attributes of human nature, but to the impress on the mind of the individual of a specific cultural pattern, which imparts characteristic 'ways of thinking and feeling'. In adopting a sociological view of kinship systems, different of course to that of Rivers, Radcliffe-Brown's concern was not with affection and cognition, but with practical action (1952:59–62). The person, in his capacity as a kinsman, is the part he plays in this system of action. Although neither Kroeber nor Radcliffe-Brown attributed much to human agency, Kroeber's individual is a repository for cultural elements (of which kinship terms form but a small subset), whereas Radcliffe-Brown's kinship system is a working arrangement (of which the person forms but one small component). This difference of approach was fundamental to the subsequent split between cultural and social anthropology.

13 Here Lévi-Strauss reiterates a point made many years previously: 'Both history and ethnography are concerned with societies *other* than the one in which we live. Whether this *otherness* is due to remoteness in time . . . or to remoteness in space, . . . is of secondary importance compared to the basic similarity of perspective' (1968:16). Elsewhere, of course, he completely contradicts this point by identifying history (as opposed to ethnography) with the continuous, oriented and cumulative sense of time characteristic of progressive evolutionism (see chapter 4).

14 Ever since the formulation of Heisenberg's indeterminacy principle, it has been evident to atomic physicists that the absolute separation of observer and observed is a theoretical impossibility. As Bohm puts it, both 'are merging and interpenetrating aspects of one whole reality' (1980:9). One would have thought that the life sciences—biology, psychology and above all anthropology—would have been the first to recognize this. But ironically, so great has been their concern to emulate supposedly 'hard' science, and so backward has been their appreciation of it, that they remain largely committed to an objectivism that is already obsolescent. And as far as anthropology is concerned, this commitment has actually been strengthened by the dominant attitude of cultural relativism.

Chapter 4

1 Darwin himself left his readers in no doubt about this, going out of his way to dispel possible misinterpretation: 'The mere lapse of time by itself does nothing, either for or against natural selection. I state this because it has been erroneously asserted that the

element of time has been assumed by me to play an all-important part in modifying species, as if all forms of life were necessarily undergoing change through some innate law' (1872:76).

2 To this list we should also add Whitehead, whose view of the universe as 'a creative advance into novelty' was considerably influenced by Bergson's philosophy. According to Whitehead, the order of nature is never complete, 'it is always passing beyond itself'. And the creative principle forever immanent in this advance corresponded to his conception of God (Whitehead 1929:314, 420; see Eisendrath 1971:206).

3 This idea will be familiar to social anthropologists from the literature on lineage systems. It is expressed most explicitly by Fortes, in his work on the Tallensi of northern Ghana: 'Among the Tallensi the lineage system enables us to see the operation of the time factor in social structure in a very concrete way. We see how the lineage structure at a given time incapsulates all that is structurally relevant of its past phases and at the same time continually thrusts its growing-points forward. The dynamic equilibrium of the lineage is an equilibrium in time' (Fortes 1945:224).

4 In the 'comparative method' of evolutionary ethnology, the superfluity of dates is taken to such an extreme that there ceases to be any correspondence at all between chronological and historical contemporaneity. Societies, it is assumed, may be glimpsed at the same point in a single historical process at moments widely apart in chronological time, and vice versa. Thus when White (1945a:230) claims that 'the evolutionist process is concerned with *classes* of events independent of specific time and place', he is referring to *chronological* time and *geodesic* space. The aim, then, of evolutionary ethnology is to reunite in real time what in abstract time has become separated.

5 The author of this phrase was, of course, William James, and the passage in which he leads up to it bears repeating: 'Consciousness . . . does not appear to itself chopped up in bits. . . . It is nothing jointed; it flows. A 'river' or 'stream' are the metaphors by which it is most naturally described. In talking of it hereafter, let us call it the stream of thought, of consciousness, or of subjective life' (James 1890, 1:239). Bergson's view was essentially the same.

6 We should note here one consequence of our rejection of Saussurian essentialism: that synchronic relations do not obtain beyond the boundaries of the individual. Different individuals, albeit of the same population and chronologically contemporary, represent different states and are therefore to be conceived as so many points in a network of diachronic relations whose links are forged in the transmission of those elements composing each state.

7 Criticizing Radcliffe-Brown's conception of the organic analogy, Leach writes: 'The entities which we call societies are not naturally existing species, neither are they man-made mechanisms. But the analogy of a mechanism has quite as much relevance as the analogy of an organism' (1961:6). How, then, do mechanism and organism differ? In one respect alone: The organism *lives*. And it was precisely this idea of social *life,* as opposed to society as an *entity,* that Radcliffe-Brown derived from the analogy.

8 This might be the appropriate point to take stock of the rather idiosyncratic classification of functions of time presented in an influential paper by Fortes: (a) time as *duration,* extrinsic, a background or container in which things happen, as they are recounted in history books; (b) time as *continuity* (or its opposite, discontinuity), intrinsic, 'an index of forces and conditions that remain more or less constant over a stretch of time; or else of those that give way precipitately to new forces and conditions'; and (c) time intrinsic to *genetic* or 'growth processes', as opposed to mere sequence, compounded from the forces of continuity and non-reversible modification (Fortes 1949:54–5). It seems clear that the third sense (c) corresponds to Bergson's 'duration', and to the curved trajectory of Fig. 4.3. Fortes uses the antinomies of continuity and discontinuity to mean persistence (constancy) and change (precipitate modification): Therefore the second sense (b) corresponds to the stepwise sequence in Fig. 4.3. Finally, time in sense (a) is an abstract, 'empty' thread, divisible into chronological segments on which we can hang the narrative of events.

9 The clarity of Geertz's argument is not enhanced by his tendency to oscillate between these two concepts of the person. Thus having explained that the everyday world of the Balinese is populated by 'determinate persons positively characterized and appropriately labeled'—that is by *dramatis personae*—he then goes on to describe his project as the description and analysis of 'the experience of persons' (1975:363–4). Labels, however, do not have experiences; it is the selves to whom they are attached that do.

10 This is a point recognized by Waddington, who also deals briefly with the relation between time-scales and forms of explanation in biology. He distinguishes between the short scale of physiological reactions, the medium scale of individual ontogeny and the longest scale of Darwinian evolution. But he notes that it is by taking the longest and shortest scale *together,* and omitting the medium term, that we arrive at the theory of natural selection (Waddington 1957:6–7).

Chapter 5

1 Besides Monod (1972), see the volume edited by Lewis (1974), and papers by Skolimowski, Birch and Dobzhansky, as well as the response by Monod, in Ayala and Dobzhansky (1974). Some of the issues involved have been recently addressed in Birch and Cobb (1981). For a sceptical review, see Toulmin (1982:140–55).

2 In an argument ostensibly similar to Monod's, Bateson compares epigenesis to the development of a complex tautology, 'in which nothing is added after the axioms and definitions have been laid down'. Thus 'in contrast with epigenesis and tautology, which constitute the worlds of replication, there is the whole realm of creativity, art, learning and evolution, in which the ongoing processes of change *feed on the random.* The essence of epigenesis is predictable repetition; the essence of learning and evolution is exploration and change' (Bateson 1980:57–8). And again, 'epigenesis is to evolution as the working out of a tautology is to creative thought' (1980:176).

3 This point receives further confirmation in a paper on 'organic design' by the zoologist C. F. A. Pantin. Likening natural selection to an engineer, he uses precisely the same analogy to characterize its products that Goudge applies to mechanistically created things. The organism, Pantin writes, is 'like a model made from a child's engineering constructional set: a set consisting of standard parts with unique properties, of strips, plates and wheels which can be used for various functional objectives' (1951:144).

4 A rather similar kind of confusion is contained in the contention of Lévi-Strauss, in his *Race and history,* that 'the true contribution of a culture consists, not in the list of inventions which it has personally produced, but in its difference from others' (1953:42). The very idea that a *culture* can produce things in *person* is a contradiction in terms, conflating the objective with the subjective, created goods and creative good. Perhaps it was merely a slip of the pen on Lévi-Strauss's part. But if so, the slip was a highly revealing one.

5 In the original French: 'Nous ne prétendons donc pas montrer comment les hommes pensent dans les mythes mais comment les mythes se pensent dans les hommes, et à leur insu' (Lévi-Strauss 1964:20). There is some debate as to how this should best be translated.

6 See Tylor (1871, 1:354). A corpus of myth, then, is rather like a library, being an accumulation of works from which it is possible to read something of the way their authors lived and thought. It is instructive to compare the views of Boas and Lévi-Strauss on the anonymity of myth with the conclusion to which Tylor moves: 'Myth is the history of its authors, not its subjects; it records the lives, not of superhuman heroes, but of poetic nations' (1871, 1:376).

7 This might be the appropriate point to mention the recent and highly provocative attempt by Webster and Goodwin to apply a structuralist approach to the classic problem of the origin of species. In their view, every species is the realization of one possibility out of a very large number of possibilities constituting a logically structured set, all of whose members may be generated through the manipulation of a system of transformations. Evolution, then, is an *exploratory* process that—although a result of the interplay of chance

and necessity—'provides a "revelation" of the system and its possibilities and, therefore, its laws. . . . Living organisms are devices which use the contingent "noise" of history as a "motor" to explore the set of structures, perhaps infinitely large, which are possible for them' (Webster and Goodwin 1982:46). If this view is well founded (and it is too early to say), the analogy between mythical and organic projects as works of *bricolage* would be even closer than I have ventured to suggest.

8   Saussure and Chomsky differ in their respective formulations of the relation between freedom and structure. For Saussure, the concatenation of words in sentences is a matter of individual free creation since it lies *outside* the sphere of linguistic structure (*la langue*). For Chomsky, on the other hand, the structure is not opposed to freedom but is its very condition, underwriting the capacity of the individual to generate ever-novel sentence types (Chomsky 1968:17; Hymes 1971:52–4).

9   'A causeless, indeterminate will', Bidney writes, 'is incompatible with scientific argument.' Nevertheless he goes on to argue, somewhat paradoxically, that mind may be 'determined and free simultaneously. . . . Freedom and causality are not mutually exclusive but rather complementary factors' (1963a:29–30). There is a similar complementarity, of course, between chance and necessity, diachrony and synchrony, and change and persistence. But none of these dichotomies present us with anything more than a reconstructed *approximation* to reality.

10   The creativity that we attribute to the mind, Bourdieu attributes to something he calls the *habitus,* which is likewise the condensation of a history of social relations. As to what the habitus actually is, and how if at all it differs from mind, I confess to being utterly bewildered. Bourdieu nowhere defines his terms, preferring to bombard his readers with some of the most contorted doublespeak ever to have appeared in recent anthropology. For example: '. . . being the product of a chronologically ordered series of structuring determinations, the habitus, which at every moment structures in terms of the structuring experiences which produced it the structuring experiences which affect its structure, brings about a unique integration . . .' (1977:86–7).

Whatever this may mean (and it could mean anything, making criticism impossible), we cannot accept Bourdieu's elevation of habitus as a system of dispositions 'common to all members of the same group or class', of whose collective history 'the history of the individual is never anything other than a certain specification' (1977:86). That seems to be a lapse into just the kind of Durkheimian essentialism that Bourdieu is otherwise so concerned to avoid.

11   See, for example, Bonner (1980) and the extensive list of references provided by Bock (1980:223 n. 28).

12   It is clear from other contexts that Marx uses the term 'species' as a synonym for 'social', to connote relations of intersubjectivity. Thus he writes that the life of man is 'an expression and confirmation of *social life.* Man's individual and species life are not *different'* (1964a:138). By this he means that social ('species') life is not the life of a hypostatized society as opposed to that of individual subjects, but rather an intersubjective process, i.e. the social life of persons. We return to Marx's views on this crucial point in the next chapter.

13   This was not so, it should be noted, for Engels, whose 'dialectic of nature' was not between Subject and Object, but a reciprocal interaction between objects, that is organisms and their environment (Venable 1945:70). To this, the fact that humans are *'self-conscious* organisms' appeared almost incidental (Engels 1934:237; Schmidt 1971:191). The same, of course, goes for much recent thinking in ecological anthropology (e.g. Rappaport 1971).

Chapter 6

1   Compare Boas: 'In place of a simple line of evolution there appears a multiplicity of converging and diverging lines which it is difficult to bring under one system. Instead of uniformity, the striking feature seems to be diversity' (1974:34); and Durkheim: '[Each society] constitutes a new individuality, and all such distinct individualities,

being heterogeneous, cannot be absorbed into the same continuous series, and above all not into one single series. The succession of societies cannot be represented by a geometrical line; on the contrary, it resembles a tree whose branches grow in divergent directions' (1982[1895]:64).

2 Sorokin, introducing his massive *Society, culture and personality* with a section on 'the superorganic world', takes a view broadly similar to that of Kroeber. Superorganic phenomena, the subject of study for the social sciences, 'are found only in man and the man-made world'. They include language, science, religion, art, law, custom, technology, architecture, plant and animal husbandry and social organization. 'These are all superorganic phenomena because they are the articulations of mind in various forms; none of them arise mainly in response to blind reflexes or instincts.' And again, superorganic traits 'are not inherited biologically but are learned from other human beings' (Sorokin 1947:3–5). Elsewhere, however, he veers towards the view that the source of the superorganic lies not in the mental processes of individuals but in emergent properties of the supraindividual matrix within which they are embedded (Bidney 1953:332–3).

3 One reason why Kroeber preferred to substitute 'social' for 'cultural' in writing about the superorganic was, apparently, that the German *Kultur* had become a catchword of the wartime propaganda of the period, attracting all kinds of bogus connotations that had nothing to do with the proper meaning of the term. 'It is not that Kroeber was ignorant of culture in 1917 but that he feared to be misunderstood outside of anthropology if he used the word' (Kroeber and Kluckhohn 1952:29 n. 78).

4 In a particularly candid and outspoken presentation of this point, Murdock has consigned a century of anthropological theorizing to the realms of mythology: 'Culture, social system, and all comparable supraindividual concepts, such as collective representations, group mind, and social organism, are illusory conceptual abstractions inferred from observations of the very real phenomena of individuals interacting with one another and with their natural environments.... As reified abstractions, they cannot legitimately be used to explain human behaviour' (1972:19). It should perhaps be added that Murdock is objecting to the concept of culture only when it is employed to denote a supraindividual emergent, i.e. in the sense in which it becomes synonymous with social structure.

5 We should perhaps mention one significant exception. This is the ethological definition of society proposed by Wynne-Edwards. As an advocate of group selection (see this volume, chapter 2 n. 10, and the discussion of altruism in the final part of this chapter), Wynne-Edwards feels that although social organization has adaptive consequences that promote its establishment under natural selection, these consequences are for the local population as a whole rather than for its expendable, individual members. Society, then, sets the goals for which individuals compete and lays down the rules of the game in such a way that the entire group benefits from the competition itself. Wynne-Edwards defines the society as 'an organization of individuals capable of providing conventional competition among its members and adapted to secure the survival of the stock'. And since individuals may, amongst other things, be competing for private space, Wynne-Edwards holds that sociality *per se* 'has no special connection with gregariousness' (1972:60).

6 In his critique of sociobiology, Sahlins correctly observes that, for its advocates, 'social organization is ... nothing more than the behavioural outcome of the interaction of organisms having biologically fixed inclinations. There is nothing in society that was not first in the organisms'. What he *fails* to note is that for much of cultural anthropology too, society is similarly reducible to the behavioural propensities of individuals, its organization resulting directly from the interaction of human beings having *culturally* fixed inclinations. In rejecting such a reductionist view of social organization, Sahlins gives a thinly veiled approval to the cultural superorganicism of Durkheim and the early Kroeber (Sahlins 1976a:5–6).

7 We owe one of the most bizarre interpretations of this passage to Marvin Harris. Relations of production are independent of human will, he claims, because they are determined by the technical nature of the prevailing apparatus of production. Since technological development follows a pre-ordained 'order of progression', which 'does

not admit of deviations or leaps', it follows that human beings can but fall in with the requirements of the technology that is prevalent in the particular 'stage of development' they happen to find themselves in (Harris 1968:232).

8 Habermas has recently attempted to accommodate this shift in Marx's understanding of co-operation by distinguishing two 'levels'. We must, he writes, 'separate the level of communicative action from that of the instrumental and strategic action combined in social co-operation' (1979:145). This is not a satisfactory solution and only further obscures the fundamental distinction between social and material relations. For one thing, as sociobiologists have clearly recognized, co-operative action is no less instrumental or strategic for being communicative. For another, that which is instrumental or strategic, hence by definition dependent on human will, cannot be included under the rubric of social relations that *constitute* the will.

9 When it comes to the delineation of cultural ecology as a subject of study, Steward vacillates—very much as did Kroeber—between contrary images of the superorganic. Man, he asserts, 'enters the ecological scene ... not merely as another organism which is related to other organisms in terms of his physical characteristics. He introduces the super-organic factor of culture, which also affects and is affected by the total web of life' (1955:31).

The focus of ecological investigation is normally the population, a local aggregate of individuals, and the ecologist studies the behaviour these individuals exhibit both amongst themselves and in the course of interaction with other elements of their environment. If culture is understood in the Boasian sense as a property of individual human beings, then a cultural ecology would likewise be concerned with 'behaviour patterns' manifested in populations of culture-bearers in their adaptation to determinate environmental conditions. Evidently, it is these that Steward sets out to elucidate. However, in demarcating cultural from biological ecology, he withdraws culture from the human individual, leaving the latter as but a genetically constituted thing. Whereas biological ecologists study the interrelations of these things, in terms of their innate (physical) characteristics, cultural ecologists are enjoined to study 'how culture is affected by its adaptation to environment' (Steward 1955:31). Culture has here become a reified, supraindividual entity with a life of its own, and its adaptation a process analogous to, but separate from, that of human individuals. Hence the two ecologies are supposed to deal with the environmental relations of biological organisms and cultural superorganisms respectively.

10 Mumford calls it the *megamachine,* consisting of a large body of individuals rigorously co-ordinated in their activities for a predetermined and calculated purpose. Defining the machine, in general terms, as 'a combination of resistant parts, each specialized in function, operating under human control to utilize energy and perform work', Mumford notes that the 'great labour machine' amply fulfils these definitional criteria: 'all the more because its components, though made of human bone, nerve and muscle, were reduced to their bare mechanical elements and rigidly standardized for the performance of their limited tasks' (Mumford 1967:191).

11 The fact that Mauss uses the keyword 'total' in two quite different senses has been a source of considerable confusion. In the first sense it is employed to characterize the general phenomenon of gift exchange, which is 'total' in that it registers at every level of societal functioning. But in the second sense, it demarcates a particular subclass of such exchange, namely 'prestation'. In this context, Mauss distinguishes 'total prestations' (between corporations sole or aggregate such as chiefs or clans) from 'gift exchange' (here limited to exchanges between particular *individuals*), and suggests that the latter represents an intermediary phase in an evolutionary development from primitive or archaic societies in the stage of 'total prestation' to modern society based on 'pure individual contract, the money market, sale proper, fixed price, and weighed and coined money' (1954[1925]:45, 68).

12 Of commodity fetishism, Marx wrote that 'the distinctive relations into which [people] enter in the course of production in society appear as the specific properties of a thing', or more precisely 'as the relations of things to one another and of things to people'

(1970[1859]:34, 49). For the determinist, too, social relations are supposed to manifest the properties of a *thing called culture,* and cultures, in the words of Sahlins, 'are meaningful orders of persons and things' (1976b:x).

13 A classic discussion of how the exchange of commodified cultural values in successive individual transactions leads to and upholds their integration into a consistent system is that of Barth (1966:12–21).

14 Thus Fortes takes exception to the view of P. J. Wilson that food-sharing in hunting and gathering societies 'does not constitute altruistic behaviour but . . . is obligatory' (Wilson 1975:12), a view that clearly implies the spontaneity of altruism. For Fortes, obligation is the essence of sharing—not, however, a contractual obligation between individuals but a moral obligation imposed by society. Thus 'human altruism is not a private virtue but a public, social office, . . . a service, kindness or attention given to others out of a sense of duty reflecting moral obligation' (Fortes 1983:44 n. 19).

15 Kantorowicz uses the image of the robot to make the point that simply to abide by jurally constituted rules is not to act as a moral subject: 'We could then imagine theoretically that a mechanical model could be constructed which, although deprived of any mental life, could behave exactly like a human being. The response of the mechanism to the appropriate external stimuli would be exactly the response prescribed by the law and this *homme-machine* would be a perfect, perhaps the only perfect, law-abiding citizen. Morally viewed, however, his conduct would be quite indifferent' (1958:47).

Chapter 7

1 Consciousness, according to Wilson, is the action of organic machinery in the brain, and 'consists of immense numbers of simultaneous and co-ordinated symbolic representations by the participating neurons of the brain's neocortex'. The fact that the workings of consciousness constitute 'the cardinal mystery of neurobiology' does not appear to shake Wilson's conviction that it will, ultimately, be completely solved (1978:74–5).

2 I do not wish to take sides here on the question of the intellectual and linguistic capabilities of chimpanzees. If it were demonstrated conclusively that they can achieve some elementary competence with language, given an appropriate medium and training, and that they can develop a corresponding aptitude for conceptual thought, we may have to move the Rubicon to put them on our side, but the basic argument concerning the dependence of thought on language would remain unaffected. Moreover we would still be left with the puzzle of explaining why the same abilities do not appear among chimpanzees observed under 'natural' conditions. There may be something in Marler's argument that animals living in small, intimate groups, familiar with one another from a long history of involvement, have little or no need for such a specialized instrument as language. But then the same could be said of primary human groups. 'Indeed it is conceivable', Marler remarks, 'that other [non-linguistic] types of communication . . . play a much more important role in our own biology than we are inclined to acknowledge' (1977:66). The point is well taken.

3 See, for example, Harré (1979:190–2, 224). Harré justifies his adoption of what he calls the 'dramaturgical model' of social life on the grounds that what humans do is primarily expressive rather than practical. 'I shall devote no space', he declares, 'to a discussion of the practical activities of mankind since I believe that they bear only tangentially on social life during most of human history' (1979:206). Such a preposterous assertion could only issue from the topmost turret of an ivory tower. By and large, advocates of the dramatic metaphor are inclined to adopt a pretty jaundiced view of the human condition, and Harré is no exception—as evidenced by the following remark, apparently meant in all seriousness: 'Marx said that it was in the nature of man to work. Not at least as the human race is presently constituted. It is in the nature of men to slip off to the pub to display their *machismo*' (1979:8).

4 This view has a clear precedent in the writings of Boas: 'Tradition manifests itself in an action performed by the individual. The more frequently this action is repeated, the more firmly it will become established, and the less will be the conscious equivalent accompanying the action; so that customary actions which are of very frequent repetition become entirely unconscious' (1911:242).

5 The failure to recognize this distinction underlies a famous and perfectly pointless argument between Schneider and Geertz over the question of whether culture can be comprehended 'in its own terms', purely as a system of symbols, apart from the actual flow of conduct in which it is manifested. Schneider thinks that it can be isolated in this fashion, yielding 'culture-as-constituted' rather than 'culture-as-lived', an opposition that has its linguistic analogue in the Saussurian dichotomy of *langue* and *parole* (1980:125–36). To this, Geertz objects that to abstract culture from conduct is to drain it of meaning, to leave it vacant. Describing a culture, for Geertz, means 'tracing the curve of social discourse', unravelling the intentions and purposes of people in saying what they say and doing what they do (1975:17–19). Obviously this requires more than a knowledge of the formal code, in terms of which anything might have been said or done. Schneider, to his credit, never denies this; his point is simply that one has to crack the code before being able to follow the conversation—the second problem cannot be tackled until the first has been overcome (1980:129). Geertz merely confuses the issue by persistently referring to an intersubjective *process* ('the curve of social discourse', 'the flow of social action', 'an ongoing pattern of life', etc.) as a pansubjective *entity,* namely a culture or 'cultural form'. Evidently the meaning that he considers to inhere in conduct, and which cannot be recovered within the terms of Schneider's opposition between symbolic structure and manifest behaviour, corresponds to the movement of intentionality-in-action, and as such is intransitive. Such meaning pertains to the consciousness that presents conduct, not to the culture that represents it. Mistaking consciousness for culture, Geertz confounds intransitive and transitive senses of meaning by assuming that whatever conveys meaning must be symbolic. That symbolic meaning is always transitive is clearly recognized by Schneider, who defines a symbol simply as 'something which stands for something else' (1980:1); hence the meaning that inheres in conduct *cannot* be symbolic. Had Geertz been less hooked on the concept of culture, and less verbose in his argumentation, he might have realized that to render an account of the process of social life is to do *just that,* and not to describe a culture; that such an account does not at all preclude the formalization of culture as a system of symbols; and moreover that since culture is a vehicle for social life (as is language for conversation), one must master the former in order to interpret the latter.

6 This is, in fact, a reverse extension. The notion of behaviour was, according to Ardener, of fifteenth-century coinage, adopted to express 'a certain conception of deportment, or socially prescribed or sanctioned conduct'. This of course survives in everyday English, where 'to behave' means to be 'good' or 'polite', according to prevailing standards of etiquette (something that we may also expect of our quasi-human, domestic animals). Only in the mid-nineteenth century were the terms 'behave' and 'behaviour' transferred to scientific discourse, originally in the field of chemistry, where one spoke of the behaviour of inorganic reagents when experimentally combined. It is from the latter usage, extended to the organic domain, that contemporary sociobiological notions of animal and human behaviour are derived (Ardener 1973:152–3).

7 In this connection, it is worth noting that the concept of the cultural 'survival', which occupies a central place in Tylor's scheme, makes sense only in the context of an identification of the cultural with the artificial. For in so denoting the class of objects that have outlived their usefulness and linger on in tradition, it is implicitly assumed that all objects were originally adopted by their users *for a purpose,* in accordance with some criterion or criteria of rational selection. Spencer likewise includes all the components of Tylor's 'Culture' (knowledge, belief, art, morals, law, custom, etc.) in the category of 'super-organic products which we commonly distinguish as artificial' (1876, I:14).

8 A confusion between these two kinds of exteriorization is evident in this otherwise perceptive comment by P. J. Wilson: 'The salient characteristic of human culture is that it is extrasomatic, and we therefore have to explain how it was possible for individuals, populations, and species to develop skills that enable them to *control things outside their bodies, to use their bodies self-consciously as instruments* to transform environments' (1980:39). The two phrases I have emphasized here have quite different meanings. The first refers to extrasomatic objects, harnessed as means to somatic (individual) projects; the second refers to the harnessing of the soma as a means to extrasomatic (conscious) projects.

9 It might be said that *Homo faber* and *Homo loquens* are but two aspects of *Homo cogitans* (Hallowell 1960b:323 n. 45).

10 Toulmin in fact adduces two more senses of adaptation, in addition to the developmental and populational. These are 'calculative' and 'homeostatic'. Calculative adaptation refers to the process of rational decision-making in the adjustment of means to ends; it therefore relates to the *artificial* selection of ideas and concepts in the course of self-conscious design, a process we take to be unique to humans (as it requires symbolic intelligence) and which can be linked to learning through *teaching*. Homeostatic adaptation refers to the maintenance of internal equilibrium and normal functioning in a system such as the living body, in the face of external environmental changes. As a form of learning, this cannot readily be distinguished from adaptation in the developmental sense (Toulmin 1981:179–81).

11 That culture should take this corpuscular form is, of course, a requirement of the theory Cloak is advocating. However, he goes so far as to claim empirical support for the assumption: 'On the basis of *various natural experiments and observations,* I believe that culture is acquired in tiny, unrelated snippets, which are specific interneural instructions culturally transmitted from generation to generation' (1975:167–8; my emphasis). These unspecified experiments and observations, of which absolutely no details are revealed, add an aura of scientific respectability to an argument which in fact rests on no sound evidence whatsoever. Had they been conducted, and had they actually demonstrated what Cloak claims, they would be of extraordinary significance—especially since the weight of ethnographic evidence points in the opposite direction.

12 A useful review and summary of the various models of gene–culture coevolution available in the literature, and their precursors, is provided by Lumsden and Wilson (1981:256–65).

13 Examples are almost too numerous to cite, and I list here only a few of the more prominent ones, many of which will be familiar from the discussion in this and preceding chapters: Alexander (1979:73–82), Bateson (1980:193–203), Campbell (1965, 1975), Cavalli-Sforza and Feldman (1981), Childe (1951:162–75), Cloak (1975), Cohen (1981:203–5), Dawkins (1976:203–15; 1982:109–10), Diener (1980), Durham (1976,1979), Emerson (1960, 1965), Emlen (1976,1980), Gerard, Kluckhohn and Rapoport (1956), Habermas (1979:171–7), Harré (1979:364–83; 1981a), Hayek (1978), Hill (1978), Huxley (1956), Ingold (1979:284–90; 1983a:14), Kroeber (1948:259–61), Murdock (1945; 1971[1956]; 1959), Rappaport (1971), Rensch (1972:115–25), Ruyle (1973), Sahlins and Service (1960), Simpson (1958b:534–5) and Wynne-Edwards (1971).

14 I shall not deal with the theory of group selection, currently much out of favour, in this context. Let it be noted, however, that in relation to mankind this is normally presented as a process by which culture-bearing populations are subjected to *natural* selection (Wynne-Edwards 1971:277). The assumption seems to be that groups that lack the customs that would serve to regulate population size around an ecologically sustainable optimum would eventually succumb, carrying their defective tradition with them and leaving the field clear for other groups in which the requisite altruistic conventions had somehow become established. Apart from all the other difficulties that attend the theory, even when applied to precultural species, this scenario poses the additional question of why the selective elimination of maladaptive tradition should actually have to await the reproductive failure of the group, or why indeed the latter should lead to its elimination at all.

BIBLIOGRAPHY

Alexander, C. 1964. *Notes on the synthesis of form*. Cambridge, Mass.: Harvard University Press.

Alexander, R. D. 1974. The evolution of social behaviour. *Annual Review of Ecology and Systematics* 5:325–83.

—— 1975. The search for a general theory of behaviour. *Behavioural Science* 20:77–100.

—— 1979. *Darwinism and human affairs*. Seattle: University of Washington Press. Althusser, L., and E. Balibar. 1970 *Reading Capital*, trans. B. Brewster. London: New Left Books.

Altmann, S. A. 1965. Sociobiology of rhesus monkeys, II: Stochastics of social communication. *Journal of Theoretical Biology* 8:490–522.

Ardener, E. 1971. Social anthropology and the historicity of historical linguistics. In *Social anthropology and language*, ed. E. Ardener (Association of Social Anthropologists Monograph 10). London: Tavistock.

—— 1973. Behaviour: A social anthropological criticism. *Journal of the Anthropological Society of Oxford* 4:152–4.

—— 1980. Some outstanding problems in the analysis of events. In *Symbol as sense: New approaches to the analysis of meaning*, ed. M. L. Foster and S. H. Brandes. London: Academic Press.

Avineri, S. 1968. *The social and political thought of Karl Marx*. Cambridge: Cambridge University Press.

Ayala, F. J. 1974. The concept of biological progress. In *Studies in the philosophy of biology*, ed. F. J. Ayala and T. Dobzhansky. London: Macmillan. Ayala, F. J., and T. Dobzhansky, eds. 1974. *Studies in the philosophy of biology*. London: Macmillan.

Baer, K. E. von. 1828. *Entwicklungsgeschichte der Thiere: Beobachtung und Reflexion*. Königsberg: Bornträger.

Bailey, G. 1981. Concepts, time-scales and explanations in economic prehistory. In *Economic Archaeology*, ed. A. Sheridan and G. Bailey (British Archaeological Reports International Series 96). Oxford: BAR.

—— 1983. Concepts of time in quaternary prehistory. *Annual Review of Anthropology* 12:165–92.

Barash, D. P. 1977. *Sociobiology and behaviour*. London: Heinemann.

Barnes, J. A. 1971. Time flies like an arrow. *Man* (N.S.)6:537–52.

Barnett, S. A. 1983. Humanity and natural selection. *Ethology and sociobiology* 4:35–51.

Barth, F. 1966. *Models of social organization* (Royal Anthropological Institute Occasional Paper 23). London: RAI.

Bartholomew, G. A., and J. B. Birdsell. 1953. Ecology and the protohominids. *American Anthropologist* 55:481–98.

Bastian, J. 1968. Psychological perspectives. In *Animal Communication,* ed. T. A. Sebeok. Bloomington: Indiana University Press.

Bateson, G. 1973. *Steps to an ecology of mind.* New York: Ballantine.

—— 1980. *Mind and nature.* London: Fontana.

Baxter, P. T. W., and U. Almagor. 1978. *Age, generation and time: Some features of East African age organizations.* London: Hurst.

Beattie, J. H. M. 1980. On understanding sacrifice. In *Sacrifice,* ed. M. F. C. Bourdillon and M. Fortes. London: Academic Press.

Beck, B. B. 1980. *Animal tool behavior.* New York: Garland STPM Press.

Benedict, R. 1935. *Patterns of culture.* London: Routledge & Kegan Paul.

Berg, L. S. 1926. *Nomogenesis, or evolution determined by law.* London: Constable.

Bergson, H. 1911. *Creative evolution,* trans. A. Mitchell. London: Macmillan.

Berlin, I. 1976. *Vico and Herder: Two studies in the history of ideas.* London: Hogarth Press.

Bertalanffy, L. von. 1952. *Problems of life.* London: Watts.

Beurton, P. 1981. Organismic evolution and subject-object dialectics. In *The philosophy of evolution,* ed. U. J. Jensen and R. Harré Brighton: Harvester Press.

Bhaskar, R. 1981. The consequence of socio-evolutionary concepts for naturalism in sociology: Commentaries on Harré and Toulmin. In *The philosophy of evolution,* ed. U. J. Jensen and R. Harré. Brighton: Harvester Press.

Bidney, D. 1953. *Theoretical anthropology.* New York: Columbia University Press.

—— 1963a. The varieties of human freedom. In *The concept of freedom in anthropology,* ed. D. Bidney. The Hague: Mouton.

—— 1963b. Preface, *The concept of freedom in anthropology,* ed. D. Bidney. The Hague: Mouton.

Birch, C. 1974. Chance, necessity and purpose. In *Studies in the philosophy of biology,* ed. F. J. Ayala and T. Dobzhansky. London: Macmillan.

Birch, C., and J. B. Cobb. 1981. *The liberation of life.* Cambridge: Cambridge University Press.

Bloch, M. 1977. The past and the present in the present. *Man* (N.S.)12:278–92.

Blum, H. F. 1955. *Time's arrow and evolution.* Princeton, N.J.: Princeton University Press.

—— 1963. On the origin and evolution of human culture. *American Scientist* 51:32–47.

Boas, F. 1898. Introduction, *Traditions of the Thompson River Indians of British Columbia,* by J. Teit (Memoirs of the American Folklore Society 6). Boston: Houghton Mifflin.

—— 1911. *The mind of primitive man.* New York: Macmillan.

—— 1948. *Race, language and culture.* New York: Free Press.

—— 1974. *A Franz Boas reader: The shaping of American anthropology 1883–1911,* ed. G. W. Stocking, Jr. Chicago: University of Chicago Press.

Bock, K. E. 1955. Darwin and social theory. *Philosophy of Science* 22:123–34.

—— 1980. *Human nature and history: A response to sociobiology.* New York: Columbia University Press.

Boesiger, E. 1974. Evolutionary theories after Lamarck and Darwin. In *Studies in the philosophy of biology,* ed. F. J. Ayala and T. Dobzhansky. London: Macmillan.

Bohm, D. 1980. *Wholeness and the implicate order.* London: Routledge & Kegan Paul.

Bonner, J. T. 1980. *The evolution of culture in animals.* Princeton, N.J.: Princeton University Press.

Bourdieu, P. 1977. *Outline of a theory of practice,* trans. R. Nice. Cambridge: Cambridge University Press.

Bowler, P. J. 1975. The changing meaning of 'evolution'. *Journal of the History of Ideas* 36:95–114.

Braudel, F. 1972. *The Mediterranean and the Mediterranean world in the age of Philip II*, trans. S. Reynolds. London: Collins.

Burghardt, G. M. 1970. Defining 'communication'. In *Communication by chemical signals* (*Advances in Chemoreception*, vol. I), ed. J. W. Johnston, Jr., D. G. Moulton and A. Turk. New York: Appleton–Century–Crofts.

Burrow, J. W. 1966. *Evolution and society: A study in Victorian social theory*. Cambridge: Cambridge University Press.

Bury, J. B. 1932. *The idea of progress*. London: Macmillan.

Calhoun, J. B. 1971. Space and the strategy of life. In *Behavior and environment: The use of space by animals and men*, ed. A. H. Esser. New York: Plenum.

Campbell, D. T. 1965. Variation and selective retention in sociocultural evolution. In *Social change in developing areas: A reinterpretation of evolutionary theory*, ed. H. R. Barringer, G. I. Blanksten and R. W. Mack. Cambridge, Mass.: Schenkman.

—— 1974. Unjustified variation and selective retention in scientific discovery. In *Studies in the philosophy of biology*, ed. F. J. Ayala and T. Dobzhansky. London: Macmillan.

—— 1975. On the conflicts between biological and social evolution and between psychology and moral tradition. *American Psychologist* 30:1103–26.

Carneiro, R. L. 1967. Editor's introduction to *The evolution of society* (selections from H. Spencer's *The principles of sociology*). Chicago: University of Chicago Press.

—— 1973. The four faces of evolution: Unilinear, universal, multilinear and differential. In *Handbook of social and cultural anthropology*, ed. J. J. Honigmann. Chicago: Rand McNally.

Carr, E. H. 1961. *What is history?* New York: Random House.

Carr-Saunders, A. M. 1922. *The population problem: A study in human evolution*. Oxford: Clarendon.

Cassirer, E. 1944. *An essay on man*. New Haven, Conn.: Yale University Press.

Cavalli-Sforza, L. L. 1971. Similarities and dissimilarities of sociocultural and biological evolution. In *Mathematics in the archaeological sciences*, ed. F. R. Hodson, D. G. Kendall and P. Tautu. Edinburgh: Edinburgh University Press.

Cavalli-Sforza, L. L., and M. W. Feldman. 1981. *Cultural transmission and evolution: A quantitative approach*. Princeton N.J.: Princeton University Press.

Cherry, C. 1957. *On human communication*. Cambridge, Mass.: MIT Press.

Childe, V. G. 1951. *Social evolution*. London: Fontana.

Chomsky, N. 1964. *Current issues in linguistic theory*. The Hague: Mouton.

—— 1966. *Cartesian linguistics*. New York: Harper & Row.

—— 1968. *Language and mind*. New York: Harcourt Brace Jovanovich.

Clark, S. R. L. 1982. *The nature of the beast*. Oxford: Oxford University Press.

Cloak, F. T. 1975. Is a cultural ethology possible? *Human Ecology* 3:161–82.

—— 1977. Comment on W. H. Durham: 'The adaptive significance of cultural behaviour'. *Human Ecology* 5:49–52.

Cohen, G. A. 1978. *Karl Marx's theory of history: A defence*. Oxford: Clarendon.

Cohen, R. 1981. Evolutionary epistemology and human values. *Current Anthropology* 22:201–18.

Collingwood, R. G. 1946. *The idea of history*. Oxford: Clarendon.

Crook, J. H. 1971. Sources of co-operation in animals and man. In *Man and beast: Comparative social behavior*, ed. J. F. Eisenberg and W. S. Dillon. Washington, D.C.: Smithsonian Institution Press.

—— 1980. *The evolution of human consciousness*. Oxford: Clarendon.

Dahrendorf, R. 1968. *Essays in the theory of society*. London: Routledge & Kegan Paul.

Darlington, C. D. 1953. *The facts of life.* London: Allen & Unwin.

—— 1969. *The evolution of man and society.* New York: Simon & Schuster.

—— 1972. Race, class and culture. In *Biology and the human sciences,* ed. J. W. S. Pringle. Oxford: Clarendon.

Darwin, C. 1862. *On the various contrivances by which British and Foreign Orchids are fertilized by insects.* London: John Murray.

—— 1872. *The origin of species.* 6th ed. London: John Murray.

—— 1874. *The descent of man and selection in relation to sex.* 2nd ed. London: John Murray.

—— 1881. *The formation of vegetable mould, through the action of worms, with observations on their habits.* London: John Murray.

—— 1889. *Journal of researches into the natural history and geology of the countries visited during the voyage of H.M.S. "Beagle" round the world.* 3rd ed. London: Ward, Lock.

—— 1950. *The origin of species* (reprint of first edition of 1859). London: Watts.

Darwin, F. 1888. *The life and letters of Charles Darwin.* Vol. II. London: John Murray.

Davis, R. T., R. W. Leary, M. D. C. Smith and R. F. Thompson. 1968. Species differences in the gross behaviour of nonhuman primates. *Behaviour* 31:326–38.

Dawkins, R. 1976. *The selfish gene.* Oxford: Oxford University Press.

—— 1982. *The extended phenotype: The gene as the unit of selection.* San Francisco: Freeman.

Diener, P. 1980. Quantum change, macroevolution and the social field: Some comments on evolution and culture. *Current Anthropology* 21:423–43.

Diener, P., D. Nonini and E. E. Robkin. 1980. Ecology and evolution in cultural anthropology. *Man* (N.S.)15:1–31.

Dobzhansky, T. 1962. *Mankind evolving.* New Haven, Conn.: Yale University Press.

—— 1974a. Chance and creativity in evolution. In *Studies in the philosophy of biology,* ed. F. J. Ayala and T. Dobzhansky. London: Macmillan.

—— 1974b. Two contrasting world views. In *Beyond chance and necessity,* ed. J. Lewis. Atlantic Highlands, N.J.: Humanities Press.

Driesch, H. 1914. *The history and theory of vitalism.* London: Macmillan.

Dumont, L. 1957. For a sociology of India. *Contributions to Indian Sociology* 1:7–22.

—— 1972. *Homo hierarchicus.* London: Paladin.

Durham, W. H. 1976. The adaptive significance of cultural behaviour. *Human Ecology* 4:89–121.

—— 1979. Towards a coevolutionary theory of human biology and culture. In *Evolutionary biology and human social behavior: An anthropological perspective,* ed. N. A. Chagnon and W. Irons. North Scituate, Mass.: Duxbury Press.

Durkheim, E. 1933[1893]. *The division of labour in society,* trans. G. Simpson. London: Macmillan.

—— 1938. *L'évolution pedagogique en France.* Paris: Alcan.

—— 1952[1897]. *Suicide: A study in sociology,* trans. J. A. Spaulding and G. Simpson. London: Routledge & Kegan Paul.

—— 1960[1914]. The dualism of human nature and its social conditions. In *Emile Durkheim, 1858–1917,* ed. K. H. Wolff. Columbus: Ohio State University Press.

—— 1961[1925]. *Moral education,* trans. E. K. Wilson and H. Schnurner. New York: Free Press.

—— 1976[1915]. *The elementary forms of the religious life,* trans. J. W. Swain (2nd ed.). London: Allen & Unwin.

—— 1982[1917]. *The rules of sociological method,* trans. W. D. Halls, ed. S. Lukes. London: Macmillan.

Eccles, J. C. 1974. Cerebral activity and consciousness. In *Studies in the philosophy of biology,* ed. F. J. Ayala and T. Dobzhansky, London: Macmillan.

Eisendrath, C. R. 1971. *The unifying moment: The psychological philosophy of William James and Alfred North Whitehead*. Cambridge, Mass.: Harvard University Press.

Elton, G. R. 1967. *The practice of history*. Sydney: Sydney University Press.

Emerson, A. E. 1958. The evolution of behavior among social insects. In *Behavior and evolution*, ed. A. Roe and G. G. Simpson. New Haven, Conn.: Yale University Press.

—— 1960. The evolution of adaptation in population systems. In *Evolution after Darwin, I: The evolution of life*, ed. S. Tax. Chicago: University of Chicago Press.

—— 1965. Human cultural evolution and its relation to organic evolution of insect societies. In *Social change in developing areas: A reinterpretation of evolutionary theory*, ed. H. R. Barringer, G. I. Blanksten and R. W. Mack. Cambridge, Mass.: Schenkman.

Emlen, S. T. 1976. An alternative case for sociobiology. *Science* 192:736–8.

—— 1980. Ecological determinism and sociobiology. In *Sociobiology: Beyond nature/nurture?*, ed. G. W. Barlow and J. Silverberg. Boulder, Colo.: Westview Press.

Engels, F. 1934. *Dialectics of nature*, trans. from German by C. Dutt. Moscow: Progress.

—— 1972[1884]. *The origin of the family, private property and the state*. New York: Pathfinder Press.

Evans-Pritchard, E. E. 1940. *The Nuer*. Oxford: Oxford University Press.

—— 1950. Social anthropology: Past and present. *Man* 50:118–24.

—— 1951. *Social anthropology*. London: Cohen & West.

—— 1961. *Anthropology and history*. Manchester: Manchester University Press.

Fabian, J. 1983. *Time and the other*. New York: Columbia University Press. Fernandez, J. 1979. On the notion of religious movement. *Social Research* 46:36–62.

Folsom, J. K. 1928. *Culture and social progress*. New York: Longmans.

Fortes, M. 1945. *The dynamics of clanship among the Tallensi*. London: Oxford University Press.

—— 1949. Time and social structure. In *Social structure: Essays presented to A. R. Radcliffe-Brown*, ed. M. Fortes. Oxford: Clarendon.

—— 1969. *Kinship and the social order*. London: Routledge & Kegan Paul.

—— 1983. *Rules and the emergence of society* (Royal Anthropological Institute Occasional Paper 39). London: RAI.

Foucault, M. 1970. *The order of things: An archaeology of the human sciences*. London: Tavistock.

Freeman, D. 1970. Human nature and culture. In *Man and the new biology*. Canberra: Australian National University Press.

—— 1974. The evolutionary theories of Charles Darwin and Herbert Spencer. *Current Anthropology* 15:211–37.

Frisch, K. von. 1950. *Bees: Their vision, chemical sense and language*. Ithaca, N.Y.: Cornell University Press.

Galton, F. 1874. *English men of science: Their nature and nurture*. London: Macmillan.

Geertz, C. 1975. *The interpretation of cultures*. New York: Basic Books.

Gellner, E. 1964. *Thought and change*. London: Weidenfeld & Nicolson.

Gennep, A. van. 1960[1909]. *The rites of passage*, ed. S. T. Kimball. London: Routledge & Kegan Paul.

George, W. 1964. *Biologist philosopher: A study of the life and writings of Alfred Russel Wallace*. London: Abelard-Schuman.

Gerard, R. W., C. Kluckhohn and A. Rapoport. 1956. Biological and cultural evolution: Some analogies and explorations. *Behavioral Science* 1:6–34.

Ghiselin, M. T. 1969. *The triumph of the Darwinian method*. Berkeley: University of California Press.

Giddens, A. 1979. *Central problems in social theory*. London: Macmillan.

Gillespie, C. S. 1959. Lamarck and Darwin in the history of science. In *Forerunners of Darwin: 1745–1859,* ed. B. Glass, 0. Temkin and W. L. Straus, Jr. Baltimore, Md.: Johns Hopkins University Press.

Glasersfeld, E. von. 1976. The development of language as purposive behavior. In *Origins and evolution of language and speech,* ed. H. B. Steklis, S. R. Harnad and J. Lancaster. Annals of the New York Academy of Sciences, vol. 280.

Gluckman, M. 1968. The utility of the equilibrium model in the study of social change. *American Anthropologist* 70:219–37.

Glucksmann, M. 1974. *Structural analysis in contemporary social thought.* London: Routledge & Kegan Paul.

Godelier, M. 1972. *Rationality and irrationality in economics,* trans. B. Pearce. London: New Left Books.

Goldenweiser, A. A. 1917. The autonomy of the social. *American Anthropologist* 19:447–9.

—— 1933. *History, psychology and culture.* New York: Knopf.

Goudge, T. A. 1961. *The ascent of life.* Toronto: University of Toronto Press.

Gould, S. J. 1980. *Ever since Darwin: Reflections in natural history.* Harmondsworth: Penguin.

—— 1983. *The panda's thumb.* Harmondsworth: Penguin.

Gould, S. J., and E. S. Vrba. 1982. Exaptation—a missing term in the science of form. *Paleobiology* 8:4–15.

Gregory, C. 1983. Kula gift exchange and capitalist commodity exchange: A comparison. In *The kula: New perspectives on Massim exchange,* ed. J. W. Leach and E. R. Leach. Cambridge: Cambridge University Press.

Griffin, D. R. 1976. *The question of animal awareness: Evolutionary continuity of mental experience.* New York: Rockefeller University Press.

—— 1977. Expanding horizons in animal communication behavior. In *How animals communicate,* ed. T. A. Sebeok. Bloomington: Indiana University Press.

Gruber, H. E. 1974. *Darwin on man: A psychological study of scientific creativity.* New York: Dutton.

Habermas, J. 1979. *Communication and the evolution of society,* trans. T. McCarthy. London: Heinemann.

Haldane, J. B. S. 1932. *The causes of evolution.* London: Longmans.

—— 1956a. Time in biology. *Science Progress* 44:385–402.

—— 1956b. The argument from animals to men: An examination of its validity for anthropology. *Journal of the Royal Anthropological Institute* 36:1–14.

Hallowell, A. I. 1960a. Personality structure and the evolution of man. *American Anthropologist* 52:159–73.

—— 1960b. Self, society and culture in phylogenetic perspective. In *Evolution after Darwin, II: The evolution of man,* ed. S. Tax. Chicago: University of Chicago Press.

Hamilton, W. D. 1964. The genetical evolution of social behaviour. *Journal of Theoretical Biology* 7:1–52.

Harlow, H. F. 1958. The evolution of learning. In *Behavior and evolution,* ed. A. Roe and G. G. Simpson. New Haven, Conn.: Yale University Press.

Harré, R. 1979. *Social being.* Oxford: Blackwell.

—— 1981a. The evolutionary analogy in social explanation. In *The philosophy of evolution,* ed. U. J. Jensen and R. Harré. Brighton: Harvester Press.

—— 1981b. On the problem of self-consciousness and the origins of the expressive order: Commentaries on Döbert, Ruben and Keiler. In *The philosophy of evolution,* ed. U. J. Jensen and R. Harré Brighton: Harvester Press.

Harris, M. 1968. *The rise of anthropological theory.* New York: Crowell.

Hatch, E. 1973. *Theories of man and culture.* New York: Columbia University Press.

Hawthorn, G. 1976. *Enlightenment and despair: A history of sociology*. Cambridge: Cambridge University Press.

Hayek, F. A. 1978. *The three sources of human values* (L. T. Hobhouse Memorial Trust Lecture 44). London: London School of Economics and Political Science.

Hempel, C. G. 1965. *Aspects of scientific explanation*. New York: Free Press. Herskovits, M. J. 1948. *Man and his works*. New York: Knopf.

Higgs, E. S., and M. R. Jarman. 1975. Palaeoeconomy. In *Palaeoeconomy*, ed. E. S. Higgs. Cambridge: Cambridge University Press.

Hill, J. 1978. The origin of sociocultural evolution. *Journal of Social and Biological Structures* 1:377–86.

Hinde, R. A., ed. 1972. *Non-verbal communication*. Cambridge: Cambridge University Press.

Hirst, P. Q. 1973. Morphology and pathology: Biological analogies in Durkheim's 'The rules of sociological method'. *Economy and Society* 2:1–34. 1976. *Social evolution and sociological categories*. London: Allen & Unwin.

Hoagland, H. 1964. Science and the new humanism. *Science* 143:111–14.

Hockett, C. F. 1959. Animal 'languages' and human language. In *The evolution of man's capacity for culture*, ed. J. N. Spuhler. Detroit: Wayne State University Press.

—— 1960. The origin of speech. *Scientific American* 203:88–111.

—— 1963. The problem of universals in language. In *Universals of language*, ed. J. H. Greenberg. Cambridge, Mass.: MIT Press.

Hockett, C. F., and S. A. Altmann. 1968. A note on design features. In *Animal communication*, ed. T. A. Sebeok. Bloomington: Indiana University Press.

Hodges, H. A. 1944. *Wilhelm Dilthey: An introduction*. London: Routledge & Kegan Paul.

Holloway, R. L. 1969. Culture, a human domain. *Current Anthropology* 10:395–412.

Howard, J. 1982. *Darwin*. Oxford: Oxford University Press.

Hull, D. 1981. Units of evolution: A metaphysical essay. In *The philosophy of evolution*, ed. U. J. Jensen and R. Harré. Brighton: Harvester Press.

Humphrey, N. K. 1976. The social function of intellect. In *Growing points in ethology*, ed. P. P. G. Bateson and R. A. Hinde. Cambridge: Cambridge University Press.

Huxley, J. S. 1942. *Evolution: The modern synthesis*. London: Allen & Unwin.

—— 1954. The evolutionary process. In *Evolution as a process*, ed. J. S. Huxley, A. C. Hardy and E. B. Ford. London: Allen & Unwin.

—— 1956. Evolution, cultural and biological. In *Current anthropology*, ed. W. L. Thomas. Chicago: University of Chicago Press.

—— 1957. *New bottles for new wine*. London: Chatto & Windus.

—— 1960. The emergence of Darwinism. In *Evolution after Darwin, I: The evolution of life*, ed. S. Tax. Chicago: University of Chicago Press.

Huxley, T. H. 1984. *Man's place in nature, and other essays*. London: Macmillan.

Hymes, D. 1971. Sociolinguistics and the ethnography of speaking. In *Social anthropology and language*, ed. E. Ardener (Association of Social Anthropologists Monograph 10). London: Tavistock.

Ingold, T. 1979. The social and ecological relations of culture-bearing organisms: An essay in evolutionary dynamics. In *Social and ecological systems*, ed. P. C. Burnham and R. F. Ellen (Association of Social Anthropologists Monograph 18). London: Academic Press.

—— 1980a. *Hunters, pastoralists and ranchers*. Cambridge: Cambridge University Press.

—— 1980b. The principle of individual autonomy and the collective appropriation of nature. In *2nd International Conference on Hunting and Gathering Societies, 19 to 24 September 1980*. Quebec: Université Laval, Département d'Anthropologie.

—— 1983a. The architect and the bee: Reflections on the work of animals and men. *Man*(N.S.)18:1–20.

—— 1983b. Gathering the herds: Work and co-operation in a northern Finnish community. *Ethnos* 48:133–59.

—— 1984. Time, social relationships and the exploitation of animals: Anthropological reflections on prehistory. In *Animals and archaeology, III: Early herders and their flocks,* ed. J. Clutton-Brock and C. Grigson (British Archaeological Reports International Series 202). Oxford: BAR.

Isaac, G. L. 1976. Stages of cultural elaboration in the Pleistocene: Possible archaeological indicators of the development of language capabilities. In *Origins and evolution of language and speech,* ed. H. B. Steklis, S. R. Harnad and J. Lancaster. Annals of the New York Academy of Sciences, vol. 280.

Jacob, F. 1977. Evolution and tinkering. *Science* 196:1161–6.

James, W. 1890. *The principles of psychology.* 2 vols. London: Macmillan. 1898. *The will to believe, and other essays in popular philosophy.* New York: Longmans.

Jensen, U. J., and R. Harré, eds. 1981. *The philosophy of evolution.* Brighton: Harvester Press.

Kantorowicz, H. 1958. *The definition of law,* ed. A. H. Campbell. Cambridge: Cambridge University Press.

Keith, A. 1916. On certain factors concerned in the evolution of human races. *Journal of the Royal Anthropological Institute* 46:10–34.

Kitahara-Frisch, J. 1980. Symbolising technology as a key to human evolution. In *Symbol as sense,* ed. M. L. Foster and S. H. Brandes. London: Academic Press.

Klineberg, O. 1935. *Race differences.* New York: Harper.

Kluckhohn, C. 1946. Review of A. L. Kroeber, 'Configurations of culture growth'. *American Journal of Sociology* 51:336–41.

—— 1949. *Mirror for man.* New York: McGraw-Hill.

Koestler, A. 1969. Beyond atomism and holism: The concept of the holon. In *Beyond reductionism: New perspectives in the life sciences,* ed. A Koestler and J. R. Smythies. London: Hutchinson.

Koestler, A., and J. R. Smythies, eds. 1969. *Beyond reductionism: New perspectives in the life sciences.* London: Hutchinson.

Kristeva, J. 1969. *Sēmeiōtike: Recherches pour une sémanalyse.* Paris: Seuil.

Kroeber, A. L. 1915. Eighteen professions. *American Anthropologist* 17:283–8.

—— 1948. *Anthropology.* Rev. ed. New York: Harcourt Brace Jovanovich.

—— 1952. *The nature of culture.* Chicago: University of Chicago Press.

—— 1963. *An anthropologist looks at history.* Berkeley: University of California Press.

Kroeber, A. L., and C. Kluckhohn. 1952. *Culture: A critical review of concepts and definitions.* Papers of the Peabody Museum of American Archaeology and Ethnology, Harvard University, vol. XLVII, no.1. Cambridge, Mass.

Kropotkin, P. 1902. *Mutual aid: A factor of evolution.* London: Heinemann.

Kubler, G. 1962. *The shape of time: Remarks on the history of things.* New Haven, Conn.: Yale University Press.

Langer, S. K. 1942. *Philosophy in a new key.* Cambridge, Mass.: Harvard University Press.

—— 1972. *Mind: An essay on human feeling.* Vol. 2. Baltimore, Md.: Johns Hopkins University Press.

Leach, E. R. 1961. *Rethinking anthropology.* London: Athlone Press.

—— 1964[1954]. *Political systems of highland Burma.* Reprint. London: Athlone Press.

Leacock, E. B. 1963. Introduction to Part I. In *Ancient Society* by L. H. Morgan, ed. E. B. Leacock. Cleveland, Ohio: World.

Lee, D. 1959. *Freedom and culture.* Englewood Cliffs, N.J.: Prentice-Hall.

Lee, D. E., and R. N. Beck. 1954. The meaning of historicism. *American Historical Review* 59:568–77.

Lenneberg, E. H. 1960. Language, evolution and purposive behavior. In *Culture in history*, ed. S. Diamond. New York: Columbia University Press.

Leopold, J. 1980. *Culture in comparative and evolutionary perspective: E. B. Tylor and the making of Primitive Culture*. Berlin: Dietrich Reimer Verlag.

Lesser, A. 1952. Evolution in social anthropology. *Southwestern Journal of Anthropology* 8:134–46.

—— 1961. Social fields and the evolution of society. *Southwestern Journal of Anthropology* 17:40–8.

Levine, D. P., and L. S. Levine. 1975. Social theory and social action. *Economy and Society* 4:162–93.

Lévi-Strauss, C. 1950. Introduction a l'oeuvre de Marcel Mauss. In M. Mauss, *Sociologie et Anthropologie*. Paris: Presses Universitaires de France.

—— 1953. *Race and history*. Paris: UNESCO.

—— 1961. *A world on the wane*, trans. J. Russel. New York: Criterion Books.

—— 1966a. *The savage mind*. London: Weidenfeld & Nicolson.

—— 1966b. Overture to 'Le cru et le cuit'. *Yale French Studies* 36/7:41–65 (original 1964 *Mythologiques I: Le cru et le cuit*. Paris: Plon).

—— 1968. *Structural anthropology*. Harmondsworth: Penguin (original 1957 *Anthropologie structurale*. Paris: Plon).

—— 1978. *Myth and meaning*. London: Routledge & Kegan Paul.

Lewis, J., ed. 1974. *Beyond chance and necessity*. Atlantic Highlands, N.J.: Humanities Press.

Locke, J. 1894[1690]. *An essay concerning human understanding*. 2 vols. Oxford: Clarendon.

Lorenz, K. 1966. *On aggression*, trans. M. Latzke. London: Methuen.

Lotka, A. J. 1945. The law of evolution as a maximal principle. *Human Biology* 17:167–94.

—— 1956[1924]. *Elements of mathematical biology*. New York: Dover.

Lovejoy, A. O. 1936. *The great chain of being*. Cambridge, Mass.: Harvard University Press.

—— 1959. Buffon and the problem of species. In *Forerunners of Darwin: 1745–1859*, ed. B. Glass, O. Temkin and W. L. Straus, Jr. Baltimore, Md.: Johns Hopkins University Press.

Lowie, R. H. 1921. *Primitive society*. London: Routledge & Kegan Paul. 1937. *The history of ethnological theory*. London: Harrap.

Luckmann, T. 1979. Personal identity as an evolutionary and historical problem. In *Human ethology*, ed. M. von Cranach, K. Foppa, W. Lepenies and D. Ploog. Cambridge: Cambridge University Press.

Lumsden, C. J., and E. O. Wilson. 1981. *Genes, mind and culture*. Cambridge, Mass.: Harvard University Press.

Lyell, C. 1830–3. *Principles of geology, being an attempt to explain the former changes in the earth's surface, by reference to causes now in operation*. 3 vols. London: John Murray.

Maitland, F. W. 1936. *Selected essays*, ed. H. D. Hazeltine. Cambridge: Cambridge University Press.

Malinowski, B. 1922. *Argonauts of the western Pacific*. London: Routledge & Kegan Paul.

—— 1923. The problem of meaning in primitive languages. Supplement I, in *The meaning of meaning*, by C. K. Ogden and I. A. Richards. London: Routledge & Kegan Paul.

—— 1944. *A scientific theory of culture, and other essays*. Chapel Hill: University of North Carolina Press.

Mandelbaum, M. 1971. *History, man and reason*. Baltimore, Md.: Johns Hopkins University Press.

Marett, R. R. 1920. *Psychology and folklore*. London: Methuen.

Marler, P. 1977. The evolution of communication. In *How animals communicate*, ed. T. A. Sebeok. Bloomington: Indiana University Press.

Marx, K. 1930[1867]. *Capital*, vol. I, trans. E. and C. Paul from 4th German edition of *Das Kapital* (1890). London: Dent.

—— 1963[1869]. *Eighteenth Brumaire of Louis Bonaparte*. New York: International Publishers.

—— 1964a. *The economic and political manuscripts of 1844*, trans. M. Milligan, ed. D. J. Struik. New York: International Publishers.

—— 1964b. *Pre-capitalist economic formations*, trans. J. Cohen, ed. E. J. Hobsbawm. London: Lawrence & Wishart.

—— 1970[1859]. *A contribution to the critique of political economy*, trans. S. W. Ryazanskaya. Moscow: Progress.

—— 1973. *Grundrisse*, trans. M. Nicolaus. Harmondsworth: Penguin.

Marx, K., and F. Engels. 1977. *The German ideology*, ed. C. J. Arthur. London: Lawrence & Wishart.

Mason, O. T. 1887. The occurrence of similar inventions in areas widely apart. *Science* 9:534–5.

Mauss, M. 1954[1925]. *The gift*, trans. I. Cunnison. London: Routledge & Kegan Paul.

—— 1979[1950]. *Sociology and psychology: Essays*, trans. B. Brewster. London: Routledge & Kegan Paul.

Maynard Smith, J. 1964. Group selection and kin selection. *Nature* 201:1145–7.

Mayr, E. 1976. *Evolution and the diversity of life*. Cambridge, Mass.: Harvard University Press (Belknap).

—— 1982. *The growth of biological thought*. Cambridge, Mass.: Harvard University Press (Belknap).

McGrew, W. C., and C. E. G. Tutin. 1978. Evidence for a social custom in wild chimpanzees? *Man* (N.S.)13:234–51.

Medawar, P. B. 1957. *The uniqueness of the individual*. London: Methuen.

—— 1960. *The future of man*. London: Methuen.

—— 1967. *The art of the soluble*. London: Methuen.

Meillassoux, C. 1981. *Maidens, meal and money*. Cambridge: Cambridge University Press.

Midgley, M. 1978. *Beast and man: The roots of human nature*. Ithaca, N.Y.: Cornell University Press.

—— 1980. Rival fatalisms: The hollowness of the sociobiology debate. In *Sociobiology examined*, ed. A. Montagu. Oxford: Oxford University Press.

—— 1983. *Animals and why they matter*. Harmondsworth: Penguin.

Mitchell, J. C. 1969. The concept and use of social networks. In *Social networks in urban situations*, ed. J. C. Mitchell. Manchester: Manchester University Press.

Monod, J. 1972. *Chance and necessity*, trans. A. Wainhouse. London: Collins.

Montagu, A. 1976. Toolmaking, hunting and the origin of language. In *Origins and evolution of language and speech*, ed. H. B. Steklis, S. R. Harnad and J. Lancaster. Annals of the New York Academy of Sciences, vol. 280.

Montalenti, G. 1974. From Aristotle to Democritus via Darwin. In *Studies in the philosophy of biology*, ed. F. J. Ayala and T. Dobzhansky. London: Macmillan.

Morgan, C. L. 1923. *Emergent evolution*. London: Williams & Norgate. 1933. *The emergence of novelty*. London: Williams & Norgate.

Morgan, L. H. 1868. *The American beaver and his works*. Philadelphia: J. B. Lippincott.

—— 1963[1877]. *Ancient society*, ed. E. B. Leacock. Cleveland, Ohio: World.

Morris, C. 1946. *Signs, language and behavior*. New York: Braziller.

Moscovici, S. 1976. *Society against nature*, trans. S. Rabinovitch. Brighton: Harvester Press.

Mumford, L. 1967. *The myth of the machine: Technics and human development*. London: Secker & Warburg.

Murdock, G. P. 1945. The common denominator of cultures. In *The science of man in the world crisis*, ed. R. Linton. New York: Columbia University Press.

—— 1959. Evolution in social organization. In *Evolution and anthropology: A centennial appraisal*, ed. B. J. Meggers. Washington D.C.: The Anthropological Society of Washington.

—— 1971[1956]. How culture changes. In *Man, culture and society*. 2nd ed., ed. H. L. Shapiro. Oxford: Oxford University Press.

—— 1972. Anthropology's mythology. *Proceedings of the Royal Anthropological Institute for 1971*:17–24.

Murphy, R. F. 1970. Basin ethnography and ethnological theory. In *Languages and cultures of western North America*, ed. E. H. Swanson, Jr. Pocatello: Idaho State University Press.

—— 1977. The anthropological theories of Julian H. Steward. Introduction to J. H. Steward, *Evolution and ecology: Essays on social transformation*, ed. J. C. Steward and R. F. Murphy. Urbana: University of Illinois Press.

Nagel, T. 1979. *Mortal questions*. Cambridge: Cambridge University Press.

Needham, J. 1943. *Time: The refreshing river*. London: Allen & Unwin.

Oakely, K. P. 1950. *Man the tool-maker*. London: British Museum.

—— 1951. A definition of man. *Science News* 20:69–81.

—— 1954. Skill as a human possession. In *A history of technology, I: From early times to the fall of ancient empires*, ed. C. Singer, E. J. Holmyard and A. R. Hall. Oxford: Clarendon.

—— 1957. Tools makyth man. *Antiquity* 31:199–209.

Oldroyd, D. R. 1980. *Darwinian impacts*. Milton Keynes: Open University Press.

Opler, M. 1964. Causes, process and dynamics in the evolutionism of E. B. Tylor. *Southwestern Journal of Anthropology* 20:123–44.

Ortega y Gasset, J. 1941. *History as a system, and other essays towards a philosophy of history*. New York: Norton.

Osborn, H. F. 1934. Aristogenesis: The creative principle in the origin of species. *American Naturalist* 68:193–235.

Pace, D. 1983. *Claude Lévi-Strauss: The bearer of ashes*. London: Routledge & Kegan Paul.

Pantin, C. F. A. 1951. Organic design. *Advancement of Science* 8:138–50.

Parsons, T. 1937. *The structure of social action*. New York: McGraw-Hill.

—— 1977. *The evolution of societies*. Englewood Cliffs, N.J.: Prentice-Hall.

Peacock, J. L. 1975. *Consciousness and change: Symbolic anthropology in evolutionary perspective*. Oxford: Blackwell.

Peel, J. D. Y. 1972. Editor's introduction, *On social evolution*, selected writings of Herbert Spencer. Chicago: University of Chicago Press.

Pittendrigh, C. S. 1958. Adaptation, natural selection and behavior. In *Behavior and evolution*, ed. A. Roe and G. G. Simpson. New Haven, Conn.: Yale University Press.

Polanyi, K. 1957. The economy as an instituted process. In *Trade and market in the early empires*, ed. K. Polanyi, C. Arensberg and H. Pearson. Glencoe, Ill.: The Free Press.

Popper, K. R. 1957. *The poverty of historicism*. London: Routledge & Kegan Paul.

—— 1972. *Objective knowledge: An evolutionary approach*. Oxford: Clarendon.

—— 1974. Scientific reduction and the essential incompleteness of all science. In *Studies in the philosophy of biology*, ed. F. J. Ayala and T. Dobzhansky. London: Macmillan.

Popper, K. R., and J. C. Eccles. 1977. *The self and its brain*. Berlin: Springer International.

Pulliam, H. R., and C. Dunford. 1980. *Programmed to learn: An essay on the evolution of culture*. New York: Columbia University Press.

Pumphrey, R. J. 1953. The origin of language. *Acta Psychologica* 9:219–39.

Radcliffe-Brown, A. R. 1947. Evolution, social or cultural? *American Anthropologist* 49:78–83.

—— 1951. The comparative method in social anthropology. *Journal of the Royal Anthropological Institute* 81:15–22.

—— 1952. *Structure and function in primitive society*. London: Cohen & West.

—— 1953. Letter to Lévi-Strauss. In *An appraisal of anthropology today*, ed. S. Tax. Chicago: University of Chicago Press.

—— 1957. *A natural science of society*. Chicago: Free Press.

Rappaport, R. A. 1971. Nature, culture and ecological anthropology. In *Man, culture and society*. 2nd ed., ed. H. L. Shapiro. Oxford: Oxford University Press.

—— 1977. Normative models of adaptive processes: A response to Anne Whyte. In *The evolution of social systems*, ed. J. Friedman and M. J. Rowlands. London: Duckworth.

Reed, E. S. 1981. The lawfulness of natural selection. *American Naturalist* 118:61–71.

Renfrew, C. 1982. *Towards an archaeology of mind*. Cambridge: Cambridge University Press.

Rensch, B. 1971. *Biophilosophy*. New York: Columbia University Press.

—— 1972. *Homo sapiens: From man to demigod*, trans. C. A. M. Sym. London: Methuen.

—— 1974. Polynomistic determination of biological processes. In *Studies in the philosophy of biology*, ed. F. J. Ayala and T. Dobzhansky. London: Macmillan.

Resek, C. 1960. *Lewis Henry Morgan: American scholar*. Chicago: University of Chicago Press.

Reynolds, P. C. 1981. *On the evolution of human behavior: The argument from animals to man*. Berkeley: University of California Press.

Reynolds, V. 1976. *The biology of human action*. Reading: Freeman.

Richerson, P. J., and R. Boyd. 1978. A dual inheritance model of the human evolutionary process, I: Basic postulates and a simple model. *Journal of Social and Biological Structures* 1:127–54.

Ricoeur, P. 1974. *The conflict of interpretations: Essays in hermeneutics*, ed. D. Ihde. Evanston, Ill.: Northwestern University Press.

Rivers, W. H. R. 1968[1914]. *Kinship and social organization*. London: Athlone Press.

Ruse, M. 1979. *The Darwinian revolution*. Chicago: University of Chicago Press.

Ruyle, E. E. 1973. Genetic and cultural pools: Some suggestions for a unified theory of biocultural evolution. *Human Ecology* 1:201–15.

—— 1977. Comment on W. H. Durham, 'The adaptive significance of cultural behaviour'. *Human Ecology* 5:53–5.

Ryle, G. 1949. *The concept of mind*. London: Hutchinson.

Sahlins, M. D. 1960. Evolution: Specific and general. In *Evolution and culture*, ed. M. D. Sahlins and E. R. Service. Ann Arbor: University of Michigan Press.

—— 1972. *Stone Age economics*. Chicago: Aldine.

—— 1976a. *The use and abuse of biology*. London: Tavistock.

—— 1976b. *Culture and practical reason*. Chicago: University of Chicago Press.

Sahlins, M. D., and E. R. Service, eds. 1960. *Evolution and culture*. Ann Arbor: University of Michigan Press.

Salzman, P. C. 1981. Culture as enhabilmentis. In *The structure of folk models*, ed. L. Holy and M. Stuchlik (Association of Social Anthropologists Monograph 20). London: Academic Press.

Sapir, E. 1917. Do we need a superorganic? *American Anthropologist* 19:441–7.

Saussure, F. de. 1959. *Course in general linguistics*. New York: Philosophical Library.

Schmidt, A. 1971. *The concept of nature in Marx*, trans. B. Fowkes. London: New Left Books.

Schneider, D. M. 1980. *American kinship: A cultural account*. 2nd ed. Chicago: University of Chicago Press.

Schrempp, G. 1983. The re-education of Friedrich Max Müller: Intellectual appropriation and epistemological antinomy in mid-Victorian evolutionary thought. *Man(N.S.) 18:90–110*.

Schrödinger, E. 1944. *What is life?* Cambridge: Cambridge University Press.

Schutz, A. 1962. *The problem of social reality* (collected papers I, ed. M. Natanson). The Hague: Nijhoff.

—— 1970. *On phenomenology and social relations*, ed. H. R. Wagner. Chicago: University of Chicago Press.

Scriven, M. 1959. Explanation and prediction in evolutionary theory. *Science* 130:477–82.

Searle, J. R. 1979. The intentionality of intention and action. *Inquiry* 22:253–80.

Sebeok, T. A., ed. 1977. *How animals communicate*. Bloomington: Indiana University Press.

Simpson, G. G. 1949. *The meaning of evolution*. New Haven, Conn.: Yale University Press.

—— 1953. *The major features of evolution*. New York: Columbia University Press.

—— 1958a. The study of evolution: Methods and present status of theory. In *Behavior and evolution*, ed. A. Roe and G. G. Simpson. New Haven, Conn.: Yale University Press.

—— 1958b. Behavior and evolution. In *Behavior and evolution*, ed. A. Roe and G. G. Simpson. New Haven, Conn.: Yale University Press.

—— 1974. The concept of progress in organic evolution. *Social Research* 41:28–51.

Smith, M. G. 1962. History and social anthropology. *Journal of the Royal Anthropological Institute* 92:73–85.

Smythies, J. R. 1969. Aspects of consciousness. In *Beyond reductionism: New perspectives in the life sciences*, ed. A. Koestler and J. R. Smythies. London: Hutchinson.

Sorokin, P. A. 1947. *Society, culture and personality: Their structure and dynamics*. New York: Harper.

Spencer, H. 1864. *Principles of biology*. New York: Appleton.

—— 1870. *The principles of psychology*, 2 vols. London: Williams & Norgate. 1874. *Essays: Scientific, political, speculative*, vol. 3. London: Williams and Norgate.

—— 1876. *The principles of sociology I*. London: Williams & Norgate.

—— 1882. *The principles of sociology II*. London: Williams & Norgate.

—— 1907[1879]. *The data of ethics*. London: Williams & Norgate.

—— 1972. *On social evolution* (selected writings edited and introduced by J. D. Y. Peel). Chicago: University of Chicago Press.

Stanner, W. E. H. 1965. The dreaming. In *Reader in comparative religion*, ed. W. A. Lessa and E. Z. Vogt. New York: Harper & Row.

—— 1968. A. R. Radcliffe-Brown. *International Encyclopaedia of the Social Sciences* 13:285–90. New York: Crowell Collier and Macmillan.

Steadman, P. 1979. *The evolution of designs: Biological analogy in architecture and the applied arts*. Cambridge: Cambridge University Press.

Stebbins, G. L. 1950. *Variation and evolution in plants*. New York: Columbia University Press.

—— 1969. *The basis of progressive evolution*. Chapel Hill: University of North Carolina Press.

Stern, B. J. 1929. Concerning the distinction between the social and the cultural. *Social Forces* 8:265–71.

Steward, J. H. 1955. *Theory of culture change*. Urbana: University of Illinois Press.

Stocking, G. W. 1968. *Race, culture and evolution*. New York: Free Press.

—— 1974. Introduction: The basic assumptions of Boasian anthropology. In *A Franz Boas Reader: The shaping of American anthropology 1883–1911*, ed. G. W. Stocking. Chicago: University of Chicago Press.

Swanson, C. P. 1973. *The natural history of man*. Englewood Cliffs, N.J.: Prentice-Hall.

Teggart, F. J. 1972. *Theory and processes of history*. Gloucester, Mass.: Peter Smith.

Teilhard de Chardin, P. 1959. *The phenomenon of man*. New York: Harper.

Teleki, G. 1981. The omnivorous diet and eclectic feeding habits of chimpanzees in Gombe National Park, Tanzania. In *Omnivorous primates: Gathering and hunting in human evolution*, ed. R. S. O. Harding and G. Teleki. New York: Columbia University Press.

Terray, E. 1972. *Marxism and "primitive" societies*, trans. M. Klopper. New York: Monthly Review Press.

—— 1977. Event, structure and history: The formation of the Abron kingdom of Gyaman (1700–1780). In *The evolution of social systems*, ed. J. Friedman and M. J. Rowlands. London: Duckworth.

Thompson, D. W. 1961[1917]. *On growth and form* (abridged), ed. J. T. Bonner. Cambridge: Cambridge University Press.

Thompson, W. R. 1958. Social behavior. In *Behavior and evolution,* ed. A. Roe and G. G. Simpson. New Haven, Conn.: Yale University Press.

Thorpe, W. H. 1956. *Learning and instinct in animals.* London: Methuen.

—— 1972. The comparison of vocal communication in animals and man. In *Non-verbal communication,* ed. R. A. Hinde. Cambridge: Cambridge University Press.

Toulmin, S. 1972. *Human understanding, I.* Oxford: Clarendon.

—— 1981. Social adaptation. In *The philosophy of evolution,* ed. U. J. Jensen and R. Harré. Brighton: Harvester Press.

—— 1982. *The return to cosmology: Postmodern science and the theology of nature.* Berkeley: University of California Press.

Toulmin, S., and J. Goodfield. 1965. *The discovery of time.* London: Hutchinson.

Trigger, B. 1978. *Time and traditions.* Edinburgh: Edinburgh University Press.

Trivers, R. L. 1971. The evolution of reciprocal altruism. *Quarterly Review of Biology* 46:35–57.

Turner, V. W. 1967. Betwixt and between: The liminal period in rites of passage. In *The forest of symbols.* Ithaca, N.Y.: Cornell University Press.

Tylor, E. B. 1871. *Primitive culture.* 2 vols. London: John Murray.

—— 1875. Anthropology. *Encyclopaedia Britannica.* 9th ed. Vol. 2:107–23. London: Funk and Wagnalls.

—— 1881. *Anthropology: An introduction to the study of man and civilization.* London: Macmillan.

Vaihinger, H. 1924. *The philosophy of 'as if'.* London: Kegan Paul, Trench, Trubner.

Venable, V. 1945. *Human nature: The Marxian view.* New York: Knopf.

Vico, G. B. 1948[1744]. *The new science,* trans. T. G. Bergin and M. H. Fisch. Ithaca, N.Y.: Cornell University Press.

Voegelin, C. F. 1951. Culture, language and the human organism. *Southwestern Journal of Anthropology* 7:357–73.

Voget, F. W. 1967. Progress, science, history and evolution in eighteenth- and nineteenth-century anthropology. *Journal of the History of the Behavioural Sciences* 3:132–55.

Waddington, C. H. 1942. *Science and ethics.* London: Allen & Unwin.

—— 1957. *The strategy of the genes: A discussion of some aspects of theoretical biology.* London: Allen & Unwin.

—— 1960. Evolutionary adaptation. In *Evolution after Darwin, I: The evolution of life,* ed. S. Tax. Chicago: University of Chicago Press.

—— 1969. The theory of evolution today. In *Beyond reductionism: New perspectives in the life sciences,* ed. A. Koestler and J. R. Smythies. London: Hutchinson.

Wagner, R. 1975. *The invention of culture.* Englewood Cliffs, N.J.: Prentice-Hall.

Walker, S. 1983. *Animal thought.* London: Routledge & Kegan Paul.

Wallace, A. R. 1870. *Contributions to the theory of natural selection.* London: Macmillan.

Washburn, S. L., and R. Moore. 1974. *Ape into man: A study of human evolution.* Boston: Little, Brown.

Weber, M. 1947. *The theory of social and economic organization,* ed. T. Parsons. New York: Free Press.

Webster, G., and B. C. Goodwin. 1982. The origin of species: A structuralist approach. *Journal of Social and Biological Structures* 5:15–47.

Weiss, P. 1969. The living system: Determinism stratified. In *Beyond reductionism: New perspectives in the life sciences,* ed. A. Koestler and J. R. Smythies. London: Hutchinson.

White, L. A. 1945a. History, evolutionism and functionalism: Three types of interpretation of culture. *Southwestern Journal of Anthropology* 1:221–48.

—— 1945b. Diffusion v. evolution. *American Anthropologist* 47:339–56.

—— 1949. *The science of culture: A study of man and civilization*. New York: Grove Press.

—— 1959a. The concept of evolution in cultural anthropology. In *Evolution and anthropology: A centennial appraisal*, ed. B. J. Meggers. Washington, D.C.: Anthropological Society of Washington.

—— 1959b. *The evolution of culture*. New York: McGraw-Hill.

—— 1959c. The concept of culture. *American Anthropologist* 61:227–51.

Whitehead, A. N. 1929. *Process and reality: An essay in cosmology*. Cambridge: Cambridge University Press.

—— 1938[1926]. *Science and the modern world*. Reprint. Harmondsworth: Penguin.

Whitrow, G. J. 1975. *The nature of time*. Harmondsworth: Penguin.

Whyte, L. L. 1965. *Internal factors in evolution*. London: Tavistock.

Wieman, H. N. 1946. *The source of human good*. Chicago: University of Chicago Press.

—— 1961. *Intellectual foundations of faith*. London: Vision Press.

Wiener, N. 1961. *Cybernetics: Or control and communication in the animal and the machine*. 2nd ed. Cambridge, Mass.: MIT Press.

Williams, G. C. 1966. *Adaptation and natural selection: A critique of some current evolutionary thought*. Princeton, N.J.: Princeton University Press.

Williams, R. 1976. *Keywords*. London: Fontana.

Wilson, E. O. 1978. *On human nature*. Cambridge, Mass.: Harvard University Press.

—— 1980. *Sociobiology: The new synthesis* (abridged ed.). Cambridge, Mass.: Harvard University Press (Belknap).

Wilson, P. J. 1975. The promising primate. Man(N.S.)10:5–20.

—— 1980. *Man, the promising primate*. New Haven, Conn.: Yale University Press.

Wiltshire, D. 1978. *The social and political thought of Herbert Spencer*. Oxford: Oxford University Press.

Winterhalder, B. 1980. Environmental analysis in human evolution and adaptation research. *Human Ecology* 8:135–70.

Woodburn, J. 1982. Egalitarian societies. *Man(N.S.)17:431–51*.

Wright, S. 1964. Biology and the philosophy of science. In *Process and divinity*, ed. W. L. Riese and E. Freeman. La Salle, Ill.: Open Court.

—— 1967. Comments on the preliminary working papers of Eden and Waddington. In *Mathematical challenges to the neo-Darwinian interpretation of evolution*, ed. P. S. Moorhead and M. M. Kaplan (Wistar Institute Symposium Monograph 5). Philadelphia: Wistar Institute Press.

Wynne-Edwards, V. C. 1963. Intergroup selection in the evolution of social systems. *Nature* 200:623–6.

—— 1971. Space use and the social community in animals and men. In *Behavior and environment: The use of space by animals and men*, ed. A. H. Esser. New York: Plenum.

—— 1972. Ecology and the evolution of social ethics. In *Biology and the human sciences*, ed. J. W. S. Pringle. Oxford: Clarendon.

Zirkle, C. 1946. The early history of the idea of the inheritance of acquired characters and pangenesis. *Transactions of the American Philosophical Society* 35:91–151.

NAME INDEX

SUBJECT INDEX